Advanced Grammar in Use

A self-study reference and practice book for advanced learners of English

with answers

SECOND EDITION

Martin Hewings

CAMBRIDGE
UNIVERSITY PRESS

CAMBRIDGE UNIVERSITY PRESS
Cambridge, New York, Melbourne, Madrid, Cape Town, Singapore, São Paulo

Cambridge University Press
The Edinburgh Building, Cambridge CB2 2RU, UK

www.cambridge.org
Information on this title: www.cambridge.org/9780521532914

First published 2005
3rd printing 2006

Printed in the United Kingdom at the University Press, Cambridge

A catalogue record for this publication is available from the British Library

ISBN-13 978-0-521-53291-4 Edition with answers
ISBN-10 0-521-53291-4 Edition with answers

ISBN-13 978-0-521-53292-1 Edition without answers
ISBN-10 0-521-53292-2 Edition without answers

ISBN-13 978-0-521-61403-0 Edition with CD-ROM
ISBN-10 0-521-61403-1 Edition with CD-ROM

ISBN-13 978-0-521-61402-3 CD-ROM
ISBN-10 0-521-61402-3 CD-ROM

ISBN-13 978-0-521-61404-7 Network CD-ROM
ISBN-10 0-521-61404-X Network CD-ROM

ISBN-13 978-3-12-534134-0 Klett Edition with answers
ISBN-10 3-12-534134-5 Klett Edition with answers

ISBN-13 978-3-12-534147-0 Klett Edition with CD-ROM
ISBN-10 3-12-534147-7 Klett Edition with CD-ROM

Contents

Thanks   vii

To the student   viii

To the teacher   ix

Tenses

1 Present continuous and present simple (1)

2 Present continuous and present simple (2)

3 Past simple and present perfect

4 Past continuous and past simple

5 Past perfect and past simple

6 Present perfect continuous and present perfect

7 Past perfect continuous, past perfect and past continuous

8 Present and past time: review

The future

9 **Will** and **be going to**

10 Present simple and present continuous for the future

11 Future continuous and future perfect (continuous)

12 **Be to** + infinitive

13 Other ways of talking about the future

14 The future seen from the past

Modals and semi-modals

15 **Can, could, be able to** and **be allowed to**

16 **Will, would** and **used to**

17 **May** and **might**: possibility

18 **Must** and **have (got) to**

19 **Need(n't), don't need to** and **don't have to**

20 **Should, ought to** and **had better**

Linking verbs, passives, questions

21 Linking verbs: **be, appear, seem; become, get,** etc.

22 Forming passive sentences (1)

23 Forming passive sentences (2): verb + **-ing** or **to-infinitive**

24 Using passives

25 Reporting with passive verbs; **It is said that...**

26 **Wh**-questions with **who, whom, which, how** and **whose**

27 Negative questions; echo questions; questions with **that-clauses**

Verb complementation: what follows verbs

28 Verbs, objects and complements

29 Verb + two objects

30 Verb + **-ing** forms and infinitives (1)

31 Verb + **-ing** forms and infinitives (2)

IF YOU ARE NOT SURE WHICH UNITS YOU NEED TO STUDY, USE THE **STUDY GUIDE** ON PAGE 240.

iii

Reporting

32 Reporting people's words and thoughts
33 Reporting statements: **that-clauses**
34 Verb + **wh-clause**
35 Tense choice in reporting
36 Reporting offers, suggestions, orders, intentions, etc.
37 Modal verbs in reporting
38 Reporting what people say using nouns and adjectives
39 **Should** in **that-clauses**; the present subjunctive

Nouns

40 Agreement between subject and verb (1)
41 Agreement between subject and verb (2)
42 Agreement between subject and verb (3)
43 Compound nouns and noun phrases

Articles, determiners and quantifiers

44 **A/an** and **one**
45 **A/an, the** and **zero article** (1)
46 **A/an, the** and **zero article** (2)
47 **A/an, the** and **zero article** (3)
48 **Some** and **any**
49 **No, none** (of) and **not any**
50 **Much** (of), **many** (of) **a lot of, lots** (of), etc.
51 **All** (of), **whole, every, each**
52 **Few, little, less, fewer**

Relative clauses and other types of clause

53 Relative pronouns
54 Other relative words: **whose, when, whereby,** etc.
55 Prepositions in relative clauses
56 Other ways of adding information to noun phrases (1): additional noun phrases, etc.
57 Other ways of adding information to noun phrases (2): prepositional phrases, etc.
58 Participle clauses with adverbial meaning (1)
59 Participle clauses with adverbial meaning (2)

Pronouns, substitution and leaving out words

60 Reflexive pronouns: **herself, himself, themselves,** etc.
61 **One** and **ones**
62 **So** and **not** as substitutes for clauses, etc.
63 **Do so; such**
64 More on leaving out words after auxiliary verbs
65 Leaving out **to-infinitives**

IF YOU ARE NOT SURE WHICH UNITS YOU NEED TO STUDY, USE THE STUDY GUIDE ON PAGE 240.

Adjectives and adverbs
66 Position of adjectives
67 Gradable and non-gradable adjectives (1)
68 Gradable and non-gradable adjectives (2)
69 Participle adjectives and compound adjectives
70 Adjectives + **to-infinitive, -ing, that-clause, wh-clause**
71 Adjectives and adverbs
72 Adjectives and adverbs: comparative and superlative forms
73 Comparative phrases and clauses
74 Position of adverbs (1)
75 Position of adverbs (2)
76 Adverbs of place, direction, indefinite frequency, and time
77 Degree adverbs and focus adverbs
78 Comment adverbs and viewpoint adverbs

Adverbial clauses and conjunctions
79 Adverbial clauses of time
80 Giving reasons: **as, because,** etc.; **for** and **with**
81 Purposes and results: **in order to, so as to,** etc.
82 Contrasts: **although** and **though; even though/if; while, whilst** and **whereas**
83 **If** (1)
84 **If** (2)
85 **If I were you...; imagine he were to win**
86 **If...not** and **unless; if** and **whether;** etc.
87 Connecting ideas in a sentence and between sentences

Prepositions
88 Prepositions of position and movement
89 **Between** and **among**
90 Prepositions of time
91 Talking about exceptions
92 Prepositions after verbs
93 Prepositions after nouns
94 Two- and three-word verbs: word order

Organising information
95 **There is, there was,** etc.
96 **It...** (1)
97 **It...** (2)
98 Focusing: **it-clauses** and **what-clauses**
99 Inversion (1)
100 Inversion (2)

Grammar review   202
Glossary   219

IF YOU ARE NOT SURE WHICH UNITS YOU NEED TO STUDY, USE THE **STUDY GUIDE** ON PAGE 240.

v

Appendix 1   Passive verb forms   224
Appendix 2   Basic question forms   225
Appendix 3   Quoting what people think or what they have said   226
Appendix 4   Irregular verbs   227

Additional exercises   229

Study Guide   240
Key to Exercises   252
Key to Additional exercises   278
Key to Study guide   281

Index   282

IF YOU ARE NOT SURE WHICH UNITS YOU NEED TO STUDY, USE THE **STUDY GUIDE** ON PAGE 240.

Thanks

I was given considerable help by many people in writing the first edition of *Advanced Grammar in Use*, and their influence will still be seen in this new edition. In particular, I would like to thank Jeanne McCarten at Cambridge University Press, and my colleagues and students in the English for International Students Unit at the University of Birmingham.

For this new edition, I have been equally lucky in the support I have received from a number of knowledgeable, professional, and generous people. Alison Sharpe had guided the project to completion with constant encouragement and great diplomacy. Also at Cambridge University Press I would like to thank Kerry Maxwell, Xanthe Sturt Taylor, Jean Hudson, and Anna Teevan. Drafts of the reference material were also read by Sylvia Chalker, Frances Eaves-Walton, Carmina Gregori Signes, Carita Paradis, Richard Smith. Their comments were invaluable in helping me to revise and clarify this part of the book.
Thanks to Gillian Martin, Roger Penwill and Lisa Smith for the illustrations and to Kamae Design for their work on the finished product. I would also like to thank Cambridge University Press for allowing me access to the Cambridge International Corpus.

A number of students and teachers who used the first edition sent me suggestions on how it might be improved, and these have been very useful in preparing this new edition. Thank you for using the book and taking the trouble to write to me.

Finally, my gratitude, as always, to Ann, David and Suzanne.

To the student

Who the book is for

The book is intended for advanced students of English. It is written mainly as a self-study book, but might also be used in class with a teacher.

How the book is organised

There are 100 units in the book. Each one looks at a particular area of grammar. Some sections within each unit focus on the particular use of a grammatical pattern, such as *will be + -ing* (as in *will be travelling*). Others explore grammatical contrasts, such as whether to use *would* or *used to* to report past events, or when we use *except* or *except for*. The 100 units are grouped under a number of headings such as *Tenses* and *The future*. You can find details of this in the Contents pages.

Each unit consists of two pages. On the left hand page are explanations and examples; on the right are practice exercises. The letters next to each exercise show you which sections of the left hand page you need to understand to do that exercise. The Grammar Review presents examples and explanations on areas of grammar that you are likely to have studied already at earlier stages of learning English. Although terms to describe grammar have been kept to a minimum some have been included, and you can find explanations of these terms in the Glossary. Four Appendices tell you about passive verb forms, basic question forms, quotation, and irregular verbs. A number of Additional Exercises are included for further practice of particular areas. You can use the Study Guide to help you decide which units to study and which areas of grammar to revise in the Grammar Review. You can check your answers to the practice exercises, Additional Exercises and Study Guide in the Key. The Key also comments on some of the answers. To help you find the information you need there is an Index at the back of the book.

How to use the book

It is not necessary to work through the units in order. If you know what grammar points you have difficulty with, go straight to the units that deal with them, using the Contents or Index to help you find the relevant unit. If you think that it would be useful to revise more basic information before you read the reference material in a unit and do the exercises, many units have links at the bottom of the reference page pointing you to the section of the Grammar Review where you can find this. In some units you will also find links to the Grammar Review in the explanations; for example '(see GR:B1)'.

You can use the units in a number of ways. You might study the explanation and examples first, do the exercises on the opposite page, check your answers in the key, and then look again at the explanations if you made any mistakes. If you just want to practise an area of grammar you think you already know, you could do the exercises first and then study the explanations for any you got wrong. You might of course simply use the book as a reference book without doing the exercises.

To the teacher

Advanced Grammar in Use was written as a self-study grammar book but teachers might also find it useful for supplementing or supporting their classroom teaching.

The book will probably be most useful for advanced level students for reference and practice. The Grammar Review towards the back of the book is a reference-only section which presents basic knowledge on a number of areas of grammar. This will be useful for students who wish to revise a particular area before moving on to the more advanced material in the units.
No attempt has been made to order the units according to level of difficulty. Instead you should select units as they are relevant to the syllabus that you are following with your students, or as particular difficulties arise.

There are many ways in which you might use the book with a class. You might, for example, present the explanations on the left hand page of a unit, and use the exercises for classroom practice or set them as consolidation material for self-study. Alternatively, you might want to begin with the exercises and refer to the left hand page only when students are having problems. You could also set particular units or groups of units (such as those on *Articles* or *The future*) for self-study if individual students are having difficulties.

There is a set of Additional Exercises, most of which can be used to provide practice of grammar points from a number of different units.

A 'classroom edition' of *Advanced Grammar in Use* is also available. It has no key and some teachers might prefer to use it with their students.

Advanced English Grammar in Use *Second Edition*

If you have already used the first edition of *Advanced Grammar in Use*, you will see some major changes in this new edition. The more basic areas of grammar have been moved out of the units into a reference section at the back, called the Grammar Review. All of the reference pages have been revised, some substantially, and some new units have been added. Most of the exercise pages have entirely new exercises or many new questions.

The book is now available with or without a CD-ROM. On the CD-ROM you will find more exercises on all of the units (different from those in the book). There are also hundreds of test questions, and you can make your own tests. The CD-ROM can also be bought separately.

Advanced Grammar in Use

Present continuous and present simple (1)

A

We can use the present continuous with some state verbs (e.g. **attract, like, look, love, sound**) when we want to emphasise that a situation is temporary or for a period of time around the present. Compare:

☐ Jean stays with us quite often. The children **love** having her here. *and*
☐ Jean's with us at the moment. The children **are loving** having her here.

State verbs which we rarely use with the present continuous include **believe, consist of, doubt, own.** (For more examples see **GR:A4.**)

B

Some verbs have different meanings when they are used to talk about states and when they describe actions. With their 'state' meanings, they usually take simple rather than continuous forms. With their 'action' meanings, they may take simple or continuous forms, depending on context. Compare:

☐ The new treatment for influenza **doesn't appear** to work. (appear: *state* = seem) *and*
☐ Madonna **is** currently **appearing** in a musical on Broadway./ She often **appears** in musicals. (appear: *action* = take part)
☐ **Do** you **think** it's a good idea? (think: *state* = about an opinion) *and*
☐ **I'm thinking** of going in August./ Your trouble is you **think** too much. (think: *action* = consider)

Other verbs like this include **anticipate, cost, expect, feel, fit, have, imagine, measure, weigh.**

C

With some verbs describing *mental* states (e.g. **find, realise, regret, think, understand**) we can use the present continuous to emphasise that we have recently started to think about something or that we are not sure about something. Compare:

☐ I **regret** that the company will have to be sold. (= I have made the decision and I am sorry about it) *and*
☐ **I'm regretting** my decision to give her the job. (= I am increasingly aware that it was the wrong decision)

When it means 'think carefully about' the verb **consider** is only used with the present continuous:

☐ He's **considering** taking early retirement. (*not* He considers taking early retirement.)

Some other verbs describing preferences and mental states (e.g. **agree, believe, conclude, know, prefer**) are rarely used with the present continuous:

☐ I **believe** you now. (*not* I'm believing you now.)

D

We use the present simple with verbs which perform the action they describe:

☐ I **admit** I can't see as well as I used to.
☐ We **apologise** for not replying earlier.

Other verbs like this (sometimes called *performatives*) include **acknowledge, advise, beg, confess, congratulate, declare, deny, forbid, guarantee, name, order, permit, predict, promise, refuse, remind, request, thank, warn.** Some verbs used as performatives in affirmative (= positive) sentences (**apologise, deny, guarantee, promise, suggest**) have a similar meaning with either the present simple or the present continuous in negative sentences:

☐ I **don't deny**/ **I'm not denying** taking the books, but Andy said it would be okay.

Note that we can use modals with performatives, often to make what we say more tentative or polite:

☐ We **would advise** you to arrive two hours before the flight leaves.
☐ I **must beg** you to keep this a secret.

Grammar review: present continuous → A1–A2; present simple → A3–A5

Exercises

1.1 Complete the sentences with the verbs given, using negatives or questions where necessary. Use the same verb for each sentence in the pair. Choose the present continuous if possible; if not, use the present simple. Use ⋏ to add any words outside the space and use contracted forms where appropriate, as in 1. (A & B)

attract consist of doubt feel fit have like ~~look~~ measure sound

1 a I hear you're having your house repainted. How⋏ it _'s looking_? (*or* How⋏ it _does look_?)

b I bought this new dress today. How⋏ it _does look_?

2 a A: What are you doing with that ruler? B: I .... the area of the kitchen.

b The garden .... 12 by 20 metres.

3 a I .... whether I'll get another chance to retake the exam.

b I suppose she might be at home tonight, but I .... it.

4 a The new science museum currently .... 10,000 visitors a month.

b Flowers .... bees with their brightly coloured petals.

5 a Mike won't work at the top of the 20-storey building because he .... heights.

b A: How's the new job? B: Well, at the moment, I .... it at all.

6 a My car's in the garage today. They .... new brakes.

b I bought this jumper for Sue, but it .... her so I'll have to take it back.

7 a What's your shirt made from? It .... like silk.

b I won't be coming to work today. I .... very well.

8 a The roof of the house .... only plastic sheets nailed down in a few places.

b Their school uniform .... black trousers and a dark green jumper.

9 a Simon has been practising the song for days. It .... quite good, but he doesn't think he's ready yet to perform it in public.

b A: What's that noise? B: It .... like a bird stuck in the chimney.

10 a I had a postcard from Joanne on holiday in Spain. It sounds like she .... a really good time.

b My sister .... long blonde hair. You're bound to recognise her.

1.2 Cross out any improbable answers. (C & D)

1 *I'm understanding/ I understand* biology a lot better now that we've got a new teacher.

2 I went to see a Formula One race last week, but *I admit/ I'm admitting* that I don't know much about cars.

3 *Do you find/ Are you finding* it difficult to concentrate on your work with this music on?

4 We'll do our best to get the computer repaired by next week, but *we're not guaranteeing/ we don't guarantee* it.

5 I've just started to learn how to drive. Now *I'm knowing/ I know* how difficult it is, I'll never criticise your driving again.

6 She says that she wasn't in the kitchen when the bottle smashed, but *I refuse/ I'm refusing* to believe her.

7 *I'm certainly agreeing/ I certainly agree* with you that people shouldn't drink and drive.

8 I know the company has made a loss this year, but *I'm not apologising/ I don't apologise* for that.

9 It's very difficult for us to get jobs here, so *we're considering/ we consider* emigrating to Canada.

3

Unit 2 — Present continuous and present simple (2)

A

We often use the present simple and present continuous in stories and jokes in informal spoken English to create the impression that events are happening now. This can make them more direct and exciting and hold people's attention:

- ☐ She **goes** up to this man and **looks** straight into his eyes. He's not **wearing** his glasses, and he **doesn't recognise** her...
- ☐ This man**'s playing** golf when a kangaroo **bounds** up to him, **grabs** his club and **hits** his ball about half a mile...

The main events are usually described in sequence using the present simple and longer background events are described using the present continuous.

In narratives and anecdotes the present simple can be used to highlight an event. Often it is used after past tenses and with a phrase such as **suddenly** or **all of a sudden**:

- ☐ I was sitting in the park, reading a newspaper, when *all of a sudden* this dog **jumps** at me.

B

We also use the present simple and present continuous in live commentaries (for example, on sports events) when the report takes place at the same time as the action:

- ☐ King **serves** to the left-hand court and Adams **makes** a wonderful return. She**'s playing** magnificent tennis in this match....

C

We can use the present simple in phrases such as **It says here, I hear, I gather, I see, I understand** and **They say, (Someone) says, (Someone) tells me** to introduce news that we have heard, read, seen (e.g. on television), or been told. We can also use past tenses (e.g. **It said here, I heard**):

- ☐ I **gather** you're worried about Ken.   ☐ Jane **tells me** you're thinking of emigrating.
- ☐ Professor Otto is at the conference and I **hear** she's an excellent speaker.

D

The present simple is often used in newspaper headlines to talk about events that have recently happened:

> QUAKE *HITS* CENTRAL IRAN   FOREIGN MINISTER *RESIGNS*

> SCIENTISTS *FIND* BRIGHTEST STAR   FIRE *BREAKS* OUT IN HOTEL ROOM

We can use the present simple to refer to the contents of books, films, newspapers, etc:

- ☐ Thompson **gives** a list of the largest European companies in Chapter Six.
- ☐ At the beginning of the book, three men **find** $4 million in a crashed plane.
- ☐ In the film, Joan Smithson **takes** the role of a private detective.

E

We can use the present continuous with adverbs such as **always, constantly, continually** or **forever** to emphasise that something is done so often that it is characteristic of a person, group or thing:

- ☐ A: I think I'll stay here after all.   B: You **are** *constantly* **changing** your mind.
- ☐ Tony is a really kind person. He**'s** *always* **offering** to help me with my work.

We often use this pattern to indicate disapproval. The past continuous is used in a similar way with these adverbs (e.g. **Was** Kath *always* **asking** you for money, too?).

We can use the present continuous to describe something we regularly do at a certain time:

- ☐ At 8 o'clock I**'m** usually **driving** to work, so phone me on my mobile.
- ☐ 7 o'clock is a bit early. We**'re** generally **eating** then.

F

We can use the present (or past) continuous rather than the present (or past) simple with the verb **wonder** if we want to be especially friendly or polite, particularly if we are unsure about the other person's feelings towards something or how they will react to what we say:

- ☐ You said that there were only 50 books in the boxes. I**'m** just **wondering**/ I **was** just **wondering** whether you counted them all? (*more polite than* 'I just wonder...?')

Grammar review: present continuous → A1–A2; present simple → A3–A5

Exercises

2.1 Complete these sentences using the verbs in brackets. Choose the present simple or present continuous. (A & B)

1 Beckham ....*passes*.... to Giggs who .... just over the bar. Manchester United .... much more in this half... (*pass – shoot – attack*)

2 A man .... home late one night after the office Christmas party. His wife .... for him, and she .... to him... (*arrive – wait – say*)

3 I went to a concert yesterday in the Town Hall. In the middle of it, while the orchestra .... this man suddenly .... on his seat and .... to conduct them. (*play – stand – start*)

2.2 Complete what each person says about the news they have read or heard using the present tense phrases in C. (C)

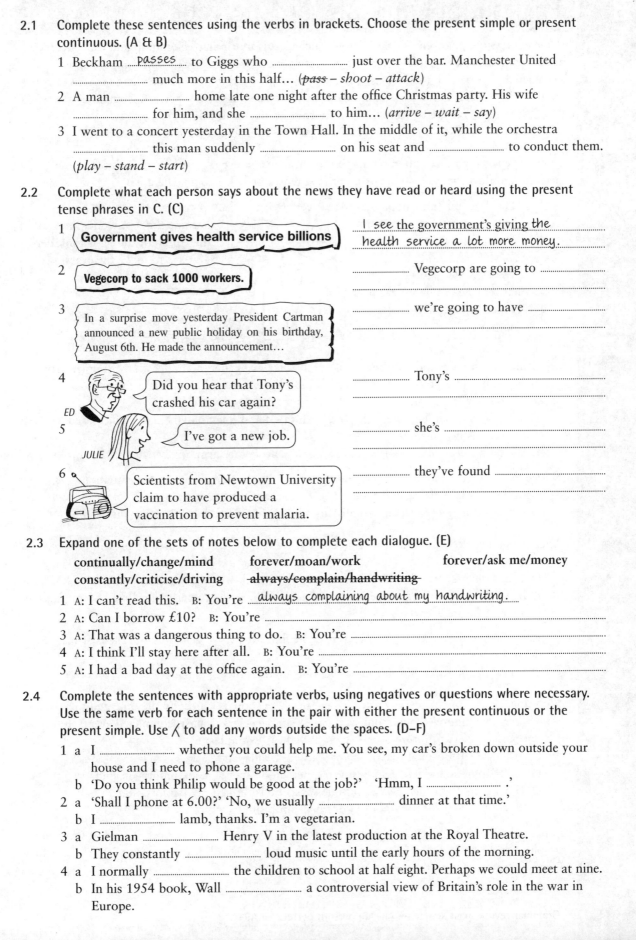

1 **Government gives health service billions**

I see the government's giving the health service a lot more money.

2 **Vegecorp to sack 1000 workers.**

.... Vegecorp are going to ....

3 In a surprise move yesterday President Cartman announced a new public holiday on his birthday, August 6th. He made the announcement...

.... we're going to have ....

4 *ED* Did you hear that Tony's crashed his car again?

.... Tony's ....

5 *JULIE* I've got a new job.

.... she's ....

6 Scientists from Newtown University claim to have produced a vaccination to prevent malaria.

.... they've found ....

2.3 Expand one of the sets of notes below to complete each dialogue. (E)

continually/change/mind   forever/moan/work   forever/ask me/money
constantly/criticise/driving   ~~always/complain/handwriting~~

1 A: I can't read this. B: You're ....*always complaining about my handwriting*....

2 A: Can I borrow £10? B: You're ....

3 A: That was a dangerous thing to do. B: You're ....

4 A: I think I'll stay here after all. B: You're ....

5 A: I had a bad day at the office again. B: You're ....

2.4 Complete the sentences with appropriate verbs, using negatives or questions where necessary. Use the same verb for each sentence in the pair with either the present continuous or the present simple. Use ⅄ to add any words outside the spaces. (D–F)

1 a I .... whether you could help me. You see, my car's broken down outside your house and I need to phone a garage.

  b 'Do you think Philip would be good at the job?' 'Hmm, I ....'

2 a 'Shall I phone at 6.00?' 'No, we usually .... dinner at that time.'

  b I .... lamb, thanks. I'm a vegetarian.

3 a Gielman .... Henry V in the latest production at the Royal Theatre.

  b They constantly .... loud music until the early hours of the morning.

4 a I normally .... the children to school at half eight. Perhaps we could meet at nine.

  b In his 1954 book, Wall .... a controversial view of Britain's role in the war in Europe.

A Time expressions that refer to the present, such as **this morning/week/month** and **today**, can be used with either past simple or present perfect verbs. If we think of **this morning** (etc.) as a past, completed time period, then we use the past simple; if we think of **this morning** (etc.) as a time period which includes the present moment, then we use the present perfect. Compare:

- ☐ I **didn't shave** *this morning*. (= the morning is over and I didn't shave) *and*
- ☐ I **haven't shaved** *this morning*. (= it is still the morning and I might shave later)

B In news reports, you will often read about or hear recent events introduced with the present perfect, and then the past simple or other past tenses are used to give details:

- ☐ 'The film star Jim Cooper **has died** of cancer. He **was** 68 and **lived** in Texas...'

- ☐ 'A teacher from Oslo **has become** the first woman to cross the Antarctic alone. It **took** her 42 days to make the crossing with her dog team...'

- ☐ 'The US space shuttle Atlantis **has returned** safely to earth. It **landed** in Florida this morning...'

C In a sentence which includes a time clause with *since*, we generally prefer a past simple verb in the time clause and a present perfect verb in the main clause. The time clause refers to a particular point in the past:

- ☐ *Since* Mr Hassan **became** president, both taxes and unemployment **have increased**. (*rather than* ...has become...)
- ☐ She **hasn't been able** to play tennis *since* she **broke** her arm. (*rather than* ...has broken...)

Notice, however, that we use the present perfect in the time clause if the two situations described in the main clause and time clause extend until the present:

- ☐ **Have** you **met** any of your neighbours *since* you**'ve lived** here? (*not* ...you lived...)

D After the pattern **It/This/That** *is/will be* **the first time**... we generally use the present perfect in the next clause:

- ☐ *That's the first time* I**'ve seen** Jan look embarrassed. (reporting a past event)
- ☐ *It won't be the first time* she **has voted** against the government in her long career. (talking about a future event)

Notice, however, that after **It/This/That** *was* **the first time**... we generally use the *past* perfect (see **Unit 5**):

- ☐ *It was the first time* I**'d talked** to Ella outside the office.

E With time clauses introduced by **after**, **when**, **until**, **as soon as**, **once**, **by the time** and the time expressions **the minute/second/moment** the past simple refers to past, completed events and the present perfect refers to future events. Compare these examples:

- ☐ *After* she **left** hospital (past), she had a long holiday. *and*
- ☐ *After* Dominic **has left** school (future), he will be spending six months in India.
- ☐ *The minute* I **got** the news about Sue (past) I telephoned my parents. *and*
- ☐ I'll contact you *the minute* I**'ve got** my exam results. (future)

In the time clause in sentences like this it is possible to use the past perfect instead of the past simple (e.g. After she **had left**...) and the present simple instead of the present perfect (e.g. After Dominic **leaves**...) with the same meaning (see also **Unit 5**).

Grammar review: past simple → A6–A8; present perfect → A9–A12

Exercises

3.1 Choose a verb to complete the sentence. Use the present perfect or past simple. (A)

   have   go   oversleep   read   spend   wear

1 I .... a lot this week, but I have to get the book completely finished by this weekend.

2 A: Shall I make us some dinner? It's already 8 o'clock. B: No thanks. I .... to the dentist this afternoon and my mouth hurts too much to eat anything.

3 I .... three lectures today and I still have two more later this afternoon.

4 It was so hot today that I .... shorts and a T-shirt at work.

5 We .... £200 on food this month and there's another week to go before I get paid.

6 A: Do you want a lift home? B: No, I .... this morning because my alarm clock didn't go off, so I need to work late.

3.2 Complete the sentences with these pairs of verbs. (Note that the verb pairs are not always in sentence order.) Choose the most appropriate tense – present perfect or past simple. (C)

   be able – feel   happen – speak   improve – be   not want – fall   rescue – be
   work – not have

1 Maria .... to go swimming since she .... in the river.

2 Since she .... at the company she .... a day off through illness.

3 Since he .... the girl from the frozen pond, he .... on TV almost every day.

4 A lot .... since I last .... to you.

5 Since I .... to drive I .... much more independent

6 Robert's reading .... enormously since he .... at school.

3.3 Choose a verb that can complete both sentences in each pair. Use the present perfect in one and the past simple in the other. Use ∧ to add any words outside the spaces. (E)

   finish   get   hear   sign

1 a Remember that after you .... the contract you won't be able to change your mind.

   b Carlo's injury only became apparent after he .... to play for Real Madrid.

2 a As soon as I .... college I want to travel around Australia.

   b I didn't have time to check the composition. I handed it in as soon as I .... it.

3 a By the time Sarah .... to work the meeting had finished.

   b I'll probably have finished breakfast by the time the children .... up.

4 a I recognised her the moment I .... her laugh.

   b I'll tell you what time we're coming the moment I .... from Frank.

3.4 Here are some extracts from a television news report. Choose the more appropriate tense – present perfect or past simple – for the verbs given. (B & D)

1 In tonight's World Cup match, France are currently beating Germany 2–1 with five minutes of the match to go. If the score remains the same it will be the first time Germany .... (*lose*) to France since 1998.

2 The Victoria Hospital in Milltown .... (*close*) to new patients after more cases of food poisoning. Three elderly patients .... (*die*) last week in the outbreak.

3 In last night's final Mark Peters .... (*defeat*) Ed Myers in three sets. It was the first time in six attempts that Peters .... (*beat*) the world champion.

4 Nearly 600 laptops .... (*steal*) from Ministry of Defence staff over the past five years. However, a spokesperson .... (*insist*) that there had been no security problems as none of the computers .... (*hold*) secret information.

Unit 4

Past continuous and past simple

A When we talk about two events or activities that went on over the same period of past time, we can often use the past continuous or the past simple for both:

- ☐ Sally **was reading** to the children while Kevin **was washing up**. (*or* ...read...washed up.)

Using the past continuous emphasises that the event or activity ('was reading') was in progress during the past period of time ('while Kevin was washing up'). Compare:

- ☐ When I **was learning/ learned** to drive I was living with my parents.

Was learning emphasises that the activity was in progress ('I had lessons during this time') and **learned** emphasises completion ('I passed my test during this time').

When we talk about two or more past completed events that followed one another, we use the past simple, not the past continuous, for both (see also **Unit 5C**):

- ☐ She **got** up when the alarm clock **went** off.
- ☐ He **jumped** out of bed and **ran** to see who the parcel was for.

B We usually use the past simple rather than the past continuous to talk about repeated past actions:

- ☐ We **went** to Spain three times last year.
- ☐ **Did** you **drive** past her house every day?

However, we can use the past continuous, particularly in spoken English, when we want to emphasise that repeated actions went on for a limited and temporary period of past time:

- ☐ When Carlo was in hospital, we **were visiting** him twice a day. (*or* ...we visited...)
- ☐ To lose weight before the race, I **wasn't eating** any sweets or biscuits for weeks. (*or* ...I didn't eat...)

or to talk about something that happened surprisingly often:

- ☐ Last week I **was having to** bring work home every night to get it all done. (*or* ...had...)
- ☐ When the builders were here I **was making** them cups of tea all the time. (*or* ...made...)

C We often use the past simple in a narrative (e.g. a report or a story) to talk about a single complete past event and the past continuous to describe the situation that existed at the time. The event might have interrupted the situation, or happened while the situation was in progress:

- ☐ Erika **dropped** her bag while she **was getting** into her car.
- ☐ She **was shaking** with anger as she **left** the hotel.

D We can use either the past continuous or past simple (or past perfect; see **Unit 5E**) to talk about things we intended to do but didn't:

- ☐ We **were meaning** to call in and see you, but Jane wasn't feeling well. (*or* We meant...)

Other verbs used like this include: **consider + -ing; expect to; hope to; intend to; plan to/on + -ing; think about + -ing/of + -ing; want to**. These verbs (with the exception of **mean** and **expect**) and **wonder about** can also be used with the present and past continuous to report what we might do in the future. The past continuous is less definite than the present continuous:

- ☐ I **was thinking of** going down to London next weekend, but it depends how much money I've got. (*less definite than* **I'm thinking of** going...)
- ☐ We **were wondering about** inviting Kay over tomorrow. (*less definite than* We're wondering about...)

Grammar review: past continuous → A13; past simple → A6–A8

Exercises

4.1 Complete the sentences using these pairs of verbs. Use the past simple in one space and the past continuous in the other. (A–D)

come – show   ~~get – go~~   hope – give   live – spend   look – see   play – break
start – check in

1 Just as I ....*was getting*.... into the bath all the lights ....*went*.... off.
2 I .... to go away this weekend, but my boss .... me some work that I have to finish by Monday.
3 When I .... in Paris, I .... three hours a day travelling to and from work.
4 A friendly American couple .... chatting to him as he .... at the hotel reception.
5 I bumped into Mary last week. She .... a lot better than when I last .... her.
6 My boss .... into the office just as I .... everyone my holiday photos.
7 I .... badminton four times a week before I .... my ankle.

This time, use the *same* tense in both spaces.

add – taste   go off – light   not listen – explain   push – run   not watch – dream

8 The smoke alarm .... when he .... a cigarette underneath it.
9 I can't remember how to answer this question. I must confess that I .... while the teacher .... it to us.
10 She .... more salt to the soup, and then it .... much better.
11 Although the television was on, I .... it. Instead I .... about my holidays.
12 She .... open the door and .... into the room.

4.2 Look again at numbers 1, 4, 7 and 11 in 4.1. Which of these could *also* be in the past simple? What difference in meaning, if any, would there be?

4.3 Complete this text with either the past simple or the past continuous form of the verbs in brackets. Where alternatives are possible, think about any difference in meaning. (A–C)

Send Now | Send Later | Save as Draft | Add Attachments | Signature ▾ | Options ▾ | Rewrap

I (1) .... (*buy*) a new alarm clock the other day in Taylor's the jewellers, when I actually (2) .... (*see*) somebody shoplifting. I'd just finished paying for my clock and as I (3) .... (*turn*) round, an elderly woman (4) .... (*slowly put*) a silver plate into a bag that she (5) .... (*carry*). Then she (6) .... (*walk*) over to another part of the shop and (7) .... (*pick up*) an expensive-looking watch a number of times. When she (8) .... (*think*) that nobody (9) .... (*look*), she (10) .... (*drop*) it into the bag. Before I (11) .... (*have*) a chance to tell the staff in the shop, she (12) .... (*notice*) that I (13) .... (*watch*) her and (14) .... (*hurry*) out. Unfortunately for her, two police officers (15) .... (*walk*) past just at that moment and she (16) .... (*run*) straight into them.

9

Past perfect and past simple

A When we give an account of a sequence of past events we usually put these events in chronological order using the past simple. If we want to refer to an event out of order – that is, an event which happened *before* the last event in the sequence we have written or spoken about – we can use the past perfect. Study the use of the past perfect and past simple in the text on the right:

> Don José was a wealthy Cuban landowner who **emigrated** to Mexico in 1959. The agricultural reforms **had begun** a few months before this. He **moved** again in 1965 and made his home in the United States. He **had made** his fortune in growing sugar cane as a young man in Cuba, and he brought his expertise to his new home.

Order of events:	1 made fortune 2 reforms began 3 emigrated to Mexico 4 moved to U.S.
Order events are mentioned:	1 emigrated to Mexico 2 reforms **had begun** (*out of order*) 3 moved to U.S. 4 **had made** fortune (*out of order*)

B When we understand that we are talking about events before another past event, we don't have to continue using the past perfect:
- We **bought** a new car last month. We'd **driven** my parents' old car for ages, but it **started** (*or* **had started**) to fall apart. We **put** (*or* **had put**) a new engine in it, but that **didn't solve** (*or* **hadn't solved**) the problems we were having.

C If the order of past events is clear from the context (for example, if time expressions make the order clear) we can often use either the past perfect or the past simple:
- *After* Ivan **had finished** reading, he put out the light. (*or* ...Ivan **finished**...)
- They were given help and advice *before* they **had made** the decision. (*or* ...they **made**...)
- The two leaders agreed to meet, even though *earlier* talks **had failed** to reach an agreement. (*or* ...talks **failed**...)

D The past perfect is often used in reporting what was originally said or thought in the present perfect or past simple (see also Unit 35):

Talking about a past event	Reporting this past event
☐ 'I **have met** him before.' ☐ 'The village **hasn't changed** much.'	☐ I was sure that I **had met** him before. (*not* ...I met him...) ☐ On my last visit to Wixton I found that the village **hadn't changed** much. (*not* ...the village didn't change...)
☐ 'Smithers **drowned** in the recent floods.' ☐ 'She **stole** the watch.'	☐ Police were convinced Smithers **had drowned** in the recent floods. (*or* ...**drowned**...) ☐ She admitted that she **had stolen** the watch. (*or* ...**stole**...)

E We can use either the past perfect or past simple (and often past continuous and past perfect continuous; see Units 4 and 7) when we talk about things that we intended to do, but didn't or won't now do in the future:
- I **had hoped** to visit the gallery before I left Florence, but it's closed on Sundays. (*or* I **hoped**..., I **was hoping**..., I **had been hoping**...)
- Bill **planned** to retire at 60, but we have persuaded him to stay for a few more years. (*or* Bill **had planned**..., Bill **was planning**..., Bill **had been planning**...)

Other verbs used like this include: **consider** + -ing; **expect to**; **intend to**; **mean to**; **think about** + ing/of + -ing; **want to**.

Grammar review: past perfect → A14–A15; past simple → A6–A8

5.1 A number of the events in the text are listed on the right. List the events (i) in the order in which they occurred (or were thought to occur), and (ii) the order in which they are mentioned. Comparing these two lists, consider why the past perfect was used where it is marked. (A & B)

From an account of how a house was bought

When I first saw the old house I *had* just *moved* to the area. It *had been* empty for about a year and was beginning to need some repairs, but the house was exactly what I wanted. But by the time I *had put together* enough money I learnt that a property developer *had bought* it and planned to turn it into a hotel. Six months later I *had* nearly *given up* hope of finding anywhere to live in the village when I heard that the house was for sale again. The property developer *had decided* to invest his money in a new housing development on the edge of the village. I bought the house immediately and I've lived there happily ever since.

Events

I moved…
I learnt…
The property developer decided…
I heard…
I first saw the old house
A property developer bought it
I nearly gave up…
I put together enough money…
It was empty

5.2 Underline the correct answers. In some cases only one is correct, and in others both are correct. (C & D)

1 As Geoff was introduced to Mrs Snape, he realised that he *had met/ met* her before.
2 During the previous week, I *had been/ went* to the gym every evening.
3 He denied that he *had taken/ took* the money from the office.
4 I didn't know the marking would take so long until I *had read/ read* the first couple of essays.
5 The boy told me that he *had lost/ lost* his train ticket and didn't know how he would get home.
6 At the conference, scientists reported that they *had found/ found* a cure for malaria.
7 The teacher guessed that some of the children *had cheated/ cheated* in the exam.
8 Thomas explained that he *had gone/ went* home early because he felt ill.
9 The waiter took my plate away before I *had finished/ finished* eating.
10 Jane didn't want any dinner. She *had eaten/ ate* already.

5.3 Expand these sets of notes using the past perfect to begin each sentence. (E)

I/expect/operation/painful   ~~I/hope/leave/by 9.00~~   He/not mean/insult/her
Lucy/not intend/become/dentist   I/not think of/cook rabbit

1 ___I had hoped to leave by 9.00___, but I overslept and missed the train.
2 _____; she always wanted to be a vet.
3 _____, but I didn't feel a thing.
4 _____, until Derek told me how tasty it was.
5 _____, but Daphne was very offended.

Unit 6

Present perfect continuous and present perfect

A

We use the present perfect continuous to express the idea of an activity (a task, piece of work, etc.) in progress until recently or until the time of speaking:

- ☐ **Have** you **been working** in the garden *all day*? You look exhausted.
- ☐ She's **been writing** the book *since she was in her twenties* and at last it's finished.

Notice that we often use time expressions to say how long the activity has been in progress.

We don't use the present perfect continuous with verbs such as **belong, know, (dis)like**, and **understand** that describe unchanging states:

- ☐ **Have** you **known** each other long? (*not* Have you been knowing...)
- ☐ I **haven't liked** ice cream since I ate too much and was sick. (*not* I haven't been liking...)

When we talk about situations (general characteristics or circumstances) that exist until the present we often use either the present perfect or present perfect continuous:

- ☐ 'Where's Dr Owen's office?' 'Sorry, I don't know. I **haven't been working** here for long.' (*or* I **haven't worked** here for long. Present perfect continuous emphasises the *activity* of working; present perfect emphasises the *state* of having a job.)
- ☐ We've **been looking forward to** this holiday for ages. (*or* We've **looked forward to**.... Present perfect continuous emphasises a mental *process*; present perfect emphasises a mental *state*.)

B

We often use the present perfect or the present perfect continuous to talk about something that has recently finished if we can still see its results. However, we generally use the present perfect continuous with verbs that suggest extended or repeated activity. Compare:

- ☐ He's **broken** his finger and is in a lot of pain. (*not* He's been breaking...) *and*
- ☐ He's **been playing** football all afternoon and needs a shower! (*more likely than* He's played...)

We use the present perfect continuous rather than the present perfect when we draw a conclusion from what we can see, hear, etc. We often use this form to complain or criticise:

- ☐ Who's **been messing** around with my papers? They're all over the place.
- ☐ You've **been eating** chocolate, haven't you? There's some on your shirt.

When we talk about the *result* of circumstances or an activity, we use the present perfect, rather than the present perfect continuous. When we focus on the *process* we often use either the present perfect or the present perfect continuous. Compare:

- ☐ Prices **have decreased** by 7%. (*not* Prices have been decreasing by 7%.) *and*
- ☐ Prices **have been decreasing** recently. (*or* Prices **have decreased**...)
- ☐ I've **used** three tins of paint on the kitchen walls. (*not* I've been using three tins of paint on the kitchen walls.) *and*
- ☐ I've **been using** a new kind of paint on the kitchen walls. (*or* I've **used**...)

C

We use the present perfect continuous to emphasise that an activity is ongoing and repeated, while the present perfect suggests that the activity happened only once or on a specified number of occasions:

- ☐ Joseph **has been kicking** a football against the wall all day. (*more likely than* ...has kicked...)
- ☐ He **has played** for the national team in 65 matches so far. (*not* He has been playing for the national team in 65 matches so far.)

Compare:

- ☐ The workers **have been calling** for the chairman's resignation. (= emphasises a number of times, probably over an extended period) *and*
- ☐ Workers **have called** for management to begin negotiations on pay. (= maybe a number of times or only once.)

---

12   Grammar review: present perfect continuous → A16–A17; present perfect → A9–A12

Exercises

6.1 Complete the sentences with appropriate verbs, using the same one for each sentence in the pair. Use the present perfect in one sentence and the present perfect continuous in the other. Use negative forms where appropriate. (A–C)

disappear   give   move   put   read   stay   stop   swim

1 a Maria Harris .... in a rented flat since returning to Liverpool.
   b We .... at this hotel a couple of times before.
2 a With their win yesterday, Italy .... into second place in the table.
   b As house prices in the cities have risen, people .... into the countryside.
3 a All day, the police .... motorists to question them about the accident.
   b Good, the noise .... I can start concentrating on my work again.
4 a I .... any of Dickens' novels.
   b I .... this book on astrophysics for hours and I'm still only on page 6.
5 a Dr Fletcher .... the same lecture to students for the last ten years.
   b Mr Goldman .... nearly a million pounds to the charity this year.
6 a I did 20 lengths of the pool today. I .... that far since I was at school.
   b I .... and I feel exhausted.
7 a In recent years, Brazilian companies .... a lot of money into developing advanced technology.
   b The South African coal company .... the Calverton Mine up for sale.
8 a An important file .... from my office.
   b Plants and vegetables .... from my garden since we had new neighbours.

6.2 The government has just announced that it is cutting the money it gives to the Influenza Research Centre. Complete these texts about it with an appropriate form of the verb given. Use the present perfect continuous if possible; if not, use the present perfect or past simple. Indicate where more than one of these tenses is possible. (A–C and Unit 3)

a *Dr Petra Adams, the Director of the Centre, talks to a reporter:*
It's remarkable to think that since 1950 influenza (1) .... (*claim*) more than 50,000 lives in this country, and in 1957 alone around 6,000 people (2) .... (*die*). But over the last 20 years we at the Centre (3) .... (*make*) considerable progress on understanding the illness. We (4) .... (*produce*) over a hundred books and articles reporting the results of our research and in 1995 they (5) .... (*award*) the Nobel Prize for medicine to one of my colleagues. In our more recent work we (6) .... (*look*) into the effects of influenza on heart disease and we (7) .... (*also explore*) a possible link between climate change and the recent increase in the number of cases of influenza. It is a tragedy that the government (8) .... (*make*) this decision now.

b *Kenneth Sparks, the Opposition spokesperson for science, talks to a television interviewer:*
The previous government (1) .... (*invest*) huge amounts of money into the Centre and I think it's terrible that the present government (2) .... (*announce*) this cut when the number of cases of influenza (3) .... (*increase*). The Centre (4) .... (*run*) successfully for many years. But this decision is just typical of this government. It (5) .... (*neglect*) health research ever since it was elected, and (6) .... (*cut*) back on spending on science generally. Although the government says that the cut is necessary because of the recent world economic problems, I (7) .... (*find*) evidence that they (8) .... (*plan*) this for some time. I (9) .... (*speak*) to the Minister about this yesterday and (10) .... (*also write*) to the Prime Minister demanding that the decision should be reversed.

13

Unit 7

Past perfect continuous, past perfect and past continuous

A

We use the past perfect continuous to talk about something that was in progress recently before or up to a past point in time, and the past perfect when we talk about a finished activity before a past time:

- □ I'**d been finishing** some work in the garden when Sue arrived, so I didn't hear her come in. (*not* I'd finished some work in the garden when Sue arrived, so I didn't hear her come in.) *and*
- □ I'**d finished** all the ironing so I started cleaning the windows. (*not* I'd been finishing all the ironing so I started cleaning the windows.)

Sometimes we can use either the past perfect continuous or the past perfect with a very similar meaning:

- □ I'**d been working/I'd worked** hard all year, so I felt that I deserved a holiday.

B

If we talk about *how many* times something happened in a period up to a particular past time, we use the past perfect, not the past perfect continuous:

- □ How many times **had** you **met** him before yesterday? (*not* How many times had you been meeting...)
- □ I **had stayed** in the hotel twice in the 1980s. (*not* I had been staying in the hotel twice...)

C

The past perfect continuous can be used to talk about a situation or activity that went on before a particular past time and (i) finished at that time, (ii) continued beyond it, or (iii) finished shortly before it:

- □ (i) We'**d been driving** for about an hour when the engine suddenly stopped.
- □ (ii) She felt terrible during the interview because she **had been suffering** from flu since the previous day.
- □ (iii) When I last saw John, he'**d been running** and was out of breath.

If we are not interested in how long the activity went on, we can use the past continuous instead of the past perfect continuous. Compare:

- □ When the merger was announced it became apparent that the two companies **had been discussing** the possibility *since last year*. *and*
- □ A friend told me about a conversation she'd recently overheard. Two women **were discussing** their holiday plans...
- □ I first met Steve and Jane when they **had been going out** together *for five years*, and they didn't get married for another three years after that. *and*
- □ Emma met Graham when she **was going out** with his best friend.

D

Remember that we don't describe states with continuous tenses (see Unit 1), and we use the past perfect, not the past perfect continuous, even when we focus on the length of a situation up to a particular past time:

- □ We **had owned** the car for 6 months before we discovered it was stolen. (*not* We had been owning the car for 6 months...)

E

The past perfect continuous is mainly used in written texts and is less common in speech. Here are two examples of the past perfect continuous used in newspaper stories:

- □ The body of a climber who went missing in the Alps was finally found yesterday. Carl Sims **had been climbing** alone in the dangerous area of Harz Waterfall, which has claimed many lives in the past.
- □ A spokesman for the company said Morgan **hadn't been working** for them long and wasn't familiar with safety procedures: 'It was an unfortunate incident...'

Grammar review: past perfect continuous → A18; past perfect → A14–A15; past continuous → A13

Exercises

7.1 Complete the sentences with one of these verbs, using the same verb for each sentence in the pair. Use the past perfect continuous if possible; if not, use the past perfect. (A)

   apply   carry   fly   smoke   work

   1 a She .... for the company since she left school, so I wasn't surprised when she took a new job in London.
      b She .... finally .... her way up from trainee to a management position, and she celebrated her promotion with a big party.
   2 a The avalanche .... them 500 metres down the mountain but no-one was hurt.
      b She took a bottle from the bag she .... all the way from home.
   3 a Michael .... all his cigarettes and had to borrow some from Kate.
      b By the smell in the room and his guilty expression I could tell that Alex ....
   4 a We .... for visas early, but still hadn't got them by the week before the holiday.
      b She .... for jobs, without success, since leaving university.
   5 a He .... all the way from New York to be at yesterday's meeting.
      b When the plane was diverted, shortly after take-off, it .... from London to Frankfurt.

Look again at the sentences where you have used the past perfect continuous and decide when you could use the past simple instead of the past perfect in these sentences. (You may need to study Unit 5 again.)

7.2 Choose the past perfect continuous form of the verb if appropriate; if not, use the past perfect. (B–D)

   1 Mrs Bishop .... to have children for years; then she finally became pregnant at the age of 45. (*try*)
   2 This was the first time we had been to the castle, even though we .... Edinburgh a few times before. (*visit*)
   3 She bought her first watch at the age of 8. It .... two pounds. (*cost*)
   4 Meg James .... children's stories for 10 years when she got her first book published. (*write*)
   5 For some time Mark .... about passing the exams and eventually decided to change the course he was taking. (*worry*)
   6 My teacher was really annoyed with me. It was the third time I .... late for school that week. (*arrive*)
   7 I .... always .... it would be easy to get a job, and was disappointed to be rejected. (*believe*)
   8 We .... about Sue when, to our amazement, she walked through the door. (*talk*)

In which one of the sentences where you have used the past perfect continuous do you think the past continuous is more likely? (C)

7.3 Study this conversation extract. If the underlined verbs are correct, write ✓. If they are wrong, correct them using either the past perfect (active or passive) or past perfect continuous. (A–E)

   A: How was your weekend?
   B: Not great, actually. I (1) <u>'d really been looking</u> forward to a relaxing couple of days. But early on Saturday morning Mum phoned to say that Dad (2) <u>had been taking</u> ill.
   A: Oh, no! What (3) <u>had happened</u>?
   B: She (4) <u>had just been hearing</u> that he (5) <u>had been flown</u> by helicopter to hospital in Edinburgh from a village called Contin where he (6) <u>had fished</u> with my Uncle Mark.
   A: And is he okay? What's wrong with him?
   B: Well, Uncle Mark said that Dad (7) <u>had been complaining</u> of a bad headache most of yesterday, but he (8) <u>hadn't been wanting</u> to go back to the hotel and spoil the day. But then in the evening, just as they (9) <u>had stopped</u> fishing for the day, he (10) <u>had been collapsing</u>...

Present and past time: review

A Continuous and simple

When we focus on an activity itself, starting before and continuing up to (and possibly beyond) a particular point of time, rather than focusing on actions as completed events, we use *continuous* forms:

- □ Janet can't come to the phone. She's **washing** her hair.
- □ As you're **not using** your car at the moment, can I borrow it?
- □ This time yesterday I **was flying** over the Pacific.
- □ **Was** she **wearing** that red dress when you saw her?

We use *simple* forms to talk about general situations, habits, and things that are or were always true:

- □ When I **worked** as a postman I **got up** at 3 o'clock every morning.
- □ Miguel **doesn't play** golf very well.
- □ These birds **build** their nests on the ground.
- □ The earthquake **struck** the area at midday yesterday. (past simple for completed events)

We use simple forms with verbs that describe unchanging states; that is, things that stay the same:

- □ She **intends** to work hard at school and go on to university.
- □ **Did** you **understand** the instructions we were given?

However, we can use continuous forms with these verbs when they describe something happening or changing:

- □ She **was intending** to talk to Tony about the idea, but she didn't get the opportunity.
- □ I'm **understanding** physics much better now that Mr Davies is teaching us.

B Perfect

We use *perfect* verb forms to describe one event or state from the point of view of a later time. The present perfect suggests a connection between something that happened in the past and the present time. Notice, however, that the situation or event does not have to continue until the time of speaking, only to have some connection or relevance to the present time:

- □ I've **finished** the new Harry Potter book now, so you can borrow my copy if you like.
- □ **Have** you **turned** the gas off? I don't like it to be on when I'm not at home.
- □ Your nose is bleeding. **Has** somebody **hit** you?

The past perfect is used to locate a past event before another past event:

- □ I invited him out to dinner, but he said he **had** already **eaten**.
- □ By the time I picked up the phone, they **had rung off**.

C Combinations of perfect and continuous

We combine the perfect and continuous forms in the present perfect continuous to describe an activity in progress either at or recently before the time of speaking, and possibly beyond it:

- □ I **have been following** the discussions with great interest.

We can also use the present perfect continuous to talk about activities that have recently finished with some result that can be seen, heard, etc.:

- □ Look at the dirt on your clothes! **Have** you **been digging** in the garden again?

The past perfect continuous has a similar meaning. However, the point of reference is not 'now' (as it is with the present perfect continuous) but a point in the past:

- □ When we met Simon and Pat, they **had been riding**.
- □ It **had been snowing** heavily for hours and when I went to the door I couldn't open it.

Grammar review: Section A

8.1 Complete this letter from Australia using the following verbs. Use the present simple, present continuous, past simple or past continuous. (A)

In 1–10 use: **arrive**   **feel** (×2)   **get**   **go**   **know**   **spend**   **wait**   **write** (×2)

In 11–20 use: **ask**   **complain**   **enjoy**   **get**   **(not) get on**   **hear**   **look** (×2) **seem**   **start**

Dear Mum and Dad

I (1) .....*am writing*..... this letter in a hotel room in Perth. I (2) .... here a couple of hours ago after a long coach journey from Adelaide. I (3) .... pretty tired so this will only be a short note before I (4) .... to sleep.

As you (5) ...., I (6) .... last week in Adelaide with Jean and David. I (7) .... to them a month or so ago to tell them when I would be arriving, and they (8) .... at the airport for me when I (9) .... there. For the first few days I (10) .... quite jet-lagged, but I soon (11) .... over that after a few days of lazing around on the beach.

Jean and David (12) .... living in Adelaide a lot, although Jean (13) .... for a new job just now. It (14) .... that she (15) .... very well with her colleagues. Apparently they constantly (16) .... about the working conditions and it (17) .... to annoy Jean. They (18) .... me to pass on their best wishes to you.

So now I (19) .... forward to exploring Perth. I (20) .... it's a wonderful place. I'll write again in a few days.

Love, Abigail

8.2 Complete this extract from a newspaper article with the verbs given. Use the past simple, present perfect or past perfect. (B)

RONSON SACKED IN UNITED CUTS

Aston United (1) .....*have sacked*..... (*sack*) their manager, Neil Ronson. The former England football international (2) .... (*say*) that he (3) .... (*hear*) the news when he (4) .... (*return*) from a three-week holiday in Spain and that it (5) .... (*come*) as a complete shock. "There (6) .... (*be*) no hint of any problem when I (7) .... (*leave*) for the holiday."

Aston United (8) .... (*appoint*) Ronson as manager two years ago and last season they (9) .... (*finish*) second in the First Division. However, they (10) .... (*win*) only five matches so far this season.

The Chairman of the club, Peter White, last night (11) .... (*accuse*) Ronson of lack of commitment to the club. "Neil's attitude (12) .... (*disappoint*) us recently. Over the last few months he (13) .... (*spend*) more time on Spanish beaches than working with the players in Aston."…

8.3 In Unit 7 (Exercise 7.3) you read the beginning of a conversation. Here is the rest of it. If the verb in the underlined section is correct, write ✓. If it is wrong, correct it using the past simple, present perfect, past perfect, present perfect continuous or past perfect continuous as appropriate. (A–C)

A: (1) <u>Did he have</u> any health problems recently?

B: Well, he (2) <u>'s been suffering</u> from high blood pressure for some time, but we (3) <u>have thought</u> a fishing holiday in Scotland would be relaxing for him. He (4) <u>worked</u> too hard for months now, and we (5) <u>'ve been trying</u> to persuade him to have a break for ages before he finally agreed.

A: So (6) <u>have you gone</u> up to Scotland when you (7) <u>have heard</u>?

B: No, Mum (8) <u>has gone</u> up to be with him, but the doctors (9) <u>have checked</u> him over and (10) <u>had been saying</u> that it's not too serious. They (11) <u>gave</u> him some medicine to bring down his blood pressure and (12) <u>had told</u> him that he needs complete rest for a couple of months. So Mum's driving him back in the car tomorrow.

A: Well, send him my best wishes when you speak to him.

B: Thanks, I will do.

Unit 9 — Will and be going to

A
We can use either **will** or **be going to** to talk about something that is planned, or something that we think is likely to happen in the future:

- ☐ We **will** study climate change in a later part of the course. (*or* We **are going to** study...)
- ☐ Where **will** you stay in Berlin? (*or* Where **are you going to** stay...?)
- ☐ The south of the city **won't** be affected by the power cuts. (*or* ...**isn't going to be** affected...)

We often prefer **be going to** in informal contexts (see also **D**).

B
We use **will** rather than **be going to** to make a prediction based on our opinion or experience:

- ☐ Why not come over at the weekend? The children **will** enjoy seeing you again.
- ☐ 'Shall I ask Sandra?' 'No, she **won't** want to be disturbed.'

We use **be going to** rather than **will** when we make a prediction based on some present evidence:

- ☐ The sky has gone really dark. There's **going to** be a storm.
- ☐ 'What's the matter with her?' 'It looks like she's **going to** faint.'

C
To predict the future we often use **will** with **I bet** (informal), **I expect, I hope, I imagine, I reckon** (informal), **I think, I wonder,** and **I'm sure,** and in questions with **think** and **reckon:**

- ☐ *I imagine* the stadium **will** be full for the match on Saturday.
- ☐ That cheese smells awful. *I bet* nobody **will** eat it.
- ☐ When *do* you *think* you'll finish work?   ☐ *Do* you *reckon* he'll say yes?

Be going to can also be used with these phrases, particularly in informal contexts.

D
We use **will** when we make a decision at the moment of speaking (see **GR:B1**) and **be going to** for decisions about the future that have already been made (see **GR:B5**). Compare:

- ☐ I'll pick him up at 8.00. (an offer; making an arrangement now) *and*
- ☐ I'm **going to** collect the children at 8.00. (this was previously arranged)
- ☐ 'Pineapples are on special offer this week.' 'In that case, I'll buy two.' *and*
- ☐ When I've saved up enough money, I'm **going to** buy a digital camera.

However, in a formal style, we use **will** rather than **be going to** to talk about future events that have been previously arranged in some detail. Compare:

- ☐ **Are** you **going to** talk at the meeting tonight? *and*
- ☐ The meeting **will** begin at 9.00 a.m. Refreshments **will** be available from 8.30 onwards.

E
We can use **will** or **be going to** with little difference in meaning in the main clause of an *if-*sentence when we say that something (often something negative) is conditional on something else:

- ☐ If we go on like this, we'll/we're **going to** lose all our money.
- ☐ You'll/You're **going to** knock that glass over if you're not more careful.

When the future event does not depend on the action described in the *if*-clause, we use **be going to**, not **will**. This kind of sentence is mainly found in spoken English. Compare:

- ☐ I'm **going to** open a bottle of lemonade, if you want some. (= I'm going to open a bottle of lemonade. Do you want some?) *and*
- ☐ I'll open a bottle of lemonade if you want some. (= If you say you want some, I'll open a bottle.)

However, we use **will**, not **be going to**, when the main clause refers to offers, requests, promises, etc. and ability:

- ☐ If Jack phones I'll let you know. (= an offer; '..., I'm going to let you know' suggests 'I intend to let you know when Jack phones')
- ☐ If you look to your left, you'll see the lake. (= you'll be able to see; '...you're going to see...' suggests 'I know this is what you can see when you look to your left')

and when one thing is the logical consequence of another:

- ☐ If you don't switch on the monitor first, the computer **won't** come on.

Grammar review: *will* → B1–B4; *be going to* → B5

Exercises

9.1 Complete the text using the verbs given. Choose **will** ('**ll**) or **(be) going** to with each verb, depending on which is more appropriate. (A–D)

1 A: I can't come over during the day.

   B: I .... you tomorrow evening, then. (*see*)

2 The method is quite simple, and I'm sure it .... familiar to most of you already. (*be*)

3 Have you seen Karen recently? She .... another baby. (*have*)

4 A: Did you get the theatre tickets?

   B: No, I forgot all about them. I .... them tomorrow. (*book*)

5 Wherever you go in Brazil, you .... the people very friendly. (*find*)

6 John says he .... a politician when he grows up – and he's only 5 years old! (*be*)

7 Are these new skis yours? .... you .... skiing? (*take up*)

8 It's getting very humid – we .... a thunderstorm. (*have*)

9 A: We've got small, medium and large. What size do you want?

   B: I .... a large one, please. (*have*)

10 A: Shall I give Ian another ring?

    B: Yes, I expect he .... home by now. (*be*)

11 A: What are all those bricks for?

    B: I .... a wall at the side of the garden. (*build*)

12 I hear you .... your car. How much do you want for it? (*sell*)

13 You can't play football in the garden. I........................... the grass. (*cut*)

14 A: What's the matter with Paula?

    B: She says she ....

    A: She .... better with some fresh air. (*be sick – feel*)

15 A: I've been offered a new job in Manchester, so I........................... Camco.

    B: When .... your boss?

    A: I'm not sure. Perhaps I .... to see him later today. (*leave – tell – try*)

16 A: Did I tell you I .... dinner with Ken on Thursday?

    B: But we .... a film with Ray and Mary on Thursday. You've known about it for weeks.

    A: Sorry. In that case, I .... a different day with Ken. (*have – see – sort out*)

9.2 Complete the sentences with **will** ('**ll**) or **(be) going to** and an appropriate verb. If both will and **be going to** are possible, write them both. (E)

1 If you want me to, I ....'ll explain.... how the equipment works.

2 If you listen carefully, you .... an owl in the trees over there.

3 You .... your back if you try to lift that box.

4 If I give you the money .... you .... me some oranges when you're out?

5 If you press the red button, the machine ....

6 I .... Jane this weekend, if you'd like to come too.

7 He's been told that if he's late once more he ....

8 If you want to help us, we .... those trees at the bottom of the garden.

Present simple and present continuous for the future

Present simple

A

We can often use either the present simple or **will** to talk about future events that are part of some timetabled or programmed arrangement or routine. However, we prefer the present simple for fixed, unchangeable events. Compare:

- ☐ **Does** the sale **finish** on Thursday or Friday? (*or* **Will** the sale **finish**...?) *and*
- ☐ The sun **rises** at 5.16 tomorrow. (*more likely than* The sun will rise...)

We avoid the present simple when we talk about less formal or less routine arrangements, or predictions. Instead we use **will**, **be going to**, or the present continuous:

- ☐ **Are** you just **staying** in to watch TV tonight, or **are** you **coming** dancing? (*not* Do you just stay to watch TV tonight, or do you come...)
- ☐ It's only a problem in Britain now, but it **will affect** the rest of Europe soon. (*not*... but it affects the rest of Europe soon.)

B

We use the present simple, not **will**, to refer to the future –

☆ in time clauses with conjunctions such as **after**, **as soon as**, **before**, **by the time**, **when**, **while**, **until**:

- ☐ *When* you **see** Dave, tell him he still owes me some money. (*not* When you will see Dave...)
- ☐ I should be finished *by the time* you **get** back. (*not* ...by the time you will get back.)

☆ in conditional clauses with **if**, **in case**, **provided**, and **unless**:

- ☐ *Provided* the right software **is** available, I should be able to solve the problem.
- ☐ I'll bring some sandwiches *in case* we **don't find** anywhere decent to eat.

☆ when we talk about possible future events with **suppose**, **supposing**, and **what if** at the beginning of a sentence. Notice that the past simple can be used with a similar meaning:

- ☐ *Suppose* we **miss** the bus – how will we get home? (*or Suppose* we **missed**...)
- ☐ *What if* the train's late? Where shall I meet you then? (*or What if* the train **was** late?)

Present continuous

C

We can often use either the present continuous or **be going to** with a similar meaning to talk about planned future events. This use of the present continuous indicates that we have a firm intention or have made a definite decision to do something, although this may not already be arranged:

- ☐ **Are** you **seeing** the doctor again next week? (*or* **Are** you **going to see**...?)
- ☐ I'm **not asking** Tom to the party. (*or* I'm **not going to ask**...)

However, we don't use the present continuous for the future –

☆ when we make or report predictions about activities or events over which we have no control (we can't arrange these):

- ☐ I think it's **going to rain** soon.
- ☐ Scientists say that the satellite **won't cause** any damage when it falls to Earth some time this afternoon.

☆ when we talk about permanent future situations:

- ☐ People **are going to live/will live** longer in the future.
- ☐ Her new house **is going to have/will have** three floors.

D

Many people avoid **be going to + go/come** and use the present continuous forms of **go** and **come** instead:

- ☐ I'm **going** to town on Saturday. (*rather than* I'm going to go to town...)
- ☐ **Are** you **coming** home for lunch? (*rather than* Are you going to come...?)

Grammar review: present simple for the future → B6; present continuous for the future → B7

10.1 Use the present simple of one of these verbs to complete the sentences if possible. If not, use will + infinitive. (A–C)

accept	change	get	give out	go	lend	look after
miss	play	rain	read	start	stop	want

1 We .... our exam results on the 20th August.
2 Jack .... our cats while we're away next week.
3 I think I'll take an umbrella in case it ....
4 There is a reading list to accompany my lecture, which I .... at the end.
5 The new drug .... on sale in the USA next year.
6 The concert .... at 7.30, not 7.15 as it says in the programme.
7 Provided it .... raining, we'll go for a walk this afternoon.
8 What if I .... my plans and decide to stay in Taiwan longer? Will I need to renew my visa?
9 We .... Sue when she leaves, but she says she'll keep in touch.
10 Unless my parents .... me some money, I won't be able to go on holiday this year.
11 Tonight France .... Germany in a match important for both teams.
12 It is unlikely that the government .... the court's decision.
13 Supposing I .... to transfer a file from one computer to another? How do I do that?
14 By the time you .... this letter, I should be in New Zealand.

10.2 Cross out any answers that are wrong or very unlikely. If two answers are possible, consider the difference in meaning, if any, between them. (C, D and Unit 9)

1 It's not a deep cut, but it .... a scar.
   (a) will leave   (b) is going to leave   (c) is leaving
2 Did you know I .... a new car next week?
   (a) will buy   (b) am going to buy   (c) am buying
3 'I'm not sure how I'll get to the concert.' 'We can take you. We .... you up at 8.00.'
   (a) will pick   (b) are going to pick   (c) are picking
4 I'm sorry I can't come for dinner. I .... to York tonight.
   (a) will drive   (b) am going to drive   (c) am driving
5 The new road .... the journey time between the cities significantly.
   (a) will cut   (b) is going to cut   (c) is cutting
6 I have to go now. I .... you back later today.
   (a) will call   (b) am going to call   (c) am calling
7 Don't go out now. I .... lunch and it'll be cold by the time you get back.
   (a) will serve   (b) am going to serve   (c) am serving
8 Unless help arrives within the next few days, thousands ....
   (a) will starve   (b) are going to starve   (c) are starving

10.3 Complete these texts with either present simple for the future or present continuous for the future with the verbs given. If neither of these is correct, use will or be going to. (Units 9 & 10)

1 A: Alan Johnson (1) .... (*join*) us for dinner. You know, the novelist.
   B: Yes, I've read some of his books.
   A: I'm sure you (2) .... (*like*) him. His latest book (3) .... (*come*) out at the end of this week. If you want, I'm sure he (4) .... (*give*) you a signed copy.

2 A: Have you heard that BWM (1) .... (*sack*) 300 workers?
   B: That's bad news. Supposing they (2) .... (*close*) completely – that would be awful.
   A: But I've heard that they (3) .... (*build*) a new factory in Ireland. If you read today's local newspaper, you (4) .... (*see*) a long article on it.

Future continuous and future perfect (continuous)

Future continuous: I will be doing

A

We can use the future continuous to talk about something that is predicted to start before a particular point of future time, and that may continue after this point. Often it is the result of a previous decision or arrangement:

- ☐ This time next year this part of the garden **will be looking** beautiful.
- ☐ She **will be taking up** her place at university in October.
- ☐ When it goes into orbit, the spacecraft **will be carrying** 30 kilos of plutonium.

We can also use the future continuous to talk about a future activity that is part of the normal course of events or that is one of a repeated or regular series of events:

- ☐ Dr Jones **will be giving** the same talk in room 103 at 10.00 next Thursday.
- ☐ **Will you be driving** to Glasgow, as usual?

We can often use either the future continuous or the present continuous when we talk about arranged activities or events in the future (see also Unit 10). Compare:

- ☐ We **will be leaving** for Istanbul at 7.00 in the evening. (timetabled; *or* ...are leaving...) *and*
- ☐ When the race starts later this afternoon the drivers **will be hoping** for drier weather than last year. (*not* ...are hoping...; not reporting the details of a programme or timetable)

B

The future continuous is sometimes used to indicate that a future activity is pre-arranged. Using **will** can indicate willingness, intention, invitation, etc. Compare:

- ☐ Ann **will be helping** us to organise the party. (suggests a previous arrangement) *and*
- ☐ Ann**'ll help** us organise the party. (suggests she is willing to help)

When we don't want to indicate willingness, intention, invitation, etc., we prefer to use the future continuous instead of **will**. For example, if guests have stayed longer than you wanted, and you don't know when they are leaving, you might ask:

- ☐ **Will** you **be staying** with us again tonight? (asking about their plans) *rather than*
- ☐ **Will** you **stay** with us again tonight? (they might think this is an invitation)

Future perfect and future perfect continuous: I will have done and I will have been doing

C

We use the future perfect to say that something will be ended, completed, or achieved by a particular point in the future:

- ☐ *By the time you get home* I **will have cleaned** the house from top to bottom.
- ☐ I'm sure his awful behaviour **will** *soon* **have been forgotten**. (= passive form)

We use the future perfect continuous to emphasise the duration of an activity in progress at a particular point in the future:

- ☐ *On Saturday*, we **will have been living** in this house for a year.
- ☐ *Next year* I **will have been working** in the company for 30 years.

With both the future perfect and future perfect continuous we usually mention the future time (*By the time you get home...*, *On Saturday...*, etc.).

D

The future continuous, future perfect and future perfect continuous can also be used to say what we believe or imagine is happening around now:

- ☐ We could ask to borrow Jim's car. He **won't be using** it today – he went to work by bike.
- ☐ Most people **will have forgotten** the fire by now.
- ☐ Tennis fans **will have been queuing** at Wimbledon all day to buy tickets.

We can use the future perfect continuous to say what we think was happening at a point in the past:

- ☐ Motorist Alan Hesketh **will have been asking** himself whether speed cameras are a good idea after he was fined £100 last week for driving at 33 mph in a 30 mph zone.

Grammar review: future continuous → B8

Exercises

11.1 Choose a verb that can complete both sentences in the pair. Use the future continuous (will/won't be + –ing) in one sentence and will/won't + infinitive in the other. (A & B)

give   leave   move   use   work

1 a I'm sorry that the train is delayed, ladies and gentlemen, but we .... the station as soon as the driver arrives.
  b Without more cheap housing, families .... the village and find homes in town.
2 a .... you .... late at the office again? I want to know when to cook.
  b 'We need to get this order sent out before Monday.' 'Well, I .... over the weekend if that will help.'
3 a I .... my car until next week, so you can borrow it if you like.
  b My father .... a computer. He says he's very happy with his old typewriter for letters and doesn't want to change now.
4 a Is your suitcase very heavy? I .... you a hand with it if you like.
  b Dr Sankey .... evidence at the trial of James Morgan next week.
5 a He's parked his car across our drive and says he .... it. Shall I call the police?
  b The company's headquarters closes in June, when most of the staff .... to its new building in Madrid.

11.2 Use a beginning from (i), an ending from (iii), and a verb from (ii) to make sentences, as in 1. Use either the future perfect or the future perfect continuous. (C & D)

(i)	(ii)	(iii)
1 The weather forecast says that the rain…	act	…the objective we set ourselves when we took over.
2 If the company is making a profit by the end of the year then we…	achieve	…by the morning and tomorrow will be dry.
3 In two years' time Morneau…	~~clear~~	…for 50 years, and shows no sign of retiring from the theatre.
4 I am confident that I…	finish	…the report before the end of the week.
5 This book on Proust is really difficult. On Saturday I…	discover	…it for a month, and I'm still only half way.
6 Whether I've finished the report or not, by 9 o'clock I…	read	…for 12 hours without a break and I'm going home.
7 As delegates who arrived early…	work	…there have been some late changes to the conference programme.

1   The weather forecast says that the rain will have cleared by the morning and tomorrow will be dry.

11.3 Here is part of a letter from Jane to her friend Rosa, a teacher in England. Underline the correct alternative. (A–D)

Darwin, 20th December

Dear Rosa

Hope this finds you all well. I suppose by now school (1) will close/ will have closed for Christmas and you (2) will be enjoying/ will have been enjoying a rest. It's hard to believe that Tim's already 18 and that it's only a few months until he (3) will be leaving/ will have been leaving school for college.

My main news is that my brother, John, and his family (4) will have been arriving/ will be arriving next Friday as part of their big trip around the world. By the time they get here they (5) will be going/ will have been to California and New Zealand. No doubt John's children (6) will have been planning/ will plan it all out for months! They (7) won't be spending/ won't have spent all their time with me. John has to go to Perth on business, so I (8) will have kept/ will be keeping the rest of the family entertained while he's away. Then they (9) will all be going/ will all have been going to Sydney …

Be to + infinitive

A

Be to + infinitive is commonly used in news reports to talk about events that are likely to happen in the near future:

- □ Police officers **are to visit** every home in the area.
- □ The main Rome to Naples railway line **is to be reopened** today. (passive form)

It is used to talk about formal or official arrangements, formal instructions, and to give orders:

- □ You **are not to leave** the school without my permission.
- □ The European Parliament **is to introduce** a new law on safety at work.
- □ Children **are not to be left** unsupervised in the museum. (passive form)

Passive forms are often used to make orders and instructions more impersonal.

Notice that we only use **be to + infinitive** to talk about future events that can be controlled by people. Compare:

- □ In the next few years, thousands of speed cameras **are to appear** on major roads.
  (*or* ...**will appear**...) *and*
- □ Scientists say they can't predict when or where the disease **will appear** again. (*not* ...the disease is to appear again; the appearance of the disease can't be controlled)
- □ The President **is to return** to Brazil later today. (*or* ...**will return**...) *and*
- □ The comet **will return** to our solar system in around 500 years. (*not* The comet is to return...; the movement of the comet can't be controlled)

However, when **be to + infinitive** refers to the future from the past (see **Unit 14B**), we often use it to describe what happened to someone, whether they were able to influence events or not:

- □ Matthew Flinders sailed past Tasmania in 1770, but it **was to be** a further 30 years before he landed there.
- □ Clare Atkins **was to write** two more books about her experiences in Africa before her death in 1967.

B

We often use **be to + infinitive** in *if*-clauses to say that something must happen first (in the main clause) before something else can happen (in the *if*-clause):

- □ *If* the human race **is to survive**, we must look at environmental problems now.
- □ The law needs to be revised *if* justice **is to be done**. (passive form)

Compare the use of **be to + infinitive** and the present simple for the future in *if*-clauses:

- □ If Jones **is to win** gold at the next Olympics, he needs to work on his fitness. *and*
- □ If Jones **wins** gold at the next Olympics, he has said that he will retire from athletics.

Notice how the order of cause and effects in *if*-sentences is reversed with these two tenses:

- □ If Jones **is to win** gold... (= effect), he needs to work... (= cause) *and*
- □ If Jones **wins** gold... (= cause), he has said that he will retire... (= effect)

C

We can use **be about to + infinitive** to say that something will (not) happen in the very near future:

- □ I'm **about to start** work on my second novel.
- □ Appearing on TV might make her famous, but it's **not about to make** her rich.

Notice that while **be to + infinitive** is mainly used in news reports and formal contexts, we often use **be about to + infinitive** in conversation:

- □ We're just **about to eat**. Do you want to join us?
- □ I **was about to go** to bed when my brother turned up.

12.1 Complete these newspaper extracts using the verbs given. Use **be to + infinitive** if possible and **will + infinitive** if not. Use active or passive forms as necessary. (A)

1 John Stobbard has written his first new play for 15 years. Its first performance .... (*stage*) at the New Victoria Theatre.

2 The new safety system .... (*stop*) trains automatically if they pass a danger signal.

3 Stafford Boys' School .... (*merge*) with the nearby Stoke Girls' School to form a new co-educational establishment.

4 There are fears that sea levels .... (*rise*) catastrophically in the next 50 years.

Now use these verbs to do the same in 5 to 9.

become   create   increase   receive   replace   retire

5 Managing director Robin Oakland, 59, ... this summer a year early. He .... by Chris Clarke, who joined the company last year.

6 As the temperatures fall with the onset of winter, the refugee crisis .... more severe.

7 Production line staff at the Heathcote garden furniture factory in Northam .... a pay rise following a big new order from Italy.

8 Seventy new posts .... at the factory following a major investment by the parent company in the United States.

9 The recent rapid rise in house prices in the south east .... the demand for higher salaries among lower-paid workers.

12.2 Underline the correct answers. In some cases both alternatives are possible. (B & C)

1 You need to work much harder if you *have/ are to have* any chance of passing the exam.

2 My sister *is to start/ is about to start* a PhD in Physics.

3 Mrs Patel is likely to become the Foreign Minister if the party *wins/ is to win* power at the next election.

4 If you *enjoy/ are to enjoy* romantic comedies, then this is a film you must see.

5 'Can you type this letter for me?' 'Sorry, I'*m just to go/ 'm just about to go* home. It'll have to wait until tomorrow.'

6 If Beckman *recovers/ is to recover* from a foot injury, it seems certain that he will play in Saturday's match against Spain.

7 If the university *keeps/ is to keep* its international reputation, it must first invest in better facilities for students.

8 Jim Brandon has denied that he *is to resign/ is about to resign* as marketing manager.

9 If the railway system *is improved/ is to be improved*, the government should invest substantial amounts of money now.

Other ways of talking about the future

A Some phrases are commonly used to refer to actions or events in the future with a meaning similar to **be about to + infinitive** (see Unit 12C). We can use **be on the verge of.../ brink of.../ point of...** (+ -ing or noun) to say that something will happen soon:

- ☐ People **are on the verge of** starvation as the drought continues.
- ☐ Scientist **are on the brink of** making major advances in the fight against AIDS.
- ☐ I looked for my car everywhere in the car park but couldn't find it. I **was on the point of** phoning the police, when I remembered that I'd walked to work that morning.

Be on the brink of usually refers to something important, exciting, or very bad.

We use **be due to** (+ **infinitive**) to say that something is expected to happen at a particular time, **be sure/bound to** (+ **infinitive**) to say that something is likely or certain to happen, and **be set to** (+ **infinitive**) to say that something is ready to happen.

- ☐ The company's chief executive **is due to** retire next year, but following today's announcement of further losses she **is sure to** be asked to leave sooner.
- ☐ 'Will there be somewhere to get a coffee at the station?' 'Oh, yes, there's **bound to** be.'
- ☐ Her new film **is set to** be a great success.

Notice that we use **due to + noun** to give the reason for something, not to talk about the future (e.g. **Due to illness**, Pavarotti is unable to perform tonight).

Note that past tense forms of **be** can be used with these phrases to talk about future events seen from the past:

- ☐ It was his 64th birthday in 1987 and he **was due to** retire the following year.

B We use some verbs with a **to-infinitive** to talk about intentions:

- ☐ **Do you mean** to work any harder in your second year at college?
- ☐ We **guarantee** to refund your money if you are dissatisfied with the computer.

Other verbs like this include **agree, aim, expect, hope, intend, plan, promise, propose, resolve, undertake,** and **want**. The **present continuous + to-infinitive** or **present simple + to-infinitive** can be used with **aim, expect, hope, intend, plan, propose,** and **want** to talk about intentions:

- ☐ I'm **aiming** to get to Bangkok by the end of June. (or I **aim** to get...)

Some people, particularly in speech and in journalism, use **be looking + to-infinitive** to mean planning a course of action:

- ☐ We're **looking** to create 3,000 jobs in the city over the next year.

When these verbs are used with past tense forms, they are concerned with future events seen from the past (see also Unit 14):

- ☐ Jack **had resolved** to become fluent in Spanish before his 30th birthday.
- ☐ She **was expecting** to inherit her father's fortune when he died.
- ☐ The new management **had been looking** to create 20 new jobs.

C Some people use **shall** (and **shan't**) instead of **will** (and **won't**) in statements about the future with I and we. However, it is more common to use **will** (particularly its contracted form **'ll**) and **won't**:

- ☐ He was a good friend and we **shall** miss him greatly. (more commonly ...we'll miss...)
- ☐ I definitely intend to visit Canada, but I **shan't** go for the next five years. (more commonly ...I won't...)

In current English we don't usually use **shall/shan't** with other subjects (it, she, they, etc.) to talk about the future, although this is found in formal rules and in older literary styles:

- ☐ The match referee **shall** be the sole judge of fair play.
- ☐ All people of the world **shall** live together as brothers.

Exercises

13.1 Expand the notes to complete the sentences, using the phrases in A.

due – announce	verge – become	bound – forget	brink – go	set – make
point – phone	~~sure – prove~~	set – rise	brink – sign	point – turn back
verge – quit	due – undergo			

1 The government's tax increases are ......*sure to prove*...... unpopular, especially among low-paid workers.

2 The snow was getting heavier, and I was .... when I saw lights from a house across the fields.

3 I have always wanted to own a sports car, and now my dream is .... a reality.

4 The Finance Minister is .... his economic plans for the year to the public later today.

5 The number of new jobs in London is increasing and is .... even more dramatically in the next few years.

6 We were .... a multi-million dollar contract with the oil company when it was taken over by its main rival.

7/8 Can you bring some paper plates when you come to the party tonight? I was .... Kate to ask her to bring some, but you know how unreliable she is. She's .... them.

9/10 Tennis star Sancho Gomez is .... a second operation on his injured shoulder. He was .... tennis earlier this year after a first operation was unsuccessful.

11/12 EU agriculture ministers are .... an important announcement on increasing support to farmers when they meet in Brussels on Monday. 'Many farmers are .... out of business,' said the Italian representative, 'and the matter must be decided very soon.'

13.2 Complete the sentences with these verb pairs. Use either the present simple or present continuous for the first verb. If both tenses are possible, write them both. (B)

aim – to study	expect – to finish	~~look – to replace~~	intend – to move
propose – to deal	resolve – to give up	guarantee – to find	

1 My computer is now 5 years old, and I ....*'m looking to replace*.... it with a faster one.

2 In the first half of the course we'll study microbiology, and in the second half I .... with genetic engineering.

3 We haven't completed the work yet, but we .... it later this week.

4 I haven't done much work at college so far, but I .... harder during the rest of the course.

5 Every New Year he .... smoking, but by February he has started again.

6 We can't provide the spare parts ourselves, but we .... a supplier who can.

7 At the moment I commute for over three hours a day, but I .... closer to my work in the next few months.

13.3 Underline the possible answers. (C)

1 I have passed your letter on to the head of department who *shall/ will* reply as soon as possible.

2 Sorry, but I *shan't/ won't* be able to give you a lift after all.

3 I think your parents *shall/ will* be very happy with your decision.

4 Only people over the age of 18 on 31st December *shall/ will* be eligible to vote in the referendum.

5 You *shan't/ won't* want to eat your dinner tonight after all that chocolate.

The future seen from the past

There are a number of ways of talking about an activity or event that was in the future at a particular point in the past. In order to express this idea, we can use the past tenses of the verb forms we would normally use to talk about the future. These forms are often used in reporting (see **Units 32–36**). Compare the following sentences:

The future from now...	*The future from the past...*
□ I haven't got much money, so I think I'll **stay** at home this summer.	□ Maureen decided that she **would stay** at home for the summer.
□ I'm **not going to say** anything about the exams today, because I don't have time.	□ I **wasn't going to say** anything about the exams, but the students asked me to.
□ I'm **having** a meeting with my tutor tomorrow to discuss my work.	□ I couldn't go to the match because I **was having** a meeting with my tutor.
□ **Will** you **be going** alone, or is Jane going with you?	□ At the time, I thought I **would be going** alone, but then Tom said he wanted to come.
□ The exam **will have finished** by 3 o'clock, so I'll see you then.	□ The exam was so easy that most people **would have finished** after 30 minutes.
□ There **is to be** a meeting of ministers this evening.	□ It was announced that there **was to be** a meeting of ministers that evening.
□ When the school closes, all the teachers and children **are to be moved** to one nearby.	□ As she approached retirement she heard that she **was to be moved** to a post in a nearby school.
□ As the bell **is about to go** for the end of the lesson, you can pack your books away.	□ The bell **was about to go** when all the children started to pack their books away.

If the future seen from the past is still in the future for the speaker, then either form is possible:
- □ It was announced this morning that there **is/was to be** a statement this evening.

In some cases we don't know whether the activity or event happened or not. Compare:
- □ I didn't phone to give him the news because we **were seeing** each other later. He was very upset when I told him. (= we saw each other) *and*
- □ We **were seeing** each other later that day, but I had to phone and cancel. (= we didn't see each other)
- □ They left the house at 6.00 a.m. and **would reach** Edinburgh some 12 hours later. (= they reached Edinburgh) *and*
- □ He was sure that the medical tests **would show** that he was healthy. (= we don't know whether he was healthy or not)

To talk about an activity or event that was in the future at a particular point in the past, we can use **was/were to + infinitive** (for things that actually happened) and **was/were to have + past participle** (for things that were expected, but didn't happen):
- □ At the time she was probably the best actor in the theatre company, but in fact some of her colleagues **were to become** much better known.
- □ He **was to find out** years later that the car he had bought was stolen.
- □ The boat, which **was to have taken** them to the island, failed to arrive.
- □ There **was to have been** a ban on smoking in restaurants, but restaurant owners have forced the council to reconsider.

Note, however, that in less formal contexts we would often more naturally use **be supposed to**:
- □ I **was supposed to help**, but I was ill. (*more natural than* I was to have helped...)

and that **was/were to + infinitive** can be used informally to talk about things that didn't happen:
- □ We **were to see** each other that day, but I had to phone and cancel. (*or* We **were to have seen**.../We **were supposed to see**...)

14.1 Write ✓ if the underlined parts are correct. If they are wrong, correct them. (A)

1 I'm going to do the washing, but we'd run out of washing powder.

2 The concert tonight would be over by about 9.30. We could eat after that.

3 When we were passing Mike's house, we thought we'd drop in and see him.

4 'Where shall I hang my coat?' 'Sorry, I thought Dawn will have shown you. The cloakroom is through there.'

5 The manager of Newtown United said that the team is to be announced at 9.00 tomorrow.

6 The second half was about to start, so shall we go back to our seats now?

7 I knew that by the morning I would be feeling exhausted, but I just couldn't refuse her invitation to go dancing.

8 'Where's Alan? He is supposed to be here yesterday, and there's still no sign of him.' 'I'm about to ask the same question.'

9 I didn't phone Tom this morning because I was going to see him when I've finished work.

10 DNA testing was to be used by police in the search for the missing Dublin schoolboy. His parents have welcomed the news.

11 We are meeting at 7.00 in the Globe coffee bar. Can you be there, too?

12 We didn't expect that having a rabbit as a pet will cause so many problems.

In which *three* cases can we use either a past or present tense form in the underlined parts?

14.2 Choose the more appropriate alternative, (a) or (b), to complete these sentences. (B)

1 The meeting was to have taken place in the hall,...
   a but had to be cancelled at the last moment.   b and was well attended.

2 She was to have appeared with Elvis Presley in his last film...
   a and was a tremendous success.   b but the part went to her sister.

3 Later, in Rome, I was to meet Professor Pearce...
   a but he left before I got there.
   b and was very impressed by his knowledge of Italian culture.

4 The twenty police officers who were to have gone off duty at 8.00...
   a went to the Christmas party.   b had to remain in the police station.

5 It was to take 48 hours to get to Japan...
   a and we were exhausted when we arrived.   b but we managed to do it in only a day.

6 After the war he was to teach at London University...
   a but no money was available to employ him.   b for 10 years.

7 The bridge was to have been completed this year...
   a but a number of accidents have led to delays.
   b and is to be opened by the president next month.

8 The new road was to have a major impact on traffic in the busy town centre,...
   a making life much easier for commuters.   b but the crowded roads continued.

9 The construction of the cathedral was to have begun in 1650...
   a but a shortage of labour delayed the start for a further 20 years.
   b and go on for over 80 years.

10 We were to stay with Vince in Lisbon...
   a many times before he moved to Madrid.   b but he moved to Madrid.

Can, could, be able to and be allowed to

Can, could and be able to: talking about ability

A We sometimes use **be able to** instead of **can** and **could** to talk about ability. However, we avoid **be able to** –

☆ when we talk about something that is happening as we speak:
  □ Watch me, Mum; I **can** stand on one leg. (*not* ...I'm able to stand on one leg.)

☆ before passives:
  □ CDs **can** now *be copied* easily. (*rather than* CDs are now able to be copied...)

☆ when the meaning is 'know how to':
  □ **Can** you cook? (*rather than* Are you able to cook?)

B If we talk about a single achievement, rather than a general ability in the past, we usually use **be able to** rather than **could**. Compare:
  □ Sue **could** play the flute quite well. (*or* ...was able to...; a general ability) *and*
  □ She swam strongly and **was able to** cross the river easily, even though it was swollen by the heavy rain. (*not* She swam strongly and could cross...; a specific achievement)

However, **could** is usually more natural –

☆ in negative sentences:
  □ I tried to get up but I **couldn't** move. (*rather than* ...I wasn't able to move.)

☆ with verbs of the senses – e.g. **feel, hear, see, smell, taste** – and with verbs of 'thinking' – e.g. **believe, decide, remember, understand**:
  □ I **could** *remember* the crash, but nothing after that. (*rather than* I was able to remember...)

☆ after the phrases **the only thing/place/time**, and after **all** when it means 'the only thing':
  □ *All* we **could** see were his feet. (*rather than* All we were able to...)

☆ to suggest that something almost didn't happen, particularly with **almost, hardly, just, nearly**:
  □ I **could** *nearly* touch the ceiling. (*rather than* I was nearly able to...)

Can and could: talking about possibility

C To talk about the theoretical possibility of something happening we use **could**, not **can**. However, we use **can**, not **could**, to say that something is possible and actually happens. Compare:
  □ It **could** be expensive to keep a cat. (= if we had one, it could or it may not be expensive) *and*
  □ It **can** be expensive to keep a cat. (= it can be, and it sometimes is)

We use **can't**, not **couldn't**, to say that something is theoretically or actually impossible:
  □ There **can't** be many people in the world who haven't watched television.
  □ The doctor **can't** see you this morning; he's busy at the hospital.

D We use **can** to indicate that there is a very real possibility of a future event happening. Using **could** suggests that something is less likely or that there is some doubt about it. Compare:
  □ We **can** stay with Jim in Oslo. (= we will be able to stay) *and*
  □ We **could** stay with Jim in Oslo. (= it's possible; if he's there)

Could and be allowed to: talking about permission

E To say that in the past someone had *general* permission to do something – that is, to do it at any time – we can use either **could** or **was/were allowed to**. However, to talk about permission for one *particular* past action, we use **was/were allowed to**, but not **could**. Compare:
  □ Anyone **was allowed to** fish in the lake when the council owned it. (*or* ...could fish...) *and*
  □ Although he didn't have a ticket, Ken **was allowed to** come in. (*not* ...could come in.)

In negative sentences, we can use either **couldn't** or **wasn't/weren't allowed to** to say that permission was not given in general *or* particular situations:
  □ We **couldn't/weren't allowed to** open the presents until Christmas morning.

Grammar review: *can, could* → C1–C4; *be able to* → C5–C6; *be allowed to* → C7

15.1 Underline the correct or more natural answer. If both answers are possible, underline them both. (A & B)

1 Valuables *can/ are able to* be left in the hotel safe. Please ask at the reception desk.
2 We *could/ were able to* finish the football match before it started snowing too heavily.
3 The rebels *could/ were able to* draw on the support of over 20,000 soldiers.
4 *Could you/ Were you able to* understand Professor Larsen's lecture? I found it really difficult.
5 'Do you want a game?' 'Sorry, I *can't/ 'm not able to* play chess.'
6 Look at me, I *can/ 'm able to* ride my bike without any help.
7 When the fire officers arrived they *could/ were able to* put out the flames in a couple of minutes.
8 The air was so polluted in the city centre, I *could hardly/ was hardly able to* breathe.
9 I knew John had been smoking. I *could/ was able to* smell the cigarettes when I came into the room.
10 *Can you/ Are you able to* drive without your glasses?
11 No changes *can/ are able to* be made to this rail ticket after purchase.
12 He *could/ was able to* untie the ropes without the guards noticing.
13 She looked all over the house, but *couldn't/ wasn't able to* find her keys anywhere.
14 I was very busy at work, but I *could/ was able to* have a couple of days off last week.

15.2 Complete these texts with **can, could** and **be allowed to**. Use negative forms where necessary. Where two answers are possible, give them both. (A–E)

a

We went camping in the north of Spain last July. As you probably know, it
(1) .... rain a lot on the coast, even in mid-summer, and the day we
arrived we (2) .... believe how heavy the rain was. Eventually we found
a place to camp, in a field next to a beach. We had a new tent – the
advertisement for it said, 'This tent (3) .... be assembled in two minutes
with no previous experience.' What a joke! Now, there (4) .... be many
people who haven't had difficulty putting up a tent at some time, but it took us
more than two hours. And then, just as it was finished, a man came along and
said that we (5) .... camp there – it was private property. So we had to
take the tent down again. Then Sue just said, 'Well, we (6) .... stay here
all night. Let's go to that hotel in the last village we drove through.' Unfortunately,
when we got there they were full. But they were very kind and we (7) ....
camp at the end of their garden!

b

It is often said that sports coaches (1) .... be strict, but athlete Peter Black's
was incredibly hard on him in the year before the Olympic Games. For instance, Peter
(2) .... stay up later than 9.00, although on his birthday he (3) ....
watch television until 10.00 as it was a special occasion! Of course, all Peter
(4) .... think of was going out with his friends in the evening, and he
(5) .... hardly wait for the Games to finish and get back to a normal life. When
he complained, his coach just said, 'Trust me and you'll win gold – you (6) ....
lose!' And his coach was right. He won a gold medal in the 400 metres in a world record
time. And on the night of his victory Peter (7) .... celebrate – by staying up
until 11 o'clock! 'But no later,' said his coach. 'The World Championships are only two
years away.'

Unit 16 — Will, would and used to

A   We can use **will** (for the present) and **would** (for the past) to talk about characteristic behaviour or habits:

- Every day Dan **will** come home from work and turn on the TV.
- At school she **would** always sit quietly and pay attention.

and about things that are or were always true:

- Cold weather **will** kill certain plants.
- During the war, people **would** eat all kinds of things that we don't eat now.

(For the use of **will** to talk about the future, see **Unit 9**.)

We don't use **will** or **would** in this way to talk about a *particular* occasion. Compare:

- Each time I gave him a problem he **would solve** it for me. *and*
- Last night I gave him a problem and he **solved** it for me. (*not* Last night I gave him a problem and he would solve it for me.)

However, we can use **will not** (**won't**) and **would not** (**wouldn't**) in either case. Compare:

- He **would/wouldn't** walk the 5 miles to his place of work. (characteristic behaviour) *and*
- She **wouldn't** say what was wrong when I asked her.

B   In speech, we can stress **will** or **would** to criticise people's characteristic behaviour or habits. It often suggests that criticisms have been made before but ignored:

- She just <u>won't</u> do the washing up when I ask her.
- I was happy when Sam left. He <u>would</u> talk about people behind their backs.

We can also criticise a person directly or express disapproval of something they have done or do regularly using **will**:

- 'I feel sick.' 'Well, if you <u>will</u> eat so much, I'm not surprised.' (indicating disapproval)

C   We can use use **will** to draw conclusions or state assumptions about things that are the case now (see also **Unit 9B**):

- Jack **will** be at home by now. Let's go and see him.
- You **will** know that John and Sandra are engaged. (= I believe you already know)

D   When we talk about repeated events in the past that don't happen now we can use either **would** or **used to + infinitive**. However, we can use **would** only if the time reference is clear. Compare:

- We **used to play** in the garden. (*not* We would play...; time reference not given) *and*
- Whenever we went to my uncle's house, we **would/used to play** in the garden.

We can use **used to** but not **would** when we talk about past states that have changed:

- The factory **used to** be over there.   Didn't you **use to** smoke at university?

We don't use either **used to** or **would** when we say exactly how many times in total something happened, how long something took, or that a single event happened at a given past time:

- We **visited** Switzerland four times during the 1970s. (*not* We would/used to visit...)
- She **went** to Jamaica last month. (*not* She would/used to go to Jamaica last month.)

E   To talk about an *unreal past* situation – that is, an imaginary situation or a situation that might have happened in the past, but didn't – we use **would have + past participle**:

- I **would have been** happy to see him, but I didn't have time.
- My grandmother **wouldn't have approved** of the exhibition.

However, when we want to indicate that we think a past situation actually happened, we prefer **will have + past participle**:

- As you **will have noticed**, he's got new glasses. (*rather than* ...would have noticed...)
- Most people **won't have seen** last night's lunar eclipse. (*rather than* ...wouldn't have seen...)

   Grammar review: *will* and *would* → C8–C12; *used to* → C13–C14

Exercises

16.1 If possible, complete these sentences with **will** (or **won't**) or **would** (or **wouldn't**) followed by one of these verbs. If it is not possible to use **will** or **would**, use a verb in the past simple. (A & C)

come   decide   eat   help   invite   keep   remember

1 Amy works really hard. Every afternoon she .... home from school at 4.15 and do an hour of piano practice.

2 Richard phoned yesterday and .... me out for dinner.

3 When Dominic was young he .... any green vegetables.

4 The creaking noises in the old house .... me awake until I became accustomed to them.

5 I'm sure that many people .... seeing Sarah Thomas on television in the 1980s.

6 Whenever I had a problem with my maths homework, Sam .... me.

7 After standing on the bathroom scales, I .... that I needed to lose some weight.

16.2 If necessary, correct these sentences using **would** or **used to**. If neither **would** nor **used to** is correct, use a past simple verb form. (D)

1 I would enjoy studying Latin when I was at school.

2 Orwell would spend winters in Spain and summers in England.

3 We would live in a bungalow on the south coast, and then we moved to a flat in London.

4 You used to teach at Halston University, didn't you?

5 On Saturdays and Sundays the ferry used to take tourists across to the island.

6 The committee would meet four times last week, but still no decision has been reached.

16.3 Complete these sentences with **will have** or **would have** and the past participle of one of these verbs. (E)

buy   **hear**   **hurt**   **notice**   **prefer**   **say**   **record**

1 'I wanted to watch *The Simpsons* last night, but I missed it.' 'I'm certain Derek .... it. We can go over to his place to see it.'

2 Don't accept lifts from strangers – as my mother ....

3 I don't think the dog .... anyone, but I was still glad when the owner took it away.

4 I'm sure by now you .... about yesterday's robbery at the supermarket.

5 My parents weren't very affectionate towards me. I always thought they .... a daughter.

6 Sampras's rivals .... the difficulties he had with his shoulder in the tournament last week.

7 'Did you like the present Joan gave you for your birthday?' 'Well, an umbrella stand isn't something I .... myself, but I suppose it might be useful.'

16.4 Suggest completions to these responses as in the last example of **B**. Show that you are criticising or expressing disapproval. (B)

'I think I'm putting on weight.' 'Well, if you **will** .... ,'

'I've got a headache.' 'Well, if you **will** .... ,'

'I'm really hot.' 'Well, if you **will** .... ,'

May and might: possibility

A **May** and **might** often have a similar meaning when we talk about possibility. However, we prefer **may** in academic or formal language to talk about the characteristics or behaviour of something:

☐ The seeds from the plant **may** grow up to 20 centimetres in length.

and in speech we prefer **might** to say what we will possibly do in the future:

☐ I **might** paint the kitchen purple.

B We don't use **may** to ask questions about the possibility of something happening. Instead we use, for example, **could(n't)** or the phrase **be likely**:

☐ **Could** it be that you don't want to leave? (*not* May it be that you ...?)

☐ **Are** you **likely** to be in Spain again this summer? (*not* May you be in Spain...?)

It is possible to use **might** in this type of question, but it is rather formal:

☐ **Might** they be persuaded to change their minds?

Note that we can use **may** in formally asking for permission and offering help:

☐ **May** I leave now?　　　　　　　☐ **May** I help you?

C **Might** (not 'may') + **bare infinitive** is sometimes used to talk about what was *typically* the case in the past. This is a formal or literary use:

☐ During the war, the police **might** *arrest* you for criticising the king.

☐ Years ago children **might** *be sent* down mines at the age of six. (passive form)

We can also use **could** + **bare infinitive** in examples like this to talk about past ability (see Unit 15). For example, 'During the war, the police could arrest you...' means that the police were legally able to arrest you.

D When we say that a person or thing compensates to some extent for a limitation or weakness by having another characteristic, we can use a pattern with **may/might not** + **bare infinitive** ...but... or **may/might not have** + **past participle**...but...:

☐ The painting **may not** *be* a masterpiece, **but** you've got to admit that the colours are striking.

☐ She **might not** *have danced* very gracefully, **but** she had a lot of energy and enthusiasm.

E We use **may/might** (not 'can') + **have** + **past participle** and **may/might** (not 'can') + **be** + **-ing** to talk about possible events in the past, present and future:

☐ Do you think Jean **may/might have completed** the report by now? (past)

☐ His maths **may/might have improved** by the time the exam comes round. (future)

☐ Malcolm isn't in his office. He **may/might be working** at home today. (present)

☐ When I go to Vienna I **may/might be staying** with Richard, but I'm not sure yet. (future)

Note that **could** can be used in the same patterns instead of **may** or **might**:

☐ Do you think Jean **could have completed** the report by now?

We can use **may/might have been** + **-ing** to talk about possible situations or activities that went on over a period of past time:

☐ David didn't know where the ball was, but he thought his sister **might have been playing** with it before she left for school.

F We can use **might/could** + **have** + **past participle** to criticise someone because they didn't do something we think they should have:

☐ She's gone without us. She **might/could have waited**!

☐ You **might/could have done** the ironing instead of leaving it all to me.

We usually stress **might** or **could** in sentences like this.

Grammar review: → C15–C19

17.1 Complete the sentences with either **may** or **might**, whichever is more likely. If neither is possible, suggest an alternative completion. (A & B)

1 We .... go to Majorca for our holiday this summer.
2 The planet Venus .... be seen clearly in the night sky during this month.
3 .... you see Becky this weekend?
4 I feel really sore after playing tennis. I think I .... have a bath.
5 'Someone's left their coat.' '........................ it be Ken's?'
6 Exceeding the stated dose .... cause drowsiness.

17.2 Complete the sentences with **may** or **might** followed by one of the following forms of the verb in brackets: **be + past participle**, **have + past participle**, **be + –ing**, **have been + –ing**. If both **may** and **might** are possible, indicate this. (C & E)

1 There's a man lying down on the pavement over there. Do you think he .... himself? (*hurt*)
2 I .... you this before. I can't remember. (*tell*)
3 Is that John's car that just stopped? He .... for us. (*wait*)
4 In the early 19th century a person .... to Australia for stealing as little as a loaf of bread. (*send*)
5 'Ann looks exhausted.' 'I suppose she ....' (*run*)
6 I've heard that the newsagent's is losing a lot of money and it .... down. (*close*)
7 Real Madrid started well and .... an early lead when Figo hit the post, but Barcelona scored first after 20 minutes. (*take*)
8 As little as 50 years ago a worker still .... for being ill. (*dismiss*)
9 'When will the painting be ready?' 'Well, I .... it by this evening.' (*finish*)
10 The race had to be stopped because the oil on the track .... an accident. (*cause*)

17.3 Complete these sentences in any appropriate way. (D)

1 He may not be the best singer in the world, but ....
2 Hugh's old car might not be terribly comfortable, but ....
3 Her English grammar may not be very accurate, but ....

Now expand these notes to complete the sentences.

sound/ exciting   agree/ him   express/ feelings openly   ~~work/ quickly~~

4 _He may/might not work very quickly_ , but at least he's very reliable.
5 .... , but his opinions on architecture certainly make you think.
6 .... , but the new museum of fishing is actually very good.
7 .... , but she is really very fond of you.

A We use **must** and **must not** in formal rules and regulations and in warnings:
- ☐ Bookings **must** be made at least seven days before departure.
- ☐ The government **must not** be allowed to appoint judges.

In spoken English we often use **must** and **mustn't** (= must not) to propose a future arrangement, such as a meeting or social event, without making detailed plans:
- ☐ We **must** get together more often. ☐ We **mustn't** leave it so long next time.

We can also use I **must**... to remind ourselves to do something:
- ☐ I **must** phone Steve when I get home. I said I'd call him last night, but I forgot.

B To draw a conclusion about –
- ☆ something that happened in the past we use **must + have + past participle**:
  - ☐ That's not Kate's car. She **must have borrowed** it from her parents.
- ☆ something happening at or around the time of speaking we use **must be + -ing**:
  - ☐ I can't hear anyone moving around upstairs. You **must be imagining** things.
- ☆ something that is likely to happen in the future we use **must be going to** or **must be + -ing**:
  - ☐ 'What are all those workmen doing?' 'I think they **must be going to** dig up the road.'
  - ☐ I was wrong about the meeting being today. It **must be happening** <u>next</u> Friday.
- ☆ a present situation we use **must be**, or **have (got) to be** in informal speech:
  - ☐ Their goalkeeper **has got to** be at least two metres tall! (*or* ...**must be**...)

We can use **must have to** to say that we conclude something based on what we know about a present situation and **must have had to** to conclude something about a past situation:
- ☐ I can't start the computer. You **must have to know** a password. (= a password is necessary)
- ☐ John wasn't at home when I went round. He **must have had to go** out unexpectedly.

Note that we can't say 'must've to' or 'must have got to/ must've got to' (but we can say **must've had to**).

C In questions that hope for or expect a negative answer we prefer **have (got) to**, although in formal contexts **must** is sometimes used:
- ☐ Do we **have to** answer <u>all</u> the questions? (*or* **Have** we **got to**...?; **Must** we...? is also possible but rather formal)

We use **have to** in questions that imply a criticism. **Must** can also be used, although some people think this is rather old-fashioned. We usually stress **have** and **must** in sentences like this:
- ☐ Do you <u>have</u> to play your trumpet here? It's deafening me! (*or more formally* <u>**Must**</u> you play...?)

D Sometimes we can use either **have to** or **have got to**. However –
- ☆ we use **have to** with frequency adverbs such as **always, never, normally, rarely, sometimes**, etc:
  - ☐ I *often* **have to** work at the weekend to get everything done.
- ☆ with the past simple we use **had to** especially in questions and negative sentences:
  - ☐ When **did** you **have to** give it back? (*not* When had you got to give it back?)
  - ☐ We **didn't have to** wait too long for an answer. (*not* We hadn't got to wait too long...)
- ☆ if **have** is contracted (e.g. I've, He's, It'd) then we must include **got**:
  - ☐ The experiment has failed twice before, so it**'s got to** work this time. (*not* ...so it's to work this time.)
- ☆ we don't use **have got to** with other modal verbs:
  - ☐ Employees *will* **have to** accept the new conditions or be dismissed. (*not* Employees will have got to accept...)

Notice also that **have got to** is often preferred in informal speech.

Grammar review: → C20–C24

18.1 Complete these sentences with one of these forms: **must have + past participle; must + bare infinitive; must be + –ing; or must have (had) to.** Use the verbs given. (B)

1 When I left my laptop on the train I thought I'd never see it again. But someone .... it and handed it in to the lost property office. (*find*)

2 Janine owns a big car and a yacht. She .... incredibly rich. (*be*)

3 'Everyone's going into the hall.' 'The meeting .... soon. Let's go.' (*start*)

4 Without things like washing machines and dishwashers our grandparents .... much harder in the kitchen than we do today. (*work*)

5 'Where's the camera?' 'If it's not in the cupboard, Ken .... it. He said he was going to take some photos of the city centre today.' (*use*)

6 The children are putting balloons outside their house. They .... a party. (*have*)

7 I didn't think Bob was coming to the meeting. He .... his mind. (*change*)

8 'I wonder how you get permission to go into the building.' 'I suppose you .... some form of identification.' (*show*)

9 'I thought Paul would be home.' 'He .... Jenny to work. He said he would.' (*take*)

10 Look at all those birds. There .... at least a thousand of them. (*be*)

18.2 Write new sentences with a similar meaning. Use **have/has got to** where it is possible or preferable; otherwise use **have/has to.** (D)

1 It is necessary to do all of this photocopying before lunchtime. _All of this photocopying has got to be done/has to be done before lunchtime._

2 It is rarely necessary to ask Suzanne to tidy her room. _Suzanne_

3 Is it necessary for us to hand in the homework tomorrow? _Have_

4 It wasn't necessary for me to go to the hospital after all. _I_

5 Was it necessary for Ben to go alone? _Did_

6 It is sometimes necessary for Don to start work at 6.30. _Don_

7 It is necessary to extend the college to accommodate the growing number of students. _The college_

8 It may be necessary for us to cancel our holiday because my mother is ill. _We_

18.3 Where necessary, make corrections in the underlined parts of this email message. (A–D)

From:	wendys@nex.net.uk
To:	marge@ex.com.uk
Subject:	A break in!
Attachments:	*none*

Hello Marge

Sorry I haven't been in touch for a while. You (1) <u>must have been wondering</u> what's been happening. Well, I must admit I've had a pretty awful week. When I got home from work last Monday, the front door was wide open. The door's very stiff, and I (2) <u>always have got to pull</u> it very hard to shut it. My neighbour's always saying, "(3) <u>Have you to bang</u> the door so hard?" When I went in I found that the house had been burgled. They (4) <u>must have climbed</u> over the fence in the back garden. None of the windows and doors were damaged, so someone very small (5) <u>must have to squeeze</u> through the tiny window in the kitchen. I suppose I (6) <u>must leave</u> it open, but I didn't expect anyone to be able to get in. Then they (7) <u>must have come</u> through the house and opened the front door for the others. Of course, the first thing I did was to call the police and I (8) <u>mustn't wait</u> very long for them to get here. Fortunately, the only thing that was taken was my television. I think the burglars (9) <u>must be disturbed</u>, perhaps when the postman came. So now (10) <u>I've to get</u> a new lock for the front door and replace the television, and I (11) <u>must put</u> some locks on the windows. I suppose I (12) <u>may must get</u> a burglar alarm, too. I must say I've never really wanted one, but needs must!

Anyway, (13) <u>I've to go</u>. Hope the family is well. Julie (14) <u>must get</u> ready to go back to university. And you (15) <u>must be busy</u> with the new school year just about to start. When you have time, we (16) <u>have to get</u> together for a weekend.

All the best for now,
Wendy

Can you find three other common expressions with **must**?

Need(n't), don't need to and don't have to

We can use **need** as an ordinary verb or as a modal verb (followed by a bare infinitive). As a modal verb it doesn't change its tense and doesn't add '-s' for the third person singular. Compare:

    ☐ I **needed** to leave early. *or*   ☐ She's thirsty. She **needs** a drink. (= ordinary verb) *and*
    ☐ You **needn't** *speak* so loudly. (= modal verb)

When it is a modal verb **need** is most commonly used in negative sentences, often with verbs like **bother, concern, fear, panic, worry**:

    ☐ I've already cleaned the car so you **needn't** *bother* to do it.
    ☐ Judges in England **need not** *retire* until they are 75.
    ☐ I was very nervous before the interview, but I **needn't** *have worried*. Everyone was very friendly and I got the job.

It is sometimes used in questions, but we prefer to use **need** as an ordinary verb or **have to**:

    ☐ **Need** you **go** so soon? (= modal verb; less common and rather formal)
    ☐ **Do** you **need to go** so soon? (= ordinary verb) *or*   ☐ **Do** you **have to go** so soon?

It is rarely used in affirmative sentences (that is, not questions or negatives), but is sometimes found in written English, particularly in fiction:

    ☐ We **need** *have* no fear for Nicole, she can take care of herself.

In other styles of formal written English it is used in this way with negative words such as **hardly, never, nobody/no-one**, and **only**:

    ☐ The changes **need** *only* be small to make the proposals acceptable. (*less formally* The changes only need to be...)
    ☐ *Nobody* ever **need** know about the money. (*less formally* Nobody ever needs to know...)
    ☐ 'I don't want my parents to know.' 'They **need** *never* find out.' (*less formally* They never need to find out.)

To give permission not to do something we can use either **needn't** or **don't need to**:

    ☐ You **needn't cut** the grass, I'll do it later. (*or* You **don't need to cut** the grass...)

To talk about a general necessity, we prefer **don't need to**:

    ☐ You **don't need to be** over 18 to get into a disco. (*rather than* You needn't be...)

We can often use either **needn't** or **don't have to** with little difference in meaning to say that it is unnecessary to do something:

    ☐ You **needn't** whisper. Nobody can hear us. (*or* You **don't have to**...)

However, some people prefer **needn't** when it is the speaker who decides the lack of necessity, and **don't have to** when external rules or somebody else's actions make something unnecessary. Compare:

    ☐ As you worked late yesterday you **needn't** come in until 10.00 tomorrow morning. (the speaker's decision) *and*
    ☐ We've been told that we **don't have to** be at work until 10.00 tomorrow. (reporting someone else's decision.)

We can use **needn't** (or **don't have to**) to say that something is not necessarily true. We don't use **mustn't** in this way (see also Unit 18C):

    ☐ Volcanoes **needn't** erupt constantly to be classified as 'active'. (*or* Volcanoes **don't have to** erupt...; *not* Volcanoes mustn't erupt...)
    ☐ Nowadays it **needn't** cost a fortune to own a powerful computer. (*or* Nowadays it **doesn't have to** cost...; *not* Nowadays it mustn't cost...)

19.1 Match the sentence beginnings and ends. Join them with **needn't** and the bare infinitive of one of the following verbs. (A)

bother   change   concern   panic   worry

1 I'll give you a lift to the station so you...   ...the details on the form.

2 The questions are in the book so you...   ...yourself with his safety.

3 All the windows have screens so you...   ...to copy them down.

4 Your son is being looked after by friends so you...   ...about booking a taxi.

5 The new tax laws don't come into force until next year so you...   ...about being bitten by mosquitoes.

19.2 Rewrite the following in a formal style using **need**. (A)

1 It is hardly necessary for us to remind you that the money is now due.

We need hardly remind you that the money is now due.

2 It is only necessary for us to look at the population projections to see the seriousness of the problem.

3 With such a lead in the opinion polls it is hardly necessary for the Democrats to bother campaigning before the election.

4 It is not necessary for anyone to know who paid the ransom to the kidnappers.

5 After such a huge lottery win, it is not necessary for him to work again.

19.3 Underline the more likely answer. If they are equally likely, underline them both. (B)

1 In most developed countries, people *needn't/ don't need to* boil water before they drink it.

2 You *needn't/ don't need to* walk. I'll give you a lift.

3 There'll be a handout at the end of the lecture so you *needn't/ don't need to* take notes.

4 You *needn't/ don't need to* have a university degree to become a police officer.

5 You *needn't/ don't need to* buy me a birthday present.

6 In most cities you *needn't/ don't need to* pay to get into the galleries and museums.

19.4 Here are some extracts from a speech made by the managing director of a company to her employees. Correct any mistakes. (A–D)

1 You needn't to worry about losing your jobs.

2 Need we make any changes in company policy? We are always happy to hear your views.

3 Changes in technology mustn't be a problem, but could be seen as a great opportunity.

4 I don't have to remind you that we are competing with two other companies.

5 I need hardly to tell you how important it is that we get this order.

6 You don't have to cancel your holiday plans.

7 We mustn't allow our speed of production to drop.

8 The present financial difficulties mustn't mean that people will lose their jobs.

Should, ought to and had better

A We can often use either **should** or **ought to** to talk about obligations and recommendations (e.g. You **should/ought to** finish your homework before you go out) and probability (e.g. It **should/ought to** be ready by now) although in general **should** is used more frequently. **Ought to** is used particularly in speech and most often to talk about obligation rather than probability.

Notice also the following details –
☆ we prefer **should** when we say what an outside authority recommends:
  □ The manual says that the computer **should** be disconnected from the power supply before the cover is removed. (*rather than* ...ought to be disconnected...)
☆ we use **should** (or **would**), not **ought to**, when we give advice with I...:
  □ I **should** leave early tomorrow, if I were you. (*or* I **would** leave...; *or* I'd leave...)
☆ we prefer **should** in questions, particularly *wh*-questions:
  □ What **should** I do if I have any problems?   □ **Should** I ring you at home?
  Some people might use 'What ought I to do...?' and 'Ought I to...?', but this is rather formal.

Note that when we conclude, on the basis of some evidence we have, that something is certain or very likely we can use **must** (see Unit 18) but not **should/ought to**:
  □ It's the third time she's been skating this week. She **must** really enjoy it.

B We use **should/ought to + have + past participle** to talk about something that didn't happen in the past and we are sorry that it didn't:
  □ We **should/ought to have waited** for the rain to stop. (I'm sorry we didn't)
We often use this pattern to indicate some regret or criticism and the negative forms **shouldn't/oughtn't to have** are almost always used in this way.

We also use **should/ought to + have + past participle** to talk about an expectation that something happened, has happened, or will happen:
  □ If the flight was on time, he **should/ought to have arrived** in Jakarta early this morning.
  □ The builders **should/ought to have finished** by the end of the week.

C We can use **should** in questions that are offers or that request confirmation or advice:
  □ **Should** I phone for a taxi for you?   □ Who **should** I pass the message to?
Note that in sentences like these we can also use **shall** with a very similar meaning, and **ought to** is also used in questions, although less commonly.

Compare the use of **shall** and **should** in sentences such as the following, where 'I shall' means 'I intend to' and 'I should' means 'I ought to':
  □ I **shall** read the script on the train tomorrow. (*or* I'll read...)
  □ I **should** read the script on the train tomorrow but I know that I'll be too tired.

D We can use **had better** instead of **should/ought to**, especially in spoken English, to say that we think it is a good idea to do something:
  □ If you're not well, you'**d better** ask Ann to go instead. (*or*... you **should/ought to**...)
although we don't use it to talk about the past or to make general comments:
  □ You **should/ought to** have caught a later train. (*not* You had better have caught...)
  □ I don't think parents **should/ought to** give their children sweets. (*not* I don't think parents had better give their children sweets.)

We prefer **had better** if we want to express particular urgency and in demands and threats:
  □ There's someone moving about downsrs. We'**d better** call the police, quickly.

Notice that the negative form is **had better not**. In question forms the subject comes after **had**, although many people avoid questions with **had better**:
  □ He'**d better not** be late again or he'll be in trouble.
  □ **Hadn't** we **better** get a taxi? (*or* **Shouldn't** we get...?)

Grammar review: *should* and *ought to* → C29–C32

20.1 Complete these sentences with **should/ought to + infinitive** (active), **should/ought to be + past participle** (passive), or **should/ought to have + past participle** using each of these verbs once only. (A & B)

> answer   arrive   be   go   put   remove   resign   send   take   visit   wear   win

1 He is running so well at the moment that Thomas .... the 800 metres easily.

2 Where .... I .... the cheese? In the fridge?

3 The tickets .... a couple of weeks before we go on holiday.

4 Payment for the full amount .... with this application form.

5 You really .... the exhibition before it closes. There are some wonderful paintings.

6 Don told us not to take this road. We .... his advice.

7 All packaging .... before switching on the printer for the first time.

8 It's important to look smart at the interview. You .... a suit.

9 There are many people who think the President .... years ago.

10 .... we .... the questions in English or in French?

11 If you want my advice, I .... by train rather than car.

12 I can't imagine what's happened to Kathy. She .... here by now.

20.2 In which sentences can you use **should** or **must** and in which can you only use **must**? Where both are possible, consider the difference between **should** and **must**. (A)

1 A timetable .... be set for withdrawing the army.

2 Les isn't home yet. He .... have been held up at work.

3 'I wonder how old Mike is?' 'Well, he went to school with my mother, so he .... be well over 50.'

4 If you smell gas, you .... phone the emergency number.

5 You .... try to visit Nepal – it's a beautiful country.

6 'I know I'm always complaining that my house is small, but it's very convenient for work.' 'Yes, it .... be handy living so close to your office.'

20.3 Where necessary correct these sentences using **should/ought to**, **must**, **shall**, or **had better**, or write ✓. (A, C & D)

1 Cyclists had better not be allowed to ride on pavements, even where roads are very busy.

2 'There's something wrong with David's computer yet again.' 'He should wish he'd never bought it.'

3 The concert starts at 7.45. I'd better make a note of that.

4 I shall take my library books back today, but I don't think I'll have time.

5 'The children from next door have been throwing stones at our windows.' 'Well, they shouldn't do it again, otherwise I'll call the police.'

6 'I'm freezing.' 'You'd better have worn a thicker coat.'

7 We have to be in Bristol by 4.00. I think we'd better get started.

8 I should phone Gary this evening, but it will probably be too late by the time I get home.

9 'I've looked all over the house and can't find the car keys.' 'Well, if they're not here, they must still be in the car.'

10 We believe that parents had better pay grandparents to look after their children.

Linking verbs: be, appear, seem; become, get, etc.

A When an adjective or noun phrase is used after a verb to describe the subject or say what or who the subject is, the adjective or noun phrase is a *complement* and the verb is a *linking verb*:
- Ian **is** *a doctor*.   □ She **seemed** *unable to concentrate*.   □ The house **became** *Peter's* in 1980.

The most common linking verb is **be**. Others are to do with 'being', e.g. **keep, prove, remain, stay**; 'becoming', e.g. **become, come, end up, grow, turn out**; and 'seeming', e.g. **appear, look, seem, sound**. Most of these verbs can be followed by either an adjective or noun phrase (e.g. It **sounds nice/a nice place**). However, when they are used as linking verbs, **come** and **grow** (e.g. **come to know, grow thoughtful**) can't be followed by a noun phrase, and **keep** is only followed by a noun if an adjective follows it (e.g. It **kept him awake**).

B After the verbs **appear** (= seems true), **look** (= seem), **prove**, **seem**, and **turn out** we can often either include or omit **to be**:
- The room **appears** (**to be**) *brighter* than when I last saw it.
- She **proved** (**to be**) *an extremely enthusiastic teacher*.

However, following these verbs **to be** is usually included before the adjectives **alive, alone, asleep**, and **awake**, and before the **-ing** forms of verbs:
- I didn't go in because **she appeared to be** *asleep*. (*not* ...she appeared asleep.)
- The roads **seem to be** *getting* icy so drive carefully. (*not* The roads seem getting...)

Before a noun we include **to be** when the noun tells us what the subject is, but can often leave it out when we give our opinion of the person or thing in the subject. We tend to leave out **to be** in more formal English. Compare:
- He walked into what **seemed to be** *a cave*. (*not* ...what seemed a cave.) *and*
- She **seems** (**to be**) *a very efficient salesperson*.

C We use the linking verb **become** to describe a process of change. A number of other linking verbs can be used instead of **become**, including **come, get, go, grow, turn** (**into**).

We use **get** rather than **become**: in informal speech and writing before **difficult, ill, interested, pregnant, suspicious, unhappy**, and **worried**; in imperatives; and in phrases such as **get changed** (clothes), **get dressed, get married/divorced**:
- I first **got** *suspicious* when he looked into all the cars. (*more formally* ...became *suspicious*...)
- *Don't* **get** *upset* about it!   □ Where did you live before you **got** *married*?

We prefer **become** to talk about a more abstract or technical process of change with words such as **adapted, apparent, aware, convinced, infected, irrelevant, obvious**, and **recognised**:
- He **became** *recognised* as an expert.   □ Their bodies **have become** *adapted* to high altitudes.

We use **become**, not **get**, if there is a noun phrase after the linking verb:
- Dr Smith **became** *an adviser* to the government.   □ She **became** *a good tennis player*.

D We use **go** or **turn**, not usually **get** or **become**, when we talk about colours changing:
- The traffic lights **turned/went** *green* and I pulled away.

We often use **go** to talk about changes, particularly to unwanted situations. We use **go**, not **turn** or **get**, with **deaf, blind, bald**, or to say that someone behaves in a mad or excited way; and also with **go bad/off/mouldy/rotten** (about old food), **go bust** (= a company closes because it has run out of money), **go dead** (= when a telephone stops working), **go missing**, and **go wrong**:
- The children **went** completely **crazy** at the party.   □ My computer's **gone wrong** again.

Notice, however, some common exceptions: **get ill, get old, get tired**.

After the verbs **come, get**, and **grow** (but not after **become**) we can use a *to*-infinitive. **Come** and **grow** are often used to talk about gradual change:
- I eventually **came/grew** *to appreciate* his work. (*not* ...became to appreciate his work.)
- I soon **got** *to know* their names. (*not* ...became to know their names.)

Exercises

21.1 Put brackets around **to be** in these sentences if it can be left out. (B)

1 The job turned out to be far easier than I'd expected.
2 When I looked through the window, Charles appeared to be alone.
3 What he called his 'little cottage in the country' proved to be a castle.
4 Hasan proved to be an excellent source of information about the town.
5 She appeared to be satisfied with the work I'd done.
6 I've adjusted the aerial and the television seems to be working okay now.
7 When I picked the crab up I thought it was dead, but it turned out to be alive and bit me.
8 With only five minutes of the match left, Spain look to be heading to victory.
9 'We've decided to buy a Ford.' 'That seems to be a very good choice.'
10 He only looked to be about 10 years old, but I knew he must be a lot older.

21.2 Complete the sentences with an appropriate form of **become** or **get**. Use the correct or more likely alternative. (C)

1 Give me a few minutes to .... changed, and then I'll be ready to go.
2 The condition of the railways .... a major political issue during the last election campaign.
3 The welfare reforms will help single women who .... pregnant.
4 The reasons for my decision will .... clear at the next meeting.
5 Don't .... annoyed with me, but I've lost the car keys.
6 I didn't finish the book. I just couldn't .... interested in it.
7 After the strange events in the house she .... convinced that it was haunted.
8 I had just .... divorced when I met Marianne.
9 It's easy to find your way to the foot of the mountain, but after that things .... difficult.

21.3 Complete the sentences with an appropriate form of one of the verbs in brackets and one of the following words or phrases. (D)

~~berserk~~   blind   bust   dead   to know   to like   red   tired

1 I was at a zoo once when an elephant ___went berserk___ and attacked its keeper. (*go/ turn*)
2 A few seconds later the line .... and Graham replaced the receiver. (*go/ turn*)
3 After the spider bit Rachel her ankle .... and started to swell up. (*go/ get*)
4 He's actually quite friendly when you .... him. (*become/ get*)
5 Cutting that wood looks like hard work. I'll take over from you when you .... (*get/ go*)
6 We soon .... each other and have been great friends ever since. (*become/ come*)
7 The doctor told me that without immediate treatment I might .... (*go/ turn*)
8 The engineering firm Malco .... during the economic recession of the late 1990s. (*go/ get*)

21.4 Where necessary, suggest corrections in the underlined parts of this text. (A–D)

The morning we were going on holiday everything seemed to (1) <u>turn wrong</u>. The taxi was due at 8.00 to take us to the airport. When I looked in on Tom at 7.00 he (2) <u>seemed awake</u>, so I went downstairs to make breakfast. When I opened the fridge I found that the milk (3) <u>had gone off</u>, so there was no breakfast for us. Then Tom (4) <u>seemed taking</u> a long time to come down, so at 7.30 I went back upstairs and he still (5) <u>hadn't become dressed</u>. He said he wasn't feeling well, but I just shouted, "You can't (6) <u>get ill</u> when we're going on holiday!" After that the keys to the luggage (7) <u>got missing</u>, but Tom eventually found them in his jacket pocket. By 8.30 the taxi hadn't arrived and I was starting (8) <u>to become worried</u>. It was (9) <u>getting obvious</u> that we were going to miss our plane if we didn't leave soon. But just then the taxi arrived and we made it to the airport with minutes to spare. Surprisingly, after such a bad start, it (10) <u>turned out to be</u> an excellent holiday.

A Verbs such as **give** take both a direct object (DO) and an indirect object (IO) in two patterns:
V + IO + DO or **V + DO + preposition + IO**. These verbs have two corresponding passives:

active pattern: **V+IO+DO/ V+DO+prep+IO**	passive
Alice gave us that vase. ✓ Alice gave that vase to us. ✓	We were given that vase (by Alice). ✓ That vase was given (to) us (by Alice). ✓

The passive form you choose depends on which is more appropriate in a particular context. If
we specify an agent (see **Appendix 1**), this follows **by** at the end of the clause. Note that in
informal contexts 'to' can be left out in the second passive pattern. Many of these verbs are to
do with 'giving', e.g. **award, hand, lend, offer, send, throw**, and 'telling' e.g. **ask, read, teach**.

Verbs that can't be followed by IO + DO in the active have only one of these passive forms:

active pattern: **V + DO + prep + IO**	passive
~~He explained me the problem.~~ ✗ He explained the problem to me. ✓	~~I was explained the problem.~~ ✗ The problem was explained to me. ✓

Many of these verbs are to do with reporting what was said or thought, including **announce,
demonstrate, describe, introduce, mention, propose, report, suggest**.

B Verbs followed by **object + complement** (see Glossary) in the active have one passive form:

active pattern: **V + object + complement**	passive
They elected her president.	She was elected president.

Other verbs like this are to do with giving someone a particular position, e.g. **appoint, declare,
make, nominate, vote**, and 'naming', e.g. **call, name, title**.

C Some verbs that are followed by **object + bare infinitive** (= an infinitive without 'to') in the
active are followed by a **to-infinitive** in the passive.

active pattern: **V + object + bare infinitive**	passive
They have made him **return** the money.	He has been made **to return** the money.

Other verbs like this include **feel, hear, help** ('help' can also be followed by V + object +
to-infinitive in the active), **observe, see** (see also Unit 23A).

D We can make a passive form of many transitive two- and three-word verbs (see also Unit 94).

active	passive
Kathy **looks after** him. They **put** the accident **down to** bad luck.	He is looked after (by Kathy). The accident was put down to bad luck.

Other examples include: **carry out** (= put into practice), **disapprove of, hold over** (= delay), **talk
down to** (= patronise). However, some transitive two- and three-word verbs are not used in the
passive (e.g. **brush up on** (= revise), **cast (your mind) back** (= try to remember), **come up against**
(= encounter), **get (something) down** (= write), **take after** (= resemble)):

□ We **came up against** a problem. (*not* A problem was come up against)

or only used in the passive in certain senses when it may not be important to mention the
subject (e.g. **call (someone) up** (= ordered to join the army, etc., passive possible; = telephone,
no passive), **call (someone) back** (= ask to return, passive possible; = telephone, no passive), **let
in** (= allow into a place, passive possible; = allow rain, etc. in, no passive), **let out** (= allow to
leave, passive possible; = let out a sound, no passive), **put out** (= put out a statement/light/fire,
passive possible; = put out a hand/arm/foot/tongue, no passive)):

□ I **put out** a hand to steady myself. (*not* A hand was put out...) *but*

□ They **put out** the fire. (*or* The fire **was put out**.)

Grammar review: → Section D & Appendix 1

22.1 Make one corresponding passive sentence or two, if possible, as in 1. Look carefully at the tense in the sentences given. (A)

1 Someone handed me a note. _I was handed a note./ A note was handed to me._

2 Someone offered her a second-hand bicycle. _____

3 Someone has proposed improvements to the developers. _____

4 Someone suggested some interesting changes to me. _____

5 Someone awarded him a prize. _____

6 Someone will announce the President's arrival to the waiting journalists. _____

7 Someone had mentioned the password to the thieves. _____

8 Someone has lent me some skis. _____

9 Someone is sending him threatening letters. _____

10 Someone is going to explain the changes to the students. _____

22.2 Choose an appropriate form of one of these verbs to complete the sentences and write a corresponding passive sentence starting with the word(s) given. Use each verb once only. (A, B, C)

appoint   bring   declare   demonstrate   ~~help~~   introduce   see   tell

1 People __helped__ Bobby to his feet after the accident.
   Bobby was helped to his feet after the accident.

2 Tony _____ me to Mrs Jennings at his birthday party. __I__
   _____

3 Has anyone _____ Chris this morning? _Has Chris_ _____?

4 The Romans may _____ rabbits to Britain as a source of food. _Rabbits_
   _____

5 People _____ the story of Father Christmas to young children to explain the presents they receive. _The story of Father Christmas_ _____

6 They _____ Martin Johnson team captain for the whole of the World Cup.
   Martin Johnson _____

7 I am certain that Sarah _____ her suitability as company director to those who still have any doubt. _I am certain that Sarah's suitability as company director_ _____

8 They _____ Alan Watson winner of the election after a recount. _Alan Watson_ _____

22.3 If possible, make a corresponding sentence with a passive form of the underlined two- or three-word verb, as in 1. If it is not possible, write 'No passive'. (D)

1 Children often <u>look up to</u> strict teachers.
   Strict teachers are often looked up to by children.

2 The company <u>phased out</u> the product over a period of three years.
   _____

3 The students <u>got</u> the information <u>down</u> as fast as they could.
   _____

4 The decision has <u>deprived</u> many people <u>of</u> the right to vote.
   _____

5 People often <u>brush up on</u> a foreign language just before a holiday.
   _____

6 John <u>called</u> Mrs Jones <u>back</u> as soon as he got home.
   _____

7 The chairman <u>held over</u> the last two items until the next committee meeting.
   _____

8 The farmer <u>prevented</u> walkers <u>from</u> crossing the field after he <u>fenced</u> it <u>off</u>.
   _____

Forming passive sentences (2): verb + -ing or to-infinitive

Active patterns with verb + -ing

A The active pattern **verb + object + -ing** is made passive with 'be' + past participle + -ing:
- They **saw** *the monkey* **climbing** over the fence. (= active)
- *The monkey* **was seen climbing** over the fence. (= passive)

Other verbs in this pattern include **bring, catch, hear, find, keep, notice, observe, send, show**:
- Everyone **was brought running** into the room by her screams.
- In the security video the burglars **are seen entering** the bank through a window.

B Some verbs that can be followed by an **-ing** form can be used with a passive form **being + past participle**:
- I really **love being given** presents.
- The children **enjoyed being taken** to the zoo.

Other verbs like this include **avoid, deny, describe, dislike, face, hate, (not) imagine, like, remember, report, resent**.

C Verbs which in the active are followed by an object consisting of a noun phrase and **-ing** clause usually have no passive:
- I dread **him** (*or* **his**) **finding out**. (*but not* He is dreaded finding out)

Other verbs like this include **anticipate, appreciate, dislike, forget, hate, imagine, like, (not) mind, recall, remember**.

Active patterns with verb + to-infinitive

D The active pattern **verb + object + to-infinitive** is made passive with 'be' + past participle + to-infinitive. Compare:
- Mr Price **has taught** *Peter* **to sing** for many years. *and*
- Peter **has been taught to sing** (by Mr Price) for many years.

Other verbs in this pattern include **advise, allow, ask, believe, consider, expect, feel, instruct, mean, order, require, tell, understand**.

Notice that in some contexts it is possible to make both verbs passive:
- Changes to the taxation system **are expected to be proposed**. (*compare the active* We **expect** the government **to propose** changes to the taxation system.)

Some verbs followed by an **object + to-infinitive** in the active have no passive:
- Susan **liked Tom to be** there. (*but not* Tom was liked to be there.)

Verbs like this are to do with 'liking' and 'wanting', and include (**can't**) **bear, hate, love, need, prefer, want, wish**.

E The active pattern **verb + to-infinitive + object** is made passive with **verb + to be + past participle**. Compare:
- Supermarkets **started to sell** *fresh pasta* only in the 1990s. *and*
- *Fresh pasta* **started to be sold** by supermarkets only in the 1990s.

Other verbs in this pattern include **appear, begin, come, continue, seem, tend**; also **agree, aim, arrange, attempt, hope, refuse, want**. The verbs in the first group (and **start**) have corresponding meanings in active and passive sentences, but the verbs in the second group do not. Compare:
- People have come to regard her as the leading violinist of her generation. (active) *corresponds to*
- She has come to be regarded as the leading violinist of her generation. (passive)
- Mr Smith wanted to help me. (active) *does not correspond to*
- I wanted to be helped by Mr Smith. (passive)

23.1 Complete these sentences using one of these pairs of verbs. Use either **was/were + past participle + -ing** or **past simple + being + past participle**. (A & B)

avoid – take	deny – involve	face – expel	find – wander	~~keep – wait~~
leave – hold	observe – hide	remember – bite	resent – give	send – tumble

1 Inger ...*was kept waiting*.... for over three hours when she went for her dental appointment.
2 When the police first questioned him, Wayne .... in the robbery.
3 I .... the baby while Karen went to answer the phone.
4 When I woke up in hospital, I .... by the snake but nothing after that.
5 They .... prisoner by pretending to be dead.
6 The man .... a suspicious package under a seat in the train.
7 When the bike hit her, Ann .... to the ground.
8 Two teenagers yesterday .... from school after they were found with over a hundred stolen mobile phones.
9 The woman was taken to hospital when she .... lost and alone in the forest.
10 Adam had worked in the company for 30 years and he rather .... orders by people who had been there only weeks.

23.2 If possible, complete the sentences using the pair of verbs given. Make passive forms with **past participle + -ing, past participle + to-infinitive**, or **past simple + being + past participle**. If no passive is possible, write 'No passive'. (A–D)

1 Robert always ...*hated being teased*.... by other children. (hate – tease)
2 We .... our passports at the border. (ask – show)
3 You .... in two copies of the customs declaration. (require – fill)
4 The children .... science lessons at school. (want – enjoy)
5 Jack and Martha could .... in the next room. (hear – argue)
6 He .... money out of the cash box. (catch – take)
7 I .... me decorate the bedroom. (need – help)
8 I .... furious when they found out the window was broken. (anticipate – be)
9 She phoned the police and .... outside her home. (report – attack)
10 The pop concert .... over 20,000 people. (expect – attract)

23.3 Make passive sentences beginning with the underlined word(s). Does the sentence you have written have a corresponding meaning to the original, or a different meaning? Look carefully at the tense in the sentences given. (E)

1 Kay's questions began to irritate <u>Malcolm</u>.

....

2 The team captain hopes to select <u>Kevin</u>.

....

3 Alan arranged to take <u>Kathy</u> to the station.

....

4 Critics have come to recognise <u>Galdos</u> as one of Spain's greatest novelists.

....

5 The south coast continues to attract <u>holidaymakers</u>.

....

6 Harris has agreed to interview <u>the finance minister</u>.

....

Unit 24

Using passives

A Here are some situations where we typically choose a passive rather than an active.

☆ In an active sentence we need to include the agent as subject; using a passive allows us to omit the agent by leaving out the prepositional phrase with **by**. Consequently, we prefer passives when the agent:
- is not known: ☐ My office **was broken into** when I was on holiday.
- is 'people in general': ☐ An order form **can be found** on page 2.
- is unimportant: ☐ He **is thought** to be somewhere in Russia.
- is obvious: ☐ She **is being treated** in hospital. (the agent is clearly 'medical staff')

☆ In factual writing, particularly in describing procedures or processes, we often wish to omit the agent, and use passives:
- ☐ Nuclear waste will still be radioactive even after 20,000 years, so it **must be disposed of** very carefully. It **can be stored** as a liquid in stainless-steel containers which **are encased** in concrete. The most dangerous nuclear waste **can be turned** into glass. It **is planned** to store this glass in deep underground mines.

☆ In informal contexts, particularly in conversation, we often use active sentences with a subject such as **people, somebody/someone, something, they, we,** or **you** even when we do not know who the agent is. In more formal contexts, we often prefer to use a passive so that we can avoid any mention of an agent. Compare:
- ☐ **Somebody** will give you the questions a week before the exam. *and*
- ☐ You **will be given** the questions a week before the exam. (*or* The questions **will be given** to you…) (*both more formal*)
- ☐ **They're installing** the new computer system next month. *and*
- ☐ The new computer system **is being installed** next month. (*more formal*)

B Notice also that some verbs have related nouns which express the same meaning. These nouns can be used as the subject of passive sentences, with a new passive verb introduced. Compare the example above *and*:
- ☐ The **installation** of the new computer system **will be completed** by next month.

C In English we usually prefer to put the topic (what is already being talked about) at the beginning of a sentence (or clause) and a comment on that topic at the end. Choosing the passive often allows us to do this. Compare these two texts and notice where the topic (in *italics*) is placed in the second sentence of each. The second text uses a passive where the emphasis is on the equipment:
- ☐ The three machines tested for the report contained different types of safety valve. The Boron Group in Germany manufactured *all the equipment*.
- ☐ The three machines tested for the report contained different types of safety valve. *All the equipment* was manufactured by the Boron Group in Germany.

It is often more natural to put long subjects at the end of a sentence. Using the passive allows us to do this. So, for example:
- ☐ **I was surprised** by Don's decision to give up his job and move to Sydney.
is more natural than '*Don's decision to give up his job and move to Sydney* surprised me', although the choice can depend on considerations of style and context.

D Instead of making a *that*-clause the subject of a passive sentence, it is normal to use an *it*-clause (see also **Unit 25**):
- ☐ **Everybody believed** (that) the plan would fail. (*active*)
- ☐ **It was believed** that the plan would fail. (*passive*) *is more natural than*
- ☐ *That the plan would fail* **was believed** by everybody. (*passive*)

Grammar review: → Section D & Appendix 1

24.1 Rewrite these sentences. Instead of using 'people', 'somebody', or 'they', write one corresponding passive sentence or two if possible (as in 1), beginning with the underlined words. Use an appropriate verb form and make any other necessary changes. (A & Appendix 1)

1 They presented <u>Maria Svensson</u> with <u>the award</u> last night. _Maria Svensson was presented with the award last night./The award was presented to Maria Svensson last night._

2 People are blaming <u>climate change</u> for the <u>recent flooding</u>.

3 Somebody has described <u>Keith Jones</u> as the world's greatest guitarist.

4 Somebody had stolen <u>the painting</u> from the gallery.

5 They will have cleared <u>the litter</u> from <u>the pitch</u> before the match starts.

6 People were watching <u>the game</u> outside the stadium on a huge screen.

7 Somebody will spray <u>the walls</u> with <u>green paint</u>.

8 Somebody should have offered <u>Mary</u> <u>a drink</u> when she arrived.

9 People will provide <u>you</u> with <u>food</u> for the journey.

10 They have planted <u>the fields</u> with <u>cotton</u>.

24.2 Rewrite these sentences beginning with **(The) + noun** formed from the underlined verb and a passive verb. Use the verb given, and make any other necessary changes. (B)

1 They will <u>consider</u> the issue at next week's meeting. (*give*) _Consideration will be given to the issue at next week's meeting._

2 They will <u>appoint</u> a new managing director next week. (*make*)

3 People have <u>accused</u> the local council of corruption. (*make*)

4 They <u>demolished</u> the building in only two days. (*complete*)

5 They will <u>present</u> the trophy after the speeches. (*make*)

6 Local residents will certainly <u>resist</u> the proposed new industrial area. (*show*)

24.3 Use appropriate forms of the verbs given to complete this text. In each case, decide whether an active or passive form is needed. (A–D)

Slowly but surely the coastline of Britain (1) _is being worn away_ (*wear away*) by an advancing sea. The country which once 'ruled the waves' now (2) .... (*rule*) by them, with huge forces threatening to destroy vast areas of human and wildlife habitat. Already some of Britain's last wild, natural areas (3) .... (*disappear*), and experts (4) .... (*fear*) that this is just the beginning. It (5) .... (*estimate*) that there will be a 38–55 cm rise in average sea levels by the year 2100. According to the Department of the Environment, during the next 50 years at least 10,000 hectares of farmland (6) .... (*turn into*) mud flats and salt marshes by the increases in sea levels. Rather than trying to prevent the erosion, the present government (7) .... (*use*) a method of 'managed retreat' by creating new defences further inland and allowing low-lying coastal farm land (8) .... (*abandon*) to the sea. However, many of the country's major cities could also (9) .... (*affect*). London, Bristol and Cardiff all (10) .... (*expect*) severe flooding as our sea defences (11) .... (*destroy*) by the rising tides.

Reporting with passive verbs; It is said that...

A We often use a passive to report what people say, think, etc., particularly if it is not important to mention who is being reported:

☐ People in the area **have been told** that they should stay indoors.
☐ Everyone **was asked** to bring some food to the party.

B Another common way of reporting what is said by an unspecified group of people is to use **it + passive verb + that-clause** (see Unit 33 for more on *that*-clauses). Using this pattern can allow us to put important information at the end of the sentence (see Unit 24C):

☐ **It is reported** *that* the damage is extensive. (*compare* The damage is extensive, according to government sources.)
☐ **It has been acknowledged** *that* underfunding contributed to the problem.
☐ **It can be seen** *that* prices rose sharply in September.

Other verbs that can be used in this pattern include:

> agree, allege, announce, assume, believe, calculate, claim, consider, decide, demonstrate, discover, establish, estimate, expect, feel, find, hope, intend, know, mention, plan, propose, recommend, reveal, say, show, suggest, suppose, think, understand.

Notice that many other verbs connected with reporting are *not* used in this pattern, including **encourage, inform, persuade, reassure, remind, tell, warn**, but can be used as in A:

☐ We **have been informed** that we have to leave the building. (*but not* It has been informed us...)

These verbs need a personal object before the *that*-clause in an active form (e.g. They have informed us that...).

C An alternative to **it + passive verb + that-clause** is to use **subject + passive verb + to-infinitive** if we want the subject to be the topic of the sentence (see Unit 24C). Compare:

☐ **It is reported** *that* the damage is extensive. *and*
☐ **The damage is reported** *to be* extensive.
☐ **It has been acknowledged** *that* underfunding contributed to the problem. *and*
☐ **Underfunding has been acknowledged** *to have contributed* to the problem.

Most of the verbs listed in the box in B can also be used in this pattern except for **announce, decide, mention, propose, recommend, suggest**.

We can only use **tell** in this pattern when it means 'order'. So we can say:

☐ **I was told** (= ordered) **to go** with them to the railway station.

but not 'The accident was told (= said) to have happened just after midnight'.

D With the verbs **discover, establish, explain, find, know, reveal, show, understand** we can also use **it + passive verb + wh-clause** to report information given or found out:

☐ **It has now been revealed** *who* was responsible for the accident.
☐ The decision to build the bridge was taken before **it was established** *whether* it was actually needed.

E When a **that-clause** begins **that + there...**, we can make a corresponding passive form **there + passive verb + to be/to have been**. Compare:

☐ **It is thought** (that) there are too many obstacles to peace. *and*
☐ **There are thought to be** too many obstacles to peace.
☐ In 1981 **it was believed** (that) there were only two experts on the disease in the country. *and*
☐ In 1981 **there were believed to be** only two experts on the disease in the country.

We can use the same verbs in this pattern as with **subject + passive verb + to-infinitive** (see C).

25.1 Which of the verbs can complete the sentence? Underline one or both. (B & D)

1 It is .... to employ 500 people in the factory. (*expected/ intended*)

2 It has been .... that the crash was the result of pilot error. (*proposed/ shown*)

3 It was .... that Mrs Ho would chair the meeting. (*hoped/ explained*)

4 It has been .... to appoint Dr Smithers as head teacher. (*decided/ suggested*)

5 It has not yet been .... who was responsible for the error. (*claimed/ explained*)

6 It has now been .... that the president broke the law in sending troops into the city. (*established/ revealed*)

7 It was .... to hold new negotiations next month. (*agreed/ announced*)

8 It is .... to close the library permanently from next April. (*planned/ recommended*)

9 It is .... that another Moon landing will take place next year. (*assumed/ thought*)

10 It has been .... how spiders are able to travel across the sea. (*discovered/ said*)

25.2 If possible, rewrite these newspaper headlines as passive sentences with the pattern **It + passive verb + that-clause**, as in 1. If this is not possible, write ✗ after the headline. (A & B)

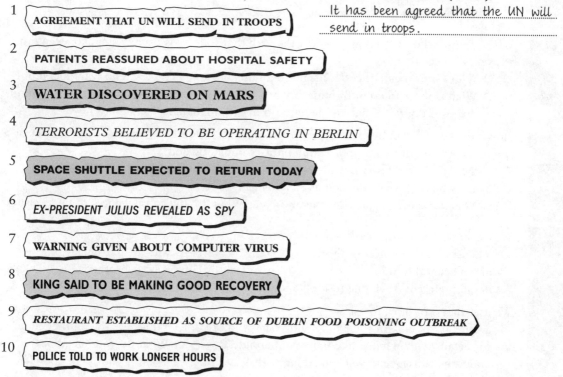

1 AGREEMENT THAT UN WILL SEND IN TROOPS — *It has been agreed that the UN will send in troops.*

2 PATIENTS REASSURED ABOUT HOSPITAL SAFETY

3 WATER DISCOVERED ON MARS

4 TERRORISTS BELIEVED TO BE OPERATING IN BERLIN

5 SPACE SHUTTLE EXPECTED TO RETURN TODAY

6 EX-PRESIDENT JULIUS REVEALED AS SPY

7 WARNING GIVEN ABOUT COMPUTER VIRUS

8 KING SAID TO BE MAKING GOOD RECOVERY

9 RESTAURANT ESTABLISHED AS SOURCE OF DUBLIN FOOD POISONING OUTBREAK

10 POLICE TOLD TO WORK LONGER HOURS

25.3 If possible, write two corresponding impersonal sentences from the pieces of information in the text using **it + passive verb + that-clause** in one and **subject + passive verb + to-infinitive** in the other, as in 1. In some cases the second pattern is not possible. (C)

(1) We have discovered that a mechanical fault caused the problem. (2) We don't think that the fault is serious. (3) We expect that it will take several weeks to correct the fault. (4) We have decided to postpone the next rocket launch, and (5) we suggest that the next launch should take place in May.

1 *It has been discovered that a mechanical fault caused the problem./ A mechanical fault was discovered to have caused the problem.*

....

....

....

....

....

A

Who refers to people, and can be used as subject, object or complement:

☐ **Who** owns that car?　　☐ **Who** did you meet?　　☐ **Who** was her father?

Whom is used as a formal alternative to **who** as object, and also directly after prepositions:

☐ **Whom** did you meet?　　☐ **To whom** were you talking?

Which is used to refer to people when we want to identify somebody in a group (for example, in a crowded room or on a photograph):

☐ '**Which** is your brother?' 'The one next to Ken.'

and we can use **which** instead of **who** to talk about particular classes of people:

☐ **Which** do you think earns more, a teacher or a police officer? (*or* **Who** do you think...?)

B

We usually use **which**, rather than **who** or **what**, in questions before **one(s)** and **of**, as **which** is commonly used to ask or talk about a choice between one or more things:

☐ I've decided to buy one of these sweaters. **Which** *one* do you think I should choose?

☐ **Which** *of* you would like to go first? (*rather than* Who of...?)

C

When we use **who** or **what** as *subjects*, the verb that follows is usually singular, even if a plural answer is expected:

☐ **Who** *wants* a cup of coffee? (said to a number of people; *not* Who want a cup of coffee?)

☐ **What** *is* there to do in Birmingham at Christmas? (expects an answer giving a number of things to do; *not* What are there to do in Birmingham at Christmas?)

However, the verb can be plural in echo questions (see **Unit 27E**) after a plural subject or a subject consisting of two or more noun phrases joined by **and**:

☐ 'Mr Smith and his family are here to see you.' '**Who** *are* here?' (*or* Who's here?)

and when **who** and **what** function as *complements*:

☐ **Who** *are* those people over there?　　☐ **What** *are* the consequences of the decision?

D

We use **how**, not **what**, to ask –

☆ a general opinion on something:　　　　　　☐ **How** was the journey?

☆ about general health:　　　　　　　　　　☐ **How** is your brother?

☆ about preferences relating to food and drink:　☐ **How** do you like your coffee?

We use **what**, not **how**, to ask –

☆ a general opinion on something with **What...like?**　☐ **What** was the journey **like**?

☆ for details with **What... like/hate** (etc.) **about...?**　☐ **What** do you **like about** the job?

☆ about the consequences of something with **What if...?**　☐ **What if** your plan doesn't work?

☆ about the naming of something in the question　☐ **What's** it **called**?

We use either **what** or **how** –

☆ to make a suggestion with **What/How about...?**　☐ **How/What** about having a swim?

☆ to ask for more information in the question **How/What do you mean?**

☐ 'There's something wrong with the car.' 'Something wrong? **How/What** do you mean?'

E

We can use **whose** to ask about the person that owns or is responsible for something. **Whose** can be used either before a verb (as a pronoun):

☐ **Whose** *are* these boots?

or before a noun or noun phrase (as a determiner) introducing direct or indirect questions:

☐ **Whose** *boots* are these?　　　　　☐ She asked me **whose** *coat* I was wearing.

In formal contexts we can use a preposition before **whose** (see also **Unit 55B**):

☐ *In* **whose** desk was it found? (*less formally* **Whose** desk was it found *in*?)

However, in questions without a verb a preposition comes before **whose**:

☐ 'We're meeting at nine.' '*In* **whose** house?' (*not* Whose house in?)

26.1 Underline the correct word. If both are possible, underline them both. (A & B)

1 To *whom/ who* should the documents be sent?
2 *Which/ Who* of you is Dr Jameson? I have a message for you.
3 'Here's a photo of our children at the fancy dress party.' '*Who/ Which* is Wendy?'
4 'Is your sister at home?' '*What/ Which* one do you want to speak to?'
5 *Whom/ Who* do you hold responsible for the damage?
6 *Who/ Which* will captain the team if Nick isn't available?
7 *Which/ Who* would you rather be – a doctor or a vet?
8 *Who/ Whom* translated the book?

26.2 Complete the sentences with an appropriate present simple form of the verb in brackets. (C)

1 What .... those cakes made from? (*be*)
2 Who .... you for Maths and English? (*teach*)
3 What .... there to see on the island? (*be*)
4 Who .... the major decisions in the company? (*take*)
5 'The Turners are in France.' 'Who .... in France?' (*be*)
6 Who .... their textbook with them? Put your hands up. (*have*)

26.3 First, complete the sentences with **how**, **what**, or **how/what** if both are possible. Then choose an appropriate answer for each question. (D)

1 '..................................... do you like about your new job?'   a 'It's really boring.'
2 '..................................... if Tom calls while you're out?'   b 'I'd love one.'
3 '..................................... about a coffee?'   c 'I mean you've got to wear a suit.'
4 '..................................... are your parents these days?'   d 'Tell him I'll call back.'
5 '.....................................'s your boss like?'   e 'It was great.'
6 '..................................... do you like your new job?'   f 'Janet Gibbs.'
7 '..................................... was the camping trip?'   g 'It's never boring.'
8 '.....................................'s your boss called?'   h 'Quite well, thanks.'
9 '..................................... do you mean, 'Smart clothes'?'   i 'We had an excellent time.'
10 '..................................... was the camping trip like?'   j 'She works us really hard.'

26.4 If necessary, suggest corrections in the underlined parts of these sentences or make them sound more natural. If the sentence is already correct, write ✓. (B, C & E)

1 <u>Who's</u> caravan were you staying in? ....
2 <u>Whose are</u> all these books? ....
3 He asked us <u>who's</u> car was parked in front of his house. ....
4 '<u>Who live</u> in the flat upstairs?' 'The Thompson family.' ....
5 <u>Whose</u> going with you to Canada? ....
6 <u>About whose</u> travels in Nepal did Nigel Smith write a book? ....
7 <u>What</u> one of the following statements is true? ....
8 <u>Who</u> of us has not wanted to own an expensive sports car at some time in our lives?
   ....
9 'Ants have got into the fridge!' '<u>What has</u> got into the fridge?' ....
10 'Can you post the books to us?' '<u>Whose address to</u>?' ....

Negative questions; echo questions; questions with **that-clauses**

Negative questions

A

We usually make a negative **yes/no** or **wh-question** with an auxiliary verb (*have, did, would,* etc.) + **-n't** to suggest, persuade, criticise, etc. (see also GR:E4–E6):

☐ **Wouldn't** it be better to go tomorrow?　　☐ Why **don't** we go out for a meal?

In formal contexts, or when we want to give some special emphasis to the negative (perhaps to show that we are angry, very surprised, or to strongly persuade someone), we can use **not** after the subject in negative questions. This happens particularly in *yes/no* rather than *wh-*questions:

☐ **Did** *she* **not** realise that she'd broken it? (*less emphatically* **Didn't** *she* realise that…?)
☐ **Can** *you* **not** get there a bit earlier? (*less emphatically* **Can't** *you*…?)

B

We sometimes use negative words other than **-n't** such as **never, no, nobody, nothing, nowhere**:

☐ Why do you **never** help?　　☐ Have you **nowhere** to go? (*or* Do you have **nowhere** to go?)

or less emphatically or more informally:

☐ Why don't you **ever** help?　　☐ **Haven't** you got anywhere to go? (*or* **Don't** you have anywhere…?)

C

We can make a suggestion with **Why not + verb** or **Why don't/doesn't…** (*but not* Why do not/does not…):

☐ **Why not** *decorate* the house yourself? (*or* **Why don't** you decorate…?)
☐ **Why not** *give* her what she wants?' (*or* **Why don't** we give her …?)

Why didn't… isn't used to make a suggestion, but can show that we think an action was wrong. For example, depending on intonation and context, it can be used to criticise someone:

☐ **Why didn't** you decorate the house yourself? (I think you should have done)
☐ **Why didn't** you tell me that in the first place? (I'm annoyed that you didn't)

D

Negative question forms are used in exclamations giving opinions:

☐ **Haven't** you grown!　　☐ **Doesn't** she look lovely!　　☐ **Didn't** it snow a lot!

Exclamations like this are usually said with a falling intonation.

Echo questions

E

Echo questions are used when we haven't understood what has been said or to check that we heard correctly, perhaps because we found it very surprising. We might repeat, usually with a rising intonation, the whole of what was said:

☐ 'Jane's lost her job.' 'Jane's lost her *job?*'

or focus on part of what was said using a stressed *wh-*word or a phrase with **how**:

☐ 'Tom's arriving at 6.30.' '*When's* Tom arriving?/Tom's arriving *when?*'
☐ 'We paid £3,000 for the painting.' '*How much* did you pay?/You paid *how much?*'

We can use **what** or 'do' **what** to focus on the verb or part of the sentence beginning with the verb:

☐ 'We paid £3,000 for the painting.' 'You *what?*' (*or* 'You *did what?*')
☐ 'I think she's having a sleep.' 'She's *what?*' (*or* 'She's *doing what?*'

Questions with **that-clauses**

F

A *wh-*question can refer to a following *that-*clause, particularly after verbs such as **expect, hope, reckon, say, suggest, suppose,** and **think.** We can leave out **that** in these questions:

☐ **When** do you *reckon* (that) you'll finish the job?
☐ **Why** did they *suggest* (that) we should buy new computers for the library?

However, when the *wh-*word is the subject, object or complement of the verb in the subordinate clause, we do not use **that**:

☐ **What** did you *think* was in the box? (*not* What did you think that was in the box?)
☐ **Who** do you *suppose* did it? (*not* Who do you suppose that did it?)

27.1 Write an appropriate negative question for each situation, using –n't in your answer. (A)

1 Can you lend me £10?
Again? _Haven't you got any money left?_ (*...money left?*)

2 I'm annoyed that you didn't come to the meeting.
Why? .... (*...my letter/ on holiday?*)

3 I've had to bring the children with me.
Why? .... (*...babysitter?*)

4 I'll just finish my homework before I go to school.
But .... (*...be supposed to/ last night?*)

5 I've put my bike in the sitting room.
The sitting room! .... (*...outside?*)

6 I'm taking the coach to Vienna.
But that will take ages. .... (*...rather/ train?*)

27.2 Expand the notes and write two alternative negative questions in each situation. In the first use –n't; in the second choose **never, no, nobody, nothing** or **nowhere**. (B)

1 (*ever/ considered you might/ wrong*) _'Haven't you ever considered you might be wrong?'/_
'Have you never considered you might be wrong?' 'No, I'm sure I'm right.'

2 (*you/ any interest/ Maths at all*) '..?' 'No, I've always hated the
subject.'

3 'I spent the night in the railway station.' (*could/ find anywhere else/ sleep*)
'..?'

4 (*can/ remember anything about/ accident*) '..?' 'Not after
getting into the car, no.'

5 (*why/ ever do well/ exams*) '..?' 'Perhaps you don't revise
enough.'

6 (*there anybody/ you can ask/ help*) '..?' 'I can't think of anyone.'

27.3 Complete the echo questions using appropriate question words or phrases. Give a number of
possible answers. (E)

1 'Jim's going to Chile.' 'He's going _where?_ / He's doing _what?_ / He's _what?_ '

2 'He's leaving at the end of next week.' 'He's leaving ....?/ He's doing ....?/
He's ....?'

3 'He'll be away for three months.' 'He'll be away for ....?/ He'll ....?'

4 'It will cost about £5,000.' 'It'll cost ....?/ It'll ....?'

5 'He's sold his house to pay for the trip.' 'He's sold ....?/ He's done ....?/
He's ....?'

6 'He's going climbing in the Andes.' 'He's going climbing ....?/ He's doing
........................?/ He's ....?'

27.4 Expand the notes to form questions. Write **(that)** where **that** may be included. (F)

1 (*why/ suppose/ left all/ money/ Charles*) _Why do you suppose (that) she left all her_
money to Charles? 'He was her favourite brother.'

2 (*who/ say/ vegetarian*) '..?' 'Mary's sister.'

3 (*what/ suggest/ get/ her birthday*) '..?' 'How about a pair of
earrings?'

4 (*how long/ expect/ you'll be/ Istanbul*) '..?' 'Two or three
weeks.'

5 (*what/ he think/ the problem*) '..?' 'A pipe needs replacing.'

6 (*who/ suppose/ lives there now*) '..?' 'I think the house is empty.'

7 (*when/ she say/ she/ be arriving*) '..?' 'In a couple of hours.'

A Some verbs can be either transitive or intransitive, allowing us to focus on either the person or thing performing the action, or the person or thing affected by the action. Compare:

- □ She **closed** *the door*. (transitive)   *and*   The door **closed**. (intransitive)
- □ I've **ripped** *my shirt*. (transitive)   *and*   My shirt **has ripped**. (intransitive)

Verbs like this are often used to talk about some kind of change. Other examples are **begin, bend, break, burn, change, decrease, drop, finish, increase, move, open, shut, start, vary, wake.**

B Some transitive verbs don't need an object when the meaning is clear from the context:

- □ He has **smoked** (*cigarettes*) since he was 10.
- □ She **plays** (*the saxophone*) beautifully.

Other verbs like this include **answer, ask, change, cook, dance, drink, drive, eat, fail, park, phone, read, sing, study, wash, wash up, wave, win, write.**

C After some verbs we usually add a *complement* – a phrase which completes the meaning of a verb, noun or adjective – which is an adverb or prepositional phrase:

- □ The disease **originated** *in Britain*. (*not* The disease originated. We need to add something about where or how it originated.)

Other verbs commonly have a complement but may not. Compare:

- □ He **paused** *for a few moments*.   *and*   He **paused**. (no complement needed)

D Some verbs are commonly followed by a particular preposition or prepositions and then an object (see also Unit 94):

- □ We had to **deal with** *hundreds of complaints*. (*not* We had to deal.)
- □ I'm sure that blue car **belongs to** *Matthew*. (*not* I'm sure that blue car belongs.)

Here are some more verbs with the prepositions which usually follow them: **adhere to, aspire to, culminate in/with, detract from, differentiate between, incline to/towards, specialise in.**

E Some verbs are usually followed by an **object + prepositional phrase** complement:

- □ I always **associate** *pizza with Italy*.   (*not* I always associate pizza.)
- □ She **put** *the report on the floor*.   (*not* She put the report.)

Here are some more verbs with the prepositions which usually begin the complement: **attribute ...to, base...on/upon, equate...with, inflict...on, mistake...for, regard...as/with, remind...of.**

F Some verbs are often followed by an **object + adjective** (or **adjective phrase**) complement:

- □ The people of this country will **hold** *the government responsible*.
- □ Beckman **pronounced** *himself fit for the match*.

Other verbs that can be followed by an **object + adjective** complement include **assume, believe, consider, declare, find, judge, prove, report, think.** The object after **declare, find, pronounce** and **prove** is often a reflexive pronoun (*himself*, etc.).

Notice that when these verbs are used with an **object + adjective** complement the sentence is usually rather formal. Less formal alternatives can be made by adding **to be** after the object or by using a *that*-clause:

- □ Dr Adams argues that house prices will fall, but other economists **believe** *the opposite true*. (*or less formally* ...believe the opposite to be true. *or* ...believe that the opposite is true.)

G Note that many of the verbs in this unit can be followed by a number of patterns, sometimes associated with different meanings. Compare, for example:

- □ She **found** *her ring*.   *and*   □ She **found** *herself in an embarrassing situation*.

Grammar review: transitive and intransitive verbs → F1–F3

Exercises

28.1 If it is possible to leave out the object (*in italics*) after the verbs (<u>underlined</u>), put brackets around it, as in 1. (B)

Jill was (1) <u>reading</u> *(a book)* when the telephone rang. It was Val. She said, "I called you earlier, but nobody (2) <u>answered</u> *the phone*. Would you like to come over to (3) <u>eat</u> *dinner* tonight with me and Tom? Is 8.00 okay?" Jill (4) <u>thanked</u> *Val* and said that she'd love to come. At about 7.00 Jill started to get ready. She (5) <u>washed</u> *herself* and (6) <u>brushed</u> *her hair*. Then she (7) <u>changed</u> *her clothes* and (8) <u>put on</u> *some makeup*. After that, she (9) <u>drove</u> *her car* to Malstowe, the village where Val and Tom lived. Val was gardening when Jill (10) <u>reached</u> *their house* and she (11) <u>waved</u> *her hand* when saw Jill. Jill (12) <u>parked</u> *her car* on the drive and walked over to Val. Val said, "Tom's still (13) <u>cooking</u> *dinner*, so I thought I had time (14) <u>to pick</u> *some flowers*. By the way, my sister Kate is staying with us. She's (15) <u>studying</u> *French* at university, but is on holiday at the moment. I forgot to (16) <u>mention</u> *her* when I spoke to you earlier. I'll (17) <u>introduce</u> *you* when we go inside." Jill (18) <u>enjoyed</u> *the evening* very much. The food was excellent. The others shared a bottle of wine, but Jill didn't (19) <u>drink</u> *alcohol* and had orange juice instead. They talked a lot about their holiday plans. Jill hoped to go to Canada, but wasn't sure yet that she could (20) <u>afford</u> *it*. Before she left, Jill helped (21) <u>wash up</u> *the dishes*. As she drove home, she decided that she must (22) <u>invite</u> *Val and Tom* for a meal at her house very soon.

28.2 Complete these sentences with: a **verb + preposition + noun phrase** (for 1–5); and **verb + noun phrase + preposition** for 6–10. Use verbs from (i) (with an appropriate form), prepositions from (ii), and noun phrases from (iii). (C–E)

(i)			(ii)			(iii)	
adhere	~~aspire~~	attribute	between		for	the black car	~~national leadership~~
base	culminate		in	in	on	his success	the discovery of penicillin
differentiate		equate	on		~~to~~	to	fantasy and reality	the rise in crime
inflict	mistake		to		with	a surprise defeat	seafood
specialise						the 1998 agreement	her new novel

1 Electors deserve more from a political party that ...*aspires to national leadership*... .
2 Years of research by Fleming ....
3 Her mental condition makes it difficult for her to ....
4 All the countries involved in the trade dispute confirmed that they would
....
5 There's a great restaurant by the harbour which ....
6 The team of amateur footballers .... the first division leaders.
7 It is too simplistic to .... the decrease in the number of police officers.
8 After Lewis's victory, he .... the advice of his new trainer.
9 It was dark and raining and she .... a taxi.
10 Paula Wills has .... events that took place in 16th century Denmark.

28.3 Complete these sentences with any appropriate adjective. (F)

1 The scientific evidence proved him ...*guilty*... .
2 She declared herself .... with the result.
3 They considered the food ....
4 I'm surprised the plumber hasn't turned up. I've always found him ....
5 We believed her .... at school.

Now make less formal alternatives to these sentences using either **to be** after the object or a **that-clause**.

1 *The scientific evidence proved him to be guilty./ The scientific evidence proved that he was guilty.*

Verb + two objects

A Some verbs can be followed by two objects. Usually the first object (= the *Indirect Object* (IO)) is a person or group of people and the second object (= the *Direct Object* (DO)) is a thing:

- ☐ Can you **bring** *me* (= IO) *some milk* (= DO) from the shops?
- ☐ I **read** *Suzanne* (= IO) *a story* (= DO).
- ☐ He **made** *himself* (= IO) *a cup of coffee.* (= DO).

Many verbs that can have two objects may also be used with a DO only (e.g. I read a story).

With many verbs that can have two objects, it is possible to reverse the order of the objects if we put **for** or **to** before the IO (this is then called a *prepositional object*). Compare:

- ☐ I built my daughter a doll's house. *and* ☐ I built a doll's house **for** my daughter.
- ☐ Can you pass me that bandage? *and* ☐ Can you pass that bandage **to** me?

We often use this pattern if we want to focus particular attention on the object after **for/to**. We also use it if the IO is a lot longer than the DO:

- ☐ Jasmin taught music **to** a large number of children at the school. (*not* Jasmin taught a large number of children at the school music.)

We use **for** + object with verbs such as **book, build, buy, catch, choose, cook, fetch, find, get, make, order, pour, save. For** suggests that the IO receives and benefits from goods or services. We use **to** + object with verbs such as **award, give, hand, lend, offer, owe, pass, show, teach, tell, throw. To** suggests a transfer of the DO to the IO.

If the DO is a pronoun, a pattern with **DO + preposition + IO** is usual. Patterns without a preposition are avoided because they are considered to be bad style:

- ☐ I gave them **to** Tim. (*rather than* I gave Tim them./I gave them Tim.)
- ☐ We bought it **for** them. (*rather than* We bought them it./We bought it them.)

B The verbs **bring, leave, pay, play, post, read, sell, send, sing, take,** and **write** can be used with either **for** or **to**. Often there is a difference in meaning: **to** suggests that there is a transfer of something to someone, and **for** suggests that someone benefits from something. Compare:

- ☐ I hadn't got time to visit Ann, so I **wrote** a letter **to** her. *and*
- ☐ Ann had broken her wrist and couldn't hold a pen, so I **wrote** a letter **for** her.

Sometimes, however, the meaning is very similar:

- ☐ He **played** the piece **to** (*or* **for**) me.   ☐ Can you **sing** that song again **to** (*or* **for**) us?

Notice that when **object + object** is used after these verbs it usually has a similar meaning to the verb with **object + to + object.** For example:

- ☐ I sold him the car. (*means* I sold the car **to** him, *not* I sold the car **for** him.)

C Some verbs that are followed by two objects cannot have their objects reversed with **for/to:**

- ☐ We all **envied** him his lifestyle. (*but not* We all envied his lifestyle for/to him.)

Other verbs like this include **allow, ask, cost, deny, forgive, guarantee, permit, refuse.**

D Some verbs can *only* have a second object if this is a prepositional object with **to** (see also Unit 22A). Compare:

- ☐ She **described** the situation. *or*
- ☐ She **described** the situation **to** me. (*but not* She described me the situation.) *and*
- ☐ She **told** this joke. *or* She **told** this joke **to** me. *or* She **told** me this joke.

Other verbs like **describe** include **admit, announce, demonstrate, explain, introduce, mention, point out, prove, report, say, suggest.**

Some verbs can *only* have a second object if this is a prepositional object with **for.** Compare:

- ☐ He **fixed** the tap.   *or*   ☐ He **fixed** the tap **for** me. (*but not* He fixed me the tap.) *and*
- ☐ I **booked** a room.   *or*   ☐ I **booked** a room **for** her.   *or*   ☐ I **booked** her a room.

Other verbs like **fix** include **collect, mend,** and **repair.**

Exercises

29.1 Complete these sentences with a suitable form of one of the following verbs and either **to** or **for**. Write **to/for** if either can be used with little difference in meaning. Put these in appropriate places, as in 1. (A & B)

> build   choose   offer   pass   ~~pay~~   post   read   save   sell   take   teach

1 Tom hasn't got any money so I'll have to ....pay.... the bill ^for him.
2 Keith hates going shopping. I have to .... his clothes him.
3 You're staying with Sue at the weekend, aren't you? Can you .... this present her?
4 I can't reach the salt. Could you .... it me, please?
5 When Mr Jenkins bought the house, we .... all the carpets him as well.
6 He's a got a very rewarding job. He .... sports disabled children.
7 I haven't got my glasses. Can you .... these instructions me, please?
8 Jane .... the letter me on her way to work because I had flu and couldn't go out.
9 I .... my old bike him, but he said he wanted something more modern.
10 I'll be in late tonight. Can you .... some dinner me, please?
11 My parents are coming to live with us, so we .... a flat them at the top of the house.

29.2 If necessary, correct these sentences. If the sentence is already correct, write ✓. (C & D)

1 He kindly collected me some library books.
2 He admitted his error for his colleagues.
3 I have to prepare a report for the meeting.
4 Can I ask a favour to you?
5 A special ticket allows entry for people to all the museums in the city.
6 I'd like to introduce you to my sister.

29.3 Complete these texts with objects chosen from the list below. Give all possible word orders and add prepositions where necessary. (A–D)

the problem/our teacher	her photograph/me	the glass/him
another half an hour/us	his sister/me	three bedtime stories/him
~~a letter/ him~~	his broken car/him	the money/me
a drink/John	a paper aeroplane/him	~~the problem/him~~
a fortune/you	an Irish jig/us	the flute/him

1 'Harry phoned. He wants to come and stay with us at the beginning of September.' 'But that's when my parents will be with us. I'll have to write _him a letter/ a letter to him_ to explain _the problem to him_ .'
2 When he described .... I didn't think I knew her, but when he showed .... I realised that I had seen her at work.
3 I handed .... and said, 'Can you play .... ? I feel like dancing.'
4 The clock on the wall was wrong. When we pointed out ...., she allowed .... to finish the exam.
5 My three-year-old nephew, Daniel, always keeps me busy when I babysit. Last night I first had to make ...., then I had to mend .... and after that he insisted that I read ....
6 'Your new motorbike must have cost ....' 'Well, actually, my parents lent ....'
7 I poured .... and gave ....

Verb + -ing forms and infinitives (1)

A Some verbs can be followed either by an **object + -ing** or a **possessive + -ing** with a similar meaning, although the **possessive + -ing** form is usually considered to be rather formal:

☐ I resented **Tom** winning the prize. (*more formally* I resented **Tom's** winning the prize.)

☐ Mary recalled **him** buying the book. (*more formally* Mary recalled **his** buying the book.)

Other verbs like this include verbs of '(dis)liking' such as **detest, (dis)approve of, (dis)like, hate, love, object to**, and verbs of 'thinking' such as **forget, imagine, remember, think of**. Notice that we only use a possessive form (Tom's, his) here to talk about a person or a group of people:

☐ I remembered **the horse** winning the race. (*but not* ...the horse's winning...)

B Some verbs can be followed by **to + -ing** where **to** is a preposition:

☐ She **confessed to** *stealing* the money.   ☐ You **don't object to** *working* late tonight, do you?

Other verbs like this include **adapt, adjust, admit, look forward, own up, resort**. Note that these verbs can also be followed by **to + noun phrase**:

☐ She **confessed to** *the crime*.   ☐ You **don't object to** *the work*, do you?

C Other verbs can be followed by different prepositions + -ing. For example:

☆ **by + -ing** (begin, close, end, finish (off/up), open, start (off/out))

☐ Can you **begin by** *cleaning* the floors, and then do the windows?

☆ **on + -ing** or **on + object + -ing** (concentrate, count, depend, focus, insist, rely)

☐ Clare **insisted on** (*Jack*) *wearing* a suit to the party.

☆ **of + -ing** or **of + object + -ing** (approve, hear, know, speak, talk, tell)

☐ I don't **approve of** (*them/ their*) *hunting* animals for sport.

☆ **object + from + -ing** (deter, discourage, keep, prevent, prohibit, stop)

☐ The noise from next door **prevented me from** *sleeping*.

D Some verbs (**feel, hear, notice, observe, overhear, see, watch**) can be followed by an object and then either by an **-ing** form or a **bare infinitive**, but their meanings may be slightly different. An **-ing** form suggests that an action is in progress, while a **bare infinitive** suggests a completed action. Compare:

☐ I **saw** *them playing* football from my window.   *and*   ☐ I **saw** *him smash* the bottle.

Also, an **-ing** form can suggest that we watch, hear, etc. some of an action, but not from start to finish, while a **bare infinitive** suggests that we watch, hear, etc. the whole action from start to finish. Compare:

☐ I was able to **watch** *them building* the new car park from my office window. *and*

☐ I **watched** *him climb* through the window, and then I called the police.

E After the verbs **dare** and **help** we can use either a **bare infinitive** or **to-infinitive**:

☐ I was angry with him, but I **didn't dare** (*to*) *say* anything.

☐ We hope the poster campaign will **help** (*to*) *raise* awareness of the problem.

When **dare** has an object, we can only use a **to-infinitive**. Compare:

☐ I **dared** *him to cross* the river. (*not* I dared him cross...) *and*   ☐ I **helped** *them* (*to*) *pack*.

After **have, let** and **make** we can use an **object + bare infinitive** but not **to-infinitive**:

☐ His exam results might **make** *him work* harder. (*not* ...might make him to work...)

☐ I **had** *Beth clean* up her bedroom before I **let** *her go* out to play.

F We use a bare infinitive after **make** and **let** in the phrases **make do** (= to manage to deal with a situation by using what is available) and **let go** (= to stop holding something):

☐ Jim had borrowed my new bike, so I had to **make do** with my old one.

☐ 'Don't **let go**!'

Grammar review: → F4–F13

Exercises

30.1 If possible, rewrite these sentences using the possessive form of the object, as in 1. If it is not possible, write ✗. (A)

1 I really hate you having to be away from home so much. <u>I really hate your having to be away from home so much</u> .

2 We don't approve of the developer locating the factory so close to houses.

3 I have always detested the dog jumping up at me when I come home.

4 No-one heard the man shouting for help.

5 It is difficult to imagine him accepting the decision without any objection.

6 No-one in the crowd that day will forget Ashe fighting so hard to win the match.

7 I remember them arguing a great deal when they were children.

8 The police investigated him stealing cars from the city centre.

30.2 Complete these sentences using an appropriate form of a verb from (i), a preposition from (ii) (you will need to use some of these more than once), and an **-ing** form from (iii). (B & C)

(i)	(ii)	(iii)
adjust close ~~concentrate~~ hear own up rely start out stop	by from of ~~on~~ to	closing driving ~~getting~~ playing sailing smoking thanking winning

1 I need to hand in the essay tomorrow, so I've got to ..... <u>concentrate on getting</u> ..... it finished today.

2 I'd like to .... all those responsible for organising what has been a very successful conference.

3 Many visitors to Britain find it difficult at first to .... on the left.

4 The injury .... him .... tennis for 6 months.

5 Charles Hall .... a small dinghy on the local lake, and he has now completed a single-handed yacht journey around the world.

6 You shouldn't .... the lottery to solve your financial problems.

7 The first I .... the factory .... was on the radio last night.

8 Although they first denied it, the boys eventually .... in the school playground.

30.3 Consider which verb form is more likely and why, and underline it. (D)

1 I heard the tyre *burst/ bursting* and then the lorry skidded across the road.

2 Karl noticed someone *watch/ watching* him from an upstairs window.

3 She felt the bee *sting/ stinging* her just before she brushed it off her arm.

4 With a good telescope you can see the eagles *feed/ feeding* their chicks in the nest.

30.4 Match the sentence beginnings and endings, adding an appropriate object where necessary and write (to) where this might be included. (E & F)

1 When Sue thought of going on the roller-coaster it made...
2 The new course is intended to help...
3 I forgot to buy any bread so we had to make...
4 Scientists hope the new drug will help...
5 The puppy isn't well trained yet, so if you let...
6 We didn't agree with the decision, but we didn't dare...
7 When John arrives, have...
8 The dial on the left lets...

a go of his lead, he'll run away.
b feel quite ill.
c prevent hay fever.
d control the speed of the fan.
e wait outside my office.
f understand modern art.
g do with coffee for breakfast.
h protest against it.

1 + b <u>When Sue thought of going on the roller-coaster it made her feel quite ill.</u>

Unit 31 · Verb + –ing forms and infinitives (2)

A

After some verbs we need to include an object before a **to-infinitive** in active sentences:

- ☐ The police **warned** *everyone* **to stay** inside with their windows closed. (*not* The police warned to stay...)
- ☐ My teachers **didn't encourage** *me* **to work** hard at school. (*not* My teachers didn't encourage to work...)

There are many other verbs like this including **advise, allow, believe, cause, command, encourage, entitle, force, invite, order, persuade, remind, show, teach, tell**.

After other verbs, however, such as **agree, consent, fail, hope, manage, offer, pretend, refuse, start, threaten, volunteer**, we can't include an object before a **to-infinitive**:

- ☐ The shop **refused to accept** his cheque. (*not* The shop refused him to accept his cheque.)
- ☐ We've **decided to leave** early. (*not* We've decided us to leave early.)

B

After some verbs, including **apply, arrange, ask, campaign, plan**, and **wait**, we have to put a preposition, usually **for**, immediately after the verb before an **object + to-infinitive** (see also Unit 29):

- ☐ We *waited* **for** *the taxi to come* before saying goodbye. (*not* We waited the taxi to come...)
- ☐ They *arranged* **for** *Jane to stay* in London. (*not* They arranged Jane to stay...)

After **apply, ask** and **campaign**, the **to-infinitive** is often passive:

- ☐ They **applied** for the court appearance **to be postponed**.

Other verbs can be followed by different prepositions + **object + to-infinitive**. For example:

☆ **at + object + to-infinitive** (**go on** (= to criticise continually), **keep on** (= to talk about something many times), **scream, yell**)
- ☐ I *shouted* **at** *the man to open* the door.

☆ **on + object + to-infinitive** (**call** (= to officially ask someone to do something), **count, prevail, rely**)
- ☐ We*'re depending* **on** *you to find* a solution soon.

☆ **to + object + to-infinitive** (**appeal, gesture, motion**)
- ☐ He closed the door and *signalled* **to** *the pilot to take off*.

C

A number of other **to-infinitive** and **-ing** forms can also follow verbs –

☆ verb + negative **to-infinitive** and negative **-ing** forms:
- ☐ We **decided not to go** to Paris after all. (*compare* The people **didn't decide to go** to war, it was their political leaders.)
- ☐ Some of my friends **have considered not going** to college because of the cost. (*compare* I **haven't considered going** to college – I don't want to go on studying after school.)

☆ verb + **to have** + past participle. Compare:
- ☐ Can you hear that strange noise? It **seems to happen** every time I turn on the tap. *and*
- ☐ The accident **seems to have happened** at around 1.00 p.m. yesterday.

This form is often used to give an opinion (with verbs like **seem** and **appear**) about a past event, or to report what is or was said (with passive verbs like **is/was alleged, believed, said, thought**) about past events:
- ☐ Simons **is alleged to have assaulted** a police officer.

☆ verb + **having** + past participle. The **verb + -ing** and **verb + having + past participle** forms have a similar meaning with these verbs. Compare:
- ☐ I now **regret buying** the car. *and*   ☐ I now **regret having bought** the car.

This form is most often used with the verbs **admit, deny, forget, recall, regret** and **remember**.

62

Grammar review: → F4–F13

31.1   Choose one of the verbs in brackets to complete each sentence. (A)

1   a   My mother .... me to throw away my old toys.   (*threatened/ told*)

     b   My mother .... to throw away my old toys.

2   a   They .... to visit Janet in hospital.   (*allowed/ offered*)

     b   They .... us to visit Janet in hospital.

3   a   I .... to carry the heavy boxes up the stairs.   (*managed/ persuaded*)

     b   I .... Nigel to carry the heavy boxes up the stairs.

4   a   She .... Jack to help in the garden.   (*agreed/ encouraged*)

     b   She .... to help in the garden.

5   a   I .... her to tidy up the house.   (*pretended/ reminded*)

     b   I .... to tidy up the house.

6   a   Brian .... to study economics at university.   (*advised/ hoped*)

     b   Brian .... me to study economics at university.

31.2   Complete the sentences with a preposition in the first space and one of the following verbs in the second. Use either a **to-infinitive** or passive form of the **to-infinitive**. (B)

     bring   **do**   **finish**   **get off**   ~~lend~~   **lose**   **provide**   **release**   **stay**

1   I knew I could count ...*on*... you ...*to lend*... me some money.

2   Mary felt ill and she longed .... the meeting .... so that she could go home.

3   I will never give up campaigning .... my brother .... from prison. I know he is innocent.

4   He signalled .... the waiter .... the bill.

5   She kept on .... me .... weight, so I've gone on a diet.

6   The earthquake has left many thousands homeless and the government has appealed .... aid agencies .... tents, blankets and food.

7   I screamed .... the children .... the railway line.

8   The shower isn't working in my hotel room. I'll have to ask .... something .... about it.

9   Following the fire at the chemical factory, the police called .... people .... in their houses with their windows closed.

31.3   Use the verbs in brackets to complete the sentences with one of the patterns in C. Give alternatives where possible.

1   I .... anyone Jack's new address. (*agree – not tell*)

2   The prisoners .... through a broken window last night. (*think – escape*)

3   I .... him at the conference. (*not recall – see*)

4   He .... any stolen property. (*deny – receive*)

5   He .... as the person who donated the money. (*ask – not name*)

6   The Etruscans .... in Italy in the 8th or 9th century BC. (*believe – arrive*)

7   I am sure my purse was on the table a few minutes ago, but now it .... (*seem – disappear*)

8   She .... all the way back home. (*not feel like – walk*)

Quoting and reporting in our own words

A When we report what people think or what they have said, we often report in our own words when the information they convey is more important than their exact words. When we do this we can use sentences that have a *reporting clause* and a *reported clause* (see also Units 33 to 39):

reporting clause	reported clause
She explained	(that) she couldn't take the job until January.
He didn't ask me	where to put the boxes.

B If their exact words are important or if we want to create some dramatic effect, we might report their actual words. In writing this is done in a *quotation* (see also Appendix 3):

- □ 'I suppose you've heard the latest news,' she said.
- □ 'Of course,' Carter replied, 'you'll have to pay him to do the job.'

The *reporting clause* can come before, within, or at the end of the quotation.

In the English used in stories and novels, the *reporting verb* (e.g. **say**, **reply**, **think**) is often placed before the subject when the *reporting clause* comes after the quotation:

- □ 'When will you be back?' asked Arnold. (*or* ...Arnold asked.)

However, we don't use this order when the subject is a pronoun (except in a literary style):

- □ 'And after that I moved to Italy,' she continued. (*not* ...continued she.)

Negatives in reporting

C To report what somebody **didn't** say or think, we make the reporting verb negative:

- □ He **didn't tell me** how he would get to London.

If we want to report a negative sentence, then we usually report this in the *reported clause*:

- □ 'You're right, it **isn't** a good idea.' → He **agreed** that it **wasn't** a good idea.

although it may be reported in the *reporting clause*, depending on meaning:

- □ 'I disagree. It's not a good idea at all.' → He **didn't agree** that it was a good idea.

However, with some verbs, to report a negative sentence we usually make the verb in the *reporting clause* negative:

- □ 'I expect he won't come.'/ 'I don't expect he will come.' → She **didn't expect** him to come.
  (*rather than* She expected he wouldn't come.)

Other verbs like this include **believe**, **feel**, **intend**, **plan**, **propose**, **suppose**, **think**, **want**.

Reporting questions

D To report a **wh-question** we use a *reporting clause* and a clause with a *wh*-word:

- □ She asked me **what** the problem was.   □ I asked him **where** to go next.

When we report a **yes/no question** we use a *reporting clause* followed by a clause beginning with either **if** or **whether** (but note that we can't use **if + to-infinitive**; see Unit 34):

- □ Liz wanted to know **if/whether** we had any photos of our holiday.

The usual word order in a *wh*-, *if*-, or *whether*-clause is the one we would use in a statement:

- □ 'Have you seen Paul recently?' → She wanted to know if I *had seen* Paul recently.

However, if the original question begins **what**, **which**, or **who** followed by **be + complement** we can put the complement before or after **be** in the report:

- □ 'Who was the winner?' → I asked who *the winner was*. (*or* ...who *was the winner*.)

Notice that we don't use a form of **do** in the *wh*-, *if*-, or *whether*-clause:

- □ She asked me where I found it. (*not* ...where did I find it./...where I did find it.)

However, if we are reporting a negative question, we can use a negative form of **do**:

- □ He asked (me) why I **didn't** want anything to eat.

Grammar review → G1–G7 & Appendix 3

Exercises

32.1 Report what was said, quoting the speaker's exact words with one of the following reporting verbs, as in 1. Put the **reporting clause** after the quotation and give alternative word orders where possible. (B & Appendix 3)

boast   chorus   ~~command~~   confess   explain   grumble   suggest   wonder

1 Come in out of the rain now. (*her mother*) *'Come in out of the rain now,' commanded her mother/her mother commanded.*
2 Why don't we stop for a coffee? (*she*)
3 All right Sean, it was me. (*he*)
4 My novel is more exciting than an Agatha Christie thriller. (*she*)
5 I always carry two umbrellas with me because I'm always losing them. (*Mary*)
6 Oh, no, it's raining again. (*Dick*)
7 Good morning, Miss. (*the children*)
8 Have I done the right thing? (*I*)

32.2 Choose a pair of verbs to complete the reports of what was said, using appropriate forms of the verbs. Make the verb negative in the **reporting clause** (as in 1) or the **reported clause**, whichever is more likely. (C)

announce – go   expect – be   feel – could   ~~intend – hurt~~   insist – be
promise – would   think – would   threaten – repay

1 'I didn't mean to upset Astrid.' → He _didn't intend_ _to hurt_ her feelings.
2 'I won't give you the money back if you keep on at me.' → He _____ _____ the money if she kept on at him.
3 'I can't ask my parents to help me again.' → He _____ that he _____ ask his parents to help him again.
4 'I wasn't anywhere near the school at the time of the break-in.' → He _____ that he _____ anywhere near the school at the time of the break-in.
5 'I'm not going back to college.' → She _____ that she _____ back to college.
6 'I was surprised that Mum was so angry.' → He _____ his mother _____ so angry.
7 'John won't mind waiting a bit longer.' → She _____ John _____ mind waiting a bit longer.
8 'I won't be late again.' → She _____ that she _____ be late again.

32.3 Report these questions using a **wh-, if-** or **whether-clause**, as appropriate. Make any necessary changes to verb tense, pronouns, etc. (Study also Units 34 and 35 if necessary.) (D)

1 'When are you leaving?' _She asked me when I was leaving._ (or _...when I am leaving_ .)
2 'Do you remember David?' She wanted to know _____
3 'Who is the girl in the photo?' She wondered _____
4 'Can we stop at the next village?' She asked me _____
5 'How do you spell 'chaos'?' She didn't know _____
6 'How many brothers and sisters have you got?' She asked me _____
7 'Where did you put the eggs?' She wondered _____
8 'Do you want a hot or a cold drink?' She asked _____
9 'Why didn't you go with Jack?' She asked me _____
10 'Which is mine?' She couldn't remember _____
11 'Are you ready to leave?' She wanted to know _____
12 'What was your grandmother's maiden name?' She asked _____

Reporting statements: that-clauses

A

When we report statements, we often use a **that-clause** in the *reported clause* (see Unit 32):

☐ He **said (that)** he was enjoying his work.
☐ The members of the Security Council **warned that** further action may be taken.

After the more common reporting verbs such as **agree**, **mention**, **notice**, **promise**, **say**, and **think**, we often leave out **that**, particularly in informal speech. However, it is less likely to be left out –

☆ after less common reporting verbs such as **complain**, **confide**, **deny**, **grumble**, **speculate**, **warn** (and after the common reporting verbs **answer**, **argue**, and **reply**)

☆ in formal writing

☆ if the **that-clause** doesn't immediately follow the verb:

☐ She **agreed** *with her parents and brothers* **that** it would be safer to buy a car than a motorbike. (*rather than* ...and brothers it would be safer...)

B

Some reporting verbs which are followed by a **that-clause** have an alternative with an **object + to-infinitive** (often **to be**), although the alternatives are often rather formal. Compare:

☐ I **felt that** the results were satisfactory.   *and*   ☐ I **felt** the results to be satisfactory.
☐ They **declared that** the vote was invalid. *and*   ☐ They **declared** the vote to be invalid.

Other verbs like this include **acknowledge**, **assume**, **believe**, **consider**, **expect**, **find**, **presume**, **report**, **think**, **understand**.

C

If we use a **that-clause** after the verb **notify** in an active form, then we must include an object between the verb and the *that*-clause, and this object can't be a prepositional object (see **D** below):

☐ I **notified the bank that** I had changed my address. (*but not* I notified that I .../I notified to the bank that I ...)

Other verbs like this include **assure**, **convince**, **inform**, **persuade**, **reassure**, **remind**, **tell**.

With the verbs **advise**, **promise**, **show**, **teach**, and **warn**, an object before a *that*-clause is not always necessary:

☐ They **promised (me) that** they would come to the party.
☐ The government **has advised that** tourists should leave the country immediately. (*or* The government **has advised tourists that** they should leave the country immediately.)

D

After some verbs we can use a **that-clause** with or without a personal object before the *that*-clause. However, if we *do* include an object, we put a preposition before it.

☆ After some verbs we use **to**:

☐ She **admitted (to me) that** she was seriously ill.
☐ I **pointed out (to the driver)** that he had parked across the entrance.

Other verbs like this include **announce**, **complain**, **confess**, **explain**, **indicate**, **mention**, **propose**, **recommend**, **report**, **say**, **suggest**.

☆ After some verbs we use **with**:

☐ We **agreed (with Susan) that** the information should go no further.
☐ I **checked (with them) that** they were free on Thursday.

Other verbs like this include **argue**, **disagree**, **joke**.

☆ After the verbs **ask**, **demand** and **require** we use **of**:

☐ The club **asks (of its members) that** they pay their fees by 31st December.
☐ The company **demands (of its staff) that** they should be at work by 8.30.

This pattern is usually used in formal contexts. Less formally we can use a **to-infinitive clause** after **ask** and **require** (e.g. The club asks its members to pay their fees by 31st December). However, we can't use a *to*-infinitive clause after **demand** (*not* The company demands its staff to...).

33.1 Underline the correct verb. If both are possible, underline them both. (C)

1 The doctors *advised/ persuaded* that I should rest for 3 months.
2 The police *assured/ promised* local residents that everything possible was being done to catch the car thieves.
3 A spokesperson for the company *reminded/ warned* that there may be delays on the railways this summer due to major engineering work.
4 We should *inform/ teach* children that diet is of vital importance to health.
5 Russian scientists *have shown/ have convinced* that honey can prevent the growth of bacteria.
6 The company *has reassured/ has advised* customers that cars ordered before 1ˢᵗ August would be delivered by the end of the month.
7 Jack *told/ promised* that he would be home before midnight.

33.2 If possible, rewrite these sentences in a more formal way with a **to-infinitive clause**, as in 1. If it is not possible to rewrite the sentence in this way, write ✘. (B)

1 Two days after the launch Houston reported that the satellite was missing. <u>Two days after</u> <u>the launch Houston reported the satellite to be missing.</u>
2 The employees argued that the reduction in wages was unlawful.
3 The judge thought that his explanation was unconvincing.
4 I expected that her plans would fail.
5 She stressed that her stories were aimed primarily at children.
6 Peter acknowledged that his chances of winning the race were slim.
7 We found that the football supporters were very well behaved.
8 The president's spokesman commented that the election result was a victory for democracy.

33.3 Complete the sentences with an appropriate form of one of the following verbs and **to, with**, or **of**. In some cases more than one verb is possible, but use each verb at least once. (D)

announce   complain   disagree   joke   mention   require

1 Mick .... the shop assistant that the computer he'd bought there was faulty.
2 She .... her neighbours that their dog was keeping her awake at night.
3 He .... his friends that he'd won the lottery and was leaving for Barbados that evening.
4 The minister .... shocked journalists that she was to resign immediately.
5 The college .... its students that they attend all classes.
6 I .... Mr Jacobs that the students were lazy. I thought they were very enthusiastic.
7 I forgot to .... Chris that I'd be home late.

33.4 Suggest corrections to the italicised text in this newspaper article. (A, C & D)

PIK TO CUT WORKFORCE

PIK, the toy manufacturer, (1) *has warned they are to make* over 100 employees redundant over the next month. Managing Director Beth Edwards yesterday (2) *explained employees that* a national fall in demand for traditional toys is to blame. She (3) *confessed her audience that* management had been surprised by the downturn, but she (4) *denied management* had been incompetent. When asked whether staff would receive redundancy pay, Ms Edwards (5) *replied an announcement* would be made within a few days, but (6) *reassured that* they would receive financial compensation. She (7) *went on to complain government help* for small businesses was insufficient and (8) *demanded ministers* that they provide more support. She (9) *asked staff that* they continue to work as normal until details of the redundancies were given. She (10) *reassured that* the company would not close completely.

Verb + wh-clause

A

Some verbs can be followed by a clause beginning with a *wh*-word (**how**, **what**, **when**, **where**, **which**, **who**, or **why**):

- That might **explain** *why* he's unhappy.
- Let's **consider** *how* we can solve the problem.
- I couldn't **decide** *which* train to catch.

Verbs like this include **arrange, calculate, check, choose, debate, determine, discover, discuss, establish, find out, forget, guess, imagine, know, learn, notice, plan, realise, remember, say, see, talk about, think (about), understand, wonder.** Many of these verbs can also be followed by –

☆ a **that-clause** (see Unit 33):   ☐ I **decided** *that* I ought to leave.

☆ a **wh-clause** (except 'why') + **to-infinitive**:   ☐ Did you **find out** *where to go*?

Notice that if we add a subject in the *wh*-clause we don't use a *to*-infinitive:

- I can't **imagine** what **he** likes about jazz.

B

Some verbs must have an object before the **wh-clause**:

- She *reminded* me *what* (I had) to do.
- I *told* Linda *how* to get to my house.

Other verbs like this include **advise, inform, instruct, teach, warn.** The verbs **ask** and **show** often have an object before a *wh*-clause, but not always:

- I *asked* (**him**) *how* I could get to the station, and he told me.

These verbs can also be followed by **object + wh-word + to-infinitive**:

- She **taught me** *how to play* chess.
- I **showed her** *where to put* her coat.

C

We can often use **the way** instead of **how** referring to either the route or the means:

- Go back **the way** (that/by which) you came. (*or informally* Go back **how** you came.)
- Have you noticed **the way** (that/in which) he spins the ball? (*or* …noticed **how** he spins…?)

Notice that we don't use 'the way how'. (e.g. *not* 'Go back the way how you came'.)

Whether

D

We can use **whether** as the *wh*-word in a *wh*-clause when we want to show possible choices. **Whether** has a similar meaning to 'if' (see Unit 86):

- He couldn't remember **whether/if** he had turned the computer off.

Whether is commonly followed by a **to-infinitive** to talk about the choice between two or more possibilities. Notice that 'if' is never used before a *to*-infinitive:

- You have 14 days to *decide* **whether to keep** it or not. (*not* …to decide if to keep it…)

Verbs that are often followed by **whether + to-infinitive** are concerned with talking or thinking about choices, and include **choose, consider, debate, decide, determine, discuss, know** (in questions and negatives), **wonder.** Some other verbs to do with talking or thinking are not used with **whether + to-infinitive**, including **ask, conclude, explain, imagine, realise, speculate, think.**

E

Notice the difference between these pairs of sentences. The first in each pair has a **wh-clause** with **whether** and the second has a **that-clause** (see Unit 33):

- I didn't know **whether** the shop was shut. (= if the shop was shut or not)
- I didn't know **that** the shop was shut. (suggests that the shop was shut)
- They haven't decided yet **whether** the airport should be closed. (the *wh*-clause says what the choice is)
- They decided **that** the airport should be closed. (the *that*-clause says what was decided)

F

In rather formal contexts, particularly in writing, we can use **as to** with a meaning similar to 'about' or 'concerning' before a *wh*-clause. This is most common before **whether**:

- Opinion was divided **as to whether** the findings from the study were representative of the population as a whole. (*or less formally* …divided whether…)

34.1 Choose an appropriate sentence ending and choose a **wh**-word to connect them, as in 1. Use each ending once only. If necessary, also add an appropriate object. (A & B)

1 Before the meeting finished they arranged…
2 He took my hands and showed…
3 I explained carefully so that the students understood…
4 Anna was new in the office and I had to keep reminding…
5 I saw Sarah leave the building, but I didn't notice…
6 When I saw Steve alone at the party I wondered…
7 As we walked over the hills the guide warned…
8 After I'd dismantled the motor I couldn't remember…
9 To win a prize you had to guess…
10 As the guests came in Peter told…

a …how to fit the parts back together.
b …where she went after that.
c …where to put their coats.
d …when to meet next.
e …why Helen wasn't with him.
f …how many sweets were in the jar.
g …what they had to do in the test.
h …where the path was dangerous.
i …who everyone was.
j …how to hold the golf club properly.

1 + d *Before the meeting finished they arranged when to meet next.*

34.2 Underline the correct or more appropriate verb. (D)

1 She was *thinking/ debating* whether to invite Jeremy over for dinner.
2 The council is meeting this morning to *discuss/ ask* whether to increase local taxes.
3 Apparently Ray and Mary are *considering/ speculating* whether to emigrate to Australia.
4 I have to *imagine/ choose* whether to get a job or apply to go to college.
5 Scientists will have to *decide/ conclude* soon whether to start testing the new drugs on people.

34.3 When Peter Miles got back from mountain climbing in the Andes he wrote a book about his experiences. Here are some extracts. Correct any mistakes you can find. (A–F)

> The villagers warned what the conditions were like at higher altitudes, and advised to take enough food for a week. There was some discussion through the day as whether the snow would arrive before my descent from the mountain, but I never imagined how hard the conditions would be. In the morning they showed me the way how to get to the track up the mountain.

> When the snow started falling it was very light, and I couldn't decide if to carry on or go back down. Soon, however, I couldn't see where to go.

> I wondered if to retrace my steps and try to find the track again, but by the time I decided whether I should go back, the track had disappeared.

> As the snow got heavier I began to realise whether my life was in danger. Fortunately, my years in the Andes had taught what to do in extreme conditions. I knew that there was a shepherd's hut somewhere on this side of the mountain that I could shelter in, but I didn't know that it was nearby or miles away.

Tense choice in reporting

Verb tense in the *reported* clause

A

When the situation described in the *reported* clause (see Unit 32) is in the *past* when we are reporting it, we use a past tense (past simple, past continuous, etc.):

- □ 'I'm leaving!' → Bob **announced** that he **was leaving**.
- □ 'I don't want anything to eat.' → Mark **said** that he **didn't want** anything to eat.
- □ 'Are you going to London? → Connie **asked** me if I **was going** to London.

When the situation described in the *reported* clause was *already* in the past when it was spoken about originally, we often use the past perfect to report it:

- □ 'We have found the missing girl.' → Last night police **said** that they **had found** the missing girl.

However, if it is clear from the context that one event took place before another, then it may not be necessary to indicate this by using the past perfect and we use the past simple instead:

- □ 'I've sent out the invitations. I did it well before the wedding.' → She **reassured** me that she **sent** out the invitations well before the wedding. (*or* ...**had sent**...)

B

When the situation described in the *reported* clause is a *permanent/habitual situation*, or still exists or is relevant at the time we are reporting it, then we use a present tense (or present perfect) if we also use a present tense for the verb in the *reporting* clause:

- □ Dr Weir **thinks** that he **spends** about 5 minutes on a typical appointment with a patient.
- □ US scientists **claim** that they **have developed** a new vaccine against malaria.

Note that the present perfect focuses attention on the *result* of the action, not the action itself.

However, when we use a past tense in the *reporting* clause we can use either a present or past tense (or present perfect or past perfect) in the *reported* clause:

- □ She **argued** that Carl **is/was** the best person for the job.
- □ They **noted** that the rate of inflation **has/had slowed** down.

Choosing a present tense (or present perfect) in the *reported* clause emphasises that the situation being reported still exists or is still relevant when we report it.

If we want to show we are not sure that what we are reporting is necessarily true, or that a situation may not still exist now, we prefer a *past* rather than a present tense. Compare:

- □ Sarah told me that she **has** two houses. (= might suggest that this is true) *and*
- □ Sarah told me that she **had** two houses. (= might suggest either that this is perhaps not true, or that she once had two houses but doesn't have two houses now)

Verb tense in the *reporting* clause

C

When we report something that was said or thought in the past, the verb in the *reporting* clause is often in a *past* tense:

- □ Just before her wedding, she **revealed** that she had been married before.

When we report current news, opinions, etc. we can use a present tense for the verb in the *reporting* clause. In some cases, either a present or past tense is possible, although we prefer a present tense to emphasise that what was said is true or still relevant when we report it:

- □ She **says** that she'll have to close the shop unless business improves. (*or* ...**said**...)

We often prefer a present rather than a past tense –

☆ to report information that we have been told or heard, but don't know whether it is true:
- □ I **hear** you're unhappy with your job.

☆ to report what is said by some authority:
- □ The law **says** that no-one under the age of 16 can buy a lottery ticket.

☆ to report what many people say:
- □ Every teacher I've spoken to **tells** me that standards of spelling are in decline.

Grammar review → G1–G7

35.1 Change the sentences into reported speech. Choose the most appropriate verb from the list, using the past simple for the verb in the reporting clause and either the past simple or past perfect for the verb in the **that-clause**. If more than one answer is possible, give them both. (A)

     alleged   conceded   ~~denied~~   estimated   recalled   repeated

     1 'I have never been in love with James.' → _She denied that she had ever been/ was_
        ever in love with James.

     2 'Thomas has stolen jewellery from my house.' → She ....

     3 'I think the vase is around 250 years old.' → She ....

     4 'I've told you once. I've already seen the film.' → She ....

     5 'Well, perhaps you're right. Maybe I did treat Jane unkindly.' → She ....

     6 'I seem to remember that Michael's great grandfather was from Spain.' → She ....

35.2 Underline the more appropriate verb. If they are both possible, underline both. (B)

     1 Engineers hope that they *solved/ have solved* the problems with the bridge now that new supports have been built, and they plan to reopen it next week.

     2 The current law *states/ stated* that an employee has the right to appeal against dismissal.

     3 After he read the novel, he commented that the plot *is/ was* difficult to follow.

     4 In the interview, Mr Brown acknowledged that he *wishes/ wished* to be prime minister.

     5 Simon is already a good tennis player, but he accepts that he still *has/ had* a lot to learn.

     6 I *understand/ understood* that you want to buy a second-hand car. Your brother just told me.

     7 Health officials warn that anyone who *looks/ looked* directly at the sun during an eclipse may put their sight at risk.

     8 They reassured us that the path *is/ was* perfectly safe.

35.3 Jim Barnes and Bill Nokes have been interviewed by the police in connection with a robbery last week. Study the verb tenses in the **that-clauses** in these extracts from the interview reports. Correct them if necessary, or write ✓. Suggest alternatives if possible. (A–C)

1

When I mentioned to Nokes that he had been seen in a local shop last Monday, he protested that he is at home all day. He swears that he didn't own a blue Ford Escort. He claimed that he had been to the paint factory two weeks ago to look for work. Nokes alleges that he is a good friend of Jim Barnes. He insisted that he didn't telephone Barnes last Monday morning. When I pointed out to Nokes that a large quantity of paint had been found in his house, he replied that he is storing it for a friend.

2

At the beginning of the interview I reminded Barnes that he is entitled to have a lawyer present. He denied that he knew anyone by the name of Bill Nokes. Barnes confirmed that he is in the area of the paint factory last Monday, but said that he is visiting his mother. He admitted that he is walking along New Street at around 10.00. He maintains that he was a very honest person and would never be involved in anything illegal.

Reporting offers, suggestions, orders, intentions, etc.

Verb + (object) + to-infinitive clause

A When we report offers, suggestions, orders, intentions, promises, requests, etc. we can follow some verbs in the *reporting clause* (see Unit 33) with –

☆ a **to-infinitive clause**:
- □ 'I'll take the children into town.' → She **offered to take** the children into town. (*not* She offered me to take the children…)
- □ 'The theatre will be built next to the town hall.' → They **propose** *to build* the theatre next to the town hall. (*not* They propose them to build…)

Other verbs followed directly by a **to-infinitive** clause include **agree, demand, guarantee, promise, swear, threaten, volunteer.**

☆ an **object + to-infinitive** clause:
- □ 'You should take the job, Frank.' → She **encouraged** *Frank* **to take** the job.
- □ 'Don't worry about the air fare – we'll pay.' → We **told** *her* **not to worry** about the air fare.

The object usually refers to the person who the offer, suggestion, etc. is made to; that is, the person who performs that action in the *reported* clause (see Unit 33). Other verbs followed by an **object + to-infinitive** include **advise, ask, call on, command, instruct, invite, order, persuade, recommend, remind, request, urge, warn.**

Compare the use of **ask** with and without an object before a **to-infinitive** clause:
- □ We **asked** *to leave* our bags outside the exam room. (= this is something we wanted) *and*
- □ They **asked** *us to leave* our bags outside the exam room. (= this is something they wanted)

Verb + that-clause *or* verb + to-infinitive clause

B After some verbs we can use a **that-clause** instead of a **to-infinitive clause**:
- □ He **promised** *to arrive* on time.   *or* □ He **promised** *that* he would arrive on time.
- □ Kathy **demanded** *to be* allowed in. *or* □ Kathy **demanded** *that* she (should) be allowed in.

Verbs like this include **agree, expect, guarantee, hope, propose, request, vow.** With a *that*-clause the person promising, etc. and the person referred to in the *reported* clause may be different:
- □ He **promised** *that* he wouldn't be late. ('He…' and '…he…' may refer to different people)
- □ **Kathy** demanded *that* John should be allowed in.

Verb + that-clause (*not* verb + to-infinitive clause)

C After the verbs **insist, order, say** and **suggest** we use a **that-clause** but not a **to-infinitive clause**:
- □ The team captain **said** *that* I had to play in goal. (*not* …said to play…)
- □ There were cheers when he **suggested** *that* we went home early. (*not* …suggested to go…)

Advise and **order** can be used with an **object + to-infinitive clause** (see A) or a **that-clause**:
- □ I **advised** *that* she should accept. (*or* I **advised** *her to accept*.; *but not* I advised to accept…)

Verb + to-infinitive clause (*not* verb + that-clause)

D After some verbs we use a **to-infinitive** but not a **that-clause**:
- □ Carolyn **intends** *to return* to Dublin after a year in Canada. (*not* …intends that…)
- □ The children **wanted** *to come* with us to the cinema. (*not* …wanted that…)

Other verbs like this include **long, offer, refuse, volunteer.**

E When we report a suggestion, either what the person reported might do themselves, or what someone else might do, we can use a *reporting clause* with **advise, propose, recommend,** or **suggest** followed by an *-ing* clause rather than a *that*-clause:
- □ The lecturer **recommended** *reading* a number of books before the exam. (*or* …recommended *that* the students should read a number of books before the exam.)

Exercises

36.1 Report each sentence using the verbs below and a **to-infinitive clause**. Use each verb once only. If necessary, add an appropriate object after the verb. (A)

~~advise~~   agree   ask   call on   expect   hope   order   urge   vow

1 'If I were you, I'd read the exam questions very carefully.' → *He advised us to read the exam questions very carefully.*

2 'Okay, I'll collect David from school.' → He ....

3 'Be quiet!' → He ....

4 'Please stay for a few more days.' → He ....

5 'I will fight the ban on smoking in public places.' → He ....

6 'I imagine I'll see Olivia at the party.' → He ....

7 'Can you lend me ten pounds?' → He ....

8 'The government should do more to help the homeless.' → He ....

9 'If I leave early I'll avoid the heavy traffic.' → He ....

36.2 Underline the correct verb. If either is possible, underline them both. (B, C & D)

1 The committee *agreed/ suggested* to postpone the meeting until 11th August.

2 Emma *insisted/ said* that we should bring the children along.

3 The prime minister *insisted/ wanted* to discuss transport policy in the interview.

4 She *said/ offered* that she would call me back.

5 He *expected/ advised* to leave at 5.30 in the morning.

6 The shop *has guaranteed/ has promised* that it will deliver the chairs by the end of the week.

7 She *offered/ suggested* to wait for the children to get ready.

8 Terry *wanted/ suggested* that I should stand in the student elections.

9 She *refused/ requested* that her brother should be invited too.

10 He *longed/ promised* to go back home and see his parents.

36.3 Complete the sentences in any appropriate way using a clause beginning with an **-ing** form of a verb. (E)

1 To avoid the road works, police have advised *leaving the motorway at junction 3.*

2 To encourage people to use public transport the council proposed ....
....

3 Richard said the play was very entertaining and he recommended ....
....

4 To find my way around London, Les suggested ....

5 I'd been feeling unwell for a few days and my mother advised ....
....

6 London urgently needs a new airport, and the government proposes ....
....

7 I've been putting on weight and my doctor has recommended ....
....

8 It was a lovely morning and Emma suggested ....

Can any of these sentences be rewritten with a **to-infinitive clause** *without* an object?

Modal verbs in reporting

A

When there is a modal verb in the original statement, suggestion, etc., it sometimes changes when we report what was said or thought. The changes are summarised here:

modal verb in original	modal verb in report
could, would, should, might, needn't, ought to, used to, could have, should have, etc.	**could, would, should, might, needn't, ought to, used to,** (*i.e. no change*) **could have, should have,** etc.
will, can, may	**would, could, might** **will, can, may** (existing or future situations and *present* tense verb in reporting clause) **will** or **would, can** or **could, may** or **might** (existing or future situations and *past* tense verb in reporting clause)
shall	**would, should** (offers, suggestions, etc.)
must (= necessity) **must** (= conclude; see Unit 18B) **mustn't**	**must** or **had to** **must** **mustn't**

B

We sometimes use a modal verb in a report when there is no modal verb in the original:
- □ 'You're not allowed to smoke here.' → She told me that I **mustn't** smoke there.
- □ 'My advice is to look for a new job now.' → She said that I **should** look for a new job now.

C

The verbs **could, would, should, might, needn't, ought to, used to,** and **could have, should have,** etc. don't change in the report:
- □ 'I **could** meet you at the airport.' → He said that he **could** meet us at the airport.
- □ 'You **should have** contacted me earlier.' → She said I **should have** contacted her earlier.

D

Will usually changes to **would, can** to **could,** and **may** to **might.** However, if the situation we are reporting still exists or is still in the future and the verb in the *reporting clause* has a *present* tense, we use **will, can,** and **may** in the *reported clause* (see Unit 32). Compare:
- □ 'I'll be in Paris at Christmas.' → She **tells** me she'**ll** be in Paris at Christmas. *and*
- □ 'Careful! You'll fall through the ice!' → I **warned** him he **would** fall through the ice.

If the situation we are reporting still exists or is still in the future and the verb in the *reporting clause* has a *past* tense, then we can use either **would** or **will, can** or **could,** or **may** or **might** in the *reported clause*:
- □ 'The problem can be solved.' → They **said** the problem **can/could** be solved.

E

When **shall** is used in the original to talk about the future, we use **would** in the report:
- □ 'I **shall** (I'll) call you on Monday.' → She told me she **would** call me on Monday.
However, when **shall** is used in offers, requests for advice and confirmation, etc. then we can use **should** in the report, but not **shall** or **would:**
- □ 'Where **shall** I put this box?' → He asked where he **should** put the box.

F

When **must** is used in the original to say that it is necessary to do something, we can usually use either **must** or **had to** in the report, although **had to** is more natural in speech:
- □ 'You **must** be home by 9 o'clock.' → She said I **must/had to** be home by 9 o'clock.
However, when **must** is used in the original to conclude that something (has) happened or that something is true, then we use **must,** not **had to,** in the report:
- □ 'I keep forgetting things. I **must** be getting old.' → Neil said he **must** be getting old.

If **mustn't** is used in the original, we can use **mustn't** in the report but not **didn't have to:**
- □ 'You **mustn't** tell my brother.' → He warned me that I **mustn't** tell his brother.

Exercises

37.1 Report what was said using a sentence with a **that-clause**. Use an appropriate modal verb in the **that-clause**, and give alternative modal verbs where possible. (B)

1 It's vital that you attend the meeting. → _She said that I had to/ must attend the meeting._

2 If you want to travel with us, that's fine. → She said that ....

....

3 I'm not prepared to answer his questions → She said that ....

....

4 Karl's likely to be back soon. → She said that ....

5 There's a possibility that I'll have to move to Milan. → She said that ....

....

6 I refuse to accept that John is dishonest. → She said that ....

....

7 Maria is sure to be disappointed if you leave without seeing her. → She said that ....

....

37.2 Underline the more appropriate verb. If both are possible, underline them both. (D)

1 The doctor says that he *will/ would* see you in twenty minutes.
2 In her letter, Elizabeth revealed that she *may/ might* be getting married soon.
3 Peter tells me that he *can/ could* come for dinner with us tonight after all.
4 Maggie promised that she *will/ would* be at home by 9.00, so I phoned her shortly after that.
5 The mechanic admitted that he *can't/ couldn't* repair the radiator and had to replace it instead.
6 Sue reckons that she *can/ could* save enough money to go on holiday to Canada.
7 Mario explained that he *will/ would* be living in Austria for the next six months.

37.3 Complete the sentences to report what was said using a **that-, wh-** or **if-clause**. (E–F)

1 'I'm sure that we shall be there soon.' → _He reassured us that we would be there soon._
2 'You mustn't forget your credit card.' → He reminded ....
3 'I shall miss the bus if I don't hurry.' → He worried ....
4 'Who shall I send the letter to?' → He wondered ....
5 'It must be cold outside. There's frost on the window.' → He thought ....

....

6 'You must come home at once.' → He said ....
7 'Shall I open a window?' → He asked ....
8 'I must have made a mistake in the calculations.' → He admitted ....

37.4 Complete the sentences to report what was said using a **that-clause** with a modal verb. (A & D)

1 'If all goes to plan, I'll study medicine.' → He hoped _that he would study medicine but_ instead he became a vet.
2 'I won't be late.' → She promised .... and she kept her word.
3 'Perhaps we can go to Paris for the weekend.' → He suggested .... but I was busy.
4 'I can get you there in good time.' → She guaranteed .... but I didn't believe her.
5 'I'll pay for the meal.' → He insisted .... and I accepted, of course.

Look again at the sentences you have written. Which of them have an alternative with a **to-infinitive** clause (without a modal verb)? (36B)

1 _He hoped to study medicine._

Unit 38 | Reporting what people say using nouns and adjectives

Reporting using nouns

A

We sometimes report people's words and thoughts using a **noun** in the reporting clause followed by a reported clause beginning with *that*, a *to*-infinitive-, or *wh*-word. Most of these nouns are related to reporting verbs (acknowledgement – acknowledge, statement – state, etc.). Notice that when we report using **nouns** and **adjectives** (see **C**) the exact words that were said are not necessarily reported. Instead we might report what was said in our own words, or report that something was said without reporting *what* was said.

☆ Nouns followed by a *that*-clause include **acknowledgement, advice, allegation, announcement, answer, argument, claim, comment, conclusion, decision, explanation, forecast, guarantee, indication, observation, promise, recommendation, reply, speculation, statement, suggestion, threat, warning**:

  □ The **claim** is often made *that* smoking causes heart disease.
  □ The jury came to the **conclusion** *that* the woman was guilty.

Notice that we don't usually leave out **that** in sentences like this (see Unit 33).

☆ Nouns followed by a *to*-infinitive clause include **decision, encouragement, instruction, invitation, order, promise, recommendation, refusal, threat, warning**:

  □ I accepted Louisa's **invitation** *to visit* her in Rome.
  □ He was delighted with his portrait and gave me every **encouragement** *to take up* painting again.

Notice that some of these nouns can also be followed by a *that*-clause:

  □ They carried out their **threat** *to dismiss* workers on strike. (*or* ...their **threat** *that* they would dismiss workers on strike.)

☆ Nouns followed by a *wh*-clause include **explanation, discussion, issue, problem, question**. We usually use **of** after these nouns in reporting:

  □ John raised the **question of** *when* the money would be collected.
  □ Our previous meeting looked at the **issue of** *how* to increase income.

B

After many of the nouns listed in **A** we can use **as to** + *wh*-clause or **as to** + *wh*-word + *to*-infinitive to introduce the subject of a question or topic discussed or thought about (see also Unit 34F). Notice that an alternative preposition can usually be used instead of **as to**:

  □ She asked my *advice* **as to** *what* subject she should study at university. (*or* ...advice **on**...)
  □ There was some *discussion* **as to** *whether* the price included tax or not. (*or* ...discussion **of**...)
  □ Before we left we gave them strict *instructions* **as to** *how to cook* it. (*or* **about** how to...)

Reporting using adjectives

C

A number of adjectives can be used to report a speaker's feelings or opinion about a situation. Some are followed by a *that*-clause. These include **adamant, agreed, angry, annoyed, certain, grateful, insistent, sure**:

  □ The builders are **certain** *that* they'll be finished by the end of the week.

Adjectives expressing uncertainty are usually followed by a *wh*-clause. These include **doubtful** (usually + **whether**), **uncertain, not certain, unsure, not sure**:

  □ Scientists aren't **sure** *where* the remains of the spacecraft will come to land.

Some are usually followed by a preposition (followed by a noun phrase). Here are some examples together with the most common preposition(s) following them: **apologetic, complimentary, insulting, tactful** (+ **about** something); **critical, dismissive, scornful** (+ **of** somebody/something); **abusive, sympathetic** (+ **to/towards** somebody):

  □ Today's newspapers are very **critical of** the President's decision to appoint Mr Walters.
  □ When I asked him what he thought of my new suit, he was quite **insulting about** it.

38.1 Complete the sentences with one of these nouns and then expand the notes in brackets. Use a **that-**, **to-infinitive** or **wh-clause**. Suggest alternatives where you can, as in 1. (A)

announcement	~~decision~~	encouragement	explanation	invitation
issue	observation	promise	question	warning

1 The turning point in his life came when he took the ___*decision to become an actor./ ...that*___
    ___*he would become an actor.*___   (*become – actor*)
2 He failed to address the...   (*who – pay – repairs – building*)
3 I was delighted to get an...   (*spend Christmas – them – Scotland*)
4 I think it was Aristotle who made the...   (*no such thing – bad publicity*)
5 Amazingly the police accepted Rudi's...   (*taken -- wallet – mistake*)
6 On the TV programme they debated the...   (*assisted suicide – criminal offence*)
7 The letter from the company gave a final...   (*pay – bill by – end of – week*)
8 The government has broken its...   (*reduce – rate – income tax*)
9 The positive reaction to my work gave me considerable...   (*take up photography – career*)
10 Waiting passengers were angry when they heard the...   (*flight – cancelled*)

38.2 Report what was said by completing the sentences. Use one of the following nouns + **as to** and then a **wh-word**. (B)

~~advice~~	argument	explanation	indication	speculation	suggestions

1 I was given lots of ___*advice as to what*___ clothes to take with me to Malaysia.
2 Smith's latest injury has prompted _____ long he can carry on playing tennis.
3 We were all very happy when the company won the award, but there has been a great deal of
_____ should get the prize money.
4 A number of very good _____ have been put forward _____
the King's 50th birthday should be celebrated in the village.
5 Mr Johnson resigned last week but gave no _____ he was leaving.
6 We were told to deliver the wardrobe to the house, but there was no _____
exactly to put it.

38.3 Complete the sentences with one of the following adjectives and then either **that**, a **wh-word**, or
a **preposition**. (C)

abusive	adamant	agreed	angry	apologetic	not certain
complimentary	dismissive	~~doubtful~~	unsure		

1 The climbers were ___*doubtful whether*___ the clothes would be warm enough at high altitudes.
2 My boss is very unsympathetic and was _____ my complaints about the new
software.
3 The company is _____ the child car seats are safe.
4 Sue tried to pick up the rabbit, but was _____ to hold it.
5 She was very _____ the window had been broken.
6 Rachel is normally very reliable and was extremely _____ turning up late.
7 Jack left for New York in September but he was _____ he would return.
8 The court heard that Hughes became _____ a police officer and was arrested.
9 Amanda doesn't normally like spicy food, but was quite _____ my fish curry.
10 All the players are _____ the game should go on despite the snow.

Unit 39

Should in that-clauses; the present subjunctive

A

We can sometimes report advice, orders, requests, suggestions, etc. about things that need to be done or are desirable using a **that-clause** with **should + bare infinitive**:

- ☐ They have proposed that Jim **should** *move* to their London office.
- ☐ We advised **that** the company **should not** *raise* its prices.

After **should** we often use **be + past participle** (passive) or **be + adjective**:

- ☐ They directed **that** the building **should** *be pulled down*.
- ☐ We insist **that** the money **should** *be available* to all students in financial difficulties.

B

In formal contexts, particularly in written English, we can often leave out **should** and use only the base form of the verb (that is, the form you would look up in a dictionary). This form is the *present subjunctive* (see Unit 85A for the *past subjunctive*) and is used when we talk about bringing about the situation expressed in the *that*-clause. Note that although they are called 'present' and 'past' subjunctive, they do not refer to present and past time:

- ☐ They have proposed that Jim **move** to their London office.
- ☐ They directed that the building **be pulled down**.

To make a negative form, we use **not** (*not* 'do not') before the verb:

- ☐ We advised that the company **not raise** its prices.

In less formal contexts we can use ordinary forms of the verb instead of the subjunctive. Compare:

- ☐ I suggested that he **should give up** golf. (*negative*: ...that he **shouldn't** give up...)
- ☐ I suggested that he **give up** golf. (more formal) (*negative*: ...that he **not** give up...)
- ☐ I suggested that he **gives up** golf. (less formal) (*negative*: ...that he **doesn't** give up...)

C

Other verbs that can be used in a *reporting clause* before a **that-clause** with either **should** or the **subjunctive** include **advise, ask, beg, command, demand, direct, insist, instruct, intend, order, prefer, propose, recommend, request, require, stipulate, suggest, urge, warn**. Notice that we can also use *that*-clauses with **should** after *reporting clauses* with nouns related to these verbs:

- ☐ The police issued an **order** that all weapons (should) be handed in immediately.
- ☐ The weather forecast gave a **warning** that people (should) prepare for heavy snow.

D

We can also use **should** or sometimes the subjunctive in a **that-clause** after **it + be + adjective** such as **advisable, appalling, (in)appropriate, (in)conceivable, crucial, essential, imperative, important, obligatory, (un)necessary, urgent, vital**:

- ☐ **It is inappropriate** that he (*should*) *receive* the award again. (*or* ...that he *receives*...)

E

We can use **should** in a **that-clause** when we talk about our own reaction to something we are reporting, particularly after **be + adjective** (e.g. **amazed, amused, anxious, astounded, concerned, disappointed, shocked, surprised, upset**). Compare:

- ☐ *I am concerned* that she **should think** I stole the money *and*
- ☐ *I am concerned* that she **thinks** I stole the money. (*not* ...that she think I stole...)

Notice that when we leave out **should** in sentences like this we use an ordinary tense, not a subjunctive. There is usually very little difference in meaning between sentences like this with and without **should**. We leave out **should** in less formal contexts.

F

We can use **should** in a **that-clause** to talk about both a situation that exists now:

- ☐ It's not surprising that they **should** *be seen* together – they're brothers.

or one that may exist in the future:

- ☐ We believe it is important that she **should** *take* the exam next year.

If we are talking about an intention or plan, we can often use a *subjunctive* rather than **should**:

- ☐ I've arranged that she **come** to the first part of the meeting. (*or* ...that she **should come**.../ ...that she **comes**.../ ...for her **to come**...)

39.1 Here are some of the things that were said at a recent board meeting of the Spanit Engineering Company. Report them using a **that-clause** with **should** (either **should + bare infinitive** or **should + be + past participle**). (A–C)

1 Mr Leeson said: "I think it's important to expand our business in South America."
Mr Leeson felt <u>that business in South America should be expanded.</u>

2 Mr Leeson said: "Philip Whittaker would make an excellent export manager. Let's promote him." *Mr Leeson urged* ....

3 Mrs Appleby said: "It would be valuable for us to send a sales representative to South Africa."
Mrs Appleby recommended ....

4 Mrs Appleby said: "The Delaware Bridge project ought to be completed by August next year."
Mrs Appleby reported ....

5 The Chairman said: "It is vital to keep to our work schedules." *The Chairman insisted*
....

6 The Chairman said: "I'd like all monthly reports sent to me directly." *The Chairman instructed* ....

7 Ms Wells said: "Perhaps we could involve trade union representatives in major decisions."
Ms Wells suggested ....

8 Ms Wells said: "Our head office must remain in London." *Ms Wells declared*
....

9 Mr Clarke said: "It's okay for us to sponsor the European chess league for the next three years." *Mr Clarke agreed* ....

10 Mr Clarke said: "In future, all claims for travel expenses are to be made in US dollars."
Mr Clarke announced ....

39.2 Look again at the sentences you have written in 39.1. In which ones is it possible to leave out **should** and still have a correct sentence? Write 'yes' if it is possible and 'no' if it isn't. (A–C)

1 ~~Mr Leeson felt that business in South America be expanded.~~ ....No....

39.3 Expand the notes to report these suggestions, requests, advice, etc. Add one of the following adjectives where ... is written. In most cases, more than one word is possible, but use each word once only. Use a **that-clause** with **should** in your report. (D & E)

amused	appalling	astounded	imperative
~~inconceivable~~	shocked	upset	urgent

1 It is .../ she/ marry Simon.
   <u>It is inconceivable that she should marry Simon.</u>

2 I am .../ Paul/ behave so badly.
   ....

3 I am .../ anyone/ vote for him.
   ....

4 It is .../ he/ return home immediately.
   ....

5 I am .../ he/ take his appearance so seriously.
   ....

6 I am .../ they/ think I had cheated them.
   ....

7 It is .../ they/ allowed to go free.
   ....

8 It is .../ we/ act now to avoid war.
   ....

Agreement between subject and verb (1)

A If a sentence has a singular subject it is followed by a singular verb, and if it has a plural subject it is followed by a plural verb; that is, the verb *agrees with* the subject. Compare:
- **She** *lives* in China. *and* □ **More people** *live* in Asia than in any other continent.

When the subject of the sentence is complex the following verb must agree with the main noun in the subject. In the examples below the subject is underlined and the main noun is circled. Notice how the verb, in italics, agrees with the main noun:
- Many leading (members) of the opposition party *have* criticised the delay.
- The only (excuse) that he gave for his actions *was* that he was tired.

The verb must agree with the subject when the subject follows the verb (see **Units 99 & 100**):
- Among the people invited *was* **the mayor**. (*compare* The mayor *was* among…)
- Displayed on the board *were* **the exam results**. (*compare* The exam results *were* displayed…)

B If the subject is a clause, we usually use a singular verb:
- To keep these young people in prison *is* inhuman.
- Having overall responsibility for the course *means* that I have a lot of meetings.
- Whoever took them *remains* a mystery.
- That Rangers won both matches *was* a great achievement.

However, if we use a *what*-clause as subject (see **Unit 98B**), we use a singular verb if the following main noun is singular, and either a singular or a plural verb if the following main noun is plural (although a plural verb is preferred in more formal contexts):
- What worries us *is* the poor selection **process**.
- What is needed *are* additional **resources**. (*or more colloquially* …needed *is*…)

C Some nouns with a singular form, referring to groups of some kind, can be used with either a singular or plural form of the verb:
- **The council** *has* (or *have*) postponed a decision on the new road.

We use a singular verb if the focus is on the institution or organisation as a whole unit, and a plural verb if the focus is on a collection of individuals. Often you can use either with very little difference in meaning, although in formal contexts (such as academic writing) it is more common to use a singular verb. Other words like this, sometimes called *collective nouns*, include **army, association, audience, class, club, college, committee, community, company, crew, crowd, department, electorate, enemy, family, generation, government, group, jury, opposition, orchestra, population, press, public, school, team, university**, and the names of specific organisations such as **the Bank of England, the BBC, IBM, Sony, the United Nations**.

In some contexts a plural form of the verb is needed. We would say:
- The committee usually **raise** their hands to vote 'Yes'. (*not* The committee usually raises its hands…)

as this is something that the individuals do, not the committee as a whole. In others, a singular form is preferred. We would say:
- The school **is** to close next year. (*not* The school are to close…)

as we are talking about something which happens to the school as a building or institution, not to the individuals in the school.

D When names and titles ending in -s refer to a single unit we use a singular verb. Examples include countries; newspapers; titles of books, films, etc.; and quoted plural words or phrases:
- At this time of the year *the Netherlands* **is** one hour ahead of the UK.
- *The Los Angeles Times* **lists** Derek Jones as the fifth richest man in the world.
- *The Machine Gunners* **was** one of Robert Westall's most successful books.
- '*Daps*' **is** the word used in the south west of the country for sports shoes.

Grammar review → H1–H3

40.1 Complete the sentences with a singular or plural form of the verb in brackets. Use present tense forms. (A & B)

1 Keeping large animals as pets in a small house .... cruel. (*be*)

2 An investigation of the circumstances surrounding her death .... that she was murdered. (*suggest*)

3 What amazes me .... his ability to hit the ball so hard. (*be*)

4 The main reasons for his lack of progress .... to be his poor motivation and inability to concentrate. (*appear*)

5 The cost of housing in the southern parts of the country .... risen dramatically in the last year. (*have*)

6 That he was the best of the many talented golfers of his generation .... indisputable. (*seem*)

7 The village's first new houses for 20 years .... to be built next to Grove Farm. (*be*)

8 Among the many valuable paintings in the gallery .... a self-portrait by Picasso. (*be*)

9 What I particularly enjoy about the film .... the scenes in Australia. (*be*)

40.2 Complete the sentences with one of the following nouns and an appropriate form of the verb in brackets. If a singular and plural verb form are possible, give both. (C)

audience	class	crew		jury	orchestra
press	~~team~~	the United Nations		university	

1 The .....team...... ....play/plays.... its first match of the season at its home ground. (*play*)

2 If the .... to host the conference, I just don't know where we will be able to hold it. (*refuse*)

3 The world-wide television .... for tomorrow's cup final .... expected to be 200 million. (*be*)

4 The .... classical concerts throughout the year. (*perform*)

5 The Waterman's Junior Book Prize .... three adults and three children. (*include*)

6 The .... all passed the end-of-year exam. (*have*)

7 The .... a picture of chaos in our schools, but it's just not like that at all. (*present*)

8 .... ordered an investigation of the capture of members of its peace-keeping force in eastern Africa. (*have*)

40.3 Correct any mistakes in these sentences or write ✓ if they are already correct. (A–D)

1 The United States come top of the list of countries ranked by economic performance.

2 The people I know who have seen the film say that it's really good.

3 A report in the *Sunday Times* detail the crimes of a 14-year-old boy in Southcastle.

4 *Northern Lights* are one of Suzanne's favourite books.

5 The stairs leading to the first floor were steep and poorly lit.

6 Chequers is the country house of the British Prime Minister.

7 Whoever made all the mess in the kitchen have to clear it up.

8 The phrase 'men in white coats' are used to talk about psychiatrists.

9 The public needs to be kept informed about progress in the peace talks.

10 Musical chairs are a party game where everyone dashes for a seat when the music stops.

A

With **any of, each of, either of, neither of,** or **none of** and a **plural noun/pronoun** we can use a *singular* or *plural* verb. However, we are more likely to use a singular verb in careful written English.	☐ I don't think **any of** them *knows* (or *know*) where the money is hidden. ☐ **Neither of** the French athletes *has* (or *have*) won this year.
With **a/the majority of, a number of, a lot of, plenty of, all** (of), or **some** (of) and a **plural noun/pronoun** we use a *plural* verb. But if we say **the number of**, we use a singular verb.	☐ **A number of** refugees *have* been turned back at the border. ☐ **The number of** books in the library *has* risen to over five million.
After **one of** and a **plural noun/pronoun** we use a *singular* verb. However, after **one of** + plural noun/pronoun + **who** we can often use either a singular or plural verb, although a plural verb is more grammatical.	☐ **One of** the reasons I took the job *was* that I could work from home. ☐ He's **one of** those teachers who *insist/insists* on pupils sitting silently in class.
With **any of, none of, the majority of, a lot of, plenty of, all** (of), **some** (of) and an **uncountable noun** we use a *singular* verb.	☐ **All** the furniture *was* destroyed in the fire. ☐ **None of** the equipment *appears* to be damaged.
With **every** or **each** and a **singular noun** or **co-ordinated noun** (x *and* y) we use a *singular* verb. (For **each of**, see above.)	☐ **Every** room *looks* over the harbour. ☐ **Every** boy and girl *takes* part in the activity. ☐ **Each** child *has* drawn a picture. *but* ☐ The children *have* **each** drawn a picture.
With **everyone, everybody, everything** (and similar words beginning **any-, some-** and **no-**) we use a *singular* verb.	☐ Practically **everyone** *thinks* that Phil should be given the job.

B

When a subject has two or more items joined by **and**, we usually use a plural verb:
  ☐ **Jean and David** *are* moving back to Australia.

However, phrases connected by **and** can also be followed by singular verbs if we think of them as making up a single item:
  ☐ **Meat pie and peas** *is* Tom's favourite at the moment. (*or* …*are*…)
  ☐ **The lorry, its cargo and passengers** *weighs* around 35 tonnes. (*or* …*weigh*…)

C

When a subject is made up of two or more items joined by (**either**)…**or**… or (**neither**)…**nor**… we use a singular verb if the last item is singular (although a plural verb is sometimes used in informal English), and a plural verb if the last item is plural:
  ☐ **Either the station or the cinema** *is* a good place to meet. (*or* …*are*… in informal English)
  ☐ **The President or his representatives** *are* to attend the meeting.
If the last item is singular and previous item plural, we can use a singular or plural verb:
  ☐ **Either the teachers or the principal** *is* to blame for the accident. (*or* …*are* to blame…)

D

In **there + be/have** (see Unit 95) we use a singular verb form with singular and uncountable nouns and a plural form with plural nouns. However, in informal speech we often use a shortened singular form of **be** or **have** (= **There's**) with plural nouns:
  ☐ Over the last few years **there** *have* been many **improvements** in car safety.
  ☐ **There's** been lots of good films on lately. (*or* **There've** been…)

We often do the same with **how/here/where + be/have**:
  ☐ **How's** your mum and dad these days? (*or* **How** *are*…?)

41.1 For each set of sentences, choose an appropriate noun or phrase from (i) and a verb from (ii). Use the present simple for the verb, active or passive as appropriate. If both singular and plural verb forms are possible, give them both. (A)

(i)
his early paintings	~~my children~~
Dr Jones's acquaintances	the food

(ii)
know	remain	~~remember~~	taste

1 a I'd be surprised if any of ....my children remember/ remembers.... my birthday.
   b It's unlikely that any of .... It seems that he destroyed most of the work he produced during the 1930s.
   c I don't think any of .... particularly good. In fact, the restaurant is rather disappointing.
   d An investigation is underway to discover whether any of .... where he is.

(i)
other museums	vegetarians
victims	medicines

(ii)
charge	exceed	expect	relieve

2 a Mainly because of the recent health scares involving beef and chicken, the number of .... to rise dramatically in the next five years.
   b You can still go into the National Museum for free, although a number of .... in the capital .... people for entry.
   c A number of .... the symptoms of influenza, but none can cure it.
   d It is estimated that the number of .... of the flooding .... a hundred thousand, and further deaths are anticipated.

(i)
player	the cars	the pieces
these factors		

(ii)
influence	last	test	try

3 a The whole concert includes 20 short items from young musicians. Each of .... about 5 minutes.
   b There are four major influences on exchange rates: price levels, tariffs, preference for imported goods, and productivity. Here we investigate how each of .... the exchange rate.
   c The aim of the game is quite simple. Each .... to buy as many properties on the board as possible.
   d Each of .... for safety, fuel economy and reliability.

41.2 Complete the sentences with present simple forms of the verb in brackets. If both a singular and plural form are possible, give them both. (A–D)

1 Plenty of European football clubs .... interested in signing Nilsen from Rowham City, but the Rowham manager has said that no-one at the club .... Nilsen to leave. (be/ want)
2 The majority of those questioned .... that the government's economic polices have failed, although neither the Prime Minister nor the Education Minister .... indicated that these policies will change. (think/ has)
3 "It's the first time that either of us .... been to China, but everyone we've met here .... been very welcoming and helpful." (have/ have)
4 Professor Smith and Dr Peters .... that the wreck of the ship and its cargo .... a danger to local people fishing near the island. (claim/ constitute)
5 "Oh, good, sausages and chips .... my favourite." "Sorry, all the sausages .... gone, but there .... plenty of chips left if you want some." (be/ has/ be)

Unit 42 · Agreement between subject and verb (3)

A Some nouns are usually plural and take a plural verb. These include **belongings, clothes, congratulations, earnings, goods, outskirts, overheads, particulars** (= information), **premises** (= building), **riches, savings, stairs, surroundings, thanks**. The noun **whereabouts** can be used with either a singular or a plural verb. The nouns **police** and **people** always take a plural verb, and the noun **staff** usually does:

- ☐ The company's **earnings** *have increased* for the last five years.
- ☐ **Police** *believe* that Thomas is in Brazil, although his exact **whereabouts** *are/is* unknown.
- ☐ **Staff** *say* that the new computer system has led to greater levels of stress in their work.

B Some nouns always end in -s and look as if they are plural, but when we use them as the subject they have a singular verb:

- ☐ The **news** from the Middle East *seems* very encouraging.

Other words like this include **means** (= 'method' or 'money'); some academic disciplines, e.g. **economics, linguistics, mathematics, phonetics, physics, politics, statistics**; some sports, e.g. **athletics, gymnastics**; and some diseases, e.g. **diabetes, measles, rabies**. However, compare:

academic subject	general use
☐ **Politics** *is* popular at this university.	☐ Her **politics** *are* bordering on the fascist. (= political belief)
☐ **Statistics** *was* always my worst subject.	☐ **Statistics** *are* able to prove anything you want them to. (= numerical information)
☐ **Economics** *has* only recently been recognised as a scientific study.	☐ The **economics** behind their policies *are* unreasonable. (= the financial system)

C Although the words **data** and **media** (= newspaper, television, etc.) are plural (with singular forms **datum** and **medium**), they are commonly used with a singular verb. However, in formal contexts such as academic writing a plural verb is preferred. Notice that other similar plurals such as **criteria** and **phenomena** (with singular forms **criterion** and **phenomenon**) are always used with plural verbs. Compare:

- ☐ All the **data** *is* available for public inspection. (*or* ...*are* available...) *and*
- ☐ I agree that the **criteria** *are* not of equal importance. (*not* ...the criteria is not...)

D With a phrase referring to a measurement, amount or quantity we usually prefer a singular verb:

- ☐ Only **three metres** *separates* the runners in first and second places. (*rather than* ...separate...)
- ☐ The **fifty pounds** he gave me *was* soon spent. (*rather than* ...were...)

and a singular verb must be used when the complement is a singular noun phrase (e.g. a long time):

- ☐ **Three hours** *seems* a long time to take on the homework. (*not* Three hours seem...)

After **per cent** (also **percent** or **%**) **(of)** we use a singular verb if the **per cent** phrase refers to a singular or uncountable noun and a plural verb if it refers to a plural noun. Compare:

- ☐ **An inflation rate** of only 2 per cent *makes* a big difference to exports. *and*
- ☐ I would say that about 50 per cent **of the houses** *need* major repairs.

However, where we use a singular noun that can be thought of as either a whole unit or a collection of individuals, we can use either a singular or plural verb:

- ☐ Some 80 per cent of **the electorate** *is* expected to vote. (*or* ...*are* expected...)

42.1 Make any necessary corrections to the underlined verbs. (A–D)

1 Dr Jones's whereabouts <u>has</u> been kept a closely guarded secret by his family.
2 Bill Clinton's politics <u>was</u> inspired by John Kennedy.
3 Phenomena such as sun spots <u>have</u> puzzled scientists for centuries.
4 Some 30 per cent of the milk drunk in the country <u>are</u> imported.
5 When the soldiers got lost in the jungle, their only means of survival <u>were</u> to eat berries.
6 Over the last decade the company's overheads <u>has</u> increased dramatically.
7 The research data <u>was</u> collected during the period 12th–29th July 2002.
8 You don't need much sugar for this pudding; ten grams <u>are</u> enough.
9 Modern linguistics <u>is</u> often said to have begun at the start of the 20th century.
10 Congratulations <u>goes</u> to Richard Branch for his excellent exam results.
11 The coastal surroundings of the village <u>is</u> particularly attractive.
12 Nowadays politics <u>seem</u> to be more about saving money than changing society for the better.
13 He feels that the media <u>have</u> criticised him unfairly.
14 I know people often have to wait for hospital treatment, but two years <u>seems</u> ridiculously long.
15 Measles <u>have</u> killed a large number of children in the Nagola region.
16 Further particulars about the house <u>are</u> available from the owner.
17 Around 90 per cent of the concert audience <u>was</u> over 60 years old.
18 Ten kilometers <u>are</u> a long way to run if you're not fit.
19 If athletics <u>are</u> neglected in schools, this will have a big impact on future national teams.
20 People <u>says</u> the house is haunted.
21 Recent statistics <u>provide</u> firm evidence of a rapid increase in living standards in Asia.
22 About 60 per cent of the people questioned <u>wants</u> cars to be banned from the town centre.

42.2 Complete these extracts from newspaper articles with a singular or plural form of the verbs in brackets. If both singular and plural forms are possible, give them both. (A–D; also Unit 40)

1 The outskirts of our cities .... (*have*) benefited from the new out-of-town shopping centres that .... (*have*) recently been built.
2 On average, 25 litres of water .... (*be*) used each day by each household and it is anticipated that as the population .... (*expect*) higher living standards, this figure will rise.
3 It has been found that some 30 per cent of the office space in London .... (*be*) presently empty and the Department of Employment .... (*blame*) high property prices.
4 Three centimetres .... (*be*) all that separated the first two runners in last night's 10,000 metres and the sports club .... (*have*) declared the race a dead-heat.
5 The research group now .... (*admit*) that the criteria they used in the work .... (*be*) not totally reliable.
6 Following last week's major art theft from the Arcon Art Gallery, the premises .... (*be*) searched by police last night and the owner's belongings .... (*have*) been taken away for further inspection.
7 A survey of the opinions of British students .... (*show*) that economics .... (*be*) the least popular subject studied at university. However, 90 per cent of all those economics students surveyed .... (*believe*) that their courses are well taught.
8 Sufferers from diabetes .... (*have*) welcomed the launch by Federex of a new drug to combat the disease. The company .... (*say*) that earnings from the drug .... (*be*) to be put back into further research.

Compound nouns and noun phrases

A

In a compound consisting of **noun + noun**, often the second noun gives the general class of things to which the compound belongs and the first noun indicates the type within this class. The first noun usually has a singular form:

☐ **an address book** (= a book for addresses; *not* an addresses book)

However, there are a number of exceptions. These include –

☆ when the first noun only has a plural form:

☐ **a savings account   a customs officer   a clothes shop** (compare **a shoe shop**)
the arms trade (arms = weapons)   **a glasses case** (glasses = spectacles. Compare 'a glass case' = a case made of glass)   **an arts festival** (arts = music, drama, film, dance, painting, etc. Compare 'an art festival'; art = painting, drawing and sculpture)

☆ when we refer to an institution (an industry, department, etc.), such as

☐ **the building materials industry   the publications department**
which deals with more than one kind of item or activity (different types of building material, different forms of publication).

Notice that to make a compound noun plural we usually make the second noun plural:

☐ **coal mine(s)   office-worker(s)   tea leaf/tea leaves**

B

Sometimes a **noun + noun** is not appropriate and instead we use **noun + -'s + noun** (possessive form) or **noun + preposition + noun**. In general, we prefer **noun + -'s + noun** –

☆ when the first noun is the user (a person or animal) of the item in the second noun:

☐ **a baby's bedroom   a lion's den   a women's clinic   a girls' school   birds' nests**

☆ when the item in the second noun is produced by the thing (often an animal) in the first:

☐ **goat's cheese   duck's eggs   cow's milk**
(Note, however, **lamb chops** and **chicken drumsticks** (= the lower part of a chicken's leg))

☆ when we talk about parts of people or animals; but we usually use **noun + noun** to talk about parts of things. Compare:

☐ **a woman's face   a boy's arm**   *but*   **a pen top   a computer keyboard**

We prefer **noun + preposition + noun** –

☆ when we talk about some kind of container together with its contents. Compare:

☐ **a cup of tea** (= a cup with tea in it)   *and*   **a tea cup** (= a cup for drinking tea from)

☆ when the combination of nouns does not refer to a well-known class of items. Compare:

☐ **income tax** (a recognised class of tax)   *and*   **a tax on children's clothes** (*rather than* 'a children's clothes tax')

☆ in the phrases **bird of prey   rule of thumb   Chief of Staff   commander-in-chief   sister-in-law**
Notice that we usually make a plural form of these phrases by making the first noun plural (e.g. **birds of prey**). However, we can say either **sisters-in-law** or **sister-in-laws** (and **brothers-in-law** or **brother-in-laws**, etc.).

C

Some compound nouns are made up of verbs and prepositions or adverbs, and may be related to a two- or three-word verb (see Unit 94). Compare:

☐ Mansen **broke out** of the prison by dressing as a woman. (= escaped) *and*
☐ There was a major **break-out** from the prison last night. (= prisoners escaped)

Countable compound nouns like this have a plural form ending in -s:

☐ **read-out(s)   push-up(s)   intake(s)   outcome(s)**

However, there are exceptions. For example:

☐ **looker(s)-on** (*or* **onlooker(s)**)   **runner(s)-up   passer(s)-by   hanger(s)-on**

D

We can form other kinds of hyphenated phrases that are placed before nous to say more precisely what the noun refers to:

☐ a **state-of-the-art** (= very modern) computer   **day-to-day** (= regular) control

Grammar review → compound nouns H4–H6; possessive forms H7–H12

43.1 Study the italicised text and make corrections where necessary. (A & B)

1 Tom worked for a long time in (a) *the parks department*, but a few years ago he retrained, and now he's (b) *a computers programmer*. Of course, what he really wants to be is (c) *a films star!*

2 I was waiting at (a) *the bus stop* this morning when a cyclist on her way to the (b) *girl school* up the road got knocked off her bike. Someone got out of a car without looking and (c) *the car's door* hit her. She was very lucky not to be badly hurt, although she did have (d) *a head cut*.

3 I shouldn't be long at (a) *the corner shop*. I've just got three things on my (b) *shopping list* – (c) *a milk bottle*, (d) *a biscuit packet*, and (e) *some teethpaste*. I'll also look for (f) *some goat's cheese*, but I don't think they'll have any.

4 The tracks on his latest CD range from (a) *love songs* to (b) *pollution songs*.

5 Mary hated going into her grandfather's old (a) *tools shed*. It was full of (b) *spider webs*.

6 When Sue was cleaning her (a) *armschair*, she found a lot of things that had slipped down the back. There was an old (b) *pen top*, a piece from (c) *the 500-pieces jigsaw puzzle* that her daughter had been doing, and her (d) *glass case* with her sunglasses inside.

43.2 First underline the two-word verbs in sentences 1–5, then complete sentences 6–10 with appropriate compound nouns related to these two-word verbs. (C)

1 Dennis tried to cover up the fact that he had gambled and lost most of his money.

2 It is reported that cholera has broken out in the refugee camp.

3 I'm flying to Sydney, but I'm stopping over in Singapore for a few days on the way.

4 On the first Friday of each month, a few of us get together and play ten-pin bowling.

5 We set out from the camp early in the morning, hoping to reach the summit by midday.

6 The minister was taken ill in Iceland during a short .... on his way back to Canada.

7 We didn't have a big party for Jane's 50th birthday, just a family ....

8 Allegations of a .... of a major leak of radioactive waste from the nuclear power plant have been strongly denied by the Energy Ministry.

9 Only two years ago there was a serious .... of malaria in the town.

10 Even at the .... of the expedition, they knew they had little chance of crossing the desert.

43.3 Complete the phrases in (i) with a word from (ii) and then use them in the sentences below. To help you, the meaning of the phrase is given in brackets. (D)

(i)

day-to-	down-to-	larger-than-
man/woman-in-the-	once-in-a-	step-by-
middle-of-the-	round-the-	

(ii)

clock	day	earth
life	lifetime	road
step	street	

1 Although the Managing Director of Transcom was involved in major decisions, she left the ....*day-to-day*.... running of the company to her staff. (*routine*)

2 The Party will never regain power unless it can persuade .... voters that it has rid itself of corruption. (*not politically extreme*)

3 Since the attempt to assassinate him last year, the Defence Minister has been given .... protection by the police. (*all day and all night*)

4 The bookcase came with simple, ... instructions on how to assemble it. (*progressing from one stage to the next*)

5 When the comet passes close to Earth next week, scientists will have a .... opportunity to study its effects on our atmosphere. (*very rare*)

6 Terry has a refreshing, ... approach to management. He's much less concerned with theory than with getting things done in the most efficient way possible. (*practical*)

7 The .... isn't interested in the finer points of the government's tax policy. They just want to know if they are going to take home more or less pay. (*ordinary person*)

8 Her father was a .... character who was well known throughout the village for his eccentric way of dressing and outspoken views. (*more exaggerated than usual*)

Unit 44 — A/an and one

A

We use **a** before nouns and noun phrases that begin with a consonant sound. If the noun or noun phrase starts with a vowel *letter* but begins with a consonant *sound*, we also use **a**:

- **a** u**niversity** (/ə juːn.../)   **a E**uropean (/ə juər.../)   **a o**ne-parent family (/ə wʌn.../)

We use **an** before words that begin with a vowel sound:

- **an** orange   **an** Italian   **an** umbrella

These include words that begin with a silent letter 'h':

- **an** hour   **an** honest child   **an** honour   **an** honorary degree

and abbreviations said as individual letters that begin with A, E, F, H, I, L, M, N, O, R, S or X:

- **an MP** (/ən em piː/)   **an FBI** agent (/ən ef biː aɪ.../)   **an IOU** (/ən aɪ əʊ juː/)

But compare abbreviations said as words:

- **a NATO** general (/ə neɪtəʊ.../) **a FIFA** official (ə fiːfə.../) *but* **an OPEC** meeting (/ən əʊpek.../)

Notice that we say

- **a history** (book)   *but* **an** (*or* a) **historical** (novel)

B

We use **a/an** (not **one**) to talk about a particular but unspecified person, thing or event:

- I really need **a** cup of coffee.
- You never see **a** police officer in this part of town, do you?

We also use **a/an**, not **one**, in number and quantity expressions such as:

- three times **a** year   half **an** hour   **a** quarter of **an** hour   **a** day or so (= 'about a day')
  50 cents **a** (= each) litre (notice we can also say '50 cents for one litre')
  a week or two (= somewhere between one and two weeks; notice we can also say 'one or two weeks')
  a few   **a** little   **a** huge number of...

We use **a** rather than **one** in the pattern **a...of...** with possessives, as in:

- She's **a** colleague **of** mine.
- That's **a** friend **of** Bill's.

C

Before a singular countable noun **one** and **a/an** both refer to one thing:

- We'll be in Australia for **one** year. (*or* ...**a** year.)
- Wait here for **one** minute, and I'll be with you. (*or* ...**a** minute...)

Using **one** in sentences like these gives a little more emphasis to the length of time, quantity, amount, etc.:

- He weighs **one** hundred and twenty kilos! Would you believe it! (using **one** emphasises the weight more than using **a**)

However, we use **one** rather than **a/an** if we want to emphasise that we are talking about *only* one thing or person rather than two or more:

- Do you want **one** sandwich or two?
- Are you staying only **one** night?
- I just took **one** look at her and she started crying.

We use **one**, not **a/an**, in the pattern **one...other/another**:

- Close **one** eye, and then the **other**.
- Bees carry pollen from **one** plant to **another**.

We also use **one** in phrases such as **one day**, **one evening**, **one spring**, etc. to mean a particular, but unspecified day, evening, spring, etc.:

- Hope to see you again **one** day.
- **One evening**, while he was working late at the office...

Grammar review: articles → 16–17

44.1 Write **a** or **an** in the spaces. (A)

1 .... unpaid bill
2 .... DIY shop
3 .... MA in Russian
4 .... Euro
5 .... MiG fighter plane
6 .... Olympic medal
7 .... AGM

8 .... U-turn
9 .... heirloom
10 .... NASA space launch
11 .... UN decision
12 .... SOS message
13 .... F grade
14 .... hero

44.2 Change **a/an** or **one** in these sentences if necessary, or write ✓. In which sentences are both **a/an** and **one** possible? (B & C)

1 I usually go to the gym four times one week.
2 There's more than one way to solve the problem.
3 I phoned the council to complain, but just got passed on from a person to another.
4 The rate of pay is really good here. You can earn over £20 one hour.
5 Maybe we could go skiing one winter.
6 The apples are 50 cents one kilo.
7 Are you hungry? Would you like one piece of cake?
8 The rules say that there is only one vote per member.
9 You can get seven hours of recording on one disc.
10 'What would Nick like for his birthday?' 'Why don't you ask Emma? She's one good friend of his and will have some ideas.'
11 There's one pen on the floor. Is it yours?
12 The library books are due back in one month.
13 Do you want some of my chips? There are too many here for a person.
14 I'm going to London for one day or two.
15 Either I'll work late tonight or I'll come in early tomorrow, but the report's got to be finished by lunchtime a way or another.
16 It will take more than one morning to finish the decorating.

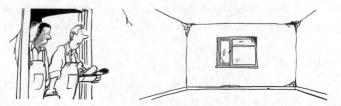

44.3 Which is more appropriate, **a/an** or **one**? If both **a/an** and **one** are possible, write them both. (B & C)

1 If you wait .... second I'll get my coat and come too.
2 I want to see the river .... last time before I leave.
3 The Queen is visiting the city .... day in November.
4 It was announced that the plane would be approximately .... hour late.
5 I could hear the sound of .... helicopter in the distance.
6 I'd just like to say .... thing before I go.
7 Martha's baby is .... year old already.
8 Dinner should be ready in .... hour or so.
9 Paul came over .... evening last week.
10 I've painted .... wall already and I'll do the other tomorrow.
11 I'd like to make .... point here, Ken, if I may.
12 .... large number of people had gathered in the square.

Unit 45

A/an, the and zero article (1)

A

We usually use **the** when we talk about things which are unique – there is only one of them (or one set of them):

- the world   the sky   the atmosphere   the sun   the ground   the climate   the sea
  the horizon   the human race   the environment   the travel industry   the arms trade

We also refer to general geographical areas with **the** as in:

- the beach   the country   the countryside   the town   the seaside   the forest

where 'the country' or 'the countryside' means 'the area where there are no towns'. We also talk about:

- the past   the present   the future

Notice, however, that some nouns like this can be used with **zero article** (i.e. no article) to refer to a concept in general:

- **Climate** is one of the many factors involved in changing farming methods. (*or* The climate...)
- The flowers grow best in sandy soil and **sun**. (= sunshine)
- In autumn the temperature difference between **land** and **sea** reduces. (*or* ...the land and the sea...)

If we want to describe a particular instance of these we can use **a/an**. Compare:

- I could see the plane high up in **the sky**. *and*
- When I woke up there was **a bright blue sky**.
- What are your plans for **the future**? *and*
- She dreamt of **a future where she could spend more time painting**.

B

We can use **the** when we make generalisations about classes of things using singular countable nouns. (See also Unit 47A.) Compare the use of **the** and **a/an** in these sentences:

- **The computer** has revolutionised publishing. (this refers to computers in general) *but not*
  A computer has revolutionised publishing. (computers *in general* have done this, not an individual computer)
- **The computer** is an important research tool. *and*   □ **A computer** is an important research tool. (this statement is true of both the general class and the individual item)

As an alternative to **the + singular countable noun** we can use a plural countable noun to talk about a class of things:

- **Computers** are an important research tool.

Notice that if **the** is used with plural and uncountable nouns we refer to a specific thing or group:

- **The computers** have arrived. Where shall I put them?
- **The music** was wonderful. I could have listened to the orchestra all night.

When we define something or say what is typical of a particular class of people or things, we generally use **a/an** rather than **the**:

- **A corkscrew** is a gadget for getting corks out of bottles.
- **A garden** is there to give you pleasure, not to be a constant worry.

C

Some nouns can be used uncountably when we talk about the whole substance or idea, but countably when we talk about an instance or more than one instance of it. When these nouns are used countably we can use **a/an** (and plurals). Compare:

- I don't drink **coffee**.   *and*   □ Would you like **a coffee**? (= a cup of coffee)
- She's got blonde **hair**.   *and*   □ There's **a hair** in my soup!
- He shook with **fear**.   *and*   □ He has **a fear** of heights.

There are many other nouns like this, including **conversation, grammar, importance, iron, pleasure, shampoo, sound**. (For more see **GR:H2 & H3**.) Some of these nouns (e.g. **grammar, iron**) have different meanings when they are used countably and uncountably (see **GR:H3**).

Grammar review: articles → I1–I9; countable and uncountable nouns → H1–H3

45.1 Choose one of the following words to complete these sentences. Use the same word in each pair. Add **the** or **a/an** in an appropriate place. (A)

> beach   future   past   world

1 a I think the best Australian wine is as good as any in ....
   b As a child, Ethel would often daydream about travelling forward in time to ....
      very different from the one she lived in.
2 a If we are elected, we will build our policies on the simple belief that our purpose is to create
      bright .... for our children rather than achieving short-term goals for ourselves.
   b Although our current financial position is worrying, we have many new orders for our
      products and .... is bright.
3 a As I get older, I seem to remember .... better than things that happened
      very recently.
   b At the age of 98, Johnson has .... that goes back to the start of the last century.
4 a If you want to get away from it all, you can take a small boat to deserted ....
      on one of the islands.
   b Dear Mum and Dad, We're having a great holiday. The weather's wonderful and we're
      spending most of our time on ....

45.2 Underline the correct or more likely answer. If both answers are possible, underline them both. (B)

1 We get some strange requests in our shop. We had *the customer/ a customer* in the other day
   who wanted to buy chocolate-covered ants.
2 It sometimes seems that *the individual/ an individual* can have little impact on the decisions
   that governments take.
3 The invention of *a car/ the car* is normally attributed to the German engineer Gottlieb Daimler.
4 *The television/ A television* has changed the way we obtain information more than any other
   modern invention.
5 The campaign against smoking in public places argues that its harmful effects are not confined
   to *the smoker/ a smoker*.

45.3 Use each of these nouns twice to complete the sentences. Where necessary, add **a/an** at an appropriate place in the sentence. (C)

> conversation   grammar   importance   iron   pleasure   shampoo   sound

1 My sisters were clearly having ᵃ⟨serious ___conversation___ so I didn't like to disturb them.
2 It now gives me great .... to introduce that marvellous ventriloquist, Marco Lutman.
3 The Nile is of critical .... to the social and economic life of Egypt.
4 As we walked through the jungle we heard .... we weren't expecting – the ring of
   a mobile phone.
5 The failure to teach .... in schools has caused an overall decline in people's ability
   to write well.
6 Most red meat is relatively high in ....
7 Within a day of washing my hair it starts to feel greasy. I have yet to find ....
   to solve this problem.
8 .... travels at different speeds, depending on the temperature of the air.
9 I got .... in my eye this morning in the shower and it's made it really sore.
10 It's real .... to travel by rail in Sweden. The trains are clean and punctual.
11 I have .... of English printed in 1890 on very thin paper.
12 Because the central government has relocated there, the town of Paraga has taken on
    .... out of all proportion to its size.
13 Although he's got .... he never seems to use it. His shirts are always creased.
14 As she walked into the party, ... ceased and everyone in the crowded room stared
    at her.

A/an, the and zero article (2)

A We use **a/an** to say what a person's job is, was, or will be:
- □ She was **a company director** when she retired.
- □ Against her parents' wishes, she wants to be **a journalist**.

However, when we give a person's job title, or their unique position, we use **the** or **zero article** (i.e. no article), not **a/an**. Compare:
- □ She's been appointed (**the**) **head of the company.** *and*
- □ I'm **a production manager** at Fino. (= there may be more than one production manager)

After **the position of, the post of,** or **the role of** we use **zero article** before a job title:
- □ Dr Simons has taken on **the position of** Head of Department.

B We usually use **zero article** (i.e. no article) before the name of an individual person or place. However, we use **the** –
- ☆ when there are two people with the same name and we want to specify which one we are talking about:
  - □ That's not **the Stephen Fraser** I went to school with.
  - but compare 'There was **a Stephen Fraser** in my class.' (= a person named Stephen Fraser)
- ☆ when we want to emphasise that the person we are referring to is the most famous person with that name. Used this way, **the** is stressed and pronounced /ðiː/:
  - □ Do they mean *the* **Ronald Reagan**, or someone else?
- ☆ with an adjective to describe a person, or another noun which tells us their job:
  - □ **the late Buddy Holly**   □ **the artist William Turner**
- ☆ when we talk about a family as a whole:
  - □ **The Robinsons** are away this weekend.

C Notice that **a/an**, or sometimes **zero article**, is used with a name when referring to the particular excellent qualities of the person named:
- □ Jane plays tennis well, but she'll never be (**a**) **Steffi Graf**.

We also use **a/an** when we refer to an individual example of a product made by a particular manufacturer (e.g I've just bought **a Mercedes**) or a work by a particular artist (e.g. Do you think it could be **a** Van Gogh/**a** Rembrandt?).

You can use **a/an** before a person's name if you don't know the person yourself. Compare:
- □ Dr Perch is here for you. (= I know Dr Perch) *and*
- □ There's **a Dr Kenneth Perch** on the phone. (= I haven't heard of him before) Do you want to talk to him?

D In stories and jokes in conversation, **this** is commonly used instead of **a/an** to introduce a new person or thing. Using **this** highlights the person or thing as the topic of what is to come next:
- □ As I was walking along, **this** spider (= 'a spider') landed on my head, and...
- □ **This** man (= 'a man') goes into a chemist and he says...

E We use **the** before a *superlative adjective* (**the biggest, the most expensive,** etc.) when the superlative adjective is followed by a noun or defining phrase:
- □ He is **the finest** *young player* around at the moment.

However, we can often leave out **the**, particularly in an informal style, when there is no noun or defining phrase after the superlative adjective. Compare:
- □ A: Why did you decide to stay in this hotel?
- B: It was (**the**) **cheapest.** *and* It was **the cheapest** I could find.

46.1 Put **a/an**, **the** or zero article (–) in the spaces. Give all possible answers. (A–C)

1 A special award was given to .... novelist Ian McMurphy.
2 I've been offered the position of .... Director of Personnel.
3 I've always wanted to meet .... Michael Owen.
4 'What make is your computer?' 'It's .... Mac.'
5 I'm .... marketing adviser at Unifleet.
6 Let me introduce you to .... Paula Cox.
7 We met our good friend .... Jean Wools when we were in .... Plymouth.
8 I found myself talking to .... George Bush! Not .... George Bush, of course, but someone with the same name.
9 Brian's .... manager of the local football team.
10 I didn't even know Joan was interested in art until I heard that she owns .... Van Gogh.
11 When Jennie was young she knew .... Picasso.
12 She was determined to be .... author.
13 He has been appointed .... Minister for Industry.
14 She recently became .... minister in the new government.
15 We're going on holiday with .... Smiths.
16 He's really keen on playing football. He likes to think of himself as .... Ronaldo.
17 .... Linda Green is outside. Do you want to see her?

46.2 If the underlined **the** can be left out of these sentences, put brackets around it. (E)

1 It's <u>the</u> best ice-cream I've ever tasted.
2 Jack's boat wasn't the most elegant in the harbour, but it was certainly <u>the</u> biggest.
3 I thought the second competitor was <u>the</u> best, even though he didn't win a prize.
4 This is by far <u>the</u> most valuable painting in the collection.
5 'Why did you ask Jim to go first?' 'Because he's <u>the</u> oldest.'
6 Sapphires occur in a variety of colours, but blue ones are <u>the</u> most valuable.
7 The Pacific is <u>the</u> biggest ocean in the world.
8 It's supposed to be <u>the</u> oldest post office in the country.

46.3 Complete the text with **a/an**, **the**, zero article or **this**. Give alternatives where possible. (Units 45 & 46)

Send Now | Send Later | Save as Draft | Add Attachments | Signature ▾ | Options ▾ | Rewrap

Something very strange happened to me the other night. As I was going home (1) .... man came up to me. He had (2) .... untidy hair and (3) .... paint all over his clothes. He told me that he was (4) .... head of the local council and that he was offering me a job as (5) .... road sweeper. He said that (6) .... road sweeper earns a great deal of money and that I would have (7) .... responsibility for miles of roads. Well, I just said 'No thanks' and walked on. When I looked back he had stopped (8) .... woman. He was telling her that he was (9) .... President of the United States and that he wanted her to be (10) .... Defence Secretary…

A/an, the and zero article (3)

A With plural and uncountable nouns, **zero article** (i.e. no article) is used to talk generally, without definite people or things in mind. **The** is used when we assume the listener or reader will understand who or what we are referring to, or when other words in the noun phrase make the reference specific. Compare:

- □ The government has promised not to tax **books**. (= books generally) *and*
- □ **The books** have arrived. (= the books you ordered)
- □ **Music** played an important part in his life. (= music generally) *and*
- □ I thought **the music** used in the film was the best part. (= this particular music)

B We often use **zero article** with the names of holidays, special times of the year, months, and days of the week including **Easter, Ramadan, New Year's Day**. But compare:

- □ I'll see you on **Saturday**. (= next Saturday) □ We met on **Saturday**. (= last Saturday)
- □ They arrived on **a Saturday** as far as I can remember. (we are only interested in the day of the week, not which particular Saturday)
- □ They arrived on **the Saturday** after my birthday. (a particular Saturday, specifying which one)

With **winter, summer, spring, autumn**, and **New Year** (meaning the holiday period), we can use either **zero article** or **the**:

- □ In (**the**) **summer** I try to spend as much time as I can in the garden.

We use **the** when it is understood or we go on to specify which summer, spring, etc. we mean:

- □ I'd like to go skiing in **the autumn**. (= this year) □ I first went skiing in **the spring** of 1992.

We say 'in the New Year' to mean near the beginning of next year:

- □ I'll see you again in **the New Year**.

When we want to describe the features of a particular holiday, season, or other period of time and say that it was somehow special when compared with others, we can use **It/That was... + a/an + noun + modifying phrase**. Compare:

- □ That was **a winter** I'll never forget. (= compared to other winters it was unforgettable) *and*
- □ That was **the winter** we went to Norway. (= a statement about a particular winter)

C We use **zero article** with times of the day and night such as **midnight, midday**, and **noon**:

- □ If possible, I'd like it finished by **midday**. □ **Midnight** couldn't come quickly enough.

But notice that we can say either **the dawn** or **dawn**:

- □ He got back into bed and waited for (**the**) **dawn**.

We use **the + morning/afternoon/evening** for a day which is understood or already specified:

- □ I enjoyed **the morning**, but in **the afternoon** the course was boring. But compare:
- □ **Morning** is the time I work best. (= mornings in general; **The morning**... is also possible)
- □ I'll be there by (**the**) **morning/evening**. (*but* ...**by the afternoon**, *not* ...by afternoon)
- □ I waited **all morning**. (*more usual than* all the morning/afternoon, etc.)
- □ 'You look upset.' 'Yes, I've had **a terrible morning**.' (= compared to other mornings)

D We use **by + zero article** to talk about means of transport and communication, including **go/travel** *by* **car/taxi/bus/plane/train/air/sea**; **contact/communicate** *by* **post/email/phone**. Compare:

- □ I generally go **by bus** to work. *and* □ I generally take **the bus** to work.

E We often use **zero article** in patterns where repeated or related words are joined by a preposition and used with a general meaning:

- □ The government makes grants according to criteria that differ from **region to region**.

Other examples include **person to person, back to back, end to end, face to face, side by side, start to finish, day by day, put pen to paper**.

Grammar review: articles → 11–19

47.1 Complete these sentences using one of these words. Use **the** where necessary. Use the *same* word in both (a) and (b) in each pair. (A)

agriculture   children   fire   holidays   islands   money   parents   rain

1 a .... as young as ten are working in the clothing industry.
 b While you're painting the sitting room, I'll take .... over to the park.
2 a As the soil quality deteriorated, so too did .... on which the region depended.
 b Around 60% of the labour force in the county is supported by ....
3 a Around the world .... are being threatened by rising sea levels.
 b .... off the east coast of Malaysia are beautiful.
4 a I've been really busy at work, so I'm really looking forward to ....
 b .... in the Brazilian rainforests are now becoming popular with adventurous travellers.
5 a Farmers will be hoping for .... in the next few weeks.
 b Last night .... was torrential.
6 a I've left .... I owe you on your desk.
 b It is said that .... is the root of all evil.
7 a Using the new software, ... will be able to monitor their children's use of the Internet.
 b .... of Paul Thomas claimed that he was at home at the time of the robbery.
8 a It isn't known how .... started.
 b Animals fear .... more than anything else.

47.2 Write **a/an**, **the** or **zero article (–)**, whichever is more likely, in the spaces in these sentences. Where more than one answer is possible, consider any difference in meaning. (B, C & D)

1 a Do you remember when Mark and Julie came over and had that terrible row? That was .... day I wouldn't want to go through again.
 b I couldn't go to Jane's party. It was .... day I was babysitting for Derek and Linda.
2 a 'Shall we go out walking on .... Sunday?' 'No, I'm busy this weekend.'
 b I know the meeting will be on .... Sunday in June, but I don't know the exact date yet.
3 a Are you talking about .... Christmas we spent in Sweden?
 b I'll see you again after .... Christmas.
4 a The exam results will be sent by .... post on 24th August.
 b The application forms came in .... post this morning.
5 a I'd been working in the garden all .... afternoon and my back ached.
 b I've spent .... afternoon on the phone to my mother.
6 a That old coat of yours won't be warm enough for .... winter.
 b 'I haven't seen Jack for months.' 'He's been away in South Africa for .... winter.'
7 a The early train to Cambridge was cancelled so I had to go by .... car.
 b It's raining so I think I'll take .... car.

47.3 Complete the sentences using one of the phrases in E. (E)

1 They sat .... on the bench looking out over the countryside.
2 She was in hospital for several weeks, but .... her health improved.
3 Tiger Woods is celebrating .... victories in his last three golf tournaments.
4 The island is so small you can walk from .... in about an hour.
5 The disease is easily spread from ....

Some

A Before plural and uncountable nouns we sometimes use **some** or **zero article** (i.e. no article) with very little difference in meaning:

- ☐ 'Where were you last week?' 'I was visiting (**some**) friends.'
- ☐ Before serving, pour (**some**) yoghurt over the top.

With both **some** and **zero article** we are referring to particular people or things but in an indefinite way. When it is used in this way, **some** is usually pronounced /səm/.

We don't use **some** to make general statements about whole classes of things or people (GR:I8 & I9):

- ☐ **Furniture** can be an expensive item when you buy your first home.
- ☐ **Babies** need lots of care and attention.

B **Some** is used before a number to mean 'approximately':

- ☐ **Some** eighty per cent of all residents took part in the vote. (= approximately eighty per cent; beginning 'Eighty per cent...' suggests a more precise figure)

When it is used in this way, **some** is usually pronounced /sʌm/.

C When we can't say exactly which person or thing we are talking about because we don't know, can't remember, or want to emphasise that it is not important, we can use **some** instead of **a/an** with a singular noun. When it is used in this way, **some** is usually pronounced /sʌm/.

- ☐ He was interrupted twice by **some** troublemaker in the audience.

We use the phrase **some(thing) or other** in a similar way:

- ☐ I bought them from **some** shop **or other** in New Street. (*not* ...from a shop or other...)

Any

D We usually use **any** not **some** (and **anyone**, **anything**, etc. not **someone**, **something**, etc.) –

- ☆ in non-affirmative contexts; that is, lacking positive, affirmative meaning.
- ☆ to refer to non-specific, unspecified things.

For example, we generally use **any** in sentences with a negative meaning when they include negative adverbs such as **barely, hardly, never, rarely, scarcely, seldom**; negative verbs such as **deny, fail, forbid, prevent, prohibit, refuse**; negative adjectives such as **impossible, reluctant, unable, unlikely**; and the preposition **without**:

- ☐ There's *hardly* **any** sugar left. We must get some when we go shopping.
- ☐ I boarded up the windows to *prevent* **any** damage during the storm.
- ☐ It was *impossible* to see **anything** in the dark.
- ☐ We didn't have tickets, but we got into the stadium *without* **any** difficulty.

However, we use **some** with these negative words–

- ☆ when **some** (pronounced /sʌm/) has the implication 'not all' (see I13):
  - ☐ We were able to *prevent* **some** damage to the house. (= but not all of it)
  - ☐ I talk to colleagues *before* I take **some** decisions, but this one I had to decide on my own.
- ☆ when the basic meaning is positive:
  - ☐ **Somebody** isn't telling the truth. (= There is some person (who isn't telling the truth))
- ☆ when we are talking about a particular but unspecified person or thing:
  - ☐ I was *reluctant* to repeat **something** so critical of Paul. (= a specific criticism)

E We often use **any** in clauses that begin with **before**, and with comparisons:

- ☐ I cleared up the mess *before* **anyone** saw it. ('...before someone saw it' suggests that I have a particular person in mind who might see it)
- ☐ She has as good a chance *as* **anybody** of winning the race.
- ☐ The material felt *softer than* **anything** she had ever touched before.

Grammar review: *some* → I10–I14, *any* → I15–I19, *anyone, someone*, etc. → I20–I21

Exercises

48.1 Complete the sentences with **some** or zero article (–). If both **some** and **zero article** are possible with little difference in meaning, write (some). (A & GR I10–I14)

1 There have been .... allegations of corruption in the government.
2 If you're going to the library, could you take back .... books that I've finished reading?
3 The price of .... coffee is at an all-time low.
4 The door kept flying open in the wind so I tied it up with .... string.
5 I'm going into town to buy .... clothes.
6 Tony knows more about .... jazz than anyone I've every met.
7 It costs much more to make .... films today than 10 years ago.
8 I need to get .... bread from the supermarket.

48.2 Rewrite these newspaper headlines in your own words using **some** to mean 'approximately'. The first is done for you. (B)

1 │ **250 people charged with assault following Molton riots** │

    Some 250 people have been charged with assault following the Molton riots.

2 │ **30% OF ALL CITY BUSES FOUND TO BE UNSAFE** │

3 │ **Unexploded bomb found 5 miles from Newham centre** │

4 │ **25% OF ELECTRICITY FROM WIND BY 2020** │

5 │ **200 jobs to be lost at Encon steel works** │

48.3 Complete the sentences in any appropriate way using **some + singular noun** or **some + singular noun + or other**. The first is done for you. (C)

1 I don't know where I got the information from. I must have heard it *on some radio programme (or other).*
2 I don't know where Richard is. He's probably ....
3 I don't know where the book is. Maybe I lent it ....
4 I don't know where Maggie works. I think it's in ....
5 I don't know why Ken is still at work. Perhaps he's got to ....

48.4 Complete these sentences with **some, someone, something, any, anyone** or **anything**. Where both **some(one/thing)** or **any(one/thing)** are possible, write them both and consider any difference in meaning. (D & E)

1 John worked hard at learning Japanese but failed to make .... real progress.
2 I was unable to eat .... of the food.
3 I always offer to help organise school concerts, but there is seldom .... for me to do.
4 Janet Jones is .... I rarely see these days.
5 He denied that he had done .... wrong.
6 I always get to work before .... else.
7 The theatre is unlikely to have .... tickets left for tonight's performance.
8 Despite rowing as hard as we could, we had progressed barely .... distance from the shore.
9 .... parents never seem to have time to sit down and talk to their children.
10 The regulations of the game forbid .... ball to rise above shoulder height.
11 When I last lent my laptop to a friend it came back damaged, so I'm reluctant to lend it to .... else.
12 She valued friendship more than .... in the world.

A We can use **no** and **none (of)** instead of **not a** or **not any** for particular emphasis. Compare:
- There isn't a train until tomorrow. *and* There's **no** train until tomorrow. (more emphatic)
- She didn't give me **any** help at all. *and* She gave me **no** help at all.
- Sorry, there isn't **any** left. *and* Sorry, there's **none** left.
- He didn't have **any** of the usual symptoms. *and* He had **none of** the usual symptoms.

We use other pairs of negative words and phrases in a similar way:
- There isn't **anyone/anybody** here. *and* There's **no-one/nobody** here. (more emphatic)
- I haven't got **anything** to wear for the party. *and* I've got **nothing** to wear for the party.
- She wasn't **anywhere** to be seen. *and* She was **nowhere** to be seen.
- Why don't you **ever** call me? *and* Why do you **never** call me?

B We don't usually use **not a/any**, **not anyone**, etc. in initial position in a sentence or clause, or straight after **and**, **but** or **that** at the beginning of a clause. Instead we use **no**, **none of**, **no-one**, etc.:
- **No** force was needed to make them move. (*not* Not any force was needed...)
- Most players are under 16 *and* **none of** them is over 20. (*not* ...and not any of them...)
- We arranged the meeting, *but* **no-one** came. (*not* ...but not anyone...)
- I'm sure *that* **nothing** can go wrong. (*not* ...that not anything can...)

C In a formal or literary style we can use **not a** in initial position or after **and**, **but** or **that** (see also Unit 100):
- **Not a** sound came from the room. (*less formally* There wasn't a sound from the room.)
- She kept so quiet *that* **not a** soul in the house knew she was there.

D After **no**, we can often use either a singular or a plural noun with little difference in meaning, although a singular noun is usually more formal:
- **No answers** could be found. (*or more formally* **No answer**...)
- We want to go to the island but there are **no boats** to take us. (*or more formally* ...there is **no boat**.)

However, we use a *singular* noun in situations where we would expect one of something, and a *plural* noun where we would expect more than one. Compare:
- I phoned Sarah at home, but there *was* **no answer**. (*not* ...but there were no answers.) *and*
- He seems very lonely at school, and *has* **no friends**. (*not* ...no friend.)

E We can give special emphasis to **no** or **none of** using phrases like **no amount of** with uncountable nouns, **not one.../ not a single...** with singular countable nouns, and **not one of...** with plural nouns:
- The company is so badly managed that **no amount of** *investment* will make it successful.
- It was clear that **no amount of** *planning* could have improved the situation.
- **Not one** *person* remembered my birthday. (*or* **Not a single** *person*...)
- **Not one of** *the families* affected by the noise wants to move.

F Some phrases with **no** are commonly used in informal spoken English: **No wonder** (= it's not surprising); **No idea** (= I don't know); **No comment** (= I have nothing to say); **No way**, **No chance** (= emphatic ways of saying 'no', particularly to express refusal to do or believe something); **No problem**, **No bother** (= it isn't/wasn't difficult to do something):
- 'The computer's not working again.' '**No wonder**. It's not plugged in!'
- 'Thanks for the lift.' '**No problem**. I had to go past the station anyway.'

Grammar review: *no, none* → 129–134

49.1 Complete the sentences with a word or phrase from (i) followed by a word or phrase from (ii). Use each word or phrase once only. (A–C)

(i)

no	~~none~~	none of
no-one	nothing	nowhere
never	not	

(ii)

a drop	else	going to get
heard	the hotels	~~in the cupboard~~
point	wrong	

1 Where are the biscuits? There's _none in the cupboard._

2 We left the house as quietly as possible and .... us.

3 .... was spilt as she poured the liquid into the flask.

4 Jack was determined to leave and I knew that there was .... in protesting.

5 The door was locked and he had .... to go.

6 I found that .... in the city centre had any rooms left.

7 Tom's so lazy. Is he .... a job?

8 The doctors reassured Emily that they could find .... with her.

49.2 Look again at the sentences in 49.1. Which of them can you rewrite to make less emphatic using **not (n't) any/anyone**, etc.? (A–B)

49.3 If necessary, suggest changes to any parts of these sentences that are unlikely. (D)

1 There were no televisions in the hotel room so I went out to see a film.

2 I was surprised to find that there were no books on football in the library.

3 The car was very old and had no seatbelt.

4 I returned the cheque to Mr Wallis because there were no signatures on it.

5 The park was just a large area of grass with no tree.

6 When I opened the packet I found there was no sweet in it.

7 I phoned Dr Owen this morning, but there was no reply.

8 When I got to the shop there was no newspaper left.

49.4 Complete these sentences in any appropriate way beginning **not one (of)** or **no amount of**. (E)

1 I made lots of cakes for the party but _not one of the children liked them._

2 Mr Carlson didn't want to sell the painting, and ....

3 I sent job applications to over a hundred companies, but ....

4 Smallpox used to be common all over the world but since 1978 ....

5 The floor had dirty black marks all over it, and ....

49.5 Choose one of the **No...** phrases in F to complete these sentences. (F)

1 'Can you give me a lift to the station?' '... I'll pick you up at 8.00.'

2 'I've got a headache.' '... You've been in front of that computer screen for hours.'

3 'Do you think Kim will pass her maths?' '... She just doesn't work hard enough.'

4 'Where's Barry?' '... Last time I saw him he was in the kitchen.'

5 'I'm from the *Daily News*, Dr James. Do you have anything to say about the accusation that you stole from your patients?' '... Goodbye.'

A

In affirmative sentences we generally use **a lot of** and **lots (of)** rather than **much (of)** and **many (of)**, particularly in informal contexts. However, there are a number of exceptions –

☆ In formal contexts, such as academic writing, **much (of)** and **many (of)** are often preferred. We can also use phrases such as **a large/considerable/substantial amount of** (with uncountable nouns), or **a large/considerable/great/substantial number of** (with plural nouns):

- ☐ **Much** debate has been heard about Thornton's new book.
- ☐ There could be **many** explanations for this.
- ☐ **Much of** her fiction describes women in unhappy marriages.
- ☐ **A large amount of** the food was inedible. (*or* **Much of…**)
- ☐ The book contains **a large number of** pictures, many in colour. (*or* …many…)

☆ In formal contexts we can use **much** and **many** as pronouns:

- ☐ There is no guarantee of a full recovery. **Much** depends on how well she responds to treatment.
- ☐ The government's policies have done **much** to reduce unemployment.
- ☐ **Many** (= many people) have argued that she is the finest poet of our generation.
- ☐ Not once did I see a tiger in the jungle, although I heard **many**. (referring back to 'tiger(s)')

☆ We usually use **many** rather than **a lot of** or **lots of** with time expressions (**days, minutes, months, weeks, years**) and **number + of** (e.g. **thousands of voters, millions of pounds**):

- ☐ We used to spend **many** *hours* driving to Melbourne and back.
- ☐ He was the founder of a company now worth **many** *millions of pounds*.

B

We can use **many** following **the, my, its, his, her**, etc. and plural countable nouns:

- ☐ Among *the* **many** *unknowns* after the earthquake is the extent of damage to the foundations of buildings.
- ☐ The gallery is exhibiting some of *his* **many** *famous paintings of ships*.

We can use the phrase **many a** with a singular noun to talk about a repeated event or a large number of people or things:

- ☐ The manager must have spent **many a** *sleepless night* worrying about his team selection.
- ☐ **Many a** *pupil* at the school will be pleased that Latin is no longer compulsory.

C

To emphasise that we are talking about a large number we can use **a good/great many** with a plural noun:

- ☐ She has **a good/great many** *friends* in New Zealand.

To emphasise that we are talking about a large amount we can use **a good/great deal of** with a singular or uncountable noun:

- ☐ **A good/great deal of** *the exhibition* was devoted to her recent work.

D

We use **far** (not 'much' or 'many') before **too many + a plural countable noun** or **too much + an uncountable noun**:

- ☐ **Far too many** *students* failed the end-of-year maths exam. (*not* Much/Many too many…)
- ☐ **Far too much** *time* is wasted filling in forms. (*not* Much/Many too much time…)

E

We often use **plenty of** instead of **a lot of** or **lots of** with uncountable and plural countable nouns. However, **plenty of** means 'enough, or more than enough' and is therefore not likely in certain contexts. Compare:

- ☐ We took **lots of** food and drink on our walk through the hills. (*or* …**plenty of**…) *and*
- ☐ Jim doesn't look well. He's lost **a lot of** weight. ('plenty of' is unlikely here)

Grammar review: *much (of), many (of), a lot of, lots (of)* → 138–142

50.1 Make corrections or improvements to these extracts from conversations (1–3) and from academic writing (4–6). (A, C, D & E)

1 Sheila's had many problems with her back for a lot of years. She's having an operation next week and she won't be back at work for a good deal of weeks afterwards.

2 'There's bound to be much traffic on the way to the station. Perhaps we should leave now.' 'Don't worry, there's plenty time left, and at this time of day many people will already be at work.'

3 Many think that hedgehogs are very rare nowadays, but when I was in Wales I saw many.

4 A lot have claimed that Professor Dowman's study on current attitudes to politics is flawed. One criticism is that much too many people questioned in the survey were under 18.

5 A lot of research has been conducted on the influence of diet on health, with a lot of studies focusing on the relationship between fat intake and heart disease. However, a lot remains to be done.

6 While it is true that a lot of thousands of jobs were lost with the decline of the northern coal and steel industries, a lot of advantages have also followed. Much too many cases of lung disease were recorded in the region, but with lower levels of pollution the number has declined. In addition, a great deal of hi-tech companies have moved in to take advantage of the newly available workforce.

50.2 Complete the sentences with either **the/my/its/his/her many** or **many a/an** and then one of the following. (B)

coffee shops	expeditions	~~German relatives~~	golf courses
letters	ship	sunny afternoon	teacher

1 She went to stay in Munich with one of ...... *her many German relatives.* ......

2 I spent .... sitting on the terrace looking out over the hills.

3 .... has been lost in the treacherous waters off the south coast of the island.

4 The town is most famous for .... that attract players from all over the world.

5 Since the end of last year he has refused to speak to me on the phone or answer

....

6 Jo Granger accompanied Colonel Smithers on .... to the Himalayas and the Andes.

7 .... will be looking forward to the start of the school holidays at the end of the week.

8 I walked into the first of .... along the High Street and ordered an espresso.

50.3 Write **plenty of** if it is appropriate in these sentences. If not, use **a lot of**. (E)

1 It will be very hot on the journey, so make sure you bring .... drinking water.

2 .... staff at the hospital have come down with a mysterious illness.

3 He didn't have .... money left, so he decided to catch the bus rather than take a taxi.

4 We were surprised when .... students failed to attend the lecture.

5 I'm looking forward to a relaxing holiday, and I'm taking .... books to read.

All (of), whole, every, each

All (of)

A

We sometimes use **all** after the noun it refers to:

- *His songs* **all** sound much the same to me. (*or* **All** (of) *his songs* sound...)
- *We* **all** think Ann's working too hard. (*or* All of *us* think...)

Notice that we usually put **all** after the verb **be** and after the first auxiliary verb if there is one:

- They *are* **all** going to Athens during the vacation. (*not* They all are going...)
- You *should* **all** have three question papers. (*not* You all should have...; however, note that we can say 'You <u>all</u> should have...' for particular emphasis in spoken English)

B

To make negative sentences with **all** (of) we usually use **not all** (of) rather than **all...not** (although **all...not** is sometimes used in informal spoken English):

- **Not all** (of) the seats were taken. *or* The seats were **not all** taken.

Note that **not all** and **none of** have a different meaning. Compare:

- **Not all** my cousins were at the wedding. (= some of them were there) *and*
- **None of** my cousins were at the wedding. (= not one of them was there)

All and whole

C

Before singular countable nouns we usually use **the whole** rather than **all the**:

- They weren't able to stay for **the whole** concert. (*rather than* ...for all the concert.)

However, we can also say **all** + **day/week/night/month/winter**, etc. (*but not usually* all October/ 2001/ 21st May, etc.; **all Monday/Tuesday**, etc. are only usually used in informal contexts); **all the time, all the way**; and in informal speech we can use **all the** with things that we see as being made up of parts (**all the world/house/city/country/department**, etc.):

- She spent **the whole** *winter* in the south of Spain. (*or* ...**all** *winter*...)
- After the fire **the whole** *city* was covered in dust. (*or* ...**all** *the city*... in informal speech)

Notice that we can use **entire** instead of **whole** immediately before a noun:

- The **whole/entire** building has recently been renovated.

Before plural nouns we can use **all** (of) or **whole**, but they have different meanings. Compare:

- **All** (of) **the towns** had their electricity cut off. (= every town in an area) *and*
- After the storm, **whole towns** were left without electricity. (= some towns were completely affected; note that we don't say '...whole the towns...')

Every and each

D

Often we can use **every** or **each** with little difference in meaning. However, we use **every** –

☆ with **almost, nearly, virtually**, etc. to emphasise we are talking about a group as a whole:
- *Almost* **every** visitor stopped and stared. (*not* Almost each visitor...)

☆ with a plural noun when **every** is followed by a number:
- I go to the dentist **every** six months. (*rather than* ...each six months.)

☆ in phrases referring to regular or repeated events such as: **every other** (kilometre), **every single** (day), **every so often, every few** (months), and **every now and again** (= occasionally)

☆ with abstract uncountable nouns such as **chance, confidence, hope, reason**, and **sympathy** to show a positive attitude to what we are saying. Here **every** means 'complete' or 'total':
- She has **every** *chance* of success in her application for the job.

We use **each** –

☆ when we are talking about both people or things in a pair:
- I only had two suitcases, but **each** one weighed over 20 kilos.

☆ as a pronoun:
- I asked many people and **each** gave the same answer. (*or* ...**each/every** one gave...)

Grammar review: *all (of)* → 143-144; *each/every* → 145-146

51.1 Put **all** in the more appropriate space in each sentence. (A)

1 They .... were .... sitting around the table waiting for me.
2 You .... can .... stay for dinner if you want.
3 It .... had .... happened so quickly, I couldn't remember much about it.
4 We .... are .... going to be late if we don't hurry.
5 .... the children .... started to speak at once.
6 We have .... been .... involved in the decision.

51.2 Underline the more appropriate answer. If both are possible, underline them both. (C)

1 *All the process/ The whole process* takes only a few minutes.
2 *All areas of the country/ Whole areas of the country* have been devastated by the floods, although others haven't had rain for months.
3 *All the trip/ The whole trip* cost me less than $1000.
4 The new rail network links *all of the towns/ whole towns* in the region.
5 When I picked up the book I found that *all of the pages/ whole pages* had been ripped out. There wasn't a single one left.
6 The new heating system makes *all the building/ the whole building* warmer.
7 *All the room/ The whole room* was full of books.

51.3 Complete these sentences with **every** or **each**, whichever is more appropriate. If you can use either **every** or **each**, write them both. (D)

1 I had .... reason to believe that she would keep my secret.
2 The ten lucky winners will .... receive £1000.
3 We've discussed the problem in virtually .... meeting for the last year.
4 Hugh sends us a postcard from .... place he visits.
5 In a rugby league game .... side has 13 players.
6 They had to take out .... single part of the engine and clean it.
7 Antibiotics were given to .... child in the school as a precaution.
8 The two girls walked in, ... one carrying a bouquet of flowers.
9 .... household in the country is to be sent a copy of a booklet giving advice on first aid.
10 There is a small picture on .... page of the book.
11 You should take two tablets .... four hours.
12 The exam is three hours in total and we have to answer six questions, so we have about half an hour for .... answer.

51.4 Find any mistakes in the italicised parts of this text and suggest corrections. (A–D)

(1) *Each so often* I like to invite (2) *my entire family* – my parents, six brothers and their families – over for dinner on Saturday evening. My parents are quite old now, so I like to see them (3) *each few weeks*. It's quite a lot of work and I usually spend (4) *all Friday* shopping and cooking. Some of my family are fussy about what they eat, so I generally have to cook different things for (5) *every of them*. Fortunately, (6) *all the food doesn't* usually get eaten, so I have plenty left for the rest of the week. (7) *None of my brothers always come*, but the ones who live locally usually do. This time (8) *Neil and his family all were on holiday* so they couldn't make it. (9) *We had all a great time* and we spent (10) *the whole evening* talking about when we were children.

Unit 52

Few, little, less, fewer

A

We often use (a) **few** and (a) **little** with nouns. However, we can also use them as pronouns:

- □ **Little** is known about the painter's early life.
- □ It is a part of the world visited by **few**. (= few people)
- □ Do you want a chocolate? There's still **a few** left. (= a few chocolates)
- □ The password is known by only **a few**. (= a few people)
- □ 'Do you know anything about car engines?' '**A little**.' (= I know a little about car engines)

Note that **quite a few** means 'quite a large number':

- □ She's been away from work for **quite a few** weeks.

B

We can use **the few** and **the little** followed by a noun to suggest 'not enough' when we talk about a group of things or people (with **few**) or part of a group or amount (with **little**):

- □ It's one of **the few** shops in the city centre where you can buy food.
- □ We should use **the little** time we have available to discuss Jon's proposal.

Instead of **the few/little** we can use **what few/little** to mean 'the small (number/amount)':

- □ She gave **what little** money she had in her purse to the man. (*or* ...**the little** money...)
- □ **What few** visitors we have are always made welcome. (*or* **The few** visitors...)

Notice that we can also say 'She gave **what/the little** she had...' and '**What/The few** we have...' when it is clear from the context what is being referred to.

We can use **few** (but rarely **little**) after personal pronouns (**my**, **her**, etc.) and **these** and **those**:

- □ I learned to play golf during **my few** days off during the summer.
- □ She put **her few** clothes into a bag, and walked out of the house for ever.
- □ **These few** miles of motorway have taken over ten years to build.

C

In speech and informal writing, it is more usual to use **not many/much** or **only/just... a few/little** instead of **few** and **little** to talk about a small amount or number, and we often use **a bit (of)** in informal speech instead of **a little**:

- □ Sorry I haven't finished, I **haven't** had **much** time today. (*rather than* ...I had little time...)
- □ I won't be long. I've **only** got **a few** things to get. (*rather than* ...I've got few things...)
- □ Want **a bit** of chocolate? (*rather than* ...a little chocolate?)

In more formal contexts, such as academic writing, we generally prefer **few** and **little**:

- □ The results take **little** account of personal preference. (*rather than* ...don't take much...)

D

less (than) and fewer (than)

We use **less** with uncountable nouns and **fewer** with plural countable nouns:

- □ You should eat **less pasta**.   □ There are **fewer cars** on the road today.

Less is sometimes used with a plural countable noun (e.g. ...**less cars**...), particularly in conversation. However, this is grammatically incorrect.

We use **less than** with a noun phrase indicating an amount:

- □ I used to earn **less than** *a pound a week* when I first started work.

Less than is sometimes also used with a noun phrase referring to a group of things or people, particularly in conversation. However, some people think this is incorrect, particularly in formal contexts, and that **fewer than** should be used instead:

- □ There were **fewer than** *twenty students* present. (*or informally* ...less than...)

When we talk about a distance or a sum of money we use **less than**, not **fewer than**:

- □ The beach is **less than** a mile away.

To emphasise that a number is surprisingly large we can use **no less than** or **no fewer than**:

- □ The team has had **no fewer than** ten managers in just five years. (*or* ...no less than...)

Notice that we prefer **no less than** with percentages, periods of time and quantities:

- □ Profits have increased by **no less than** 95% in the last year. (*rather than* ...no fewer than...)

Grammar review: *few, little, less* → 147–152

Exercises

52.1 Complete the sentences with (a) few, (a) little, the few, the little, what few or what little, giving alternatives where possible. (A & B)

1 Thomas was named sportsman of the year, and .... would disagree with that decision.
2 .... remains of the old castle walls except the Black Gate.
3 She called her .... remaining relatives together and told them she was leaving.
4 Simpson is among .... foreign journalists allowed into the country.
5 .... evidence we have so far suggests that the new treatment will be important in the fight against AIDS.
6 'Has my explanation helped?' '..........................., yes.'
7 .... belongings she had were packed into a small suitcase.
8 .... will forget the emotional scenes as Wilson gave his farewell performance in front of a huge audience.
9 The announcement will come as .... surprise.
10 Tony hasn't been looking well recently, and I'm .... worried about him.
11 'Have there been many applications for the job?' 'Yes, quite ....'
12 The children weren't well so I had to take .... days off.
13 I don't have much money, but I'm happy to lend you .... I have.
14 The tax reforms will mean less income for the majority of people and more for ....

52.2 If necessary, suggest changes to the italicised text in these examples from conversations (1–4) and from academic writing (5–8). (C)

1 'Did you do anything last night?' 'I just watched *a little TV* and then went to bed.'
2 Take some sweets if you want, although *there are few left*.
3 I've tried to help her, but *there's little more* I can do.
4 See that old car over there? There's *few* left now.
5 The country *hasn't had many* female politicians since independence.
6 It is thought that the two leaders *didn't exchange many words* on their first meeting.
7 Teachers were found to be *a bit more confident* after the extra training.
8 *There doesn't seem to be much prospect* of ever recovering the missing manuscript.

52.3 A survey of British university students was conducted in 1980 and recently repeated. Some of the results are given below. Comment on them in sentences using fewer (than) or less (than). (D)

1 Do you have a part-time job?
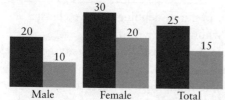
Fewer students had a part-time job in 1980 than now.

3 Do you walk to the university?

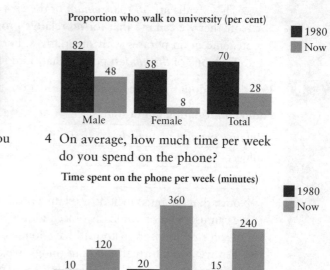

Proportion with part-time jobs (per cent)

Male 27 / 55 Female 9 / 69 Total 18 / 62

Proportion who walk to university (per cent)

1980 / Now

Male 82 / 48 Female 58 / 8 Total 70 / 28

2 What proportion of your money do you spend on books?

Proportion of money spent on books (per cent)

Male 20 / 10 Female 30 / 20 Total 25 / 15

4 On average, how much time per week do you spend on the phone?

Time spent on the phone per week (minutes)

1980 / Now

Male 10 / 120 Female 20 / 360 Total 15 / 240

Are there any results that surprise you? Comment on them using no less than or no fewer than.

A   *Defining* and *non-defining relative clauses* (see also **GR: J1–J2**) begin with a *relative pronoun*, which can sometimes be omitted:

☐ We went to a beach (**which/that**) Jane had recommended to us.

Here the relative pronoun refers to 'a beach', and the subject of the relative clause is 'Jane'. Compare:

☐ I know a man **who/that** ran in the New York Marathon last year.

where the relative pronoun refers to 'a man', and the subject of the relative clause is also 'a man'. In this case, the relative pronoun can't be omitted.

B   When we use *a defining relative clause*, the relative pronoun can be either the subject or the object of the relative clause. When it is the *subject* the word order is subject + verb + object:

☐ I have *a friend* **who/that** *plays guitar*. (a friend = subject, plays = verb, guitar = object)

When the relative pronoun is the *object* the word order is object + subject + verb:

☐ He showed me *the rocks* (**which/that**) *he had collected*. (the rocks = object, he = subject, had collected = verb)

C   Relative pronouns are used to add information in *defining relative clauses* as follows:

adding information about things

Relative pronoun	which	that	no relative pronoun
subject	✓	✓	✗
object	✓	✓	✓

adding information about people

Relative pronoun	who	that	no relative pronoun	whom
subject	✓	✓	✗	✗
object	✓	✓	✓	✓

☆ When we add information about things, we can use **that** (or **no relative pronoun**) as object in conversation and **which** in more formal contexts:

☐ Decorating's a job (**that**) I hate. (*rather than* '...which...' *in this informal context*)

☆ When we add information about people, we generally prefer **that** (or **no relative pronoun**) as object in informal contexts rather than **who** or **whom**:

☐ That's the man (**that**) I met at Alison's party (*rather than* ....who/whom I met...)

☆ **whom** is very formal and rarely used in spoken English:

☐ The boy **whom** Elena had shouted at smiled. (*less formally* **that**, **no relative pronoun** *or* **who**)

☆ We use **that** as subject after: **something** and **anything**; words such as **all**, **little**, **much**, and **none** used as pronouns; and noun phrases that include superlatives. **Which** is also used as subject after **something** and **anything**, but less commonly:

☐ These walls are *all* **that** *remain* of the city. (*not* ... which remain of the city.)

☆ Note that we can use **that** (or **no relative pronoun**) as object after **something/anything**; **all**, etc.; and noun phrases with superlatives. For example:

☐ She's one of *the kindest* people (**that**) I know. (*not* ...one of the kindest people who I know.)

D   Relative pronouns are used to add information in *non-defining relative clauses* as follows:

adding information about things

Relative pronoun	which	that
subject	✓	✓
object	✓	✓

adding information about people

Relative pronoun	who	whom
subject	✓	✗
object	✓	✓

☆ Notice that we must include a relative pronoun in a non-defining relative clause.

☆ We can use **who** or **whom** as object, although **whom** is very formal:

☐ Professor Johnson, **who(m)** I have long admired, is to visit the University next week.

☆ When we add information about things, we can use **which** as subject or object. **That** is sometimes used instead of **which**, but some people think this is incorrect:

☐ The Master's course, **which** I took in 1990, is no longer taught. (*or* ...that I took...)

53.1 Put brackets around the underlined relative pronoun if it can be omitted from these sentences. (A)

1 We talked about the party <u>which</u> Sarah wants to organise for my birthday.
2 To get to Frank's house, take the main road <u>that</u> bypasses the village.
3 The paintings <u>which</u> Mr Flowers has in his house are worth around £100,000.
4 Let's go through the main points <u>that</u> he made in his lecture.
5 He received a low mark for his essay, <u>which</u> was only one page long.
6 Mrs Richmond, <u>who</u> is 42, has three children.
7 Don is a friend <u>who</u> we stayed with in Australia.
8 In the shop window there's a sign <u>that</u> says 'Ten per cent off'.
9 The couple <u>who</u> live next to us have sixteen grandchildren.
10 There was little <u>that</u> we could do to help her.

53.2 Write the information in brackets as a relative clause (defining or non-defining) in an appropriate place in the sentence. Give alternative relative pronouns if possible. (Use – to indicate 'no relative pronoun'.) (C & D)

1 Susan said something. (I couldn't hear it clearly) <u>Susan said something that/ which/ – I couldn't hear clearly.</u>

2 Julia's father has just come back from a skiing holiday. (he is over 80)

3 The problems faced by the company are being resolved. (I'll look at these in detail in a moment)

4 She was greatly influenced by her father. (she adored him)

5 He pointed to the stairs. (they led down to the cellar)

6 These drugs have been withdrawn from sale. (they are used to treat stomach ulcers)

7 The singer had to cancel her concert. (she was recovering from flu)

8 The minister talked about the plans for tax reform. (he will reveal them next month)

9 I have two older sisters. (I love them very much)

53.3 If necessary, correct or make improvements to these sentences. If they are already correct, write ✓. (A–D)

1 There's something which I should tell you.
2 The doctor whom Ingrid went to see was very thorough.
3 Yesterday was the hottest day I can remember.
4 There isn't much can go wrong with the machine.
5 Thieves whom stole paintings from Notford art gallery have been arrested in Paris.
6 It may be the most important decision which you will ever take.
7 The boy took the photograph was paid £100.
8 I heard many different accents in the room, but none which I could identify as British.
9 There's this dream which I have every night about falling downstairs.
10 He just said anything which came into his head.

Unit 54

Other relative words: whose, when, whereby, etc.

A Clauses with whose

We use a relative clause beginning with the relative pronoun **whose + noun**, particularly in written English, when we talk about something belonging to or associated with a person, animal or plant:

- ☐ Stevenson is an architect **whose designs** have won international praise.
- ☐ Sue was taking care of a rabbit **whose ears** were badly damaged in a fight with a cat.

We can use **whose** in both *defining* and *non-defining relative clauses* (see **GR: J1–J2**).

We generally avoid using **whose** to talk about something belonging to or associated with a *thing*:

- ☐ I received a letter, and its poor spelling made me think it was written by a child. (*more natural than* 'I received a letter, **whose** poor spelling made me think…')

However, we sometimes use **whose** when we talk about towns, countries, or organisations:

- ☐ The film was made in *Botswana*, **whose wildlife parks** are larger than those in Kenya.
- ☐ We need to learn from *companies* **whose trading** is more healthy than our own.

In academic writing **whose** is used to talk about a wide variety of 'belonging to' relationships:

- ☐ Students are encouraged to use an appropriate theory in order to solve *problems* **whose** geographical limits are clear.

B Clauses with when, whereby, where and why

We can begin relative and other clauses with **when** (referring to time), **whereby** (method or means; used mainly in formal contexts), and **where** (location). In formal English in particular, a phrase with **preposition + which** can often be used instead of these:

- ☐ He wasn't looking forward to the time **when** he would have to leave. (*or* …the time **at which** …)
- ☐ Do you know the date **when** we have to hand in the essay? (*or* …the date **on/by which**…)
- ☐ The government is to end the system **whereby** (= 'by which means') farmers make more money from leaving land unplanted than from growing wheat. (*or* …the system **in/by which** farmers…)
- ☐ This was the place **where** we first met. (*or* …the place **at/in which** we…)

In academic English, we can also use **where** to refer to relationships other than location, particularly after words such as **case, condition, example, situation, system**:

- ☐ Later in this chapter we will introduce *cases* **where** consumer complaints have resulted in changes in the law. (*or more formally* …cases **in which**…)

We can also use **a/the reason why** or **a/the reason that** or just **a/the reason**:

- ☐ I didn't get a pay rise, but this wasn't **the reason why** I left. (*or* …the reason (that) I left.)

C Clauses with who and what; whatever, whoever and whichever

Some clauses beginning with a *wh*-word are used like a noun phrase in a sentence. These are sometimes called *nominal relative clauses*:

- ☐ Can you give me a list of **who's** been invited? (= the people who have been invited)
- ☐ I didn't know **what** I should do next. (= the thing that I should do next)

Notice that we can't use **what** in this way after a noun:

- ☐ I managed to get all the *books* **that** you asked for. (*not* …all the books what you asked for.)

We use clauses beginning with **whatever** (= anything *or* it doesn't matter what), **whoever** (= the person/group who *or* any person/group who), or **whichever** (= one thing or person from a limited number, to talk about things or people that are indefinite or unknown:

- ☐ I'm sure I'll enjoy eating **whatever** you cook.
- ☐ **Whoever** wins will go on to play Barcelona in the final.
- ☐ **Whichever** one of you broke the window will have to pay for it.

Grammar review: relative clauses → J1–J3

54.1 Combine a sentence from **i** with a sentence from **ii** to make new sentences with **whose**, as in 1. (A)

i

1 Dr Rowan has had to do all his own typing.
2 The newspaper is owned by the Mears group.
3 Parents are being asked to take part in the survey.
4 Children do better in examinations.
5 My aunt is now manager of a department store.
6 I enjoy growing plants in my garden.
7 The new regulations are part of a broader strategy.

ii

a Its chairperson is Sir James Bex.
b Their diets contain high levels of protein.
c Their flowers are attractive to bees.
d ~~His secretary resigned two weeks ago.~~
e Their objectives are to increase fish stocks.
f Her first job was filling shelves in a supermarket.
g Their children are between four and six.

1   _Dr Rowan, whose secretary resigned two weeks ago, has had to do all his own typing._

54.2 Define these items using **whose** (1–3) and **in which** (4–6). You may need to use a dictionary. (A)

1 A lexicographer is a person _whose job is to write dictionaries._
2 A widow is a woman ....
3 An actuary is a person ....
4 A furnace is a container ....
5 A gazebo is a small garden building ....
6 Polo is ....

54.3 Choose one of the following phrases and then either **when**, **whereby**, **where** or **why** to complete these sentences. (B)

     the area   **an agreement**   **a condition**   **a method**   **moments**   **the reason**

1 During the performance there were .... she found it difficult not to laugh.
2 The two governments reached .... the border would be patrolled by troops from a third country.
3 The land is very fertile in .... Jack has bought his farm.
4 I think .... we get on so well is that we both enjoy talking.
5 Freeze drying is .... water is rapidly evaporated from frozen food in order to preserve it.
6 Hypoglycemia is .... the level of sugar in the blood drops suddenly.

54.4 If the underlined word is correct, write ✓. If not, suggest another word. (C)

1 I think <u>whatever</u> was responsible for damaging the trees should be fined or sent to prison.
2 Do they really understand <u>that</u> they are doing?
3 I don't envy <u>whoever</u> buys that house. It's in a terrible condition.
4 Now that I no longer have to wear a school uniform, I'll be able to wear <u>which</u> I want.
5 I think the government should improve the health service, <u>whichever</u> the cost.
6 It's a question <u>that</u> I've been asking for many years.
7 The clock makes a noise <u>what</u> keeps me awake at night.
8 I'm sure that Keith will do well at university, <u>which</u> one he goes to.
9 We kept a note of <u>who</u> we met as we travelled around Africa and wrote to them when we got home.

A In formal styles **noun + of which** is often preferred to **whose + noun** when we talk about things:

☐ A huge amount of oil was spilled, *the effects* **of which** are still being felt.

☐ The end of the war, *the anniversary* **of which** is on the 16th November, will be commemorated in cities throughout the country.

We can use **of which** and **of whose**, but not usually **which** or **whose**, after **all, both, each, many, most, neither, none, part, some, a number** (one, two, etc.; the first, the second, etc.; half, a third, etc.) and **superlatives** (the best, the biggest, etc.):

☐ Lotta was able to switch between German and Russian, **both of which** she spoke fluently. (*not* ...both which she spoke fluently.)

☐ She joined the local tennis club, **most of whose** members were at least 60.

In formal contexts, **of which** can be used instead of **that/which...of** in relative clauses:

☐ The school **that/which** she is head **of** is closing. (*or more formally* The school **of which** she...)

☐ The book **that/which** he's most proud **of**... (*or more formally* The book **of which** he...)

B In formal, mainly written, English **whose** can come after a preposition in a relative clause. However, it is more natural to put the preposition at the end of the clause in less formal contexts and in spoken English:

☐ The council is in discussion with Lord Thomas, **on whose** land most of the village is built. (*or less formally* ...Lord Thomas, **whose** land most of the village is built **on**.)

☐ I now turn to Freud, **from whose** work the following quotation is taken. (*or less formally* ...Freud, **whose** work the following quotation is taken **from**.)

C When a preposition is needed with the relative pronouns **which** and **whom** we usually put it before the relative pronoun in formal styles:

☐ The rate **at which** a material heats up depends on its chemical composition.

☐ Her many friends, **among whom** I like to be considered, gave her encouragement.

After a preposition we usually use **whom** rather than **who** in formal styles:

☐ Is it right that politicians should make important decisions without consulting the public **to whom** they are accountable? (*rather than* ...the public to who they are accountable.)

and we don't use **that** or **no relative pronoun**:

☐ The valley **in which** the town lies is heavily polluted. (*not* The valley in that the town lies is heavily polluted.; *not* The valley in the town lies is heavily polluted.)

In less formal English we usually put the preposition later in the relative clause rather than at the beginning:

☐ The office **that** Graham took us **to** was filled with books.

and we prefer **who** (or **that**) rather than **whom** (see also Unit 26A):

☐ The playground wasn't used by the children **who** it was built **for**.

D If the verb in the relative clause is a two-word verb (e.g. **come across, fill in, look after, take on**) we don't usually put the preposition before the relative pronoun:

☐ The Roman coins, **which** a local farmer **came across** in a field, are now on display in the National Museum. (*not* ...coins, across which the local farmer came, are...)

With three-word verbs, we only put the preposition before the relative pronoun in a very formal or literary style, and many people avoid this pattern:

☐ She is one of the few people **to whom** I **look up**. (*or less formally* ...**who** I **look up to**.)

55.1 Rewrite these sentences so that they are more appropriate for formal written English. Use **preposition + which** or **preposition + whose**, as appropriate. (A & B)

1 Fleming's discovery of penicillin, which he was awarded the Nobel Prize for, had a major influence on the lives of people in the 20th century.

   Fleming's discovery of penicillin, for which he was awarded the Nobel Prize, had a major influence on the lives of people in the 20th century.

2 He was the uncle of Ann Boleyn, whose execution in 1542 he lost power after.
3 It is her unmarried name which she is better known by.
4 Mr Marks, whose farm the stream flows across, is unhappy about the plans for the new dam.
5 The election result, which there can be no doubt about, is a great disappointment.
6 The building which Mr Marcus emerged from was little more than a ruin.
7 It is a medieval palace, whose tower the king hid in during the civil war.
8 I am grateful to Alan Mackie, whose book on the history of the bicycle this information comes from.

55.2 Join the sentence halves using **which** or **whom** after an appropriate preposition. (C)

the furniture is to be delivered.	she was divorced in 1995.	he had shown his novel.
~~I had great respect.~~	it was named.	the printer was supplied.
most world trade was conducted.	you should be aware.	

1 My English teacher, Mrs Brookes, was someone _for whom I had great respect._
2 Until 1914 the pound sterling was the currency ....
3 They have changed the date ....
4 Pasteurisation was discovered by the French chemist Louis Pasteur, ...
5 He was persuaded to stay in England by Charles Dickens, ...
6 There are a number of safety procedures ....
7 Details are in the instruction manual ....
8 Ms Peters was left the money by her former husband, ...

55.3 How would you express the sentences you have written in 55.2 in a less formal way, putting the preposition at the end of the relative clause? (A)

1 _My English teacher, Mrs Brookes, was someone who/that/– I had great respect for._

55.4 Suggest corrections or improvements to these sentences or write ✓ if they are already correct. (A, C & D)

1 The house into which the thieves broke is owned by Peter Brown.
2 The school has been given 20 computers, half of which are brand new.
3 JKL Motorbikes sells six different models, the first which they started making in 1985.
4 It was the perfect tree under that to sit on a hot, sunny day.
5 The party, to which I've been looking forward all week, is at Mary's house.
6 The water that she fell into was freezing cold.
7 I have heard her on the violin and clarinet, both which she plays extremely well.
8 The film was made at Tulloch Castle, part which dates back to 1466.
9 The college is home to 30 students from Nepal, almost all of who are studying economics.

Other ways of adding information to noun phrases (1): additional noun phrases, etc.

A We sometimes add information about a person or thing referred to in one noun phrase by talking about the same person or thing in a different way in a following noun phrase:

- □ *A hooded cobra, one of the world's most dangerous snakes,* has escaped from Dudley Zoo.
- □ *Dr Alex Parr, director of the State Museum,* is to become the government's arts adviser.
- □ When Tom fell off his bike we gave him *arnica, a medicine made from a flower,* for the bruising.

In writing, the items are usually separated by a comma, and in speech they are often separated by a pause or other intonation break. However, when the second item acts like a defining relative clause, when it is usually a name, there is usually no punctuation in writing or intonation break in speech:

- □ *My friend Jim* has moved to Sweden. (*rather than* My friend, Jim, ...)
- □ The current champion is expected to survive her first-round match with *the Italian Silvia Farina.* (*rather than* ...the Italian, Silvia Farina.)

B We can add information to a noun phrase with a conjunction such as **and** or **or**:

- □ Kurt Svensson, her teacher **and** *well-known concert pianist,* thinks that she has great talent. (= her teacher is also a well-known concert pianist)
- □ My business partner **and** *great friend* Tom Edwards is getting married today.
- □ Phonetics **or** *the study of speech sounds* is a common component on courses in teaching English as a foreign language.

C The adverb **namely** and the phrase **that is** are used to add details about a noun phrase:

- □ This side-effect of the treatment, **namely** *weight gain,* is counteracted with other drugs.
- □ The main cause of global warming, **that is** *the burning of fossil fuels,* is to be the focus of negotiations at the international conference.

D We can also add information to a noun phrase using a participle clause beginning with an **-ing**, **-ed** or **being + -ed** verb form. These are often similar to *defining relative clauses* (see **GR: J1–2**):

- □ Any passengers *travelling to Cambridge* should sit in the first two carriages of the train. (*or* Any passengers who are travelling...)
- □ The people *living next door* come from Italy. (*or* The people who are living next door...)
- □ The weapon *used in the murder* has now been found. (*or* The weapon that was used..)
- □ The book *published last week* is his first novel. (*or* The book that was published last week...)
- □ The prisoners *being released* are all women. (*or* The prisoners who are being released...)
- □ The boys *being chosen* for the team are under 9. (*or* The boys who are being chosen...)

Notice that **-ing** participle clauses correspond to defining relative clauses with an active verb, while **-ed** and **being + -ed** clauses correspond to defining relative clauses with a passive verb.

We can also use a **to-infinitive clause**, as in:

- □ Have you brought a book **to read**? (= you bring it and you read it)
- □ Have you brought a book for Kevin **to read**? (= you bring it and Kevin reads it)
- □ My decision **to resign** *from the company* was made after a great deal of thought.
- □ I thought that the decision of the committee, **to increase** *staff holidays,* was a good one.

E In written English, particularly in newspapers, **-ing** and **-ed** clauses are also used instead of *non-defining relative clauses*. These are usually written between commas or dashes (–):

- □ The men, *wearing anoraks and hats,* made off in a stolen Volvo estate.
- □ The proposals – *expected to be agreed by ministers* – are less radical than many employers had feared.

56.1 Add the information given below to the sentences and rewrite them in an appropriate way, using the examples in **A** and **B** as models.

> Klaus Schmidt is the current European champion
> Andy Todd is head of Downlands Hospital
> Beluga caviar is among the most expensive food in the world
> Tonya's father has also been her trainer for the last 10 years
> Paul Jennings is Australian   My colleague is Paul
> ~~Gofast Technology is part of the Maddison Enterprises Group~~
> Another name for rubella is German measles
> The German 10,000 metres record holder is also the current European champion

1 Gofast Technology has launched its new generation of high-speed trains.
   Gofast Technology, part of the Maddison Enterprises Group, has launched its new generation of high-speed trains.
2 I went on an IT training course with my colleague.
3 Rubella is still a common childhood disease in many countries.
4 Four kilos of Beluga caviar has been ordered for James and Stephanie's wedding party.
5 One of the most popular modern writers for children is Paul Jennings.
6 Tonya's father was in the crowd to watch her victory.
7 Dr Andy Todd has criticised government plans to cut health funding.
8 Klaus Schmidt is running in the Stockholm Marathon.

56.2 Match the sentence beginnings (in **i**) and endings (in **ii**) and add appropriate information (from **iii**) after **namely** or **that is**. The first is done for you. (C)

i
1 Leo Tolstoy's most celebrated novel,
2 The two countries having land borders with the USA,
3 The three most popular pets in Britain,
4 The capital of Estonia,
5 The largest island in the world,
6 The 'consumers' of education,

ii
a are found in 25% of households.
b covers over 2 million square kilometres.
c should have ways of complaining about poor teaching.
d have complained to the President about the new customs regulations.
e ~~was published in 1869.~~
f is situated on the Gulf of Finland.

iii
| Tallinn | students | cats, dogs and rabbits | ~~War and Peace~~ |
| Mexico and Canada | Greenland | | |

1+ e *Leo Tolstoy's most celebrated novel, namely War and Peace, was published in 1869.*

56.3 Complete the sentences with an **-ing**, **-ed** or **being + -ed** form of these verbs. Then rewrite the sentence using a relative clause instead of the participle clause. (D)

| build | ~~drive~~ | educate | elect | flow | hold |
| introduce | need | print | say | take | tell off |

1 The man _driving_ the bus is my brother. *The man who is driving the bus is my brother.*
2 I went to a reunion for students _____ in the physics department during the 1980s.
3 As my aunt told me what she thought, I felt like a schoolboy _____ by his headmaster.
4 There is a sign on the gate _____ 'Entry forbidden'.
5 Across the river were some of the deer _____ into the park in the 19th century.
6 Rivers _____ into the Baltic Sea are much cleaner now than ten years ago.
7 The booklets _____ as we speak will be on sale later this afternoon.
8 Anyone _____ further information can see me in my office.
9 Mary O'Brien, the Democrat _____ to the council only last week, has resigned.
10 We live in a house _____ in 1906.
11 The protest march _____ next week is expected to attract over 100,000 people.

Unit 57

Other ways of adding information to noun phrases (2): prepositional phrases, etc.

A

We commonly add information about a thing or person using a prepositional phrase. Often these have a meaning similar to a relative clause:

- ☐ What's the name of the *man* **by** the window? (*or* ...the man **who's** by the window?)
- ☐ It's in the *cupboard* **under** the stairs. (*or* ...the cupboard **that's** under the stairs.)
- ☐ She lives in the *house* **with** the red door. (*or* ...the house **which has** the red door.)

In some cases, however, these prepositional phrases do not have a corresponding relative clause:

- ☐ You need to keep a careful *record* **of** what you spend.
- ☐ There is likely to be an *increase* **in** temperature tomorrow.

We often prefer a relative clause rather than a prepositional phrase in non-defining relative clauses with **be + preposition** or with **have** as a main verb:

- ☐ *Johnson*, **who was in** the store at the time of the robbery, was able to identify two of the men. (*rather than* ...Johnson, in the store...)
- ☐ *Jim Morton*, **who has** a farm in Devon, has decided to grow only organic vegetables. (*rather than* Jim Morton, with a farm in Devon, has...)

B

In written English, particularly in academic writing, a series of prepositional phrases and relative clauses is often used to add information about a previous noun phrase. Note that prepositional phrases can also be used with an adverbial function (e.g. '...taken the drug *in the last 6 months*' in the sentence below):

- ☐ Doctors are contacting patients (with diabetes) (who have taken the drug in the last 6 months.)

- ☐ Scientists (in Spain) (who have developed the technique) are optimistic that it will be widely used in laboratories within the next decade.

We can also use participle clauses and noun phrases (see **Unit 56**) in a series of clauses/phrases which add information to the preceding noun phrase:

- ☐ The waxwing is the only bird (found in Britain) (with yellow and red tail feathers.)

- ☐ Mr Bob Timms, (leader of the Democratic Party,) (MP for Threeoaks,) has announced his resignation.

C

Notice that adding a series of prepositional phrases can often lead to ambiguity. For example:
- ☐ The protesters were demonstrating against the mistreatment of animals on farms.
could mean either that the place the protesters were demonstrating was 'on farms' or that the animals were 'on farms'. We could make the sentence unambiguous with, for example:
- ☐ The protesters were demonstrating on farms against the mistreatment of animals. *or*
- ☐ The protesters were demonstrating against the mistreatment of animals kept on farms.

57.1 Match the sentence halves, adding an appropriate preposition, as in 1. (A)

1 Jane's the girl...	a ...green shirts.
2 She's in the photograph...	b ...the back garden.
3 I plan to cut down the tree...	c ~~...blonde hair.~~
4 There's a team of people...	d ...the canal.
5 I walked along the footpath...	e ...the piano.
6 The children can't get over the fence...	f ...Paris to Lyons.
7 Go along the lane...	g ...the houses.
8 Jack's a boy...	h ...New Zealand.
9 Follow the main road...	i ...the pool.
10 She's a teacher...	j ...a quick temper.

1 + c   _Jane's the girl with blonde hair._

57.2 Rewrite the sentences in 57.1 with defining relative clauses. (A)

1   _Jane's the girl who has blonde hair._

57.3 Complete the sentence by adding the pieces of information given. Use relative clauses (see **Unit 53**), additional noun phrases and participle clauses (**Unit 56**) and prepositional phrases (**Unit 57**).

1 Police are questioning men...   _between 25 and 30 living in the village, known to have a criminal record._
(The men are between 25 and 30. They live in the village. They are known to have a criminal record.)

2 Teachers...
(The teachers work at Queen's College. Queen's College is in the city centre. The teachers went on strike last week. They have appointed Jacqui Smith as their spokesperson. She is the head of English.)

3 Marge Scott...
(Marge Scott has died. She was aged 95. She was educated at Marston College. She was the first woman to be educated there. Marston College is in south Wales.)

4 The conference...
(The conference was held in Singapore. It approved the world trade agreement. The agreement was drawn up by European and Asian states. The conference has now ended.)

5 A book...
(The book is on gardening. It is called *All about Plants*. Mary wanted to borrow it. It wasn't available in the library.)

6 A painting...
(The painting was found in a second-hand shop. It was found by Beth Sands. She is an antique dealer. She is from York. The painting is thought to be by J.M.W. Turner. Turner was a British landscape artist.)

57.4 Why are these sentences ambiguous? Can you rewrite them to remove the ambiguity? (C)

1 A man was talking with a grey suit.

....

2 A lorry was stopped by a police officer carrying thousands of stolen cigarettes.

....

3 I discussed my plan to decorate the room with my parents.

....

Participle clauses with adverbial meaning (1)

A We can use **present participle** (-ing) and **past participle** (-ed) clauses with an adverbial meaning. (See also **Unit 59**.) Clauses like these often give information about the timing, causes, and results of the events described:

- ☐ *Opening her eyes*, the baby began to cry. (= When she opened her eyes...)
- ☐ *Faced with a bill for £10,000*, John has taken an extra job. (= Because he is faced...)
- ☐ *Looked after carefully*, the plant can live through the winter. (= If it is looked after...)
- ☐ *Having completed the book*, he had a holiday. (perfect; = When/Because he had completed...)
- ☐ The fruit was expensive, *being imported*. (simple passive; = ...because it was imported)
- ☐ *Having been hunted close to extinction*, the rhino is once again common in this area. (perfect passive; = Although it had been hunted close to extinction...)

B The implied subject of a participle clause (that is, a subject known but not directly mentioned) is usually the same as the subject of the main clause:

- ☐ *Arriving* at the party, we saw Ruth standing alone. (= When **we** arrived...**we** saw...)

However, sometimes the implied subject is not referred to in the main clause:

- ☐ *Having wanted* to drive a train all his life, this was an opportunity not to be missed.

In careful speech and writing we avoid different subjects for the participle and main clause:

- ☐ *Turning round quickly*, the door hit me in the face. (first implied subject = 'I'; second subject = 'the door')

C In formal English, the participle clause sometimes has its own subject, which is often a pronoun or includes one:

- ☐ The collection of vases is priceless, **some** *being over two thousand years old*.
- ☐ **Her voice** *breaking with emotion*, Jean spoke about her father's illness.

We use a present participle (-ing) clause to talk about something happening at the same time as an event in the main clause, or to give information about the facts given in the main clause.

D When we use **not** in a participle clause it usually comes before the participle. However, it can follow the participle, depending on the part of the sentences affected by **not**. Compare:

- ☐ *Wishing* **not** to go out that night, I made an excuse. ('not' relates to 'to go out that night'; the sentence means 'I didn't want to go out on that particular night') *and*
- ☐ **Not** *wishing* to go out that night, I made an excuse. ('not' relates to 'wish to go out that night'; the sentence could mean 'going out on that particular night wasn't my wish')

E We use a clause beginning with **having + past participle** rather than a present participle if the action in the main clause is the consequence of the event in the participle clause:

- ☐ **Having won** every major judo title, Mark retired from international competition. (*or* **After winning**...; *not* Winning every major judo title...)
- ☐ **Having broken** her leg the last time she went, Brenda decided not to go on the school skiing trip this year. (*or* **After breaking** her leg...; *not* Breaking her leg...)

We can use either a **present participle** (-ing) clause or a **having + past participle** clause with a similar meaning when the action in the participle clause is complete before the action in the main clause begins. Compare:

- ☐ **Taking off** his shoes, Ray walked into the house. (*Having taken off*...has a similar meaning) *and*
- ☐ **Running** across the field, I fell and hurt my ankle. (= While I was running...; 'Having run...' would suggest that I fell *after* I had run across the field)

Grammar review: *-ing* clauses and *-ed* clauses → J4–J8

58.1 Rewrite the sentences beginning with one of the clause forms shown in A and D.

1 When she saw the dog coming towards her, she quickly crossed the road.
   Seeing the dog coming towards her, she quickly crossed the road.

2 As she was dressed all in black, she couldn't be seen in the starless night.

3 As I don't have a credit card, I found it difficult to book an airline ticket over the phone.

4 Keith spent a lot of time filling in job application forms because he was unemployed.

5 Because I was walking quickly, I soon caught up with her.

6 The house was built of wood, so it was clearly a fire risk.

7 I was eager to catch the bus in good time because I had been told off the day before for arriving late.

8 She didn't know where the theatre was, so she asked for directions at the hotel reception.

9 As she was a nurse, she knew what to do after the accident.

10 He had spent his childhood in Oslo so he knew the city well.

58.2 Where the implied subject of the two clauses is the same write S and where it is different write D. In the sentences where it is different, rewrite the sentence to make it more acceptable. (B)

1 Waiting for the bus, a car went through a puddle and splashed water all over me.

2 Known mainly as a writer of novels, James has now written a successful biography.

3 Keeping a careful eye on the spider, Suzanne hurried out of the bathroom.

4 Looking down from the hill, the town spread out before us towards the coast.

5 Feeling rather sick, the boat ploughed through the huge waves.

6 Found only in the Andes, the plant is used by local people to treat skin diseases.

58.3 Choose the more appropriate position for **not** in these sentences. (D)

1 .... wishing .... to boast, she said nothing about her success.

2 .... pretending .... to notice that people were staring at me, I carried on looking on the floor for my lost contact lens.

3 .... determined .... to be beaten, she put all her energy into the serve.

4 .... feeling .... well, she went home early.

5 .... bothering .... to put on his coat, he left the house.

6 .... trying .... to cry, she waved to Mark as the train pulled out.

58.4 Complete the sentences with either **having + past participle** or the **-ing** form of one of these verbs. In which is it also possible to use either form with a similar meaning? (E)

     move   park   suffer   wait   walk

1 .... the car about a kilometre from the stadium, I walked the rest of the way.

2 .... out of the city, she felt much happier.

3 .... through the tunnel, I banged my head on the low roof.

4 .... six months for the washing machine to be delivered, I decided to cancel the order.

5 .... from depression himself as a teenager, Kevin could understand how his son was feeling.

A We can use prepositions such as **after, before, besides, by, in, on, since, through, while, with,** and **without** with a present participle (-ing) clause with an adverbial meaning (see also Unit 58):

- ☐ **While understanding** her problem, I don't know how I can help. (= Although I understand...)
- ☐ **After spending** so much money on the car, I can't afford a holiday.
- ☐ **Before being changed** last year, the speed limit was 70 kph. (passive form)

Less formal alternatives have a clause with a verb that can change according to tense and subject. Compare:

- ☐ **Since moving** to London, we haven't had time to go to the theatre. *and*
- ☐ **Since we moved** to London, we haven't had time to go to the theatre. (less formal)

B **by, in, on + -ing**

☐ **By working** hard, she passed her maths exam. ☐ They only survived **by eating** roots and berries in the forest.	= the **-ing** clause indicates 'the method or means used'
☐ **On returning** from Beijing, he wrote to the Chinese embassy. ☐ John was the first person I saw **on leaving** hospital.	= the **-ing** clause indicates 'when'
☐ **In criticising** the painting, I knew I would offend her. ☐ **In choosing** Marco, the People's Party has moved to the left.	= the **-ing** clause indicates 'cause'

We can often use **by + -ing** or **in + -ing** with a similar meaning, although **by + -ing** is preferred in informal contexts:

- ☐ **In/By writing** the essay about Spanish culture, I came to understand the country better. ('In writing...' = the consequence of writing was to understand...; 'By writing...' = the method I used to understand the country better was to write...)

But compare:

- ☐ **By telephoning** every hour, she managed to speak to the doctor. (*not* In telephoning...; the method, not the consequence)

C **with -ing; without -ing**

With + -ing often introduces a reason for something in the main clause. This use is fairly informal. Notice that a subject has to come between **with** and **-ing**:

- ☐ **With Louise living** in Spain, we don't see her often. (= Because Louise lives in Spain...)
- ☐ **With sunshine streaming** through the window, Hugh found it impossible to sleep. (= Because the sunshine was streaming...)

With and what with can also be used with a noun phrase to introduce a reason:

- ☐ **With** *my bad back* I won't be able to lift a heavy suitcase.
- ☐ **What with** *the traffic* and *the heavy rain*, it's no wonder you were late.

We can use **without + ing** to say that a second action doesn't happen:

- ☐ I went to work **without eating** breakfast.   ☐ They left **without paying**.

Often, however, it has a similar meaning to 'although...not' or 'unless':

- ☐ **Without meaning** to, I seem to have offended her. (= Although I didn't mean to...)
- ☐ **Without seeing** the photo, I can't judge how good it is. (= Unless I see the photo...)

D Adverbial meanings can also be added by a clause beginning with a conjunction or adjective but with no verb, having the same meaning as a clause beginning with a **conjunction + subject + be**. This is used in fairly formal English. More informal alternatives are given in brackets:

- ☐ **While in Poland,** they will play two concerts in Warsaw. (*or* **While** they are in Poland...)
- ☐ **Although just two feet apart,** they didn't speak. (*or* **Although** they were just...)
- ☐ I try to use public transport **whenever possible**. (*or* ...**whenever** it is possible.)
- ☐ **Unhappy with the decision,** Johnson swore at the referee. (*or* **Because** he was unhappy...)
- ☐ James relaxed, **pleased with his day's work.** (*or* ...**because** he was pleased...)

Grammar review: *-ing* clauses and *-ed* clauses → J4–J8

59.1 Complete these sentences with a preposition from (i) and a verb from (ii). Use an **–ing** form of the verb or **being + past participle**, as appropriate. You will need to use some of the words from (i) more than once. (A)

i

after	before	since
through	while	

ii

~~come~~	interview	leave	overthrow
sell	take	welcome	work

1 _Since coming_ out of hospital, I have been to the gym every day.
2 .... on TV last night, the minister mentioned that she would be retiring soon.
3 .... the back off the computer, make sure it is unplugged.
4 .... the government's new policy, I think it should have been introduced months ago.
5 .... in a military takeover, the king has been under house arrest.
6 .... with young children for the last 40 years, she has come to understand their behaviour better than most.
7 .... in supermarkets, most milk is pasteurised.
8 .... Oxford University in 1953, Painter spent three years teaching at a local school.

59.2 Match the items on the left with those on the right. Then write sentences beginning **by + –ing**, **on + –ing**, or **in + –ing**, as in the example. (B)

1 She returned home.	a She soon began to lose weight.
2 She gave up sugar.	b She saved over a hundred pounds a month.
3 She turned down the job.	c She knew that she might offend him.
4 She moved to a smaller flat.	d ~~She found Dave waiting outside her front door.~~
5 She entered the classroom.	e She gave up the possibility of a huge salary.
6 She criticised her father.	f She was surprised when all the children stood up quietly.

1+ d _On returning home, she found Dave waiting outside her front door._

59.3 Rewrite these sentences beginning **With... –ing** or **Without... –ing**. (C)

1 We couldn't go on holiday because Kathy had flu.

....

2 I won't be able to advise you unless I have more information.

....

3 He had solved the problem, although he didn't realise it.

....

4 I couldn't wait for Ken any longer as time was running out before the train left.

....

59.4 Match the sentence halves and write new sentences with a reduced clause, as in the examples in D.

1 When you are in Madrid,...
2 Because he was popular with his fellow pupils,...
3 Although she was exhausted,...
4 As she was determined to do well in the concert,...
5 Since they are attractive to butterflies,...
6 Where it is necessary,...

a ...she continued to climb.
b ...the flowers are a welcome addition to any garden.
c ...she practised for hours every day.
d ...students can refer to their dictionary.
e ...he was elected head boy at the school.
f ~~...you must visit the Prado Museum.~~

1+ d _When in Madrid, you must visit the Prado Museum._

Reflexive pronouns: herself, himself, themselves, etc.

A In addition to the usual reflexive pronouns (**myself, yourself,** etc.; see GR: K1–K2) some people use **themselves** to refer to the person who is the subject of the sentence, to avoid saying whether the subject is male or female:

- □ *The author of the letter* describes **themselves** as 'a senior government official'.
- □ *Who* wants to go through life by **themselves**, without friends?

Oneself (or less formally **yourself**) is used to refer to people in general:

- □ I think *one* has to have the courage to be **oneself** and say whatever comes naturally. (*less formally* I think *you* have to have the courage to be **yourself**...)

B We can use reflexive pronouns for emphasis in various ways (see GR: K2). We also use reflexive pronouns to emphasise that the subject caused a certain action:

- □ When Tom and Jack saw the robbery they called the police, but then they *got arrested*.
- □ When Tom and Jack saw the robbery they called the police, but *got* **themselves** *arrested*. (emphasises that Tom and Jack did something to make the police arrest them)
- □ When Tom and Jack saw the robbery they called the police, but they *got arrested* **themselves**. (emphasises that Tom and Jack were arrested, not the robbers)

C If the object of a transitive verb refers to the same person or thing as the subject, then that object must be a reflexive pronoun. Compare:

- □ He walked around the golf course to *familiarise* himself *with* it. *and*
- □ We walked around to *familiarise* **the children** *with* their new surroundings.

Other verbs commonly used in this way include **absent...from, avail...of, busy...with, concern...with, occupy...with, pride...on, tear...away from, trouble...about/with.**

With some verbs we can use a reflexive pronoun or leave it out with little difference in meaning:

- □ We are confident that both sets of fans will **behave (themselves)** at the match.

Other verbs like this include **acclimatise, adapt, (un)dress, hide, move, prepare, shave, wash.** We include the reflexive pronoun if we want to emphasise particularly that the person or thing referred to in the subject is affected by the action:

- □ Although he helped other athletes in their preparations for competing at high altitudes, he found it difficult to **acclimatise himself**.

D When the subject and object (after a preposition) refer to the same person or thing we use a reflexive pronoun after the preposition:

- □ He was pleased *with* **himself**. (*not* ...pleased with him.)

If the verb has a direct object we use a personal pronoun, not a reflexive pronoun:

- □ I remember closing *the door behind* me. (*not* ...closing the door behind myself.)

However, if the clause has a direct object and we need to make it clear that the subject and prepositional phrase refer to the same person or thing, we use a reflexive pronoun:

- □ **She** bought *the bracelet for* **herself**. ('...for her' suggests it was bought for someone else)

E **Myself** is sometimes used after **and** and **or** rather than 'I' or 'me', although some people consider this use incorrect and avoid it:

- □ I believe that Tony **and myself** have done a pretty good job.
- □ When you've finished the job can you send the bill either to Mrs Smith **or myself**?

Using **myself** reduces focus on the speaker or writer and so sounds less forceful or more polite.

F When we want to contrast someone's characteristics with how they were or usually are we can use a possessive pronoun with **self** or **selves**:

- □ Colin was very cheerful this morning. He didn't seem at all like **his** usual miserable **self**.
- □ The image that people have of famous actors may not coincide with **their** real **selves**.

Exercises

60.1 Complete the sentences with one of these verbs in an appropriate form followed by a reflexive pronoun and, if necessary, a preposition. If the reflexive pronoun can be omitted, put brackets around it. (C)

absent   adapt   ~~concern~~   dress   hide   occupy   prepare   pride   trouble

1 She works for a charity which ....*concerns itself with*.... the welfare of children in developing countries.
2 She .... for the interview by reading the job description again.
3 It is a town with a long history, that .... being civilised and sophisticated.
4 While I was working, the children .... reading and drawing.
5 When you get to Tokyo, it will take you some time to .... to the pace of life there.
6 Jack just expects to be given a job without making any effort. He won't even .... filling in any application forms.
7 When Marjorie broke her arm she couldn't .... properly, so I had to go round each morning to help.
8 I could see my brother coming through the park, so I .... behind a tree and waited to surprise him.
9 Peter arranged to .... the company for the first time in his life so that he could spend time with his father in hospital.

60.2 Underline the correct answer. If both answers are possible, notice the difference in meaning. (D)

1 Can you post this letter for *myself/ me*, please?
2 All my friends were away, I was bored, and I just didn't know what to do with *myself/ me*.
3 We put the tape recorder on the table between *ourselves/ us*.
4 They dragged the tree behind *themselves/ them* all the way to the trailer.
5 Now that you're a well-known novelist, you must hear a lot about *yourself/ you* on TV and in the newspapers.
6 He ought to be ashamed of *himself/ him*, being rude to his parents like that.
7 She should take care of *herself/ her* better. She's looking really ill.
8 I opened the window in front of *myself/ me* and took a deep breath of fresh air.

60.3 Study the underlined parts of this email. Make corrections if necessary or write ✓. Give alternatives where possible. (A–F)

Send Now	Send Later	Save as Draft	Add Attachments	Signature ▾	Options ▾	Rewrap

From: Maggie
To: Jane
Subject: Tony
Attachments: none

Default Font ▾ | Text Size ▾ | **B** *I* U T | ≡ ≡ ≡ | ≟ ≡ ≢ ≢ | A ▾ ✏ ▾

Hi Jane

Yes, Tony's a lot better, thanks. Pretty much back to (1) <u>his old himself</u>. We (2) <u>got vaccinated ourselves</u> against hepatitis before we went to West Africa, so Tony was just unlucky to get it. He went into work after we got back although he was feeling bad, and some of his colleagues were worried about (3) <u>getting it themselves</u>. I know that some of them (4) <u>had checked themselves</u> by their doctors. By coincidence, his boss said that (5) <u>he'd caught himself hepatitis</u> when he was in Africa a few years ago. When he's completely recovered, (6) <u>Tony and myself</u> are off to Paris for a few days, and (7) <u>we're going to occupy us</u> with looking at the galleries and having a rest.

Must go now. The children have just shouted that they want some juice and (8) <u>they can't reach it themself</u>.

Will be in touch, Maggie

One and ones

A We can use **one** instead of repeating a singular countable noun and **ones** instead of repeating a plural noun when it is clear from the context what we are talking about:

- □ 'Can I get you a drink?' 'It's okay, I've already got **one**.' (= a drink)
- □ I think his best poems are his early **ones**. (= poems)

We don't use **one/ones** instead of an uncountable noun:

- □ If you need any more paper, I'll bring you some. (*not* ...I'll bring you one/ones.)
- □ I asked him to get apple juice, but he got orange. (*not* ...but he got orange one/ones.)

We can't use **ones** without defining precisely which group of things we are talking about. Instead, we use **some**. Compare:

- □ 'We need new curtains.' 'Okay, let's buy *green* **ones** this time./...**ones** *with flowers on*/...*those* **ones**.' *and*
- □ 'We need new curtains.' 'Okay, let's buy **some**.' (*not* Okay, let's buy ones.)

B We don't use **one/ones** after nouns used as adjectives:

- □ I thought my key was in my trouser pocket, but it was in my **coat** pocket.
  (*not* ...my coat one.)

Instead of using **one/ones** after possessive determiners (**my, your, her,** etc.) we prefer **mine, yours, hers,** etc. However, a possessive determiner + **one/ones** is often heard in informal speech:

- □ I'd really like a watch like **yours**. (*or* '...like your one' in informal speech)

We usually use **ones** to refer to things rather than people:

- □ We need two people to help. We could ask those men over there. (*not* ... ask those ones...)

However, **ones** is more likely to be used in comparative sentences to refer to groups of people:

- □ Older students seem to work harder than younger **ones**. (*or* ...than younger students.)

Notice also that we use **ones** to refer to people in **the little ones** (= small children), (**your**) **loved ones** (= usually close family), (**one of**) **the lucky ones**.

C We can leave out one/ones –

☆ after **which**:

- □ When we buy medicines, we have no way of knowing *which* (**ones**) contain sugar.

☆ after superlatives:

- □ Look at that pumpkin! It's the *biggest* (**one**) I've seen this year.

☆ after **this, that, these,** and **those**:

- □ The last test I did was quite easy, but some parts of *this* (**one**) are really difficult.
- □ Help yourself to grapes. *These* (**ones**) are the sweetest, but *those* (**ones**) taste best.
  (Note that some people think 'those/these ones' is incorrect, particularly in formal English.)

☆ after **either, neither, another, each, the first/second/last,** (etc.):

- □ Karl pointed to the paintings and said I could take *either* (**one**). (*or* ...either of them.)
- □ She cleared away the cups, washed *each* (**one**) thoroughly, and put them on the shelf.

D We don't leave out one/ones –

☆ after **the, the only, the main,** and **every**:

- □ When you cook clams you shouldn't eat *the* **ones** that don't open.
- □ After I got the glasses home, I found that *every* **one** was broken.

☆ after adjectives:

- □ My shoes were so uncomfortable that I had to go out today and buy some *new* **ones**.
  However, after colour adjectives we can often leave out **one/ones** in answers:
- □ 'Have you decided which jumper to buy?' 'Yes, I think I'll take the *blue* (**one**).'
  and we don't include **ones** when we use adjectives in place of nouns to refer to groups of people, as in **the affluent, the disadvantaged, the elderly, the homeless, the low-paid, the poor, the privileged, the rich, the wealthy, the young,** etc. (But when these are ordinary adjectives, we can use **ones**, e.g. These are the **privileged ones**; the other children aren't so lucky.)

61.1 If necessary, correct these sentences. If they are already correct, write ✓. (A)

1 Chris brought in the wood and put ones on the fire.
2 Normally I don't like wearing a scarf, but it was so cold I put one on.
3 'We've run out of potatoes.' 'I'll get ones when I go to the shops.'
4 We haven't got lemon tea, but you could have mint one instead.
5 Those aren't your gloves. You must have picked up the wrong ones.
6 'What kind of cakes do you like best?' 'Ones with cream inside.'
7 I couldn't fit all the boxes in the car, so I had to leave ones behind and pick it up later.
8 Most of the trees in our garden are less than 10 years old but ones are much older than that.

61.2 If appropriate, replace the underlined words or phrases with **one** or **ones**. If it is not possible or is unlikely, write **No** after the sentence. (A & B)

1 I answered most of the questions, but had to miss out some very difficult <u>questions</u>.
2 The female violinists in the orchestra outnumber the male <u>violinists</u> by about three to one.
3 He used to work for a finance company, but he's moved to an insurance <u>company</u>.
4 The issue discussed at the meeting was an extremely complicated <u>issue</u>.
5 'I'll just clean my shoes before we go out.' 'Can you do my <u>shoes</u>, too, please?'
6 Many people are happy about the new road being built, but there are some angry <u>people</u>, too.
7 'Was it these earrings you wanted?' 'No, the <u>earrings</u> on the left of those, please.'
8 Dave is really good at taking photos of old buildings. There's an excellent <u>photo</u> of a local church in his office.
9 'Are you picking Jo up at the train station?' 'No, she's arriving at the bus <u>station</u>.'
10 On one channel was a war film and on the other was a horror <u>film</u>, so I turned the TV off.
11 There are lots of gloves here. Are these your <u>gloves</u>?

61.3 If the sentence is correct without the underlined **one/ones**, put brackets around it (as in 1). If it is not correct without **one/ones**, write ✓(as in 2). (C & D)

1 The children had eaten all the pizza and were still hungry so I had to make them another (<u>one</u>).
2 I drove around the houses, looking for the <u>ones</u> with 'For Sale' notices outside. ✓
3 I'm not keen on those <u>ones</u> with the cherry on top. I think I'll have a chocolate biscuit instead.
4 I like both of these jackets. I don't know which <u>one</u> to choose.
5 The vases are all handmade and every <u>one</u> looks different.
6 Each winter seemed to be colder than the last <u>one</u>.
7 There are many excellent food markets in town but the main <u>one</u> is near the port.
8 She tried on lots of pairs of shoes and finally chose the purple <u>ones</u>.
9 The books were so disorganised that I soon lost track of which <u>ones</u> I had already counted.
10 I went to a lot of interesting talks at the conference, but the best <u>one</u> was given by a Chinese professor.
11 Mark drove because he was the only <u>one</u> who knew where the restaurant was.
12 Can you remember where you bought this <u>one</u>? I'd like to get one myself.
13 You can buy quite a good guitar for under €200, but the most expensive <u>ones</u> cost thousands.
14 He's just bought a new bike and has offered to give me his old <u>one</u>.

A

We can use **so** instead of repeating an adjective, adverb, or a whole clause:
- □ The workers were angry and they had every right to be **so**. (= angry)
- □ John took the work seriously and Petra perhaps even more **so**. (= took the work seriously)
- □ Bob's giving us a lift. At least I presume **so**. (= that he's giving us a lift)

B

We often use **so** instead of a clause after verbs concerned with thinking, such as **be afraid** (expressing regret), **appear/seem** (after 'it'), **assume, believe, expect, guess, hope, imagine, presume, suppose, suspect, think**; and also after **say** and after **tell** (with an indirect object):
- □ 'Is Tony going back to Scotland to see his parents this summer?' 'I've no idea, but I would **imagine so**. He goes most years.'
- □ I found it ridiculous, and **said so**./...and **told them so**. (= that I found it ridiculous)

Notice that we don't use **so** after certain other verbs, including **accept, admit, agree, be certain, doubt, hear, know, promise, suggest, be sure**:
- □ Liz will organise the party. She **promised** (that) she would. (*not* She promised so.)
- □ 'Will Ken know how to mend it?' 'I **doubt** it./ I **doubt** (that) he will.' (*not* I doubt so.)

In informal English, particularly in an argument, we can use 'I **know so**'.

C

In negative sentences, we use **not** or **not...so**:
- □ Is the Socialist Party offering anything new in its statement? It would *appear* **not**.
- □ They want to buy the house, although they did**n't** *say* **so** directly.

We can use *either* **not** or **not...so** with **appear, seem, suppose**:
- □ 'I don't suppose there'll be any seats left.' 'No, I don't *suppose* **so**.' (*or* ...I *suppose* **not**.)

We prefer **not...so** with **believe, expect, imagine, think**. With these verbs, **not** is rather formal:
- □ 'Will we need to show our passports at the border?' 'I don't *think* **so**.' (*rather than* I think **not**.)

We use **not** with **be afraid** (expressing regret), **assume, guess** (in the phrase 'I guess...', = 'I think...'), **hope, presume, suspect**:
- □ 'You'd better do it yourself. Brian won't help.' 'No, I **guess not**.' (*not* No, I don't guess so.)

Compare the use of **not** (**to**) and **not...so** with **say**:
- □ 'Do we have to do all ten questions?' 'The teacher *said* **not**.' (= the teacher said that we didn't have to) *or* 'The teacher *said* **not to**.' (= the teacher said that we shouldn't)
- □ 'Do we have to do all ten questions?' 'The teacher did**n't** *say* **so**.' (= the teacher didn't say that we should do all ten, but perhaps we should)

D

We can use **so** in a short answer, instead of a short answer with 'Yes, ...', when we want to say that we can see that something is true, now that we have been told, particularly if we are surprised that it is true. In answers like this we use **so + pronoun + auxiliary verb** (*be, can*, etc.):
- □ 'Jack and Martha are here.' '**So they are**.' (*or* Yes, they are.) (= I can see that, too, now)

However, to indicate that we already know something we use 'Yes, ...', not 'So..'. Compare:
- □ 'Your bike's been moved.' '**So it has**./Yes, it has. I wonder who did it.' (= I didn't know before you told me) *and*
- □ 'Your bike's been moved.' '**Yes, it has**. Philip borrowed it this morning.' (= I knew before you told me; *not* So it has.)

E

We can use **so** in a similar way in short answers with verbs such as **appear** (after 'it'), **believe, gather, hear, say, seem, tell** (e.g. So she tells me.), **understand**. However, with these verbs, the pattern implies 'I knew before you told me':
- □ 'The factory is going to close.' '**So I understand**.' (= I've heard that news, too)
- □ 'I found that lecture really boring.' '**So I gather**. (= I knew that) I saw you sleeping.'

Grammar review → K10–K12

62.1 Complete the sentences with **so**, as in 1. If it is not possible, complete the sentences with an appropriate **that–clause**, as in 2. **(B)**

1 'Is Don ill again?' ' Well, he hasn't come to work, so I assume ....so.... .'
2 'Will we need to pay to get in?' 'I doubt ....that we will.... .'
3 'Will you be able to come over this weekend?' 'I hope ....'
4 'Can you give me a lift to work?' 'I suppose ....'
5 'Is this one by Van Gogh, too?' 'I think ....'
6 'Apparently Carol's getting married again.' 'Yes, I hear ....'
7 'The weather's awful, so we'll need to take a taxi.' 'I guess ....'
8 'Will the decorator be finished this week?' 'He says ....'
9 'You will remember to pick me up at 1.00, won't you?' 'I promise ....'
10 'I hope I'll be able to get a ticket.' 'I'm sure ....'

62.2 Complete the answers using the verb in brackets with **not**, or **not (n't)...so**. If two answers are possible, give them both. **(B & C)**

1 'Do you know where the post office is?' 'I....'m afraid not.... .' (*be afraid*)
2 'Karl's drawing is wonderful, but he's certainly no artist. He must have had some help.' 'When I asked him he...................................... .' (*say*)
3 'With the children being ill I haven't had time to do much housework.' 'No, I ....' (*suppose*)
4 'Did I leave my handbag in your car yesterday?' 'I ....' (*think*)
5 'Will Alex be staying with us for the whole summer?' 'I ....' (*expect*)
6 'I'm sure the bank has charged me too much. Will they refund the money?' 'I ....' (*suspect*)
7 'Didn't Alice hear you?' 'It ....' (*appear*)
8 'The test results were terrible. Do you think the students understood the questions?' 'I ....' (*assume*)
9 'What did you think of Amanda's work?' 'Well, I thought it was pretty awful, although I ....' (*say*)

62.3 Complete these conversations with an appropriate short answer beginning Yes, ... Give an alternative answer with So... if possible. **(D)**

1 'That horse is walking with a limp.' '....Yes, it is.... (or ....So it is.....) Perhaps we should tell the owner.'
2 'The children from next door are taking the apples from our trees.' '...................................... . I said they could come round and get them.'
3 'The cassette player's gone again.' '...................................... . Dr Adams has probably borrowed it.'
4 'I told you I'd be late for work today.' '......................................, I agree. But you didn't say *how* late – it's nearly 2.00.'

62.4 Choose any appropriate short answer beginning So... to respond to the comments below, saying that you already knew what is being said. Use the verbs in E opposite.

1 'My car won't start again.' ....So I hear....
2 'Eva's not very well.' ....
3 'The class has been cancelled again.' ....
4 'I see income tax is going up.' ....
5 'Bob's moving to Berlin.' ....

Do so

A

We use **do so** (or **does so**, **did so**, **doing so**, etc.) instead of repeating a verb phrase (a verb and what follows it to complete its meaning) when it is clear from the context what we are talking about:

- ☐ She won the competition in 1997 and seems likely to **do so** (= win the competition) again this year.
- ☐ Dr Lawson said, 'Sit down.' Katia **did so** (= sat down), and started to talk about her problems.
- ☐ The climbers will try again today to reach the summit of the mountain. Their chances of **doing so** (= reaching the summit of the mountain) are better than they were last week. (In very formal English we can also use **so doing**.)
- ☐ When he was asked to check the figures, he claimed that he **had** already **done so**. (= checked the figures)

Do so is most often used in formal spoken and written English. In informal English we can use **do it** or **do that** instead:

- ☐ Mrs Bakewell waved as she walked past. She **does so/it/that** every morning.
- ☐ Ricardo told me to put in a new battery. I **did so/it/that**, but the radio still doesn't work.

We can also use **do** alone rather than **do so** in less formal English, especially after modals or perfect tenses (see also **B**):

- ☐ 'Will this programme work on your computer?' 'It *should* **do**.'
- ☐ I told you that I'd finish the work by today, and I *have* **done**. ('have' is stressed here)

B

We can use **do so** instead of verbs that describe *actions*, but we avoid **do so** with verbs that describe *states* and *habitual actions*. Compare:

- ☐ 65% of the members voted for Ken Brown this time, whereas 84% **did so** last year.
- ☐ Kenyon confessed to the murder, although he only **did so** after a number of witnesses had identified him as the killer.
- ☐ I gave her the medicine, and I take full responsibility for **doing so**. *and*
- ☐ Stefan doesn't like Porter's films but Bridget **does**.
- ☐ He earned a lot more than I **did**.
- ☐ I don't have time to go swimming every day, but I *usually* **do**.

C

Such

We can use **such** + (**a/an**) + **noun** to refer back to something mentioned before, with the meaning 'of this/that kind'. We use **such** + **noun** when the noun is uncountable or plural, and **such** + **a/an** + **noun** when the noun is countable and singular. **Such** is used in this way mainly in formal speech and writing:

- ☐ The students refer to teachers by their first names and will often criticise them for badly-prepared lessons. **Such behaviour** is unacceptable in most schools. (*more informally* Behaviour like this...)
- ☐ When asked about rumours that the company is preparing to lose more than 200 jobs, a spokeswoman said: 'I know of no **such plans**.' (*more informally* ...no plans of this kind.)
- ☐ They needed someone who was both an excellent administrator and manager. **Such a person** was not easy to find. (*more informally* A person like this...)
- ☐ We allow both men and women to have time off work to bring up children. We were the first department to introduce **such a scheme**. (*more informally* ...a scheme like this.)

63.1 Make the two sentences into one, joining them with either **and** or **but** as appropriate. In the second part of the sentence use a form of **do** followed by **so** instead of repeating the **verb + object/ complement**. (A)

1 Johnson never won an Olympic medal. He twice came close to winning an Olympic medal.
   Johnson never won an Olympic medal, but twice came close to doing so.

2 She was asked to teach more classes. She was happy to teach more classes.

3 My French hosts gave me snails to eat. I ate them very reluctantly.

4 The company wanted to build a new dam on the site. They were prevented from building the dam by local opposition.

5 All EU countries agreed to implement the new regulations on recycling plastic. So far only Finland and Austria have implemented the new regulations.

6 The water freezes in the cracks in rocks. As it freezes, it expands.

63.2 Complete these sentences with a form of **do** followed by **so** only if possible. (B)

1 If you have not already handed in the form, then please .... without delay.

2 Tom drives much faster than you ....

3 He jumped down from the window, but in .... twisted his ankle.

4 I know that many people don't enjoy Felipe's films, but I ....

5 Anyone crossing the railway .... at their own risk.

6 I thought Pete was joking when he said these apples smell like oranges. But they ....!

7 When we play tennis Kathy usually wins, and she gets upset if I ....

8 She pointed to the old box, her hand shaking as she ....

63.3 Complete the sentences with **such** or **such a/an** followed by one of these words. Use a singular or plural form of the word as appropriate. (C)

   claims   destruction   ~~device~~   project   research   tactics

1 Manufacturers often claim that their washing machines have built-in computers, but is there really a computer in _such a device_ ?

2 After Professor Jones spoke about his work on climate change, he called on the government to put more money into ....

3 Television is sometimes said to harm children's social development, yet the evidence for .... is often lacking.

4 The new power station would undoubtedly create new jobs, but has the environmental impact of .... been considered fully?

5 The earthquake demolished nearly all the houses in the town. The country has rarely seen .... before.

6 United played very defensively in the second half, but .... were criticised by the team's supporters.

63.4 Rewrite the sentences in 63.3 to make them less formal, as in 1. (C)

1 _...but is there really a computer in a device like this?_ (or _...like that_ ?)

Unit 64

More on leaving out words after auxiliary verbs

A

To avoid repeating words from a previous clause or sentence we use an auxiliary verb (**be**, **have**, **can**, **will**, **would**, etc.) instead of a whole verb group (e.g. 'has finished') or instead of a verb and what follows it (e.g. 'like to go to Paris'):

- □ She says she's finished, but I don't think she **has**. (*instead of* ...has finished.)
- □ 'Would any of you like to go to Paris?' 'I **would**.' (*instead of* I would like to go to Paris.)

If there is more than one auxiliary verb in the previous clause or sentence, we leave out all the auxiliary verbs except the first instead of repeating the main verb. Alternatively, we can use two (or more) auxiliary verbs:

- □ Alex **hadn't been** invited to the meal, although his wife **had**. (*or* ...**had been**.)
- □ 'They **could have been** delayed by the snow.' 'Yes, they **could**.' (*or* ...**could have** (been).)

B

If there is no auxiliary verb in the previous clause or sentence, or if the auxiliary is a form of **do**, we can use a form of **do** instead of repeating the main verb. We use **do** when the main verb is a present simple form and **did** when it is a past simple form:

- □ Monica **plays** golf on Saturdays, and I **do** too. (*instead of* ...and I play golf on Saturdays too.; '...and so do I' is also possible)
- □ 'I **didn't steal** the money.' 'No-one thinks that you **did**.' (*instead of* ...thinks that you stole it.; 'No-one thinks so' is also possible.)

If **be** is the main verb in the previous clause or sentence, we repeat a form of the verb **be**:

- □ 'The children **are** noisy again.' 'They always **are**.'

If **have** or **have got** is the main verb in the previous clause or sentence, we can usually use a form of either **do** or **have**:

- □ 'Do you think I **have** a chance of winning?' 'Yes, I think you **have**.' (*or* ...you **do**.; 'Yes, I think so' is also possible.)
- □ Even if he **hasn't got** a map himself, he may know someone who **has**. (*or* ...who **does**.)

However, if we use **have** + **noun** in the previous clause or sentence to talk about actions (**have a shower**, **have a shave**, **have a good time**, etc.) we prefer **do**:

- □ I wasn't expecting to *have a good time* at the party, but I **did**.

Notice that sometimes we can use either **do**, **be** or **have** with a similar meaning (see also **C**):

- □ I asked Suzie to tidy her room, and she **has/did**. ('has' replaces 'has tidied her room'; 'did' replaces 'tidied her room'.)

C

If we use **have** as an auxiliary verb, we can often follow it with **done** instead of repeating the main verb. This happens particularly in spoken English:

- □ 'She's never made a mistake before.' 'Well, she **has** (**done**) this time.'

However, this is usually not possible when the verb being substituted is intransitive:

- □ 'They've already gone.' 'I don't think Bob **has**.' (*not* ...Bob has done.)

Similarly, after a *modal* auxiliary verb (**can**, **could**, **may**, **might**, **must**, **ought to**, **shall**, **should**, **will**, **would**) we can use **do**, particularly in spoken English:

- □ 'Will you be seeing Tony today?' 'I **might** (**do**).'

Sometimes we can use **be** instead of **do** with a similar meaning (see also **D**):

- □ 'Will you be seeing Tony today?' 'I **might** (**do/be**).' ('do' replaces 'see Tony today'; 'be' replaces 'be seeing Tony today'.)

D

If we use **be** as an *auxiliary* verb in the previous clause or sentence, we can use **be** after a modal:

- □ 'Is Ella staying for lunch?' 'Yes, I think she **will** (be).' (*or* ...she will **do**.)

However, if **be** is used as a *main* verb in the previous clause or sentence, or as an auxiliary verb within a passive, we can usually leave out **be** after a modal in informal contexts only. Compare:

- □ 'John's late again.' 'I thought he **might** (be).' *and*
- □ It has been found that the comet is made entirely of gas, as it was predicted it **would be**.

Exercises

64.1 By omitting parts of the sections in italics, you can leave short answers. Indicate which parts you would leave out. Give all answers if more than one is possible. (A)

1 'Have you ever played squash before?' 'Yes, I *have* ~~*played squash before.*~~'

2 'I suppose we should have booked tickets in advance.' 'Yes, we *should have booked tickets in advance.*'

3 'Do you think you'll be staying in New Zealand permanently?' 'Yes, *we might be staying in New Zealand permanently.*'

4 'All the parking places will probably have been taken by now.' 'Yes, I'm sure they *will have been taken by now.*'

5 'Have you had dinner yet?' 'No, I *haven't had dinner yet.*'

6 'Are you going to Steve's party?' 'Yes, I *am going to Steve's party.*'

7 'If Diane hadn't given you a lift you would have missed the train.' Yes, I *would have missed the train.*'

8 'Can you see Joe anywhere?' 'No, I *can't see him anywhere.*'

9 'Did you see that cyclist go through the red light? He couldn't have been looking.' 'No, he *couldn't have been looking.*'

64.2 Complete the sentences with an appropriate form of **do**, **be** or **have**. If more than one answer is possible, give them both. Put brackets around the word you have written if it can be left out, and write (**done**) after a form of **have** to show in which sentences this might be added. (B & C)

1 As a child I always enjoyed watching cartoons on TV, and I still ....

2 I haven't finished doing the translation yet, but I will .... by tomorrow morning.

3 Paul keeps promising to write, but he never ....

4 Have a shower if you want, but take a towel from the cupboard when you ....

5 'It costs a fortune to rent a flat in the city centre.' 'I'm sure it must ....'

6 I was hoping Derek had an electric drill that I could borrow, but he ....

7 I'm not a member of the tennis club myself, but I know someone who ....

8 I told the class that they had to hand in their books by 9.00 and they all ....

9 'Have you got a copy of *Great Expectations*?' 'Yes, I think I ....'

10 'I've got a hundred pounds with me. Will that be enough to pay for the meal?' 'It should ....'

64.3 Complete the sentences with **might**, **should**, **will** or **would** as appropriate, giving alternatives where possible. If necessary, write **be** after the modal, or (**be**) if it is possible to either include it or leave it out. (D)

1 It's not snowing at the moment, but they say it ...*will/ might (be)*... later.

2 'My photograph was awarded first prize.' 'I thought it ....'

3 'Are they staying for lunch?' 'They .... I'll ask them.'

4 'Are you revising a lot for the exams?' 'Not as much as I .... , I'm afraid.'

5 The wreck of the ship was just a few metres from the shore, as it was claimed it ....

6 Bill says he's very sorry – as he ....

7 The book is a bestseller, as we hoped it ....

8 Chris was cleaning the house when I got home, as I hoped he ....

Leaving out to-infinitives

A

We can sometimes use **to** instead of a clause beginning with a **to-infinitive** when it is clear from the context what we are talking about:

- ☐ I wanted to come with you, but I won't be able **to**. (*instead of* ...to come with you.)
- ☐ 'I can't lend you any more money.' 'I'm not asking you **to**.' (*instead of* ...to lend me any more money.)
- ☐ It might have been better if Rosa had asked for my help, but she chose **not to**. (*instead of* ...chose not to ask for my help.)

However, when we use the verb **be** in the previous sentence or clause the **to-infinitive** form of **be** is repeated in the next clause or sentence:

- ☐ Simon **was** frightened – or maybe he just pretended **to be**. (*not* ...just pretended to.)
- ☐ The report **is** very critical and is clearly intended **to be**. (*not* ...clearly intended to.)

B

After most nouns and adjectives that can be followed by a **to-infinitive** clause, we can leave out the **to-infinitive** clause or use **to**:

- ☐ I'm not going to write another book – at least I don't have any **plans** (**to**). (*or* ...plans to write another book.)
- ☐ 'Could you and Tom help me move house?' 'Well, I'm **willing** (**to**), and I'll ask Tom.'

Other nouns and adjectives like this include **chance, idea, opportunity, promise, suggestion; afraid, delighted, determined.**

We can also leave out a **to-infinitive** or use **to** with verbs such as **agree, ask, begin, forget, promise, refuse, start, try:**

- ☐ Robert will collect us by 10 o'clock. He **promised** (**to**).
- ☐ 'You were supposed to buy some sugar.' 'Sorry, I **forgot** (**to**).'

After verbs which must have a complement (i.e. a phrase which completes the meaning of the verb) we can't leave out **to:**

- ☐ I admit that I took her watch, but I didn't **mean to**.
- ☐ 'Please suggest changes to the plans if you want.' 'I **intend to**.'
- ☐ Have you thought about getting vaccinated against cholera before going there? I'd certainly **advise** you **to**.

Other verbs like this include **afford, be able, choose, deserve, expect, fail, hate, hope, love, need, prefer.**

C

After **want** and **would like** in *if*-clauses and *wh*-clauses we can often leave out a **to-infinitive** or use **to:**

- ☐ You're welcome to dance *if* you'**d like** (**to**).   ☐ You can do *whatever* you **would like** (**to**).
- ☐ Call me Fred **if** you **want** (**to**).   ☐ Come and see us *when* you **want** (**to**).

In other clauses (not *if*- and *wh*-clauses) we include **to:**

- ☐ I was planning to see you tomorrow, and I **would** still **like to**.
- ☐ They offered to clean your car because they really **want to**, not because they hope to be paid.

In *if*-clauses and *wh*-clauses we usually leave out **to** after **like**. Compare:

- ☐ You can have one if you **like**. *and* You can have one if you'**d like** (**to**).
- ☐ Leave whenever you **like**. *and* Leave whenever you'**d like** (**to**).

However, we include **to** with negative forms of **want, would like,** and **like,** including in *if*-clauses and *wh*-clauses:

- ☐ 'Shall we go and visit Julio?' 'I **don't** really **want to**.'
- ☐ I should have phoned Jo last night, but it was so late when I got home I **didn't like to**.
- ☐ 'He won't mind you asking him for a loan.' 'Oh, no, I **wouldn't like to**.'

Exercises Unit 65

65.1 Complete the sentences with one of the following words and then either **to** or **to be**. Use the same word in each sentence in the pair. Use **to** in one sentence and **to be** in the other. (A)

  appeared   claims   expected   need   used

1 a Is she really as good at tennis as she ___claims to be___ ?
  b The present government doesn't represent the majority of people, although it
  _____ .

2 a We don't get paid to work overtime, but we're _____ anyway.
  b The Pantheon in Rome wasn't anything like I _____ it _____ .

3 a She occupies a much less important role in the company than she _____ .
  b Derek has lost a lot of weight. He's much thinner than he _____ .

4 a 'I'm really worried about taking my driving test.' 'There's no _____,
     you're an excellent driver.'
  b 'Shall I bring a calculator to the exam?' 'No, you don't _____ . They'll
     be provided.'

5 a Some people thought that Katie was lazy, but she studied much harder than she
  _____ .
  b Tom was working hard at the computer – or at least he _____ .

65.2 Complete the sentences. Write **to** if it must be used; write **(to)** if it can be either included or left out. (B)

1 I've always wanted to go white-water rafting, but I've never had the opportunity _____ before.
2 James had to admit that he'd failed, even though he obviously hated _____ .
3 When the police officer told the crowd to leave the square they refused _____ .
4 I don't have to walk to work. I do it because I choose _____ .
5 We didn't want Pam to leave college, but she was determined _____ .
6 Spain won 3–nil, and deserved _____, after a fine performance.
7 'Shall we ask Dad before we borrow the car?' 'Yes, it might be a good idea _____ .'
8 'Would you present the prizes for the competition?' 'I'd be delighted _____ .'
9 'Would you like to travel first class?' 'Well, yes, I'd certainly prefer _____ .'
10 I was hoping to go to Russia this year, but I can't afford _____ .

65.3 If necessary, correct the responses (B's parts) in these conversations. If they are already correct, write ✓. (C)

1 A: Can I have a biscuit?   B: Take more than one if you like to.
2 A: When shall we start playing the music?   B: Whenever you'd like.
3 A: Will Rosa be able to play?   B: I asked her, but she says she doesn't want.
4 A: I can't come out tonight, I'm seeing Emma. B: She can join us, if she'd like to.
5 A: Where are you going to in Norway?   B: I haven't decided yet. I'll just go where I want.
6 A: I don't think I'll go after all.   B: That's okay. You don't have to if you don't want.
7 A: Can the children come too?   B: Yes, of course, if they want.
8 A: Shall we go out walking tomorrow?   B: Yes, I'd like very much.
9 A: Could I ask you a personal question? B: Of course. Ask anything you like to.
10 A: Did you ask Dr Jones to help you?   B: No, he was very busy, so I didn't like.
11 A: Where shall I put this painting?   B: You choose. Put it where you want to.

Position of adjectives

A Many adjectives can be used either before the noun they describe, or following linking verbs such as **appear, be, become, feel, get,** and **seem** (see Unit 21). Compare:

☐ The **high** *price* surprised him. *and* ☐ The price **seemed** *high*.

B Some adjectives are seldom or never used before the noun they describe. These include –

☆ some adjectives formed by adding a prefix '**a-**', often to a noun or verb: **afraid, alike, alive, alone, ashamed, asleep, awake, aware:**

☐ The horse *was* **alone** in the field. (*but not* The alone horse...)

Some of these adjectives with an '**a-**' prefix have related adjectives that can be used either before a noun or after a linking verb. Compare:

☐ The animal was **alive**. *and* A **living** animal. (*or* A **live** animal./ The animal was **living**.)

Other pairs like this include **afraid – frightened, alike – similar, alone – lone, asleep – sleeping.**

☆ some adjectives used to describe health and feelings: **content, fine, glad, ill** (but note '**ill** health'), **sorry, (un)sure, upset** (but 'an **upset** stomach'), **(un)well** (but 'He's not a **well** man'):

☐ My son *felt* **unwell**. (*but not* My unwell son...)

These adjectives are sometimes used between an adverb and noun e.g. 'a terminally **ill** patient'.

C *Emphasising adjectives* are used to emphasise your feelings about something. Compare:

☐ I felt a fool. *and* ☐ I felt a **complete** fool. (for emphasis)

Some emphasising adjectives (such as **complete**, and also **absolute, entire, mere, sheer, total, utter**) are seldom or never used after a linking verb:

☐ It was a **total** failure. (*but not usually* 'The failure was total.')

Classifying adjectives are used to say that something is of a particular type. For example, we can talk about '**democratic** decisions', where '**democratic**' distinguishes them from other types of decision. Other classifying adjectives include **atomic, chemical, cubic, digital, environmental, medical, phonetic; annual, general, occasional, northern** (etc.), **maximum, minimum, underlying.** Classifying adjectives are seldom or never used after a linking verb:

☐ a **nuclear** explosion (*but not usually* 'The explosion was nuclear', unless we particularly want to emphasise a contrast with other kinds of explosion)

Qualitative adjectives are used to give the quality that a thing or person has. We use them either directly before a noun or after a linking verb. Compare:

☐ a **beautiful** sunset *and* ☐ The sunset was **beautiful**.

Note that some classifying adjectives can also be used with different meanings as qualitative adjectives and placed after a linking verb. Compare:

☐ The country's **economic** *reforms*. *and* ☐ The *process* isn't **economic**. (= not profitable)

Other adjectives like this include **academic, conscious, educational, (il)legal, scientific.**

D Many adjectives can be used immediately after a noun, at the beginning of a reduced relative clause (see Unit 69B). For example –

☆ adjectives before a *to-*infinitive, or a prepositional phrase as part of the adjective phrase:

☐ It was a *speech* **calculated** *to appeal* to the unions.

☐ He is a *manager* **capable** *of taking* difficult decisions.

☆ some -*ible* and -*able* adjectives such as **available, imaginable, possible, suitable.** However, we use these adjectives immediately after a noun *only* when the noun follows **the** or when the noun is made definite by what follows in a relative clause:

☐ This was *the* most difficult *decision* **imaginable**.

☐ It is a *treatment* **suitable** *for all children with asthma*.

☆ the adjectives **concerned, involved, opposite, present, proper, responsible.** These words have different meanings when they are used *before* a noun and immediately after it. Compare:

☐ All the *people* **present** (= who were there) approved of the decision. *and*

☐ I was asked for my **present** *address*. (= my address now)

66.1 Suggest corrections to these sentences, or write ✓ if they are already correct. (B)

1 After the accident I tried to comfort the upset driver of the car.
   After the accident I tried to comfort the driver of the car, who was upset.

2 In the distance I could see an alone figure walking towards me.

3 It wasn't a great surprise when Ken died as he hadn't been a well man for years.

4 I remember her as a glad person who was always smiling.

5 He stood at the bedroom door, looking at his asleep daughter.

6 The fire on the ship is now under control, but there are still a lot of afraid passengers on board.

7 She spent most of her life nursing seriously ill children in the hospital.

8 The two children were of an alike age.

9 We were unsure which way to go.

10 The sorry girls apologised to their teacher for their behaviour.

66.2 Choose one pair of words to complete each pair of sentences. In some sentences, you can use either adjective in the pair, in which case write them both; in others you can use only one of them. (C)

> domestic – unsafe   educational – entertaining   inevitable – utter
> legal – stupid   serious – underlying

1 a The experiment was a/an .... failure.
   b After Dr Owen left the project, its failure was ....

2 a None of the equipment in the warehouse is ....
   b All .... equipment should be switched off at the end of the day.

3 a The trip to the wildlife park was a/an .... experience.
   b The toys were .... and the children played with them for hours.

4 a The fault in the computer system is .... enough to disrupt all the work in the office.
   b The .... problem has not yet been solved.

5 a He was involved in a .... argument with his neighbour over some trees in the garden.
   b It's completely .... to charge a fee for entry into the museum.

66.3 Write the word given in brackets in one of the spaces in each sentence, either before or after the noun. If both positions are possible, indicate this. (D)

1 The party was excellent, and I'd like to thank all the .... people .... (*concerned*)

2 As the .... minister .... for the health service, I think he should resign. (*responsible*)

3 The new machinery was intended to increase output, but it seems to have had the .... effect .... (*opposite*)

4 The pond on the village green was filled in with the .... approval .... of most local residents. (*apparent*)

5 Children are only admitted when accompanied by a/an .... adult .... (*responsible*)

6 It's the only .... room .... in the hotel that night. (*available*)

7 I live on one side of the road and my mother lives in the .... house .... (*opposite*)

8 Cars drive too fast past the school and .... teachers .... have complained to the police. (*concerned*)

9 There is .... financial advice .... if you need it. (*available*)

Gradable and non-gradable adjectives (1)

A

If an adjective is *gradable* it can be used with adverbs such as **very** or **extremely** to say that a thing or person has more or less of a particular quality. Here are some examples of adjectives used as gradable in their most common meanings:

| *Grading adverbs* | a bit, dreadfully, extremely, hugely, immensely, intensely, rather, reasonably, slightly, very | + | angry, big, busy, clever, common, deep, fast, friendly, happy, important, low, popular, quiet, rich, strong, weak, young | *Gradable adjectives* |

- □ She was *extremely* **rich**.
- □ The people there are *reasonably* **friendly**.

Non-gradable adjectives are not used with adverbs such as **very** or **extremely** because we don't usually imagine degrees of the quality referred to. With non-gradable adjectives we can use adverbs which emphasise their extreme or absolute nature, such as **absolutely, completely**, etc. Many classifying adjectives (see Unit 66) are usually non-gradable. Adverbs such as **almost, exclusively**, etc., which indicate the extent of the quality, are commonly used with classifying adjectives. Here are some examples of adjectives used as non-gradable in their most common meanings:

| *Non-grading adverbs* | absolutely, completely, entirely, perfectly, practically, simply, totally, utterly, virtually; almost, exclusively, fully, largely, mainly, nearly, primarily | + | awful, excellent, huge, impossible, superb, terrible, unique, unknown, whole; domestic, environmental (see Unit 66C) | *Non-gradable adjectives* |

- □ She gave us a *completely* **impossible** problem to solve.
- □ It was *absolutely* **superb**.

Gradable adjectives are sometimes used with non-grading adverbs such as **absolutely** and **totally**, and non-gradable adjectives are sometimes used with grading adverbs such as **extremely**, **rather** and **very**, particularly when we want to give special emphasis or when we are being humorous (see also Unit 68):

- □ What you're asking isn't just difficult – it's *extremely* **impossible**! (*grading adverb + non-gradable adjective*)
- □ You've won a hundred pounds? Wow, you're *virtually* **rich**! (*non-grading adverb + gradable adjective*)

Note that not all the adverbs can go with all the adjectives given in each of the tables above. For example, we can say 'absolutely huge', but we wouldn't usually say 'completely huge' unless it was for particular emphasis or for humour.

B

The adverbs **fairly** (= to quite a large degree, but usually less than 'very'), **really** (= 'very (much)') and **pretty** (= similar to 'fairly'; used in informal contexts) are commonly used with both gradable and non-gradable adjectives:

- □ She's *fairly* **popular** at school.
- □ I'm *really* **busy** at the moment.
- □ It's a *pretty* **important** exam.
- □ It was a *fairly* **awful** film.
- □ The flooding was *really* **terrible**.
- □ The bill was *pretty* **huge**.

However, notice that we don't generally use **fairly** (or **very**) with gradable adjectives such as **essential, invaluable, perfect, superb, tremendous** and **wonderful** which indicate that something is very good or necessary:

- □ Some experience is *really/pretty* **essential** for the job. (*not* …fairly essential…)
- □ The weather that day was *really/pretty* **perfect**. (*not* …fairly perfect.)

67.1 Write **very** in the spaces before gradable adjectives. (There are 5 of these.) Before the non-gradable adjectives write the following adverbs. Try to use a different one each time. (A)

> absolutely   almost   completely   exclusively   largely   mainly   practically

1 The bridge is now .... complete.
2 He acted in a/an .... professional way.
3 The material is .... cotton.
4 The food was .... excellent.
5 Her explanation was .... clear.
6 Their actions were .... illegal.
7 The new restaurant is .... popular.
8 I was in a/an .... permanent state of suspense.
9 I thought she was .... attractive.
10 Until last year the club was .... male.
11 Small black cars are not .... visible.
12 The railway is .... underground.

67.2 Use an adverb + adjective in your response, as in 1. (A) How would you feel if...

1 a friend said s/he had just won a million pounds? _I'd be absolutely delighted._
2 your best friend told you s/he was emigrating to Australia?
3 someone broke a window in your house or flat?
4 a complete stranger told you that you were very beautiful/handsome?
5 you lost some airline tickets you had just bought?

67.3 Make corrections to the italicised parts of this text where necessary. (A)

Dear Alan

I'm writing this letter from my new flat in Stratford. It's in an (1) *absolutely old* building which was (2) *totally renovated* last year. Fortunately, I didn't have to do much decorating when I moved in. As you know, I'm (3) *hugely useless* at DIY so I was (4) *absolutely happy* about that. The building is (5) *reasonably unique* in this part of Stratford, as most others around are (6) *rather modern*, and the view across the river from my sitting room is (7) *simply superb*. The flat's (8) *simply small*, but (9) *completely comfortable* for me.

My neighbours are (10) *very friendly* and usually (11) *fully quiet*. The only problem is that the woman upstairs plays the trumpet and I find it (12) *a bit impossible* to read when she's playing. I get (13) *slightly angry* about this, but she doesn't play for long each time, so it's not an (14) *extremely terrible* problem.

I know that the weather has been (15) *dreadfully awful* recently, so it's been difficult to for you to get here, but you must come over one evening. There's an (16) *absolutely marvellous* restaurant nearby that we could go to.

Hope all is well,
Eva

67.4 Cross out any incorrect or unlikely alternatives. (B)

1 Her advice was *fairly/ really* invaluable.
2 Our neighbours are *really/ fairly* friendly.
3 I thought his performance as Hamlet was *fairly/ really* tremendous.
4 The children kept *pretty/ very* quiet during the concert.
5 The view from the window was *very/ pretty* wonderful.
6 Their co-operation is *pretty/ very* essential if we want the project to go ahead.
7 The weather was *really/ fairly* perfect for a long walk.
8 In this photograph she looked *really/ very* young.
9 The workmanship in the furniture was *pretty/ very* superb.
10 The disease is *fairly/ pretty* common in this part of the country.

Gradable and non-gradable adjectives (2)

A

Some adjectives have both gradable and non-gradable senses.

(i) Some adjectives have different senses when they are gradable and non-gradable. Compare:

- ☐ Smith is a *very* **common** name. (= frequently found; gradable) *and*
- ☐ We have a lot of **common** interests. (= shared; non-gradable; not *very*)
- ☐ The house is *very* **old**. (= existed many years; gradable) *and*
- ☐ I met my **old** politics professor the other day. (= former; non-gradable; not *very*)
- ☐ Sue's shoes are *very* **clean**. (= not dirty; gradable) *and*
- ☐ He left the town because he wanted to make a **clean** break with the past. (= starting again in different circumstances; non-gradable; not *very*)

Other adjectives like this include **civil, clean, critical, electric** (= 'exciting' when gradable), **empty, false, late, odd, original, particular, straight**.

(ii) Some adjectives have similar meanings when they are gradable and non-gradable. However, when they are gradable we talk about the quality that a person or thing has (i.e. they are *qualitative* adjectives and therefore can be used with an adverb), and when they are non-gradable we talk about the category or type they belong to (i.e. they are *classifying* adjectives). Compare:

- ☐ I don't know where he came from, but he sounded *slightly* **foreign**. (= not from this country; gradable) *and*
- ☐ She is now advising on the government's **foreign** policy. (= concerning other countries; non-gradable)
- ☐ They had a *very* **public** argument. (= seen/heard by a lot of people; gradable) *and*
- ☐ He was forced to resign by **public** pressure. (= from many people in the community; non-gradable)
- ☐ She had a *rather* **wild** look in her eyes. (= uncontrolled or frightened; gradable) *and*
- ☐ Even if it is raised by humans, a lion will always be a **wild** animal. (= not tame; non-gradable)

Other adjectives like this include **academic, adult, average, diplomatic, genuine, guilty, human, individual, innocent, mobile, private, professional, scientific, technical, true**.

(iii) When nationality adjectives are non-gradable we mean that a person or thing comes from a particular country; when they are gradable we mean that they have supposed characteristics of that country. Compare:

- ☐ There's a shop around the corner that sells **Italian** bread. *and*
- ☐ Giovanni has lived in Britain for 20 years, but he's still *very* **Italian**.

B

In spoken English in particular, we can use **good and...**, **lovely and...**, and **nice and...** followed by another gradable adjective in order to emphasise the second adjective. Possible patterns include: **good and ready** and more colloquially **good and proper/relaxed/strong** (but not usually 'good and beautiful/rich/tall'); **lovely and cosy/dry/sunny/warm** (but not usually 'lovely and decent/empty short'); **nice and bright/clean/cold/comfortable/early/fresh/quiet/simple/ soft/tidy/warm** (but not usually 'nice and interesting/handsome/exciting'):

- ☐ If you're all feeling **good and relaxed** after the break, let's get on with the meeting.
- ☐ It's **lovely and warm** in here. Freezing outside, though.
- ☐ 'Shall we get some strawberries?' 'Yes, they look **nice and fresh**.'

We can also link comparative adjectives (see Unit 72) with **and** to talk about an increasing degree of the quality described in the adjective. We use **more and more + adjective** in a similar way:

- ☐ As she got **more and more excited**, her voice got **higher and higher** and **louder and louder**.
- ☐ The taxi driver just drove **faster and faster and faster** until I told him to stop, and I got out.

68.1 Choose from these adjectives to complete the sentences. Use each of the adjectives twice, once with a gradable sense and once with a non-gradable sense. With a gradable sense, write **very** before the adjective. It may help to use a dictionary for this exercise. (Ai)

> critical   empty   false   late   original   straight

1 The novel was praised by the judges for its ....<u>very original</u>.... use of language.
2 I wasn't frightened by the manager's warning that I would be dismissed if I came late again. It was just a/an .... threat that she had used before.
3 The train is .... again. I wonder if the bad weather has delayed it.
4 The report was .... of the police officers involved in the investigation.
5 I had a/an .... choice between working for my father and having no job at all.
6 She was accused of giving .... information during the trial.
7 After such a long period without rain, the reservoirs are now ....
8 The driver of the overturned lorry was in a/an .... condition in hospital last night.
9 I was given the oil painting by my .... uncle Simon.
10 The .... fireplaces had been removed and replaced by more modern ones.
11 The path to the summit of the hill was .... and steep.
12 Many of the people I met were quite sincere, but some seemed ...., so that I could never be sure if they meant what they said.

68.2 Complete the sentences with these adverb + adjective phrases. Use the same adjective in each pair of sentences, but include the adverb in only one. The first pair is done for you. (Aii)

> (largely) academic   (fairly) average   (extremely) diplomatic
> (very) human   (intensely) private   (highly) technical

1 a The ....<u>average</u>.... temperature on the island is a pleasant 23.4°C.
   b Brecston is a/~~an~~ ....<u>fairly average</u>.... town in the south of England.
2 a The instructions were .... and clearly meant for an expert.
   b Paul got a job providing .... support for people having computing problems.
3 a Being frightened in this situation is a .... response and nothing to be ashamed of.
   b Near the top of the mountain there were signs of .... habitation, perhaps centuries old.
4 a I found it difficult to understand the .... talk that Professor Downs gave.
   b The .... standards at the school are very high.
5 a He worked hard to afford a .... education for his three children.
   b She was a/an .... person and had few close friends.
6 a After Mary left university she worked in the .... service for a number of years.
   b When he was asked to comment on the French President's decision he gave a/an .... answer, not wanting to appear critical.

68.3 Suggest a phrase to complete each sentence. Begin with **good/lovely/nice + and** ... and then choose an appropriate adjective, as in 1. (B)

1 Now that the room is painted yellow, it looks ....<u>lovely and bright.</u>
2 I've put you in the spare room at the back of the house, so it'll be ....
3 'Have you felt the material my new coat's made of?' 'Oh, it's ....'
4 The oranges looked quite old, but when I cut into them they were ....
5 There's no point in trying to persuade Tom. He won't make up his mind until he's
....

Unit 69

Participle adjectives and compound adjectives

A

Some **-ing forms** (present participles) and **-ed forms** (past participles) of verbs can be used as adjectives. Most of these *participle adjectives* can be used before the noun they describe or following linking verbs (see Unit 21):

- The hotel had a **welcoming** *atmosphere*.
- I found this **broken** *plate* in the kitchen cupboard.
- The students' tests results *were* **pleasing**.
- My mother *seemed* **delighted** with the present.

B

We can use many participle adjectives *immediately* after nouns when they identify or define the noun. This use is similar to **defining relative clauses** (see GR: J1–J2) and they are often called 'reduced relatives':

- I counted the number of *people* **waiting**. (*or* ...*people* **who were waiting**.)
- We had to pay for the *rooms* **used**. (*or* ...the *rooms* **that were used**.)

Some of these are rarely used before the noun:

- None of the *candidates* **applying** was accepted. (*but not* ...the applying candidates...)
- My watch was among the *things* **taken**. (*but not* ...the taken things.)

Participle adjectives like this include **caused, found, included, provided**.

Others can be used before *or* immediately after nouns. For example, we can say:

- Rub the *area* **infected** with this cream. *or* Rub the **infected** *area* with this cream.
- The *crowd* **watching** grew restless. *or* The **watching** *crowd* grew restless.

Participle adjectives like this include **affected, alleged, allocated, broken, chosen, identified, interested, remaining, resulting, stolen**.

C

In formal English, **that** and **those** can be used as pronouns before a participle adjective:

- The office temperature is lower than **that required** by law. (= the temperature which is required)
- The quality of the motors is lower than **those manufactured** elsewhere. (= the motors which are manufactured elsewhere)

Notice that **those** can mean 'people':

- Here is some advice for **those** (= people) **preparing** to go on holiday.

D

Many *compound adjectives* include a participle adjective. Common patterns are:

adverb + -ed participle	They are **well-behaved** children.
adverb + -ing participle	China's economic boom is generating a **fast-growing** market at home.
adjective + -ed participle	She seems to live on **ready-made** frozen meals.
adjective + -ing participle	He's the **longest-serving** employee in the company.
noun + -ed participle	The public square was **tree-lined**.
noun + -ing participle	I hope it will be a **money-making** enterprise.
-ed participle + particle (from two-word verbs)	Did it really happen, or was it a **made-up** story?

We can use some participle adjectives **only** in adjective compounds. For example, we can't say '...behaved children' or '...a making enterprise' as the sense is incomplete without the adverb or noun. Other compounds like this include **London-based, Paris-born, brick-built, easy-going, peace-keeping, long-lasting, good-looking, home-made, hair-raising, far-reaching, well-resourced, sweet-smelling, strange-sounding, soft-spoken, sour-tasting, nerve-wracking**.

Notice that many other compound adjectives do not include participle adjectives:

- The problem is **short-term**. □ It was just a **small-scale** project.

69.1 Replace the underlined parts of these sentences with a present or past participle adjective formed from one of the following verbs. Give alternative positions for the adjective if possible. (B)

~~cause~~   identify   include   interest   provide   remain   result

1 I offered to pay for any damage <u>that was the result</u>. ....*caused*.... (*not* …any caused damage.)
2 Steps are being taken by telephone engineers to solve the problems <u>which have been noticed</u>.
3 Visitors <u>who want to find out more</u> can buy a booklet with further information.
4 Please answer the questions on the sheet <u>that has been given to you</u>.
5 The holiday cost £1200, with flights <u>which were part of the total</u>.
6 Although he didn't want to appear on TV, the publicity <u>that was the consequence</u> was good for his business.
7 Just before serving the pasta, sprinkle over any cheese <u>that is left over</u>.

In which of the sentences can the participle adjective you have written be placed before the noun?

69.2 Complete the sentences with either **that** or **those** followed by an appropriate participle adjective. (C)

1 Her time for the 10,000 metres was four seconds faster than .... by the winner of last month's European Championship.
2 Vegetables from the east of the country are generally cheaper than .... in the west.
3 The company claims that its electric goods are more reliable than .... by its competitors.
4 The top wind speed was even higher than .... in the great storm of 1987.
5 Levels of heart disease among people in rural areas are considerably lower than among .... in urban areas.

69.3 Complete the second sentences using a compound adjective from D to replace the underlined information in the first sentences. (D)

1 The company <u>is organised from</u> New York. It is a ...*New York–based company*... .
2 The school <u>has all the things it needs</u>, with sufficient books and computers. The school is .... , with sufficient books and computers.
3 I found that the whole experience <u>made me tense and worried</u>. I found the whole experience ....
4 The proposed changes will <u>have a major influence on a large number of people</u>. The proposed changes will be ....

69.4 Combine the following words to make compound adjectives to replace the underlined parts of these sentences. Make any other necessary changes. (D)

| clean | eye | ~~ill~~ | wide | catching | ~~equipped~~ | ranging | shaven |

1 At the age of 16 children <u>do not have the ability or experience</u> to take on the role of parents. ....*are ill-equipped*.... .
2 The discussions between the presidents <u>dealt with a great variety of topics</u>.
   ....
3 I almost didn't recognise Mark. When I last saw him he had a beard and moustache, but now he <u>has no beard or moustache</u>.
   ....
4 The advertisements for the new car are <u>very noticeable</u>.
   ....

A

When an adjective comes after a linking verb (e.g. **appear, be, become, seen**; see Unit 21) we can use a number of patterns after the adjective including a **to-infinitive, -ing, that-clause,** and **wh-clause.** (For It + linking verb + adjective, see B.)

	adjective +	*example adjectives used in this pattern*
i	**to-infinitive** ☐ You're **free** *to leave* at any time you want.	(un)able, careful, crazy, curious, difficult, easy, foolish, free, good, hard, impossible, inclined, mad, nice, prepared, ready, stupid, welcome, willing
ii	**-ing** ☐ He was **busy** *doing* his homework.	busy, crazy, foolish, mad, stupid; (after the verb feel) awful, awkward, bad, good, guilty, terrible
iii	**that-clause** ☐ He became **worried** (*that*) she might leap out from behind a door.	afraid, alarmed, amazed, angry, annoyed, ashamed, astonished, aware, concerned, disappointed, glad, (un)happy, pleased, shocked, sorry, upset, worried; certain, confident, positive, sure
iv	**wh-clause** ☐ I'm not **certain** (of/ about) *why* he wants to borrow the money	afraid, not aware/unaware, not certain/ uncertain, doubtful, not sure/unsure, worried
v	**to-infinitive** *or* **that-clause** ☐ She was **afraid** *to say* anything. ☐ I was **afraid** *that* I would be late.	the adjectives in *iii* above, except **aware, confident** and **positive**
vi	**to-infinitive** *or* **-ing** ☐ He'd be **stupid** *to leave* now. ☐ He'd be **stupid** *giving up* the job.	crazy, foolish, mad, stupid
vii	**-ing** *or* **that-clause** ☐ She felt **awful** *leaving* him with all the clearing up. ☐ She felt **awful** *that* she wasn't able to help.	(after the verb feel) awful, awkward, bad, good, guilty, terrible

B

It + linking verb + adjective
We can sometimes use **it + linking verb + adjective + to-infinitive** as an alternative to **subject + linking verb + adjective + to-infinitive** (see also Units 96 and 97). Compare:
   ☐ She is **easy** *to understand.*   *and*   **It is easy** *to understand* her.
   ☐ The fireworks were **amazing** *to watch.*   *and*   **It was amazing** *to watch* the fireworks.
Notice that in informal speech we can use an **-ing** form instead of a **to-infinitive:**
   ☐ **It is easy** *understanding* her.   ☐   **It was amazing** *watching* the fireworks.
Other adjectives that can be used in this pattern include **annoying, awkward, easy, good, interesting, lovely, simple, terrific, wonderful.** Notice that we can use a similar pattern with adjective + *wh-* or *that-*clause (see Unit 96A):
   ☐ It is not **clear** *why* he did it.   ☐   It was **odd** *that* she left so suddenly.

After certain adjectives we often include **of + subject** between the adjective and a **to-infinitive:**
   ☐ It was rude (**of them**) to criticise her. (*or* They were rude to criticise her.)
Other adjectives which often take **of + subject** in this pattern include **brave, kind, mean, thoughtful, unprofessional, unreasonable.**

When we talk about how somebody reacts to a situation we can use **it + make** with an adjective and **to-infinitive, -ing** or **that-clause:**
   ☐ **It made me angry** (*to discover*) that so much money was wasted. (*or* **It made me angry** *discovering* that...; *or* **I was angry** *to discover* that...)
Other adjectives used in this way include **ashamed, furious, glad, miserable, nervous, sad, tired, uncomfortable.**

70.1 Choose an appropriate verb to complete these sentences. Use a **to-infinitive** or **–ing** form, giving alternatives where possible. (A)

cheat	earn	know	leave	open	panic
reduce	resign	see	talk	turn	underestimate

1 I'm afraid I can't afford that much. Would you be prepared .... the price if I pay cash?
2 Jack was stupid .... in the exam. He was bound to get caught.
3 He felt good .... that he had helped solve the problem.
4 Don't feel that you need to stay to the very end of the conference. You're free .... at any time.
5 I hadn't been to Wolverton since I was a child, and I was curious .... how it had changed.
6 Anyone trying to climb the mountain would be foolish .... the challenge facing them.
7 People told me I was crazy .... a shop in this part of the city, but it's been very successful so far.
8 She was too busy .... on the phone to notice that Dave had come into the room.
9 She felt guilty .... such a lot when so many people in the country were living in poverty.
10 It's so difficult to get a job at the moment you'd be mad ....
11 Some people would be inclined .... if they smelt smoke in the house.
12 I felt awful .... people away from the concert, but there just wasn't any more room.

70.2 Here is part of a letter in which Sarah is describing her holiday in Thailand with Mark. Where necessary, correct the italicised text. (A)

…After a couple of days Mark announced that he was going walking in the hills near the hotel. I thought he was (1) *stupid that he would go* alone and that it was dangerous. But he said that he was (2) *confident not to get lost*. We ended up arguing and finally he stormed off, saying he (3) *wasn't sure when* he'd be back. I went into town, but I felt a bit (4) *guilty to shop* all day. On the bus on the way back to the hotel I got talking to a local woman and (5) *was concerned learning* that it got very cold in the hills at night. I started (6) *to get worried that* he might be in danger, but I (7) *wasn't certain what* to do. But when I got back to the hotel, there was Mark (8) *busy to drink* orange juice by the pool. He'd decided not to go walking after all! He said he (9) *was sorry upsetting me*. At first I was angry and said he was stubborn and that he just (10) *wasn't prepared admitting* that I'd been right. But really I was just (11) *pleased that* he was safe…

70.3 Rewrite these sentences using **It + be + adjective**... If possible, use **of + a personal pronoun** after the adjective (as in 1). (B)

1 She was brave to spend the night in the old house alone.
   <u>It was brave of her to spend the night in the old house alone.</u>
2 Such a magnificent performance was wonderful to hear.
3 You were mean to eat all the cake and not leave any for me.
4 They were unreasonable to complain about the exam results.
5 The top of the jar was awkward to get off.
6 The shelves were simple to put up.
7 He was unprofessional to criticise the head teacher in front of the staff.
8 You were kind to give birthday presents to the children.

70.4 Complete these sentences with **It made me...** and any appropriate adjective. (B)

1 <u>It made me angry</u> to hear how she had been insulted.
2 .... listening to his lies.
3 .... that we wouldn't be working together again.
4 .... to learn how badly we treated immigrants in the 1950s.
5 .... hearing the dentist's drill as I sat in the waiting room.

A

Some adverbs of manner (saying how something is done) are formed from an **adjective + -ly**: **sudden** → **suddenly**, **happy** → **happily**, etc. When an adjective already ends in **-ly** (e.g. **cowardly, elderly, friendly, kindly, lively, lonely, lovely**) we don't add **-ly** to it to make an adverb. Instead we can use a prepositional phrase with **fashion, manner,** or **way**:

☐ He smiled at me in a **friendly way**. ☐ She waved her hands around in **a lively fashion**.

Most participle adjectives ending in **-ed** (see **Unit 69**) don't have an adverb form and so we use a prepositional phrase instead:

☐ They rose to greet me in **a subdued manner**. (*not* …subduedly.)
☐ He faced the court in **a dignified fashion**. (*not* …dignifiedly.)

or we use a preposition and a related noun if there is one:

☐ She looked at me **in amazement**. (*not* …amazedly.)
☐ He was overwhelmed **with confusion**. (*not* …confusedly.)

However, some do have an adverb form with **-ly**. Compare:

☐ The storm was **unexpected**. *and* ☐ The weather turned **unexpectedly** stormy.

Other adverbs like this include **agitatedly, allegedly, deservedly, determinedly, disappointedly, excitedly, hurriedly, pointedly, repeatedly, reportedly, reputedly, supposedly, worriedly**.

B

Some adverbs have two forms, one ending in **-ly** and the other not. We can sometimes use either of the two forms of the adverb without changing the meaning, although the form ending in **-ly** is grammatically correct and more usual in a formal style:

☐ She ran **quick/quickly** towards the door. ('quick' is less formal)

and must be used if the adverb comes immediately before the verb:

☐ She **quickly** *ran* towards the door. (*not* She quick ran…)

Other words like this include **cheap(ly), clean(ly), clear(ly), fine(ly), loud(ly), slow(ly), thin(ly)**.

C

In other cases there is a difference in the meaning of the adverb with and without **-ly**. Compare:

☐ She gave her time **free**. (= for no money) *and* She gave her time **freely**. (= willingly)
☐ I arrived **late** for the concert. (= not on time) *and* I haven't seen John **lately**. (= recently)

Here are some other pairs of adverbs that can have different meanings. Compare:

☐ He wandered **deep** into the forest and got lost. (= a long way)	☐ He felt **deeply** hurt by his criticisms. (= very) ☐ They loved each other **deeply**. (= very much)
☐ 'You don't have to change trains.' 'You can go **direct**.' (= without stopping)	☐ I'll be with you **directly**. (= very soon) ☐ He saw Susan **directly** ahead. (= straight)
☐ It sounded awful – one of the choir members was singing **flat**.	☐ This time I **flatly** refused to lend him any money. (= definitely; completely)
☐ He kicked the ball **high** over the goal.	☐ Everyone thinks **highly** of her teaching. (= they think her teaching is very good)
☐ 'Is Bob here yet?' 'He's **just** arrived.' ☐ She looks **just** like her mother.	☐ You can be **justly** proud of your musical achievements. (= rightly; justifiably)
☐ Which of these cheeses do you like **most**?	☐ Her novels are now **mostly** out of print. (= most of them) ☐ We **mostly** go on holiday in France. (= usually)
☐ They cut **short** their holiday when John fell ill. (= went home early)	☐ The speaker will be arriving **shortly** (= soon). Please take your seats.
☐ The door was **wide** open so I just went straight in. (= completely)	☐ You won't have any problems getting the book. It's **widely** available. (= in many places)

71.1 Replace the underlined parts of these sentences using the participles below. If possible, use a **-ly** form. If it is not possible, use either a prepositional phrase or a preposition and a related noun. **(A)**

agitated	anticipated	despaired	determined	disappointed
organised	relaxed	repeated	reputed	satisfied

1 I warned him <u>again and again</u> of the dangers on the mountain, but he insisted on going ahead with the climb.

2 The class was completely out of control and the teacher put his hands to his head <u>feeling that he could do nothing</u>.

3 As his mother took the roast chicken out of the oven, Rod licked his lips <u>because he was excited about what was going to happen</u>.

4 St Enedoc's is <u>said to be, although no-one knows for certain,</u> the smallest church in the country.

5 'Still no news from Paul,' she said <u>in a sad way</u>.

6 He ran the company <u>in a calm way</u> and rarely let anything annoy him.

7 She shook her head <u>as if she had made a firm decision</u>.

8 When he had finished the painting, he stepped back and looked at it <u>in a way that showed he was happy</u>.

9 Vicky runs the office <u>carefully and tidily</u>, so I don't think we should change things now.

10 Caroline paced about <u>in an anxious way</u> as she waited to go into the interview.

71.2 Use the adverbs discussed in **C** to complete the sentences. Use the form with **-ly** in one of the pairs and the form without **-ly** in the other.

1 a What she hated .... was having to get up at 5.30 every morning.
  b We don't go out much in the evening. We .... watch television.

2 a The company paid compensation, but stopped .... of admitting they were to blame.
  b The book is due to be published ....

3 a I'm not in my office at the moment, but if you leave your name and number I'll get back to you .... *[Message on a telephone answering machine]*
  b I used to have to change at Amsterdam to get to Moscow, but now I can fly ....

4 a Even though I got very little sleep on the flight I felt .... awake when I arrived in Tokyo.
  b French is .... spoken in North Africa.

5 a She is one of the most .... regarded researchers in the university.
  b We could just see the plane flying .... overhead.

71.3 Find the mistakes and correct them. If there are no mistakes, write ✓. (A–C)

1 The rise in car crime in the area is deeply worrying.

2 She waved friendlily to me.

3 Cut the onions up finely and fry them with garlic.

4 I asked the boys to move their bicycles off the football pitch but they flat refused.

5 I couldn't understand what he was saying. He didn't speak very clearly.

6 He was accused of behaving cowardlily in the battle.

7 Pierre Evene manufactured the glass for which the town became just renowned.

8 I called Jim and he slow turned to face me.

9 Spread some butter on the bread as thin as possible.

10 The prime minister was loud applauded by her audience.

Adjectives and adverbs: comparative and superlative forms

Comparatives: -er vs more/less...than

A

We usually add **-er** to one-syllable adjectives and adverbs to make their comparative form. However, we use **more + adjective** –

☆ with one-syllable past participle adjectives (see Unit 69) such as **bored, creased, pleased, worn**:
  □ After I'd ironed my shirt it looked **more creased** than before. (*not* ...creaseder...)

☆ with **fun, real, right** and **wrong**:
  □ I expected the film to be rather dull, but I couldn't have been **more wrong**. (*not* ...wronger.)

☆ when we are comparing two qualities:
  □ 'Don't you think Carl was brave to go bungee jumping?' 'Personally, I thought he was **more mad** than **brave**.'
  □ Although the paint was called 'Sky blue', I thought it was **more green** than **blue**.
  We can also use '...he wasn't so much *brave* **as** mad' and '...it was *blue* **rather than** *green*'.

We can sometimes use **more** as an alternative to the -er form to emphasise the comparison:
  □ You might think it's dark here but it's **more dark** in the cellar. (*or* ...darker...)
Other adjectives used like this include **clear, cold, fair, rough, soft, true**.

B

Some adjectives with two syllables are most commonly used with **more/less**, particularly **participle adjectives** (e.g. **worried, boring**); adjectives ending in **-ful** and **-less** (e.g. **careful, careless**); **afraid, alert, alike, alone, ashamed, aware**; and some other adjectives, including **active, cautious, certain, complex, direct, eager, exact, formal, frequent, modern, special, recent**. Most two-syllable adjectives ending **-y, -ow, -er** and **-ure** can take either an **-er** or the **more + adjective** form, although the **-er** form is more frequently used.

Some adjectives (such as **complete, equal, favourite, ideal, perfect, unique**) have a comparative or superlative meaning so they are not often used with **-er/-est** or **more/less/most/least**. However, we can use comparative or superlative forms for special emphasis or for a particular communicative purpose:
  □ The weather today was good, but **less perfect** than yesterday.

Superlatives

C

We usually use **the**, a possessive form (with **-'s**), or a possessive pronoun before a superlative adjective or adverb. In informal contexts we sometimes leave out **the** before an **-est** or **most + adjective** superlative after a linking verb, particularly when the superlative is at the end of a sentence:
  □ 'Why did you go by bus?' 'It was **(the) cheapest**.'   □ Which was **(the) most expensive**?
However, we can't leave out **the** when we go on to say what group of things is being compared:
  □ 'Why did you buy these oranges?' 'They were **the cheapest** *ones I could find*.' (*not* They were cheapest ones...)

When **most + adjective/adverb** is used without **the**, **most** means something like 'very':
  □ Did you see how she looked at you? It was **most peculiar**. (= very peculiar)
  □ I checked the form **most carefully** (= very carefully) but didn't notice the mistake.

D

After a superlative we use **of + a plural noun phrase** to name the objects being compared:
  □ John's *the oldest* **of my three brothers**.
Notice that we can put the of-phrase at the beginning to emphasise it:
  □ **Of my three brothers**, John's *the oldest*.

When we give the location or context within which the comparison is made we usually use **in + a singular noun phrase**:
  □ It was *the tallest tree* **in the forest**. (*not* ...the tallest tree of the forest.)

Grammar review: → L7–L8

72.1 Underline the correct or more likely alternative. If both are possible, notice the difference between them. (A)

1 It was almost as if the wolf was *more scared/ scareder* of us than we were of it.
2 The river was *more deep/ deeper* than I expected so I decided to turn back.
3 I think I'd describe her as *more pretty/ prettier* than beautiful.
4 He had always seemed unfriendly, but now they were alone he seemed even *more cold/ colder*.
5 I bought this tennis racket because it's *more strong/ stronger*.
6 As a politician I often receive threats, but some are *more real/ realer* than others.
7 There were two routes up the hill, but as we had lots of time we took the *more long/ longer*, *more winding/ windinger* one.
8 Sam isn't a bad boy really. He's *more naughty/ naughtier* than dishonest.
9 Although a different speaker began to talk, I felt even *more bored/ boreder* than before.
10 The exam was *more hard/ harder* than I thought it would be.
11 We need to take responsibility for elderly neighbours, and in a cold winter like this it is *more true/ truer* than ever.
12 If the critics were wrong about Willis's first novel, they couldn't have been *more right/ righter* about her second.

72.2 Complete the sentences with an appropriate comparative adjective, using an **-er** or **more +** **adjective** form. Indicate where both forms are possible. (B)

alert	clever	complex	dirty	exciting	pleasant
powerful	recent	useless	wealthy	worried	

1 I may not be much of a cook, but Brian is even .... in the kitchen than I am.
2 Most research in this area uses simple interviews, but we used a .... methodology.
3 I didn't do well at school, and my fellow students all seemed .... than me.
4 The film starts slowly, but gets .... after the first half hour.
5 Neil is already rich, but his aim in life seems to be to become even ....
6 I was concerned when John didn't phone to say he'd be late, but I was even .... when he didn't come at all that night.
7 'This painting is from the 17th century.' 'Really? It looks .... than that.'
8 The walk was quite enjoyable, but if the sun had been shining it would have been ....
9 When I took the washing out of the machine it looked .... than when it went in.
10 For an extra $500 you could buy a much .... motorbike.
11 Curiously, many people say they feel mentally .... if they eat very little for a day.

72.3 Put brackets around **the** if it can be left out in these sentences. (C)

1 It was the sweetest orange I'd eaten for ages.
2 Ann and Clara were both excellent musicians, but Clara was the most creative.
3 He's the fastest runner in his class.
4 We get lots of birds in our garden, but blackbirds are the most common.
5 'Shall we go by train or car?' 'Well, going by bus is actually the easiest.'

72.4 Complete the sentences with **in** or **of**. (D)

1 The building is said to be the highest .... Europe.
2 The Democrats are the smallest .... the four main political parties.
3 The hotel enjoys the most spectacular setting .... any on the south coast.
4 For many people, it is the most important day .... the whole year.
5 She's without doubt the best swimmer .... my school.

Comparative phrases and clauses

A We use **as + adjective/adverb + as** to say that something or someone is like something or someone else, or that one situation is like another:

- ☐ Was the film **as funny as** his last one? ☐ I came round **as quickly as** I could.

Negative forms of sentences like this can use either **not as** or **not so**. In formal speech and writing it is more common to use **less + adjective + than**:

- ☐ The gap between the sides is **not as/so wide as** it was. (*or* ...is **less wide than** it was.)

B If we put a singular countable noun between an adjective and the second **as**, we use **a/an** in front of the noun:

- ☐ Despite his disability, he tried to lead **as normal a life as** possible. (*not* ...as normal life as...)
- ☐ She was **as patient a teacher as** anyone could have had. (*not* ...as patient teacher as...)

The negative form of sentences like this can use either **not as** or sometimes **not such**:

- ☐ It's **not as quiet a place** (*or* ...**not such a quiet place** ...) **as** it used to be.

Notice that we use **not as + adjective + a/an + noun** but **not such a/an + adjective + noun**.

We can use **how, so** and **too** followed by an adjective in a similar way:

- ☐ **How significant a role** did he play in your life?
- ☐ It's not quite **so straightforward a problem as** it might at first seem.
- ☐ 'Conspiracy' is perhaps **too strong a word**. ☐ **How big a piece** do you want?

C We also use **as much/many as** or **as little/few as** to say that a quantity or amount is larger or smaller than expected. **Many** and **few** are preferred before numbers; **much** and **little** are preferred with amounts (e.g. $5, 20%) and distances (e.g. 3 metres):

- ☐ There are a small number of people involved, possibly **as few as** twenty.
- ☐ Prices have increased by **as much as** 300 per cent.

D We can use **not + adjective/adverb + enough + to-infinitive** to mean that there isn't as much as is necessary to do something:

- ☐ I'm not **tall enough** *to reach*. ☐ He didn't speak **loudly enough** *to be heard*.

We can use **sufficiently** before adjectives to express a similar meaning to **enough**. **Sufficiently** is often preferred in more formal contexts:

- ☐ She didn't play **sufficiently well** to qualify. (*or* ...**well enough** to qualify.)

E We can use **too + adjective/adverb + to-infinitive** to mean 'more than necessary, possible, etc.' to do something:

- ☐ They arrived **too late** *to get* seats. ☐ It moved **too fast** *to see* it clearly.

If we need to mention the things or people involved in the action, we do this with **for...**:

- ☐ The suitcase was **too small** (*for him*) *to get* all his clothes in.

In rather formal English we can use **too + adjective + a/an + noun**:

- ☐ I hope you haven't had **too tiring a day**. (*not* ...a too tiring day.)

(In a less formal style we might say 'I hope your day hasn't been too tiring.')

F We can use **so + adjective/adverb + that-clause** to say that something existed or happened to such a degree that a specified result occurred (see also Unit 81):

- ☐ It's **so simple** *that* even I can do it. ☐ He came in **so quietly** *that* I didn't hear him.

Less often we use **so + adjective/adverb + as + to-infinitive** with a similar meaning. Compare:

- ☐ The difference was **so small** *that* it wasn't worth arguing about. *and*
- ☐ The difference was **so small** *as to not be* worth arguing about. (= Because the difference was so small, it wasn't worth arguing about)

We can use **go so/as far as + to-infinitive** to talk about actions that are surprising or extreme:

- ☐ One furious woman **went so/as far as** *to throw* tomatoes at the minister.

Exercises

73.1 Complete these sentences with **as...as** or **not as/such...as**. Sometimes two answers are possible. Use the words in brackets and add any other necessary words. (B)

1 It's <u>not such a polluted city now as/not as polluted a city now as</u> it was 10 years ago. (*not/ polluted/ city* now)
2 The Downtown Hotel is .... Strand Hotel. (*not/ pleasant/ place to stay*)
3 The President's address to the nation is .... he is ever likely to make in his career. (*important/ speech*)
4 It was .... I first thought. (*not/ big/ problem*)
5 Theresa's dog is .... I've ever seen. (*ferocious/ animal*)
6 She's .... she claims to be. (*not/ fluent/ Greek speaker*)

73.2 Complete these sentences with **as much as, as many as, as little as,** or **as few as**. (C)

1 When it was really hot I was having .... four showers a days.
2 The elephant population may soon fall to .... 1,000 from 5,000 10 years ago.
3 At the end of the 200-metre race there was .... 50 metres between the first and second runners.
4 .... 5,000 people phoned in to complain about last night's TV programme.
5 Lit continuously, the life of a light bulb varies from .... two weeks to three months.
6 Some days there were .... three or four students at his lectures.
7 We don't use much electricity. Sometimes our bill is .... £20 a month.
8 The country spends .... 25% of its income on defence.

73.3 Match the sentences to make ones using **so + adjective + as + to-infinitive**, as in 1. (F)

1 The noise from the factory was loud.
2 Her handwriting was untidy.
3 The bookcase was heavy.
4 The CD was badly scratched.
5 The plot of the novel was complicated.
6 The difference between the results was small.

a It was nearly illegible.
b It was insignificant.
c It was unplayable.
d ~~It prevented me sleeping.~~
e It was almost impossible to move it.
f It was completely incomprehensible.

1+d <u>The noise from the factory was so loud as to prevent me sleeping.</u>

73.4 Here is part of an interview with the manager of a football team. His best player, Alan Green, has just suffered a serious injury. Correct any mistakes in the underlined text. (A–F)

INTERVIEWER: (1) <u>How serious injury</u> is it? Is it (2) <u>so serious as</u> has been claimed in the newspapers? Some people are saying Alan Green will never play international football again.

MANAGER: Well, it's certainly (3) <u>enough bad to</u> keep him out of football for at least 6 months. He's obviously (4) <u>not so fit as</u> he used to be and even he would admit that he's (5) <u>not such good player as</u> he was in his 20s. But I wouldn't (6) <u>go so far to say</u> that he'll never play for the national team again. I know him (7) <u>sufficiently well enough</u> to say that he will consider his future carefully before making any major decisions.

INTERVIEWER: Well, we all wish him (8) <u>as speedy recovery as</u> possible...

Position of adverbs (1)

A

There are three main positions for adverbs which modify a verb: *end*, *front* and *mid* position.

☆ In *end position*, the adverb is placed after the verb – either immediately after it or later in the clause:

- □ They *played* **quietly** all day.   □ He *tried to leave* **quietly**.   □ He *sat* in the corner **quietly**.

☆ In *front position* the adverb is placed before the subject:

- □ **Finally** *he* could stand the noise no longer.   □ **Sometimes** *I* feel like going home.

☆ In *mid position* the adverb is placed between the subject and verb, immediately after **be** as a main verb, or after the first auxiliary verb:

- □ *He* **usually** *plays* better than this.   □ *She is* **usually** here by 10.00.
- □ They *would* **usually** *come* by car.

Many adverbs can go in any of these positions, depending on context or style. For example:

- □ He turned round **slowly**. (*end*)   □ **Slowly** he turned round. (*front*)
- □ He **slowly** turned round. (*mid*)

End position

B

In end position, we usually put an adverb *after* an object if there is one rather than immediately after the verb:

- □ We considered *the problem* **briefly**. (*not* We considered briefly the problem.)

However, if an object is very long other positions are possible:

- □ We considered **briefly** *the long-term solution to the problem*. (*or* We **briefly** considered...)

C

We avoid putting an adverb between a main verb and a following **-ing** form or **to-infinitive**:

- □ He began running **quickly**. *or* He **quickly** began running. (*not* He began quickly running.)
- □ She tried to leave **quietly**. *or* She **quietly** tried to leave. (*not* She tried quietly to leave.)

The position of the adverb can change the meaning of the sentence (see **Unit 75A**). Compare:

- □ I recall telling him **clearly** that he had won. (= I told him clearly; 'clearly' modifies 'telling him') *and*
- □ I **clearly** recall telling him that he had won. (= I clearly recall it; 'clearly' modifies 'recall'.)

'I recall **clearly** telling him that he had won' is also possible, but is ambiguous; it can have either of the two meanings given above. In speech, the meaning intended is usually signalled by intonation.

D

When there is more than one adverbial (see Glossary) in end position, the usual order in written English is **adverbial of manner** (= saying *how* something is done), **place**, and then **time**:

- □ In the accident she was thrown **violently forwards**. (= manner + place)
- □ We arrived **here on Saturday**. (= place + time)

For special emphasis we can move an adverbial to the end:

- □ In the accident she was thrown **forwards, violently**.

If one adverbial is much longer than another then it is usually placed last:

- □ They left **at 3.00 with a great deal of noise**. (= time + manner)

An adverb usually comes before a prepositional phrase when these have the same function (i.e. when they both describe manner, or place, or time):

- □ She went **downstairs to the cellar**. (= place + place)

E

End position is usual for many adverbials of **place**, **definite frequency**, and **definite time** (including adverbial prepositional phrases):

- □ They live **upstairs**. (*not* They upstairs live.)   □ She goes **weekly**. (*not* She weekly goes.)
- □ Have you heard the good news? Jane had a baby **in May**. (*not* Jane in May had a baby.)

However, adverbs of indefinite time usually go in mid position (see Unit 75).

Notice that in journalism, other adverbs of time are often used in mid position, where we would normally place them in end (or front) position:

- □ The government **yesterday** announced an increase in education spending.

74.1 Write the adverb in brackets in the sentence in an appropriate position. In some cases both positions are possible. (C)

1 I .... expect Sue to win the race .... (*easily*)

2 He .... regretted missing the concert .... (*greatly*)

3 I .... hated playing the piano ...., although my parents thought I loved it. (*secretly*)

4 He .... started to walk .... across the bridge over the gorge. (*calmly*)

5 She .... offered to do the work .... (*kindly*)

6 Ray .... finished speaking .... and sat down. (*hurriedly*)

7 I .... don't remember putting it down .... (*simply*)

8 We .... look forward to hearing from you .... (*soon*)

9 They .... tried to ignore me .... (*deliberately*)

10 I don't .... pretend to understand the instructions .... (*completely*)

74.2 Complete the sentences. Put the words and phrases in brackets in the most likely order for written English. (B & D)

1 He hid Nancy's ..present in the wardrobe. (*in the wardrobe/ present*)

2 She waited .... (*nervously/ until her name was called*)

3 The road climbed .... (*through the mountains/ steeply*)

4 As a punishment, she had to be at school .... (*for the next two weeks/ early*)

5 As I left, I locked .... (*the door/ securely*)

6 We're travelling .... (*during the summer/ around Australia*)

7 The house is by the river, just .... (*from the bridge/ downstream*)

8 She was able to describe .... (*the exact details of the house where she had lived as a baby/ accurately*)

9 In hospital she had to lie .... (*with her right leg suspended in mid air/ for a week*)

10 He swam .... and then got out of the pool. (*rapidly/ for a few minutes*)

11 If you leave now, you should be .... (*by nine o'clock/ at home*)

12 They enjoyed .... (*at the party/ themselves/ immensely*)

74.3 If necessary, improve these sentences by putting the italicised word or phrase in a more appropriate position. If no improvement is needed, write ✓. (B–E)

1 I try to visit *every week* my parents. ..I try to visit my parents every week... *or* ..Every week I try to visit my parents...

2 Next, beat the eggs *vigorously* in a small bowl.

3 I thought I'd locked *securely* the luggage.

4 I stopped *regularly* playing tennis after I broke my wrist.

5 Rafter was *easily* beaten in the final.

6 Sarah never eats in the canteen at work. She always brings *from home* sandwiches.

7 'Do the Simpson family still live next door?' 'No, they moved last year *away*.'

8 The local residents welcomed the decision to introduce a new bus service from their village into the nearby town *warmly*.

9 We have to hand the homework in *on Tuesday*.

Position of adverbs (2)

Front position

A Most types of adverb commonly go in front position in a clause (see Unit 74A). In particular –

☆ *connecting adverbs* (e.g. **as a result**, **similarly**) which make immediately clear the logical relation to the previous sentence:
   □ The value of the yen has fallen. **As a result**, Japan faces a crisis.

☆ *time* and *place adverbs* (e.g. **tomorrow**, **nearby**) which give more information about a previous reference to a time or place, or show a contrast:
   □ The last few days have been hot. **Tomorrow** the weather will be much cooler.

☆ *comment* and *viewpoint adverbs* (e.g. **presumably**, **financially**) which highlight the speaker's attitude to what they are about to say (see Unit 78):
   □ She has just heard that her sister is ill. **Presumably**, she will want to go home.

However, other positions are possible for these adverbs.

Some words can be used both as comment adverbs or adverbs of manner. As comment adverbs they usually go in front position (but can go in other positions) and relate to the whole of the clause; as adverbs of manner they usually go in end position and modify the verb. Compare:
   □ **Naturally**, I'll do all I can to help.   *and*   □ The gas *occurs* **naturally** in this area.
Other adverbs like this include **clearly, curiously, frankly, honestly, oddly, plainly, seriously**.

Note that for special emphasis or focus, adverbs that usually go in mid position (see B) and end position (see also Units 74 and 76) can sometimes be put in front position:
   □ **In May**, Jane had a baby.   □ **Regularly**, Kim works on several paintings at once.

Mid position

B The following types of adverb usually go in mid position (see Unit 74A) –

☆ *degree adverbs* (e.g. **almost, hardly, nearly, quite, rather, scarcely**):
   □ The street lighting was so bad that *we* **almost** *missed* the turning.
   although some (e.g. **completely, enormously, entirely, greatly, slightly**) can go in end position:
   □ I **greatly** *admire* your work. (*or* I *admire* your work **greatly**.)

Notice, however, that some degree adverbs are not usually used in mid position with some verbs. For example, **enormously** is not usually used in mid position with **develop, differ, go up** or **vary**; **greatly** is not normally used in mid position with **care** or **suffer**.

☆ *adverbs which indicate the order of events*, such as **first, last** and **next**. These can also go in end position, but if there is a phrase giving the time of an event they usually go before this:
   □ I **first** *met* her in 1987. (*or* I met her **first** in 1987.)
   We don't usually put these in front position, except when we use them to list actions (when we usually follow them with a comma in writing; see also Unit 76B):
   □ **Next**, add three teaspoons of sugar.

☆ *adverbs of frequency* which say in an indefinite way how often something happens, including **hardly ever, often, rarely, regularly, seldom** (see also Unit 76B); and also the frequency adverbs **always** and **never**:
   □ We **hardly ever** *see* Derek nowadays, he's so busy at the office.

Notice, however, that adverbial phrases of indefinite frequency (e.g. **as a rule, on many occasions, from time to time, every so often**) usually go in front or end position:
   □ **As a rule**, I go every six months. (*or* every six months, **as a rule**; *not* 'I as a rule go…')

C We rarely put long adverbials (including clauses (see Units 58 and 59), and prepositional and noun phrases) in mid position. Usually they go in end position or front position for emphasis:
   □ She phoned home, **anxious for news**. (*or* **Anxious for news**, she phoned home.)
   □ He picked up the vase **with great care**. (*or* **With great care** he picked up the vase.)
   □ I'd seen Jack **the day before**. (*or* **The day before** I'd seen Jack.)

Exercises

75.1 Use one of these adverbs in each pair of sentences. In one, add the adverb in front position (as a comment adverb); in the other, add the adverb in end position (as an adverb of manner). (A)

clearly   ~~curiously~~   frankly   honestly   plainly   seriously

1 a ...Curiously..., the house has three chimneys ...., even though there are only two fireplaces.

  b ...., Esther looked at him ...curiously..., trying to work out whether he was being serious or not.

2 a ...., I was brought up to earn money ...., not to steal it from others.

  b ...., I'm perfectly capable of putting up the shelf myself ....

3 a ...., she admitted .... that she felt she wasn't doing a good job.

  b .... I went to sleep during his lecture........................, it was so boring.

4 a 'Thanks for looking after the children for me.' 'That's okay.' '........................, I don't know what I'd have done .... if you hadn't been around to help.'

  b ...., I tried to speak .... to him about his bad behaviour, but he kept making me laugh.

5 a The chief executive of Eclom has phoned me every day this week to ask whether I've made my mind up. ...., he wants me to take the job ....

  b ...., I'd had very little sleep the night before and was having difficulty thinking ....

6 a Robert fidgeted in his seat and kept looking nervously at the door. ...., he was feeling ill at ease ....

  b .... she always dressed .... at work in a white blouse and grey skirt.

75.2 Cross out any adverbs or adverbials that are incorrect or unlikely in these sentences. (B & Unit 74E)

1 Asthma rates in cities do not *enormously/ significantly* differ from those in rural areas.

2 Now that Megan has moved to Liverpool, I *from time to time/ rarely* see her.

3 I could see them *easily/ scarcely* in the bright sunshine.

4 It was snowing and I was *almost/ by an hour* late for the interview.

5 I met Mick at a party and then saw him a couple of days later *next/ at the bus stop on College Road.*

6 Carmen had *often/ on many occasions* spoken at meetings before so it was no surprise when she stood up.

7 I play chess with Tim *hardly ever/ every week.*

8 Although he had to lift heavy boxes in the factory, he *greatly/ rarely* suffered from backache.

9 I forgot about the meeting *nearly/ entirely* and my boss was really angry with me.

75.3 Which of the positions indicated [1], [2] or [3] can the adverb or adverbial in brackets go in? (A–C)

1 [1] He [2] moved to New Zealand [3]. (*the following year*)

2 [1] The children [2] walked along the road [3]. (*in single file*)

3 [1] We [2] see Tom [3] any more. (*seldom*)

4 [1] He [2] complained to his physics teacher [3] . (*unhappy with the result*)

5 [1] I [2] agree with you [3]. (*entirely*)

6 [1] I [2] meet [3] Emma at school. (*often*)

Adverbs of place, direction, indefinite frequency, and time

A

Adverbs of **place** and **direction** (or adverbials, particularly prepositional phrases) usually go in end position, but we can put them in front position to emphasise the location. The effect may also be to highlight what comes at the end (e.g. 'a body' in the example below). This order is found mainly in formal descriptive writing and reports. Compare:

- The money was eventually found **under the floorboards**. (= end) *and*
- The police searched the house. **Under the floorboards** they found a body. (= front)

If we put an adverb of place in front position we put the subject *after* the verb **be** (see also Unit 99A):

- **Next to the bookshelf** *was* a fireplace. (*or less formally* **Next to the bookshelf** there *was* a fireplace; *not* Next to the bookshelf a fireplace was.)

Note that this doesn't apply when the subject is a pronoun. For example, we can't say 'Next to the bookshelf was it.'

We can also put the subject after the verb with intransitive verbs (except with a pronoun subject) used to indicate being in a position or movement to a position, including **hang, lie, live, sit, stand; come, fly, go, march, roll, run, swim, walk**:

- Beyond the houses **lay** *open fields*. (*but compare* Beyond the houses *they* **lay**.)
- Through the town **marched** *the band*. (*but compare* Through the town *it* **marched**.)

Note that '...open fields lay', '...the band marched' (etc.) might be used in a literary style.

However, we don't usually put the subject after the verb when we talk about actions: if one of these intransitive verbs is followed by an adverb of manner; with other intransitive verbs; or with transitive verbs:

- Through the waves the boy **swam** *powerfully*. (*rather than* ...swam the boy powerfully.)
- Outside the church the choir **sang**. (*rather than* ...sang the choir.)
- In the garden John **built** *a play house* for the children. (*not* In the garden built John...)

B

When we put certain adverbs of time in front position the subject must come *after* an auxiliary verb or a main verb **be** (see also Unit 100):

- **At no time** would *he* admit that his team played badly. (*not* At no time he would admit...)
- **Not once** was *she* at home when I phoned. (*not* Not once she was...)

If the main verb is not **be** and there is no auxiliary, we use **do**, although inversion is not necessary in this case:

- **Only later** did *she* realise how much damage had been caused. (*or* Only later she realised...)

Adverbs like this include negative time adverbials such as **at no time, hardly ever, not once, only later, rarely**, and **seldom**. Notice also that we can put **first, next, now** and **then** in front position with the verb **come** to introduce a new event, when the subject follows the verb. But if a comma (or an intonation break in speech) is used after **first** (etc.) the verb follows the subject. Compare:

- At first there was silence. **Then** *came* a voice that I knew. (*not* Then a voice came...) *and*
- At first there was silence. **Then**, a voice *came* that I knew.

C

Adverbs of **time** which indicate a definite point or period in time or a definite frequency, usually go in end position, or front position for emphasis, but not in mid position. Note that when these adverbs are in front position there is no inversion of subject and verb:

- I went to Paris **yesterday**. (*or* **Yesterday** I went to Paris.)
- We meet for lunch **once a week**. (*or* **Once a week** we meet for lunch.)

Note that the adverbs **daily, hourly, monthly, weekly, annually, quarterly** (= four times a year), etc. only go in end position:

- The train leaves **hourly**. (*not* Hourly the train leaves; *not* The train hourly leaves.)
- I pay my subscription **annually**. (*not* Annually I pay...; *not* I annually pay...)

Exercises

76.1 Rewrite the sentences with the underlined adverbs of place or direction at the front of the clause. If possible, invert the order of subject and verb. (A)

1 A dark wood was <u>at the bottom of the garden</u>.
    At the bottom of the garden was a dark wood.

2 The car stopped suddenly and Nick jumped <u>out</u>.

3 Two small children stood <u>outside the door</u>.

4 The boys were playing cricket <u>in the park</u>, despite the muddy conditions.

5 The choir was singing one of my favourite carols <u>inside the church</u>.

6 A jade necklace hung <u>around her neck</u>.

7 The horse ran <u>down the hill</u> quickly.

8 The man released the monkey and it climbed <u>up the tree</u>.

9 The door burst open and a delegation from the striking workers marched <u>in</u>.

10 I tripped over the cat, dropped the tray, and it flew <u>across the room</u>.

11 While Nigel was looking around for his net the fish swam <u>away</u>.

12 Most of the furniture was modern, but a very old grandfather clock was <u>in the corner</u>.

13 She drove <u>around the town</u> for hours looking for the gallery, until she spotted the place <u>in a side street</u>.

14 Megan watched sadly <u>through the window</u>.

15 Ann found it difficult to concentrate <u>in the office</u>, but she worked more efficiently <u>at home</u>.

16 They saw a volcano erupting <u>in Japan</u>, and they experienced an earthquake <u>in Indonesia</u>.

17 A 16th century church is <u>on one side of the village green</u> and a 15th century pub stands <u>opposite</u>.

76.2 If possible, rewrite the underlined parts of these sentences with the time adverbial in front position. Where you can, invert the order of subject and verb, and make any other necessary changes. (B & C)

1 I trusted Dan completely, and <u>I realised only later that he had tricked me</u>.
    I trusted Dan completely, and only later did I realise that he had tricked me.

2 After working so hard all summer, <u>I had a holiday last week</u>.

3 Professor Coulson was to give the initial paper at the conference, but <u>a welcoming address came first by the head of the organising team</u>.

4 The area was cleared before the explosion, and <u>members of the public were in danger at no time</u>.

5 I've got high blood pressure and <u>I have to take tablets daily</u> for it.

6 When it became clear that he was in danger of losing the election, <u>a politician can seldom have changed his views so quickly as Beckett</u>.

7 After a few days of relative calm, <u>a blizzard came next, preventing us from leaving the hut</u>.

8 It's hard to imagine that <u>we'll be in Japan by next Friday</u>.

9 You won't have long to wait as <u>trains for Rome leave hourly</u>.

10 My grandfather was a gentle man, and <u>I hardly ever heard him raise his voice in anger</u>.

11 I walk to work for the exercise, and <u>I play squash twice a week</u>.

12 If you take the job, <u>your salary will be paid quarterly</u> into your bank account.

Degree adverbs and focus adverbs

A

Degree adverbs can be used before adjectives, verbs, or other adverbs to give information about the extent or level of something:

- □ They're **extremely** *happy*.
- □ I **really** *hate* coffee.
- □ He **almost** *always* arrived late.

Some degree adverbs, such as **almost, largely, really** and **virtually**, are usually used before the main verb, and others, such as **altogether, enormously, somewhat,** and **tremendously**, are usually used after the main verb. Degree adverbs are rarely used in front position (see Unit 75B).

Focus adverbs draw attention to the most important part of what we are talking about. Some (e.g. **especially, even, mainly, mostly, particularly, specifically**) make what we say more specific:

- □ There is likely to be snow today, **particularly** in the north.

and others (e.g. **alone, just, only, simply, solely**) limit what we say to one thing or person:

- □ Many people offered to help me invest the money, but I **only** trusted Peter.

B

Much and very much

In affirmative sentences in formal contexts, **much** can be used as a degree adverb before the verbs **admire, appreciate, enjoy, prefer** and **regret** to emphasise how we feel about things:

- □ I **much** *enjoyed* having you stay with us.
- □ Their music *is* **much** *admired*.

Much is used in this way particularly after **I** and **we** and (with **admire** and **appreciate**) in passives. Note that we don't usually use this pattern in questions (e.g. *not* 'Did you much enjoy…?').

We can use **very much** in a similar way before these verbs and also before **agree, doubt, fear, hope, like** and **want**. Notice, however, that we don't use **much** before this last group of verbs. Compare:

- □ I **much** *prefer* seeing films at the cinema than on television. (*or* I **very much** prefer…) *and*
- □ We **very much** *agree* with the decision. (*or* We agree very much…; *but not* …much agree…)

We can also use **much** or **very much** before a past participle which is part of a passive:

- □ The new by-pass *was* (**very**) **much** needed.

We don't use **much** but can use **very much** before past participle adjectives (see Unit 69A):

- □ She was (**very**) *interested* in the news. (*or* … **very much** *interested*…; *but not* much interested…)

and we don't use either **much** or **very much** before present participle adjectives:

- □ The hotel was (**very**) *welcoming*. (*but not* The hotel was (very) much welcoming.)

In negative sentences in informal contexts we can use (**very**) **much** before verbs such as **appreciate, enjoy, like,** and **look forward to** to emphasise a negative feeling about something:

- □ I didn't (**very**) **much** *enjoy* the film.

C

Very and too

Before an adjective or another adverb we use **very** when we mean 'to a high degree', and **too** when we mean 'more than enough' or 'more than is wanted or needed'. Compare:

- □ The weather was **very** hot in Majorca. Perfect for swimming. (*not*…too hot…) *and*
- □ It's **too** hot to stay in this room – let's find somewhere cooler. (*not* …very hot…)

In negative sentences in informal spoken English we can use **not too** to mean 'not very':

- □ I'm **not too** bothered about who wins. (*or* I'm **not very** bothered…)

D

Even, only and alone

Even and **only** usually go in mid position (see Unit 75), but if they refer to the subject they usually come before it. Compare:

- □ My mother has **only** brought some food. (= She hasn't brought anything else) *and*
- □ **Only** my mother has brought some food. (= My mother and nobody else)
- □ Sue can **even** speak French. (= in addition to everything else she can do) *and*
- □ **Even** Sue can speak French. (= you might not expect her to) (*rather than* Sue even…)

When **alone** means that only one thing or person is involved, it comes *after* a noun:

- □ *You* **alone** should decide what is right for you.

77.1 Which of these can go in the spaces: **very, much, very much?** (B)

1 We .... hope that the striking workers will now resume negotiations.

2 Thanks for organising the refreshments on school sports day. Your help was .... appreciated.

3 I felt .... intimidated by some of the questions in the interview.

4 I had always .... admired her work, and it was a great experience to meet her personally.

5 There was a time when I .... wanted a lot of children, but I'm perfectly happy now with the one child we have.

6 I would .... prefer to be remembered as someone who was kind rather than just as someone who was wealthy.

7 It was .... thrilling to get Eva's news.

8 When I was travelling in India I became .... interested in regional foods.

9 Jack says that he wants to go into politics, but I .... doubt that he's serious.

10 I .... regret not being able to hear Dr Jackson speak when she came to the university.

77.2 Write **very, too,** or **very/too** if either is possible. (C)

1 The old bridge in town was .... narrow for the coach to drive across, so we had to go an extra 50 miles to the new one.

2 Kay has agreed to start work earlier, but she's not .... enthusiastic about it.

3 The instructions are .... easy. You'll have no trouble understanding them.

4 It was .... alarming to learn that one of the plane's engines had stopped.

5 We'll be at the cinema well before the film starts. It won't take .... long to get there.

6 It was snowing .... heavily for us to climb further up the mountain.

7 He revised .... hard and did well in his exams.

8 Joanna was in a wheelchair as she was still .... weak from her operation to walk far.

77.3 Put **even, only** or **alone** in the most appropriate place in each sentence. (D)

1 Mark offered to let me stay with him while I was in Glasgow, and .... he .... offered to pick me up from the station.

2 .... I will .... be in my office on Monday next week as I'm going to Poland for a business meeting on Tuesday.

3 You are unlikely to buy the car you really need if you choose one on the basis of .... price ....

4 Every penny the charity raises helps the homeless, and .... the smallest donation .... can make a vital difference.

5 Ron seems to have invited everyone to the party. .... he has .... asked Claire, and they haven't spoken to each other for years.

6 .... John .... knew where the keys were kept, and nobody else.

7 .... advertising .... won't persuade people to buy. You need to have a quality product.

8 The theme park is really expensive. .... admission .... costs £25 and then you have to pay £5 for each of the rides.

Comment adverbs and viewpoint adverbs

A We use some adverbs to make a *comment* on what we are saying.

some comment adverbs...	example
indicate how likely we think something is	apparently, certainly, clearly, definitely, obviously, presumably, probably, undoubtedly
indicate our attitude to or opinion of what is said	astonishingly, frankly, generally, honestly, interestingly, luckily, naturally, sadly, seriously, surprisingly, unbelievably
show our judgement of someone's actions	bravely, carelessly, foolishly, generously, kindly, rightly, stupidly, wisely, wrongly

Comment adverbs often apply to the whole sentence and are most frequently used in front position (see **Unit 75A**), although they can also be used at the end of the sentence and in other positions. At the beginning and end of sentences we usually separate them from the rest of the sentence by a comma in writing or by intonation in speech:

- ☐ **Presumably**, he didn't hear me when I called.
- ☐ The book was based on his experience in China, **apparently**.
- ☐ Jackson believes that child development can be slowed down by poor nutrition. This is **undoubtedly** the case.

Comment adverbs which show judgement usually follow the subject, although they can be put in front position for emphasis:

- ☐ He **kindly** offered to take me to the station. (*or* **Kindly**, he offered... *to emphasise* 'Kindly')

If comment adverbs apply to only part of the sentence they can be used in other positions. Compare:

- ☐ **Astonishingly**, she did well in the exam. (= I was surprised that she did well)
- ☐ She did **astonishingly** well in the exam. (= she did very well)
- ☐ You've had a major operation. **Obviously**, it will be very painful for a while. (= I expect you to know this already)
- ☐ When he stood up it was **obviously** very painful. (= the pain was clear to see)

B Some adverbs are used to make clear what *viewpoint* we are speaking from; that is, identifying what features of something are being talked about:

- ☐ **Financially**, the accident has been a disaster for the owners of the tunnel.
- ☐ The brothers may be alike **physically**, but they have very different personalities.

Other examples include **biologically, environmentally, financially, ideologically, industrially, logically, medically, morally, outwardly, politically, technically, visually.**

A number of phrases are used in a similar way. For example:

politically **speaking**	in political **terms**	in terms of politics
from a political **point of view**	as far as politics **are concerned**	

- ☐ **Politically/In political terms**, this summer is a crucial time for the government.
- ☐ **Financially/From a financial point of view**, it is a good investment.

Some adverbs or phrases are used to say *whose* viewpoint we are expressing:

- ☐ The head of National North Bank is to receive, **according to newspaper reports**, a 50% salary increase.
- ☐ **In my view**, the Foreign Minister should resign immediately.

Other examples include **to my/his/her** (etc.) **knowledge, from my/his/her** (etc.) **perspective, personally, in my/his/her** (etc.) **opinion.**

Exercises

78.1 Choose a comment adverb to replace the underlined part. Consider possible positions in the sentence for the adverb. (A)

~~astonishingly~~	bravely	carelessly	generously
interestingly	obviously	presumably	rightly

1 It was very surprising indeed that no paintings were destroyed by the fire in the gallery.
   Astonishingly, no paintings were destroyed by the fire in the gallery.

2 As you drive off the ferry, there are lots of different flags flying by the side of the road.
   It seems likely that the idea is to welcome visitors from other countries.

3 Acting more kindly than they needed to, the builders agreed to plant new trees to replace the
   ones they had dug up.

4 Most people believe in a correct way that the prisoners should be released.

5 It was easy to see that she knew more about the robbery than she told the police.

6 He broke the window when he was painting because he wasn't paying attention to what he
   was doing.

7 She picked up the spider and put it outside, showing no fear.

8 I found it strange that this was the only map I could find that includes the village of
   Atherstone.

78.2 Complete the sentences with an appropriate viewpoint adverb from (i) and an ending from (ii). (B)

(i)

environmentally	financially
industrially	~~medically~~
outwardly	politically
technically	visually

(ii)

...we'd be much better off if we moved there.
...the performance was stunning.
...it is relatively undeveloped.
...she looked remarkably calm.
...she could be sent to prison.
~~...the doctors can't find anything wrong.~~
...it is no longer the problem it once was.
...he claims to be a socialist.

1 Sam says that he is still getting severe headaches, although...
   medically the doctors can't find anything wrong.

2 As she stepped onto the stage she felt terrified, but...

3 Now that lead is no longer added to most petrol,...

4 The country earns most of its income from agriculture and...

5 The band didn't play terribly well, and the singing was awful, but...

6 The cost of living is much lower in Northumberland, so...

7 Edwards is one of the richest men in the country, although...

8 Val is likely to be fined for failing to pay her gas bill, although...

78.3 Suggest an appropriate noun, adjective or adverb and one of the phrases in the box in B to complete these sentences. Use a different phrase each time. You could use the following words (or adjectives or adverbs formed from them) or suggest your own.

architecture   democracy   geology   grammar   history

1 _Historically speaking_, in what ways has disease affected the development of Western
   civilisation?

2 _____ limestone is a relatively new rock.

3 The building is similar to the opera house in Milan _____ .

4 _____ the essay was well written, but its style was inappropriate.

5 The election was clearly rigged and the result is a severe blow to the country _____ .

A As, when and while

We can often use **as**, **when** or **while** to mean 'during the time that', to talk about something that happens when something else takes place:

- ☐ **As/When/While** Dave was eating, the doorbell rang.

We use **when** (*not* as or while) to introduce a clause which talks about –
- ☆ an event that takes place at the same time as some longer event (in the main clause):
  - ☐ They were playing in the garden **when** they heard a scream.
- ☆ the circumstances in which the event in the main clause happens:
  - ☐ **When** they are fully grown these snakes can be over two metres long.

We also use **when** to mean 'every time':
- ☐ I still feel tired **when** I wake up in the morning.

and we prefer **when** to talk about past periods of our lives:
- ☐ His mother called him Robbie **when** he was a baby.

We prefer **when** to emphasise that one event happens immediately after another, particularly if one causes the other:
- ☐ You'll see my house on the right **when** you cross the bridge.
- ☐ **When** the lights went out, I lit some candles.

In the first sentence, 'as' or 'while' would suggest 'during the time that' and the continuous would be more likely ('...as/while you are crossing...'). In the second sentence 'as' or 'while' would be very unlikely because lights usually go out instantaneously.

We prefer **as** to say that when one thing changes, another thing changes at the same time:
- ☐ **As** the cheese matures, its flavour improves. (*rather than* When the cheese...)

We can also use 'While...', particularly with a continuous tense: 'While the cheese is maturing...'.

We prefer **while** or **as** (rather than **when**) to talk about two longer actions that go on at the same time, although **while** is more common than **as** in informal speech:
- ☐ I went shopping **while** Linda cleaned the house. (*or* ...**as** Linda cleaned...)

We use **while** or **when** (rather than **as**) to avoid ambiguity where 'as' could mean 'because':
- ☐ **While** you were playing golf, I went to the cinema. ('As you were playing golf...' could mean 'Because you were playing golf...')

B Before, after and until

We use **before** or **after** to talk about an event happening earlier or later than another event:

- ☐ I put on my coat **before** I went out.   ☐ The message arrived **after** I'd left.

We can often use either **until** or **before** when a situation continues to happen up to a time indicated in the adverbial clause:
- ☐ I had to wait six weeks **until/before** the parcel arrived.

We use **until** to talk about an action that continues to a particular time and then stops:
- ☐ They sat on the beach **until** the sun sank below the horizon, and then they went home.

and when the adverbial clause describes the *result* of an action in the main clause:
- ☐ He cleaned his shoes **until** they shone. ('shining' is the result of 'cleaning'.)

C Hardly, no sooner, scarcely

When we say that one event happened immediately after another we can use sentences with **hardly**, **no sooner**, and **scarcely** (see also Unit 100). After **hardly** and **scarcely** the second clause begins with **when** or **before**; after **no sooner** it begins with **than** or **when**:

- ☐ The concert *had* **hardly** *begun before* all the lights went out.
- ☐ I *had* **no sooner** *lit* the barbecue *than/when* it started to rain.

We often use a past perfect in the clause with **hardly**, **no sooner** or **scarcely** and a past simple in the other.

79.1 Choose **as**, **when** or **while**, whichever is correct or more likely, to complete these sentences. If there is more than one possible answer, write them both and notice any differences in meaning. (A)

1 She fell over .... she kicked the ball.
2 .... we were younger our parents had to pay for our music lessons.
3 .... I speak Spanish, I talk slowly to help people understand me.
4 .... I carefully packed all the old books into boxes, Emily wrote down their titles in a notebook.
5 She stayed at home watching television .... her brother was at school.
6 Where did you live .... you got married?
7 .... I'm older I'd love to be a dancer.
8 .... the results started to come in, it became clear that President Como had lost the election.
9 The humidity started to increase .... the day wore on.
10 .... the boy watched in fascination, the ants picked up the dead beetle and carried it off to their nest.
11 The fan makes a screeching sound .... I switch the computer on.
12 .... the meeting continued, it became clear that the two sides would not reach an agreement.
13 .... the car went by, someone waved to me through the window.
14 .... Kingsley had finished, he tidied up the room and left.
15 The snow was getting deeper and deeper .... we waited for the delayed train to arrive.
16 I was in the shower .... the phone rang.
17 .... the paint dries it changes from a light to a deep red.

79.2 Here are some extracts from a talk about the life and work of Professor Johannes Wichmann. Write **before** or **until** in the spaces or **before/until** if both are possible. (B)

1 He continued to work at London University .... he retired in 1978.
2 .... he left his native country, he learned English by listening to the radio.
3 It wasn't long .... he was appointed Professor of Chemistry.
4 He married Martha .... he moved to England in 1935.
5 .... he came to England he worked in his father's grocery shop.
6 He kept applying for university research positions .... he was appointed to a post at London University.
7 He was almost unknown outside his specialised field .... he was awarded the Nobel Prize.
8 He would work in his laboratory for days at a time .... he had gathered the results he needed.

79.3 Complete the sentences in any appropriate way. (C)

1 The paint on the sitting room wall had scarcely dried...
  before my daughter put her dirty hands all over it.
2 David had no sooner recovered from a broken ankle...
3 He had hardly put down the phone...
4 We had no sooner eaten...
5 Maggie had hardly finished speaking...
6 I had scarcely driven to the end of the street...

Giving reasons: as, because, etc.; for and with

A

We can begin a clause with **as, because, seeing that, seeing as**, or **since** to give a *reason* for a particular situation:

- ☐ **As** *it was getting late*, I decided I should go home.
- ☐ We must be near the beach, **because** *I can hear the waves*.
- ☐ **Since** *he was going to be living in Sweden for some time*, he thought he should read something about the country.
- ☐ We could go and visit Sue, **seeing that** *we have to drive past her house anyway*.

Notice that –

☆ it is also common and acceptable for **because** to begin a sentence, as in:
- ☐ **Because** *everything looked different*, I had no idea where to go.

☆ to give reasons in spoken English, we most often use **because**. **So** is also commonly used to express a similar meaning (see also Unit 81). Compare:
- ☐ **Because** *my mother's arrived*, I won't be able to meet you. ('because' introduces the reason) *and*
- ☐ *My mother's arrived*, **so** I won't be able to meet you. ('so' introduces the result.)

☆ when it means 'because', **since** is rather formal. It is uncommon in conversation, but is frequently used in this way in academic writing:
- ☐ I had to go outside **because** I was feeling awful. ('since' is unlikely in an informal context)
- ☐ The results of this analysis can be easily compared to future observations **since** satellite coverage will remain continuous. (more likely than 'because' in this formal context.)

☆ **seeing that** is used in informal English. Some people also use **seeing as** in informal speech:
- ☐ Ken just had to apologise, **seeing that/as** he knew he'd made a mistake.

B

In formal or literary written English we can also introduce reasons with **for, in that**, or, less commonly, **inasmuch as**. **For** is a formal alternative to 'because'; **in that** and **inasmuch as** introduce clauses which clarify what has been said by adding detail:

- ☐ The film is unusual **in that** *it features only four actors*. (or **In that**…, the film is…)
- ☐ Clara and I have quite an easy life, **inasmuch as** *neither of us has to work too hard but we earn quite a lot of money*. (or **Inasmuch as**…, Clara and I…)
- ☐ We must begin planning now, **for** *the future may bring unexpected changes*. (*not* For the future…, we must… – where 'for' means 'because'.)

C

The prepositions **because of, due to**, and **owing to** can also be used before a noun or noun phrase to give a reason for something:

- ☐ We were delayed **because of** an accident.
- ☐ She was unable to run **owing to/due to** a leg injury. (= because of a leg injury.)
- ☐ We have less money to spend **owing to/due to** budget cuts. (= because of budget cuts.)

Notice that we don't use **because** alone before a noun or noun phrase:
- ☐ We were delayed **because** there was an accident. (*not* …because an accident.)

In current English we usually avoid **owing to** directly after a form of **be**:
- ☐ The company's success *is* **due to** the new director. (*not* …is owing to…)

However, **owing to** is used after **be + a degree adverb** such as **entirely, largely, mainly, partly**:
- ☐ The low election turnout *was partly* **due to/owing to** the bad weather.

We can often use either **it was due to…that** or **it was owing to…that**:
- ☐ *It was* **owing to** his encouragement *that* she applied for the job. (or *It was* **due to**…*that*)

D

We can use **for** and **with** followed by a noun phrase to give a reason. **For** has a similar meaning to 'as a result of' and is common in most styles of English (compare **B** above):

- ☐ She was looking all the better **for** her stay in hospital.

With has a similar meaning to 'as a result of there being':
- ☐ **With** so many people ill, I've decided to cancel the meeting.

Exercises

80.1 Complete the sentence frames with an item from (i) and an item from (ii), in an appropriate order, as in 1. (A)

(i)
1 ~~passengers were given a full refund~~
2 Angela agreed to book tickets for us all
3 I'll buy you lunch
4 I've given up dairy products
5 we were recommended to buy the textbook second hand
6 the guest lecturer was late
7 we get on so well
8 you should never walk under a ladder

(ii)
a it's your birthday
b it was her idea to go to the theatre
c Dr Jones spoke about his research instead
d a new copy would be very expensive
e I suggested we all go on holiday together
f ~~the train was delayed for more than an hour~~
g it's supposed to be unlucky
h I'm trying to lose weight

1 + f **Since** _the train was delayed for more than an hour, passengers were given a full refund._

2 .... **as** ....
3 **Seeing as** ....
4 **Because** ....
5 .... **since** ....
6 **As** ....
7 .... **seeing that** ....
8 .... **because** ....

80.2 Complete these sentences using **due to** or **owing to** with one of these phrases. If both **due to** and **owing to** are possible, write them both. (C)

lack of interest ~~stress at work~~ **heavy cloud** **its central location** **human error**

1 She claims her illness is entirely _due to/owing to stress at work._
2 The cancellation of the competition is ....
3 The popularity of the restaurant is largely ....
4 It's likely that the mistake was ....
5 We couldn't see last night's eclipse of the moon ....

Now complete these sentences using **because** or **because of** + one of these phrases. (C)

his age **his phone was engaged** **local opposition**
the bright sunlight **there was a fly in it**

6 I had to drive in dark glasses ....
7 I couldn't speak to Tom ....
8 The council had to withdraw its plan to close the swimming pool ....
9 My grandfather couldn't do a sponsored parachute jump ....
10 He sent the soup back ....

80.3 Rewrite these sentences using **for** or **with** instead of **because (of)**. Give alternatives where possible. (D)

1 I got a job as a street sweeper because my money was running out.

With my money running out, I got a job as a street sweeper. or
I got a job as a street sweeper, with my money running out.

2 I couldn't hear what Sue was saying because of the noise.
3 Jane went to stay with her aunt because her father was in hospital.
4 I felt a lot fitter because of all the exercise I was doing.
5 Because the train drivers are on strike tomorrow, I don't think I'll go to London after all.

Purposes and results: **in order to, so as to,** etc.

A In order/so as + to-infinitive

To talk about the purpose of an action we can use **in order/so as + to-infinitive**:

- ☐ He took the course **in order to get** a better job.
- ☐ Trees are being planted by the roadside **so as to reduce** traffic noise.

In spoken English in particular it is much more common simply to use a **to-infinitive** without 'in order' or 'so as' to express the same meaning:

- ☐ He took the course **to get** a better job.

We rarely use just 'not + *to*-infinitive', but instead use **so as not to** or **in order not to**:

- ☐ He kept the speech vague **in order not** *to commit* himself to one side or the other. (*not* ...vague not to commit himself...)
- ☐ The land was bought quickly **so as not** *to delay* the building work. (*not* ...quickly not to delay...)

However, in contrastive sentences we can use **not + to-infinitive, but + to-infinitive** as in:

- ☐ I came to see you *not* (**in order/so as**) *to complain*, *but* (**in order/so as**) *to apologise*.

Notice that we can put **in order/so as** before the *to*-infinitives in sentences like this.

B In order that and so that

We also use **in order that** and **so that** to talk about a purpose. Compare:

- ☐ She stayed at work late **in order/so as** to complete the report. *and*
- ☐ She stayed at work late **in order that/so that** she could complete the report. (*not* ...in order that/so that to complete the report.)

So that is more common than **in order that**, and is used in less formal situations. Note that informally we can leave out **that** after **so**, but we always include it after **in order**.

A present tense verb in the main clause is usually followed by a present tense verb (or a modal with present or future reference – **can, will,** etc.) in the clause beginning **in order that/so that**. A past tense verb in the main clause is usually followed by a past tense verb (or a modal with past reference – **could, would,** etc.) in the clause beginning **in order that/so that**. Modal verbs are very often used after **in order that/so that**:

- ☐ Regular checks *are made* **in order that** safety standards *are maintained*.
- ☐ Advice *is given* **in order that** students *can* choose the best course.
- ☐ *Did* you give up you job **so that** you *could* take care of your mother?
- ☐ I *hid* the presents **so that** Jackie *wouldn't* find them.

C Such that and in such a way that; such...that

In formal contexts, such as academic writing, we can use **such that** to introduce a result:

- ☐ The model was designed **such that** the value of x could be calculated. (= 'in a way that has the result that...'; *or* ...in order that...; *or* ...so that...)

Less formally we can also use **in such a way that** or **in such a way as + to-infinitive** with a similar meaning:

- ☐ The advertisement is printed **in such a way that** two very different pictures can be seen depending on how you look at it.
- ☐ In fact, the tax cuts have been designed **in such a way as to leave out** the very people it is supposed to help.

We can also use **such + noun phrase + that** to introduce a result:

- ☐ It is **such** *a popular play* **that** the performance was sold out after the first day.

(For **so + adjective/adverb + that**, see Unit 73.)

81.1 Combine the two sentences in the most appropriate way using **in order (not) + to-infinitive** or **so as (not) + to-infinitive.** (A)

1 I had to borrow money from the bank.	a This was done to encourage people to use public transport.
2 He packed his suitcase with the books at the bottom.	b We wanted to prevent people walking across the grass.
3 Bus fares in the city are being cut.	c I didn't want to damage the growing crops.
4 We crept quietly towards the deer.	d ~~I did this to set up the business.~~
5 I walked around the outside of the field.	e They didn't want to disrupt traffic too much.
6 We put up a fence.	f We didn't want to frighten them away.
7 She looked down at the book in front of her.	g She wanted to avoid his gaze.
8 The roadworks were carried out at night.	h He didn't want to crush his clothes.

1 + d _I had to borrow money from the bank in order to set up the business._ (or
...so as to set up...)

81.2 Look again at the sentences you wrote in 81.1. Is it also possible to use only a **to-infinitive**, without **in order** or **so as**? Write ✓ or ✗. (A)

1 _I had to borrow money from the bank to set up the business._ ✓

81.3 Choose one of these items to complete each sentence. Decide which of the underlined parts of the item is correct. (B)

> it <u>will/ would</u> let enough light in   it <u>won't/ wouldn't</u> take up a lot of computer memory
> mosquitoes <u>can't/ couldn't</u> get in   nobody <u>will/ would</u> know it was there
> ~~people <u>can/ could</u> walk around the gardens~~   we <u>can/ could</u> see the view over the city

1 They have an open day at their house each year so that _people can walk around the
gardens._

2 I put a rug over the stain on the carpet so that ....

3 There were screens on all the windows so that ....

4 The software is designed so that ....

5 We went up to the top floor so that ....

6 The camera aperture needs to be wide on dull days so that ....

81.4 Rewrite each sentence less formally in two ways; one using **in such a way that** and the other using **in such a way as to.** (C)

1 The factory demolition was planned such that any risk to the public was avoided.

_The factory demolition was planned in such a way that any risk to the public was
avoided. / The factory demolition was planned in such a way as to avoid any risk
to the public._

2 The meeting room is designed such that everyone's voice can be heard without the use of
microphones.

....

3 The documents are written such that they are easily comprehensible.

....

4 If the dial is rotated such that the number 1 is at the top, the valve opens.

....

A Although and though

We use **although** or (less formally) **though** to say that there is a surprising contrast between what happened in the *main clause* and what happened in the *adverbial clause*:

☐ **Although/Though** Reid failed to score himself, he helped Jones to score two goals.

With a similar meaning, we can use **despite the fact that/in spite of the fact that** (e.g. 'Despite the fact that/In spite of the fact that Reid failed to score himself…') *or* **despite/in spite of + -ing** (e.g. 'Despite/In spite of Reid **failing** to score himself…').

Notice that we can use **though**, but not **although**, at the end of a clause:

☐ I eat most dairy products. I'm not keen on yogurt, **though**.

We can give special emphasis to an adjective by putting it before **though** in the pattern **adjective + though + noun/pronoun + verb** (usually a linking verb such as **appear, be, become, feel, look, seem, sound, prove**, etc.). **As** can be used instead of **though**, but notice that you can't use **although**. Compare:

☐ **Hot though** (*or* **as**) **the night air was**, they slept soundly. *and*
☐ **Although/Though** the night air **was** hot, they slept soundly.

B Even though and even if

We can use **even though** (*but not* 'even although') to mean 'despite the fact that' and **even if** to mean 'whether or not'. Compare:

☐ **Even though** Tom doesn't speak Spanish, I think he should still visit Madrid.	= Despite the fact that he doesn't speak Spanish	i.e. the speaker knows that Tom doesn't speak Spanish
☐ **Even if** Tom doesn't speak Spanish, I think he should still visit Madrid.	= Whether or not he speaks Spanish	i.e. the speaker doesn't know definitely whether Tom speaks Spanish or not

C While, whilst and whereas

In formal contexts we can use **while** or **whilst** with a meaning similar to 'although' to introduce something that qualifies what is said in the main clause or something that may seem to conflict with it. In this case, the **while/whilst** clause comes before or within the main clause, but not after it:

☐ **While/Whilst** there is no evidence that Peter cheated, we were all astonished that he passed the exam. (*not* We were all astonished that he passed the exam, while…)
☐ The diesel model of the car, **while/whilst** more expensive, is better value for money.

Note that **whilst** is a rather literary word and some people avoid using it.

We can use **while** or **whereas** (or less often **whilst**) to say that something contrasts with something in the main clause. The **while/whereas** clause may come before or after the main clause:

☐ Dave gets lots of homework from school, **while/whereas** Sue gets very little.
☐ **While/Whereas** I always felt I would pass the exam, I never thought I would get an A grade.

We don't use **whereas** where what is said in the subordinate clause makes what is said in the main clause unexpected:

☐ **Although/While** Sophie's father is from Spain, she doesn't speak Spanish. (*not* Whereas…)

D

We can use **-ing** and **past participle (-ed)** clauses after **although, though, while** and **whilst**, and also clauses with the subject and verb left out (see Unit 59D):

☐ **(Al)though** not huge, the garden needs constant attention. (= (Al)though it is not huge…)
☐ **While** welcoming the government's new funding for the health service, doctors are still unhappy about working conditions. (= While they welcome…)
☐ Some writers, **whilst** convinced that Hemingson supported the rebels, have questioned how involved he was in the fighting. (= whilst they are convinced…)

82.1 Match the sentence halves and give special emphasis to the adjective by moving it to the front of the sentence, as in 1. Use either **though** or **as**. (A)

1 it may seem amazing	a they were very useful when I looked at them in detail
2 she was frightened	b she forced herself to pick up the snake
3 food became scarce	c they had never faced such severe conditions before
4 the climbers were experienced	
5 the instructions first appeared confusing	d the company is still in financial difficulties
6 it looked disgusting	e they always found enough to share with me
7 she felt confident	f she knew the examination would not be easy
8 their new products have proved successful	g ~~my brother John has won the lottery~~
	h it was actually quite tasty

1 + g _Amazing though it may seem, my brother John has just won the lottery._ (or _Amazing as it may seem..._)

82.2 Expand the notes and rewrite the sentences using **In spite of + -ing** in 1–3 and **In spite of his/her + noun** in 4–6. (A)

1 Although she has to cope with three small children, ... (*taking – part-time MBA course*)
In spite of having to cope with three small children, she is taking a part-time MBA course.

2 Although he was much younger than the others, ... (*was – most outstanding footballer – team*)

3 Although he ate a big lunch, ... (*had – three-course meal – evening*)

4 Although she was frightened, ... (*allowed – huge spider – placed in her hands*)

5 Although she is obviously intelligent, ... (*finds – it difficult – express – ideas in writing*)

6 Although she was ill, ... (*went – walking holiday – Nepal*)

Now rewrite the sentences you have written beginning **Despite the fact that...**

1 _Despite the fact that she has to cope with three small children, she is taking a part-time MBA course._

82.3 Underline the correct phrase. (B)

1 The driver stopped to let on more passengers *even though/ even if* the bus was already full.
2 I wouldn't tell you where Gail lives *even though/ even if* I knew.
3 *Even though/ Even if* I only play one match for my country, I'll be happy.
4 *Even though/ Even if* he had just put a cigarette out, Lawrence lit another one.
5 He plays for Wales *even though/ even if* he was born in Scotland.
6 You won't see all the animals in the zoo *even though/ even if* you stay for the whole day.
7 *Even though/ Even if* I'm quite old, I still miss my parents.
8 I still couldn't afford to go to Paris, *even though/ even if* I took the cheapest route.

82.4 Match the sentence halves and join them with **While** or **Whereas** at the beginning of the sentence. In which of the sentences you write can the clause beginning **while** or **whereas** come after the main clause? (C)

1 Paula is blonde	a more and more people are taking it up
2 horse riding is an expensive pastime	b the government says it is under 500,000
3 a decade ago we used to get a lot of blackbirds in our garden	c ~~all her sisters have dark hair~~
	d it actually feels quite warm when the sun is out
4 the true number of unemployed is over a million	e we rarely see them today
5 the temperature is below freezing	

1 + c _While/ Whereas Paula is blonde, all her sisters have dark hair._ or
All her sisters have dark hair, whereas/while Paula is blonde.

Real conditionals

A

In real conditionals (see **GR note above M9**) we usually use a present tense verb in the **if-clause** to talk about the future:

☐ If you **leave** now, you'll be able to catch the 5 o'clock train. (*or* If you**'re leaving** now…)

However, in conversation we can use **be going to** instead of a present tense verb:

☐ If I**'m going to** catch the train, I'll have to leave now.

☐ We'll need more chairs if we**'re going to** invite so many people to the performance.

When we make offers, and give instructions or advice we can use an imperative in the main clause:

☐ **Take** another sandwich if you're hungry.

☐ If you have a mobile phone, **check** that it is turned off.

B

We can use *if*-clauses with a present tense verb to introduce certain conditions under which something is true:

☐ The video pauses **if** you *press* this button.

☐ **If** age-related changes *are taken* into account, the conclusion remains the same.

(Here 'if' has a meaning similar to 'when'.)

C

We can talk about possible future events with a present perfect verb in the *if*-clause and a future form (**will**, present continuous, or **be going to**) in the main clause. Sometimes present perfect or present simple can be used with a similar meaning:

☐ I**'ll** lend you *War and Peace* if I**'ve finished** it before you go on holiday. (*or* …if I **finish**…)

☐ If you **haven't paid** the bill by Friday, we**'re** *taking* the carpets back. (*or* If you **don't pay**…)

However, to focus on the future consequences of a past event, we use the present perfect. Compare:

☐ If I**'ve failed** my maths exam again, I'm going to give up the course. (suggests I have already taken the exam; I don't know the result) *and*

☐ If I **fail** my maths exam again, I'm going to give up the course. (I may or may not have taken the exam)

Unreal conditionals

D

In unreal conditionals (see **GR note above M9**) we can use **if…were + to-infinitive** rather than **if + past simple** to talk about imaginary future situations, particularly to suggest it is unlikely that the situation in the *if*-clause will happen (see also Unit 14):

☐ If the technology **were to become** available, we would be able to expand the business.

However, notice that we don't usually this pattern with verbs such as **belong, doubt, enjoy, know, like, remember,** and **understand** when they describe a state:

☐ If I **knew** they were honest, I'd gladly lend them the money. (*not* If I were to know…)

We sometimes use this pattern to make a suggestion sound more polite:

☐ Would it be too early for you **if we were to** meet at 5.30?

E

We use **if it was not for + noun phrase** (or more formally **if it were not for + noun phrase**) to say that one situation is dependent on another situation or on a person (see also Unit 85A). When we talk about the past we can also use **if it had not been for + noun phrase**:

☐ If it **wasn't/weren't for** *Vivian*, the conference wouldn't be going ahead.

☐ If it **wasn't/weren't for** *the fact that* Chloe would be offended, I wouldn't go to the party.

☐ If it **hadn't been for** *Dad*, I wouldn't have gone to college. (*or* If it **wasn't/weren't for**…)

In formal language we can also use **Were it not for…** and **Had it not been for…** (see Unit 84B):

☐ **Were it not for** Vivian…   ☐ **Had it not been for** Dad…

We can use **but for + noun** with a similar meaning, particularly in formal contexts:

☐ The village school would have been closed years ago **but for** *the determination* of teachers and parents to keep it open. (= …if it hadn't been for the determination…)

Grammar review: real and unreal conditionals → M9–M17

83.1 Suggest completions for these sentences. Add either an imperative (1–3) or an if-clause (4–6). (A)

1 There have been a lot of thefts from cars in the city centre. If you leave your car there...
   make sure it's locked. or _don't leave any valuables in it._

2 If you have any more problems with the computer, ...

3 If you see John today, ...

4 ...keep well away from them.

5 ...don't hesitate to get in touch with me again.

6 ...get off at the stop near the library.

83.2 Complete the sentences using one of the following pairs of verbs. Use the present simple or present perfect in the if-clause, and give alternatives. Notice any possible differences in meaning when these tenses are used. (C)

   not fill in – need   not help – go   leave – meet
   not arrive – give   ~~study – know~~   break – have to

1 If you _have studied/study_ Macbeth, you'll _know_ the scene with the witches.
2 If you .... home before I get there, I'll .... you at the airport.
3 If you .... the window, you'll .... pay for it.
4 If the taxi .... by 10 o'clock, I'll .... you a lift to the station.
5 If you .... in an application form, you will .... to do so before you can be considered for the job.
6 If the antibiotics .... by the end of the week, I'll .... to the hospital.

83.3 Choose from these verbs to complete the sentences, using each verb once only. If possible, use the pattern **were + to-infinitive**. If this is not possible, use the past simple form of the verb. (D)

   belong   close   doubt   hold   switch   understand

1 If they .... an election now, the Democrats would undoubtedly win.
2 If I .... his honesty, I wouldn't employ him.
3 If all cars .... to liquefied petroleum gas, air pollution levels would fall dramatically.
4 I'd sell the house immediately if it .... to me.
5 If I .... Chinese, I'd do the translation myself.
6 There would be no cinema in the town if the Odeon ....

83.4 Write new sentences with similar meanings. Begin with the word(s) given. (E)

1 It's only because he's a professor that anybody pays any attention to him. *If it wasn't*
   for the fact that he is a professor, nobody would pay any attention to him.

2 His happiness would have been complete except for his anxiety over Bridget. *If it were...*
3 The weather was terrible. Otherwise, we would have gone walking this weekend. *If it had...*
4 The strike would probably still be going on if the government hadn't intervened. *Were it...*
5 The fight could have got out of hand if the police hadn't arrived. *Had it...*
6 Everything was quiet except for the sound of birds singing. *But for...*
7 There would have been far more wars in the last 50 years without the United Nations. *If it was...*
8 We would have been here two hours ago except for the roadworks on the motorway. *If it had...*
9 Paul comes from a wealthy family. Otherwise he could not have gone to the USA to study. *Were it...*

If (2)

A

In spoken English we often use **if-clauses** without a main clause. In particular, we use them in polite requests, instructions, etc.:

- ☐ **If I might** just say a few words. (= I want to speak) I think it's important to...
- ☐ **If we could** get back to the subject of homework. Why haven't you done any for the last week? (= Let's go back to talking about homework)

and to qualify what someone else has said. In this case **if** is usually stressed:

- ☐ A: Bill won't be happy if he finds out you've taken his bike. B: **If** he finds out.
  (= s/he doesn't necessarily agree that Bill will find out, or s/he will make sure that he doesn't)

B

When the first verb in a conditional *if*-clause is **should**, **were**, or **had** we can leave out **if** and put the verb at the start of the clause (see Units 99 and 100 for more on inversion). We do this particularly in formal or literary English, and only in hypothetical conditionals (a type of unreal conditional which answers the question 'What would happen if...?'):

- ☐ **Should** any of this **cost** you anything, send me the bill. (= If any of this should **cost**...)
- ☐ It would be embarrassing, **were** she **to find out** the truth. (= ...if she were to **find** out..)
- ☐ **Had** they **not rushed** Jo to hospital, he would have died. (= If they **hadn't rushed** Jo...)

C

We don't usually use **if...will** in conditional clauses. However, we can use **if...will** –

- ☆ when we talk about a *result* of something in the main clause. Compare:
  - ☐ Open a window **if** it **will help** you to sleep. (*or* ...if it **helps** you to sleep; 'Helping you to sleep' is the result of opening the window) *and*
  - ☐ I will be angry **if** it **turns out** that you are wrong. (*not* ...if it will turn out...; 'Turning out that you are wrong' is **not** the result of being angry)
- ☆ in requests or with the meaning 'if you are willing to' (*or* **if...would** to be more polite):
  - ☐ **If you will/would** take your seats, ladies and gentlemen, we can begin the meeting.
- ☆ in real conditionals when we want to show that we disapprove of something. In this case, **will** is stressed in speech (see also Unit 16B):
  - ☐ A: I'm tired.   B: Well, **if** you **will** go to bed so late, I'm not surprised.

Notice that we can use **if...won't** when we talk about a refusal to do something:

- ☐ There's no point in trying to teach the class **if** they **won't** pay attention.

D

In a *real* conditional sentence (see GR note above M9), we use **if...happen to**, **if...should**, or **if...should happen to** to talk about something which may be possible, but is not very likely. **If...happen to** is most common in spoken English:

- ☐ **If** you **happen to** be in our area, drop in and see us. (*or* If you **should** (**happen to**) be..)

Notice that we don't usually use this pattern in *unreal* conditionals talking about states or events in the *if*-clause which the speaker perceives as highly unlikely or impossible:

- ☐ If the North Sea **froze** in winter, you could walk from London to Oslo. (*but probably not* If the North Sea happened to freeze/should (happen to) freeze in winter...)

E

In *comparison clauses* we can use **as if** followed by a **noun phrase**, **-ing** clause, **past participle** (**-ed**) clause, or **to-infinitive** to introduce a comparison with a situation described in the main clause. We do this to give an explanation or to say that something appears to be the case but is not:

- ☐ Richard walked in **as if** *nothing* had happened.
- ☐ His hands made a circular motion, **as if** *steering* a bus through a sharp bend.
- ☐ After scoring, Fowler fell to the floor **as if** *hit* by a bullet.
- ☐ **As if** *to convince* herself that Rob was really there, she gently touched his cheek.

Notice that we can use **as though** instead of **as if**, and in informal speech some people use **like** with the same meaning:

- ☐ The crowd reacted **as though** they were watching a boxing match. (*or* ...as if...)
- ☐ He walked into the room **like** nothing had happened. (*or* ...as if...)

Grammar review: real and unreal conditionals → M9–M11, M17

84.1 Write a new sentence with a similar meaning to the sentence given. Begin with the word(s) given. (B)

1 Consult your doctor again if the symptoms remain 72 hours after starting the course of medicine. *Should the symptoms remain 72 hours after starting the course of medicine, consult your doctor again.*

2 You would know what you have to do for homework, if you had not been absent from school on Friday. *Had...*

3 Clare would have been able to stay with her friends if they were still living in Brussels. *Were...*

4 The shop would not have had to shut down if the workers were prepared to accept a wage cut. *Were...*

5 We shall have to reduce the number of staff employed if the financial performance of the company doesn't improve in the near future. *Should...*

6 I might have considered taking the job if the salary had been higher. *Had...*

84.2 Are the underlined parts of the sentences correct? Correct the ones that are wrong. (C)

1 <u>If I will press this button</u>, will it start to record?
2 You're welcome to borrow my old bike, <u>if you think it will be of any use to you</u>.
3 <u>If he won't resign</u>, the Prime Minister should sack him.
4 <u>If the disease will be untreated</u>, it can lead to brain damage.
5 <u>If you'll tell me where the vacuum cleaner is</u>, I'll clean the house.
6 <u>If you'll complain about me</u>, I'll get into trouble with my teacher.
7 <u>If it'll save money</u>, I'm willing to go by public transport.

84.3 If possible, rewrite the underlined parts of these sentences with **happen to**. If it is unlikely, write ✗ after the sentence. (D)

1 <u>If I see Karen when I'm in Rome</u>, I'll send her your regards.
2 <u>If a UFO landed in the centre of London</u>, there would be mass panic.
3 The plan for a new airport to be built outside London is bad news <u>if you live nearby</u>.
4 <u>If I was the President of the United States</u>, I would order its nuclear weapons to be destroyed.
5 <u>If you are in the south of Spain next week</u>, there is a good chance of seeing a total eclipse of the sun.

84.4 Complete the sentences in any appropriate way, or use the notes for ideas. (E)

(agree – everything Julie said)   (~~I – say – shocking~~)   (it – reverse – wall)
(try – imagine – contained)   (overcome – great weariness)

1 My father raised his eyebrows as if *I had said something shocking.*
2 He folded his arms on the table and laid his head on them, as if...
3 She stared hard at the parcel as if...
4 He nodded his head slowly as if...
5 The back of the car looked as if...

If I were you...; imagine he were to win

A

In *unreal* conditional sentences (see GR note above M9) we can use **were** after any subject in the *if*-clause, including singular first and third person subjects (e.g. **I/she/he/it**). This use of **were** is sometimes called the *past subjunctive*, and is generally preferred only in formal contexts. Note that although the verb has a past form, reference is to the imagined present or future:

- ☐ **If your mother were here**, I'm sure she wouldn't let you eat all those chocolates.
- ☐ We would not be able to provide after-school sports **if it were not for** dedicated teachers like Mr Morgan.

Was can be used instead of **were** with the same meaning ('If your mother was here...', etc.). However, we prefer **were** rather than **was** when we give advice with **If I were you...**:

- ☐ **If I were you**, I'd take it back to the shop. It's got a hole in it. (*rather than* If I was you...)

B

Were is used in this way in other patterns when we talk about *imaginary situations* –

(i) when we use **were + subject + to-infinitive** or **were + subject** as a more formal alternative to **if + subject + was/were** (see also Unit 84B):

- ☐ **Were the election to be** held today, the Liberals would win easily. (*or* **If the election was/ were** held today...)
- ☐ **Were I not** in my 70s and rather unfit, I might consider taking up squash. (*or* **If I wasn't/ weren't** in my 70s and rather unfit...)

(ii) after **wish**:

- ☐ I enjoy my job enormously, but I *wish* **it were** closer to home. (*or* ...I wish it **was**...)
- ☐ Of course I'm pleased that James has been given the award. I only *wish* **he weren't** so boastful about it. (*or* ...I only wish he wasn't...)

(iii) after **if only** when we express our regret that a situation isn't different:

- ☐ 'If your job is so bad, why don't you leave?' '*If only* **it were** that simple.' (*or* If only **it was**...)
- ☐ I'd really like to do accounting. *If only* **I weren't** so poor at maths. (*or* If only **I wasn't**...)

(iv) after **would ('d) rather** and **would ('d) sooner** when we talk about preferences:

- ☐ I feel embarrassed about what happened and *would rather* **the event were** forgotten. (*or* ...was forgotten.)
- ☐ 'I've arranged a meeting for the end of July.' 'I'*d sooner* **it were** earlier, if possible. (*or* ...it was earlier.)

(v) in sentences or clauses beginning with **suppose**, **supposing** and **imagine**:

- ☐ *Suppose* **I were** to lower the price by £100. Would you consider buying the car then? (*or* Suppose **I was** to lower...)
- ☐ I know it looks rather dirty now, but *imagine* **the house were** (to be) repainted. It would look a lot more attractive. (*or* ...imagine the house **was** (to be) repainted.)

And in *comparisons* we can use **were** –

(vi) after **as if** and **as though** (see Unit 84E) and **even if**:

- ☐ I remember stepping off the boat in New York *as if* **it were** yesterday.
- ☐ Despite losing the election, she continues to act *as though* **she were** prime minister.
- ☐ It would be too late to start work on the building this year *even if* **it were** possible to find the money for it.

C

We can use the phrase **as it were** to show that we realise that something we have said may not precisely express what we mean. We often do this to be humorous or to sound less definite:

- ☐ To dismantle the machine you begin by holding it by its ears, **as it were**, these handles at the sides, and pulling the front towards you.
- ☐ Becky runs the office and Sue is her apprentice, **as it were**. (= Sue is not really her apprentice, but is learning from Becky as an apprentice might do)

Exercises

85.1 Match an item from (i) with an ending from (ii) to form a sentence. Begin with **Were...(not)**. (Bi)

(i)
1	...guilty of libel...
2	...government to increase university fees...
3	...anyone to lean against the window...
4	...not already busy in August...
5	...to see the conditions in which the refugees are living...

(ii)
a	the glass would certainly break
b	you would be horrified
c	I would gladly accept your invitation
d	there would be an outcry from students
e	~~the newspaper would face huge legal costs~~

1 + e _Were it to be found guilty of libel, the newspaper would face huge legal costs._

85.2 Expand the notes to write a sentence to go before each of the questions below. Start the new sentence with **Suppose**, **Supposing**, or **Imagine**, followed by a pronoun, noun or noun phrase and then **were**. (Bv)

1 (miss/ last train) _Supposing we were to miss the last train._ How would we get home?
2 (inherit/ million dollars) .... How would it change your life?
3 (parents/ tell you/ emigrating to Canada) .... How do you think you would react?
4 (Spain/ win/ World Cup) .... How would you celebrate?
5 (population of Britain/ all Buddhist) .... How would its society be different?

85.3 Complete the sentences with either **as if** or **even if** followed by an appropriate pronoun and then **were**. (Bvi)

1 Muller spoke slowly _as if it were_ a great physical effort.
2 Every day Mrs Green would walk around the park .... snowing.
3 She knew she wouldn't be able to eat rabbit meat .... starving.
4 Jamie completely ignored me .... not standing next to him.
5 He picked Natasha up .... no heavier than a two-year-old.
6 I don't think I would have got the job .... better qualified.
7 When Mary saw that I was stuck she laughed out loud ....not so critical...employees a joke.
8 I wouldn't accept the job .... to offer it to me.

85.4 Complete the sentences using one of the phrases in (i) with expanded notes from (ii). (A & B)

(i)
~~if it were not for~~	if I were you
wish he were	if only it were
'd rather it were	'd sooner she were

(ii)
forgotten...classmates	going...friends
not so critical...employees	
~~long nights...winter~~	as easy...that
breakfast before...leave	

1 I would be happy to live in the north of Sweden _if it were not for the long nights in the winter._
2 I'm not happy about Katie going to Thailand alone. I ....
3 'If you're unhappy with your new car, why don't you ask for your money back?' 'Well, ...,'
4 I know you haven't got much time, but ....
5 Forgetting to wear my shoes to school was embarrassing and I..
6 I'm very fond of Sebastian, but I ....

85.5 Add **as it were** to one of the possible places in each sentence. (C)

1 You could see tiredness descending upon her as her eyes began to close.
2 The virus hides behind healthy cells to prevent it being attacked.
3 After his long serious illness, Frank returned from the grave to play an important part in the performance.

If...not and unless; if and whether; etc.

If...not and unless

A

Unless is used in conditional sentences with the meaning 'except if':
- You can't travel on this train **unless you have** a reservation.

With **unless** we use present tenses when we talk about the future:
- **Unless it rains**, I'll pick you up at 6.00. (*not* Unless it will rain...)

B

In *real* conditional sentences, we can often use either **unless** or **if...not** with a similar meaning:
- **Unless** the theatre is able to raise £100,000, it will have to close. (*or* If the theatre isn't able to...; implies 'it will have to close *only if* it can't raise the money')

However, we use **if...not** but not **unless** –
☆ when we say in the main clause that an event or action in the **if**-clause is unexpected:
- I'll be amazed **if** Christie doesn't win.
☆ usually in questions:
- **If** you don't pass the test, what will you do?
☆ when the 'only if' implication does not apply:
- **If** it wasn't the best performance of *Hamlet* I've seen, it was certainly the strangest.

We usually use **if...not** rather than **unless** in *unreal* conditional sentences:
- **If** I weren't so tired, I'd give you a hand.

However, **unless** can be used in *unreal* conditional sentences when the main clause is negative:
- She wouldn't have gone to university **unless** her parents had insisted.

We use **unless** but not **if...not** –
☆ when we introduce an afterthought:
- We can leave now – **unless** you'd rather wait for Jack, of course.
☆ when a relative clause refers back to a positive phrase:
- We can walk to the cinema **unless** it's raining, in which case we'll get a taxi.

If and whether

C

We can use **if** or **whether** to say that two possibilities have been talked or thought about, or to say that people are not sure about something:
- They couldn't decide **if/whether** it was worth re-sitting the exam.
- Do you know **if/whether** Ben's at home?

Whether can usually be followed immediately by **or not**. Compare:
- I didn't know **if** Tom was coming **or not**. (*not* ...if or not Tom was coming.) *and*
- I didn't know **whether or not** Tom was coming. (*or* ...**whether** Tom was coming **or not**...)

D

We use **whether** rather than **if** –
☆ after a **preposition** (although **if** is sometimes used informally) and before a **to-infinitive**:
- We argued *about* **whether** butter or margarine was better for you. (*informally* ...if...)
- I couldn't decide **whether** *to buy* apples or bananas.
☆ in the pattern **noun/adjective + as to whether** to mean 'about' or 'concerning':
- There was some *disagreement* **as to whether** he was eligible to play for France.
Other nouns and adjectives used in this pattern include **conflict, confusion, debate, discussion, doubt, question, speculation, uncertainty; concerned, indifferent, uncertain, undecided, unsure**.

and we prefer **whether** rather than **if** –
☆ after the verbs **advise, choose, consider, depend on, discuss, talk about**, and **think about**:
- You should *consider* **whether** the car you are interested in is good value.
☆ in a clause acting as a subject or complement:
- **Whether the minister will quit over the issue** remains to be seen.
- The first issue is **whether he knew he was committing a crime**.

86.1 Match the sentence halves and write a new sentence with the same meaning, beginning each one with **Unless...** (A)

1 We'll never get to the meeting...   a ...or the farmers will lose their crops.
2 Alternative sources of funding must be found...   b ~~...if the train doesn't leave within five minutes.~~
3 If the roads haven't changed in that part of town...   c ...I'm sure I'll be able to find my way there.
4 The weather must start improving soon...   d ...or the research will not be able to continue.
5 If it isn't ridiculously expensive...   e ...I think I'll buy that painting.
6 You are only entitled to state benefit...   f ...if you have been unemployed for six months.

1 + b   *Unless the train leaves within five minutes, we'll never get to the meeting.*

86.2 Underline the correct phrase. If either is possible, underline them both. (B)

1 *Unless the infection is treated/ If the infection isn't treated* urgently, there is a real danger that she will die.
2 *Unless she had gone/ If she hadn't gone* to university, she would have gone into the army.
3 *Unless he was/ If he wasn't* so clumsy, he'd be the best person to do the work.
4 The man can't be prosecuted *unless the police can prove/ if the police can't prove* he intended to steal the jewels.
5 *Unless they were/ If they weren't* the tastiest strawberries I've every eaten, they were definitely the biggest.
6 It'll be surprising *unless Rachel passes/ if Rachel doesn't pass* her piano exam.
7 John was expecting us, but I've knocked and rung on the bell and there's no answer – *unless he's gone/ if he hasn't gone* next door to see the neighbours.
8 *Unless you get/ If you don't get* a loan from the bank, how will you pay for the house?
9 They'll go on strike *unless they get/ if they don't get* a pay rise.
10 Where will you stay *unless Louise is at home/ if Louise isn't at home*?
11 I can borrow my brother's tent *unless he's using it/ if he's not using it*, in which case I'll have to buy one.

86.3 Write **whether** or **if/whether** (if both are possible) in these sentences. (C & D)

1 I was wondering .... you'd had your exam results yet.
2 She was undecided as to .... to fly or go by train.
3 Police have refused to confirm .... or not they have arrested anyone following the robbery.
4 It is unclear .... the new regulations will affect all buildings or just new ones.
5 'How much will the computer cost?' 'That depends on .... I get one with a 15 or 17-inch screen.'
6 Harry said that he was leaving home, but I didn't know .... to believe him.
7 Have you any idea .... Ken will be at the meeting?
8 Can you remember .... the door was open or closed when you got to the house?
9 There was considerable debate as to .... chess was a game or a sport.
10 I don't know .... Clare's going to wait for us or not.
11 The government is considering .... to hold an enquiry into the accident.
12 Everyone in the village was very friendly. It didn't matter .... you'd lived there for a short or a long time.
13 Do you have any view on .... young children should be given homework from school?

Connecting ideas in a sentence and between sentences

A

Some words and phrases (*sentence connectors*) are used to connect one sentence with a previous sentence or sentences. Often (but not always) these go at the beginning of the sentence:

☐ There was no heating in the building. **As a result**, the workers had to be sent home. (*or* The workers had to be sent home **as a result**.)

Other words and phrases (*conjunctions*) are used to connect clauses *within* a single sentence:

☐ **While** I was waiting, I read a magazine.

☐ I'll be wearing a red jumper **so that** you can see me easily.

We can't use a comma to connect ideas joined by a sentence connector. However, these words and phrases can be used to connect two clauses in one sentence if the clauses are joined with **and, but, or, so**, or a **semi-colon** (;), **colon** (:), or **dash** (–):

☐ The building was extremely well constructed **and, as a result**, difficult to demolish.

☐ You could fly via Singapore; **however**, this isn't the only way.

type of connection	example sentence connectors	example conjunctions
comparing, contrasting, and indicating that a situation (in the main clause) is unexpected	after all, all the same, alternatively, anyway, by contrast, even so, however (*but see* **D**), in any case, in contrast, instead, nevertheless, on the contrary, on the other hand	although, even though, though, whereas, while, yet
reasons and results	as a consequence, as a result, consequently, for one thing, so; hence, in consequence, therefore, thus (*the last four are rather formal*)	as, because, for, in that, since, insofar as, so, so that
adding information	above all, after all, also, besides, furthermore, in addition, likewise, moreover, similarly, what's more; as well, too (*the last two are not used at the beginning of a sentence*)	
condition	if not, if so, otherwise	as long as, assuming (that), if, on condition that, provided (that), so long as, supposing (that), unless
time: one event at the same time as another	at that time, at the same time, meanwhile	as, when, whenever, while
time: one event before or after another	after, after that, afterwards, before, before that, earlier, later, previously, soon, subsequently, then	after, as soon as, before, since, until

Note that **after, before** and **so** can be both connectors and conjunctions.

B

Even though is a conjunction used to say that a fact doesn't make the rest of the sentence untrue (see also Unit 82B). It connects ideas *within* a sentence:

☐ **Even though** it was midday, I put on the light.

Even so is a sentence connector used to introduce a fact that is surprising in the context of what was just said. It connects ideas *between* sentences:

☐ It was midday. **Even so**, I put on the light.

C

However is often used as a sentence connector, but it can also be used –

☆ as an adverb when it is followed by an **adjective, adverb**, or **much/many**:

☐ We just don't have the money to do the work, **however necessary** you think it is.

☆ as a conjunction when it means 'in whatever way':

☐ **However** she held the mirror, she couldn't see the back of her neck.

87.1 Choose items from (i) and from (ii) to complete these sentences in an appropriate way. Note the punctuation at the ends of the sentences and phrases already given. (A & B)

(i)		(ii)	
alternatively	as long as	~~everybody had their fair share~~	you could poison them
for one thing	meanwhile	his face seemed familiar	it's too expensive
otherwise	~~so that~~	the rent was paid on time	the street was deserted
while	yet	the volcano continues to erupt	we were on holiday

1 Martha cut the cake carefully into slices _so that everybody had their fair share._
2 A small boy was kicking a ball against a wall; ....
3 I couldn't remember meeting him before, ...
4 A mass evacuation of islanders is taking place. ....
5 A: Why don't you like that new French restaurant?　B: ....
6 Karen came down with flu ....
7 My landlady didn't mind me having parties in my room ....
8 One way of getting rid of weeds is to dig them out. ....

87.2 Underline the correct alternative. (A, B & C)

1 Your essay is badly organised and full of spelling mistakes. *Though/ Nevertheless*, it contains some very interesting ideas.
2 To the east the trees were left standing, *while/ in contrast* to the west they were cut down.
3 I felt guilty about leaving the company *even so/ even though* I knew I had made the right decision.
4 The course taught me a lot about jewellery design. *Even though/ Even so*, there is still a lot I need to learn.
5 I had expected my mother to be happy with the news. *Instead/ Although* tears came to her eyes and she started to cry.
6 Herbs are usually grown in temperate climates, *whereas/ on the other hand* spices are mainly from tropical areas.
7 We were very short of money *so/ as a consequence* we had to spend the night on a park bench.
8 I turned the ignition, but the car refused to start. *As/ Meanwhile* the lions were getting ever closer.
9 She wrote the questions on the blackboard *while/ at the same time* the students copied them into their books.
10 *Previously/ Before* I went to Australia, I'd never seen a koala.
11 Modern farming methods have destroyed the habitat of many birds. *As a result/ So that* their numbers are in decline.
12 I'll have to buy some ladders *unless/ if not* I can borrow a pair from Ray.
13 I first met Kevin in the 1970s. *At that time/ When* he had long hair and a beard.

87.3 Use your own ideas to complete the sentences. Begin **however + adjective/adverb/many/much**. (D)

1 She is determined to be a successful artist, _however difficult it might be to achieve._
2 ...., it is difficult to lose weight without cutting down on the amount you eat.
3 ...., it is important to spend some time apart.
4 Professor Malcolm is always happy to spend time with his students,

....

Prepositions of position and movement

A | Across, over

We can use **across** or **over** to talk about a *position* on the other side of, or *moving* to the other side of a road, bridge, border, river, etc.:

☐ Mike lives in the house **across/over** *the road* from ours.
☐ The truck came towards them **across/over** *the bridge*.
☐ Once she was **across/over** *the border*, she knew she would be safe.

We use **over** rather than **across** when we talk about reaching the other side of something that is high, or higher than it is wide. Compare:

☐ He jumped **over** *the fence* into the garden. *and* ☐ He jumped **across** *the stream*.

When we are talking about something we think of as a flat surface, or an area such as a country or sea, we prefer **across** rather than **over**:

☐ He suddenly saw Sue **across** *the room*.   ☐ The figures moved rapidly **across** *the screen*.
☐ The programme was broadcast **across** *Australia*.

We prefer **all over** rather than **all across** to mean 'to or in many different parts of an area'. However, we commonly use **across**, or **right across** for emphasis:

☐ The disease has now spread **all over** the world. (*or* ...(**right**) **across** the world.)

B | Along, through

When we talk about following a line of some kind (a road, a river, etc.), we use **along**:

☐ They walked **along** the footpath until they came to a small bridge.

We use **through** to emphasise that we are talking about movement in a three dimensional space, with things all around, rather than a two dimensional space, a flat surface or area:

☐ He pushed his way **through** the crowd of people to get to her.

Through often suggests movement from one side or end of the space to the other. Compare:

☐ She walked **through** the forest to get to her grandmother's house. *and*
☐ She spent a lot of her free time walking **in** the forest.

C | Above, over; below, under; beneath, underneath; throughout

We can use either **above** or **over** when we say that one thing is at a higher level than another:

☐ **Above/Over** the door was a sign saying, 'Mind your head'.

However, we prefer **above**, when one thing is not directly over the other. Compare:

☐ They lived in a village in the mountains **above** the lake. (not directly over) *and*
☐ The bird hovered just a few metres **above/over** the lake. (directly over)

We use **over**, not **above**, when something covers something else and touches it:

☐ She put a quilt **over** the bed.

and usually when we are talking about horizontal movement at a higher level than something:

☐ I saw the helicopter fly out **over** the water, near the fishing boat.

Below is the opposite of **above**; **under** is the opposite of **over**. The differences in the uses of **below** and **under** are similar to those between **above** and **over** (see above):

☐ It's hard to believe that there is a railway line **below/under** the building. (at a lower level)
☐ Her head was **below** the level of the table so nobody noticed her. (not directly under)
☐ She hid the presents **under** a blanket. (the blanket covers and touches the presents)
☐ Esther ran **under** the bridge. (horizontal movement at a lower level)

We can use **underneath** as an alternative to **under** as a preposition of place. **Beneath** is sometimes used as a more formal alternative to **under** or **below**.

We can use **throughout** to emphasise that something is in every part of a place (see also Unit 90A):

☐ The flower is found **throughout** the island.   ☐ The same laws apply **throughout** Europe.

88.1 Complete the sentences with **across** or **over**, whichever is correct or more likely. If both are possible, write **across/over**. (A)

1 After I'd finished work I walked .... the car park to where Ruth was waiting.
2 They own a house .... the river in Richmond.
3 The gate was locked so we had to climb .... the wall.
4 You're not allowed to go .... the railway line. You have to use the bridge.
5 She was the first woman to row alone .... the Atlantic.
6 Nuclear waste continues to be transported .... the country, despite objections from campaigners.
7 The traffic was busy on the main road so we walked .... the pedestrian crossing.
8 She leaned out .... the balcony rail and looked for Philip in the square below.

88.2 Underline the correct or most appropriate word(s) in each sentence. (A & B)

1 It took several minutes to walk *across/ over/ along/ through* the corridor to the exit.
2 *Across/ Over/ Along/ Through* the table I could see Oliver looking at his watch.
3 He fell *across/ over/ along/ through* the floor into the cellar below.
4 I could see Bob *across/ over/ along/ through* the other side of the river.
5 He cycles thousands of miles each year all *across/ over/ along/ through* the country.
6 Hotels have been built *across/ over/ along/ through* the beach for about 25 kilometres north of the town.

88.3 Correct the prepositions (**above, over, below, under**) if necessary, or write ✓. (C)

1 He slept with his wallet below his pillow.
2 He broke his leg just below his knee.
3 The town stood at the top the hill, and stretching into the distance under it were huge areas of green fields.
4 She threw a coat above her shoulders and stepped out into the cold.
5 The autumn and spring equinoxes are when the sun is directly above the equator.
6 He lived in a first-floor flat above a greengrocer's in Leyton.
7 When the police got to the car they found the driver slumped above the steering wheel.
8 He always wore a vest below his shirt, even in summer.
9 I could hear the plane flying high over the clouds.
10 The palace is situated on a wooded hillside 3 kilometres over the city.

88.4 A number of common idioms include the prepositions in this unit. Match the idioms in italics and their meanings below.

1 'What's wrong?' 'I'm just feeling rather *below par*.'
2 'Her clothes look rather old-fashioned. In fact, she's never been particularly concerned about her appearance.' 'That's a bit *below the belt*, isn't it?'
3 She already has 18 books on gardening *under her belt* and she is now working on number 19.
4 He had never played well for the club and left *under a cloud*.
5 She lost her temper and went completely *over the top*, accusing him of cheating.
6 They received a bonus in December *over and above* their monthly salary.
7 We have a lot more students at college this year. They haven't just come to particular departments, the increase is right *across the board*.

a in addition to .... b successfully completed ....
c slightly unwell .... d applies equally to all areas ....
e cruel or unfair .... f with some people's disapproval ....
g extreme behaviour; indicating disapproval ....

Between and among

A

As prepositions of *place* we use **between** with two or more people or things that we see as individual or separate, and we use **among** when we see the people or things as part of a group or mass. **Among** is only used with three or more people or things:

- ☐ She held the diamond **between** her thumb and forefinger.
- ☐ Zimbabwe is situated **between** Zambia to the north, Mozambique to the east, Botswana to the west, and South Africa to the south.
- ☐ He stood **among** all his friends in the room and felt very happy.
- ☐ She eventually found her passport **among** the clothes in the drawer.

Note that **amongst** is sometimes used instead of **among**, but in more literary contexts.

B

Between and **among** are not only used as prepositions of place. For example, we can use either to talk about something divided or shared between people:

- ☐ The money is to be divided **between/among** the towns in the area.
- ☐ The prize will be shared **between/among** the first six finishers in the race.

We also use **between** –

☆ to talk about comparisons and relationships (e.g. with the words **association**, **balance**, **comparison**, **connection**, **contrast**, **correlation**, **difference**, **distinction**, **link**, **relationship**):

- ☐ There should be a better *balance* on the committee **between** the various ethnic groups.
- ☐ They are wrong to claim that there is a *link* **between** unemployment and crime.

☆ to talk about choices:

- ☐ I have to choose **between** the universities of Leeds, York and Manchester.
- ☐ He felt torn **between** his family and his friends.

☆ to talk about discussions or the results of discussions when we specify the two or more people or groups involved:

- ☐ There was a disagreement **between** Neil, John and Margaret.
- ☐ The treaty was signed **between** Great Britain and France.

☆ to say that people or things share an amount of something:

- ☐ **Between** them, Ray and Ingrid must earn about £100,000 a year.
- ☐ Last year the three companies built 30,000 houses **between** them.

We also use **among** –

☆ when we mean 'existing or happening in a particular group':

- ☐ The disease has now broken out **among** the hill tribes.
- ☐ Their music is still very popular **among** young teenagers.

☆ when we mean 'included in a particular group':

- ☐ They are **among** the best hockey players in the world.
- ☐ **Among** the capital cities of South America, Quito is the second highest.

C

There are a number of common expressions using **between** and **among**, including **among others** (= what is said applies to other people or things, too), **among other things** (= including other things), **between ourselves** (= this should be kept secret), and **between you and me** (= this should be kept secret):

- ☐ The concert features, **among others**, Karl Frisk and the Johnsons. (= other singers/groups are featured, too)
- ☐ I later found out that he had been a carpenter and a dustman, **among other things**. (= he had had other jobs, too)
- ☐ **Between ourselves** (= keep this a secret), I don't think Tom is as honest as he should be.
- ☐ I've got a maths exam next week, but **between you and me** (= but keep this a secret) I haven't done any revision yet.

89.1 Underline the correct answer. (A)

1 For a couple of days I've had a pain *between/ among* my shoulder blades.
2 He couldn't find a microphone *between/ among* all the recording equipment he had with him.
3 It would be easier to read if you put a line space *between/ among* the paragraphs.
4 In the photograph Val is standing *between/ among* her parents.
5 The lost manuscript was discovered *between/ among* the thousands of books in the cellar.
6 The buffet is towards the middle of the train *between/ among* first and second class seating.
7 She carried trays of drinks and food *between/ among* the crowd of guests in the room.
8 I couldn't see Robbie *between/ among* the audience, although he said he would be there.
9 Rebecca commutes *between/ among* her flat in London and her sister's home in Halifax.

89.2 Complete the sentences with **between** or **among** and the most likely words or phrases from those below. If you can use either **between** or **among**, write **between/among**. (B)

amateur	its clients	my closest friends	cooking
intake of refined sugar	the pupils	his remaining relatives	the striking dockers
teenagers	~~us~~		

1 I wasn't feeling very hungry, so Jo and I shared a bowl of noodles ___between us___ .
2 I bought four bars of chocolate and divided them _____ in the class.
3 The distinction _____ and professional athletes is becoming less clear.
4 It has become fashionable _____ to dye their hair in various colours.
5 When Jack died, his daughter inherited the house and the rest of his money was split
_____ .
6 The advertising company is very successful, numbering most of the big banks
_____ .
7 Researchers have found a striking correlation _____ and arthritis.
8 Given a choice _____ and washing up, I know which I'd prefer to do.
9 Neil and Ashley are _____, so I'll invite them to the wedding, of course.
10 Late last night the talks _____ and their employers broke down.

89.3 Kathy and her friend Jo recently travelled around Europe. Here is what Kathy wrote in a letter home from Rome. Fill in the gaps with **between** or **among**. (A & B)

Hello Mum and Dad!

Rome must be (1) _____ the most fascinating cities in the world. Yesterday we
visited, (2) _____ other places, the Foro Romano – the centre of ancient Rome –
and the Vatican. There is such an incredible contrast (3) _____ the old parts of
the city built up to 2000 years ago and the more recent parts. In the Vatican we
climbed the long stairs to the top of St Peter's church. The view from the top must be
(4) _____ the most incredible over any city in the world. But (5) _____
you and me, I'm a bit scared of heights and was glad to get back to ground level. Later
we went to the Pantheon, an ancient Roman temple, which is (6) _____ the
Vatican and the Foro Romano. The Italian king Umberto I and the artist Raphael are
(7) _____ the people buried there. In the evening we had a bit of an argument
(8) _____ us over where we should eat – Jo wanted pizza, but I wanted to try
some of the special local food. Eventually we found a place that did excellent pasta,
(9) _____ other things. The only problem then was choosing (10) _____
the many different types!

Kathy

Prepositions of time

During, in, over, throughout

A   We use **during** or **in** to talk about a period of time within which an event or activity occurs. The activity may continue for the whole of the period of time:

- ☐ I stayed at home **during** the summer. (*or* ...**in** the summer.)
- ☐ The population of the city has actually fallen **during** the last decade. (*or* ...**in** the last...)

or the event may happen at some time, or be repeated a number of times, in the period of time:

- ☐ We went to France **during** the summer. (*or* ...**in** the summer.)
- ☐ He suffered a number of injuries **during** his career as a footballer. (*or* ...**in** his career...)

We use **during**, rather than **in**, to mean 'at some time in the period of' before nouns such as **illness, holiday, meal, stay, treatment**, and **visit**, when we refer to an event which lasts some time:

- ☐ The President made the speech **during** *a visit* to Madrid.

and also with the phrase **the whole (of)**, emphasising duration of an entire period:

- ☐ No-one was allowed to leave the ship **during** *the whole of* its time in port.

We can use **throughout** to emphasise that something happens over the whole of a period of time:

- ☐ We had enough firewood to keep us warm **throughout** the winter. (*or* ...warm **during/ through** the winter.)

B   We can use **over** or **during** when we talk about something that goes on for a length of time within a *period of time*, either for some of that period or for the whole of it:

- ☐ Weather conditions have been improving **over/ during** *the past few days.*
- ☐ I fell, banged my head, and can't remember anything about what happened **over/ during** *the next hour or so.*

However, if we talk about a short event that happens within a period of time, we prefer **during**:

- ☐ *She sneezed* **during** the performance. (= on one or a few occasions; *not* ...over the performance.)
- ☐ **During** a pause in the conversation, *she left the room.* (*not* Over a pause...)

Note that we can use **throughout** to mean that short events happen continuously within a period of time:

- ☐ *She sneezed* **throughout** the performance.

C   **Until, by, up to**

There are a number of ways of saying when something that has continued for some time stops –

☆ We use **until** to say that something continued or will continue to a particular time, and **by** to say that something happened or will happen either before a particular time or at that time at the latest. Compare:

- ☐ We have to be at home **until** 2.30. (We must not leave home before 2.30) *and*
- ☐ We have to be at home **by** 2.30. (We must arrive home either before or at 2.30)

Note that **till** can be used instead of **until**. It is particularly common in conversation, but rarely found in formal writing.

☆ In informal contexts we can use **up to** or **up till** instead of **until**. We commonly use **up to/till** with **now** and with **then**:

- ☐ I've just bought a computer. I've always used a typewriter **up to** *now*. (*or* ...**up till** now...)
- ☐ The roadworks are likely to go on **up to** the end of May. (*or* ...**up till** the end...)

☆ We can use **until now** to talk about a situation that will not continue beyond now:

- ☐ Supermarkets say that **until now** there has been little consumer interest in buying organic produce. (The situation has changed or is going to change)

Notice, however, that we don't use **until now** for a situation that will or may continue into the future. Instead we can use **so far** or, in formal contexts, **to date**:

- ☐ It was certainly the best match of the football season **so far**.
- ☐ When the contract is signed it will be the building company's biggest order **to date**.

90.1 In which of the sentences can the word in brackets replace **during**? Write ✓ if it can replace it and ✗ if it can't. (A & B)

1 I'm going to get a cup of coffee *during* the break. (*in*)
2 She lost more than 15 kilos *during* her illness and she was off work for two months. (*in*)
3 He twisted his ankle *during* the match and had to retire injured. (*over*)
4 The weather was terrible here *during* December. (*in*)
5 The meeting will be some time *during* January. (*over*)
6 She sang in a choir *during* her childhood. (*throughout*)
7 People no longer expect to be employed in the same place *during* the whole of their working lives. (*in*)
8 Do you think standards of numeracy have fallen *during* the last twenty years? (*over*)
9 This is one of the pieces we heard *during* the concert last night. (*in*)
10 Jean will have to sleep in the spare room *during* her stay with us. (*in*)
11 The town was rebuilt *during* the early 16th century. (*over*)
12 It was impossible to buy bananas *during* the war. (*in*)
13 Harry had a phone call *during* the meal and had to leave early. (*in*)
14 He had to put up with great pain *during* his treatment for a heart condition. (*in*)
15 My stomach ache got steadily worse *during* the evening. (*over*)

90.2 Complete the sentences with **by** and **until**. Use **by** in one of the pair and **until** in the other. (C)

1 a I was feeling really hungry .... the time dinner was served.
  b We sat around the fire talking .... the time dinner was served.
2 a Sorry I'm late. I've been in a meeting .... now.
  b I thought Jack would have been here .... now.
3 a I've got to pay the money back .... the end of the month.
  b I've got .... the end of the month to pay the money back.
4 a I put on an extra pair of socks. .... then my feet were freezing cold.
  b I stood outside the cinema for an hour. .... then my feet were freezing cold.
5 a She was already a leading economist .... her early twenties.
  b She studied economics .... her early twenties and then moved into law.
6 a I hope to finish the decorating .... the weekend.
  b It will take me .... the weekend to finish the decorating.

90.3 Here is another of Kathy's letters (see Unit 89.3). Choose the correct or more likely word or phrase. In some cases, both are possible. (A–C)

Hi Peter

(1) Over/ During the last three weeks we've covered thousands of kilometres by train.
(2) So far/ Until now we've been to Stockholm, Berlin and Rome, and now we're in
Amsterdam. (3) So far/ Until now I thought Rome was the best city we'd been to, but I
think I love Amsterdam even more. We've been here for three days, and have been very
impressed with what we've seen (4) so far/ until now. We spent the first two days in
galleries, looking particularly at Van Gogh's paintings. I didn't know much about his
work (5) so far/ until now. Incidentally, we bumped into your friend Ken (6) in/
during our visit to the Van Gogh museum. We're staying here (7) until/ by Saturday
and then we're going to Paris. Must go now. We're off to The Hague for the day and
have to be at the station (8) until/ by 9.30.

Kathy

A

We use **except** or **except for** to introduce the only thing or person that a statement does not include:

- ☐ The price of the holiday includes all meals **except (for)** lunch.
- ☐ Everyone seemed to have been invited **except (for)** Mrs Woodford and me.
- ☐ I had no money to give him **except (for)** the few coins in my pocket.

We use **except**, not **except for**, with **to-infinitives**, and **that-clauses**:

- ☐ I rarely need to go into the city centre **except** *to do* some shopping.
- ☐ They look just like the real thing, **except** *that* they're made of plastic.

We usually use **except** before **prepositions**, **bare infinitives**, and **that-clauses** including where the word *that* is left out (see Unit 53). However, informally **except for** is sometimes also used, although this is grammatically incorrect:

- ☐ There is likely to be rain everywhere today **except** *in* Wales.
- ☐ There is nothing more the doctor can do **except** *keep* an eye on him.
- ☐ They look just like the real thing, **except** (*that*) they're made of plastic.

We can use **except for**, but not **except**, with the meaning 'but for' (see C below).

B

We use **except (for)** to mean that something is not included in a particular statement, but we use **besides** to mean 'as well as' or 'in addition to'. Compare:

- ☐ I don't enjoy watching any sports **except (for)** cricket. (= I enjoy only cricket) *and*
- ☐ **Besides** cricket, I enjoy watching football and basketball. (= I enjoy three sports)
- ☐ I haven't read anything by her, **except (for)** one of her short stories. *and*
- ☐ **Besides** her novels and poems, she published a number of short stories.

Apart from can be used with the same meanings as both **except (for)** and **besides**:

- ☐ I don't enjoy watching any sports **apart from** cricket. (= except for)
- ☐ **Apart from** cricket, I enjoy watching football and basketball. (= besides; as well as)

C

We can use **but** with a similar meaning to **except (for)**, particularly after negative words such as **no**, **nobody**, and **nothing**:

- ☐ Immediately after the operation he could see *nothing* **but/except (for)/apart from** vague shadows.
- ☐ There was *no* way out **but/except/apart from** upwards, towards the light.

But for has a different meaning from **except for**. We use **but for** to say what would or might have happened if the thing introduced by **but for** had not happened:

- ☐ The country would now be self-sufficient in food **but for** the drought last year. (= if there hadn't been the drought...)
- ☐ **But for** the leg injury he suffered last year, he would probably have been picked for the national team by now. (= if he hadn't injured his leg...)

However, some people use **except for** in the same way as **but for**, particularly in informal spoken English:

- ☐ I'd have got there on time **except for** the taxi being late. (*or* ...**but for** the taxi being late.)
- ☐ **Except for** the problems with my computer, I would have got the book finished weeks ago. (*or* **But for** the problems with my computer...)

D

We can use **excepted**, **apart** or **aside** after mentioning a person or thing to say that they are not included in a statement that we make:

- ☐ It has been, *1984* **excepted/apart/aside**, the hottest July for the last 100 years.
- ☐ Tom had difficulties with question two. *This* **excepted/apart/aside**, he did very well in the exam.

91.1 Complete the sentences with **except** or **except for**. Indicate where both are possible. (A)

1 He was dressed very smartly .... that his shoes were dirty.
2 I'll be able to see you any day .... Thursday when I'm in Paris.
3 I liked everything in the meal .... the cabbage.
4 I had nothing to do .... sit by the pool and relax.
5 We would have gone walking last week .... the terrible weather.
6 She had no choice .... to wait for the next train.
7 There are very few wolves left in the country .... in a small area of forest in the north.
8 All the puddings on the menu cost £3.50 .... the ice cream, which was £2.
9 I'm in the office all the time .... at lunch times.
10 She might have won the race .... hitting the last fence.
11 The plant is found on every continent .... Africa.
12 He gave no excuse for turning up late .... that he was tired.
13 I thought the cake was pretty good .... that it had too much sugar in it.
14 I drove all the way without stopping .... to buy petrol.

91.2 Where necessary, correct these sentences with **besides** or **except (for)**. If the sentence is already correct, write ✓. (B)

1 She had never been out of the country besides a week in Ireland as a child.
2 Besides being small, Denmark is very flat, with villages linked by country roads.
3 The planned new road will increase traffic in the area except for damaging an area of ancient woodland.
4 Except for his novels, Campbell wrote a number of biographies.
5 There was nothing in the fridge besides a rather mouldy piece of cheese.
6 He was unhurt in the crash except for a bruise on his forehead.

91.3 Match the sentences and rewrite them as single sentences beginning **But for the...** . (C)

1 Barry gave me excellent directions.
2 The bad weather caused interruptions.
3 The charity supplied food and medicines.
4 The trees provided shelter.
5 The EU threatened sanctions.
6 The bank gave me a loan.

  a If it hadn't, the building would have been completed by now.
  b Without this, human rights would not have improved in the country.
  c Otherwise, many more people would have died in the famine.
  d If it hadn't, I would not have been able to set up my business.
  e ~~Without these, I would have got totally lost.~~
  f Otherwise, the wind would have caused even more damage to the house.

1 + e _But for the excellent directions Barry gave me, I would have got totally lost._
2 ....
3 ....
4 ....
5 ....
6 ....

Prepositions after verbs

Some verbs are frequently followed by particular prepositions. This table shows some common verb + preposition combinations:

	about	*after*	*for*	*of*	*on*	*with*
agree	✓				✓	✓
argue	✓		✓			✓
ask	✓	✓	✓	✓		
care	✓		✓			
enquire (or *inquire*)	✓	✓				
know	✓			✓		
learn	✓			✓		
talk	✓			✓	✓	✓

about usually means 'concerning a particular thing':
  □ They began to **learn about** nutrition when they were at primary school.
We use **care about** to talk about something we are (not) concerned about:
  □ He doesn't seem to **care about** the effect smoking has on him.

after is used with **ask** and **enquire** meaning to try to get information about a person (but not a thing), particularly concerning their health. Compare:
  □ I'm phoning to **ask/enquire after** Mrs Brown in Ward 4. (*or* ...ask/enquire about...) *and*
  □ He got angry when they **asked/enquired about** his private life. (*not* ...asked/enquired after...)

for is used with **ask** to talk about what people want:
  □ He finished the drink quickly and **asked for** another.
and with **care** to talk about doing the necessary things for someone or something in order to keep them in good health or condition:
  □ Jan **cared for** her disabled mother until her death last year. (*or* Jan **took care of**...)
or to mean 'like', particularly in negative sentences, and to mean 'want' in offers. Both of these uses of **care for** are rather formal:
  □ I don't **care for** the theatre much.   □ Would you **care for** a cup of coffee?

of is used with **talk**, **know**, and **learn** to talk about discussing, having or getting information:
  □ Diane went recently to Laos and can **talk of** nothing else. (*or less formally* '...talk about...')
  □ The whole country **knew of** Churchill's love of cigars. (*or less formally* '...knew about...')
  □ I have just **learnt of** the death of Dr Brown. (*or less formally* '...learnt about...')
We use **ask of** when we make or talk about requests:
  □ I have a favour to **ask of** you and your sister.

on is used with **talk** and **agree** to mean 'concerned with a particular topic':
  □ I was asked to **talk on** my research. (*or* ...to **talk about**...)
  □ We **agreed on** a time to meet. (usually there has been previous discussion or disagreement.)
Notice that we use **agree to** to say that someone allows something to happen:
  □ Once the government **agreed to** the scheme it went ahead without delay.

with is used with **argue** and **talk** when we go on to mention the person involved:
  □ I used to **argue/talk with** Les for hours.
We use **agree with** to say that two people have the same opinion:
  □ Adam thinks we should accept the offer, and I **agree with** him.
and to say that we approve of a particular idea or action:
  □ I **agree with** letting children choose the clothes they wear. (*or* I **agree about/on**...)
or to say that two descriptions are the same:
  □ Tom's story **agreed with** that of his son.

92.1 Cross out any incorrect prepositions. (A)

1 When I phoned the hospital to enquire *after/ on/ about* Ricky, I was told that he'd gone home.

2 I only advertised the car for sale on Wednesday, but by the end of the week ten people had phoned to ask *after/ for/ about* it.

3 We can learn a great deal *after/ of/ about* the oceans by studying even a small piece of coral.

4 I didn't agree *about/ for/ with* a word of what she said.

5 Professor Owen is giving a talk *of/ with/ on* the Romans in Lecture Hall 1.

6 I had to care *for/ after/ about* my elderly parents when they both became ill.

7 For many years we have been arguing *for/ on/ with* changes in the way the college is managed.

8 She didn't know *of/ about/ on* her stepbrother's existence until her mother died.

92.2 Put in the correct or most appropriate preposition from those in A. Sometimes two answers are possible. (B)

1 'If you want to enquire .... a motor insurance quotation, please press 1.'

2 I hope you're brother's feeling better soon. When you see him, tell him I asked .... him.

3 I first learnt .... his decision to resign when it was announced on the radio last night.

4 We're going to talk .... the council about the possibility of planting some new trees in the park.

5 I don't care .... pop music at all. I much prefer classical music.

6 The teacher says we've got to do the test, so there's not point in arguing .... it.

7 The government has agreed .... a public inquiry into the helicopter crash.

8 If you know .... any reasons why you should not be given medical insurance, you must declare them here.

9 'Josh can be really stupid sometimes.' 'You shouldn't talk .... your brother like that.'

10 I'm calling to enquire .... Mr Dawes, who was operated on last night.

11 She's always arguing .... her parents about what to watch on television.

12 I know it's a lot to ask .... you, but would you look after the children while I'm in Japan on business?

13 The course was brilliant. We learnt .... using the Internet in language learning.

14 'Dan said he'll try to fix my car.' 'What does he know .... cars?'

15 I don't think the government cares enough .... nursery education to fund it properly.

16 After hours of discussion, the committee finally agreed .... the amount of money to donate.

92.3 These sentences include more verbs that are commonly followed by the prepositions in A. Can you explain the difference in meaning? Use a dictionary if necessary.

1 The police *acted on* the information very quickly./ I couldn't be at the meeting, so my solicitor *acted for* me.

2 I've been *thinking* a lot *about* your idea, and I've decided I'd like to support you./ What do you *think of* the colour in the bedroom?

3 Sam *was called after* my grandfather./ Campaigners have *called for* a referendum on the issue.

4 They say he *worked for* the CIA in the 1970s./ She *works with* computers.

5 We're *counting on* Mike to supply the food for the party./ Playing exciting football *counts for* little if the team isn't winning.

Prepositions after nouns

Many nouns are followed by the same prepositions as their related adjective or verb. Compare:

- Are you **satisfied** *with* the way that the business is being run? *and*
- The shareholders have expressed **satisfaction** *with* the way the business is being run.

A few nouns are followed by different prepositions. Compare:

- They became **fond** *of* each other at school. *and*
- Their **fondness** *for* each other grew and many years later they married.

Other nouns like this and their corresponding adjective or verb are **proud of/pride in, ashamed of/shame about/at.**

Some nouns take a preposition where their related verb does not. Compare:

- They're going to **ban** smoking in restaurants. *and*
- I would support a **ban** *on* smoking in restaurants.

Other nouns like this include **admiration for, amazement at, discussion about/on, improvement in, influence on, interview with, lack of.** Note that many other nouns are commonly followed by **of**-phrases which indicate possession, a property, or classify the noun by describing what it relates to. Compare:

- He **described** the conductor as moving his arms like a windmill. *and*
- His **description** *of* the conductor was very funny.

Some nouns can be followed by **of + -ing** but not usually a **to-infinitive:**

- He's got into the **habit** *of biting* his nails when he's nervous.

Other nouns like this include **cost, effect, fear, likelihood, possibility, probability, problem, prospect, risk, sign.**

Some nouns can be followed by a **to-infinitive** but not usually **of + -ing:**

- His unhappy childhood explains his **reluctance** *to talk* about his parents.

Other nouns like this include **ability, attempt, concern, decision, desire, determination, failure, inability, permission, proposal, reason, refusal, (un)willingness.** Note that many of these nouns can also be used with other prepositions + ing (e.g. **attempt at -ing, reason for -ing,** etc.).

Some nouns can sometimes be followed either by **of + -ing** or a **to-infinitive** with a similar meaning, usually after **the:**

- Do staff have *the* **opportunity** *of taking* unpaid leave? (*or* ...the **opportunity** *to take*...)
- *The* **aim** *of providing* clean drinking water has been achieved. (*or The* **aim** *to provide*...)

Other nouns like this include **ambition, idea, option, plan.**

However, some nouns, such as **chance, sense** and **way,** have more than one meaning and are followed either by **of + -ing** or a **to-infinitive** depending on which meaning is used. Compare:

- What's the **chance** *of throwing* five heads when you throw a coin five times?
  (= likelihood; *not* ...chance to throw...) *and*
- Will you get the **chance** *to visit* Miki in Japan? (= opportunity; *not* ...of visiting...)
- He didn't have the **sense** *to move* away from the puddle of water as the bus went past.
  (= good judgement; *not* ...sense of moving...) *and*
- Everyone was very friendly and she had a **sense** *of belonging* within a few days of moving to her new school. (= feeling; *not* ...sense to belong...)
- I've got a **way** *of cooking* rice perfectly every time. (= method; *or* ...way to cook...) *and*
- She has a really funny **way** *of speaking.* (= manner; *not* ...way to speak)

Notice also that **of +-ing** usually follows **no/every/the sole/the slightest/(not) any/with the + intention,** but that we can use either **of + -ing** or a **to-infinitive** in most other cases. Compare:

- I have **no intention** *of lending* Dan any more money. (*not* ...no intention to lend...) *and*
- He announced his **intention** *to stand* in the election. (*or* ...**intention** *of standing*...)

93.1 Complete the sentences with a noun related to one of the following adjectives and verbs followed by an appropriate preposition. Use a dictionary where necessary. (A)

admire	advise	amaze	ashamed	~~cruel~~	discuss
improve	influence	interview	lack	proud	vaccinate

1 I am against any form of ....._cruelty to_..... animals and would support a ban on hunting.
2 Maggie is still in hospital, but there has been a big .... her condition in the last couple of days.
3 Maurice took great .... his cooking, and was always eager to talk about his recipes.
4 The website is full of useful .... how to lose weight.
5 In her .... *The Daily Herald*, the Finance Minister denied that she plans to raise taxes.
6 I have the greatest .... people who work full time and also study for a university degree.
7 We had a long .... the relative merits of CDs and records.
8 He confessed his .... not having spent more time with his children when they were young.
9 I had to have a .... typhoid before entering the country.
10 Benny Carter had a significant .... the development of British jazz.
11 She stared in .... the sight that met her eyes – Dave had shaved all his hair off.
12 There is a severe .... affordable housing in the city and many people are homeless.

93.2 Complete the sentences with a noun from (i) and a word from (ii). Use either **of + –ing** or a **to-infinitive**. (B)

(i)

ability	cost	decision
failure	~~fear~~	possibility
reason	risk	sign	unwillingness

(ii)

acknowledge	allow	buy	~~fly~~
get	remember	stop	
transmit	win	worry	

1 My mother recently overcame her ...._fear of flying_.... and had a holiday in South Africa.
2 The snow has been falling now for two days and shows no ....
3 The government has defended its .... coal mining in the national park.
4 Your blood pressure is a little high, but there is no .... about it.
5 She was kept in isolation to reduce the .... the virus to other people in the hospital.
6 The exercise tests children's .... a random sequence of numbers.
7 The manager was sacked after his team's .... promotion from the second division.
8 The .... new cars in Europe is expected to fall in the next year.
9 I knew that there was little .... the job with so many applicants.
10 It is very difficult to work with Chris because of his .... that he ever makes mistakes.

93.3 Complete the sentences with an appropriate verb using either **of + –ing** or a **to-infinitive**. Give both forms if both are possible. (C)

1 Although Debbie said she would think about it, she never had the slightest intention of ...._accepting_... my suggestion.
2 It's going to be cloudy tonight so there is only a fifty-fifty chance .... the eclipse of the moon.
3 It's pouring with rain. I hope David had the sense .... an umbrella with him.
4 The head of the company repeated his intention .... on his 65th birthday.
5 When the History Department closed she was given the option .... another job.
6 Martha had a very unusual way ...., keeping her feet firmly on the floor and waving her arms around her head.

Two- and three-word verbs: word order

A The meaning of some verbs commonly used with a particular *preposition* or *adverb* (or *particle*) is often different from the meaning of their separate parts. We can call these *two-word verbs*:

- ☐ The company's debts were **mounting up**. (= increasing)
- ☐ I'll quickly **go over** the main points of the report again. (= summarise)
- ☐ She had to **let** her dress **out** because she'd put on weight. (= make it larger)

Other *three-word verbs* are commonly used with an *adverb + preposition*.

- ☐ Do you think he's really likely to **go through with** his threat? (= do it)
- ☐ The team has failed to **live up to** earlier expectations. (= achieve what was expected)

These two- and three-word verbs are sometimes also called *phrasal verbs*.

B Many two-word verbs are usually *intransitive* (see Glossary):

- ☐ He **grew up** on a farm.   ☐ When she **came to** she found herself in hospital.

Other verbs like this include **crop up, fall through, get up, move off, shop around, splash out**.

However, some two-word verbs can be used transitively or intransitively with the same meaning (e.g. **answer back, 'call back, clear away, cover up, help out, take over, tidy away, wash up**):

- ☐ I'll **call back** later.   ☐ I'll **call** *you* **back** when I get home.

and other two-word verbs can be used transitively or intransitively with a different meaning (e.g. **break in, cut out, hold out, look out, look up, pick up, split up, turn in, wind up**):

- ☐ The engine **cut out** and the car stopped.   ☐ I **cut** *the picture* **out** of the magazine

C With many *transitive* two-word verbs, the object can come before or after the verb:

- ☐ I want to **try out** *the local food*. (or ...**try** *the local food* **out**.)

However, if the object is a pronoun it must come between the verb and the adverb:

- ☐ I won't be able to go to the party. You'll have to **count** *me* **out**. (*not* ...count out me.)

and we prefer to put the object after the adverb when the object is long. Compare:

- ☐ I had to **clean** *the kitchen* **up**. (or ...**clean up** *the kitchen*.) *and*
- ☐ I had to **clean up** *the mess in the kitchen*. (*rather than* ...clean the mess in the kitchen up.)

Other verbs like this include **bring about, drink up, gather up, get down, leave out, make up, mess up, shoot down, sort out, throw away, try out, use up**.

D With some transitive two-word verbs, the object comes between the verb and the adverb:

- ☐ I just couldn't **tell** *the twins* **apart**. (*not* ...tell apart the twins)

Other verbs like this include **catch out, hear out, order about, pull to, push to, shut up, stand up**.

E With some transitive two-word verbs, the object follows the preposition:

- ☐ She **takes after** *her mother*.

Other verbs like this include **account for, act on, approve of, call on, check into, flick through, look after, provide for, result from, run into, take against**.

F With most three-word verbs, the object goes after the preposition:

- ☐ The government is to **cut back on** *spending on the armed forces*.
- ☐ He really **looks up to** *his older brother*.

Other verbs like this include **come in for, come up against, look down on, put up with**.

However, a few three-word verbs usually have the object immediately after the verb. A second noun or noun phrase goes after the preposition:

- ☐ She tried to **talk** *me* **out of** *the plan*. (= persuaded me not to do it)

Other verbs like this include **do out of, help on with, let in on, put down as, put up to, take up on**.

94.1   If possible or necessary, add an appropriate noun or pronoun in the space. (B)

1 The same problem kept cropping .... up, even though I thought I'd fixed it.
2 I'm not sure how you spell it. I'll look .... up in the dictionary.
3 I'm busy at the moment, but I can help .... out this evening.
4 If you tidy .... away, I'll do the cleaning.
5 The deal fell .... through because we couldn't agree a price.

94.2   Show where the word or phrase in brackets should go in each sentence with a ✓. If it is possible to put it in more than one place, mark these two possibilities. (C)

1 The house is really untidy, but I haven't got time to sort .... out .... now. (*it*)
2 We've introduced a training scheme to bring .... about .... (*some improvement*)
3 The strike by airline pilots messed .... up .... (*the holiday I'd spent months planning*)
4 I decided to try .... out .... for a couple of months. (*the diet*)
5 I used .... up .... to buy the car. (*all my savings*)
6 'I must get my shoes repaired again.' 'But they're so old – why don't you just throw .... away .... ? (*them*)

94.3   Choose a two-word verb from (i) and a noun phrase from (ii) to complete each sentence. If two word orders are possible, give them both. (C & D)

(i)

get down	leave out	make up
~~push to~~	hear out	shut up

(ii)

the general ideas	me	my mind
her name	the thing	~~the window~~

1 It's freezing in here. <u>Can you push the window to?</u>
2 When she filled the form in she ...., so they sent it back to her.
3 The alarm started when I opened the car door, and now I can't ....
4 There were so many desserts on the menu, I couldn't ....
5 I ...., but the lecturer spoke so quickly I couldn't follow the details.
6 I know you suspect me of cheating, but you've got to give me a chance to explain myself. At least .... before making up your mind.

94.4   If necessary, correct the word order or give a more likely word order in these sentences. If they are already correct, write ✓. (D, E & F)

1 He was always ordering about everyone, getting them to do his work for him.
2 It is assumed that parents will provide their children for until they are 18.
3 She wouldn't let in me on the secret, however hard I tried to persuade her.
4 The snow has been so heavy that the police have called motorists on to avoid unnecessary journeys.
5 I checked into the hotel at about 4.00.
6 I took up Keith on his offer and stayed in his flat while I was in London.
7 The government has come in for a lot of criticism over its decision to increase spending on arms.
8 My parents didn't approve of our engagement.
9 I had always looked Mr Brooks up to, so I was shocked to discover what he had done.

There is, there was, etc.

A

When we introduce a new person or thing into what we are saying – to say that this person or thing exists, happens, or is to be found in a particular place – we can use a sentence beginning **There + be**. In these cases, **there** is not stressed:

- ☐ **There was** a loud bang from upstairs. (*not* A loud bang was from upstairs.)
- ☐ **There's** nothing to eat. (*not* Nothing is to eat.)

We invert this pattern in questions to ask about the existence etc. of people and things:

- ☐ **Is there** anybody in here?

We can also use **there** with auxiliary and modal verbs with **be** (e.g. **has been, can be**):

- ☐ **There** *must be* some way of contacting her.

with verbs and **to be** (e.g. **used to be, is supposed to be, tends to be, appears to be, seems to be**):

- ☐ **There** *appears to be* a major disagreement between the two presidents.

and some other verbs that indicate existence (e.g. **arise, emerge, exist, remain**):

- ☐ During the 1990s **there** *arose* a demand for organic food.

Because we use **there** in this way to *introduce* topics, the noun after **there + be** often has an indefinite or non-specific meaning. So we often use **a/an**, **zero article**, **any(one)** (+ noun), or **some(thing)**, **no(body)**, etc. rather than **the, this, my, your** (+ noun), or a **name**, which give the noun a more definite or specific meaning. Compare:

- ☐ **There's** *nobody* here.   ☐ **There was** *something* strange about her.   *and*
- ☐ *The cat* was in the kitchen. (*more usual than* There was the cat in the kitchen.; *but compare* **There was** *a cat* in the kitchen.)
- ☐ *Sam* is waiting for me outside. (*more usual than* There is Sam waiting for me outside.)

When we use **there + be + the**, this is often done to show a change of topic. Choosing **the, that,** etc. + **noun** indicates that we think the topic is already known to the listener or reader:

- ☐ …And then **there is the** question of who is going to pay.

B

If the noun after **be** is singular or uncountable, the verb is singular; if the noun is plural, the verb is plural:

- ☐ **There is** a very good *reason* for my decision.
- ☐ **There were** too many *people* trying to get into the football stadium.

However, in informal speech we sometimes use **there's** before a plural noun:

- ☐ 'Anything to eat?' 'Well, **there's** *some* apples on the table.'

If the noun phrase consists of two or more nouns in a list, we use a singular verb if the first noun is singular or uncountable, and a plural verb if the first noun is plural:

- ☐ When I opened the fridge **there was** only *a bottle of milk*, some eggs, and butter.
- ☐ When I opened the fridge **there were** only *some eggs*, a bottle of milk, and butter.

C

There + be is also used with nouns followed by a *that-, wh-, to-infinitive* or *-ing* clause:

- ☐ **Is there** *a chance* (*that*) Kim could arrive this afternoon?
- ☐ **There is** *no reason* (*why*) I can't see you tomorrow.
- ☐ **There is** *a small stream which/that* runs at the bottom of the garden.
- ☐ **There was** *an attempt to resolve* the dispute at the factory.
- ☐ **There was** *a taxi waiting* outside the hotel.

We don't usually leave out a relative pronoun when it is a *subject* of the following finite verb (e.g. There is a small stream which/that runs…) except in very informal speech (e.g. There was a man (who) phoned about half eleven.), but we can leave out a relative pronoun when it is the *object* of the following finite verb (e.g. There is a small stream (that) the children play in.).

D

In formal English we can use a clause with **there being** to introduce a reason for something:

- ☐ **There being** no evidence against him, he was released. (= Because there was no evidence…)
- ☐ **There being** no reports of adverse reactions, the drug is to be sold more widely.

95.1 Rewrite these sentences using **there** *only* if the answer is likely. Consider why some answers are not likely. (A)

1 Coffee was spilt on the table. _There was coffee spilt on the table._
2 Your dinner is in the oven.
3 Is something bothering you?
4 A barrier was across the road.
5 The doctor is free to see you now.
6 My son is at university.
7 No petrol was available anywhere in the city.
8 Can anyone help me?
9 You can follow some general rules.

95.2 The sentences in this exercise are all taken from written English. Which is correct or more likely in the space – **is** or **are**? (B)

1 There .... two pubs and a church on the village green.
2 There .... other possible locations for the car park, but the area near the station is preferred.
3 There .... no direct rail link between the cities.
4 There .... further rain and strong winds forecast for the next three days.
5 There .... chocolate bars, crisps, and a bottle of lemonade in the bag if you get hungry.
6 There .... substantial evidence to suggest that the Robinsons lied to the police.
7 There .... no easy answers to the problem of global warming.
8 There .... a shower, television, and two single beds in each room.

95.3 Match the sentence halves. Join them with an appropriate relative pronoun (**that**, **which**, or **who**). Write the relative pronoun in brackets if it can be left out. (C & Unit 53)

1 There were a lot of people at the party   a   an election will be held next month.
2 There's a cake in the kitchen   b   are harder working than Julie.
3 There was never any doubt   c   I've made especially for your birthday.
4 There have been suggestions   d   I could do to prevent him falling.
5 There aren't many people alive today   e   ~~hadn't been invited.~~
6 There are still some old houses in the village   f   remember the First World War.
7 There was absolutely nothing   g   don't have electricity.
8 There are few people in the company   h   Thomas would get the job.

1 + e _There were a lot of people at the party who/that hadn't been invited._

95.4 Write new sentences with similar meanings beginning **There being....** (D)

1 As there was no food in the house, they went to a local restaurant.
There being no food in the house, they went to a local restaurant.

2 There was no further business, so the meeting closed at 12.30.

....

3 The patients were sent home because there was no doctor available.

....

4 Because the facilities were inadequate at the hotel, the conference was relocated to a nearby university.

....

A

We can use an introductory **it** at the beginning of a sentence –

☆ to place long or grammatically complex sentence elements at the end (the usual place for them in English). Compare:

    □ *To drive without a licence* is illegal. *and*   □ **It is illegal** to drive without a licence.

☆ to focus attention on a sentence element by placing this element at the end (the usual place for new or important information in English). Compare:

    □ *That she wasn't hurt* is a miracle. *and*   □ **It's a miracle** *that she wasn't hurt.*

Introductory **it** is commonly used when the subject is a *to*-infinitive or *that*-clause (as in the examples above), and also when the subject is a *wh-* or *-ing* clause (see also Unit 25):

    □ **It is clear** *why* Don decided to leave Spain.   □ **It is useless** *asking* Sue to help.

B

We often use introductory **it** with **be + adjective/noun** (as in the examples above), but other patterns with an introductory **it** are possible. Here are some common examples –

☆ **it + verb + to-infinitive clause**

    □ 'I've got a terrible headache.' '**It helps** *to lie down.*'

    □ If you want someone to help you, **it doesn't do** *to annoy* them just before you ask. ('(not) do' = (not) advisable, acceptable or enough)

Other verbs used in this pattern are **hurt** and **pay** (= give an advantage or benefit).

☆ **it + verb + object + to-infinitive clause**

    □ **It shocked** *him to see her* looking so ill.   □ **It annoys** *me to hear* James swear like that.

    □ **It costs** *a fortune to go* to the opera.   □ **It means** *a lot to get* a place at university.

Most of the verbs used in this pattern are to do with feelings, and include:

> **amaze, annoy, astonish, concern, frighten, hurt, scare, shock, surprise, upset, worry.**

After these verbs the object usually refers to a person.

We can also use **it + take + object + to-infinitive clause** when we say what is or was needed in a particular activity; for example, the time, resources or characteristics needed. Compare:

    □ **It took** (them) a week *to mend* our roof. *and*   □ To mend our roof took (them) a week.

    □ **It takes** a lot of effort *to play* the flute. *and*   □ To play the flute takes a lot of effort.

☆ **it + verb + that-clause**

    □ **It seems** *that* she has lost her memory. (*not* That she has lost her memory seems.)

    □ During the trial **it emerged** *that* Jacks had been convicted of burglary before. (*not* ...that Jacks had been convicted of burglary before emerged.)

Other verbs used in this pattern include **appear, come about, follow, happen, transpire**. Note that alternatives with the *that*-clause in initial position are not possible.

☆ **it + verb + object + that-clause**

    □ **It** suddenly **hit** *me that* Jane wanted to borrow money. (*less likely is* ...that Jane wanted to borrow money suddenly hit me.)

    □ When Bond saw Vanya taking photographs of the plane, **it dawned on** *him that* she was a spy. (*less likely is*...that she was a spy dawned on him.)

The object usually refers to a person. Other verbs used in this pattern include those in the box above and also **strike** (= occur to) and **turn out**.

C

We don't usually use an **it...** pattern as an alternative to a **noun** as subject:

    □ **Their success** was unexpected. (*not* It was unexpected their success.)

However, in informal contexts, particularly in speech, this is quite common in order to give special emphasis to the information immediately following **it...**:

    □ **It tastes really good,** this new ice cream.

and also to place a longer noun phrase at the end in order to focus attention on it:

    □ **It's ridiculous,** all the bureaucracy involved in running a school these days.

96.1 Rewrite these sentences beginning It... . Rewrite them only if the It... sentence would be appropriate in written English; otherwise write ✗ and consider why an It... sentence would be inappropriate. (A & C)

1 That we continue to monitor the situation is important.
   It is important that we continue to monitor the situation.

2 How he stared straight at me was unsettling.
3 Andrew's excellent exam result was surprising.
4 To be a qualified driver is an advantage in the job.
5 Her proposal is quite radical.
6 To put carpet on walls is highly unusual.
7 John's new car is a Ferrari.
8 Finding a good plumber is hard these days.

96.2 Complete the sentences using it... followed by a verb from (i) and an expanded form of the notes in (ii). Include an appropriate object where necessary. (B)

(i)

~~appear~~	astonish
not bother	concern
hurt	not do
pay	strike
upset	scare

(ii)

pedal/ bicycle	~~seriously injured/ back~~
see/ carrying knives	plan your journey ahead
criticise/ too much	hadn't even told/ when/ going away
everyone/ see in	discover/ also/ successful novelist
he/ jealous	hear/ offended

1 When Kate fell heavily and lay completely still,
   it appeared that she had seriously injured her back.

2 I knew that Rachel was a journalist for the local paper, but...
3 Since I broke my ankle last year,...
4 I told Peter that I had invited James, too. When he became so angry...
5 My comment about Don's baldness was only meant as a joke and...
6 There were no curtains in his house, but...
7 I didn't mind Amy not asking me to go on holiday with her, but...
8 Children need a lot of praise and...
9 The boys walked towards me in a threatening way, and...
10 You can save money by booking tickets in advance, so...

96.3 What personal or physical characteristics are needed to...? (Use It takes... in your answers.) (B)

1 play a musical instrument well
   It takes a lot of determination to play a musical instrument well.

2 build your own house

3 make a speech in front of a group of strangers

4 explain the rules of cricket to someone who doesn't know the game

Now suggest completions for these sentences.

5 It takes bravery...
6 It takes a lot of organisation to...
7 It takes a great deal of time...

A We can use a pattern with **it...** as the object of a verb where it refers forward to a clause. It can sometimes be followed directly by a *that-*, *if-* or *when-*clause after **can't bear, hate, like, love, resent** and **can't stand**, and by an *if-* or *when-*clause after **dislike, enjoy, prefer** and **understand**:

- ☐ I *hate* it *that* you can swim so well and I can't. (*not* I hate that you can swim...)
- ☐ We always *enjoy* it when they stay with us. (*not* We always enjoy when they...)

Some verbs, including **accept, admit, deny, guarantee,** and **mention,** can be followed by **it** and a *that-*clause, particularly in spoken English, or directly by a *that-*clause without **it**:

- ☐ You've just got to **accept** (**it**) *that* Jim's gone and won't be coming back.

Notice that many other verbs that can be followed by a *that-*clause or *wh-*clause are not used with **it...** in this way, including **argue, discover, emphasise, notice, predict, remember**:

- ☐ I can't **remember** *when* I last saw her. (*not* ...remember it when...)

B With other verbs used to indicate how we see a particular event or situation, **it** is followed first by an adjective or noun phrase and then a *that-*clause, *to-*infinitive clause, or clause beginning **when**. Verbs commonly used in this way include **believe, consider, feel, find** (= discover something from experience), **think**:

- ☐ Officials have said they **believe it unlikely** *that* any lasting damage to the environment has been done. (*or* ...they **believe it is unlikely** *that...*; *not* ...they believe unlikely that...)
- ☐ I **thought it a waste of money** *to throw* away so much food. (*or* I **thought it was a waste of money** *to...*; *not* I thought a waste of money to throw away...)

When we use **leave** and **owe** (= have a responsibility to) with **it...** we can use **to somebody + to-infinitive** after **it**:

- ☐ Don't bother to arrange anything. Just **leave it to me to sort out.**
- ☐ She **owed it to her parents to do** well at college.

C With the verbs **accept, regard, see, take** (= interpret something in a particular way), or **view** we use **it + as + noun** (or **adjective**) + clause:

- ☐ We **see it as an insult** *to have received no reply to our letter.*
- ☐ I **take it as encouraging** *when students attend all my lectures.*

D **It is/was no...** vs **There is/was no...**
Here are some common expressions including **It is/was no...** and **There is/was no...**:

- ☐ **It's no secret** that the President wants to have a second term of office.
- ☐ Following the popularity of his first two films, **it's no surprise** that his latest production has been successful.
- ☐ **It's no use** telling me now. I needed to know a week ago.
- ☐ **It's no good** getting angry. That won't help solve the problem.
- ☐ **It's no coincidence** (*or* **accident**) that they left the party at the same time.
- ☐ **It's no longer** necessary to have a visa to visit the country.

- ☐ **There's no denying** that he's intelligent.
- ☐ I'm afraid **there's no alternative** (*or* **choice**) but to ask her to leave.
- ☐ **There's no hope** of getting more money.
- ☐ **There's no need** to explain how it works; I'll read the instruction book.
- ☐ **There's no point** in buying an expensive computer unless you plan to use it a lot.
- ☐ **There's no question** of agreeing to his demands.
- ☐ **There's no reason** to be pessimistic.
- ☐ **There's no chance** of finding a cure if we don't fund more research.

The sentences with **It is/was no...** have alternatives in which the *that-*, *-ing* or *to-*infinitive clause is placed at the front, but the sentences with **There is/was no...** do not. Compare:

- ☐ **It's no secret** that he wants a new job. (*or* That he wants a new job is no secret.) *and*
- ☐ **There's no denying** that he's a very good footballer. (*but not* That he's a very good footballer is no denying.)

97.1 Complete these sentences with a verb in an appropriate form. If necessary, add **it**. Use each verb once only. (A & B)

> ~~can't bear~~   consider   discover   enjoy   find
> leave   owe   predict   prefer   remember

1 She ....*can't bear it*.... when people criticise her work, and she gets very upset.
2 I .... hard to understand why the film was made in black and white and not colour.
3 If you .... that you can't get to the meeting on the 16th I'll try to rearrange it.
4 We .... to our supporters to play to the best of our ability in the match.
5 I .... that the camera was on the table when I left the house.
6 I really .... when the weather's hot like this. I'd hate to live in a cold climate.
7 I can't stop you dismantling your motorbike in the kitchen, but I'd .... if you didn't.
8 I think we should .... to the children to do the washing up.
9 I .... that Jean will withdraw from the course within a month.
10 I .... a privilege to have known Roy Jennings.

97.2 John Timms has recently been appointed as managing director of the company Rexco. Here are some notes he made for his first speech to the board of directors. In the speech he expanded the notes beginning **I + (verb) + it as...**, using the verb in brackets. Write what he said. (C)

1   great honour – asked to become – managing director – Rexco   (*take*)

     I take it as a great honour to be asked to become managing director of Rexco.

2   part of my role – make Rexco household name – next 5 years   (*see*)

3   necessary evil – some people – may redundant – in next year   (*accept*)

4   important for relations with workforce – make available information – salaries of managers   (*view*)

5   unacceptable – modern company – exclude workforce – major decision-making   (*regard*)

6   something positive – employees make suggestions – how management be improved   (*regard*)

7   vital – future of company – expand into Asian market   (*see*)

8   fundamental principle of company – suppliers of raw materials – given fair price for products   (*take*)

97.3 Complete the sentences with an appropriate **it...** or **there...** phrase from **D** opposite. Suggest alternatives where possible.

1 ...*It's no coincidence*... that Karlsbad has won the ice hockey tournament for the last three years. It is a very rich club and its training facilities are excellent.
2 My contact lens must have fallen out in the snow, so .... of finding it.
3 .... that Karen and Mark have split up. Everyone in the office knows.
4 .... getting depressed about your exam results. You just need to work harder.
5 Your broken arm will take some time to mend, but .... why you shouldn't be playing tennis again by the summer.
6 As the car ferry isn't running because of the high winds, ... but to drive 100 kilometres around the lake.
7 .... possible to buy tickets on the train. You have to get them at the station.
8 Bungee jumping might be dangerous, but .... that it's very exciting.

Focusing: it-clauses and what-clauses

Focusing with it-clauses

A

We can use an **it-clause** with **be** to focus attention on the information that immediately follows *it* + (*be*). A sentence in which emphasis is given using this pattern is sometimes called a *cleft sentence*. The clause after the **it-clause** (usually a *that*-clause) contains information that is already known or considered to be less important:

- □ 'Helen bought the car from Tom.' 'No, **it was Tom** *that* bought the car from Helen.'
- □ He already plays for the national side, and **it was only last year** *that* he turned professional.
- □ I don't mind her criticising me, but **it's how she does it** *that* I object to.
- □ **It was to show her how much I cared for her** *that* I bought her the necklace.

We sometimes use **which** or **who** instead of **that**; **when** and **where** can also be used, but usually only in informal English; and note that **how** or **why** can't replace **that**:

- □ Karl was always there to help her, and **it was to him** *that/who* she now turned for support.
- □ 'Carol's seriously ill in hospital.' 'But **it was only last Sunday** *when/that* I was playing tennis with her.'
- □ **It was in Bristol** *where/that* the film was made.
- □ 'Was it by cutting staff that he managed to save the firm?' 'No, **it was by improving distribution** *that* he made it profitable.' (*not* ...how he made it profitable.)

Focusing with what-clauses

B

If we want to focus particular attention on certain information in a sentence, we sometimes use a **what-clause** followed by **be**. Sentences with this pattern are another form of *cleft sentence*. This pattern is particularly common in conversation. The information we want to focus attention on is outside the **what-clause**. Compare:

- □ We gave them some home-made cake. *and*
- □ **What we gave them** *was* some home-made cake.

We often do this if we want to introduce a new topic; to give a reason, instruction or explanation; or to correct something that has been said or done. In the following examples, the information in focus is in italics:

- □ **What I'd like you to work on is** *exercise two on page 38.*
- □ Tim arrived two hours late: **what had happened was** that *his bicycle chain had broken.*
- □ 'We've only got this small bookcase – will that do?' 'No, **what I was looking for was** something *much bigger and stronger.*'

We can often put the **what-clause** either at the beginning or the end of the sentence:

- □ **What upset me most** *was* his rudeness.   *or*   His rudeness *was* **what upset me most**.

To focus attention on an *action* performed by someone, we use a sentence with **what + subject + do + be + to-infinitive** clause. We can't use an *it*-clause to do this (see A):

- □ Dave lost his job and was short of money, so **what he did was (to) sell** his flat and move in with his brother. (*not* ...so it was (to) sell his flat that he did.)

Notice that the 'to' in the infinitive can be omitted.

C

The pattern in **B** is only usually used with **what-clauses**. Instead of placing other *wh*-clauses (beginning **how, when, where, who, why**) at the beginning of the sentence we prefer to use a noun which has a meaning related to the *wh*-word (e.g. **reason** rather than **why; place** rather than **where**) followed by a *that*- or *wh*-clause. Here are some examples:

- □ **The only reason (why/that)** I left the party early was that I was feeling unwell. (*rather than* Why I left the party early was...)
- □ **The place (where/that)** you should play football is the playground, not the classroom. (*rather than* Where you should play football is...)
- □ **Somebody (who/that)** I enjoy reading is Peter Carey. (*not* Who I enjoy reading is...)
- □ **The time (when/that)** I work best is early morning. (*rather than* When I work best is...)

98.1 Rewrite the sentences to focus attention on the underlined information. Start with it + be and use an appropriate **wh**-word or **that**. (A)

1 Mark's known for ages that his parents are coming to stay with us this weekend, but he <u>only told me yesterday</u>. *Mark's known for ages that his parents are coming to stay with us this weekend, but...* <u>it was only yesterday that/when he told me.</u>

2 Caroline has been feeling a bit depressed for some time, so I booked a holiday in Amsterdam <u>to cheer her up</u>. *Caroline has been feeling a bit depressed for some time, so...*

3 It's not that I don't want to have dinner with you tonight; I can't come <u>because I've got so much work to do</u>. *It's not that I don't want to have dinner with you tonight; ...*

4 I had my wallet when I went into the sports hall, so I lost it <u>somewhere in there</u>. *I had my wallet when I went into the sports hall, so...*

5 She doesn't find learning languages very easy, and she improved her Spanish <u>only by studying very hard</u>. *She doesn't find learning languages very easy, and...*

6 I have had great help from my parents and two brothers in doing my research, and I dedicate this thesis <u>to my family</u>. *I have had great help from my parents and two brothers in doing my research, and...*

98.2 Give responses beginning **No, what...**, correcting what was said in the question, as in 1. Use the notes in brackets to help. (B)

1 'Did you say that Bernard was going to live in Austria?' (*holiday/ Austria*)
   'No, what I said was that he was going on holiday to Austria.'

2 'Do you hope to sell your Picasso paintings?' (*be put into/ public art gallery*)

3 'Did it annoy you that Clare came so late?' (*not apologise*)

4 'Did you mean to give Erica your bike?' (*could borrow it/ until needed again*)

Now give similar responses which focus on the action, as in 5.

5 'Did you watch the football on TV last night?' (*get brother/ video it/ watch tonight*)
   'No, what I did was (to) get my brother to video it and I'll watch it tonight.'

6 'This steak tastes delicious. Did you fry it?' (*put oil and soy sauce on/ grill*)

7 'Did you buy Sue the coat she wanted?' (*give/ money towards it*)

8 'Did you fly from Sydney to Brisbane.' (*hire a car/ drive all the way*)

98.3 Write a sentence using one of the phrases in **C** opposite and the information in brackets. You need to put the information in the right order and add an appropriate form of **be**. (C)

1 'I suppose Paul got the job because of his qualifications.' (*uncle owns company*)
   'Well, actually, I think... <u>the reason why/that Paul got the job was that his uncle owns the company.</u>'

2 'Do you know anyone who could mend my computer?' (*might be able/ help/ Saleh*)
   I don't know if he's free, but...

3 'You grew up in this village, didn't you?' (*between this village and next*)
   In fact...

4 'In what period of your life do you think you were happiest?' (*lived Australia*)
   I suppose...

Unit 99   Inversion (1)

A

In statements it is usual for the verb to follow the subject, but sometimes this word order is reversed. We can refer to this as *inversion*. There are two main types of inversion: when the verb comes before the subject (inversion is often optional), and when the auxiliary comes before the subject and the rest of the verb phrase follows the subject (inversion is usually necessary):

- *Her father* **stood** in the doorway. → In the doorway **stood** *her father*. (or ... her father stood.)
- *He* **had** rarely **seen** such a sunset. → Rarely **had** *he* **seen** such a sunset. (*not* Rarely he had seen...)

Inversion brings about *fronting*, the re-ordering of information in a sentence to give emphasis in a particular place. Often this causes an element to be postponed until later in the sentence, focusing attention on it.

B

In conversation we use **Here comes + noun** and **There goes + noun**, with inversion of verb and subject, to talk about things and people moving towards or away from the speaker:

- **Here comes** the bus.
- **There goes** Nigel Slater, the footballer.

Here comes... is also used to say that something is going to happen soon, and **There goes...** is used to talk about things (particularly money) being lost and to say that something (such as a phone or door bell) is ringing:

- **Here comes** lunch.
- My bike's been stolen! **There goes** £100!
- **There goes** the phone. Can you answer it?

We also put the verb before the subject when we use adverbs expressing direction of movement, such as **along, away, back, down, in, off, out, up** with verbs such as **come, fly, go**. This pattern is found particularly in narrative, to mark a change in events:

- The door opened and **in came** the doctor. (*less formally* ... and the doctor came in.)
- As soon as I let go of the string, **up went the balloon**, high into the sky. (*less formally* ...the balloon went up...)
- Just when I thought I'd have to walk home, **along came Miguel** and he gave me a lift. (*less formally* ... Miguel came along and gave me...)

For more on inversion after adverbs of place and direction, see Unit 76A.

C

We can use clauses with inversion instead of certain kinds of *if*-clause (see Unit 83). Compare:

- It would be a serious setback, **if** *the talks* **were to fail**.	- It would be a serious setback, **were** *the talks* **to fail**.
- **If** *you* **should need** more information, please telephone our main office.	- **Should** *you* **need** more information, please telephone our main office.
- **If** *Alex* **had asked**, I would have been able to help.	- **Had** *Alex* **asked**, I would have been able to help.

The sentences with inversion are rather more formal than those with 'if'. Notice that in negative clauses with inversion, we don't use contracted forms:

- **Had** *the plane* **not been diverted**, they would have arrived early. (*not* Hadn't the plane...)

D

In formal written language we commonly use inversion after **as** and **than** in comparisons:

- The cake was excellent, **as** *was* **the coffee**. (*or* ...as the coffee was.)
- I believed, **as** *did* **my colleagues**, that the plan would work. (*or* ...as my colleagues did...)
- Research shows that parents watch more television **than** *do* **their children**. (*or* ...than their children do.)

Notice that we don't invert subject and verb after **as** or **than** when the subject is a pronoun:

- We now know a lot more about the Universe **than** *we* **did** ten years ago. (*not* ...than did we ten years ago.)

Exercises

99.1 Complete the sentences with an appropriate adverb and a form of either **come** or **go**. (B)

1 We'd just got to the top of the hill when ....._down came_..... the rain and we got thoroughly soaked.
2 Just when you've bought a computer that you think will last a lifetime, ... some new software that needs an even bigger hard disk.
3 Whenever I ask the class a question, ... their hands and they sit patiently until I choose one of them to answer.
4 I asked Dave to get three kilos of potatoes from the supermarket and he only bought one, so .... he .... to get some more.
5 After I'd been waiting for an hour, the door opened and .... the nurse, who said the dentist would be able to see me now.
6 We'd given up hope of getting the cat out of the tree, when .... a man with a ladder.
7 As soon as I'd given Jo some pocket money, ... she .... to buy sweets from the shop.

99.2 Match the most likely sentence halves and then make new sentences beginning **Were...**, **Should...**, or **Had...** (C)

1 If McGrath had not resigned as party leader, ...
2 If you do not wish to receive further information about our products, ...
3 If the plane were ever to be built, ...
4 If United win again today, ...
5 If I were to be asked to take the job, ...
6 If a car had been coming in the other direction, ...
7 If there had been a referendum on the issue, ...
8 If you are not able to afford the Rombus 2000, ...
9 If Charles Dickens were alive today, ...

a it would cut the journey time from New York to Tokyo by 4 hours.
b there are less expensive models in the range.
c ~~he would have been sacked.~~
d I would have no hesitation in accepting.
e he would be writing novels about the homeless in London.
f it is unlikely that the country would have supported the government.
g it will be their tenth consecutive victory.
h put a tick in the box.
i I might have been seriously injured.

1 + c .._Had McGrath not resigned as party leader, he would have been sacked._..

99.3 Write new sentences using **as** or **than** + **be** or **do**. (D)

1 Compared with their counterparts 20 years ago, the highly educated now receive vastly higher salaries.
   The highly educated now receive vastly higher salaries than did their counterparts 20 years ago.
2 I was opposed to the new road being built. Everyone else in the village was opposed to it, too.
   I was opposed...
3 Karen went to Oxford University. Her mother and sister went there, too.
   Karen went...
4 Compared with people in developed nations, people in poorer countries consume a far smaller proportion of the earth's resources.
   People in poorer countries...
5 Compared to 5 years ago, he is a much better teacher.
   _He is..._
6 Don is a keen golfer. His wife is a keen golfer, too.
   Don is...

A — Inversion after negative adverbials

In formal and literary language in particular, we use negative adverbials at the beginning of a clause. The subject and first auxiliary are inverted, and **do** is used with a simple tense verb after –

☆ the time adverbials **never (before), rarely, seldom; barely/hardly/scarcely...when/before; no sooner...than:**

  □ **Seldom do** *we* **have** goods returned to us because they are faulty.
  □ **Hardly had** *everybody* **taken** their seats when Dr Smith began his lecture.

☆ **only + a time expression**, as in **only after, only later, only if, only once, only then, only when:**

  □ She bought a newspaper and some sweets at the shop on the corner. **Only later did** *she* **realise** that she'd been given the wrong change.
  □ **Only once did** *I* **go** to the opera the whole time I was in Italy.
  □ **Only when she apologises will** *I* **speak** to her again.

☆ **only + other prepositional phrases** beginning **only by..., only in..., only with...,** etc.:

  □ **Only by chance had** *Jameson* **discovered** where the birds were nesting.
  □ Mary had to work in the evenings and at weekends. **Only in this way was** *she* **able to complete** the report by the deadline.

☆ expressions such as **at no time, in no way, on no account, under/in no circumstances:**

  □ **At no time did** *they* actually **break** the rules of the game.
  □ **Under no circumstances are** *passengers* **permitted** to open the doors themselves.

☆ expressions with **not...,** such as **not only, not until, not since, not for one moment** and also **not a + noun:**

  □ **Not until August did** *the government* **order** an inquiry into the accident.
  □ **Not a word had** *she* **written** since the exam had started.

☆ **little** with a negative meaning:

  □ **Little do** *they* **know** how lucky they are to live in such a wonderful house. (= 'they don't know' or 'they don't know sufficiently')
  □ **Little did** *I* **realise** that one day Michael would become famous. (= 'I didn't realise' or 'I didn't realise sufficiently')

Notice that inversion can occur after a clause beginning **only after/if/when** or **not until:**

  □ **Only when the famine gets worse will** *world governments* **begin** to act.
  □ **Not until the train pulled into Euston Station did** *Jim* **find** that his coat had gone.

B — Inversion after so + adjective... that; such + be...that; neither.../nor...

We can use **so + adjective** at the beginning of a clause to give special emphasis to the adjective. When we do this, the subject and first auxiliary are inverted, and **do** is used with a simple tense verb. Compare:

  □ Her business was so successful that Marie was able to retire at the age of 50. *and*
  □ **So successful** *was* **her business**, that Marie was able to retire at the age of 50.
  □ The weather conditions became so dangerous that all mountain roads were closed. *and*
  □ **So dangerous** *did* **weather conditions** *become*, that all mountain roads were closed.

We can use **such + be** at the beginning of a clause to emphasise the extent or degree of something. Compare:

  □ **Such** *is* **the popularity** of the play that the theatre is likely to be full every night. *and*
  □ The play is so popular that the theatre is likely to be full every night.

We use inversion after **neither** and **nor** when these words begin a clause to introduce a negative addition to a previous negative clause or sentence:

  □ For some time after the explosion Jack couldn't hear, and **neither** *could* he *see*.
  □ The council never wanted the new supermarket to be built, **nor** *did* local residents.

Notice that we also use inversion in **Neither/Nor do I, Neither/Nor does Kate** (etc.) and in **So do I, So does Becky** (etc.).

100.1 Write new sentences with a similar meaning beginning with one of these words and phrases. (A)

> only if   barely   only with   ~~rarely~~   at no time   little

1 A new film has not often before produced such positive reviews.
   Rarely has a new film produced such positive reviews.
2 The public was never in any danger.
3 He only felt entirely relaxed with close friends and family.
4 The match won't be cancelled unless the pitch is frozen.
5 I didn't know then that Carmen and I would be married one day.
6 He had only just entered the water when it became clear he couldn't swim.

Now do the same using these words and phrases. (A)

> only once   only in   on no account   hardly   not only   not for one moment

7 You must not light the fire if you are alone in the house.
8 There was never any competitiveness between the three brothers.
9 I wasn't only wet through, I was freezing cold.
10 I had only ever climbed this high once before.
11 The audience had only just taken their seats when the conductor stepped on to the stage.
12 He has only been acknowledged to be a great author in the last few years.

100.2 Complete these sentences in any appropriate way. You can use the following words in your answers. (B)

> alike   boring   complicated   dominance   ~~interest~~   strength

1 Such _is the interest in Dr Lowe's talk_ that it will be held in a bigger lecture theatre.
2 Such .... that few buildings were left standing in the town.
3 Such .... that he hasn't lost a match for over three years.
4 So .... that even their parents couldn't tell them apart.
5 So .... that it even took a computer three days to solve it.
6 So .... that most of the students went to sleep.

100.3 Correct any mistakes you find in this newspaper item. (Units 99 & 100)

TOWN EVACUATED AS FOREST FIRES APPROACH

The people of Sawston were evacuated yesterday as forest fires headed towards the town. Such the heat was of the oncoming inferno that trees more than 100 metres ahead began to smoulder. Only once in recent years, during 1994, a town of this size has had to be evacuated because of forest fires. A fleet of coaches and lorries arrived in the town in the early morning. Into these vehicles the sick and elderly climbed, before they headed off to safety across the river. Residents with cars left by mid morning, as all non-essential police officers did.

Hardly the evacuation had been completed when the wind changed direction and it became clear that the fire would leave Sawston untouched. Soon after that were heard complaints from some residents. "At no time the fires posed a real threat," said one local man. "I didn't want to leave my home, and nor most of my neighbours did." So upset some elderly residents are that they are threatening to complain to their MP. But Chief Fire Officer Jones replied, "Hadn't we taken this action, lives would have been put at risk. Only when the fires have moved well away from the town residents will be allowed to return to their homes."

Grammar review

A   TENSES (→ Units 1–8)

Present continuous (→ Units 1, 2 & 8)

A1   □ 'Who *are you phoning*?' 'I*'m trying* to get through to Helen.'
        We use the present continuous to talk about particular events or activities that have
        begun but have not ended at the time of speaking. The event or activity is in progress
        at the present time, but not necessarily at the moment of speaking.

A2   □ She*'s doing* voluntary work with young children until she starts her university course.
        We use the present continuous to suggest that an event or activity is or may be
        temporary.

        (For the present continuous for the future, see B7 & Unit 10.)

Present simple (→ Units 1, 2 & 8)

A3   □ Trees *grow* more quickly in summer than in winter.
        We use the present simple with verbs describing states or situations that are always
        true or continue indefinitely.

A4   □ This cake *tastes* wonderful. Where did you buy it?
        We use the present simple with states or situations (thoughts, feelings) that exist at the
        present moment.

        Verbs generally used to talk about states include *agree, appreciate, attract, *desire,
        *doubt, expect, hate, hope, like, love, *prefer, *regret (*to do with emotions, attitudes,
        and preferences*); anticipate, assume, *believe, consider, expect, feel, find, imagine,
        *know, realise, think, understand (*mental states*); ache, hear, *notice, see, *smell,
        sound, *taste (*senses and perception*); *belong to, *consist of, *constitute, *contain,
        cost, *differ from, have, look, *mean, measure, *own, *possess, *resemble, *seem,
        weigh ('*being*', '*having*', etc.).

        The verbs marked * are rarely used with continuous tenses (but can be if we mean
        actions rather than states).

A5   □ *Do you go* to Turkey every year for your holidays?
        We use the present simple to talk about habits or regular events or actions.

        (For the present simple for the future, see B6 & Unit 10.)

Past simple (→ Units 3, 4, 5 & 8)

A6   □ Kathy *left* a few minutes ago.

A7   □ Jim *continued* the course even though it was proving very difficult.
        We use the past simple to refer to a completed action or event in the past or to talk
        about situations that existed over a period of time in the past, but not now. We can
        either say when something happened, using a time adverbial (e.g. *a few minutes ago*:
        A6), or assume that the listener or reader already knows when it happened or can
        understand this from the context (A7).

A8   □ I *saw* my grandparents every week as a child.
        We use the past simple to talk about repeated past actions.

        (For the past simple in conditionals, see M12 & M13 and Unit 83.)

Present perfect (→ Units 3, 6 & 8)

A9   □ We can't have a meeting, because so few people *have shown* any interest.

A10   □ My ceiling *has fallen* in and the kitchen is flooded. Come quickly!

A11   □ We *have belonged* to the tennis club since we moved here.

A12   □ Lee *has represented* his country on many occasions, and hopes to go on to compete in
        the next Olympics.
        We use the present perfect to talk about a past action, event or state, when there is
        some kind of connection between what happened in the past, and the present time.

Often we are interested in the way something that happened in the past affects or is relevant to the situation that exists now (A9). However, the connection with the present may also be that the action happened recently with a consequence for the present (A10), that it continues until the present time (A11), or that a repeated event in the past may (or may not) happen again (A12).

Past continuous (→ Units 4, 7 & 8)

A13 □ When he realised I *was looking* at him, he turned away.
We use the past continuous to talk about a situation (...I *was looking at him*...) that started before a particular point in the past (...*he turned away*) and was still in progress at that point.

Past perfect (→ Units 5, 7 & 8)

A14 □ When I went into the bathroom, I found that the bath *had overflowed*.
A15 □ By 10 o'clock most people *had gone* home.
We use the past perfect to talk about a past event that took place before another past event (A14), or before or up to a particular time in the past (A15).

(For the past perfect in conditionals, see M14 & Unit 83.)

Present perfect continuous (→ Units 6 & 8)

A16 □ Since the operation two months ago, Joe *has been learning* to walk again. He can already take one or two steps unaided.
A17 □ Your eyes are red – *have* you *been crying*?
We use the present perfect continuous to talk about an activity in progress in the past for a period until now, which is still in progress (A16) or has recently finished (A17).

Past perfect continuous (→ Units 7 & 8)

A18 □ When I saw the vase in the shop window, I knew it was exactly what I *had been looking* for.
We use the past perfect continuous to talk about a situation or activity that was in progress over a period up to a particular past point in time.

B THE FUTURE (→ Units 9–14)

Will + infinitive (→ Unit 9)

B1 □ It's late. I think I'*ll* go to bed now.
B2 □ I think you'*ll* enjoy the film.
We use **will** when we state a decision made at the moment of speaking (B1) and when we say that we think something is likely to happen in the future (B2).

B3 □ I'*ll* make one of my special desserts for dinner, if you like.
B4 □ I've asked her to join us this evening, but she *won't*.
We use **will** (or '**ll**) when we talk about *willingness* to do something in the future (e.g. in offers (B3), invitations, requests, and orders) and **will not** (or **won't**) when we talk about *unwillingness* to do something in the future (e.g. reluctance, refusal (B4)).

Be going to + infinitive (→ Unit 9)

B5 □ 'Has anybody offered to look after the children?' 'Jo'*s going to* do it.'
We use **be going to** when we state a decision made some time before we report it. **Going to** is often preferred in informal spoken English (where it is often pronounced /gənə/) and **will** is preferred in more formal contexts.

Present simple for the future (→ Unit 10)

B6 □ The next train to Newcastle *leaves* at 3.45. [*station announcement*]
We use the present simple to talk about future events that are part of some official arrangement such as a timetable or programme. A time expression is usually used with the present simple for the future (...*at 3.45*) unless the time referred to is already clear from the context.

Present continuous for the future (→ Unit 10)

B7   □ We're *having* a party next Saturday. Can you come?

We use the present continuous to talk about future activities and events that are intended or have already been arranged. Usually a personal pronoun is used (*We...*) and a future time is mentioned (*...next Saturday*) or already understood.

Future continuous (→ Unit 11)

B8   □ After the operation you *won't be doing* any sport for a while.

We use the future continuous to talk about an activity or event happening at a particular time or over a particular period in the future. We usually mention the future time (*After the operation...*).

C   MODALS & SEMI-MODALS (→ Units 15–20)

The modal verbs are: **will, would, can, could, may, might, shall, should, must**. Modal verbs have meanings relating to ideas such as possibility, likelihood, prediction, necessity, permission and obligation. They do not have *to*-infinitive, *-s*, *-ing* or past participle forms. They are often followed by the bare infinitive of another verb (e.g. *She might go*) but can also be used on their own (e.g. *Yes, I can*). They cannot be followed directly by a *to*-infinitive, an *-ing* form, a past participle, or another modal verb. In questions they come before the subject (e.g. *Could you help?*) and before *not* in negatives (e.g. *He won't* (= will not) *help*). The semi-modals are: **ought to, used to, need, dare, had better, have (got) to, be able to**. These have meanings like modal verbs but not the same formal features: for example, some can be marked for tense (e.g. *have/ had (got) to*); some have non-modal uses (e.g. *She needs a rest*).

Can, could and be able to (→ Unit 15)

C1   □ A polyglot is someone who *can* speak several different languages.

C2   □ Anita *could* speak three languages before she was six.

C3   □ Martha *couldn't* swim until she was ten.

When we say that someone or something has or doesn't have the ability to do something, we use **can('t)** (for the present; C1) or **could(n't)** (for the past; C2, C3).

C4   □ 'Why isn't Tim here yet?' 'It *could* be because his mother's ill again.'

We use **could**, not **can**, to say there is a possibility of something happening or being true.

C5   □ Despite yesterday's snowfalls, we *were able to* drive home in less than an hour.

We can use **be able to** instead of **can** or **could** to talk about ability. We prefer **be able to** when we talk about a specific achievement (particularly if it is difficult, requiring some effort; C5) rather than a general ability. Where there is a choice, in speech we generally prefer **can** or **could** rather than **be able to**.

C6   □ After the trees have been cut back, we *will be able to* see more of the garden from the sitting room.

We use **will be able to**, not **can**, to say that something is possible in the future on condition that something is done first.

C7   □ We *can/are allowed to* stay up late on Fridays and Saturdays because we don't have to go to school the next day.

We use **can** for the present or the future and **could** for the past to report permission. We can also use **be allowed to**.

Will, would and used to (→ Unit 16)

C8   □ *Will/Won't* you have another biscuit? ('Won't you...?' is a very polite and rather formal offer)

C9   □ 'John wants to borrow the car.' 'He *will not*.' (a firm refusal)

C10   □ You *will* now put your pens down and pay attention. (a firm instruction)

We use **will** and **will not** (**won't**) to talk about (un)willingness (see B3–4) and also to make offers (C8), requests, refusals (C9), and to give instructions (C10).

C11 □ You should apply for the job. You *would* have a good chance of getting it.
We can use **would** to make a prediction about an imaginary situation; that is, about something that may or may not happen (see also M13).

C12 □ *Would* you like me to get you some water?
We can use **Would you like...** when we make an offer, but not 'Will you like...'. In requests, too, we can say **I would like...**, but not 'I will like...'. We can use **should** (with **I** or **we**) instead of **would** in requests like this, but this is formal.

C13 □ We *would/used to* lend him money when he was unemployed.

C14 □ I *used to* live in a flat in Paris.
To talk about things that happened repeatedly in the past, but don't happen now, we can use **would** or **used to + infinitive** (C13). **Used to** is more common in informal English. We can use **used to** but not **would** to talk about permanent past states (C14). Notice how we normally make questions and negatives with **use to** in spoken English: '*Did* your children *use to* sleep well when they were babies?'; 'I *didn't use to* like visiting the dentist when I was young.' Many people avoid using **used to** in questions and negatives without **do** ('Used you to...?', 'I usedn't to...') and in question tags (..., usedn't you?) because it sounds very formal and old-fashioned.

may, might, can and could (→ Units 15 & 17)

C15 □ If the drought goes on much longer, there *may/might/could* be water rationing before the end of the month.

C16 □ Her parents *may/might/could have influenced* her decision to resign.
In affirmative sentences (that is, sentences which are not questions or negatives) we use **may**, **might**, or **could** with a similar meaning to say that there is a possibility of something happening or being true (C15). **Can** is not used in this way. We sometimes prefer **could** to show that we are giving an opinion about which we are unsure. We use **may/might/could + have + past participle** to say that it is possible that something happened in the past (C16).

C17 □ 'While we're in Leeds shall we go and see Mark?' 'But it's been nearly 20 years since we last saw him. He *may not/might not* remember us.'

C18 □ I think I saw her go out, so she *can't/couldn't* be at home.
In negative sentences, including sentences with words like **only**, **hardly**, or **never**, we use **may not** or **might not** to say it is possible that something is not true (C17), and **can't** or **couldn't** to say that it is not possible that something is true (C18).

C19 □ Coats *may* be left in the cloakroom.
May (not 'might') is used in formal contexts to say that something is allowed. **May not** is used to say that things are not allowed (e.g. Calculators *may not* be used in the examination.).

must and have (got) to (→ Unit 18)

C20 □ That's really good news. I *must* tell Steve straight away.

C21 □ 'Can we meet on Thursday morning?' 'Sorry, no. I *have to* go to the dentist at 11.00.'
When we say that it is necessary to do something, we use **must** or **have (got) to**. Sometimes it doesn't matter which we use, although **have got to** is less formal than either **must** or **have to** and is particularly common in spoken English. However, we use **must** when we want to indicate that the *speaker* decides that something is necessary (C20) and we use **have (got) to** to suggest that *someone else* or some outside circumstances or authority makes something necessary (C21).

C22 □ She was bruised quite badly in the accident. It *must* hurt a lot.
We normally use **must**, not **have (got) to**, when we conclude that something (has) happened or that something is true .

C23 □ 'I'm seeing Dr Evans next week.' 'That *can't* be right. He's on holiday then.'
When we give a negative conclusion we rarely use **must not** or **have (got) to**. Instead, we use **can't (cannot)** or **couldn't**.

C24 □ When I went to school I *had to* learn Latin.

To say that something was necessary in the past we use **had to**, not **must**.

need(n't), don't have to and mustn't (→ Units 18 & 19)

C25 □ He didn't cook the meal himself so you *needn't/don't have to* eat it all. He won't be offended.

C26 □ You *mustn't* put anything on the shelves until the glue has set hard.

We use **needn't** (or **don't need to**) or **don't have to** to say that something is not necessary (C25) and **mustn't** to say that something is not allowed (C26).

C27 □ I *didn't have to/didn't need to have* an interview because I'd worked there before.

C28 □ I *needn't have* cooked dinner. Just as it was ready, Chris and June phoned to say that they couldn't come to eat.

When we say that it was not necessary to do something in the past, and it wasn't done, we use **didn't need to** or **didn't have to** (C27). To show that we think something that *was* done was not in fact necessary we use **need not** (**needn't**) **have** (C28).

should, ought to and be supposed to (→ Unit 20)

C29 □ You'll catch cold if you go out like that. I think you *should/ought to* take a hat.

C30 □ I enjoyed her first novel, so the new one *should/ought to* be good.

We can often use **should** or **ought to** with little difference in meaning when we talk about obligation (e.g. in giving advice, making recommendations, or talking about a responsibility, (C29) and the probability of something happening or being true (C30).

C31 □ The work *was supposed to start/should have started/ought to have started* last week.

C32 □ Walking under a ladder *is supposed to* be unlucky.

(Be) supposed to can be used instead of **should/ought to** to express a less strong obligation than **should** (C31). It is also used to report what many people think is true, but **should/ought to** are not used in this way (C32).

D | PASSIVES (→ Units 22–25)

Passive verb forms have one of the tenses of the verb **to be** and a **past participle**. Passive verb forms are summarised in Appendix 1. The choice between an active and passive sentence allows us to present the same information in two different orders. Compare:

active □ The storm damaged the roof.	*passive* □ The roof was damaged. □ The roof was damaged by the storm.
This sentence is about *the storm*, and says what it did. The subject (*The storm*) is the 'agent' and the object (*the roof*) is the 'done to'.	These sentences are about *the roof* and say what happened to it (in the first sentence) and what did it (in the second). The subject (*The roof*) is the 'done to'. If it is mentioned, the agent (*the storm*) goes in a prepositional phrase with *by* after the verb.

D1 □ The building *survived* the earthquake but then *was destroyed by* a fire.

Verbs which take an object (*transitive verbs*) can have a passive form (*...was destroyed*). Verbs which *do not* take an object (*intransitive verbs*) do not have passive forms (The child *vanished...*, but not 'The child was vanished...').

However, many verbs can be used at different times with and without objects – that is, they can be both transitive and intransitive. Compare: '**Are they meeting him** at the airport?' (*transitive*) and '**Is he being met** at the airport?' (*passive*); 'When shall we **meet**?' (*intransitive*; no passive possible)

D2 □ I'm really disappointed. I *didn't get picked/wasn't picked* for the team again.

D3 □ The house *was owned* by an elderly couple before I bought it.

In spoken language we often use **get + past participle** (*...didn't get picked...*) instead of a passive form (*...wasn't picked...*) to talk about actions or events that we see as negative (D2). Note, however, that we can also use it to talk about positive actions and events (e.g. Great news – I **got picked** for the team again!). We don't normally use **get +** **past participle** to describe states (D3).

E QUESTIONS (→ Units 26 & 27)

Question forms are summarised in Appendix 2.

E1 □ *What happened* to your eye?

If we use **what, which, who** or **whose** as the subject, we don't use **do** in the question (E1). However, notice that we can sometimes use **do** when **what, which, who** or **whose** is the subject if we want to add emphasis, or to contrast with what has been said or implied. **Do** is stressed in spoken English: 'Come on, be honest – who *did* tell you?' Don't confuse **whose** with **who's** (short for either **who is** or **who has**), which are pronounced the same.

E2 □ I've got orange juice or apple juice. *Which* would you prefer?

E3 □ He just turned away when I asked him. *What* do you think he meant?

In these questions the *wh*-word is the object. We prefer **which** when we are asking about an identified group or range of things or people (E2), and we use **what** when the possible range of reference is open (E3). Sometimes, however, we can use either **which** or **what** with little difference in meaning (e.g. *What/Which* towns do we go through on the way?).

E4 □ *Haven't you finished* your homework yet?

E5 □ *Why didn't* she pay for the meal?

E6 □ *Who wouldn't like* to own an expensive sports car?

We can use negative **yes/no** or **wh-questions** to make a suggestion, to persuade someone, to criticise, or to show that we are surprised, etc. We make a negative **yes/no** or **wh-question** with an auxiliary verb (*have, did, would*, etc.) + **-n't** (E4, E5, E6). We can also ask a negative question using a negative statement and a positive 'tag' at the end (e.g. We do*n't* have to leave just yet, *do we?*). Negative questions can be used to sound polite when giving an opinion (e.g. Should*n't* we offer her a lift?).

F VERB COMPLEMENTATION: WHAT FOLLOWS VERBS (→ Units 28–31)

F1 □ She described the attacker to the police.

F2 □ They arrived at the restaurant an hour late.

F3 □ He gave me a biscuit.

Some verbs (e.g. *describe* in F1) are followed by an object (...*the attacker*...). These are called *transitive verbs*. Other verbs that are usually transitive include **arrest, avoid, do, enjoy, find, force, get, grab, hit, like, pull, report, shock, take, touch, want, warn**. Some verbs (e.g. *arrive* in F2) are not usually followed by an object. These are called *intransitive verbs*. Other verbs that are usually intransitive include **appear, come, fall, go, happen, matter, sleep, swim, wait**. If a verb can't be followed by an object, it can't be made passive. Some verbs (e.g. *give* in F3) are commonly followed by two objects (*me* and *a biscuit* in F3). Other verbs that are commonly followed by two objects include **lend, offer, pay, sell, tell, throw**.

A good dictionary will list the meanings of verbs and for each meaning tell you whether each meaning is intransitive, transitive and, if transitive, whether it is followed by one or by two objects.

F4–13 Many verbs can be followed by another verb in the form of a **to-infinitive** (e.g. refuse *to eat*), **-ing** (e.g. avoid *working*), **bare infinitive** (e.g. help *carry*). Note that when **to** comes after a verb it can be part of a **to-infinitive** (= *to* + the base form of a verb; e.g. He wants *to go*, She hopes *to win*) or it can be a **preposition** followed by a noun phrase (e.g. He went *to the theatre*) or by an **-ing** form (e.g. He admitted *to having* a gun). An **-ing** form often behaves like an object (e.g. I regret *leaving*).

Here is a summary of common patterns together with examples of verbs that are used in this pattern. Note that many verbs can be used in several different patterns, and that some of the verbs given can be used just with an object, and may also be used intransitively (e.g. He failed to stop, He failed the test, He failed).

	F4 ☐ They won't *agree to pay* for the damage.
Verb + to-infinitive	agree, aim, ask, decline, demand, fail, hesitate, hope, hurry, manage, offer, plan, prepare, refuse, want, wish
	F5 ☐ Stevens *admitted stealing* the wallet.
Verb + -ing	admit, avoid, consider, delay, deny, detest, dread, envisage, feel like, finish, imagine, miss, recall, resent, risk, suggest
	F6 ☐ Before we *began eating/to eat* my father thanked everyone for coming.
Verb + to-infinitive *or* -ing with little difference in meaning	begin, cease, continue, start
	F7 ☐ She *came hurrying* up the path to bring us the news. **F8** ☐ How did you *come to buy* the car?
Verb + to-infinitive *or* -ing but with a difference in meaning	come, go on, mean, regret, remember, stop, try
	F9 ☐ My parents wouldn't *allow me to go* to the party.
Verb + object + to-infinitive (= there must be an object)	allow, believe, cause, command, consider, enable, encourage, entitle, force, invite, order, persuade, show, teach, tell, warn
	F10 ☐ I would *hate (her) to give* the job up.
Verb + (object) + to-infinitive (= there may be an object)	hate, help, like, love, need, prefer, want, wish,
	F11 ☐ The police *caught him driving* without a licence.
Verb + object + -ing (= there must be an object)	catch, discover, feel, find, hear, leave, notice, observe, overhear, see, spot
	F12 ☐ I *can't stand (him) wearing* a suit.
Verb + (object) + -ing (= there may be an object)	can't stand, detest, dislike, dread, envisage, hate, imagine, like, love, mind (in questions and negatives), miss, recall, regret, remember, resent, risk, start, stop
	F13 ☐ She *felt the mosquito bite/biting* her.
Verb + object + bare infinitive *or* -ing, but there is sometimes a difference in meaning	feel, hear, notice, observe, overhear, see, watch

G REPORTING (→ Units 32–39)

When we report speech in a different context from the one in which it was originally produced, we sometimes need to make changes to the original words. Of course, differences between the original speech context and the one in which it is reported will influence whether changes are needed and what they should be. Here are some possible changes:

G1 □ '*Jim's arriving* later *today*.' → She said that Jim *was arriving* later *that day*.

G2 □ 'I was sure *I'd* left it *here*.' → He said that he was sure *he'd* left it *there/on the table*.

G3 □ 'I *grew these* carrots *myself*.' → He told me that he *had grown those* carrots *himself*.
   The tense we choose for a report is one that is appropriate *at the time that we are reporting* what was said or thought. This means that we sometimes use a different tense in the report from the one that was used in the original statement (G1 & G3) and change pronouns, references to time and place, and words such as **this, that**, and **these** (G1–G3).

G4 □ Martha *told me* (that) she would be late for the meeting.

G5 □ She *said* (that) she was feeling ill.

G6 □ I *said to John* (that) he had to work harder.

G7 □ She *told me about* her holiday in Finland.
   Say and **tell** are the verbs most commonly used to report statements. We use an **object** after **tell** (...*me*..., G4), but not after **say** (G5). Notice, however, that we can use **to +** **object** after **say** (...*to John*..., G6), but not after **tell**, and that we can report what topic was talked about using **tell + object + about** (G7).

H NOUNS (→ Units 40–43)

Countable and uncountable nouns

H1 □ The *equipment* was faulty.
   Nouns can be either **countable** or **uncountable**. Countable nouns are those which can have the word **a/an** before them or be used in the plural. Uncountable nouns are not used with **a/an** or in the plural. Some nouns in English are normally uncountable (like *equipment*), while in many other languages they are countable. For example: **accommodation, advice, applause, assistance, baggage, camping, cash, chaos, chess, clothing, conduct, courage, cutlery, dancing, dirt, employment, equipment, evidence, fun, furniture, harm, health, homework, housing, housework, information, jewellery, leisure, litter, luck, luggage, machinery, money, mud, music, news, nonsense, parking, pay, permission, photography, poetry, pollution, produce, progress, publicity, research, rubbish, safety, scenery, shopping, sightseeing, sunshine, transport, underwear, violence, weather, work.**

H2 □ The company is/are doing a lot of *business* in South America.
   Sometimes a noun is used uncountably when we are talking about the whole substance or idea (e.g. *business*), but countably when we are talking about units or different kinds (e.g. *businesses*). There are many nouns like this, including **beer, coffee, water; fruit, toothpaste, washing powder; cake, chicken, land, paint, space, stone; abuse, (dis)agreement, business, difficulty, fear, improvement, language, life, pain, protest, responsibility, success, thought, war.** Here are some examples: Three **coffees** and a lemonade, please. – Brazil is a major producer of **coffee**.; Most **toothpastes** contain colourings. – Don't forget to buy some **toothpaste**.; The **chickens** have escaped. – I don't eat **chicken**.; I have a **fear** of spiders – He was trembling with **fear**.

H3 □ The use of recycled *paper* is saving thousands of trees from being cut down each year.
   Some nouns (such as *paper*) usually have different meanings when they are used countably and uncountably. Other nouns like this include **accommodation, competition, glass, grammar, iron, jam, lace, property, room, sight, speech, time, tin, work.** Here are some examples: I just don't understand **grammar**. – I looked the answer up in **a grammar** (= a reference book); I got held up in **a jam** (= traffic jam). – This **jam** is really sweet. (Note that 'jams' can also be used to mean types of jam); She made a wonderful **speech** at the wedding. – His **speech** has been affected by the illness.

Compound nouns (→ Unit 43)

H4   □ How much *pocket money* do you give to your children?

H5   □ A new *golf course/golf-course* is being built outside the town.

A *compound noun* (such as *pocket money*) is an expression made up of more than one word, which functions as a noun in a sentence. For example, we can use a **noun + noun** combination to say what something is made of, where something is, when something happens, or what someone does: **rice pudding, a glasshouse, the kitchen cupboard, hill fog, a night flight, a morning call, a language teacher, a window-cleaner.** We sometimes make compounds from nouns which consist of more than two nouns: **a milk chocolate bar, an air-traffic controller, a dinner-party conversation.**

Some compound nouns are usually written as one word (e.g. **a tablecloth**), some as separate words (e.g. **waste paper**), and others with a hyphen (e.g. **a word-processor**). Some compound nouns can be written in more than one of these ways (e.g. **a golf course** *or* **a golf-course**; H5). A good dictionary will tell you how a particular compound noun is usually written.

H6   □ She got some *chewing gum* stuck on her shoe.

Some compound nouns consist of **-ing + noun** as in: **chewing gum, a living room, drinking water, (a pack of) playing cards, a dressing gown, a turning-point, a working party.** The *-ing* form usually says what purpose the following noun has. Other compound nouns consist of a **noun + -ing**: **fly-fishing, film-making, sunbathing, risk-taking, life-saving.** These compounds usually refer to actions or processes.

The possessive form of nouns

H7   □ The *girls'* shoes were covered in mud, so I asked them to take them off before they got into *Tom's* car.

To make the possessive form of nouns in writing – referring to people or groups of people (e.g. *companies*), other living things, places, times, etc. – we add 's ('apostrophe s') to singular nouns and to irregular plurals that don't end in *-s* (e.g. **Tom's** car; the **college's** administrators; the **women's** liberation movement) and add ' (an apostrophe) to regular plurals (e.g. the **girls'** shoes; the **companies'** difficulties). To make the possessive form of names ending in *-s* pronounced /z/ we can add either ' or 's (e.g. It's Tom **Jones'** (*or* Tom **Jones's**) new sports car).

H8   □ That *old car of Jo's* is falling apart.

H9   □ It belongs to a *friend of his*.

We can use the pattern **noun + of + 's** (H8)/ *possessive pronoun* (H9) to talk about something that someone owns or about a relationship. Notice that when we are talking about relationships between people we can also use a noun without **'s** (e.g. an uncle **of** Mark's (*or* an uncle of Mark)).

H10   □ We're going to *Linda's* (house) for the evening.

The noun following a possessive form can be left out when we talk about someone's house. We don't use 'shop' when we talk about, for example, **the newsagent's/the chemist's** or **the newsagent/the chemist** (but not 'the newsagent's shop'/'the chemist's shop') where the name of the shop includes the name of the person who works there (compare 'the sweet shop', but not 'the sweet's').

H11   □ *David's guitar playing* has improved enormously.

H12   □ *The construction of the office block* was opposed by protestors.

Often we can use the possessive **'s** or **...of + noun...** with very little difference in meaning. However, in general, we are more likely to use the **possessive** form of a noun when the noun refers to a particular person or group of people (H11); and when we are talking about time (e.g. **next year's** holiday prices, *rather than* the holiday prices of next year).

We are more likely to use the **...of + noun...** form with an inanimate noun (H12); when we are talking about a process, or a change over time (e.g. *the establishment* **of the committee**, *rather than* the committee's establishment); and when the noun is a long noun phrase (e.g. She is *the sister* **of someone I used to go to school with**. *rather than* She is someone I used to go to school with's sister.).

I ARTICLES, DETERMINERS AND QUANTIFIERS (→ Units 44–52)

Determiners are words such as **this, her,** and **your** which determine or specify what a noun or noun phrase refers to. They come before the noun and at the front of the noun phrase. *Quantifiers* are words such as **some, much,** and **few** which identify the quantity of something. Some words can be both determiners and quantifiers (e.g. 'I sent out invitations to a *few* friends' [few = determiner] and 'A *few* of my friends came to the party' [few = quantifier]) while some are determiners only (e.g. 'This is *my* friend Andrew' [my = determiner]). Many determiners and quantifiers can be *pronouns*, taking the place of a noun phrase (e.g. I've invited all my friends and *most* are coming [most = pronoun]). *Articles* (**a/an** and **the**) are determiners. They also specify what the noun refers to and come at the beginning of the noun phrase. However, they cannot be quantifiers or pronouns.

The (→ Units 45–47)

I1 ☐ Dorothy took a cake and some biscuits to the party, but only *the* biscuits were eaten.

I2 ☐ Can you shut *the* door after you, please?

I3 ☐ We had a good time on holiday. *The* beaches were all beautifully clean.

I4 ☐ Give it to *the* man wearing the red coat.

I5 ☐ Look at *the* moon. It's very bright tonight.

We use **the** with singular, plural or uncountable nouns when we expect the listener or reader to be able to identify the thing or person we are referring to in the following noun. It may be that the thing has already been mentioned (I1); that it is clear from the situation which person or thing we mean (I2); that it is in some other way understandable from the context which thing or person we mean (I3; 'the beaches' = 'the beaches we went to'); that the thing or person is identified in what is said after the noun (I4; 'wearing the red coat'); or that there is only one of a particular thing (I5 and also, for example, the Great Wall of China, the North Pole, the USA, the world).

A/an (→ Units 44–47)

I6 ☐ Helen's just bought *a* house on Wilson Street.

I7 ☐ Sydney is *a* beautiful city.

We use **a/an** with singular nouns when we don't expect the listener or reader to be able to identify the thing or person we are referring to in the following noun. We often use **a/an** to introduce a new specific person or thing (I6); or when the noun refers to a class of people or things generally – for example, when we describe someone or something or say what type of thing someone or something is (I7).

Zero article (→ Units 45–47)

I8 ☐ *[–]* Water has got into my camera and damaged it.

I9 ☐ There are *[–]* examples of the present continuous tense on page 32.

We use **zero article** *[–]* with uncountable and plural nouns when we talk generally about people or things rather than about specific people or things. We might talk about a whole class of things in a general way (I8) or about an indefinite number or amount (I9).

Some (→ Unit 48)

Some and **any** are used with plural and uncountable nouns, usually when we are talking about limited, but indefinite or unknown, numbers or quantities of things.

I10 ☐ Peter gave me *some* advice.

I11 ☐ Hasn't *some* information about the proposal been sent out already? I thought I read about it last week.

I12   ☐ Shall I send you *some* details?
> We generally use **some**: in affirmative sentences (sentences which are not negatives or questions) (I10); in questions where we expect agreement or the answer 'Yes' (I11); in offers and requests in order to sound positive, expecting the answer 'Yes' (I12). If it is used in this way **some** is pronounced with its weak form /səm/.

I13   ☐ *Some* teachers never seem to get bored with being in the classroom.
> We use **some** to talk about particular, but unspecified, people or things with the implication 'some, but not all'. If it is used in this way **some** is pronounced with its strong form /sʌm/.

I14   ☐ I haven't been here for *some* years.
> We use **some** (pronounced /sʌm/) when we mean quite a large amount of, or a large number of something. Notice that we can say '*some* years, months, weeks, etc.' or just 'years, months, weeks, etc.' with a similar meaning.

Any (→ Unit 48)

I15   ☐ We haven't got *any* butter left.

I16   ☐ Do you have *any* better ideas?

I17   ☐ *Any* student could have answered the question.
> We generally use **any**: in sentences with a negative meaning (I15); in questions where we don't necessarily expect agreement or the answer 'Yes' (I16); when we mean 'all (of them), and it's not important which' (I17).

I18   ☐ If you see *any* cherries in the shop, can you buy them?

I19   ☐ *Any* questions should be sent to the manager.
> We commonly use **any**: in 'if' clauses (I18; note that 'some' is possible, but would seem to expect that you will see cherries); when **any** means 'if there is/are' (I19; = If there are questions...).

Anyone, someone, etc.

I20   ☐ Joseph lives *somewhere* in Denmark.

I21   ☐ I've never seen *anybody* that tall before.
> The rules for the use of the following words are generally the same as those given in I10–I19 for **some** and **any**: the pronouns **someone/anyone**, **somebody/anybody**, **something/anything**, (notice that **somebody** = **someone**, and **anybody** = **anyone**), and the adverbs **somewhere/anywhere**. For example, **some-** words are generally used in affirmative sentences (I20), and **any-** words are generally used in sentences with a negative meaning (I21).

Quantifiers with and without 'of': any (of), some (of), much (of), many (of), both (of), all (of) each (of), none (of), few (of), little (of) (→ Units 48-52)

I22   ☐ *Many of* Bob's closest friends are women.

I23   ☐ *Some of* my jewellery is missing.

I24   ☐ Have you seen *any of* these new light bulbs in the shops yet?

I25   ☐ Are you going to eat *all* (*of*) that cake, or can I finish it?

I26   ☐ *Both of* us were exhausted after flying to Japan.

I27   ☐ I polished *each* trophy with a soft cloth.

I28   ☐ Is there *much* orange juice left?
> We usually need to put **of** after quantifiers when there is a **possessive form** (I22), **pronoun** (I23) or **determiner** (I24) before a noun. Notice, however, that in informal contexts after **both** and **all** we can leave out **of** before **the, these, those** (and **this** or **that** with **all**; I25); **my, your, her, his**, etc.; and **mine, yours**, etc., but not before **them, you,** or **us** (I26) (or **it** with **all**). We don't use **of** after a quantifier immediately before a noun (I27/28).

No, none (of), neither (of), either (→ Unit 49)

I29   □   There's *no* train until tomorrow.

I30   □   *No* information was given about how the study was conducted.

I31   □   She had *no* shoes on.

I32   □   Have we got any more sugar? There's *none* in the kitchen.

I33   □   'How many children have you got?' '*None*.'

We use the determiner **no** to mean 'not a' or 'not any' before a singular (I29), uncountable (I30), or plural noun (I31). Before **the, my, this**, etc. we use the quantifier **none (of)** to mean 'not any' (I32). If it is clear from the context what we mean, we can use the pronoun **none** (I33).

I34   □   *None of* the furniture has arrived yet.

When we use **none of** with an uncountable noun the verb must be singular. However, when we use **none of** with a plural noun the verb can be either singular or plural (e.g. **None of** *the parcels* **have/has** arrived yet), although the singular form is more grammatical.

I35   □   *Neither of* his parents could drive.

We use **neither of** instead of **none of** when we are talking about two people or things.

I36   □   You could catch the 10.05 or the 10.32. *Either* train gets you there in good time.

I37   □   Has *either of* them passed their driving test yet?

When we use **either** as a determiner (I36), it is followed by a singular countable noun. If this is the subject of the sentence, it is followed by a singular verb. We use **either of** with plural nouns and pronouns (I37). Note that **either** can also be used as an adverbial as in 'We can **either** take the train or go by bus' and 'I had no wish to go, and Les didn't want to go **either**'.

Much (of), many (of), a lot of, lots (of) (→ Unit 50)

I38   □   There isn't *much* traffic along the street where I live.

I39   □   Will you be taking *many* suitcases on the trip?

Much and **many** are used to talk about quantities and amounts. **Much** is used with uncountable nouns (I38) and **many** with plural nouns (I39). Before **the, my, this**, etc. we use **much of/ many of**. **Much of** can also be used with a singular countable noun to mean 'a large part of' (e.g. *Much of* the national park was destroyed in the fire.). We can use **much** and **many** without a noun if the meaning is clear (e.g. Can you get some sugar when you go shopping? There isn't *much* left.). **Much** and **many** are often used after **as, how, so,** and **too** (e.g. I'd say there were twice *as many* women at the meeting as men.).

I40   □   She didn't show *much* interest in what I said.

I41   □   John offered me *a lot of* money for the car.

I42   □   *Many of* my relatives live around Wolverhampton.

Much (of) and **many (of)** are used in *negative sentences* to emphasise that we are talking about small (or smaller than expected) quantities or amounts (I40) and in *questions* to ask about quantities or amounts (e.g. Have you got *much* homework to do?). In *affirmative sentences* we often use **a lot of, lots of** or **plenty of** rather than **much (of)** and **many** to talk about large amounts and quantities, particularly in conversation and informal writing (I41). However, **many of** is common in affirmative sentences in both formal and informal contexts (I42).

All (of) (→ Unit 51)

I43   □   There is heating in *all* (*of*) the bedrooms in the house.

We use **all** or **all of** when we are talking about the total number of things or people in a group, or the total amount of something. In informal contexts we can leave out **of**.

I44   □   *Everyone* was waiting to hear the results.

In modern English we don't use **all** without a noun to mean 'everyone' or 'everything'. However, **all** can mean 'everything' when it is followed by a *relative clause* (e.g. I don't agree with *all* that he said. (= everything that he said)). We can also use **all** without a noun to mean 'the only thing' (e.g. *All* she wants to do is help.).

Each/every (→ Unit 51)

I45   □ *Every* newspaper had the same front page story.

I46   □ Following the flood, *every* building in the area needs major repair work.

We can use **each** and **every** with singular countable nouns (I45), and **each of** with plural nouns, to mean all things or people in a group of two or more (**each (of)**) or three or more (**every**). We use a singular verb (...*needs*...) after **each (of)** and **every** (I46). However, when **each** follows the noun or pronoun it refers to, the noun/pronoun and verb are plural (e.g. *Every* student *is* tested twice a year. They *are each* given a hundred questions to do.).

(A) few (of), less (of), (a) little (of) (→ Unit 52)

I47   □ *A few of* the boys were very good footballers.

I48   □ There is *little* evidence to support his claim.

We use **(a) few (of)** with plural countable nouns (I47) and **(a) little (of)** with uncountable nouns (I48).

I49   □ There's a lot *less* water in the lake than last year.

I50   □ The holiday cost *less* than I thought it would.

We use **less (of)** with uncountable nouns (I49) or in a general sense (I50).

I51   □ I've got *a few* close friends that I meet regularly.

I52   □ He has *few* close friends and often feels lonely.

We often use **a few** and **a little** in a 'positive' way (I51); for example, to suggest that a small amount or quantity is enough, or to suggest that it is more than we would expect. We often use **few** and **little** in a 'negative' way (I52); for example, to suggest that the amount or quantity is not enough, or is surprisingly low. Compare '*A few of* her songs were popular and she was very well known' (= 'positive') and '*Few of* her songs were very popular and eventually she gave up her musical career' (= 'negative'). This use of **few** and **little** is often rather formal.

J   RELATIVE CLAUSES AND OTHER TYPES OF CLAUSE (→ Units 53–59)

Relative clauses have a similar function to adjectives in that they give more information about someone or something referred to in a main clause. Participle clauses (**-ing** and **-ed** clauses) can be used like relative clauses, but can also have an adverbial function, giving information about time, cause, etc.

Relative clauses (→ Units 53–55)

J1   □ Andrew stopped the police car *that was driving past*.

J2   □ My mother, *who is in her seventies*, enjoys hill walking.

Defining relative clauses (e.g. ...*that was driving past*; J1) are used to specify *which* person or thing we mean, or which *type* of person or thing we mean. Notice that we don't put a comma between the noun and a defining relative clause.

Non-defining relative clauses (e.g. ..., *who is in her seventies*, ...; J2) are used to add extra information about a noun, but this information is not necessary to explain which person or thing we mean. We don't use them often in everyday speech, but we do use them frequently in written English. Notice that we often put a comma before and after a non-defining relative clause.

J3   □ The house, *which is to the north of the road*, is owned by the council.

After a relative clause, we don't repeat the subject with a pronoun; so, for example, we wouldn't say 'The house which is to the north of the road it is owned by the council'. However, this is sometimes found in informal speech; for example, 'A friend of mine who is a solicitor – she helped me.'

-ing clauses (= present participle clauses) (→ Units 58 & 59)

J4   □ *Glancing over his shoulder*, he could see the dog chasing him.

J5   □ *Pushing her way through the crowds*, she just managed to get on the bus as it pulled away.

J6   □ 'Wait a minute,' said Frank, *running through the door*.

We can use an **-ing** clause to talk about something that takes place at the same time as (J4) or just before (J5) an action in the main clause. We often use an **-ing** clause in written narrative after quoted speech, when we want to say what someone was doing while they were talking (J6).

Note that the understood subject of **-ing** and **-ed** (see J8) clauses should be the same as the subject of the main clause. For example, in J4, 'he' is the unstated subject of 'Glancing over his shoulder...'.

J7   □ *Knowing exactly what I wanted*, I didn't spend much time shopping.

-ing clauses can be used to talk about reasons and results. This sentence has a similar meaning to 'Because I knew exactly what I wanted, I didn't spend much time shopping'.

–ed clauses (= past participle clauses) (→ Units 58 & 59)

J8   □ *Annoyed by the boys' behaviour*, she complained to the head teacher.

We can use an **-ed** clause to talk about something that happened before an action in the main clause. Often the event in the **-ed** clause causes the event in the main clause.

K   PRONOUNS, SUBSTITUTION AND LEAVING OUT WORDS (→ Units 60–65)

Reflexive pronouns (→ Unit 60)

K1   □ 'What did you do to your hand?' 'I cut *myself* when I was chopping vegetables.'

When the subject and object of a sentence refer to the same person or thing, we use a **reflexive pronoun** as the object of a sentence rather than a personal pronoun. The singular forms of reflexive pronouns are **myself, yourself, herself, himself, itself**; the plural forms are **ourselves, yourselves, themselves**.

K2   □ We phoned the plumber and he came *himself*.

K3   □ My sister drew the picture *herself*.

K4   □ I was given this book by the author *herself*.

We can use reflexive pronouns for emphasis: for example, after an intransitive verb (K2) to emphasise the subject; after a transitive verb (K3) to emphasise that something is done without help; or after a noun to emphasise that noun (K4).

each other/one another

K5   □ They tried to avoid *each other/one another* at the party.

K6   □ John and Carmen first met (*each other/one another*) when they were working in Spain.

Some verbs, such as **avoid** (K5), can be used to describe actions in which two or more people or things do the same thing to the other(s). We use **each other** or **one another** with these. Other verbs like this include **attract, complement, face, help**, and **repel**. After the verbs **embrace, fight, kiss, marry** and **meet** we can use **each other** or **one another**, but this may be omitted when the subject is plural or has the form '...and...' (K6).

K7   □ The scheme allows students from many countries to communicate *with each other/with one another*.

K8   □ We *looked at each other/one another* and started to laugh.

With some verbs we have to use a preposition, often **with**, before **each other/one another** (K7). Verbs like this include **agree, coincide, collaborate, communicate, compete, contrast, co-operate, disagree, joke, mix, quarrel, talk**. Note that we can also use **compete against, talk to**, and **look at** before **each other/one another** (K8).

K9   □ The two children *each* blamed the *other* for breaking the window.

For emphasis we can separate **each** and **other**. This sentence is more emphatic than 'The two children blamed each other...'.

Substitution (→ Units 61–63)

K10 ☐ I had a racing bike when I was young, and *so did my brother.*

K11 ☐ 'Amy loves ice cream.' '*So do I.*'

K12 ☐ 'I didn't think much of the restaurant.' '*Neither did I.*'
   We can use **so** + **auxiliary verb** + **subject** to say that a second person does the same things as the person already mentioned (K10 & K11). The corresponding negative form uses **neither** (K12), **nor** ('Nor did I'), or **not...either** ('I didn't either'). We often use this to avoid repetition (e.g. in K12 we use 'Neither did I' rather than 'I didn't think much of the restaurant either').

L   ADJECTIVES AND ADVERBS (→ Units 66–78)

Gradable and non-gradable adjectives (→ Units 67–68)

L1 ☐ They live in a very *large* house.

L2 ☐ Our teacher gave us an absolutely *impossible* problem to solve.
   Most adjectives describe qualities that can be measured or graded, and so can be used in comparative and superlative forms and with words such as 'very' or 'extremely'. These are referred to as **gradable** adjectives (for example, 'large' in L1). Some adjectives are not gradable because they refer to qualities that are completely present or completely absent. These **non-gradable** adjectives (such as 'impossible' in L2) are not usually used in comparative and superlative forms or with words such as 'very' or 'extremely'. They can often, however, be used with words such as 'absolutely' or 'completely'.

Order of adjectives

L3 ☐ I drank some *very good Brazilian* coffee.
   When we use more than one adjective before a noun, there is often a *preferred* (although not fixed) order for these adjectives depending on what type of adjective they are: **opinion** + **size/physical quality/shape/age** + **colour** + **participle adjectives** + **origin** + **material** + **type** + **purpose** + NOUN. Here are some examples showing the most likely order: *an old plastic container* (= age + material + noun); *a hard red ball* (= quality + colour + noun); *a frightening Korean mask* (= opinion + origin + noun); *a round biscuit tin* (= shape + purpose (for holding biscuits) + noun); *a small broken plate* (= size + participle adjective + noun); *a useful digital alarm clock* (= opinion + type + purpose + noun).

   To help you to learn this order, it can be useful to remember that *gradable* adjectives (describing *opinion*, *size*, *quality*, *shape*, and *age*) usually precede *ungradable* adjectives (*participle adjective* and adjectives describing *origin*, *material*, *type* and *purpose*).

Easily confused adjectives

L4 ☐ I was *surprised* to find that the film was quite *frightening*.
   When we use the following adjectives to describe how a person feels about something or someone else, generally the **-ed** adjectives describe how the person feels (e.g. I was *surprised*...), and the **-ing** adjectives give an evaluation of the thing or other person (e.g. ...the film was quite *frightening*.): **alarmed – alarming, amazed – amazing, bored – boring, excited – exciting, frightened – frightening, interested – interesting, pleased – pleasing, surprised – surprising, tired – tiring, worried – worrying.**

Adjectives and adverbs: use (→ Unit 71)

L5 ☐ The staff in the shop always speak *politely* to customers.

L6 ☐ It was *strangely* quiet as we went into the room.
   We use an *adverb*, not an *adjective*, to say how something happened or was done (L5) or to modify adjectives (L6).

Adjectives and adverbs: comparative and superlative forms (→ Unit 72)

L7   ☐ The building was *bigger* than I'd expected.

L8   ☐ It was the *most ridiculous* thing to say.

We usually add the ending **-er** to one-syllable adjectives and adverbs to make their comparative forms (L7) and **-est** to make their superlative forms. With three or more syllables we usually add **more/less** and **most/least** (L8). With two syllables we can usually use either.

Quite

L9   ☐ I was *quite* satisfied with the result.

L10 ☐ No, you're *quite* wrong!

L11 ☐ The food here is *quite* superb.

Quite has two meanings: to a particular degree, but not 'very' (= 'fairly') (L9); and to a large degree, or 'very much' (= 'completely') (L10). When **quite** is used with non-gradable adjectives it means 'completely' (L11).

M   ADVERBIAL CLAUSES & CONJUNCTIONS (→ Units 79-87)

An adverbial clause is a type of subordinate clause, linked to a main clause. An adverbial clause adds extra information to the main clause about such things as time and conditions. Most adverbial clauses begin with a conjunction that indicates their link with the main clause. Example conjunctions are **after**, **before**, and **until** (time conjunctions); and **if** and **unless** (conditional conjunctions).

Tenses in adverbial and main clauses: general

M1 ☐ Because I'*m* overweight, my doctor *has put* me on a diet.

M2 ☐ I *felt* unwell when I *got* up this morning.

The verb in the adverbial clause is usually the same tense as the verb in the main clause. In M1 they are both present (present simple + present perfect), and in M2 they are both past (past simple + past simple).

Time clauses: tenses (→ Unit 79)

M3 ☐ Have something to eat before you *leave*.

To refer to the future after a time conjunction (...*before*...) we use present tenses.

M4 ☐ As soon as you *see/ have seen* her, come and tell me.

M5 ☐ She wrote to me after she *spoke/ had spoken* to Jim.

To talk about an action in the adverbial clause that is completed before another action described in the main clause, we can use either simple or perfect tenses (present as in M4 or past as in M5), but not **will** or **will have** + **-ed** (the future perfect).

M6 ☐ When I *saw* Kim, I asked her over for dinner.

If the actions in the main clause and the adverbial clause take place at the same time, we use simple, not perfect tenses.

M7 ☐ While the children *were swimming*, their mother kept a watchful eye on them.

M8 ☐ I read a book while I *waited*.

While is mainly used with continuous tenses (M7) and also with simple tenses (M8).

Conditional clauses (→ Units 83-86)

Real and unreal conditionals (→ Units 83 & 84)

Some conditional clauses beginning with **if** suggest that a situation is *real* – that is, the situation is or was true, or may have been or may become true (e.g. *If anyone phones*, tell them I'll be back at 11.00; *If you really want to learn Italian*, you need to spend some time in Italy). Others suggest that a situation is *unreal* – that is, the situation is imaginary or untrue. (e.g. What would you do *if you won the lottery?*; *If you had started out earlier*, you wouldn't have been so late).

Compare: *If I go to Berlin*, I'll travel by train. (= *real* conditional) and *If I went to Berlin*, I'd travel by train. (= *unreal* conditional). In the first, the speaker is thinking of going to Berlin (it is a real future possibility), but in the second, the speaker is not thinking of doing so. The second might be giving someone advice.

Real conditionals: tenses (→ Units 83 & 84)

M9   □ I'll give you a lift if it *rains*.

M10 □ If you *leave* now, you'll be home in two hours.

M11 □ If water *freezes*, it expands.

M12 □ If I *made* the wrong decision then I apologise.

       In real conditionals we use a present tense to talk about the future (M9), the present (M10) or unchanging relationships (M11), and past tenses to talk about the past (M12).

Unreal conditionals: tenses (→ Units 83 & 84)

M13 □ *If my grandfather was/ were still alive, he would be a hundred today.*

       To talk about *present* or *future* situations in unreal conditionals, we use a past tense (either simple or continuous) in the **if-clause** and **would + bare infinitive** in the main clause. In *unreal* conditionals we don't use the past simple or past perfect in the main clause. In *unreal* conditionals, we can also use **could/might (have)** instead of **would (have)** (e.g. If my grandfather *was/ were* still alive, he *might have* enjoyed looking after our garden; If I *lived* out of town, I *could* take up horse riding.). Notice that we sometimes use **if...were** instead of **if...was** (see Unit 85).

M14 □ *If I had known how difficult the job was, I wouldn't have taken* it.

       When we talk about something that might have happened in the *past*, but didn't, then we use **if + past perfect** and **would have + past participle** in the main clause. We can also use **might/could have** instead of **would have** in the main clause (e.g. They *might have found* a better hotel *if* they *had driven* a few more kilometres.).

M15 □ *If Bob wasn't so lazy, he would have passed the exam easily.*

M16 □ *If the doctor had been called earlier, Mary would still be alive today.*

       In some *unreal* conditionals we use mixed tenses. That is, a past tense in the **if-clause** and **would have + past participle** in the main clause (M15), or a past perfect in the **if-clause** and **would + infinitive** in the main clause (M16). We can use these patterns to talk about possible consequences if situations were or had been different. We can also use **might/could (have)** in the main clause instead of **would (have)** (e.g. ...he *could have* passed the exam easily.; ...Mary *might* still *be* alive today.).

M17 □ *If I had a more reliable car, I'd drive to Spain rather than fly.*

       In *unreal* conditional sentences we don't normally use **would** in an **if-clause** (but see Unit 84).

Other types of *adverbial clause* give information about *place* (M18), *contrast* (M19 and Unit 82), *cause* or *reason* (M20 and Unit 80), *purpose* (M21 and Unit 81), and *result* (M22 and Unit 81):

M18 □ Can you put it back *where you found it*, please?

M19 □ My sister is blonde, *whereas my brother has dark hair*.

M20 □ He wasn't allowed in *because he was too young*.

M21 □ We got up early *so that we could watch the sunrise*.

M22 □ He played so badly *that he was easily beaten*.

Glossary

active

In an active clause or active sentence, the grammatical subject is the person or thing that performs the action given in the verb (e.g. Geoff wrote the book). Compare PASSIVE.

adjective

A word that describes a noun (e.g. an *interesting* book) or a pronoun (e.g. a *red* one). **Gradable adjectives** can be used to say that a person or thing has more or less of this quality (e.g. She's very *happy*), while **non-gradable adjectives** can't (e.g. It's *impossible*. We can't say 'It's very impossible'). **Classifying adjectives** say that something is of a particular type (e.g. *atomic*, *initial*). **Emphasising adjectives** stress how strongly we feel about something (e.g. *complete* nonsense). **Qualitative adjectives** say what qualities a person or thing has (e.g. *big*, *rich*). See also **grading** ADVERBS and **non-grading** ADVERBS.

adjective phrase

A group of words where the main word is an adjective (e.g. it's *extremely important*; it wasn't *strong enough*).

adverb

A word that describes or gives more information (when, how, where, etc.) about a verb (e.g. He ran *quickly*), adjective (e.g. an *extremely* expensive car), another adverb (e.g. She did it *very* easily), or phrase (e.g. They live *just* across the road.). Types of adverb include: **adverbs of manner** (e.g. *slowly*, *violently*) which we use to say how something is done; **connecting adverbs** (e.g. *consequently*, *similarly*); **time adverbs** (e.g. *tomorrow*, *already*); **place adverbs** (e.g. *upstairs*, *outside*); **direction adverbs** (e.g. *backwards*, *through*); **comment adverbs** (e.g. *apparently*, *personally*) which we use to make a comment on what we are saying; **viewpoint adverbs** (e.g. *financially*, *politically*) which we use to make clear from what point of view we are speaking; **adverbs of indefinite frequency** (e.g. *always*, *never*); **degree adverbs** (e.g. *completely*, *quite*) which give information about the extent or degree of something; **focus adverbs** (e.g. *just*, *even*) which we use to focus on a particular word or phrase. **Grading adverbs** (e.g. *extremely*, *very*) are used with **gradable** ADJECTIVES. **Non-grading adverbs** (e.g. *completely*, *mainly*) are used with **non-gradable** ADJECTIVES.

adverbial

A word or group of words that says when, how, where, etc. something happens. They may consist of an ADVERB (e.g. *quietly*), a PREPOSITIONAL PHRASE (e.g. *through the door*), a NOUN PHRASE (e.g. *next week*), or an ADVERBIAL CLAUSE (e.g. *after she left*).

adverbial clause

A type of **subordinate** CLAUSE that says when, how, where, etc. something happens (e.g. *Before I went to school this morning*, I did my homework).

affirmative sentence

A statement (i.e. not a question) that is positive, not negative.

agent

The person or thing that performs the action described in a verb. Usually it is the subject in an active clause and comes after 'by...' in a passive clause.

article

The word *the* is the **definite article** and the word *a* (*an* before vowels) is the **indefinite article**. When there is no article before a noun we refer to this as the **zero article**.

auxiliary verbs

The verbs *be*, *have* and *do* when they are used with a main verb to form questions, negatives, tenses, passive forms, etc. MODAL VERBS are also auxiliary verbs.

clause

A group of words that contains a verb. A clause may be a complete sentence or a part of a sentence. A **main clause** can exist as a separate sentence, while a **subordinate clause** cannot (e.g. *If I see Tony at work* [= subordinate clause], *I'll invite him over this evening* [= main clause]). Types of clause include: **since-clause** (e.g. I haven't seen him *since we left school*); **that-clause** (e.g. She said *that she was thirsty*); **wh-clause** (e.g. I asked Sandra *where she was going*); **it-clause** (e.g. *It's not surprising* that you're feeling cold); **what-clause** (e.g. *What I want to do* is buy a better computer); **if-clause** (e.g. *If you leave now*, you'll be home by 10.00); **whether-clause** (e.g. You have to take the exam *whether you want to or not*); **to-infinitive clause** (e.g. *To become a doctor* takes years of study); **present participle (-ing) clause** (e.g. *Feeling hungry*, I went into the kitchen); **past participle (-ed) clause** (e.g. *Built during the 1950s*, the building is now in need of repair); **being + past participle (-ed) clause** (e.g. *Being unemployed*, Tom had a lot of time on his hands); **having + past participle (-ed) clause** (e.g. *Having seen the doctor*, I went straight home). See also CONDITIONAL CLAUSE, NON-FINITE CLAUSE, RELATIVE CLAUSE.

cleft sentence

A sentence in which focus is given to either the subject or object using a pattern beginning 'It...' (e.g. It was my brother who lent me the money) or 'What...' (e.g. What you need is a holiday).

complement

A word or phrase that follows a LINKING VERB and describes the SUBJECT (e.g. Linda is a *lawyer*) or OBJECT (e.g. I found the food *inedible*). A complement may also be an ADVERBIAL or PREPOSITIONAL PHRASE which completes the meaning of a verb. Some verbs need a complement (e.g. The disease originated *in Britain*; 'The disease originated' would be incomplete).

compound

A **compound noun** consists of two or more words together used as a noun (e.g. a *language school*). A **compound adjective** consists of two or more words together used as an adjective (e.g. They were *well-behaved*).

conditional

A **conditional clause** usually starts with 'if', but other patterns are possible (e.g. *Had it not rained*, England would have won). A **conditional sentence** contains a conditional clause. A distinction can be made between **real conditionals**, which suggest that the situation is or was true, or may have been or may become true (e.g. If she makes a promise, she keeps it) and **unreal conditionals**, which suggest that the situation is imaginary or untrue (e.g. If you had asked me, I would have helped).

conjunction

A word such as *and, but, if, while, after, because* which connects words, phrases, or clauses in a sentence. Compare SENTENCE CONNECTOR.

countable

A **countable noun** can be both singular and plural (e.g. *cup/cups*). An **uncountable noun** doesn't have a plural form (e.g. *electricity*, but not 'electricities').

declarative sentence

A declarative sentence is a statement. In a declarative sentence the subject is followed by the verb.

determiner

A word that goes in front of a noun to identify what the noun refers to (e.g. *this, some, the, a/an, each, all, my*). **Possessive determiners** (also called **possessive adjectives**) are words such as *my, your* and *their*.

direct speech

Speech that is written using the exact words of the speaker, without any changes. Compare REPORTED SPEECH.

dynamic verb
A verb that describes an action (e.g. *walk*, *throw*). Compare STATE VERB.

imperative
An **imperative clause** uses the **bare** INFINITIVE form of a verb for such things as giving orders and making suggestions (e.g. *Go to bed!*).

infinitive
The form of a verb that usually goes after 'to'. The form can be either the **to-infinitive** (e.g. *to sing*, *to eat*) or the **bare infinitive** (e.g. *sing*, *eat*).

intransitive verb
A verb that doesn't take an object (e.g. She *smiled*). Compare TRANSITIVE VERB.

inversion
Changing the usual word order so that the verb comes before the subject (e.g. Up *went the balloon*).

linking verb
A verb (e.g. *be*, *become*, *appear*) that connects a SUBJECT with its COMPLEMENT.

modal verbs
A group of verbs (*can*, *could*, *dare*, *may*, *might*, *must*, *need*, *ought to*, *shall*, *should*, *will*, *would*, *used to*) that give information about such things as possibility, necessity, and obligation. **Semi-modal verbs** (*ought to*, *used to*, *need*, *dare*, *had better*, *have (got) to*, *be able to*) have similar meanings to modal verbs.

non-affirmative
Referring to a lack of positive, affirmative meaning; for example, in most questions and negatives. However, questions which expect a positive reply are affirmative. The terms 'non-assertive' and 'assertive' are sometimes used for 'non-affirmative' and 'affirmative'.

non-finite clause
A clause with a non-finite VERB; either a **to-infinitive** form (e.g. I want *to leave soon*), an **-ing** (present participle) form (e.g. I caught him *stealing my camera*), or **-ed** (past participle) form (e.g. We cleared up the mess *left after the party*).

noun
A word that refers to a person, place, thing, quality, etc. A **collective noun** refers to a group of people or things (e.g. *audience*, *crowd*, *herd*). See also COUNTABLE NOUN.

noun phrase
A group of words where the main word is a noun (e.g. I've been talking to *the woman across the road*; We spoke to *several small children*).

object
The **direct object** is the person or thing affected by the action of the verb (e.g. I put *the book* [= direct object] back on the shelf). The **indirect object** is the person or thing who benefits from the action or who receives something (e.g. I gave *my mother* [= indirect object] some flowers [= direct object]). Compare SUBJECT.

participle
The **present participle** is the **-ing form** of a verb (e.g. *walking*, *singing*, *eating*) used, for example, in continuous tenses. The **past participle** is the -ed form of a verb (e.g. *walked*, *sang*, *eaten*) used, for example, in perfect tenses. A **participle adjective** is one formed from the present or past participle of a verb (e.g. the candidates *applying*, a *broken* plate). A **participle clause** has a present participle or past participle verb form (e.g. *Feeling unwell*, he went to bed; The person *appointed to the post* will have a difficult job to do).

particle

An adverb or preposition that follows a verb in TWO-WORD VERBS and THREE-WORD VERBS (e.g. What time did you *get in*? [in = adverb]; I *flicked through* the magazine [through = preposition]; She *looks up to* her mother [up = adverb, to = preposition]).

passive

In a passive clause or passive sentence, the grammatical subject is the person or thing that experiences the effect of the action given in the verb (e.g. The book was written by Geoff). Compare ACTIVE.

performative

A performative is a verb which states the action that is performed when a speaker uses the verb (e.g. I *promise* I'll do it tomorrow; I *apologise*).

phrasal verb

A verb together with a following adverb and/or a preposition that has a single meaning (e.g. *set off*, *look up to*). Compare 'I *ran across* Tanya at the concert' (= met unexpectedly; a phrasal verb) and 'She *ran across* the road' (= a PREPOSITIONAL VERB).

possessive

The possessive form of a noun ends in either -'s (e.g. *Mark's* car) or -s' (e.g. the *girls'* changing room).

preposition

A word such as *in*, *on*, or *by* that comes before a noun, pronoun, noun phrase or -**ing** form (e.g. *in* March, *above* my uncle's head, *by* investing).

prepositional phrase

A group of words that consists of a PREPOSITION and its **prepositional object** (a noun, pronoun, noun phrase or -**ing** form) (e.g. *behind our house, across it*).

prepositional verb

A verb and a following preposition (e.g. *believe in, consist of, look after*). Compare PHRASAL VERB.

pronoun

A word that is used instead of a noun or noun phrase. Pronouns include **personal pronouns** (e.g. *I, she, me*), **reflexive pronouns** (e.g. *myself, herself*), **possessive pronouns** (e.g. *my, mine, your, yours*), and RELATIVE PRONOUNS (e.g. *who, which*).

quantifier

A word or phrase that goes before a noun or noun phrase to talk about the quantity of something (e.g. *a little* water, *many of* the women in the room).

question

A **wh-question** begins with a WH-WORD (e.g. *Where are you going?*). A **yes/no question** is one that can be answered with 'yes' or 'no' (e.g. *Do you like coffee?*). An **echo question** repeats part of a previous utterance and asks for a repetition of all or part of it (e.g. 'I'm moving to Alaska.' '*You're moving where?*'). We can ask an **indirect question** by putting it into a **subordinate** CLAUSE beginning with a WH-WORD or with *if* or *whether* (e.g. Can you tell me *where you live*?).

relative clause

A kind of **subordinate** CLAUSE that describes a noun that comes before it in a **main** CLAUSE. A **defining relative clause** says which person or thing is being talked about (e.g. A friend *who lives in London* is getting married). A **non-defining relative clause** gives more information about the noun (e.g. My bicycle, *which I've left outside your house*, is over 20 years old). A **nominal relative clause** begins with a WH-WORD or *whatever, whenever*, etc. and functions as a NOUN PHRASE in a sentence (e.g. *What I need now* is a long, hot bath). A **reduced relative clause** usually begins with an -**ing** (present participle) or -**ed** (past participle) form and has a similar meaning to a relative clause (e.g. I met the people *living in our old house* [= ...who live in our old house], The new rules only affect people *born before 1950* [= ...who were born before 1950]).

relative pronoun
A pronoun such as *who*, *which*, or *that* which is used at the beginning of a relative clause.

relative word
Words including RELATIVE PRONOUNS and others (e.g. *whereby*, *why*) that can begin a RELATIVE CLAUSE.

reported speech
Speech that is reported without using the exact words of the speaker. Sometimes called 'indirect speech'.

reporting clause & reported clause
A statement that reports what people think or say is often divided into a **reporting clause** and a **reported clause** (e.g. *She said* [= reporting clause] *that the building was unsafe* [= reported clause]).

reporting verb
A verb used in a REPORTING CLAUSE that describes what people say or think (e.g. *ask*, *claim*, *say*).

sentence connector
A word or phrase that shows a connection between two separate sentences (e.g. My car isn't very comfortable. *However*, it's very cheap to run.; The house is large and has a beautiful garden. *What's more*, it's very close to the station.). Compare CONJUNCTION.

simple sentence
A sentence consisting of one clause.

state verb
A verb that is used to describe a state (e.g. *believe*, *think*) rather than an action. Compare DYNAMIC VERB.

subject
The person or thing that does the action of the verb (e.g. *Tommy* went home). Compare OBJECT.

subjunctive
The subjunctive is a set of verb forms used mainly in rather formal English to talk about possibilities rather than facts. The **present subjunctive** uses the base form of the verb (e.g. We suggest that she *leave* immediately) and the **past subjunctive** uses *were* (e.g. If I *were* you, I'd go home now).

transitive verb
A verb that takes an object (e.g. She *was holding* a bunch of flowers). Compare INTRANSITIVE VERB.

two-word verbs & three-word verbs
Verbs that are commonly used with a particular PARTICLE (adverb or preposition) are referred to here as **two-word verbs** (e.g. She *looked after* her elderly parents). Verbs that are commonly used with two particular particles (adverb + preposition) are referred to here as **three-word verbs** (e.g. He *looked up to* his older brothers). See also PREPOSITIONAL VERB and PHRASAL VERB.

verb
A **finite verb** has a tense (e.g. She *waited*; She *is waiting* for you). **Non-finite** verb forms are INFINITIVE (e.g. He came *to see* me) and PARTICIPLE forms (e.g. *Shouting* loudly, I was able to make myself heard; *Built* in 1980, the tower is still the tallest construction in Europe).

verb phrase
A group of words consisting of one or more verbs (e.g. *gives*, *is giving*, *has been giving*).

wh-words
A group of words (*who, whom, whose, where, when, why, how*) that are used in **wh-**QUESTIONS.

Appendix 1
Passive verb forms

If an agent is mentioned, it goes in a prepositional phrase with **by** after the verb (see also Unit 24).

Present simple		
Active:	**tell(s)**	John **tells** me that you're thinking of leaving.
Passive:	**am/is/are told**	I'**m told** (by John) that you're thinking of leaving.
Past simple		
Active:	**told**	John **told** me that you were leaving.
Passive:	**was/were told**	I **was told** (by John) that you were leaving.
Present perfect		
Active:	**have/has told**	John **has told** me that you are leaving.
Passive:	**have/has been told**	I **have been told** (by John) that you are leaving.
Past perfect		
Active:	**had told**	John **had** already **told** me that you were leaving.
Passive:	**had been told**	I **had** already **been told** (by John) that you were leaving.
Present continuous		
Active:	**am/is/are telling**	John is always **telling** me that you are leaving.
Passive:	**am/is/are being told**	I **am** always **being told** (by John) that you are leaving.
Past continuous		
Active:	**was/were telling**	John **was** always **telling** me that you were leaving.
Passive:	**was/were being told**	I **was** always **being told** (by John) that you were leaving.
Future simple		
Active:	**will tell**	I **will tell** John that you are leaving.
Passive:	**will be told**	John **will be told** (by me) that you are leaving.
Future perfect		
Active:	**will have told**	By tomorrow I **will have told** John that you are leaving.
Passive:	**will have been told**	By tomorrow John **will have been told** (by me) that you are leaving.
Present perfect continuous (rare in the passive)		
Active:	**has/have been telling**	John **has been telling** me for ages that you are leaving.
Passive:	**has/have been being told**	I **have been being told** (by John) for ages that you are leaving.

Other passive verb forms are very rare.

Modal verbs with passives

Active:	**should/could/might/ought to** (etc.) **tell**	You **should tell** John.
Passive:	**should/could/might/ought to** (etc.) **be told**	John **should be told**.
Active:	**should/could/might/ought to** (etc.) **have told**	You **should have told** John.
Passive:	**should/could/might/ought to** (etc.) **have been told**	John **should have been told**.
Active:	**should/could/might/ought to** (etc.) **have been telling**	You **should have been telling** John while I was outside.
Passive:	**should/could/might/ought to** (etc.) **have been being told**	John **should have been being told** while I was outside.

Other passive verb forms with modal verbs are very rare.

Appendix 2
Basic question forms

1   If a verb phrase includes an auxiliary verb, the auxiliary verb comes before the subject:
   - **Are they** leaving soon?
   - Where **will you** stay?

2   If a verb phrase includes more than one auxiliary verb, only the first comes before the subject:
   - **Has she** *been* doing her homework?
   - What **should we** *have* told Jack?

3   In present and past simple tenses of verbs (apart from **be**), we use **do** or **did**:
   - **Does he** *enjoy* school?
   - Where **did you** *go* on holiday?

4   If **be** is used in a verb phrase without another verb, the verb comes before the subject:
   - **Are you** happy at work?
   - Where **was Jack** today?

5   If we use **what, which, who** or **whose** as the subject, we use the same word order as in a statement with the subject before the verb phrase:
   - **What made** that noise?
   - **Who can tell** me the answer to question 5?

Appendix 3 Quoting what people think or what they have said

A   You put single ('...') or double ("...") quotation marks at the beginning and end of a report of someone's exact spoken or written words. This is often referred to as *direct speech*:

- □ 'It's a pity you can't come this weekend.'
- □ "I'm really hungry. I fancy a cheese sandwich."

B   If there is a *reporting clause* (e.g. **she said, exclaimed Tom**) *after* the quotation, you put a comma before the second quotation mark:

- □ "I think we should go to India while we have the opportunity," argued Richard.

If you are quoting a question or exclamation, you use a question mark or exclamation mark instead of a comma:

- □ "Can I make an appointment to see the doctor?" asked Bill.
- □ 'You must be mad!' yelled her brother.

If the reporting clause comes *within* the quotation, you put a comma before the second quotation mark of the first part of the quotation, a comma at the end of the reporting clause, and you start the second part of the quotation with a lower case (not a capital) letter:

- □ "It tastes horrible," said Susan, "but it's supposed to be very good for you."

If the second part of the quotation is a new sentence, you put a full stop at the end of the reporting clause, and start the second part of the quotation with a capital letter:

- □ "You should go home," Sandra advised. "You're looking really ill."

If the reporting clause comes *before* the quotation, you put a comma at the end of the reporting clause, and a full stop (or question or exclamation mark) at the end of the quotation:

- □ John said, "Put them all on the top shelf."

A colon is sometimes used at the end of the reporting clause instead of a comma:

- □ She stood up and shouted to the children: "It's time to go home!"

C   When you quote what a person *thinks*, you can either use the conventions described in **A** and **B**, or separate the quotation from the reporting clause with a comma (or colon) and leave out quotation marks:

- □ "Why did she look at me like that?" wondered Mary.
- □ Perhaps the door is open, thought Chris.
- □ Suddenly she thought: Could they be trying to trick me?

Appendix 4
Irregular verbs

bare infinitive	past simple	past participle (-ed form)
arise	arose	arisen
awake	awoke	awoken
be	was/were	been
bear	bore	borne
beat	beat	beaten
become	became	become
begin	began	begun
bend	bent	bent
bet	bet	bet
bind	bound	bound
bite	bit	bitten
bleed	bled	bled
blow	blew	blown
break	broke	broken
bring	brought	brought
broadcast	broadcast	broadcast
build	built	built
burn[1]	burnt	burnt
burst	burst	burst
buy	bought	bought
cast	cast	cast
catch	caught	caught
choose	chose	chosen
cling	clung	clung
come	came	come
cost	cost	cost
creep	crept	crept
cut	cut	cut
deal	dealt	dealt
dig	dug	dug
dive	dived	dived
do	did	done
draw	drew	drawn
dream[1]	dreamt	dreamt
drink	drank	drunk
drive	drove	driven
dwell[1]	dwelt	dwelt
eat	ate	eaten
fall	fell	fallen
feed	fed	fed
feel	felt	felt
fight	fought	fought
find	found	found
fit[1]	fit	fit
flee	fled	fled
fling	flung	flung
fly	flew	flown
forbid	forbade[2]	forbidden
forecast[1]	forecast	forecast
forget	forgot	forgotten
forgive	forgave	forgiven
freeze	froze	frozen
get	got	got
give	gave	given
go	went	gone
grow	grew	grown

bare infinitive	past simple	past participle (-ed form)
hang[1]	hung	hung
have	had	had
hear	heard	heard
hide	hid	hidden
hit	hit	hit
hold	held	held
hurt	hurt	hurt
keep	kept	kept
kneel[1]	knelt	knelt
knit[1]	knit	knit
know	knew	known
lay	laid	laid
lead	led	led
lean[1]	leant	leant
leap[1]	leapt	leapt
learn[1]	learnt	learnt
leave	left	left
lend	lent	lent
let	let	let
lie[4]	lay	lain
light[1]	lit	lit
lose	lost	lost
make	made	made
mean	meant	meant
meet	met	met
mow[3]	mowed	mown
pay	paid	paid
prove[3]	proved	proven
put	put	put
quit	quit	quit
read	read[5]	read[5]
ride	rode	ridden
ring	rang	rung
rise	rose	risen
run	ran	run
saw[3]	sawed	sawn
say	said	said
see	saw	seen
seek	sought	sought
sell	sold	sold
send	sent	sent
set	set	set
sew[3]	sewed	sewn
shake	shook	shaken
shear[3]	sheared	shorn
shed	shed	shed
shine	shone	shone
shoot	shot	shot
show	showed	shown
shrink	shrank	shrunk
shut	shut	shut
sing	sang	sung
sink	sank	sunk
sit	sat	sat
sleep	slept	slept
slide	slid	slid

bare infinitive	past simple	past participle (-ed form)
sling	slung	slung
smell[1]	smelt	smelt
sow[3]	sowed	sown
speak	spoke	spoken
speed[1]	sped	sped
spell[1]	spelt	spelt
spend	spent	spent
spill[1]	spilt	spilt
spin	spun	spun/span
spit	spat	spat
split	split	split
spoil[1]	spoilt	spoilt
spread	spread	spread
spring	sprang	sprung
stand	stood	stood
steal	stole	stolen
stick	stuck	stuck
sting	stung	stung
stink	stank	stunk
strike	struck	struck
strive	strove	striven
swear	swore	sworn

bare infinitive	past simple	past participle (-ed form)
sweep	swept	swept
swell[3]	swelled	swollen
swim	swam	swum
swing	swung	swung
take	took	taken
teach	taught	taught
tear	tore	torn
tell	told	told
think	thought	thought
throw	threw	thrown
thrust	thrust	thrust
tread	trod	trodden
understand	understood	understood
wake[1]	woke	woken
wear	wore	worn
weave[1]	wove	woven
weep	wept	wept
wet[1]	wet	wet
win	won	won
wind	wound	wound
wring	wrung	wrung
write	wrote	written

[1] These verbs have two past simple and two past participle forms, both the ones given and regular forms (eg burn; burnt/burned; burnt/burned).

[2] 'forbad' is also sometimes used, but is old fashioned.

[3] These verbs have two past participle forms, the one given and a regular form (eg mow; mowed; mown/ mowed).

[4] When *lie* means 'deliberately to say something untrue' it is regular ('lie/lied/lied').

[5] Pronounced /red/.

Additional exercises

1   Complete the sentences with an appropriate positive or negative form of one of these verbs, using the same verb in each pair of sentences. Choose from the *present simple, present continuous, past simple* or *past continuous*. Give all possible answers. Use ⋏ to add any words outside the space.

consider   expect   own   phone   prefer   ~~promise~~   put   read   tell   weigh

1   a   If I'm not too busy, I ....*promise*.... to help you in the garden later today.
    b   I'll try to get over on Saturday, but I .... to be there.
2   a   I made a cup of coffee while she .... the letter.
    b   As soon as the teacher told us to start, I .... through all the questions quickly.
3   a   They .... to reach the top of the mountain by evening, but the weather was too bad.
    b   We .... Jean to visit us in June if she can get a cheap flight.
4   a   Over half the population now .... a mobile phone.
    b   I grew up in Newport, where my father .... a bookshop.
5   a   I .... selling my house and buying a flat.
    b   Many people .... her to be the finest violinist in the country at the moment.
6   a   Jack .... me that you're getting married. Congratulations!
    b   Apparently Carol is seriously ill. They .... me that she never leaves her house now.
7   a   I .... the theatre four times this morning, but there was no answer.
    b   I .... my mother twice a day when my father was in hospital.
8   a   He always .... his feet up on the chairs. It's really unhygienic.
    b   I find it very annoying that she constantly .... empty milk cartons back in the fridge.
9   a   A survey has found that, surprisingly, most children .... to walk to school than be taken by car.
    b   I swam across the river, but my friends .... to walk all the way to the nearest bridge.
10 a   Jim .... over 100 kilos and really needs to take more exercise.
    b   He held the fish in his hands as if he .... it and then said, "It's about 3.5 kilos."

Present perfect, past simple, and present perfect continuous   **Units 3 & 6**

2   Match the beginnings and endings. Sometimes there is more than one possibility.

1 a I haven't had time to phone Tony today, b I didn't have time to phone Tony today,	(i) but I'll certainly contact him before I leave work. (ii) but I'll certainly contact him some time tomorrow.

2 a When she was prime minister,
     Mrs Nathan
  b Since she became prime minister,
     Mrs Nathan
	(i) has often been accused of ignoring the advice of her colleagues.
	(ii) was often accused of ignoring the advice of her colleagues.

3 a I've watched *The Sound of Music* b I've been watching *The Sound of Music*	(i) and now I keep humming the songs to myself. (ii) at least ten times already.
4 a I'd always wanted to own a Porsche b I won't know if I can afford a Porsche	(i) until I've found out how much they cost. (ii) until I found out how much they cost.
5 a Unemployment has risen b Unemployment has been rising	(i) by 58% since the present government came to power. (ii) ever since the present government came to power.
6 a As soon as I've finished the book b As soon as I finished the book	(i) I'm going to have a holiday. (ii) I started writing another one.
7 a I've been playing squash b I've played squash	(i) since my doctor advised me to lose weight. (ii) a couple of times before, but I can't get the hang of it.
8 a I haven't been back to London b I haven't eaten really good pasta	(i) since I lived in Italy. (ii) since I've lived in Italy.

Past perfect, past perfect continuous, and past simple   **Units 5 & 7**

3   Complete each sentence so that it has a similar meaning to the one given. Use a verb related to the word in italics with an appropriate tense (active or passive): *past perfect*, *past perfect continuous* or *past simple*. Give alternatives where possible.

1 The proposed new library had been under *discussion* for almost three years at the time an appropriate site became available.
   At the time an appropriate site became available, they _had been discussing the proposed new library for almost three years._

2 There had been a considerable *improvement* in his condition when I saw him in hospital last night.
   His condition ....

3 It was announced that there was a 10 minute *delay* to the York train.
   It was announced that the York train ....

4 Joe had been on a *diet* for a month when he came to stay with us, and we noticed immediately that he had already lost a lot of weight.
   Joe ....

5 There was an *expectation* that Sylvia would win comfortably, but she finished only third.
Sylvia ....

6 When I reversed the car out of the garage, I did some *damage* to the rear number plate.
When I reversed the car out of the garage, I ....

7 John received a *promotion* last week.
John ....

8 Rentpool had been under *investigation* by the tax authorities for a number of months when they arrested the chairman.
The tax authorities ....

9 The Minister made her colleagues *angry* when she criticised them during her speech yesterday.
The Minister ....

10 There had already been a *suggestion* from Christine that the money should be spent on new textbooks for the school.
Christine ....

The future

Units 9 & 10

4   Study the future references highlighted in these sentences and suggest corrections or improvements where necessary. Choose from *will, shall, going to, present continuous for the future,* and *present simple for the future.*

A A: Careful, (1) you're going to spill your coffee.
   B: Oh, no! Too late. Now (2) I'm going to have to change my trousers.

B A: What have you got all that wood for?
   B: (1) I'll build a bird table in the garden.
   A: If you need any help, let me know and (2) I'm going to give you a hand.

C A: (1) Shall you be able to come over on the 3rd? We (2) have a barbecue.
   B: Just a minute, (3) I'm going to have a look in my diary. No, I'm sorry. (4) I'm meeting some friends in London that day.

D A: Did you know that Dave (1) is going to go to New Zealand this summer?
   B: Yes, I heard. I'm really sorry he (2) doesn't come to see us.
   A: I wonder when we (3) see him again?
   B: Well, he certainly (4) won't be back before Christmas.

E A: I (1) take Aunt Joan to the station later. Do you want a lift into town, too?
   B: What time (2) does her train go?
   A: It (3) will be at 4.15. It (4) takes us about half an hour to get there if there isn't too much traffic.
   B: Well you should start out early. Apparently, (5) we'll have heavy snow this afternoon. In fact, thanks for your offer, but I think (6) I'm going to stay at home in the warm.

Modals

Units 15–20

5   Underline the best answers from each group in italics.

1 A: I've spent most of the morning trying to fix my washing machine, but I seem to have made it worse.
   B: You *ought to ask/ may ask/ ought to have asked* me to come over and take a look at it. I *would have been/ should be/ would be* happy to help. But I suppose it's too late now!

2 The taxi *needs to/ should/ would* be here in a couple of minutes. We'*d better/ 've better/ 'd better to* get ready to go.

3 My daughter *wouldn't/ won't/ may not* eat carrots. She hates the taste of them. I *don't have to/ 'm not able to/ can't* think of any way of getting her to eat them. But to tell the truth, I *could/ would/ used to* hate them when I was young, too.

4 A: We're completely lost! I'*m not able to/ can't / mustn't* find any of the street names around here on the map.

   B: We *must have/ have got to have/ can have* taken the wrong turning at the traffic lights about a kilometre back.

5 You *haven't got to/ needn't/ mustn't* go on the beach when the tide's coming in. It's very dangerous. You *can/ might/ would* play in the fields instead.

6 I was beginning to be concerned that I *won't/ mustn't/ wouldn't* get to the station for my train. But I *didn't need worry/ needn't have worried/ needn't worry*; Colin turned up in good time to give me a lift.

7 Most head teachers today feel that parents *need/ should/ had better* play a more active part in the running of schools. There was a time when parents *would/ will/ should* put a lot of effort into raising money for school projects, but those days seem to have gone.

8 A: These trousers shrank the first time I washed them.

   B: If I were you, I *ought to/ should/ can* take them back.

   A: Yes, I suppose they *can/ need/ may* give me my money back.

9 Preliminary research suggests that the bones *must/ have got to/ used to* be at least 100,000 years old, but they *would/ could/ can* be considerably older than that.

10 Apparently, in the future, airline passengers *will be able to/ can/ could* send and receive email messages without moving from their seats. Of course, by the time this is common, we *can/ must/ might* have started using even more efficient ways of communicating.

11 Both candidates for the job were very strong and it was hard to choose between them. I certainly *couldn't/ mustn't/ had got to* have decided which one to appoint. But fortunately, we *hadn't got to/ didn't have to/ mustn't* make a final decision; the management found enough money to allow us to appoint both of them.

12 You *needn't/ don't need to/ mustn't* be very fit to play badminton well. It *can/ is able to/ could* be played by anyone who is reasonably fit and who has a good sense of timing.

Passives

Units 22–25

6 Some extracts from radio news reports are given below. Rewrite them in a more appropriate way using passive forms in which the underlined word forms the subject of the clause. If 'that' is underlined, use a passive construction with *it* or *there*.

Examples:

Picasso encouraged <u>her</u> to paint. → **She was encouraged** to paint by Picasso.

People believe <u>that</u> the Prime Minister will resign tomorrow. → **It is believed** that the Prime Minister will resign tomorrow.

A People are encouraging <u>the Prime Minister</u> to sack the Environment Minister, Maggie Long, after someone revealed <u>that</u> she had received payments from a major oil company. However, in a statement today, the Prime Minister said: 'My advisors tell <u>me</u> that the company paid <u>Mrs Long</u> the money before she joined the government. I have no intention of dismissing her.'

B A tropical storm has caused severe flooding in the city of Chittagong in southern Bangladesh. Although we understand <u>that</u> there are no casualties, the floods have made <u>many thousands of people</u> homeless, and people estimate the <u>damage to property</u> as running into millions of dollars.

C Protesters have continued to block the construction of the new Newburn ring road by tying themselves to trees along the proposed route. Police say that they have given <u>the protesters</u> two days to leave the area or they will arrest <u>them</u>.

D Conservation groups have demanded that the government should close down <u>the Seafield nuclear power station</u> after a report which said that investigators have found <u>unacceptable levels of radiation</u> in the local area.

E The Chief Constable of the London police force has revealed that they have received <u>a death threat</u> against the life of President Nabon, who is visiting the capital this weekend. He says that they are taking <u>the threat</u> very seriously. People expect <u>that</u> security levels will be increased during the President's visit.

F Someone found <u>a man</u> injured on a Scottish hillside this morning. People think <u>that</u> he fell while coming down a hillside in bad weather. Medical staff are treating <u>him</u> in hospital for leg and head injuries. Someone reported <u>him</u> missing last night when he failed to return home after a day's walking.

G And now football. People expect <u>that</u> there will be a record crowd at tonight's match between Manchester United and Bayern Munich. People report <u>that</u> the club will give <u>the United players</u> a huge financial bonus if they win and people have even suggested <u>that</u> the club might pay <u>them</u> as much as £50,000 each.

Verb complementation: what follows verbs   Units 30 & 31

7   Underline the correct alternatives. Sometimes both are possible.

1 He insisted *to pay/ on paying* for the meal.
2 The interviewer started off *to ask/ by asking* me why I wanted the job.
3 I can clearly recall *his saying/ him saying* that he was meeting Sarah at eight o'clock.
4 The university has *arranged/ appointed* Dr Charles to be head of the new Medical Institute.
5 I knew I could *ask/ count* on Philip if I needed any help.
6 My parents are always going on *at me to tidy/ for to tidy* up my bedroom.
7 The ticket enables you *visiting/ to visit* both the museum and the art gallery.
8 Karen is so small that she often has to resort to *wearing children's clothes/ children's clothes* to get the right size.
9 We objected to *their cat/ their cat's* digging up our garden.
10 The government plans to bring in new laws *forcing/ making* parents to take more responsibility for the education of their children.
11 I don't approve of *her smoking/ smoking*.
12 Johnson was arrested when he failed *him to appear/ to appear* in court.
13 If you have any problems with the computer, contact Simon. It's best if you *allow/ let* him deal with it.
14 I've heard a lot about Dr James, and I'm looking forward *to hearing/ to hear* his talk tomorrow.
15 Although Patricia is a doctor herself, it doesn't *entitle her to/ entitle for her to* special treatment, and she will have to join the waiting list like everyone else.
16 We *waited/ waited for* the storm to pass before we continued.
17 When I was in the supermarket I *noticed a man to take/ noticed a man take* some food off the shelf and hide it inside his coat.
18 We *invited/ refused* Liz to come to the party.
19 I overheard her *tell/ telling* Jack that she was seriously ill.
20 She gave up work so that she could focus on *looking/ look* after her children.

21 We were unhappy in England, and even *discussed/ talked* of emigrating to New Zealand.

22 The lizard is amazingly well adapted *to live/ to living* in very dry and windy conditions.

23 An increase in the price of petrol would discourage *me from using/ from using* my car.

Reporting
Units 33, 35, 36 & 38

8 Complete the sentences to report what was said using one of the following nouns followed by a *that*-clause or *to-infinitive* clause. Give two completions where both a *that*-clause and *to-infinitive* clause are possible.

advice   complaint   conclusion   confession   decision   prediction
promise   refusal   reply   ~~statement~~   threat   warning

1 'The government has decreased taxation every year since we came to power,' stated the President.
Opposition leaders have challenged *the President's statement that the government have/had decreased taxation every year since they came to power.*

2 Karen said, 'I've decided not to go to university next year.'
We were disappointed with *Karen's decision*

3 'The Earth will pass through the tail of a comet within the next five years,' predicted Professor Adams.
Considerable media attention has been focused on ....

4 'We said that we would dismiss the strikers if they didn't return to work, and we have now done that.'
The company has carried out ....

5 'You should delegate more of your work to your secretary,' Mary was advised by her boss.
Mary decided to follow ....

6 'I'll pick you up at 10.00,' John promised.
John didn't turn up until 11.00, despite ....

7 'Professor Jones doesn't know what he's talking about,' Bob concluded.
I wasn't surprised by ....

8 'My dinner is cold!'
We decided to ignore Donald's ....

9 'We will not negotiate over the ownership of the land!'
I was astonished by ....

10 'Small children should be kept indoors until pollution levels have reduced,' the Health Minister has warned.
The Health Minister has issued ....

11 'I've never used a computer before,' she confessed.
I was surprised by ....

12 'Where's Susan?' I asked Derek. 'I don't know,' he replied.
When I asked Derek where Susan was ....

Nouns
Units 40–43

9 Choose an appropriate present simple form (singular or plural) of the verb in brackets. If both singular and plural forms are possible, give them both.

1 I've been trying to sell my car for ages, but nobody .... to buy it. (*want*)

2 A lettuce and a carrot .... all I need to make the salad. (*be*)

3 A lot of students .... in the old houses near the university. (*live*)

4 All of the scientific evidence .... to the conclusion that increasing use of pesticides in farming is damaging our health. (*point*)

5 The university .... to appoint lecturers who already have a PhD. (*prefer*)

6 She's one of those people who .... just sitting in the sun on holiday. (*love*)

7 The office staff .... that they have been treated badly by management. (*claim*)

8 All of my children .... to the same school. (*go*)

9 A lot of cheaper furniture nowadays .... in pieces inside a flat box for you to build yourself. (*come*)

10 In France, the media .... more respectful of the privacy of celebrities than in Britain. (*be*)

11 Currently, 16 per cent of the workforce .... jobless. (*be*)

12 It's a really quiet town at night. Everything .... at around 10 o'clock. (*shut*)

13 The police .... that the fire was caused deliberately. (*suspect*)

14 The majority of the children in the class .... under five years old. (*be*)

15 Although the bracelet might be worth something, none of the other jewellery .... to be of great value. (*appear*)

16 The stairs .... quite steep, so be careful how you go down. (*be*)

17 What worries me about the car .... the problems we've been having with the brakes. (*be*)

18 The United Nations .... to send a team of doctors to investigate the outbreak of TB. (*plan*)

19 One of the arguments in favour of the new airport .... that it will bring jobs to the area. (*be*)

20 Many people have speculated on the reasons for the southern population movements in the Indian sub-continent during the fifteenth century, but none of the historical records identified so far .... an answer. (*provide*)

21 It's a charity performance, so none of the actors .... a fee for taking part. (*get*)

22 Every letter and parcel .... carefully checked before posting to make sure it has the correct address. (*be*)

23 My parents want to move to Spain, but neither of them .... Spanish. (*speak*)

24 'Where are the scissors?' 'I think either Becky or Miguel .... borrowed them.' (*have*)

25 Most people would agree that the criteria .... not of equal importance. (*be*)

26 The economics of nuclear power .... become more and more difficult in the last decade. (*have*)

27 Whoever had contact with the patient .... to be found and vaccinated against polio. (*have*)

28 'I've got to walk all the way to my uncle's house, and he lives about two miles away.' 'But two miles .... far.' (*be/ not*)

29 A recent survey shows that around 10 per cent of all cars .... dangerous to drive. (*be*)

30 Phonetics .... one of the options you can take in the second year of the course. (*be*)

Articles etc.   **Units 44–48**

10   Which of the following can you use to complete the sentences correctly? Which *one* can you use to complete *all* of the sentences in each set?

      a/an   one   some   the   'zero article' (–)

    1 a   Could you look after my cat while I'm away on holiday? It's only for .... week.

       b   David lives less than .... mile from school, so he can get up at eight o'clock and still be at school by nine.

c As I walked in, Sue was sitting in .... corner of the room and Malcolm was sitting in the other. I could tell that they had been arguing.

2 a .... vulture feeds primarily on dead animals.

    b Margaret has arthritis, and her doctor has suggested that she should spend as much time as possible in .... warm climate.

    c Katherine has decided she wants to be .... accountant.

3 a A: How should I get to the town centre from here?

       B: Well, you could walk, but catching a bus is probably .... quickest.

    b The World Wide Fund for Nature organised a major campaign to save .... tiger.

    c .... washing machine has had a huge impact on people's lives since it was invented.

4 a A: Michael Jordan is visiting our school next week to talk about basketball.

       B: You mean .... Michael Jordan? Can you get his autograph for me?

    b It was hot in the house, so she opened all the windows to let in .... fresh air.

    c Large areas of Canada are still covered by .... forest.

5 a She was made .... Chief Executive Officer in 2002.

    b Do you want .... sugar in your coffee?

    c You can buy .... new microwave ovens for as little as a hundred dollars.

6 a .... 500 people were at the meeting.

    b Despite years of research, we still don't understand the significance of .... dreams.

    c It is a sad fact that .... money buys political power in many societies.

7 a .... earthquake in the south of the country has left thousands homeless.

    b I love having holidays at .... seaside.

    c Do you remember .... Wilmotts? They used to live opposite us.

8 a .... bicycle is an important means of transport for many people with no access to public transport.

    b We only stayed in Oxford for .... night, but we really liked the place.

    c Andre owns a painting that he claims is .... Picasso.

9 a I felt fine when I woke up, but by .... evening I had a high fever.

    b The temperature at .... midday reached over 40°C.

    c It's probably easiest to contact me by .... email.

10 a My history teacher at school – .... Mrs Bullenski – was always giving us advice on how to improve our examination skills.

     b I'll just spend .... day or two in Singapore and then go on to Australia for three weeks.

     c It was .... day that would remain in my memory forever.

Relative clauses   Units 53–55

11   Write the information in brackets as a relative clause in an appropriate place in the sentence. Give all possible relative pronouns, but if you can leave them out, put them in brackets. Make sure you put in commas where necessary.

    1 Later in the programme we have an interview with Peter Svensson. (last week he became the first man to row solo across the Indian Ocean) _Later in the programme we have an interview with Peter Svensson, who last week became the first man to row solo across the Indian Ocean._

    2 Carla's restaurant is very good value. (it serves a range of Mediterranean dishes)

    3 The New Zealand rugby team are clear favourites to win the match. (all of its members weigh over 100 kilos)

4 Suzie brought home a kitten. (she'd found it in the park)
5 The story is about a teenage boy. (his ambition is to become an astronaut)
6 Paul has got a job with Empirico. (its main product is electric light bulbs)
7 Politicians should give more consideration to the working people. (they represent them)
8 Among the group of people was Professor Rogers. (I had last seen him in Oxford twenty years earlier)
9 I live on a small road. (it leads down to the river)
10 Monet's earlier paintings are in a new exhibition in London. (many have never been seen in this country before)
11 Ian McIver has become managing director of Europe's largest food retailer. (his first job was selling vegetables in a market)
12 Douglas has a new girlfriend. (she works in the library)
13 My Volkswagen Golf is a very reliable car. (I bought it in 1980)
14 Brian Brookes will be present at its official opening. (the Brookes art gallery is named after him)

Substitution and leaving out words

Units 62–65

12 Underline the appropriate alternatives. Sometimes both are possible.

1 He has a shave every morning, but you wouldn't think he *did/ had*.
2 The developers pulled down the clock tower to make way for the new road. In *doing so/ so doing*, they destroyed one of the finest examples of 17th century architecture in the country.
3 'Ben won't be coming this weekend.' 'But he *promised so/ promised he would*.'
4 'It looks like Schumacher is going to win again.' 'It *appears/ appears so*.'
5 'I didn't know you cycled to work.' 'Yes, I always *do/ do so*.'
6 I don't smoke cigars, and never *have/ have done*.
7 They asked me to go fishing with them, but I *didn't want/ didn't want to*.
8 'Will it take you long to fix it?' 'Well, it might *do/ do so*. I'm not sure yet.'
9 'Do you think Ray will be up by now?' ' I *doubt that he will/ doubt so*.'
10 'Dad won't mind us borrowing the car, will he?' 'No, I *don't suppose so/ suppose not*.'
11 Just park the car wherever you *want to/ want*.
12 'Has Rachel arrived yet?' 'No, I don't think she *has done/ has*.'
13 Karl had to choose between working much longer hours and moving to another part of the country. He had never faced *such a dilemma/ a such dilemma* before.
14 He owns much more land than I *do so/ do*.
15 We'd like to go to Canada to see Ruth, but we can't *afford to/ afford*.
16 'I imagine the information is kept on computer somewhere.' 'I would *expect so/ expect*.'
17 I don't know whether my parents want me to go to Norway, but I *suspect not/ don't suspect*.
18 'Will she expect us to get the job finished by the weekend?' 'I certainly *don't hope so/ hope not*.'
19 'There's no answer. I suppose she might have left home by now.' 'Yes, I suppose she *might have/ might*.'
20 The car's in good condition. They *told so/ told me so* at the garage.
21 I didn't want Matthew to climb the mountain, but he was *determined to/ determined*.
22 'My mother was really angry.' 'But didn't you expect her *to/ to be*?'
23 'It doesn't look like the rain's going to stop soon.' 'I *don't guess/ guess not*.'
24 'Are you going to the library today?' 'I *might do/ might be*.'

| Position of adjectives, adverbs and adverbial phrases | Units 66, 69, 74 & 75 |

13 Are the italicised words and phrases in the correct position? If not, suggest a change of position or additions to improve the texts.

a I *every so often* leave work *early* and go to a performance in the local concert hall. It's very close to my office, in the *opposite* building. *Usually* they *rather* are good, but yesterday's, given by a singer and pianist, was a *total* disaster. The singer *with wonderful control* began to sing. But when the pianist started to play, it sounded awful. At first I thought he was *badly* playing, but then it became obvious that the piano *completely* was out of tune. They stopped and discussed *briefly* the problem. They couldn't continue *clearly*, and they left the stage *unhappily*. *Naturally*, all the *present* people felt sorry for them. I'm sure the *responsible* person for tuning the piano will be severely reprimanded.

b I *just* was going out to work this morning when the postman pushed *through my letterbox* a letter. It was from Maggie, who writes *from time to time*. The letter said that she has to come to Bristol to visit her *unwell* uncle. She is one of his few *remaining* relatives. She wants us to meet and asked if I could suggest a time *possible*. Well, I *for a couple of years* haven't seen her, so I was really pleased. We *first* met at university. We have *alike* interests, so *always* we find a lot to talk about. The *included* photos in the letter showed that she hadn't changed since I *last* saw her. I spent so long reading the letter that I *nearly* was late for work.

| Adverbial clauses and conjunctions | Units 79–82 & 87 |

14 Match the ideas in (i) and (ii) and use the word in brackets to write either a single sentence (as in 1) or two sentences (as in 2), as appropriate. Note that you can put the idea in (ii) first in the sentence.

i
1 I knew there was something wrong
2 prepare the remaining vegetables
3 his wife is really small
4 only about 100 people attended
5 I can't afford a coat like that
6 I'm determined to finish the report
7 you'll have to walk all the way from the station
8 I stayed until the end
9 her husband would never find it
10 I've been running about 200 kilometres a week

ii
a I found the film boring
b Jamie must weigh over 120 kilos
c to prepare for the marathon
d ~~she said she was feeling fine~~
e I don't like the style
f ~~leave the carrots to cool for a few minutes~~
g make sure you catch the last bus at 11.00
h I have to stay at work until midnight
i she hid the letter between the pages of a book
j there had been a lot of publicity about the meeting

1 (even though) (+ d) I knew there was something wrong, even though she said she was feeling fine. or Even though she said she was feeling fine I knew there was something wrong.

2 (meanwhile) (+ f) Leave the carrots to cool for a few minutes. Meanwhile, prepare the remaining vegetables.

3 (whereas)
4 (even so)
5 (besides)
6 (even if)
7 (otherwise)

8 (although)
9 (so that)
10 (in order to)

Prepositions   Units 92–94

15 Write a preposition in an appropriate place after the italicised nouns and verbs.

                            with

1 Personally, I don't *agree* ⋀ fox hunting, although I know that you *approve* it.
2 There seems to be little *likelihood* Williamson winning Wimbledon because of her *inability* play well on grass tennis courts.
3 Our plan is to *split* the organisation into a number of small units. This will improve our *prospects* competing with more specialised companies.
4 I *ran* Paul in town the other day. He *asked* you.
5 Jack takes great *pride* never *throwing* anything. He always says that one day he'll find a use for things.
6 Although Professor Watson *knows* a great deal meteorology, even he can't *account* the unusual weather we have been having over the last few weeks.
7 There has been a great *improvement* the behaviour of children in the school. This has *resulted* the headteacher's *idea* involving them in decision-making.
8 Even though Dennis didn't *act* my advice and follow a career in medicine, I'm full of *admiration* his *determination* train to be a vet.

Inversion   Units 99 & 100

16 Write new sentences with a similar meaning. In the new sentence the verb should come before the subject (inversion), and the sentences should begin with one of the following words or phrases.

Had	Hardly	~~Little~~	Not for one moment	Only if	Only in
Seldom	Should	So	Under no circumstances	Such	Were

1 I didn't imagine that the boss had called me into her office to fire me. <u>Little did I</u> <u>imagine that the boss had called me into her office to fire me.</u>
2 The police will only investigate the matter further if an official complaint is made.
3 The instructions were so complicated, that it was impossible to assemble the machine.
4 If we had known how ill Rob was, we would have taken him straight to the hospital.
5 The wind was so strong that all the trees in the park were blown down.
6 She didn't often regret her lack of formal education, although she was sometimes aware of gaps in her knowledge.
7 You should only phone for an ambulance in an emergency.
8 There was never any disagreement between us.
9 If it were not for financial assistance from the government, the museum would have closed long ago.
10 They had only just finished eating before a waiter started to clear away the plates.
11 Children should never be allowed into the room without adult supervision.
12 If the bridge is ever built, it will be welcomed by the local community.

Study guide

Use this study guide if you need help in deciding which units you should study, or which part of the *Grammar review* you should read first. Which of the four alternatives completes the sentences in the correct or most likely way? Sometimes more than one alternative is possible.

If you are not sure which alternatives are correct, study any related sections of the *Grammar review* first and then the unit(s) given on the right. You will find the correct answer in the section of the *Grammar review* or the unit highlighted.

You can find an answer key to this study guide on page 281.

TENSES		GRAMMAR REVIEW	STUDY UNIT
1.1	'Who ....?' '.................. to get through to Helen.' A do you phone...I'm trying B are you phoning...I'm trying C are you phoning...I try D do you phone...I try	A1	1, 2
1.2	.... to Turkey every year for your holidays? A Are you going B Were you going C Have you gone D Do you go	A5	1, 2
1.3	I .... I can't see as well as I used to. A am admitting B admits C admit D was admitting		1, 2
1.4	Jane .... me that you're thinking of emigrating. A told B tells C is telling D tell		2, 1
1.5	Kathy .... a few minutes ago. A has left B leaves C left D had left	A6	3, 4, 5
1.6	We .... to the tennis club since we moved here. A have belonged B belong C belonged D are belonging	A11	3, 6
1.7	After she .... hospital, she had a long holiday. A leaves B is leaving C has left D left		3, 4, 5
1.8	When he realised I .... at him, he .... away. A looked...was turning B was looking...turned C was looking...was turning D looked...turned	A13	4, 7
1.9	When the builders were here I .... them cups of tea all the time. A was making B am making C made D make		4, 7
1.10	When I went into the bathroom, I found that the bath .... A overflows B overflowed C had overflowed D is overflowing	A14	5, 7
1.11	I was sure that I .... him before. A had met B am meeting C meet D met		5, 7
1.12	Your eyes are red – .... ? A did you cry B have you been crying C have you cried D do you cry	A17	6
1.13	.... this holiday for ages. A We're looking forward to B We've been looking forward to C We look forward to D We've looked forward to		6, 3

TENSES	**GRAMMAR REVIEW**	**STUDY UNIT**

1.14 When I saw the vase in the shop window, I knew it was exactly what I ....

       A looked for   B look for   C had been looking for
       D have looked for

(A18 — 7)

1.15 .... hard all year, so I felt that I deserved a holiday.

       A I work   B I'd been working   C I'd worked
       D I'm working

(7, 4, 5)

THE FUTURE

2.1 I .... one of my special desserts for dinner, if you like.

       A make   B 'm going to make   C 'll make   D 'm making

(B3 — 9)

2.2 If Jack phones I .... you know.

       A 'm going to let   B let   C 'm letting   D 'll let

(9)

2.3 'Has anybody offered to look after the children?' 'Jo .... it.'

       A is to do   B 's going to do   C does   D will do

(B5 — 9)

2.4 The next train to Newcastle .... at 3.45. [station announcement]

       A will leave   B is leaving   C is going to leave   D leaves

(B6 — 10)

2.5 When you .... Dave, tell him he still owes me some money.

       A are going to see   B are seeing   C see   D will see

(10)

2.6 We .... a party next Saturday. Can you come?

       A 're to have   B 're having   C have   D 'll have

(B7 — 10)

2.7 After the operation you .... any sport for a while.

       A won't be doing   B aren't doing   C don't do   D won't to do

(B8 — 11)

2.8 When the race starts later this afternoon the drivers .... for drier weather than last year.

       A were hoping   B are hoping   C hope   D will be hoping

(11)

2.9 In the next few years, thousands of speed cameras .... on major roads.

       A are appear   B will appear   C are to appear
       D are appearing

(12)

2.10 .... to Bangkok by the end of June.

       A I aim getting   B I'm aiming getting   C I aim to get
       D I'm aiming to get

(13)

2.11 We .... each other later that day, but I had to phone and cancel.

       A see   B are seeing   C were seeing   D saw

(14)

MODALS		GRAMMAR REVIEW	STUDY UNIT

3.1 Despite yesterday's snowfalls, we .... home in less than an hour.

A could drive   B can drive   C were able to drive

D are able to drive

C5   15

3.2 She swam strongly and .... cross the river easily, even though it was swollen by the heavy rain.

A can   B was able to   C could   D is able to

15

3.3 .... me to get you some water?

A Would you like   B Should you like   C Shall you like

D Will you like

C12   16

3.4 We .... Switzerland four times during the 1970s.

A would visit   B used to visit   C visit   D visited

16

3.5 'While we're in Leeds shall we go and see Mark?' 'But it's been nearly 20 years since we last saw him. He .... remember us.'

A can't   B couldn't   C may not   D might not

C17   17

3.6 During the war, the police .... arrest you for criticising the king.

A may   B might   C should   D could

17

3.7 'I'm seeing Dr Evans next week.' 'That .... be right. He's on holiday then.'

A mustn't   B can't   C hasn't to   D hasn't got to

C23   18

3.8 I can't start the computer. You .... a password.

A must have got to know   B must've to know

C must have to know   D must know

18

3.9 I .... an interview because I'd worked there before.

A didn't have to have   B needn't have had

C didn't need to have   D needn't have

C27   19

3.10 Nowadays it .... cost a fortune to own a powerful computer.

A hasn't to   B needn't   C doesn't have to   D mustn't

19

3.11 Walking under a ladder .... be unlucky.

A is suppose to   B should   C ought to   D is supposed to

C32   20

3.12 It's the third time she's been skating this week. She .... really enjoy it.

A must   B should   C ought to   D had better

20

LINKING VERBS, PASSIVES, QUESTIONS

4.1 The traffic lights .... green and I pulled away.

A got   B became   C turned   D went

21

LINKING VERBS, PASSIVES, QUESTIONS	GRAMMAR REVIEW	STUDY UNIT

4.2 The building .... the earthquake but then ....
     by a fire.
     A was survived...destroyed   B survived...was destroyed
     C survived...destroyed   D was survived...was destroyed

D1 — 22, 23, 24

4.3 I'm really disappointed. I.......................... for the team again.
     A wasn't picked   B didn't pick   C didn't get picked
     D wasn't got picked

D2 — 22, 23, 24

4.4 When I asked what was wrong, ...
     A I was explained the problem
     B he explained the problem to me
     C the problem was explained to me
     D he explained me the problem

22

4.5 The children .... to the zoo.
     A were enjoyed taken   B enjoyed being taken
     C were enjoyed taking   D enjoyed taking

23 App.1

4.6 The new computer system .... next month.
     A is being installed by people   B is be installed
     C is being installed   D is been installed

24 App.1

4.7 .... that we have to leave the building.
     A They have informed us   B It has been informed
     C It has been informed us   D We have been informed

25

4.8 He just turned away when I asked him. .... he meant?
     A Which do you think   B How do you think
     C What you think   D What do you think

E3 — 26 App.2

4.9 .... to do in Birmingham at Christmas?
     A What there are   B What is there   C What are there
     D What there is

26

4.10 .... was in the box?
     A What did you think that   B What you thought
     C What did you think   D What you did think

27 App.2

VERB COMPLEMENTATION: WHAT FOLLOWS VERBS

5.1 I always associate ....
     A pizza   B pizza by Italy   C Italian pizza   D pizza with Italy

28

5.2 She described ....
     A the situation   B the situation to me   C me the situation
     D the situation me

29

5.3 Stevens .... the wallet.
     A admitted to steal   B admitted steal   C admitted stealing
     D admitted him stealing

F5 — 30, 31

VERB COMPLEMENTATION: WHAT FOLLOWS VERBS	GRAMMAR REVIEW	STUDY UNIT
5.4 My parents wouldn't .... to the party. A allow me go B allow me to go C allow me going D allow to go	F9	30, 31
5.5 She felt the mosquito .... her. A bites B to bite C bite D biting	F13	30, 31
5.6 You don't object .... late tonight, do you? A to working B to work C work D working		30
5.7 They arranged .... in London. A for Jane to stay B Jane to stay C by Jane to stay D for Jane staying		31

REPORTING		
6.1 Martha .... she would be late for the meeting. She .... she was feeling ill. A told that...said that B told that...said me that C told me that...said that D told me that...said me that	G4/5	32
6.2 She .... her holiday in Finland. A told me about B said about C said me about D told about	G7	32
6.3 'I suppose you've heard the latest .... A news,' said she B news.' she said C news', she said D news,' she said		32 App.3
6.4 I notified .... I had changed my address. A with the bank that B the bank that C that D to the bank that		33
6.5 She reminded .... A what to do B me what I had to do C what I had to do D me what to do		34
6.6 Last night police said that they .... the missing girl. A had found B have found C find D were finding		35
6.7 She encouraged .... the job. A to take the job B that Frank should take C Frank to take D to Frank to take		36
6.8 He asked where he .... put the box. A shall B ought to C will D should		37
6.9 She asked my advice .... subject she should study at university. A on to what B as to what C on what D to what		38
6.10 They directed that the building .... A be pulled down B to be pulled down C should be pulled down D should pull down		39

		GRAMMAR REVIEW	STUDY UNIT

NOUNS

7.1 The .... faulty.
A equipments are   B equipment was   C equipments were
D equipment were
H1

7.2 The company .... doing a lot of .... in South America.
A is...businesses   B are...business   C are...businesses
D is...business
H2   *40*

7.3 The .... shoes were covered in mud, so I asked them to take them off before they got into .... car.
A girl's...Tom's   B girls'...Toms'   C girls'...Tom's
D girl's...Toms'
H7   *43*

7.4 The council .... postponed a decision on the new road, and many leading members of the opposition party ....
criticised the delay.
A has...have   B has...has   C have...has   D have...have
40

7.5 .... thinks that Phil should be given the job.
A Neither of us   B The majority of my colleagues
C Practically everyone   D A number of people
41

7.6 Police .... that Thomas is in Brazil, although his exact whereabouts .... unknown.
A believes...are   B believe...are   C believes...is   D believe...is
42

7.7 A new .... is being built outside the town.
A golf course   B golfcourse   C golf's course   D golf-course
H5

7.8 The government has introduced ....
A a children's clothes tax   B a tax on children clothes
C a children clothes tax   D a tax on children's clothes
43

7.9 .... has improved enormously.
A David's guitar playing   B David guitar playing
C Davids' guitar playing   D The guitar playing of David
H11   *40*

ARTICLES, DETERMINERS AND QUANTIFIERS

8.1 I'll be with you in ....
A one quarter of an hour   B a quarter of an hour
C a quarter of one hour   D a quarter of hour
44

8.2 Look at .... It's very bright tonight.
A the moons   B moon   C the moon   D a moon
I5   *45–47*

8.3 Sydney is ....
A a beautiful city   B beautiful city   C the beautiful city
D the beautiful cities
I7   *45–47*

8.4 .... of the present continuous tense on page 32.
A There are example   B There are examples
C There are the examples   D There is example
I9   *45–47*

ARTICLES, DETERMINERS AND QUANTIFIERS	GRAMMAR REVIEW	STUDY UNIT
8.5 .... is one of the many factors involved in changing farming methods. A Climate B A climate C Climates D The climate		45
8.6 Against her parents' wishes, she wants to be .... A the journalist B journalist C a journalist D journalists		46
8.7 'You look upset.' 'Yes, I've had ....' A the terrible morning B terrible morning C some terrible morning D a terrible morning		47
8.8 I haven't been here for .... A some years B any years C years D the years	I14	48
8.9 We haven't got .... left. A a butter B any butter C the butter D some butter	I15	48
8.10 'Where were you last week?' 'I was visiting ....' A any friends B friends C the friends D some friends		48 49–51
8.11 .... my jewellery is missing. A Some of B Any of C Some D Any	I23	49
8.12 .... the furniture .... arrived yet. A None ... has B None ... have C None of ... has D None of ... have	I34, I22–28	49
8.13 I phoned Sarah at home, but .... A there were no answers B there were no answer C there was no answers D there was no answer		49
8.14 There isn't .... traffic along the street where I live. A many B much C much of D many of	I38, I22–28	50
8.15 .... the food was inedible. A A large amount of B Many of C Much of D A large number of		50
8.16 .... waiting to hear the results. A Everyone was B All was C Everyone were D All were	I44	51
8.17 Following the flood, ... in the area .... major repair work. A each of building...need B every building...needs C every building...need D each buildings...need	I46, I22–28	51
8.18 .... to Athens during the vacation. A All they are going B They are all going C They all are going D They are going all		51
8.19 There is .... evidence to support his claim. A little of B few C a few D little	I48, I22–28	52
8.20 We should use .... time we have available to discuss Jon's proposal. A the little of B the little C the few D little		52

RELATIVE CLAUSES AND OTHER TYPES OF CLAUSE	GRAMMAR REVIEW	STUDY UNIT

9.1 My mother .... enjoys hill walking.
   A who is in her seventies   B , that is in her seventies,
   C , which is in her seventies,   D , who is in her seventies,

9.2 She's one of the kindest people ....
   A that I know   B I know   C who I know   D which I know

9.3 Do you know the date .... we have to hand in the essay?
   A which   B on which   C by which   D when

9.4 The valley .... the town lies is heavily polluted.
   A in that   B in which   C in   D which

9.5 The prisoners .... are all women.
   A who being released   B are being released   C being released
   D who are being released

9.6 She lives in the house ....
   A which has the red door   B has the red door
   C with the red door   D which with the red door

9.7 'Wait a minute,' said Frank, ...
   A running through the door   B run through the door
   C ran through the door   D runs through the door

9.8 .... by the boys' behaviour, she complained to the head teacher.
   A She annoyed   B Annoyed   C She was annoyed
   D Annoying

9.9 .... at the party, we saw Ruth standing alone.
   A Arrived   B We arrived   C Arriving   D We were arriving

9.10 John was the first person I saw .... hospital.
   A by leaving   B on leaving   C in leaving   D on to leave

Study units / Grammar review references:
- 9.1 — J2 — 53
- 9.2 — 53
- 9.3 — 54
- 9.4 — 55
- 9.5 — 56
- 9.6 — 57
- 9.7 — J6 — 58, 59
- 9.8 — J8 — 58, 59
- 9.9 — 58
- 9.10 — 59

PRONOUNS, SUBSTITUTION AND LEAVING OUT WORDS

10.1 'What did you do to your hand?' 'I .... when I was chopping vegetables.'
   A cut me   B cut   C myself cut   D cut myself
   — K1 — 60

10.2 The scheme allows students from many countries to communicate ....
   A each other   B with each other   C themselves
   D with one another
   — K7

10.3 We are confident that both sets of fans will .... at the match.
   A behave itself   B behave them   C behave themselves
   D behave
   — 60

PRONOUNS, SUBSTITUTION AND LEAVING OUT WORDS	GRAMMAR REVIEW	STUDY UNIT

10.4 'We need new curtains.' 'Okay, let's buy ....'   **61**
A ones with flowers on   B some   C ones   D one

10.5 The two children .... for breaking the window.   **K9**
A each blamed other   B blamed other   C blamed each other
D each blamed the other

10.6 I had a racing bike when I was young, and **K10**   **62**
A my brother did so   B so did my brother   C so my brother
D did my brother

10.7 'I don't suppose there'll be any seats left.' 'No, I ....'   **62**
A don't suppose   B suppose   C don't suppose so
D suppose not

10.8 They needed someone who was both an excellent administrator   **63**
and manager. .... was not easy to find.
A Such person   B A such person   C Such   D Such a person

10.9 'They could have been delayed by the snow.' 'Yes, they ....'   **64**
A could have   B could   C could been   D could have been

10.10 The report is very critical and is clearly **65**
A intended to be   B intended to   C intended   D intend to be

ADJECTIVES AND ADVERBS		

11.1 He is a **66**
A capable of taking difficult decisions manager
B manager capable of taking difficult decisions
C capable manager of taking difficult decisions
D manager capable to take difficult decisions

11.2 Our teacher gave us .... problem to solve.   **L2**   **67, 68**
A a very impossible   B a completely impossible
C an absolutely impossible   D an extremely impossible

11.3 Some experience is .... for the job.   **67**
A really essential   B fairly essential   C pretty essential
D very essential

11.4 I met my .... professor the other day. She is now   **68**
advising on the government's ....
A old politics...very foreign policy
B very old politics...foreign policy
C very old politics...very foreign policy
D old politics...foreign policy

11.5 I drank some .... coffee.   **L3**
A good very Brazilian   B Brazilian very good
C very good Brazilian   D very Brazilian good

ADJECTIVES AND ADVERBS

		GRAMMAR REVIEW	STUDY UNIT

11.6 I was .... to find that the film was quite **L4**
A surprised...frightening   B surprised...frightened
C surprising...frightening   D surprising...frightened

11.7 My watch was among the **69**
A things taken   B taken things   C things stolen
D stolen things

11.8 He was busy .... his homework. **70**
A to do   B doing   C that he was doing   D he was doing

11.9 It was .... as we went into the room. **L6**   **71**
A strange quiet   B strange quietly   C strangely quiet
D strangely quietly

11.10 She .... towards the door. **71**
A quick ran   B ran quick   C ran quickly   D quickly ran

11.11 It was the .... thing to say. **L8**   **72**
A most ridiculous   B ridiculous   C ridiculousest
D most ridiculousest

11.12 'Why did you buy these oranges?' 'They were **72**
A cheapest   B the cheapest   C the cheapest ones I could find
D cheapest ones I could find

11.13 She was .... as anyone could have had. **73**
A as patient teacher   B a patient a teacher
C as patient as teacher   D as patient a teacher

11.14 Have you heard the good news? **74, 75**
A In May, Jane had a baby   B Jane had a baby in May
C Jane in May had a baby   D Jane had in May a baby

11.15 .... Derek nowadays, he's so busy at the office. **75**
A We see hardly ever   B We hardly see ever
C We hardly ever see   D Hardly we ever see

11.16 Only later .... how much damage had been caused. **76, 99, 100**
A she realised   B she did realised   C did she realise
D realised she

11.17 We .... with the decision. **77**
A agree very much   B much agree   C agree much
D very much agree

11.18 ...., this summer is a crucial time for the government. **78**
A Politics speaking   B Politically   C In political terms
D In a political point of view

ADVERBIAL CLAUSES AND CONJUNCTIONS	GRAMMAR REVIEW	STUDY UNIT
12.1 I .... unwell when I .... this morning. A felt...get up B felt...got up C feel...get up D feel...got	M2	
12.2 Have something to eat before you .... A leave B left C will leave D had left	M3	
12.3 I still feel tired .... in the morning. A when I wake up B as I wake up C when I will wake up D while I wake up		79
12.4 We were delayed .... an accident. A because B because of there was C because there was D because of		80
12.5 The land was bought quickly .... delay the building work. A so as not to B so not to C not to D in order not to		81
12.6 .... they slept soundly. A Hot though was the night air B Hot though the night air was C Hot as the night air was D Hot although the night air was		82
12.7 I'll give you a lift if it .... A is raining B will rain C rained D rains	M9	83, 84
12.8 If I had known how difficult the job was, I .... it. A won't have taken B wouldn't have taken C won't take it D mightn't have taken	M14	83, 84
12.9 If I .... a more reliable car, I .... to Spain rather than fly. A would have...would drive B had...had driven C had...would drive D would have had...would drive	M17	83, 84
12.10 If the technology .... available, we would be able to expand the business. A would become B were become C were to become D became		83
12.11 If the North Sea .... in winter, you could walk from London to Oslo. A happened to freeze B froze C should freeze D should happen to freeze		84
12.12 .... in my seventies and rather unfit, I might consider taking up squash. A Were I not B Was I not C Weren't I D If I wasn't		85
12.13 They couldn't decide .... it was worth re-sitting the exam. A if B whether or not C whether D if or not		86
12.14 It was midday. ...., I put on the light. A Even so B Although C Even D Even though		87

PREPOSITIONS

13.1   He suddenly saw Sue .... the room. He pushed his way
.... the crowd of people to get to her.
A across...through   B over...through   C across...across
D over...along

88

13.2   The concert features, ... others, Karl Frisk and the
Johnsons. Their music is still very popular .... teenagers.
A between...among   B between...between   C among...between
D among...among

89

13.3   .... a pause in the conversation, she left the room.
A In   B During   C Over   D Throughout

90

13.4   .... cricket, I enjoy watching football and basketball.
A Apart from   B Except   C Except for   D Besides

91

13.5   He got angry when they started to .... his private life.
A ask after   B ask about   C enquire about   D enquire after

92

13.6   What's the chance .... five heads when you toss a coin
five times?
A of throwing   B to throw   C of throw   D throw

93

13.7   She tried to ....
A talk me the plan out of   B talk out of me the plan
C talk me out of the plan   D talk out me of the plan

94

ORGANISING INFORMATION

14.1   .... people trying to get into the football stadium.
A There were too much   B There were too many
C It was too many   D There was too many

95, 96

14.2   When Bond saw Vanya taking photographs of the plane,
.... that she was a spy.
A dawned on him   B it dawned him   C it dawned on him
D it dawned on

96

14.3   I .... you can swim so well and I can't.
A hate   B hate it that   C hate that   D hate it

97

14.4   Dave lost his job and was short of money, so .... his flat
and move in with his brother.
A that he did was to sell   B what he did was to sell
C what he did sold   D what he did was sell

98

14.5   .... been diverted, they would have arrived early.
A Had the plane not   B Hadn't the plane
C The plane had not   D The plane not had

99

14.6   .... that Marie was able to retire at the age of 50.
A So successful her business was,   B So successful was her business,
C Her business was so successful   D So was her successful business

100

Key to Exercises

UNIT 1

1.1
2 a 'm (am) measuring
  b measures
3 a doubt b doubt
4 a is currently attracting
    ('attracts' is also possible)
  b attract
5 a doesn't like b 'm (am) not
    liking ('don't like' is also
    possible)
6 a 're (are) fitting
  b doesn't fit
7 a feels b 'm (am) not feeling
    ('don't feel' is also possible)
8 a consists of ('consists only
    of' would also be possible);
  b consists of
9 a 's (is) sounding ('sounds' is
    also possible) b sounds
10 a 's (is) having b has

1.2
1 I'm understanding/ I understand
  (both possible)
2 I admit/ I'm admitting
3 Do you find/ Are you finding
  (both possible)
4 we're not guaranteeing/ we don't
  guarantee (both possible)
5 I'm knowing/ I know
6 I refuse/ I'm refusing
7 I'm certainly agreeing/
  I certainly agree
8 I'm not apologising/ I don't
  apologise. (both possible)
9 we're considering/ we consider

UNIT 2

2.1
1 shoots, are attacking
2 arrives, is waiting, says
3 is playing ('was playing' is also
  possible), stands, starts

2.2 Possible answers
2 I gather Vegecorp are going to
  sack a thousand workers.
3 I understand we're going to
  have a new public holiday for
  the President's birthday.
4 Ed tells me Tony's crashed his
  car again.
5 Julie says she's got a new job.
6 They say they've found a new
  vaccination to prevent/ against
  malaria.

2.3
2 You're forever asking me for
  money.
3 You're constantly criticising my
  driving.
4 You're continually changing
  your mind.
5 You're forever moaning about
  (your) work.

2.4 The most likely verbs are given
1 a I'm (am) wondering/ I was
    wondering ('I wonder'/ 'I
    wondered' are also possible)
  b wonder
2 a we're (are) usually eating ('we
    usually eat' is also possible)
  b don't eat
3 a plays ('is playing' is also
    possible)
  b 're (are) constantly playing
    ('play' is also possible)
4 a I'm normally taking ('I
    normally take' is also possible.
    It would suggest, however,
    that this is the time they leave
    home. Present continuous
    suggests that they are on the
    way to school at 8.30.)
  b takes

UNIT 3

3.1
1 've (have) read
2 went
3 've (have) had
4 wore
5 've (have) spent
6 overslept

3.2
1 hasn't wanted – fell
2 has worked – hasn't had
3 rescued – has been
4 has happened – spoke
5 have been able – have felt
6 has improved – has been

3.3
1 a 've (have) signed b signed
2 a 've (have) finished
  b finished
3 a got b have got
4 a heard b 've (have) heard

3.4 The most appropriate tenses are given
1 have lost (or has lost)
2 has closed (or has been closed) –
  died
3 defeated – has beaten
4 have been stolen (present perfect
  passive) – insisted – held

UNIT 4

4.1
2 was hoping – gave
3 lived – was spending or was
  living – spent
4 started – was checking in
5 was looking – saw
6 came – was showing
7 was playing – broke
8 went off – lit
9 wasn't listening ('didn't listen' is
  also possible) – was explaining
  ('explained' is also possible)
10 added – tasted
11 wasn't watching ('didn't watch'
  is also possible) – was dreaming
  ('dreamt' is also possible)
12 pushed – ran

4.2
1 'was getting' and 'got' are both
  possible. The past simple
  suggests that one event followed
  the other: I got in and then the
  lights went off. The past
  continuous suggests that the
  lights went off as I was in the
  process of getting ready to get
  into the bath.
4 'was checking in' or 'checked in'
  are both possible with a similar
  meaning. Using the past
  continuous presents 'checking
  in' as the background event
  which was going on as the
  couple started to chat to him.
7 'was playing' and 'played' are
  both possible. The past
  continuous suggests that this
  was a temporary rather than a
  regular arrangement.
11 'didn't watch' and 'dreamt' are
  also possible. However, the past
  continuous emphasises that 'not
  watching' and 'dreaming' went
  on at the same time and seems
  more likely here.

4.3
1 was buying
2 saw
3 turned
4 was slowly putting (Past simple
  in 3 and past continuous in 4
  seem most likely here as 'turned
  round' describes a completed
  action and 'was slowly putting'
  describes the action that was
  going on at that time. However,
  past continuous is also possible
  in 3 and past simple is also
  possible in 4.)
5 was carrying
6 walked
7 picked up
8 thought
9 was looking
10 dropped
11 had
12 noticed
13 was watching
14 hurried
15 were walking or walked (similar
  meaning)
16 ran

UNIT 5

5.1

order of events	order events mentioned in text
It was empty	I first saw the old house
I moved...	I moved...
I first saw the old house	It was empty
A property developer bought it	I put together enough money...
I put together enough money...	I learnt...
I learnt...	A property developer bought it
I nearly gave up...	I nearly gave up...
The property developer decided...	I heard...
I heard...	The property developer decided...

The first past 'point of reference' is 'When I first saw the old house'. Events before this are in the past perfect: 'I had just moved'... 'It had been empty'. The second past 'point of reference' is when 'I learnt...'. Events before this are in the past perfect: 'I had put together' ... 'had bought'. Notice that we could use 'I put together' here as the order of events is made clear by 'By the time...'.
The third past 'point of reference' is '...when I heard that the house was for sale again'. Events before this are in the past perfect: 'I had nearly given up'... 'The property developer had decided...'.

5.2

1 had met
2 had been/ went
3 had taken/ took
4 had read/ read
5 had lost
6 had found
7 had cheated/ cheated
8 had gone/ went
9 had finished/ finished
10 had eaten

5.3

2 Lucy hadn't intended to become a dentist...
3 I had expected the operation to be painful...
4 I hadn't thought of cooking rabbit...
5 He hadn't meant to insult her... (or He hadn't meant it to be an insult to her...)

UNIT 6

6.1

1 a 's (has) been staying ('has stayed' is also possible)
   b 've (have) stayed
2 a have ('has' is also possible, but less likely in British English) moved
   b have been moving ('have moved' is also possible)
3 a have been stopping ('have stopped' is also possible)
   b has stopped
4 a haven't read

b 've (have) been reading ('have read' is also possible)
5 a has been giving ('has given' is also possible)
   b has given
6 a haven't swum
   b 've (have) been swimming
7 a have been putting ('have put' is also possible)
   b has (or 'have') put
8 a has disappeared
   b have been disappearing ('have disappeared' is also possible)

6.2

a
1 has claimed
2 died
3 have been making (or have made)
4 've (have) produced
5 awarded
6 've (have) been looking (or have looked, or looked)
7 've (have) also been exploring (or have also explored, or also explored)
8 has/have made
b
1 invested
2 has announced
3 has been increasing (or has increased)
4 has been running (or has run)
5 's (has) been neglecting (or has neglected)
6 has been cutting (or has cut)
7 've (have) found
8 've (have) been planning (or have planned)
9 spoke
10 've (have) also written (or wrote)

UNIT 7

7.1

1 a had been working ('had worked' is also possible)
   b had finally worked
2 a had carried
   b had been carrying ('had carried' is also possible)
3 a had smoked
   b had been smoking
4 a had applied
   b had been applying ('had applied' is also possible)

5 a had flown
   b had been flying
   (Note that the past simple could be used in 1a, 1b, 2a, 2b, 3a, 4a, 5a)

7.2

1 had been trying ('had tried' is also possible)
2 had visited
3 had cost
4 had been writing ('had written' is also possible)
5 had been worrying ('had worried' is also possible)
6 had arrived
7 had always believed
8 had been talking
The past continuous is more likely in 8 (We were talking...).

7.3

1 ✓
2 had been taken
3 ✓ (Note that 'What happened?' is also possible)
4 had just heard
5 ✓
6 had been fishing
7 ✓
8 hadn't wanted
9 ✓
10 had collapsed

UNIT 8

8.1 *The most likely verbs and tenses are given.*

2 got/ arrived
3 feel/ am feeling (Present simple and present continuous have a similar meaning here.)
4 go
5 know
6 spent
7 wrote
8 were waiting
9 got
10 felt/ was feeling (Past simple and past continuous have a similar meaning here.)
11 got
12 enjoy/ are enjoying (Present simple and present continuous have a similar meaning here, although the present continuous may suggest that they are not living in Adelaide permanently.)
13 is looking
14 seems
15 doesn't get on/ isn't getting on (Present simple and present continuous have a similar meaning here, although the present continuous suggests that this is a temporary problem.)
16 complain/ are constantly complaining (Note the word order.)
17 is starting
18 asked
19 am looking
20 hear/ heard (Present simple and past simple have a similar meaning here.)

Key to Exercises

8.2 *The most likely tenses are given.*

2 said ('has said' is also possible, but less likely here)
3 heard/ had heard
4 returned/ had returned
5 came/ had come
6 was/ had been
7 left
8 appointed
9 finished
10 have won
11 accused
12 has disappointed
13 has spent

8.3

1 'Has he had' or 'Has he been having' are more likely
2 ✓
3 thought/ had thought
4 has worked/ has been working
5 had been trying
6 did you go
7 heard
8 ✓ ('went' is also possible)
9 ✓ ('checked' is also possible)
10 have said / said
11 ✓ ('have given' is also possible)
12 have told ('told' is also possible)

UNIT 9

9.1

1 'll see (decision made at moment of speaking)
2 'll be (prediction based on opinion/ past experience)
3 's going to have (prediction based on present evidence)
4 'll book (decision made at moment of speaking)
5 'll find (prediction based on opinion/ past experience)
6 's going to be (decision already made)
7 Are you going to take up (prediction based on present evidence)
8 're going to have (prediction based on present evidence)
9 'll have (decision made at moment of speaking)
10 'll be (prediction based on opinion/ past experience)
11 'm going to build (decision already made)
12 're going to sell (prediction based on present evidence)
13 'm going to cut (decision already made)
14 's going to be sick (prediction based on present evidence); 'll feel (prediction based on opinion/ past experience)
15 'm going to leave (decision already made); will you tell *or* are you going to tell (asking about something planned); 'll try (decision made at moment of speaking)

16 'm going to have (decision already made); 're going to see (decision already made); 'll sort out (decision made at moment of speaking)

9.2 *Example verbs are given*

2 'll hear (ability)
3 'll hurt/ 're going to hurt (conditional – negative)
4 will … buy (request)
5 will start/stop. (logical consequence)
6 'm going to see (main clause action does not depend on action in the *if*-clause)
7 'll be sacked/ 's going to be sacked. (conditional – negative)
8 're going to plant (main clause action does not depend on action in the *if*-clause)

UNIT 10

10.1

1 get (fixed event; 'will get' is also possible)
2 will look after (less routine arrangement)
3 rains (with 'in case')
4 will give out (less routine arrangement)
5 goes (fixed event; 'will go' is also possible)
6 starts (fixed event; 'will start' is also possible)
7 stops (with 'provided')
8 change (with 'what if')
9 will miss (prediction)
10 lend (with 'unless')
11 play (or 'plays') (fixed event; 'will play' is also possible)
12 will accept (prediction)
13 want (with 'supposing')
14 read (with 'by the time')

10.2

1 (c) is leaving (prediction perhaps based on opinion, experience or present evidence). 'Will leave' and 'is going to leave' have a similar meaning here.
2 (a) will buy (planned future event). 'I'm going to buy' suggests an intention without a definite arrangement; 'I'm buying' suggests a definite arrangement – perhaps the speaker has bought the car and is simply picking it up next week.
3 (b) are going to pick; (c) are picking (offer; decision made at moment of speaking)
4 (a) will drive (planned future event). 'I'm going to drive' suggests a personal intention; 'I'm driving' suggests a more definite arrangement – perhaps the speaker has been told to go there by their employer.
5 (c) is cutting (permanent future situation). 'Will cut' and 'is going to cut' have a similar meaning here.

6 (b) am going to call; (c) am calling (promise; decision made at time of speaking)
7 (a) will serve (planned future event). As the present continuous for the future suggests a definite arrangement, using 'I am serving lunch' in this context suggests '…and I am not changing what I plan to do', perhaps showing some irritation or annoyance.
8 (c) are starving (no control over predicted event). 'Will starve' and 'are going to starve' have a similar meaning here. However, as 'will' is often used to talk about future facts, it may express more certainty in this context.

10.3

1

1 is joining ✓ joins ✗ (will join ✓ is going to join ✓)
2 are liking ✗ likes ✗ (will like ✓ are going to like ✓)
3 is coming ✓ comes ✓ (will come ✓ [but present continuous, present simple or 'be going to' are more natural here] is going to come ✓)
4 is giving ✗ gives ✗ (will give ✓ is going to give ✗)

2

1 is/are sacking ✓ sack ✗ (will sack ✓ [but present continuous or 'be going to' are more natural here] is/are going to sack ✓)
2 are closing ✗ close ✓ (will close ✗ are going to close ✗)
3 are building ✓ build ✗ (will build ✓ [but present continuous or 'be going to' are more natural here] are going to build ✓)
4 are seeing ✗ see ✗ (will see ✓ are going to see ✗)

UNIT 11

11.1

1 a will be leaving ('will leave' is also possible) b will leave
2 a Will you be working ('Will you work' is also possible) b 'll work
3 a won't be using ('won't use' is also possible) b won't use
4 a 'll (will) give b will be giving ('will give' is also possible)
5 a won't move b will be moving ('will move' is also possible)

11.2

2 If the company is making a profit by the end of the year then we will have achieved the objective we set ourselves when we took over.
3 In two years' time Morneau will have been acting for 50 years, and shows no sign of retiring

from the theatre. ('will have acted' is also possible)

4　I am confident that I will have finished the report before the end of the week.

5　This book on Proust is really difficult. On Saturday I will have been reading it for a month, and I'm still only half way.

6　Whether I've finished the report or not, by 9 o'clock I will have been working for 12 hours without a break and I'm going home. ('will have worked' is also possible)

7　As delegates who arrived early will have been discovering, there have been some late changes to the conference programme. ('will have discovered' is also possible)

11.3

1　will have closed
2　will be enjoying
3　will be leaving
4　will be arriving
5　will have been
6　will have been planning
7　won't be spending
8　will be keeping
9　will all be going

UNIT 12

12.1

1　is to be staged ('will be staged' is also possible)
2　will stop
3　is to merge/ is to be merged ('will merge' or 'will be merged' are also possible)
4　will rise
5　is to retire; is to be replaced ('will retire' and 'will be replaced' are also possible)
6　will become
7　are to receive ('will receive' is also possible)
8　are to be created ('will be created' is also possible)
9　will increase

12.2

1　are to have (see section B)
2　is about to start (C)
3　wins (B)
4　enjoy (B)
5　'm just about to go (C)
6　recovers (B)
7　is to keep (B)
8　is to resign/ is about to resign (C)
9　is to be improved (B)

UNIT 13

13.1

2　on the point of turning back ('was on the verge of quitting' would also be possible)
3　on the verge of becoming
4　due to announce
5　set to rise
6　on the brink of signing

7　on the point of phoning
8　bound to forget
9　due to undergo
10　on the verge of quitting
11　set to make
12　on the brink of going

13.2

2　propose/ 'm proposing to deal
3　expect/ 're expecting to finish
4　aim/ 'm aiming to study
5　resolves to give up
6　guarantee to find
7　intend/ 'm intending to move

13.3

1　will
2　shan't/ won't ('won't' is more natural)
3　will
4　shall/ will
5　won't

UNIT 14

14.1

1　was going to do
2　will be
3　✓
4　would have shown
5　✓ ('was to be announced' is also possible)
6　is about to start
7　✓
8　was supposed; was about to ask
9　✓ ('am going to see' is also possible)
10　is to be used
11　✓ ('were meeting' is also possible)
12　would cause

Past or present tense forms are possible in 5, 9 and 11.

14.2

1 a　2 b　3 b　4 b　5 a　6 b
7 a　8 a　9 a　10 a

UNIT 15

15.1

1　can (A: before passive)
2　were able to (B: single past achievement)
3　could/ were able to (A)
4　Could you (B: with 'understand'; 'could' is more natural)
5　can't (A: 'know how to')
6　can (A: happening as speaking)
7　were able to (B: single past achievement)
8　could hardly (B: with 'hardly'; 'could' is more natural)
9　could (B: with 'smell'; 'could' is more natural)
10　Can you/ Are you able to (A)
11　can (A: before passive)
12　was able to (B: single past achievement)
13　couldn't (B: negative sentence; 'couldn't' is more natural)
14　was able to (B: single past achievement)

15.2

a
1　can
2　couldn't
3　can
4　can't
5　couldn't/ weren't allowed to
6　can't
7　were allowed to
b
1　can
2　wasn't allowed to/ couldn't
3　was allowed to
4　could
5　could
6　can't
7　was allowed to

UNIT 16

16.1

1　will come
2　invited
3　wouldn't eat
4　would keep
5　will remember *or* would remember
6　would help
7　decided

16.2

1　would ✗ used to ✓ (changed past state)
2　would ✓ ('used to' is also possible)
3　would ✗ used to ✓ (changed past state)
4　used to ✓ ('would' is not possible) (changed past state)
5　used to ✓ ('would' is also possible)
6　would meet ✗ met ✓ (number of times specified)

16.3

1　will have recorded
2　would have said
3　would have hurt
4　will have heard
5　would have preferred
6　will/ would have noticed
7　would have bought

16.4 *Example answers*

'I think I'm putting on weight.' 'Well, if you *will* drive everywhere instead of walking, I'm not surprised.'
'I've got a headache.' 'Well, if you *will* spend so long in front of the television, I'm not surprised.'
'I'm really hot.' 'Well, if you *will* wear a heavy sweater when it's 30 degrees, it's not surprising.'

UNIT 17

17.1

1　might (more likely than 'may')
2　may
3　Are you likely to... (possible answer; Might you... would be rather formal)
4　might (more likely than 'may')

5 Could (possible answer; Might would be rather formal)
6 may

17.2

1 may/ might have hurt
2 may/ might have told
3 may/ might be waiting
4 might be sent ('might have been sent' is also possible)
5 may/ might have been running
6 may/ might be closing ('may/ might close' is also possible)
7 might have taken
8 might be dismissed ('might have been dismissed' is also possible)
9 may/ might have finished ('may/ might finish' is also possible)
10 might have caused

17.3 *Possible answers*
1 ... at least he's in tune.
2 ... it's never broken down.
3 ... she has a very wide vocabulary.
5 You may/ might not agree with him, ...
6 It may/ might not sound very exciting, ...
7 She may/ might not express her feelings openly, ...

UNIT 18

18.1

1 must have found
2 must be
3 must be starting ('must be going to start' and 'must start' are also possible)
4 must have had to work ('must have worked' is also possible)
5 must be using
6 must be having
7 must have changed
8 must have to show
9 must be taking ('must have taken' is also possible)
10 must be

18.2

2 Suzanne rarely has to be asked to tidy her room.
3 Have we got to hand in the homework tomorrow? ('Do we have to...' is also possible)
4 I didn't have to go to the hospital after all.
5 Did Ben have to go alone?
6 Don sometimes has to start work at 6.30. ('Don has sometimes got to start work...' is also possible)
7 The college has to be extended to accommodate the growing number of students. ('has got to be extended' is also possible, but less likely in a formal context)
8 We may/ might have to cancel our holiday because my mother is ill.

18.3

1 ✓
2 ~~always have got to pull~~ always have to pull
3 ~~Have you to bang~~ Do you have to bang ('Must you bang...' is also possible but less likely)
4 ✓
5 ~~must have to squeeze~~ must have had to squeeze *or* must have squeezed
6 ~~must leave~~ must have left
7 ✓
8 ~~mustn't wait~~ didn't have to wait
9 ~~must be disturbed~~ must have been disturbed
10 ~~I've to get~~ I've got to get *or* I have to get
11 ✓
12 ~~may must get~~ may have to get
13 ~~I've to go~~ I must go *or* I have to go *or* I've got to go
14 ~~must get~~ must be getting
15 ✓
16 ~~have to get~~ must get (more likely)

The three common expressions with 'must' are 'I must say...', 'I must admit...' (both used to emphasise the following point), and 'needs must' (meaning if something is necessary I will do it, even though I may not want to).

UNIT 19

19.1

1 I'll give you a lift to the station so you needn't worry/ bother about booking a taxi.
2 The questions are in the book so you needn't bother to copy them down.
3 All the windows have screens so you needn't panic/ worry about being bitten by mosquitoes.
4 Your son is being looked after by friends so you needn't concern yourself with his safety.
5 The new tax laws don't come into force until next year so you needn't change the details on the form.

19.2

2 We need only (*or* We only need...) look at the population projections to see the seriousness of the problem. (*less formally* We only need to look at...)
3 With such a lead in the opinion polls the Democrats need hardly bother (*or* ...the Democrats hardly need bother...) campaigning before the election. (*less formally* ...the Democrats hardly need to bother campaigning...)
4 No-one need know who paid the ransom to the kidnappers. (*less formally* No-one needs to know who paid...)

5 After such a huge lottery win, he need never work again. (*less formally* ... he never needs to work again.)

19.3

1 don't need to
2 needn't/ don't need to
3 needn't/ don't need to
4 don't need to
5 needn't/ don't need to
6 don't need to

19.4

1 You needn't worry...
2 Do we need to make... *is more likely*
3 ...needn't be a problem...
4 ✓
5 I need hardly tell you..., *or less formally* I hardly need (to) tell you...
6 some people would prefer 'needn't' in this context (see C)
7 ✓
8 ... needn't mean...

UNIT 20

20.1

1 should/ ought to win (should/ ought to have won *is also possible*)
2 should I put (*more likely than* ...ought I to put...; should I have put *is also possible*)
3 should/ ought to have arrived (should/ ought to arrive *is also possible*)
4 should be sent (*more likely than* ought to be sent)
5 should/ ought to visit
6 should/ ought to have taken (should/ ought to take *is also possible*)
7 should be removed (*more likely than* ought to be removed)
8 should/ ought to wear
9 should/ ought to have resigned
10 Should we answer (*more likely than* Ought we to answer...; Should we have answered *is also possible*)
11 should go (ought to *is not possible*)
12 should/ ought to be (should/ ought to have been *is also possible*)

20.2

1 should *or* must; 'must' gives a stronger recommendation
2 must
3 must
4 should *or* must; 'must' gives stronger advice and is perhaps more likely than 'should' in this context
5 should *or* must; 'must' gives a stronger recommendation
6 must
(2, 3 and 6 include logical conclusions, so we use 'must' not 'should')

20.3
1 ~~had better not~~ shouldn't/ ought not to be…
2 ~~should~~ must
3 ✓
4 ~~shall~~ should/ ought to
5 ~~shouldn't~~ 'd better not
6 ~~'d better~~ should/ ought to
7 ✓
8 ✓
9 ✓
10 ~~had better~~ should/ ought to

UNIT 21

21.1
1 (to be)   6 to be
2 to be   7 to be
3 to be   8 to be
4 (to be)   9 (to be)
5 (to be)   10 (to be)

21.2
1 get
2 became/ has become
3 become (more likely than 'get' in a formal context)
4 become
5 get
6 get (more likely than 'become' in an informal context)
7 became
8 got
9 get (more likely than 'become' in an informal context)

21.3
2 went dead
3 went red
4 get to know
5 get tired
6 came to like
7 go blind
8 went bust

21.4
1 go wrong
2 seemed to be awake
3 ✓
4 seemed to be taking
5 hadn't got dressed
6 ✓ ('be ill' would also be possible)
7 went missing
8 to get worried
9 becoming obvious
10 ✓

UNIT 22

22.1
2 She was offered a second-hand bicycle./ A second-hand bicycle was offered (to) her.
3 Improvements have been proposed to the developers.
4 Some interesting changes were suggested to me.
5 He was awarded a prize./ A prize was awarded to him.
6 The President's arrival will be announced to the waiting journalists.
7 The password had been mentioned to the thieves.
8 I have been lent some skis./ Some skis have been lent to me.
9 He is being sent threatening letters./ Threatening letters are being sent to him.
10 The changes are going to be explained to the students.

22.2
2 I was introduced to Mrs Jennings by Tony at his birthday party. (or ...Mrs Jennings at Tony's birthday party.)
3 Has Chris been seen (by anyone) this morning?
4 Rabbits may have been brought to Britain by the Romans as a source of food.
5 The story of Father Christmas is told to young children to explain the presents they receive.
6 Martin Johnson has been appointed (or was appointed) team captain for the whole of the World Cup.
7 I am certain that Sarah's suitability as company director will be demonstrated to those who still have any doubt.
8 Alan Watson was declared (or has been declared) winner of the election after a recount.

22.3
2 The product was phased out (by the company) over a period of three years.
3 No passive
4 Many people have been deprived of the right to vote (by the decision).
5 No passive
6 No passive
7 The last two items were held over (by the chairman) until the next committee meeting.
8 Walkers were prevented from crossing the field after it was fenced off (by the farmer).

UNIT 23

23.1
2 denied being involved
3 was left holding
4 remembered being bitten
5 avoided being taken
6 was observed hiding
7 was sent tumbling
8 faced being expelled
9 was found wandering
10 resented being given

23.2
2 were asked to show
3 are required/ will be required to fill
4 No passive
5 be heard arguing
6 was caught taking
7 No passive
8 No passive
9 reported being attacked
10 is/ was expected to attract

23.3
1 Malcolm began to be irritated by Kay's questions. (corresponding meaning)
2 Kevin hopes to be selected by the team captain. (different meaning)
3 Kathy arranged to be taken to the station by Alan. (different meaning)
4 Galdos has come be recognised as one of Spain's greatest novelists by critics. (corresponding meaning)
5 Holidaymakers continue to be attracted to the south coast. (corresponding meaning)
6 The finance minister has agreed to be interviewed by Harris. (different meaning)

UNIT 24

24.1
2 The recent flooding is being blamed on climate change./ Climate change is being blamed for the recent flooding.
3 Keith Jones has been described as the world's greatest guitarist.
4 The painting had been stolen from the gallery.
5 The litter will have been cleared from the pitch before the match starts./ The pitch will have been cleared of litter before the match starts.
6 The game was being watched outside the stadium on a huge screen.
7 The walls will be sprayed with green paint./ Green paint will be sprayed on the walls.
8 Mary should have been offered a drink when she arrived./ A drink should have been offered to Mary when she arrived.
9 You will be provided with food for the journey./ Food will be provided (for you) for the journey.
10 The fields have been planted with cotton./ Cotton has been planted in the fields.

24.2
2 The appointment of a new managing director will be made next week.
3 Accusations of corruption in/against the local council have been made.
4 The demolition of the building was completed in only two days.
5 The presentation of the trophy will be made after the speeches.
6 Resistance from local residents to the proposed new industrial area will certainly be shown.

24.3
2 is being ruled (or more naturally 'is now being ruled')
3 are disappearing/ have disappeared

4 fear
5 is estimated/ has been estimated
6 will be turned into
7 is using/ has used
8 to be abandoned
9 be affected
10 expect
11 are being destroyed/ are destroyed

UNIT 25

25.1
1 intended
2 proposed/shown
3 hoped/ explained
4 decided
5 explained
6 established/ revealed
7 agreed
8 planned
9 assumed/ thought
10 discovered

25.2
2 ✗
3 It has been discovered that there is water on Mars.
4 It is believed that terrorists are operating in Berlin.
5 It is expected that the space shuttle will return (to Earth) today.
6 It has been revealed that ex-president Julius is/was a spy.
7 ✗
8 It is said that the King is making a good recovery.
9 It has been established that a restaurant is/was the source of a food poisoning outbreak in Dublin.
10 ✗

25.3
2 It is not thought that the fault is serious. (or It is thought that the fault is not serious.)/ The fault is not thought to be serious.
3 It is expected that it will take several weeks to correct the fault.(or It is expected that the fault will take several weeks to correct.)/ The fault is expected to take several weeks to correct.
4 It has been decided to postpone the next rocket launch.
5 It is suggested that the next launch should take place in May.

UNIT 26

26.1
1 whom
2 Which
3 Which
4 Which
5 Whom/ Who ('Whom' is very formal)
6 Who
7 Which/ Who
8 Who

26.2
1 are
2 teaches (whether or not the expected answer is one person or two)
3 is
4 takes
5 are/ is
6 has

26.3
1 What + g
2 What + d
3 What/ How + b
4 How + h
5 What + j
6 How + a or g
7 How + e or i
8 What + f
9 What/ How + c
10 What + e or i

26.4
1 Whose...
2 ✓
3 whose...
4 Who lives *is more likely*
5 Who's
6 ✓ (*or less formally* Whose travels in Nepal did Nigel Smith write a book about?)
7 Which *is more likely*
8 Which *is more likely*
9 ✓ (What have *is also possible*)
10 To whose address?

UNIT 27

27.1 *Possible answers are given*
2 Didn't you get my letter saying I'd be on holiday?
3 Couldn't you get a babysitter?
4 But weren't you supposed to do that last night?
5 Can't you leave it outside?
6 Wouldn't you rather go by train?

27.2
2 Haven't you any interest in Maths at all? (*or* Don't you have any interest in Maths at all?) Have you no interest in Maths at all? (*or* Do you have no interest in Maths at all?)
3 Couldn't you find anywhere else to sleep? Could you find nowhere else to sleep?
4 Can't you remember anything about the accident? Can you remember nothing about the accident?
5 Why don't I ever do well in exams? Why do I never do well in exams?
6 Isn't there anybody you can ask for help? Is there nobody you can ask for help?

27.3
2 He's leaving when?/ He's doing what?/ He's what?
3 He'll be away for how long?/ He'll what?

4 It'll cost how much?/ It'll what?
5 He's sold (his) what?/ He's done what?/ He's what?
6 He's going climbing where?/ He's doing what?/ He's what?

27.4
2 Who did you say is/ was a vegetarian?
3 What do you suggest (that) I get for her birthday?
4 How long do you expect (that) you'll be in Istanbul?
5 What does he think is the problem? (*or* What does he think the problem is?)
6 Who do you suppose lives there now?
7 When did she say (that) she'd be arriving? (*or* ...she'll be arriving?)

UNIT 28

28.1
2 answered (the phone)
3 eat (dinner)
4 thanked Val
5 washed (herself)
6 brushed her hair
7 changed (her clothes)
8 put on some makeup
9 drove (her car)
10 reached their house
11 waved (her hand)
12 parked (her car)
13 cooking (dinner)
14 to pick some flowers
15 studying (French)
16 mention her
17 introduce you
18 enjoyed the evening
19 drink (alcohol)
20 afford it
21 wash up (the dishes)
22 invite Val and Tom

28.2
2 ...culminated in the discovery of penicillin.
3 ...differentiate between fantasy and reality.
4 ...adhere to the 1998 agreement.
5 ...specialises in seafood.
6 ...inflicted a surprise defeat on...
7 ...to equate the rise in crime with ...('to attribute the rise in crime to' is also possible)
8 ...attributed his success to...
9 ...mistook the black car for...
10 ...based her new novel on...

28.3 *Example adjectives are given*
2 She declared herself to be satisfied with the result./ She declared that she was/ is satisfied with the result.
3 They considered the food to be inedible./ They considered that the food was/ is inedible.
4 I have always found him to be reliable./ I have always found that he was/ is reliable.

5 We believed her to be happy at school./ We believed that she was/ is happy at school.

UNIT 29

29.1 *In some cases other tenses are possible*
2 I have to choose his clothes for him.
3 Can you take this present for/ to her?
4 ...pass it to me... (some people would also use '...pass it me...')
5 ...we sold all the carpets to him as well. ('...we offered all the carpets to him...' is also possible)
6 He teaches sports to disabled children.
7 Can you read these instructions to/ for me, please?
8 Jane posted the letter for me... ('Jane took the letter for me...' is also possible)
9 I offered my old bike to him...
10 Can you save some dinner for me, please?
11 ...so we're building a flat for them at the top of the house.

29.2
1 He kindly collected some library books for me.
2 He admitted his error to his colleagues.
3 ✓
4 Can I ask you a favour?
5 A special ticket allows (people) entry to all the museums in the city.
6 ✓

29.3
2 his sister to me/ me her photograph/ her photograph to me
3 him the flute/ the flute to him/ an Irish jig for (*or* to) us/ us an Irish jig
4 the problem to our teacher/ us another half hour
5 him a paper aeroplane/ a paper aeroplane for him/ his broken car for him/ him three bedtime stories/ three bedtime stories to (*or* for) him
6 you a fortune/ me the money/ the money to me
7 John a drink/ a drink for John the glass to him/ him the glass

UNIT 30

30.1
2 We don't approve of the developer's locating the factory so close to houses.
3 ✗
4 ✗ (not a verb of [dis]liking or thinking)
5 It is difficult to imagine his accepting the decision without any objection.

6 No-one in the crowd that day will forget Ashe's fighting so hard to win the match.
7 I remember their arguing a great deal when they were children.
8 ✗ (not a verb of [dis]liking or thinking)

30.2
2 close by thanking ('start out by thanking' would also be possible said at the beginning of a speech)
3 adjust to driving
4 stopped/ has stopped/ will stop him from playing ('from' could be omitted)
5 started out by sailing
6 rely on winning
7 heard of the factory closing
8 owned up to smoking

30.3
1 burst (a single, short event)
2 watching (the contexts suggests that Karl was being watched before he saw the watcher; in other words, he didn't see the whole of the event)
3 sting ('stinging' is also possible, but this would suggest that the bee stung several times)
4 feeding (this refers to a repeated event)

30.4
2 + f The new course is intended to help **people** (**to**) understand modern art.
3 + g I forgot to buy any bread so we had to make do with coffee for breakfast.
4 + c Scientists hope the new drug will help (**them**) (**to**) prevent hay fever.
5 + a The puppy isn't well trained yet, so if you let go of his lead, he'll run away.
6 + h We didn't agree with the decision, but we didn't dare (**to**) protest against it.
7 + e When John arrives, have **him** wait outside my office.
8 + d The dial on the left lets **you** control the speed of the fan.

UNIT 31

31.1
1 a told   b threatened
2 a offered   b allowed
3 a managed   b persuaded
4 a encouraged   b agreed
5 a reminded   b pretended
6 a hoped   b advised

31.2
2 for – to finish
3 for – to be released
4 to – to bring
5 at – to lose
6 to – to provide
7 at – to get off
8 for – to be done
9 on – to stay

31.3
1 agreed not to tell
2 are thought to have escaped
3 don't recall seeing/ don't recall having seen (similar meanings)
4 denied having received/ denied receiving (similar meanings)
5 asked not to be named
6 are/were believed to have arrived
7 seems to have disappeared
8 didn't feel like walking

UNIT 32

32.1 *The most likely reporting verbs are given in the answers, but others are possible.*
2 'Why don't we stop for a coffee?' she suggested.
3 'All right, Sean, it was me,' he confessed.
4 'My novel is more exciting than an Agatha Christie thriller,' she boasted.
5 'I always carry two umbrellas with me because I'm always losing them,' explained Mary./ ...Mary explained.
6 'Oh, no, it's raining again,' grumbled Dick./ ...Dick grumbled.
7 'Good morning, Miss,' chorused the children./ ...the children chorused.
8 'Have I done the right thing?' I wondered.

32.2
2 threatened – not to repay
3 didn't feel – could (*more likely than* He felt that he couldn't ask his parents to help him again.)
4 insisted – wasn't (*or* hadn't been)
5 announced – wasn't going
6 didn't expect – to be (*more likely than* He expected his mother not to be so angry.)
7 didn't think – would (*more likely than* She thought John wouldn't mind waiting a bit longer.)
8 promised – wouldn't

32.3
2 She wanted to know if/ whether I remember (remembered) David.
3 She wondered who was/ is the girl in the photo/ ...who the girl in the photo was/ is.
4 She asked me if/whether we could stop at the next village.
5 She didn't know how to spell 'chaos'.
6 She asked me how many brothers and sisters I've got. (*or* ...I had.)
7 She wondered where I (had) put the eggs.
8 She asked if/ whether I wanted a hot or a cold drink.
9 She asked me why I didn't go with Jack./ ...why I hadn't gone with Jack.

10 She couldn't remember which was (is) hers. / ...which hers was/ is.
11 She wanted to know if/whether I was ready to leave.
12 She asked what my grandmother's maiden name was./ ...what was my grandmother's maiden name.

UNIT 33

33.1
1 advised
2 assured/ promised
3 warned
4 inform/ teach
5 have shown
6 has reassured/ has advised
7 promised

33.2
2 ✗
3 The judge thought his explanation to be unconvincing.
4 I expected her plans to fail.
5 ✗
6 Peter acknowledged his chances of winning the race to be slim.
7 We found the football supporters to be very well behaved.
8 ✗

33.3 *Likely answers are given*
1 complained to
2 complained to; mentioned to; announced to
3 joked with; announced to; mentioned to
4 announced to
5 requires of
6 disagreed with
7 mention to

33.4 *Possible necessary objects are given in bold*
1 has warned that they
2 explained to employees that
3 confessed to her audience that
4 denied that management
5 replied that an announcement
6 reassured **employees/them** that
7 went on to complain that government help
8 demanded of ministers that ('demand that ministers provide' would also be possible and less formal)
9 asked of staff that ('asked staff to continue' would also be possible and less formal)
10 reassured **workers/them** that
Note that alternatives without 'that' (1 has warned they, 2 explained to employees, etc.) are grammatical, but less likely in a formal written context.

UNIT 34

34.1 *Added objects are in bold*
2 + j He took my hands and showed **me** how to hold the golf club properly.
3 + g I explained carefully so that the students understood what they had to do in the test.
4 + i Anna was new in the office and I had to keep reminding her who everyone was.
5 + b I saw Sarah leave the building, but I didn't notice where she went after that.
6 + e When I saw Steve alone at the party I wondered why Helen wasn't with him.
7 + h As we walked over the hills the guide warned **us** where the path was dangerous.
8 + a After I'd dismantled the motor I couldn't remember how to fit the parts back together.
9 + f To win a prize you had to guess how many sweets were in the jar.
10 + c As the guests came in Peter told **them** where to put their coats.

34.2
1 debating
2 discuss
3 considering
4 choose
5 decide

34.3
The villagers warned **me** what the conditions were like at higher altitudes, and advised **me** to take enough food for a week. There was some discussion through the day as **to** whether the snow would arrive before my descent from the mountain, but I never imagined how hard the conditions would be. In the morning they showed me (**the way/ how**: *one of these must be deleted*) to get to the track up the mountain. .... When the snow started falling it was very light, and I couldn't decide ~~if~~ **whether** to carry on or go back down. Soon, however, I couldn't see where to go... I wondered ~~if~~ **whether** to retrace my steps and try to find the track again, but by the time I decided ~~whether~~ **that** I should go back, the track had disappeared... As the snow got heavier I began to realise ~~whether~~ **that** my life was in danger. Fortunately, my years in the Andes had taught **me** what to do in extreme conditions. I knew that there was a shepherd's hut somewhere on this side of the mountain that I could shelter in, but I didn't know ~~that~~ **whether** it was nearby or miles away...

UNIT 35

35.1
2 She alleged that Thomas had stolen/ stole jewellery from her house.
3 She estimated that the vase was ('is' is also possible) around 250 years old.
4 She repeated that she had already seen the film.
5 She conceded that she treated/ had treated Jane unkindly.
6 She recalled that Michael's great grandfather was/ had been from Spain.

35.2
1 have solved
2 states
3 is/ was
4 wishes/ wished ('wished' might suggest that he no longer wishes to be prime minister)
5 has
6 understand
7 looks
8 is/ was

35.3
1 When I mentioned to Nokes that he **had been seen** ✓ (or **was seen**) in a local shop last Monday, he protested that he ~~is~~ **was** at home all day. He swears that he ~~didn't own~~ **doesn't own** a blue Ford Escort. He claimed that he **had been** ✓ (or **went**) to the paint factory two weeks ago to look for work. Nokes alleges that he **is** ✓ a good friend of Jim Barnes. He insisted that he **didn't telephone** ✓ (or **hadn't telephoned**) Barnes last Monday morning. When I pointed out to Nokes that a large quantity of paint **had been found** ✓ (or **was found**) in his house, he replied that he ~~is storing~~ **had been storing** (or **was storing**) it for a friend.
2 At the beginning of the interview I reminded Barnes that he **is** ✓ (or **was**) entitled to have a lawyer present. He denied that he **knew** ✓ (or **knows**) anyone by the name of Bill Nokes. Barnes confirmed that he ~~is~~ **had been** (or **was**) in the area of the paint factory last Monday, but said that he ~~is visiting~~ **was visiting** (or **had been visiting**) his mother. He admitted that he ~~is walking~~ **was walking** (or **had been walking**) along New Street at around 10.00. He maintains that he ~~was~~ **is** a very honest person and would never be involved in anything illegal.

UNIT 36

36.1 *The most likely answers are given. Possible objects are given in bold.*
2 He agreed to collect David from school.
3 He ordered **us** to be quiet.
4 He urged **me** to stay for a few more days.
5 He vowed to fight the ban on smoking in public places.
6 He expected/ hoped to see Olivia at the party.

7 He asked **me** to lend him ten pounds. (*or* He asked to borrow ten pounds.)

8 He called on **the government** to do more to help the homeless.

9 He hoped/ expected to avoid the heavy traffic (by leaving early).

36.2
1 agreed
2 insisted/ said
3 wanted
4 said
5 expected
6 has guaranteed/ has promised
7 offered
8 suggested
9 requested
10 longed/ promised

36.3 *Example answers*
2 ...reducing bus and train fares.
3 ...seeing it.
4 ...buying a guide book.
5 ...going to the doctor.
6 ...building it to the east of the city.
7 ...doing more exercise.
8 ...going for a long walk.

The verb 'propose' can be followed by a *to*-infinitive without an object (see A). For example:
2 To encourage people to use public transport the council proposed to reduce bus and train fares.
6 London urgently needs a new airport, and the government proposes to build it to the east of the city.

UNIT 37

37.1
2 She said that I could/ can travel with them.
3 She said that she wouldn't answer his questions.
4 She said that Karl would/ should/ ought to be back soon.
5 She said that she may/ might/ could have to move to Milan.
6 She said that she couldn't/ wouldn't accept that John is/ was dishonest.
7 She said that Maria would/ will be disappointed if we leave/ left without seeing her.

37.2
1 will
2 may/ might
3 can
4 would
5 couldn't
6 can/ could
7 will/ would

37.3
2 He reminded me that I mustn't forget my credit card.
3 He worried that he would miss the bus (if he didn't hurry).
4 He wondered who he should send the letter to. ('ought to send' is also possible)

5 He thought that it must be cold outside (because there is/ was frost on the window).
6 He said that I had to/ have to come home at once. ('should' is also possible; 'must' is possible, but less likely in speech)
7 He asked whether/ if he should open a window. ('ought to open' is also possible)
8 He admitted that he must have made a mistake in the calculations.

37.4
2 She promised that she wouldn't be late...
3 He suggested that we could go to Paris for the weekend...
4 She guaranteed that she could get us there in good time...
5 He insisted that he would pay for the meal...

Sentences 2 and 4 have alternatives with a *to*-infinitive clause:
2 She promised not to be late...
4 She guaranteed to get us there in good time...

UNIT 38

38.1
2 He failed to address the question/ issue of who would/ should pay for the repairs to the building.
3 I was delighted to get an invitation to spend Christmas with them in Scotland.
4 I think it was Aristotle who made the observation that there's no such thing as bad publicity.
5 Amazingly the police accepted Rudi's explanation that he had taken the wallet by mistake.
6 On the TV programme they debated the issue/ question of whether assisted suicide should be a criminal offence.
7 The letter from the company gave a final warning that I should pay the bill by the end of the week./ ...to pay the bill by the end of the week.
8 The government has broken its promise to reduce the rate of income tax./ ...that it would reduce the rate of income tax.
9 The positive reaction to my work gave me considerable encouragement to take up photography as a career.
10 Waiting passengers were angry when they heard the announcement that the flight was cancelled. (*or* ... had been cancelled).

38.2
2 speculation as to how
3 argument as to who (or more formally 'whom')
4 suggestions ...as to how
5 explanation/ indication as to why
6 indication as to where

38.3
1 unsure whether *or* not certain whether *are also possible*
2 dismissive of
3 adamant that
4 unsure how/ not certain how
5 angry that (or apologetic that)
6 apologetic about
7 not certain when/ unsure when
8 abusive to/ towards
9 complimentary about
10 agreed that/ adamant that

UNIT 39

39.1 *The most likely answers are given*
2 Mr Leeson urged that Philip Whittaker should be promoted to export manager.
3 Mrs Appleby recommended that a sales representative should be sent to South Africa.
4 Mrs Appleby reported that the Delaware Bridge project should be completed by August next year.
5 The Chairman insisted that work schedules should be kept to.
6 The Chairman instructed that all monthly reports should be sent to him directly.
7 Ms Wells suggested that trade union representatives should be involved in major decisions.
8 Ms Wells declared that the company's head office should remain in London.
9 Mr Clarke agreed that the company should sponsor the European chess league for the next three years.
10 Mr Clarke announced that in future all claims for travel expenses should be made in US dollars.

39.2
2	Yes	6	Yes	10	No
3	Yes	7	Yes		
4	No	8	No		
5	Yes	9	No		

39.3 *Possible adjectives are given in these answers*
2 I am shocked that Paul should behave so badly.
3 I am astounded that anyone should vote for him.
4 It is urgent that he should return home immediately.
5 I am amused that he should take his appearance so seriously.
6 I am upset that they should think I had cheated them.
7 It is appalling that they should be allowed to go free.
8 It is imperative that we should act now to avoid war.

Key to Exercises

UNIT 40

40.1
1 is	6 seems
2 suggests	7 are
3 is	8 is
4 appear	9 are (or more
5 has	colloquially 'is')

40.2
2 university refuse/ refuses
3 audience ... is (A singular verb form is more likely here as the focus is on the audience as a whole rather than individual members.)
4 orchestra perform/ performs
5 jury includes (A singular verb form is used here as 'include' focuses on the group as a whole rather than individual members.)
6 class have (A plural verb form is used as this is something the individuals did, emphasised by the use of 'all'.)
7 press presents/ present
8 The United Nations has/ have

40.3
1 ~~come~~ comes top
2 ✓
3 ~~detail~~ details the crimes
4 ~~are~~ is one of
5 ✓
6 ✓
7 ~~have~~ has to clear
8 ~~are~~ is used
9 ✓ ('...need to be kept...' is also possible)
10 ~~are~~ is a party game

UNIT 41

41.1
1
b any of his early paintings remains/ remain
c any of the food tastes
d any of Dr Jones's acquaintances knows ('know' is also possible, but a singular verb is perhaps more likely in the formal context that this example suggests)

2
a the number of vegetarians is expected
b a number of other museums ... charge
c A number of medicines relieve
d the number of victims ... exceeds

3
a Each of the pieces lasts/ last
b each of these factors influences ('influence' is also possible, but a singular verb is perhaps more likely in the formal context that this example suggests)
c Each player tries
d Each of the cars are/is tested

41.2
1 are – wants
2 think – has (more likely than 'have' in this formal context)
3 has or have – has

4 claim – constitutes (more likely than 'constitute' as 'the wreck of the ship and its cargo' constitute together, as a single item, a danger)
5 is or are – have – are or 's

UNIT 42

42.1
1 ✓ ('have' is also possible)	12 seems
2 were	13 ✓ ('has' is also possible)
3 ✓	14 ✓
4 is	15 has
5 was	16 ✓
6 have	17 ✓ ('were' is also possible)
7 ✓ ('were' is also possible)	18 is
8 is	19 is
9 ✓	20 say
10 go	21 ✓
11 are	22 want

42.2
1 have – have
2 is ('are' is also possible, but less likely) – expect/ expects
3 is – blames/ blame
4 was ('were' is also possible, but less likely) – has/ have
5 admit/ admits – were
6 were – have
7 shows – is – believe
8 have – says/ say – are

UNIT 43

43.1
1 a ✓ b a computer programmer c a film star
2 a ✓ b girls' school c the car door d a cut on the/ her head
3 a ✓ b ✓ c a bottle of milk d a packet of biscuits e some toothpaste f ✓
4 a ✓ b songs about pollution ('pollution songs' is not a well-known class of songs)
5 a tool shed b spiders' webs
6 a armchair b ✓ c the 500-piece jigsaw puzzle d glasses case

43.2
1 cover up
2 broken out
3 stopping over
4 get together
5 set out
6 stopover (related to 3)
7 get-together (4)
8 cover-up (1)
9 outbreak (2)
10 outset (5)

43.3
2 middle-of-the-road 3 round-the-clock 4 step-by-step 5 once-in-a-lifetime 6 down-to-earth 7 man-in-the-street (*alternatives* are: man/ woman in the street, *or* man or woman in the street (usually without hyphens)) 8 larger-than-life

UNIT 44

44.1
1 an	8 a
2 a	9 an
3 an	10 a
4 a	11 a
5 a ('MiG'	12 an
is said /mɪg/)	13 an
6 an	14 a
7 an	

44.2
1 ~~one~~ a
2 ✓
3 ~~a~~ one
4 ~~one~~ an
5 ✓
6 ~~one~~ a
7 ~~one~~ a ('one' would imply 'one and no more'; 'a' is more likely if this is a more general invitation to 'have some cake')
8 ✓ ('one' implies 'one and only one')
9 ✓ (both 'one' and 'a' are possible)
10 ~~one~~ a
11 ~~one~~ a ('one' would emphasise the number and seems less likely than 'a' in this context)
12 ✓ (both 'one' and 'a' are possible)
13 ~~a~~ one
14 ~~one~~ a
15 ~~a~~ one
16 ✓ (both 'one' and 'a' are possible)

44.3
1 one/ a	7 one/ a
2 one	8 an
3 one	9 one
4 one/ an	10 one
5 a	11 one/ a
6 one	12 A

UNIT 45

45.1
1 a the world b a world
2 a a bright future b the future
3 a the past; b a past
4 a a deserted beach b the beach ('a beach' is also possible here, meaning a particular but unspecified beach)

45.2
1 a customer
2 the individual/ an individual (similar meaning)
3 the car
4 The television
5 the smoker

45.3
2 pleasure
3 importance
4 a sound
5 grammar
6 iron
7 a shampoo (= 'a type of shampoo'; 'shampoo' is also possible)

8 Sound ('Sounds travel' would also be possible)
9 shampoo
10 a real pleasure
11 a grammar
12 an importance ('importance' is also possible)
13 an iron
14 conversation

UNIT 46

46.1
1 the
2 –
3 –
4 a
5 a/ the/ – ('a' suggests that there are a number of marketing advisers; 'the' or '–' indicate that there is only one)
6 –
7 –/ –
8 –/ the
9 the/ –
10 a
11 –
12 an
13 the/ –
14 a
15 the
16 a/ –
17 –/ A

46.2
1	the	5	(the)
2	(the)	6	(the)
3	(the)	7	the
4	the	8	the

46.3
1 this/ a
2 –
3 – ('this' would be unlikely here as the paint is not the topic of what comes next)
4 the/ –
5 a/ –
6 a
7 –
8 a/ this ('this' introduces the woman as the focus of the next part of the story)
9 the/ –
10 the/ –

UNIT 47

47.1
1 a Children (a general reference; specific children are not referred to) b the children (a specific reference, probably to my/our children)
2 a the agriculture (a reference to the agriculture in a specific area) b agriculture (a general reference)
3 a islands (reference to islands generally) b The islands (reference to a specific group of islands)

4 a the holidays (specific reference; the holidays that are coming soon) b Holidays (a general reference to holidays in this part of the world)
5 a rain (a general reference) b the rain (reference to a specific, understood period of rain)
6 a the money (reference to a specific, understood sum of money) b money (an observation on the effect of money generally)
7 a parents (= a general reference) b The parents (a specific reference to particular parents)
8 a the fire (reference to a specific fire) b fire (a general reference)

47.2
1 a a day b a/ the day ('a day' suggests one of a number of days; 'the day' suggests either that it was the only day that I babysat for them or that it was a particular day that the listener knows about)
2 a on Sunday b on a Sunday
3 a a/ the Christmas ('a Christmas' suggests that we have often spent Christmas in Sweden; 'the Christmas' suggests that we have only done it once) b after Christmas
4 a by post b in the post
5 a all afternoon (more likely than 'all the afternoon') b spent the afternoon
6 a the/ – winter ('the winter' might imply 'the coming winter' however, both 'winter' and 'the winter' might be a generalisation meaning 'any winter') b the winter
7 a by car b take the car (= my/our car; 'a car' would suggest one of a number of cars available)

47.3
1 side by side
2 day by day
3 back to back
4 end to end
5 person to person

UNIT 48

48.1
1	(some)	5	(some)
2	some	6	–
3	–	7	–
4	(some)	8	(some)

48.2 *Suggested answers are given*
2 Some 30% of all city buses have been found to be unsafe.
3 An unexploded bomb has been found some 5 miles from the centre of Newham.
4 Some 25% of electricity will come from wind energy by 2020.
5 Some 200 jobs are to be lost at the Encon steel works.

48.3 *Suggested answers are given*
2 He's probably out with some girlfriend or other.
3 Maybe I lent it to some student in my geography class.
4 I think it's in some travel agent in the High Street.
5 Perhaps he's got to finish some report or other.

48.4
1 any
2 any/ some ('any' suggests that I could eat none of the food; 'some' implies that I was able to eat some but not all of it)
3 anything
4 someone ('positive' meaning)
5 anything/ something ('anything' suggests that he said that he did nothing at all wrong; 'something' suggests that he has been accused of a particular wrong-doing but denied this)
6 anyone
7 any
8 any
9 Some (= not all)
10 any
11 anyone/ someone ('anyone' suggests that I don't want to lend it to any person; 'someone' suggests that I may have a particular person in mind (perhaps they have asked me to lend it to them))
12 anything

UNIT 49

49.1
2 ...no-one heard...
3 Not a drop...
4 ...no point...
5 ...nowhere else...
6 ...none of the hotels...
7 ...never going to get...
8 ...nothing wrong...

49.2
1 There aren't any in the cupboard.
4 ...there wasn't any point in protesting.
5 ...he didn't have anywhere else to go.
7 Isn't he ever going to get a job? (*or* Is he ever going to get a job?)
8 ...they couldn't find anything wrong with her.

49.3
1 There was no television...
2 ✓
3 ...had no seatbelts.
4 ...there was no signature on it.
5 ...no trees.
6 ...were no sweets in it.
7 ✓
8 ...there were no newspapers left.

49.4 *Possible answers*

2 Mr Carlson didn't want to sell the painting, and no amount of money/ persuading could make him change his mind.
3 I sent job applications to over a hundred companies, but not one of them invited me for an interview.
4 Smallpox used to be common all over the world but since 1978 not one case of the disease has been recorded.
5 The floor had dirty black marks all over it, and no amount of polishing could get it clean.

49.5

1 No problem./ No bother.
2 No wonder.
3 No chance. / No way.
4 No idea.
5 No comment.

UNIT 50

50.1 *Suggested corrections/ improvements are given*

1 Sheila's had ~~many~~ **a lot of** (more usual than 'many' in conversation) problems with her back for ~~a lot of~~ **many** years. She's having an operation next week and she won't be back at work for ~~a good deal of~~ a **good many** weeks afterwards.
2 'There's bound to be ~~much~~ **a lot of/ lots of** traffic on the way to the station. Perhaps we should leave now.' 'Don't worry, there's plenty of time left, and at this time of day ~~many~~ **a lot of/ lots of** people will already be at work.'
3 ~~Many~~ **A lot of/ Lots of** (more usual than 'many' in conversation) **people** think that hedgehogs are very rare nowadays, but when I was in Wales I saw ~~many~~ **a lot/ lots** (more usual than 'many' in conversation).
4 ~~A lot~~ **Many** have claimed that Professor Dowman's study on current attitudes to politics is flawed. One criticism is that ~~much~~ **far** too many people questioned in the survey were under 18.
5 ~~A lot of~~ **Much** research has been conducted on the influence of diet on health, with ~~a lot of~~ **many** studies focusing on the relationship between fat intake and heart disease. However, ~~a lot~~ **much** remains to be done. ('much' and 'many' are preferred in a written academic context).
6 While it is true that ~~a lot of~~ **many** thousands of jobs were lost with the decline of the northern coal and steel industries, ~~a lot of~~ **many**

advantages have also followed. ~~Much~~ **Far** too many cases of lung disease were recorded in the region, but with lower levels of pollution the number has declined. In addition, a ~~great deal of~~ a **great many** hi-tech companies have moved in to take advantage of the newly available workforce.

50.2

2 many a sunny afternoon
3 Many a ship
4 its/the many golf courses
5 my many letters
6 his many expeditions ('many an expedition' is also possible)
7 Many a teacher
8 the many coffee shops

50.3

1 plenty of ('a lot of' is also possible)
2 A lot of (not 'plenty of')
3 a lot of (not 'plenty of')
4 a lot of (not 'plenty of')
5 plenty of ('a lot of' is also possible)

UNIT 51

51.1

1 ...were all
2 ...can all
3 ...had all
4 ...are all
5 All the children *or* The children all (both are possible)
6 all been...

51.2

1 The whole process
2 Whole areas of the country
3 The whole trip
4 all of the towns
5 all of the pages/ whole pages ('all of the pages' means that every page had been ripped out; 'whole pages' means that some, but not all, pages had been ripped out entirely)
6 all the building/ the whole building ('all the building' suggests that we see the building as being made up of parts (a number of rooms, for example); 'the whole building' would be more likely in a formal context)
7 The whole room

51.3

1	every	7	each/ every
2	each	8	each
3	every	9	Every/ Each
4	each/ every	10	each/ every
5	each	11	every
6	every	12	each

(In 4, 7, 9, 10, 'each' emphasises that we are thinking of the places/ children/ households/ pages separately; 'every' suggests something like 'all of'.)

51.4

1 Every so often
2 ✓
3 every few weeks
4 ✓ ('all Friday' is possible in an informal context; 'the whole of Friday' would also be possible here)
5 each of them
6 not all the food usually gets eaten
7 Not all of my brothers always come
8 Neil and his family were all on holiday
9 We all had a great time
10 ✓ ('all evening' would also be possible)

UNIT 52

52.1

1 few ('a few' would mean that a small number of people would disagree. It would be more likely after 'but...' than 'and...')
2 Little
3 few
4 the few/ a few
5 The little/ What little
6 A little
7 The few/ What few
8 Few
9 little
10 a little
11 a few
12 a few
13 the little/ what little
14 the few/ a few

52.2 *Most likely changes are given*

1 '...a bit of TV...' (is perhaps more likely in this informal context)
2 ...there are only a few left. *or* ...there aren't many left.
3 .... there isn't much more... *or* ...there's not much more...
4 ...not many... *or* ...only a few...
5 ...has had few female politicians...
6 ...exchanged few words...
7 ...a little more confident...
8 There seems to be little prospect...

52.3 *Possible answers*

1 Fewer students had a part-time job in 1980 than now. ('Less students...' would also be acceptable for some people) Less (*or* Fewer) than 10% of female students had a part-time job in 1980.
2 Male students spend less money than female students on books. Students spend less on books now than they did in 1980.
3 Less (*or* Fewer) than 10% of female students walk to university now. Fewer students walk to university now than they did in 1980. ('Less students...' would also be acceptable for some people)

4 Male students spend less time on the phone now than female students.

Surprising results might be:
Female students now spend no less than 20% of their income on books. Female students spend no less than 6 hours a week on the phone.

UNIT 53

53.1
The relative pronoun can be omitted in 1, 3, 4, 7 and 10.

53.2
1 ('that' or '–' are more likely in an informal context)
2 Julia's father, who is over 80, has just come back from a skiing holiday.
3 The problems faced by the company, which I'll look at in detail in a moment, are being resolved. (some people would use 'that' as an alternative)
4 She was greatly influenced by her father, who/ whom she adored. ('whom' is formal)
5 He pointed to the stairs which/ that led down to the cellar.
6 These drugs, which are used to treat stomach ulcers, have been withdrawn from sale. (some people would use 'that' as an alternative)
7 The singer, who was recovering from flu, had to cancel her concert.
8 The minister talked about the plans for tax reform that/ which/ – he will reveal next month. ('which' is more likely in a formal context)
9 I have two older sisters whom/ who/ that/ – I love very much. ('whom' is very formal)

53.3
1 'which' is possible, but less likely than 'that' or '–'
2 'whom' seems rather formal here and less likely than 'who', 'that', or '–'
3 ✓ 'that I can' is also possible
4 ...much that can...
5 ~~whom~~ who
6 ~~which~~ 'that' or '–'
7 The boy who took the photograph was paid £100.
8 'which' is possible, but less likely than 'that'
9 'which' is possible, but less likely than 'that' or '–' in this informal context
10 'which' is possible, but less likely than 'that'

UNIT 54

54.1
2 + a The newspaper is owned by the Mears group, whose chairperson is Sir James Bex.

3 + g Parents whose children are between four and six are being asked to take part in the survey.
4 + b Children whose diets contain high levels of protein do better in examinations.
5 + f My aunt, whose first job was filling shelves in a supermarket, is now manager of a department store.
6 + c I enjoy growing plants in my garden whose flowers are attractive to bees.
7 + e The new regulations are part of a broader strategy whose objectives are to increase fish stocks.

54.2 *Example answers*
2 A widow is a woman whose husband has died and who has not re-married.
3 An actuary is a person whose job is to decide how much insurance companies should charge their customers.
4 A furnace is a container in which things are melted or burnt.
5 A gazebo is a small garden building in which people can sit to enjoy the view.
6 Polo is a sport in which horse riders hit a ball using hammers with long handles.

54.3
1 moments when ('moments where' is also possible, but less usual)
2 an agreement whereby
3 the area where
4 the reason why ('...the reason we get on...' and '...the reason that we get on...' are also possible)
5 a method whereby
6 a condition where

54.4
1 ~~whatever~~ whoever
2 ~~that~~ what
3 ✓
4 ~~which~~ whatever (or 'what')
5 ~~whichever~~ whatever
6 ✓ (or 'no relative pronoun' or 'which')
7 ~~what~~ that
8 ~~which~~ whichever/ whatever
9 ✓ (or 'whoever')

UNIT 55

55.1
2 He was the uncle of Ann Boleyn, after whose execution in 1542 he lost power.
3 It is her unmarried name by which she is better known.
4 Mr Marks, across whose farm the stream flows, is unhappy about the plans for the new dam.
5 The election result, about which there can be no doubt, is a great disappointment.

6 The building from which Mr Marcus emerged was little more than a ruin.
7 It is a medieval palace, in whose tower the king hid during the civil war.
8 I am grateful to Alan Mackie, from whose book on the history of the bicycle this information comes.

55.2
2 Until 1914 the pound sterling was the currency in/ with which most world trade was conducted.
3 They have changed the date on/ by which the furniture is to be delivered.
4 Pasteurisation was discovered by the French chemist Louis Pasteur, after whom it was named.
5 He was persuaded to stay in England by Charles Dickens, to whom he had shown his novel.
6 There are a number of safety procedures of which you should be aware.
7 Details are in the instruction manual with which the printer was supplied.
8 Ms Peters was left the money by her former husband, from whom she was divorced in 1995.

55.3
2 Until 1914 the pound sterling was the currency which/ that most world trade was conducted in.
3 They have changed the date which/ that/ – the furniture is to be delivered on/ by.
4 Pasteurisation was discovered by the French chemist Louis Pasteur, who it was named after.
5 He was persuaded to stay in England by Charles Dickens, who he had shown his novel to.
6 There are number of safety procedures which/ that/ – you should be aware of.
7 Details are in the instruction manual which/ that/ – the printer was supplied with.
8 Ms Peters was left the money by her former husband, who she was divorced from in 1995.

55.4
1 The house which the thieves broke into...
2 ✓
3 ...first of which...
4 ...under which... (*or less formally* '...tree to sit under on a hot...')
5 The party, which I've been looking forward to all week...
6 ✓
7 ...both of which...
8 ... part of which...
9 ... all of whom...

Key to Exercises

UNIT 56

56.1 *The most likely answers are given*
2 I went on an IT training course with my colleague Paul.
3 Rubella, or German measles, is still a common childhood disease in many countries.
4 Four kilos of Beluga caviar, among the most expensive food in the world, has been ordered for James and Stephanie's wedding party.
5 One of the most popular modern writers for children is the Australian Paul Jennings.
6 Tonya's father, and (her) trainer for the last ten years, was in the crowd to watch her victory.
7 Dr Andy Todd, head of Downlands Hospital, has criticised government plans to cut health funding.
8 Klaus Schmidt, the German 10,000 metres record holder and current European champion, is running in the Stockholm Marathon. (*or* Klaus Schmidt, the current European champion and (the) German 10,000 metres record holder, ...)

56.2
2 + d The two countries having land borders with the USA, namely/ that is Mexico and Canada, have complained to the President about the new customs regulations.
3 + a The three most popular pets in Britain, namely/ that is cats, dogs and rabbits, are found in 25% of households.
4 + f The capital of Estonia, namely/ that is Tallinn, is situated on the Gulf of Finland.
5 + b The largest island in the world, namely/ that is Greenland, covers over 2 million square kilometres.
6 + c The 'consumers' of education, namely/ that is students, should have ways of complaining about poor teaching.

56.3
2 educated – I went to a reunion for students who were educated in the physics department during the 1980s.
3 being told off – As my aunt told me what she thought, I felt like a schoolboy who was being told off by his headmaster.
4 saying – There is a sign on the gate which says 'Entry forbidden'.
5 introduced – Across the river were some of the deer which were introduced into the park in the 19th century.

6 flowing - Rivers which flow into the Baltic Sea are much cleaner now than ten years ago.
7 being printed – The booklets which are being printed as we speak will be on sale later this afternoon.
8 needing – Anyone who needs further information can see me in my office.
9 elected – Mary O'Brien, the Democrat who was elected to the council only last week, has resigned.
10 built – We live in a house which was built in 1906.
11 being held – The protest march which is being held next week is expected to attract over 100,000 people.

UNIT 57

57.1 *The most likely answers are given*
2 + e She's in the photograph on the piano.
3 + b I plan to cut down the tree in the back garden
4 + a There's a team of people in green shirts.
5 + d I walked along the footpath by the canal.
6 + i The children can't get over the fence around the pool.
7 + g Go along the lane between the houses.
8 + j Jack's a boy with a quick temper.
9 + f Follow the main road from Paris to Lyons.
10 + h She's a teacher from New Zealand.

57.2
2 She's in the photograph which is on the piano.
3 I plan to cut down the tree which is in the back garden.
4 There's a team of people who had/ were wearing green shirts.
5 I walked along the footpath which runs/ goes by the canal.
6 The children can't get over the fence which is around the pool.
7 Go along the lane which runs between the houses.
8 Jack's a boy who has a quick temper.
9 Follow the main road which runs/ goes from Paris to Lyons.
10 She's a teacher who is/ comes from New Zealand.

57.3 *Possible answers are given with some alternatives*
2 Teachers (who work/ working) at Queen's College in the city centre, who went on strike last week, have appointed Jacqui Smith, the head of English, as their spokesperson.
3 Marge Scott, who has died aged 95, was the first woman (to be) educated at Marston College in

south Wales. / Marge Scott, the first woman (to be) educated at Marston College in south Wales, has died aged 95.
4 The conference (held) in Singapore, which approved the world trade agreement drawn up by European and Asian states, has now ended.
5 A book on gardening, *All about Plants*, that/ which Mary wanted to borrow, wasn't available in the library./ A book on gardening called *All about Plants* that/ which Mary wanted to borrow wasn't available in the library.
6 A painting found in a second-hand shop by Beth Sands, an antique dealer from York, is thought to be by J.M.W. Turner, the British landscape artist. (*or* ...by the British landscape artist J.M.W. Turner.)

57.4
1 The sentence could mean: (i) that a man was wearing a grey suit – he was talking; (ii) (the ridiculous) that a man was talking with a grey suit. To remove the ambiguity the sentence should be: A man (who was) wearing a grey suit was talking.
2 The sentence could mean: (i) that the lorry was carrying thousands of stolen cigarettes – it was stopped by a police officer; (ii) (the ridiculous) that the police officer was carrying thousands of stolen cigarettes at the time s/he stopped the lorry. To remove the ambiguity the sentence should be: A lorry (which was) carrying thousands of stolen cigarettes was stopped by a police officer.
3 The sentence could mean: (i) that I am going to discuss the matter with my parents; (ii) that I am going to decorate the room and my parents will help decorate it with me; (iii) (the ridiculous) that I am going to use my parents as decoration in the room! To remove the ambiguity the sentence should be: I discussed with my parents my plan to decorate the room. (to mean (i)) *or* I discussed my plan to decorate the room with the help of my parents (to mean (ii)).

UNIT 58

58.1
2 Dressed (*or* Being dressed) all in black, she couldn't be seen in the starless night.
3 Not having a credit card, I found it difficult to book an airline ticket over the phone.

4 Being unemployed, Keith spent a lot of time filling in job application forms.
5 Walking quickly, I soon caught up with her.
6 Built of wood (*or* Being built of wood...), the house was clearly a fire risk.
7 Having been told off the day before for arriving late, I was eager to catch the bus in good time.
8 Not knowing where the theatre was, she asked for directions at the hotel reception.
9 Being a nurse, she knew what to do after the accident.
10 Having spent his childhood in Oslo, he knew the city well.

58.2

1 D (first implied subject = 'I'; second subject = 'a car') Waiting for the bus, I was splashed all over by a car that went through a puddle./ While I was waiting for the bus, a car went through a puddle and splashed water all over me.
2 S (subject in both clauses = 'James')
3 S (subject in both clauses = 'Suzanne')
4 D (first implied subject 'we'; second subject = 'the town') Looking down from the hill, we could see the town spread out before us towards the coast./ As we looked down from the hill, we could see the town spread out before us towards the coast.
5 D (first implied subject = 'I'; second subject = 'the boat') I was feeling rather sick as the boat ploughed through the huge waves.
6 S (subject in both clauses = 'the plant')

58.3

1 Not wishing to boast...
2 Pretending not to notice...
3 Determined not to be beaten...
4 Not feeling well...
5 Not bothering to put on his coat...
6 Trying not to cry...

58.4

1 Having parked *or* Parking (similar meanings)
2 Having moved *or* Moving (perhaps a similar meaning; however, 'Moving' could imply a move that is in progress or is anticipated)
3 Walking
4 Having waited
5 Having suffered

UNIT 59

59.1

2 While being interviewed...
3 Before taking...

4 While welcoming...
5 Since being overthrown... (*or* After being overthrown...)
6 Through working... (*or* After working...)
7 Before being sold...
8 After leaving...

59.2

2 + a By giving up sugar, she soon began to lose weight.
3 + e In turning down the job, she gave up the possibility of a huge salary. ('By turning down' is also possible. However, 'In turning down' focuses on the consequence of the action and so is perhaps more likely here.)
4 + b By moving to a smaller flat, she saved over a hundred pounds a month. ('In moving...' is also possible. However, 'By moving...' focuses on the method used to save money.)
5 + f On entering the classroom, she was surprised when all the children stood up quietly.
6 + c In criticising her father, she knew that she might offend him. ('By criticising' is also possible. However, 'In criticising' focuses on the consequence of the action and so is perhaps more likely here.)

59.3

1 With Kathy having flu we couldn't go on holiday.
2 Without having more information, I won't be able to advise you.
3 Without realising it, he had solved the problem.
4 With time running out before the train left I couldn't wait for Ken any longer.

59.4

2 + e Popular with his fellow pupils, he was elected head boy at the school.
3 + a Although exhausted, she continued to climb.
4 + c Determined to do well in the concert, she practised for hours every day.
5 + b Attractive to butterflies, the flowers are a welcome addition to any garden.
6 + d Where necessary, students can refer to their dictionary.

UNIT 60

60.1

2 prepared (herself)
3 prides itself on
4 occupied themselves with/ by ('with' and 'by' could also be omitted: 'occupied themselves reading and drawing')
5 adapt (yourself)

6 trouble himself about/ with
7 dress (herself)
8 hid (myself)
9 absent himself from

60.2

1 me
2 myself
3 us
4 them
5 yourself
6 himself ('him' is also possible if 'he' and 'him' refer to different people)
7 herself ('her' is also possible if 'she' and 'her' refer to different people)
8 me

60.3

1 his old self
2 got ourselves vaccinated or got vaccinated
3 ✓
4 had themselves checked
5 he'd caught hepatitis himself
6 ✓ (however, some people think this is incorrect and would use 'Tony and I')
7 we're going to occupy ourselves
8 they can't reach it themselves

UNIT 61

61.1

1 ~~ones~~ some   5 ✓
2 ✓   6 ✓
3 ~~ones~~ some   7 ~~ones~~ one
4 ...mint ~~one~~...   8 ~~ones~~ some
   or ...have some
   mint instead.

61.2

1 ones
2 ones
3 No
4 one
5 No ('my ones' is possible, but some people avoid it. 'Can you do mine, too, please?' is much more likely)
6 No ('ones' would be unlikely here, referring to a group of people)
7 ones
8 one
9 No
10 No
11 No ('your ones' is possible, but some people avoid it. 'Are these yours?' is much more likely)

61.3

3 (ones) Note that some people think that 'those ones' is incorrect.
4 (one)   10 (one)
5 ✓   11 ✓
6 (one)   12 (one)
7 ✓   13 (ones)
8 (ones)   14 ✓
9 (ones)

Key to Exercises

UNIT 62

62.1
2 'I doubt it' is also possible.
3 I hope so.
4 I suppose so.
5 I think so.
6 Yes, I hear (that) she is. ('So I hear' is also possible; see E)
7 I guess so.
8 He says so.
9 I promise (that) I will.
10 I'm sure (that) you will.

62.2
2 ...he said not.
3 ...I suppose not. *or* ...I don't suppose so.
4 I don't think so. ('I think not' would be rather formal here.)
5 I don't expect so. ('I expect not' is also possible, but rather formal. It also expresses a more definite belief that Alex will not be staying.)
6 I suspect not.
7 It doesn't appear so. *or* It appears not.
8 I assume not.
9 ...I didn't say so.

62.3
2 Yes, they are.
3 Yes, it has. *or* So it has.
4 Yes, you did.

62.4 *Possible answers*
2 So I understand.
3 So I gather.
4 So it appears.
5 So he tells me.

UNIT 63

63.1
2 She was asked to teach more classes, and was happy to do so.
3 My French hosts gave me snails to eat, but I did so very reluctantly.
4 The company wanted to build a dam on the site, but they were prevented from doing so by local opposition.
5 All EU countries agreed to implement the new regulations on recycling plastic, but so far only Finland and Austria have done so.
6 The water freezes in the cracks in rocks, and as it does so it expands.

63.2
1 do so
2 do (not 'do so'; habitual action)
3 doing so
4 do (not 'do so'; 'enjoy' refers to a state)
5 does so
6 do (not 'do so'; 'smell' refers to a state)
7 do (not 'do so'; habitual action)
8 did so

63.3
2 such research
3 such claims
4 such a project
5 such destruction
6 such tactics

63.4 *Example answers*
2 ...into research of this kind.
3 ...claims like this (*or* these) ...
4 ...this kind of project...
5 ...this sort of destruction...
6 ...these tactics...

UNIT 64

64.1
2 Yes, we should ~~have booked tickets in advance.~~ *or* Yes, we should have ~~booked tickets in advance.~~
3 Yes, we might ~~be staying in New Zealand permanently.~~ *or* Yes, we might be ~~staying in New Zealand permanently.~~
4 Yes, I'm sure they will ~~have been taken by now.~~ *or* Yes, I'm sure they will have ~~been taken by now.~~ *or* Yes, I'm sure they will have been ~~taken by now.~~
5 No, I haven't ~~had dinner yet.~~
6 Yes, I am ~~going to Steve's party.~~
7 Yes, I would ~~have missed the train.~~ *or* Yes, I would have ~~missed the train.~~
8 No, I can't ~~see him anywhere.~~
9 No, he couldn't ~~have been looking.~~ *or* No, he couldn't have ~~been looking.~~ *or* No, he couldn't have been ~~looking.~~

64.2
1 do
2 have (done)
3 does *or* has ('does' replaces 'he never writes'; 'has' replaces 'he has never written')
4 do
5 (do)
6 hasn't *or* doesn't
7 is
8 have (done) *or* did
9 have *or* do
10 (do) *or* (be) ('do' replaces 'pay for the meal'; 'be' replaces 'be enough to pay for the meal')

64.3
2 would/ might be
3 might/ should (be)
4 should (be)
5 might/ would be
6 should/ would be ('should' without 'be' is also possible, replacing 'says')
7 would/ might be
8 might/ would (be)

UNIT 65

65.1
1 b claims to
2 a expected to   b expected it to be
3 a used to   b used to be
4 a need to be   b need to
5 a appeared to   b appeared to be

65.2
1 opportunity (to)
2 hated to
3 refused (to)
4 choose to
5 determined (to)
6 deserved to
7 idea (to)
8 delighted (to)
9 prefer to
10 afford to

65.3
1 ...if you like to.
2 ✓ (*or* ...you'd like to.)
3 ...she doesn't want to.
4 ✓ (*or* ...if she'd like.)
5 ✓ (*or* ...where I want to.)
6 ...if you don't want to. (However, 'if you don't want' is sometimes used in colloquial speech)
7 ✓ (*or* ...if they want to.)
8 ...I'd like to very much.
9 ...you like. ('...you'd like to' is also possible)
10 ...so I didn't like to.
11 ✓ (*or* ...you want.)

UNIT 66

66.1 *Suggested corrections are given*
2 a **lone** figure *or* a figure walking **alone**
3 ✓
4 a **happy/cheerful** person *or* a person who was always **glad** and smiling
5 his **sleeping** daughter *or* his daughter, who was **asleep**
6 **frightened** passengers *or* passengers on board who are **afraid**
7 ✓
8 a **similar** age
9 ✓
10 The girls, who were sorry for their behaviour, apologised to their teacher. *or* The girls apologised to their teacher because they were sorry for their behaviour.

66.2
1 a utter/ inevitable
  b inevitable.
2 a unsafe ('domestic' would only be possible here if we wanted to emphasise that the equipment was for use in the home (i.e. domestic) rather than another kind of equipment)
  b domestic/ unsafe
3 a educational/ entertaining
  b educational/ entertaining
4 a serious
  b serious/ underlying
5 a legal/stupid   b legal/ stupid

66.3
1 all the people concerned
2 As the minister responsible
3 the opposite effect.
4 the apparent approval
5 a responsible adult.
6 the only available room *or* the only room available
7 the house opposite.
8 and concerned teachers
9 financial advice available

UNIT 67

67.1 *The most likely answers are given*
1 almost/ practically complete
2 a very professional
3 mainly cotton
4 absolutely excellent
5 very clear
6 completely illegal
7 very popular
8 an almost permanent
9 very attractive
10 exclusively/ mainly male
11 very visible
12 mainly/ completely/ largely underground

67.2 *Suggested answers:*
2 I'd be incredibly upset.
3 I'd be rather angry.
4 I'd be a bit embarrassed.
5 I'd be extremely annoyed.

67.3 *Suggested corrections are given, but others are possible*
1 extremely old
2 ✓
3 absolutely useless
4 very happy
5 'reasonably unique' is unlikely; more likely is, for example, 'almost unique'
6 ✓
7 ✓
8 quite small
9 perfectly comfortable
10 ✓
11 reasonably quiet
12 virtually impossible
13 ✓
14 really terrible
15 simply awful
16 ✓

67.4
1 ~~fairly/~~ really
2 really/ fairly (both correct)
3 ~~fairly/~~ really
4 pretty/ very (both correct)
5 ~~very/~~ pretty
6 pretty/ ~~very~~
7 really/ ~~fairly~~
8 really/ very (both correct)
9 pretty/ ~~very~~
10 fairly/ pretty (both correct)

UNIT 68

68.1 *The most likely answers are given*
2 an empty   8 a critical
3 very late   9 late
4 very critical   10 original
5 a straight   11 very straight
6 false   12 very false
7 very empty

68.2
2 a highly technical   b technical
3 a very human   b human
4 a largely academic b academic.
5 a private   b intensely private
6 a diplomatic b extremely diplomatic

68.3 *Possible answers are given*
2 ...nice and quiet.
3 ...lovely and soft.
4 ...nice and juicy.
5 ...good and ready.

UNIT 69

69.1
2 ...the problems identified. (*or* ...the identified problems.)
3 Interested visitors...
4 ...the sheet provided.
5 ...with flights included.
6 ...the resulting publicity... (*or* ...the publicity resulting...)
7 ...any remaining cheese. (*or* ...any cheese remaining.)

69.2 *Some possible participle adjectives are given*
1 that achieved/ recorded
2 those grown/ produced
3 those produced/ manufactured
4 that recorded
5 those living

69.3
2 well-resourced
3 nerve-wracking
4 far-reaching

69.4
2 were wide-ranging
3 is clean-shaven
4 eye-catching

UNIT 70

70.1
1 to reduce
2 to cheat *or* cheating
3 knowing
4 to leave
5 to see (*or* to know)
6 to underestimate *or* underestimating
7 to open *or* opening
8 talking
9 earning
10 to resign *or* resigning
11 to panic
12 turning

70.2
1 stupid going *or* stupid to go
2 confident that he wouldn't get lost
3 ✓
4 guilty shopping
5 was concerned to learn
6 ✓
7 ✓
8 busy drinking
9 was sorry to (have) upset me/ was sorry that he'd upset me ('was sorry for upsetting me' is also possible)
10 wasn't prepared to admit
11 ✓

70.3
2 It was wonderful to hear such a magnificent performance.
3 It was mean of you to eat all the cake and not leave any for me.
4 It was unreasonable of them to complain about the exam results.
5 It was awkward to get the top off the jar. (*or* ...to get the top of the jar off.)
6 It was simple to put up the shelves.
7 It was unprofessional of him to criticise the head teacher in front of the staff.
8 It was kind of you to give birthday presents to the children.

70.4 *Possible answers are given*
2 It made me furious listening to his lies.
3 It made me sad that we wouldn't be working together again.
4 It made me ashamed to learn how badly we treated immigrants in the 1950s.
5 It made me nervous hearing the dentist's drill as I sat in the waiting room.

UNIT 71

71.1
1 repeatedly
2 in/ with despair ('despairingly' is also possible)
3 in/ with anticipation
4 reputedly
5 disappointedly
6 in a relaxed way/ manner/ fashion
7 determinedly
8 in/ with satisfaction ('in a satisfied way/ manner/ fashion' are also possible)
9 in an organised way/ manner/ fashion
10 agitatedly

71.2
1 a most   b mostly
2 a short   b shortly
3 a directly   b direct
4 a wide   b widely
5 a highly   b high

71.3

1 ✓
2 ...to me in a friendly way/ manner/ fashion.
3 ✓ (or ...fine...)
4 ...flatly refused.
5 ✓ ('...very clear' is also possible in informal contexts)
6 ... in a cowardly way/ manner/ fashion...
7 ...justly renowned.
8 ...slowly turned...
9 'thinly' is grammatically correct, but some people would use 'thin' in informal contexts
10 ...loudly applauded...

UNIT 72

72.1

1 more scared
2 deeper or more deep (for emphasis)
3 more pretty
4 colder or more cold (for emphasis)
5 stronger
6 more real
7 longer; more winding
8 more naughty
9 more bored
10 harder
11 truer or more true (for emphasis)
12 more right

72.2

1 more useless
2 more complex
3 more clever or cleverer (more usual)
4 more exciting
5 more wealthy or wealthier (more usual)
6 more worried
7 more recent
8 more pleasant or pleasanter (more usual)
9 more dirty or dirtier (more usual)
10 more powerful
11 more alert

72.3

'the' can be left out in 2, 4 and 5.

72.4

1 in
2 of
3 of
4 in or of (both are possible)
5 in

UNIT 73

73.1

2 The Downtown Hotel is not such a pleasant place to stay as the Strand Hotel. or The Downtown Hotel is not as pleasant a place to stay as the Strand Hotel.
3 The President's address to the nation is as important a speech as he is ever likely to make in his career.

4 It wasn't such a big problem as I first thought. or It wasn't as big a problem as I first thought.
5 Theresa's dog is as ferocious an animal as I've ever seen.
6 She's not such a fluent Greek speaker as she claims to be. or She's not as fluent a Greek speaker as she claims to be.

73.2

1 as many as
2 as few as
3 as much as
4 As many as
5 as little as
6 as few as
7 as little as
8 as much as

73.3

2 + a Her handwriting was so untidy as to be nearly illegible.
3 + e The bookcase was so heavy as to be almost impossible to move.
4 + c The CD was so badly scratched as to be unplayable.
5 + f The plot of the novel was so complicated as to be completely incomprehensible.
6 + b The difference between the results was so small as to be insignificant.

73.4

1 How serious an injury
2 as serious as
3 bad enough to
4 ✓ or not as fit as
5 not such a good player as or not as good a player as
6 go so far as to say
7 sufficiently well or well enough
8 as speedy a recovery as possible

UNIT 74

74.1

1 I expect Sue to win the race **easily**.
2 He regretted missing the concert **greatly**. or He **greatly** regretted missing the concert.
3 I **secretly** hated playing the piano... (more likely than 'I hated playing the piano secretly, although my parents thought I loved it.' This would mean that my parents thought I loved playing the piano secretly.)
4 He **calmly** started to walk across... or He started to walk calmly across...
5 She **kindly** offered to do the work.
6 Ray **hurriedly** finished speaking and sat down. or Ray finished speaking **hurriedly** and sat down.
7 I **simply** don't remember putting it down.
8 We look forward to hearing from you **soon**.
9 They **deliberately** tried to ignore me. or They tried to ignore me **deliberately**.
10 I don't pretend to understand the instructions **completely**.

74.2

2 She waited nervously until her name was called. (manner + time)
3 The road climbed steeply through the mountains. (*more likely than* ...through the mountains steeply) (manner + place)
4 As a punishment she had to be at school early for the next two weeks. (adverb + prepositional phrase; both time)
5 As I left, I locked the door securely. (object + adverb)
6 We're travelling around Australia during the summer. (place + time)
7 The house is by the river, just downstream from the bridge. (adverb + prepositional phrase; both place)
8 She was able to describe accurately the exact details of the house where she had lived as a baby. (adverb + long object)
9 In hospital she had to lie for a week with her right leg suspended in mid air. (time (short) + manner (long))
10 He swam rapidly for a few minutes and then got out of the pool. (manner + time)
11 If you leave now, you should be at home by nine o'clock. (place + time)
12 They enjoyed themselves immensely at the party. (object + manner + place)

74.3

2 ✓ or Next, vigorously beat the eggs in a small bowl. (Both of these are more likely than Next, beat the eggs in a small bowl vigorously.)
3 I thought I'd securely locked the luggage. or I thought I'd locked the luggage securely.
4 I stopped playing tennis regularly... (more likely)
5 ✓ or Rafter was beaten easily in the final./ Rafter was beaten in the final easily.
6 She always brings sandwiches from home.
7 No, they moved away last year.
8 The local residents welcomed warmly the decision... or The local residents warmly welcomed the decision...
9 ✓

UNIT 75

75.1

2 a I was brought up to earn money **honestly**...
  b **Honestly**, I'm perfectly capable of putting up the shelf myself.
3 a She admitted **frankly**...
  b **Frankly**, I went to sleep during his lecture...

4 a **Seriously**, I don't know what I'd have done...
  b I tried to speak **seriously** to him...
5 a **Clearly**, he wants me to take the job.
  b I'd had very little sleep the night before and was having difficulty thinking **clearly**.
6 a **Plainly**, he was feeling ill at ease.
  b She always dressed **plainly**...

75.2
1 ~~enormously~~/ significantly
2 ~~from time to time~~/ rarely
3 easily/ ~~scarcely~~
4 almost/ ~~by an hour~~
5 ~~next~~/ at the bus stop on College Road
6 often/ ~~on many occasions~~
7 ~~hardly ever~~/ every week
8 ~~greatly~~/ rarely
9 ~~nearly~~/ entirely

75.3
1 [1] & [3]   4 [1] & [3]
2 [1] & [3]   5 [2] & [3]
3 [2]   6 [1] & [2]

UNIT 76

76.1
2 ...and out jumped Nick.
3 Outside the door stood two small children.
4 In the park the boys were playing cricket, despite the muddy conditions. (no inversion)
5 Inside the church the choir was singing one of my favourite carols. (no inversion)
6 Around her neck hung a jade necklace.
7 Down the hill the horse ran quickly. (more likely than 'Down the hill ran the horse quickly.')
8 ...and up the tree it climbed.
9 ...and in marched a delegation from the striking workers.
10 ...across the room it flew. (no inversion)
11 ...away swam the fish.
12 ...in the corner was a very old grandfather clock.
13 Around the town she drove (no inversion) for hours looking for the gallery, until in a side street she spotted (no inversion) the place.
14 Through the window Megan watched sadly. (more likely than 'Through the window watched Megan sadly.')
15 In the office Ann found (no inversion) it difficult to concentrate, but at home she worked (no inversion) more efficiently.
16 In Japan they saw (no inversion) a volcano erupting, and in Indonesia they experienced (no inversion) an earthquake.

17 On one side of the village green is a 16th century church and opposite stands a 15th century pub.

76.2
2 ...last week I had a holiday. (subject–verb inversion is not possible: 'last week' is an adverb of time indicating a period; does not take inversion (see C))
3 ...first came a welcoming address by the head of the organising team.
4 ...at no time were members of the public in danger.
5 No change; the adverb 'daily' can't go in front position.
6 ...seldom can a politician have changed his views so quickly as Beckett.
7 ...next came a blizzard, preventing us from leaving the hut.
8 ...by next Friday we'll be in Japan. (subject–verb inversion is not possible: 'by next Friday' is an adverb of time indicating a definite point; does not take inversion (see C))
9 No change; the adverb 'hourly' can't go in front position.
10 ...hardly ever did I hear him raise his voice in anger.
11 ...twice a week I play squash. (subject–verb inversion is not possible: 'twice a week' is an adverb of time indicating a definite frequency; does not take inversion (see C))
12 No change; the adverb 'quarterly' can't go in front position.

UNIT 77

77.1
1 very much
2 much/ very much
3 very/ very much
4 much/ very much
5 very much
6 much/ very much
7 very
8 very/ very much
9 very much
10 much/ very much

77.2
1 too   5 very/ too
2 very/ too   6 too
3 very   7 very
4 very   8 too

77.3
1 ...and he **even** offered...
2 I will **only** be...
3 ...on the basis of price **alone**.
4 ...and **even** the smallest donation can make...
5 ...he has **even** asked Claire...
6 **Only** John knew... (or John **alone** knew...)
7 Advertising **alone**...
8 Admission **alone**...

UNIT 78

78.1 *A number of positions for these adverbs are possible, depending on the wider context and the particular emphasis that the speaker/ writer wants to give. The first answer below gives perhaps the most likely position in many contexts, and then alternatives.*
2 ...**Presumably**, the idea is to welcome visitors from other countries. *or* The idea, **presumably**, is to welcome.../ The idea is, **presumably**, to welcome.../ ...other countries, **presumably**.
3 The builders **generously** agreed to plant new trees to replace the ones they had dug up. *or* **Generously**, the builders agreed.../ The builders agreed **generously** to plant...
4 Most people **rightly** believe that the prisoners should be released. *or* **Rightly**, most people.../ Most people believe, **rightly**, that...
5 **Obviously**, she knew more about the robbery than she told the police. *or* She **obviously** knew.../ ...told the police, **obviously**.
6 He **carelessly** broke the window when he was painting. *or* **Carelessly**, he broke...
7 She **bravely** picked up the spider and put it outside. *or* **Bravely**, she picked up.../ She picked up the spider **bravely**...
8 **Interestingly**, this was the only map I could find that includes the village of Atherstone. *or* This was, **interestingly**, the only map...

78.2
2 ...outwardly she looked remarkably calm.
3 ...environmentally it is no longer the problem it once was.
4 ...industrially it is relatively undeveloped.
5 ...visually the performance was stunning.
6 ...financially we'd be much better off if we moved there.
7 ...politically he claims to be a socialist.
8 ...technically she could be sent to prison.

78.3 *Suggested answers are given*
2 **In geological terms**, limestone is a relatively new rock.
3 The building is similar to the opera house in Milan **in terms of architecture**.
4 **From a grammatical point of view** the essay was well written, but its style was inappropriate.
5 The election was clearly rigged and the result is a severe blow to the country **as far as democracy is concerned**.

UNIT 79

79.1

1 as/ when ('when' emphasises a direct connection between kicking the ball and falling over – it suggests that kicking the ball caused her to then fall over; 'as' suggests 'at the same time as' – kicking and falling happened simultaneously)
2 When (more likely than 'While...'; talking about a period of our lives)
3 When
4 While/ As
5 while/ when ('as' could mean 'because' here)
6 when
7 When
8 As/ When
9 as
10 While/ As
11 when ('as' is also possible and would imply that the sound happens at the time the computer is being switched on; 'when' is more likely, however, as a sound of this kind is more likely to *follow* switching on)
12 As ('When' would be possible if 'continued' meant 'restarted')
13 As/When ('When' might suggest 'just after' the car went by)
14 When/As
15 while/ as
16 when
17 As/When ('When' suggests 'By the time the paint is dry'; 'As' emphasises a continuous change during the period it is drying)

79.2

1 until	5 Before/ Until
2 Before/ Until	6 until
3 before/ until	7 before/ until
4 before	8 until

79.3 *Possible answers are given*

2 ...than he broke his arm.
3 ...when it rang again.
4 ...than it was time to start work again.
5 ...before members of the audience started to criticise her.
6 ...when the engine cut out.

UNIT 80

80.1

2 + b Angela agreed to book tickets for us all **as** it was her idea to go to the theatre.
3 + a **Seeing as** it's your birthday, I'll buy you lunch.
4 + h **Because** I'm trying to lose weight I've given up dairy products.
5 + d We were recommended to buy the textbook second hand **since** a new copy would be very expensive.
6 + c **As** the guest lecturer was late, Dr Jones spoke about his research instead.

7 + e I suggested we all go on holiday together **seeing that** we get on so well.
8 + g You should never walk under a ladder **because** it's supposed to be unlucky.

80.2

2 ...due to lack of interest.
3 ...due to/ owing to its central location.
4 ...due to human error.
5 ...due to/ owing to heavy cloud.
6 ...because of the bright sunlight.
7 ...because his phone was engaged.
8 ...because of local opposition.
9 ...because of his age.
10 ...because there was a fly in it.

80.3

2 I couldn't hear what Sue was saying with the noise. *or* With the noise, I couldn't hear what Sue was saying. *or* I couldn't hear what Sue was saying for the noise.
3 With her father (being) in hospital, Jane went to stay with her aunt. *or* Jane went to stay with her aunt, with her father (being) in hospital.
4 With all the exercise I was doing I felt a lot fitter. *or* I felt a lot fitter with all the exercise I was doing. *or* I felt a lot fitter for all the exercise I was doing.
5 With the train drivers on strike tomorrow, I don't think I'll go to London after all. *or* I don't think I'll go to London after all, with the train drivers on strike tomorrow.

UNIT 81

81.1

2 + h He packed his suitcase with the books at the bottom **so as not to/ in order not to** crush his clothes.
3 + a Bus fares in the city are being cut **so as to/ in order to** encourage people to use public transport.
4 + f We crept quietly towards the deer **so as not to/ in order not to** frighten them away.
5 + c I walked around the outside of the field **so as not to/ in order not to** damage the growing crops.
6 + b We put up a fence **so as to/ in order to** prevent people walking across the grass.
7 + g She looked down at the book in front of her **so as to/ in order to** avoid his gaze.
8 + e The roadworks were carried out at night **so as not to/ in order not to** disrupt traffic too much.

81.2

2	✗	4	✗	6	✓	8	✗
3	✓	5	✗	7	✓		

81.3

2 ...nobody would know it was there.
3 ...mosquitoes couldn't get in.
4 ...it won't take up a lot of computer memory.
5 ...we could see the view over the city.
6 ...it will let enough light in.

81.4 *Suggested answers are given*

2 The meeting room is designed in such a way that everyone's voice can be heard without the use of microphones. / ...in such a way as to allow everyone's voice to be heard without the use of microphones.
3 The documents are written in such a way that they are easily comprehensible./ ...in such a way as to be easily comprehensible.
4 If the dial is rotated in such a way that the number 1 is at the top, the valve opens./ ...in such a way as to locate the number 1 at the top, the valve opens.

UNIT 82

82.1

2 + b Frightened though/ as she was, she forced herself to pick up the snake.
3 + e Scarce though/ as food became, they always found enough to share with me.
4 + c Experienced though/ as the climbers were, they had never faced such severe conditions before.
5 + a Confusing though/ as the instructions first appeared, they were very useful when I looked at them in detail.
6 + h Disgusting though/ as it looked, it was actually quite tasty.
7 + f Confident though/ as she felt, she knew the examination would not be easy.
8 + d Successful though/ as their new products have proved, the company is still in financial difficulties.

82.2

2 In spite of being much younger than the others, he was the most outstanding footballer in the team.
3 In spite of eating a big lunch, he had a three-course meal in the evening.
4 In spite of her fear, she allowed the spider to be placed in her hands.
5 In spite of her obvious intelligence, she finds it difficult to express her ideas in writing.

6 In spite of her illness, she went on a walking holiday in Nepal.

2 Despite the fact that he was much younger than the others, he was the most outstanding footballer in the team.

3 Despite the fact that he ate a big lunch, he had a three-course meal in the evening.

4 Despite the fact that she was frightened, she allowed the spider to be placed in her hands.

5 Despite the fact that she is obviously intelligent, she finds it difficult to express her ideas in writing.

6 Despite the fact that she was ill, she went on a walking holiday in Nepal.

82.3

1	even though	5	even though
2	even if	6	even if
3	Even if	7	Even though
4	Even though	8	even if

82.4

2 + a While horse riding is an expensive pastime, more and more people are taking it up. (*not* More and more people are taking it up, while horse riding is an expensive pastime.) 'Whereas' is not possible.

3 + e Whereas/While a decade ago we used to get a lot of blackbirds in our garden, we rarely see them today. (*or* We rarely see them today, whereas/while a decade ago we used to get a lot of blackbirds in our garden.)

4 + b Whereas/ While the true number of unemployed is over a million, the government says it is under 500,000. (*or* The government says it is under 500,000, whereas/ while the true number of unemployed is over a million.)

5 + d While the temperature is below freezing, it actually feels quite warm when the sun is out. (*not* It actually feels quite warm when the sun is out, while the temperature is below freezing.) 'Whereas' is not possible.

The clause beginning 'while' or 'whereas' can come after the main clause in 3 and 4.

UNIT 83

83.1 *Suggested answers are given*

2 ...give me a call./ ...take it back to the shop.

3 ...tell him I want to see him./ ...ask him to come and see me.

4 If you see any large, hairy spiders in the grass.../ If you come across any snakes on your walk....

5 If you're ever in Birmingham.../ If you ever need any more advice...

6 If you're coming by bus.../ If you don't want to walk far to the shops...

83.2

1 The present perfect suggests 'if you previously studied *Macbeth*...'; the present simple suggests 'if you study *Macbeth* in the future, then you will (get to) know...'.

2 leave/ have left...meet. The present perfect and the present simple have a similar meaning.

3 break/ have broken...have to. The present perfect suggests that you may have broken it (perhaps I think you have); the present simple may be a warning or threat about a possible future event.

4 doesn't arrive/ hasn't arrived...give. The present perfect and the present simple have a similar meaning.

5 haven't filled in/ don't fill in...need. The present perfect suggests 'if you previously filled in an application form'; the present simple may imply 'If you don't fill in an application form now, you will need to do so...'.

6 don't help/ haven't helped...go. The present perfect and the present simple have a similar meaning.

83.3

1	were to hold	4	belonged
2	doubted	5	understood
3	were to switch	6	were to close

83.4

2 If it weren't for his anxiety over Bridget, his happiness would have been complete.

3 If it hadn't been for the terrible weather, we would have gone walking this weekend.

4 Were it not for the intervention of the government (*or* ...for (the) government intervention...), the strike would probably still be going on.

5 Had it not been for the arrival of the police (*or* ...for the police arriving...), the fight could have got out of hand.

6 But for the sound of birds singing, everything was quiet.

7 If it wasn't/ weren't for the United Nations, there would have been far more wars in the last 50 years.

8 If it hadn't been for the roadworks on the motorway we would have been here two hours ago.

9 Were it not for the fact that he comes from a wealthy family, Paul could not have gone to the USA to study.

UNIT 84

84.1

2 Had you not been absent from school on Friday, you would know what you have to do for homework.

3 Were Clare's friends still living in Brussels, she would have been able to stay with them. (*or* Were her friends still living in Brussels, Clare would...)

4 Were the workers prepared to accept a wage cut, the shop would not have had to shut down.

5 Should the financial performance of the company not improve in the near future, we shall have to reduce the number of staff employed.

6 Had the salary been higher, I might have considered taking the job.

84.2

1	✗ If I press this button...
2	✓
3	✓
4	✗ If the disease is untreated... (*or* ...goes untreated...)
5	✓
6	✗ If you complain about me...
7	✓

84.3

1 If I happen to see Karen when I'm in Rome...

2 ✗

3 ...if you happen to live nearby.

4 ✗

5 If you happen to be in the south of Spain next week, ...

84.4 *Possible answers are given using the notes*

2 ...overcome with a great weariness.

3 ...trying to imagine what it contained.

4 ...to agree with everything Julie said. (*or* ...agreeing with...)

5 ...it had been reversed into a wall.

UNIT 85

85.1

2 + d Were the government to increase university fees, there would be an outcry from students.

3 + a Were anyone to lean against the window, the glass would certainly break.

4 + c Were I not already busy in August, I would gladly accept your invitation.

5 + b Were you to see the conditions in which the refugees are living, you would be horrified.

85.2 *Possible sentences are given*
2 Imagine you were to inherit a million dollars.
3 Suppose your parents were to tell you they were emigrating to Canada.
4 Supposing Spain were to win the World Cup.
5 Imagine the population of Britain were all Buddhist.

85.3
2 even if it were
3 even if she were
4 as if I were
5 as if she were
6 even if I were
7 as if it were
8 even if they were

85.4 *Possible answers*
2 I'm not happy about Katie going to Thailand alone. I'd sooner she were going with friends.
3 'If you're unhappy with your new car, why don't you ask for your money back?' 'Well, if only it were as easy as that.'
4 I know you haven't got much time, but if I were you I'd have breakfast before you leave.
5 Forgetting to wear my shoes to school was embarrassing and I'd rather it were forgotten by my classmates.
6 I'm very fond of Sebastian, but I wish he were not so critical of his employees.

85.5
1 ...tiredness, as it were, descending...; *or* ...tiredness descending, as it were, upon her...; *or* ...tiredness descending upon her, as it were...
2 The virus, as it were, hides...; *or* The virus hides, as it were, behind...; *or* The virus hides behind healthy cells, as it were...; *or* ...being attacked, as it were.
3 ...Frank, as it were, returned from the grave...; *or* ...Frank returned, as it were, from the grave...; *or* ...Frank returned from the grave, as it were...

UNIT 86

86.1
2 + d Unless alternative sources of funding are found, the research will not be able to continue.
3 + c Unless the roads have changed in that part of town, I'm sure I'll be able to find my way there.
4 + a Unless the weather starts improving soon, the farmers will lose their crops.
5 + e Unless it's ridiculously expensive, I think I'll buy that painting.

6 + f Unless you have been unemployed for six months, you are not entitled to state benefit.

86.2
1 Unless the infection is treated/ If the infection isn't treated
2 Unless she had gone/ If she hadn't gone
3 Unless he was/ If he wasn't
4 unless the police can prove/ if the police can't prove
5 Unless they were/ If they weren't
6 unless Rachel passes/ if Rachel doesn't pass
7 unless he's gone/ if he hasn't gone
8 Unless you get/ If you don't get
9 unless they get/ if they don't get
10 unless Louise is at home/ if Louise isn't at home
11 unless he's using it/ if he's not using it

86.3
1 if/ whether
2 whether
3 whether
4 if/ whether
5 whether (*or informally* 'if')
6 whether
7 if/ whether
8 if/ whether
9 whether
10 if/ whether
11 whether
12 if/ whether
13 whether (*or informally* 'if')

UNIT 87

87.1
2 A small boy was kicking a ball against a wall; otherwise, the street was deserted.
3 I couldn't remember meeting him before, yet his face seemed familiar.
4 A mass evacuation of islanders is taking place. Meanwhile, the volcano continues to erupt.
5 A: Why don't you like that new French restaurant? B: For one thing, it's too expensive.
6 Karen came down with flu while we were on holiday.
7 My landlady didn't mind me having parties in my room as long as the rent was paid on time.
8 One way of getting rid of weeds is to dig them out. Alternatively, you could poison them.

87.2
1 Nevertheless
2 while
3 even though
4 Even so
5 Instead
6 whereas
7 so
8 Meanwhile
9 while
10 Before
11 As a result
12 unless
13 At that time

87.3 *Example answers are given*
2 However hard you might exercise, it is difficult to lose weight without cutting down on the amount you eat.

3 However much we enjoy being together, it is important to spend some time apart.
4 Professor Malcolm is always happy to spend time with his students, however busy he might be.

UNIT 88

88.1
1 across
2 across/ over
3 over
4 across/ over
5 across
6 across
7 across
8 over

88.2
1 along/ through
2 Across
3 through
4 across/ over
5 over ('all over' is more likely than 'all across' or 'all through')
6 along

88.3
1 under
2 ✓ ('under' is also possible)
3 below
4 over
5 ✓ ('over' is also possible)
6 ✓ ('over' is also possible)
7 over
8 under
9 ✓ ('above' is also possible)
10 above

88.4
1 + c below par (or 'under par') = slightly unwell (in other contexts 'below par' means 'less than the standard expected')
2 + e below the belt = cruel or unfair
3 + b under her belt = successfully completed
4 + f under a cloud = people disapprove of someone because they think the person has done something wrong
5 + g over the top = extreme behaviour; indicating disapproval
6 + a over and above = in addition to
7 + d across the board = applies equally to all areas

UNIT 89

89.1
1 between
2 among
3 between
4 between
5 among
6 between
7 among
8 among
9 between

89.2
2 between/ among the pupils
3 between amateur
4 among teenagers
5 between/ among his remaining relatives
6 among its clients

7 between intake of refined sugar
8 between cooking
9 among my closest friends
10 between the striking dockers

89.3

1	among	6	between
2	among	7	among
3	between	8	between
4	among	9	among
5	between	10	between

UNIT 90

90.1

1	✓	6	✓	11	✗
2	✗	7	✗	12	✓
3	✗	8	✓	13	✗
4	✓	9	✓	14	✗
5	✗	10	✗	15	✓

90.2

1 a by   b until ('until' would also be possible in a. It would mean, however, that up to the time dinner was served I was hungry, and then when it was served (but before I ate it) I was not. Perhaps the food was so unappetising that I couldn't face eating it; 'by' in a simply means that I was hungry when dinner was served)
2 a until   b by
3 a by   b until
4 a Until   b By ('By' would also be possible in a)
5 a by   b until
6 a by   b until

90.3

1	Over/ During	5	until now
2	So far	6	during
3	Until now	7	until
4	so far	8	by

UNIT 91

91.1

1 except
2 except *or* except for
3 except *or* except for
4 except
5 except for (in informal contexts); more formally, 'but for' is possible
6 except
7 except *or* except for (in informal contexts)
8 except *or* except for
9 except *or* except for (in informal contexts)
10 except for (in informal contexts); more formally, 'but for' is also possible
11 except *or* except for
12 except
13 except
14 except

91.2

1 ~~besides~~ except for
2 Besides ✓
3 ~~except for~~ besides
4 ~~Except for~~ Besides

5 ~~besides~~ except (for)
6 except for ✓

91.3

2 + a But for the interruptions caused by the bad weather, the building would have been completed by now.
3 + c But for the supply of food and medicines by the charity (*or* But for the food and medicines supplied by the charity...), many more people would have died in the famine.
4 + f But for the shelter provided by the trees, the wind would have caused even more damage to the house.
5 + b But for the threat of sanctions by the EU (*or* But for the sanctions threatened by the EU...), human rights would not have improved in the country.
6 + d But for the loan from the bank (*or* But for the loan the bank gave me.../ ...given to me by the bank...), I would not have been able to set up my business.

UNIT 92

92.1

1 after/ ~~on~~/ about
2 ~~after~~/ ~~for~~/ about
3 ~~after~~/ ~~of~~/ about (both 'of' and 'about' are possible, but 'of' is more formal)
4 ~~about~~/ ~~for~~/ with
5 ~~of~~/ ~~with~~/ on
6 for/ ~~after~~/ ~~about~~
7 for/ ~~on~~/ ~~with~~
8 of/ about/ ~~on~~

92.2

1 about
2 after
3 of/ about
4 with (note that 'to' would also be possible)
5 for
6 about
7 on (note that 'to' would also be possible)
8 of ('about' is unlikely in this formal context)
9 about
10 after/ about
11 with
12 of
13 about
14 about
15 about
16 on ('about' is also possible but less natural here)

92.3

1 acted on = did what someone else advised or suggested; acted for = represented (usually a professional person such as a lawyer or accountant)

2 thinking...about = concentrating on; think of = asking about an opinion
3 was called after = was given the same name as; called for = demanded
4 worked for = was employed by; works with computers = uses computers a lot in her work
5 counting on = depending on; counts for little = is of little value

UNIT 93

93.1

2 improvement in
3 pride in
4 advice about/ on
5 interview with ('in' is also possible. 'with' highlights that staff from *The Daily Herald* conducted the interview; 'in' indicates that what is being referred to is the published article in the newspaper which comprises the interview or includes a report of it)
6 admiration for
7 discussion about/ on
8 shame at/ about
9 vaccination against
10 influence on
11 amazement at
12 lack of

93.2

2 sign of stopping
3 decision to allow
4 reason to worry
5 risk of transmitting
6 ability to remember
7 failure to win/ get
8 cost of buying
9 possibility of getting
10 unwillingness to acknowledge

93.3 *Likely verbs are given*

2 of seeing
3 to take
4 to retire/ of retiring
5 of taking/ to take
6 of dancing

UNIT 94

94.1

1 intransitive; no noun/ pronoun needed
2 ...look it up... (a noun or pronoun is necessary)
3 ...help (you) out... (a noun or pronoun is possible)
4 ...tidy (things) away... (a noun or pronoun is possible)
5 intransitive; no noun/ pronoun needed

94.2

1	.... ✓	out	....
2	.... ✓	about	.... ✓
3	....	up	.... ✓
4	.... ✓	out	.... ✓
5	.... ✓	up	.... ✓
6	.... ✓	away	....

94.3

2 left her name out/ left out her name
3 shut the thing up
4 make my mind up/ make up my mind
5 got down the general ideas/ got the general ideas down
6 hear me out

94.4

1 ~~ordering about everyone~~ ordering everyone about
2 ~~provide their children for~~ provide for their children
3 ~~let in me on the secret~~ let me in on the secret
4 ~~called motorists on~~ called on motorists
5 ✓
6 ~~took up Keith on~~ took Keith up on
7 ✓
8 ✓
9 ~~looked Mr Brooks up to~~ looked up to Mr Brooks

UNIT 95

95.1

3 Is there something bothering you?
4 There was a barrier across the road.
7 There was no petrol available anywhere in the city.
8 Is there anyone who/that can help me?
9 There are some general rules (which/ that) you can follow.
(Sentences with 'There...' are unlikely in 2, 5, and 6 because the subjects have a definite or specific meaning, indicated by 'Your', 'The', and 'My'.)

95.2

1 are	4 is	7 are
2 are	5 are	8 is
3 is	6 is	

95.3 *The most likely sentences are given*

2 + c There's a cake in the kitchen (that/ which) I've made especially for your birthday.
3 + h There was never any doubt (that) Thomas would get the job.
4 + a There have been suggestions (that) an election will be held next month.
5 + f There aren't many people alive today who/ that remember the First World War.
6 + g There are still some old houses in the village that/ which don't have electricity.
7 + d There was absolutely nothing (that) I could do to prevent him falling.
8 + b There are few people in the company who/ that are harder working than Julie.

95.4

2 There being no further business, the meeting closed at 12.30.
3 There being no doctor available, the patients were sent home.
4 There being inadequate facilities at the hotel, the conference was relocated to a nearby university.

UNIT 96

96.1

2 It was unsettling how he stared straight at me.
3 ✗ (However, in spoken English we might say 'It was surprising, Andrew's excellent exam result'.)
4 It is an advantage in the job to be a qualified driver.
5 ✗ (However, in spoken English we might say 'It's quite radical, her proposal'.)
6 It is highly unusual to put carpet on walls.
7 ✗ (However, in spoken English we might say 'It's a Ferrari, John's new car'.)
8 It is hard finding a good plumber these days. (*or* It is hard to find...)

96.2 *The most likely answers are given*

2 ...it astonished me to discover (that) she was also a successful novelist.
3 ...it hurts (me) to pedal my bicycle. / ...it has hurt (me) to pedal my bicycle.
4 ...it struck me (that) he was jealous.
5 ...it concerned me to hear (that) he was offended. (*or* ...it upset me...)
6 ...it didn't bother him (that) everyone could see in.
7 ...it upset me (that) she hadn't even told me when she was going away. (*or* ...it concerned me...)
8 ...it doesn't do to criticise them too much.
9 ...it scared me to see (that) they were carrying knives.
10 ...it pays to plan your journey ahead.

96.3 *Example answers are given*

2 It takes a lot of hard work to build your own house.
3 It takes a considerable amount of courage to make a speech in front of a group of strangers.
4 It takes patience and a lot of time to explain the rules of cricket to someone who doesn't know the game.
5 It takes bravery to stand up to a bully.
6 It takes a lot of organisation to be a good administrator.
7 It takes a great deal of time to learn to speak a foreign language well.

UNIT 97

97.1

2 find it
3 discover ('find' would also be possible)
4 owe it
5 remember
6 enjoy it
7 prefer it
8 leave it
9 predict
10 consider it

97.2

2 I see it as part of my role to make Rexco a household name in the next 5 years.
3 I accept it as a necessary evil that some people may be made redundant in the next year.
4 I view it as important for relations with the workforce to make available information about/ on the salaries of managers.
5 I regard it as unacceptable for a modern company to exclude the workforce from major decision-making.
6 I regard it as something positive when employees make suggestions on how management can be improved.
7 I see it as vital for the future of the company to expand into the Asian market.
8 I take it as a fundamental principle of the company that suppliers of raw materials should be given a fair price for their products.

97.3

2 there's no hope/ chance
3 It's no secret
4 It's no good/ use *or* There's no point
5 there's no reason
6 there's no alternative/ choice
7 It's no longer
8 there's no denying/ question

UNIT 98

98.1

2 ...it was to cheer her up that I booked a holiday in Amsterdam.
3 ...it's because I've got so much work to do that I can't come.
4 ...it was somewhere in there that/ where I lost it.
5 ... it was only by studying very hard that she improved her Spanish.
6 ...it is to my family that I dedicate this thesis.

98.2

2 'No, what I hope is that they will be put into a public art gallery.'
3 'No, what annoyed me was that she didn't apologise.'

4 'No, what I meant was that she could borrow it until I needed it again.'
6 'No, what I did was (to) put some oil and soy sauce on it and grill it.'
7 'No, what I did was (to) give her some money towards it.'
8 'No, what I did was (to) hire a car and drive all the way.'

98.3 *Suggested answers*
2 I don't know if he's free, but somebody who/ that might be able to help is Saleh. (*or* ...but Saleh is somebody who/ that might be able to help.)
3 In fact the place where/ that I grew up is between this village and the next. (*or* ...the place that I grew up in...)
4 I suppose the time when I lived in Australia was when I was happiest.

UNIT 99

99.1
1 (in a narrative 'down comes' is also possible; see Unit 2)
2 along comes
3 up go
4 back/ away he went
5 out/ in came (*or* comes)
6 along/ up came (*or* comes)
7 off/ away she went (*or* goes)

99.2
2 + h Should you not wish to receive further information about our products, put a tick in the box.
3 + a Were the plane ever (to be) built, it would cut the journey time from New York to Tokyo by 4 hours.
4 + g Should United win again today, it will be their tenth consecutive victory.
5 + d Were I (to be) asked to take the job, I would have no hesitation in accepting.
6 + i Had a car been coming in the other direction, I might have been seriously injured.
7 + f Had there been a referendum on the issue, it is unlikely that the country would have supported the government.

8 + b Should you not be able to afford the Rombus 2000, there are less expensive models in the range.
9 + e Were Charles Dickens (to be) alive today, he would be writing novels about the homeless in London.

99.3
2 I was opposed to the new road being built, as was everyone else in the village.
3 Karen went to Oxford University, as did her mother and sister.
4 People in poorer countries consume a far smaller proportion of the earth's resources than do those in developed nations.
5 He is a much better teacher now than he was 5 years ago. (no inversion with a pronoun as subject)
6 Don is a keen golfer, as is his wife.

UNIT 100

100.1
2 At no time was the public (ever) in any danger.
3 Only with close friends and family did he feel entirely relaxed.
4 Only if the pitch is frozen will the match be cancelled.
5 Little did I know then that Carmen and I would be married one day.
6 Barely had he entered the water when it became clear he couldn't swim.
7 On no account are you to light the fire if you are alone in the house. (*or* On no account should/ must you...)
8 Not for one moment was there any competitiveness between the three brothers.
9 Not only was I wet through, I was freezing cold.
10 Only once had I ever climbed this high before. *or* Only once before had I ever climbed this high.
11 Hardly had the audience taken their seats when the conductor stepped onto the stage.

12 Only in the last few years has he been acknowledged to be a great author.

100.2 *Possible answers*
2 ...was the strength of the earthquake...
3 ...is his dominance in the sport...
4 ...alike were the twins...
5 ...complicated was the equation...
6 ...boring was the lesson...

100.3 *Corrections are given in the underlined sections*
The people of Sawston were evacuated yesterday as forest fires headed towards the town. Such was the heat of the oncoming inferno that trees more than 100 metres ahead began to smoulder. Only once in recent years, during 1994, has a town of this size (*inversion is likely in this written context*) had to be evacuated because of forest fires. A fleet of coaches and lorries arrived in the town in the early morning. Into these vehicles climbed the sick and elderly (*inversion is likely in this written context*), before they headed off to safety across the river. Residents with cars left by mid morning, as did all non-essential police officers.

Hardly had the evacuation been completed when the wind changed direction and it became clear that the fire would leave Sawston untouched. Soon after that complaints were heard from some residents. "At no time did the fires pose a real threat," said one local man. "I didn't want to leave my home, and nor did most of my neighbours." So upset are some elderly residents that they are threatening to complain to their MP. But Chief Fire Officer Jones replied, "Had we not taken this action, lives would have been put at risk. Only when the fires have moved well away from the town will residents be allowed to return to their homes."

Key to Additional exercises

1
1. b 'm not promising/ don't promise/ didn't promise
2. a was reading/ read   b read
3. a were expecting/ expected   b are expecting/ expect
4. a owns ('or 'own')   b owned/ owns
5. a 'm considering/ was considering/ considered   b consider
6. a tells/ told   b tell/ told
7. a phoned   b was phoning/ phoned
8. a 's always putting/ puts;   b 's constantly putting/ puts
9. a prefer   b preferred
10. a weighs   b was weighing

2
1. a + i or ii   b + ii
2. a + ii   b + i
3. a + i or ii   b + i
4. a + ii;   b + i
5. a + i or ii   b + ii
6. a + i   b + ii
7. a + i   b + ii
8. a + ii   b + i (b + ii is also correct grammatically, but it is unlikely to be used; it suggests that it is difficult to get good pasta in Italy, which is of course not the case!)

3
1. 'had discussed' is also possible, but less likely as the duration of the discussions is emphasised
2. His condition **had improved** considerably when I saw him in hospital last night. ('improved' would be unlikely as it would suggest that his condition improved *because* I saw him last night)
3. It was announced that the York train **had been delayed** by 10 minutes. ('was delayed' is also possible with a similar meaning)
4. Joe **had been dieting** for a month when he came to stay with us, and we noticed immediately that he had already lost a lot of weight.
5. Sylvia **had been expected to win** comfortably, but she finished only third. ('was expected' is also possible with a similar meaning)
6. When I reversed the car out of the garage, I **damaged** the rear number plate.
7. John **was promoted** last week.
8. The tax authorities **had been investigating** Rentpool for a number of months when they arrested the chairman. ('had investigated' is also possible, but less likely as the duration of the investigation is emphasised)
9. The Minister **angered** her colleagues when she criticised them during her speech yesterday.
10. Christine **had already suggested** that the money should be spent on new textbooks for the school.

4A
1. ✓
2. I'll (= 'I will' or 'I shall')

4B
1. I'm going to build *or* I'm building
2. I'll give

4C
1. Will *or* Are you going to be able to *or* Are you able to
2. 're going to have *or* 're having
3. I'll
4. ✓

4D
1. is going (more likely than 'is going to go')
2. isn't (is not) coming *or* isn't (is not) going to come *or* won't come
3. 'll see *or* 're going to see
4. ✓

4E
1. 'm taking *or* 'm going to take *or* 'll take
2. ✓
3. more likely is 'It's at 4.15' as this is part of a timetable
4. 'll take
5. 'we're going to have' is more likely
6. 'I'll stay' is more likely if the decision is made at the moment of speaking

5
1. ought to have asked; would have been
2. should; 'd better
3. won't; can't; used to
4. can't; must have
5. mustn't; can
6. wouldn't; needn't have worried
7. should; would
8. should; may
9. must; could
10. will be able to; might
11. couldn't; didn't have to
12. don't need to; can

6
The agent (after 'by...') is given only where it is likely to be included. Where it might either be included or left out, it is written in brackets.

A   **The Prime Minister is being encouraged** to sack the Environment Minister, Maggie Long, after **it was revealed** that she had received payments from a major oil company. However, in a statement today, the Prime Minister said: 'I **am told** (by my advisors)/ **I am advised** that Mrs Long **was paid** the money (by the company) [*Note the word order*: not '...*by the company the money...*'] before she joined the government. I have no intention of dismissing her.'

B   A tropical storm has caused severe flooding in the city of Chittagong in southern Bangladesh. Although **there are understood to be** (*or* **it is understood that there are/ have been**) no casualties, **many thousands of people have been made homeless** (by the floods), and **the damage to property is estimated** as running into millions of dollars.

C   Protesters have continued to obstruct the construction of the new Newburn ring road by tying themselves to trees along the proposed route. (Police say that) **The protesters have been given** two days to leave the area or **they will be arrested** (by the police).

D   Conservation groups have demanded that the Seafield nuclear power station should **be closed down** (by the government) after a report which said that unacceptable levels of radiation **have been found** (by investigators) in the local area.

E   The Chief Constable of the London police force has revealed that a death threat **has been received** (by the police) against the life of President Nabon, who is visiting the capital this weekend. He says that **the threat is being taken** very seriously. **It is expected** that security levels will be increased during the President's visit.

F   A man **was found** injured on a Scottish hillside this morning. **It is thought** that he fell while coming down a hillside in bad weather. **He is being treated** in hospital for leg and head injuries. [*We can assume that medical staff would treat him in hospital, so there is no need to mention the agent here.*] **He was reported** missing last night when he failed to return home after a day's walking.

G   And now football. **There are expected to be** (*or* **It is expected that there will be**) a record crowd at tonight's match between Manchester United and Bayern Munich. **It is reported** that **the United players will be given** a huge financial bonus (by the club) if they win and **it has even been suggested** that **they might be paid** as much as £50,000 each (by the club).

7

1. on paying
2. by asking
3. his saying/ him saying
4. appointed
5. count
6. at me to tidy
7. to visit
8. wearing children's clothes/ children's clothes
9. their cat
10. forcing
11. her smoking/ smoking
12. to appear
13. let
14. to hearing
15. entitle her to
16. waited for
17. noticed a man take
18. invited
19. tell/ telling
20. looking
21. talked
22. to living
23. me from using

8

2. We were disappointed with Karen's decision not to go to university next year./ ...Karen's decision that she wouldn't go/ wasn't going/ isn't going to university next year.
3. Considerable media attention has been focused on Professor Adams' prediction that the Earth will/ would pass through the tail of a comet within the next five years.
4. The company has carried out its threat to dismiss the strikers (if they didn't return to work).
5. Mary decided to follow her boss's advice that she should delegate more of her work to her secretary./ ...her boss's advice to delegate more of her work to her secretary.
6. John didn't turn up until 11.00, despite his promise to pick me up at 10.00./ ...his promise that he would pick me up at 10.00.
7. I wasn't surprised by Bob's conclusion that Professor Jones doesn't know what he is talking about. ...Bob's conclusion that Professor Jones didn't know what he was talking about.
8. We decided to ignore Donald's complaint that his dinner was cold.
9. I was astonished by their refusal to negotiate over the ownership of the land.
10. The Health Minister has issued a warning to keep small children indoors until pollution levels have reduced./ ...a warning that small children should be kept indoors until pollution levels have reduced.
11. I was surprised by her confession that she has/ had never used a computer before.

12. When I asked Derek where Susan was, his reply was that he didn't know.

9

1. wants
2. are
3. live
4. points
5. prefer/ prefers
6. love/ loves (although a plural verb is more grammatical)
7. claim
8. go
9. comes
10. is/ are
11. is/ are
12. shuts
13. suspect
14. are
15. appears
16. are
17. is/ are (although a plural is preferred in formal contexts)
18. plan/ plans
19. is
20. provides (more likely than 'provide' in this formal context)
21. get/ gets
22. is
23. speak/ speaks
24. has/ have
25. are
26. have
27. has
28. isn't
29. are
30. is

10

1. a a/one (colloquially, we could also say '...for the week'); b a/ one; c one ('one' can complete all three sentences)
2. a A/The; b a; c an (a/an)
3. a the/–; b the; c The (the)
4. a the/–; b some/–; c – (–)
5. a the/–; b some/–; c some/– (–)
6. a –/Some; b –; c – (–)
7. a The/An; b the; c the (the)
8. a The/A; b a/one (colloquially, we could also say '...for the night...'); c a (a)
9. a the/–; b –; c – (–)
10. a a/–; b a; c a (a)

11

2. Carla's restaurant, which serves a range of Mediterranean dishes, is very good value. (some people would use 'that' as an alternative to 'which')
3. The New Zealand rugby team, all of whose members weigh over 100 kilos, are clear favourites to win the match.
4. Suzie brought home a kitten (which/that) she'd found in the park.
5. The story is about a teenage boy whose ambition is to become an astronaut.
6. Paul has got a job with Empirico, whose main product is electric light bulbs.

7. Politicians should give more consideration to the working people (who/ that/ whom) they represent.
8. Among the group of people was Professor Rogers, who/ whom I had last seen in Oxford twenty years earlier.
9. I live on a small road which/that leads down to the river.
10. Monet's earlier paintings, many of which have never been seen in this country before, are in a new exhibition in London.
11. Ian McIver, whose first job was selling vegetables in a market, has become managing director of Europe's largest food retailer.
12. Douglas has a new girlfriend who/ that works in the library.
13. My Volkswagen Golf, which I bought in 1980, is a very reliable car. (some people would use 'that' as an alternative to 'which')
14. Brian Brookes, after whom the Brookes art gallery is named, will be present at its official opening. / Brian Brookes, who(m) the Brookes gallery is named after, will...

12

1. did
2. doing so/ so doing
3. promised he would
4. appears so
5. do
6. have/ have done
7. didn't want to
8. do ('do so' is unlikely in this informal context)
9. doubt that he will
10. don't suppose so/ suppose not
11. want to/ want
12. has
13. such a dilemma
14. do
15. afford to
16. expect so
17. suspect not
18. hope not
19. might have/ might
20. told me so
21. determined to/ determined
22. to be
23. guess not
24. might do/ might be

13

Suggested improvements are given

a *Every so often* I leave work *early* (✓) (or I leave work *early every so often*) and go to a performance in the local concert hall. It's very close to my office in the building *opposite*. *Usually* (✓) they are *rather* good, but yesterday's, given by a singer and pianist, was a *total* (✓) disaster. The singer began to sing *with wonderful control*. But when the pianist started to play, it sounded awful. At first I thought he was playing *badly*,

Key to Additional exercises

but then it became obvious that the piano was *completely* out of tune. They stopped and discussed the problem *briefly* (or ...and *briefly* discussed the problem). *Clearly*, they couldn't continue (or They *clearly* couldn't continue), and they left the stage *unhappily* (✓). *Naturally* (✓), all the people *present* felt sorry for them. I'm sure the person *responsible* for tuning the piano will be severely reprimanded.

b I was *just* going out to work this morning when the postman pushed a letter *through my letterbox*. It was from Maggie, who writes *from time to time* (✓). The letter said that she has to come to Bristol to visit her uncle, *who is unwell*. She is one of his few *remaining* (✓) relatives. She wants us to meet and asked if I could suggest a *possible* time. Well, I haven't seen her *for a couple of years*, so I was really pleased. We *first* (✓) met at university. We have *similar* interests (or Our interests *are alike*), so we *always* find a lot to talk about. The photos *included* in the letter showed that she hadn't changed since I *last* (✓) saw her. I spent so long reading the letter that I was *nearly* late for work.

14

3 + b Jamie must weigh over 120 kilos, whereas his wife is really small./ Whereas Jamie must weigh over 120 kilos, his wife is really small./ His wife is really small, whereas Jamie must weigh over 120 kilos./ Whereas his wife is really small, Jamie must weigh over 120 kilos.

4 + j There had been a lot of publicity about the meeting. Even so, only about 100 people attended.

5 + e I can't afford a coat like that. Besides, I don't like the style.

6 + h I'm determined to finish the report tonight, even if I have to stay at work until midnight./ Even if I have to stay at work until midnight I'm determined to finish the report.

7 + g Make sure you catch the last bus at 11.00. Otherwise, you'll have to walk all the way from the station.

8 + a Although I found the film boring, I stayed until the end./ I found the film boring, although I stayed until the end.

9 + i She hid the letter between the pages of a book so that her husband would never find it./ So that her husband would never find it, she hid the letter between the pages of a book.

10 + c In order to prepare for the marathon, I've been running about 200 kilometres a week./ I've been running about 200 kilometres a week in order to prepare for the marathon.

15

1 ...although I know that you *approve* of it.

2 There seems to be little *likelihood* of Williamson winning Wimbledon because of her *inability* to play well on grass tennis courts.

3 Our plan is to *split* the organisation **up** into a number of small units. (or '*split* **up** the organisation into'. Note that 'split the organisation into' [without 'up'] is also possible.) This will improve our *prospects* **of** competing with more specialised companies.

4 I *ran* **into/across** Paul in town the other day. He *asked* **after/about** you.

5 Jack takes great *pride* **in** never *throwing* anything **away** ('throwing away anything' is

also possible, but less likely).

6 Although Professor Watson *knows* a great deal **about** meteorology, even he can't *account* **for** the unusual weather we have been having over the last few weeks.

7 There has been a great *improvement* **in** the behaviour of children in the school. This has *resulted* **from** the headteacher's *idea* of involving them in decision-making.

8 Even though Dennis didn't *act* **on** my advice and follow a career in medicine, I'm full of *admiration* **for** his *determination* **to** train to be a vet.

16

2 Only if an official complaint is made will the police investigate the matter further.

3 So complicated were the instructions,...

4 Had we known how ill Rob was,...

5 Such was the strength of the wind that... (or So strong was the wind that...)

6 Seldom did she regret her lack of formal education,...

7 Only in an emergency should you phone for an ambulance. (or Only if there is an emergency should you phone for an ambulance.)

8 Not for one moment was there any/ a disagreement between us.

9 Were it not for financial assistance from the government,...

10 Hardly had they finished eating before a waiter started to clear away the plates.

11 Under no circumstances should children be allowed into the room without adult supervision.

12 Should the bridge ever be built,...

Key to Study guide

Tenses
1.1	B
1.2	D
1.3	C
1.4	A, B
1.5	C
1.6	A
1.7	D
1.8	B
1.9	A, C
1.10	C
1.11	A
1.12	B
1.13	B, D
1.14	C
1.15	B, C

The future
2.1	C
2.2	D
2.3	B, D
2.4	A, D
2.5	C
2.6	B
2.7	A
2.8	D
2.9	B, C
2.10	C, D
2.11	C

Modals
3.1	C
3.2	B
3.3	A
3.4	D
3.5	C, D
3.6	B, D
3.7	B
3.8	C
3.9	A, C
3.10	B, C
3.11	D
3.12	A

Linking verbs, passives, questions
4.1	C, D
4.2	B
4.3	A, C
4.4	B, C
4.5	B
4.6	C
4.7	A, D
4.8	D
4.9	B
4.10	C

Verb complementation: what follows verbs
5.1	D
5.2	A, B
5.3	C
5.4	B
5.5	C, D
5.6	A
5.7	A

Reporting
6.1	C
6.2	A
6.3	D
6.4	B
6.5	B, D
6.6	A
6.7	C
6.8	B, D
6.9	B, C
6.10	A, C

Nouns
7.1	B
7.2	B, D
7.3	C
7.4	A, D
7.5	A, C
7.6	B, D
7.7	A, D
7.8	D
7.9	A

Articles, determiners and quantifiers
8.1	B
8.2	C
8.3	A
8.4	B
8.5	A, D
8.6	C
8.7	D
8.8	A, C
8.9	B
8.10	B, D
8.11	A
8.12	C
8.13	D
8.14	B
8.15	A, C
8.16	A
8.17	B
8.18	B
8.19	D
8.20	B

Relative clauses and other types of clause
9.1	D
9.2	A, B
9.3	B, C, D
9.4	B
9.5	C, D
9.6	A, C
9.7	A
9.8	B
9.9	C
9.10	B

Pronouns, substitution and leaving out words
10.1	D
10.2	B, D
10.3	C, D
10.4	A, B
10.5	C, D
10.6	B
10.7	C, D
10.8	D
10.9	A, B, D
10.10	A

Adjectives and adverbs
11.1	B
11.2	B, C
11.3	A, C
11.4	D
11.5	C
11.6	A
11.7	A, C, D
11.8	B
11.9	C
11.10	B (in informal speech only), C, D
11.11	A
11.12	A (in informal speech only), B, C
11.13	D
11.14	A, B
11.15	C
11.16	A, C
11.17	A, D
11.18	B, C

Adverbial clauses and conjunctions
12.1	B
12.2	A
12.3	A
12.4	C, D
12.5	A, D
12.6	B, C
12.7	A, D
12.8	B, D
12.9	C
12.10	C, D
12.11	B
12.12	A, D
12.13	A, B, C
12.14	A

Prepositions
13.1	A
13.2	D
13.3	A, B
13.4	A, D
13.5	B, C
13.6	A
13.7	C

Organising information
14.1	B
14.2	C
14.3	B
14.4	B, D
14.5	A
14.6	B, C

Index

A

a/an, the, and zero article
 generalisations about classes of
  things 90
 geographical areas 90
 holidays, seasons, days of the
  week, and festivals 94
 jobs/job titles 92
 means of transport and
  communication 94
 names of people 92
 nouns both countable and
  uncountable 90
 repeated/related words joined by
  preposition 94
 specific *versus* general 94
 with superlative adjectives 92
 with **there + be** 190
 things that are unique 90
 this, in stories and jokes 92
 times of day and night 94
a/an and one
 abbreviations 88
 in number/quantity expressions
  88
 one ...other/another pattern 88
 particular, but unspecified
  person/thing/event 88
 with possessives 88
 before singular countable nouns
  88
 before vowels/consonants 88
abbreviations 88
ability
 be able to 30
 can/could 30, 34, 204, 205
academic writing
 few and **little** 104
 may 34
 much (of), many (of) 100
 prepositional phrases 114
 such that, to introduce a result
  162
active (*versus* passive) forms 44,
 46, 48, 219, 224
adding information
 conjunctions 174
 noun phrases 112, 114
 prepositional phrases 114
 sentence connectors 174
adjectives
 and adverbs, use of 142, 216
 definition of 219
 easily confused 216
 gradable and non-gradable 134
  both senses 136
  classifying adjectives 136
  different senses 136
  **good and/lovely and/nice and ...
   + gradable adjective** 136
  grammar review 216
  more and more + adjective 136
  nationality adjectives 136
  qualitative adjectives 136
 patterns after linking verbs

**adjective + -ing/that-clause/
 to-infinitive/wh-clause** 140
**it + linking verb + adjective (+ to-
 infinitive)** 140
**it + make + adjective (+ to-
 infinitive/-ing/ that-clause)** 140
 position of
  additional exercise 238
  before/after noun 132
  classifying adjectives 132
  emphasising adjectives 132
  grammar review 216
  with linking verbs 132
  qualitative adjectives 132
  reduced relative clauses 132
 study guide 248–49
 types of 219
 see also comparative forms;
  compound adjectives; participle
  adjectives; superlative forms
adverbial clauses
 additional exercise 238
 contrasts 164
 definition of 219
 study guide 250
 tenses in 217
 of time 158
adverbial phrases, as complement
 220
adverbials
 adverb as 219
 adverbial clause as 219
 definition of 219
 inversion after negative 200
 noun phrase as 219
 participle clauses 116, 118
 prepositional phrase as 219
adverbs
 and adjectives, use of 216
 definition of 219
 formation of 142
 participle adjectives in **-ed,**
  adverbial form of 142
 particles 222
 phrasal verbs 222
 position of
  additional exercise 238
  after object 148
  comment adverbs 150, 156
  connecting adverbs 150
  degree adverbs 150, 154
  focus adverbs 154
  frequency adverbs 148, 150, 152
  long adverbials 148
  and meaning 148
  more than one adverbial 148
  order of events 150
  place and direction adverbs 150,
   152
  time adverbs 150, 152
  viewpoint adverbs 150
 prepositional phrases, adverbial
  use of 142
 study guide 248–49
 types of 219

 with and without **-ly** 142
 see also comparative forms;
  superlative forms
advice 40, 78
affirmative sentences 219, 221
agent 219
 see also passive forms
agreement, subject and verb
 clause, as subject 80
 co-ordinated nouns/phrases, as
  subject 82
 collective nouns 80
 complex subject 80
 determiners 82
 how/here/where + be/have 82
 items joined by (**either**) **... or** or
  (**neither**) **... nor** 82
 measurement/amount/quantity,
  with singular verb 84
 names/titles ending in -s 80
 nouns ending in -s 84
 subject, position of 80
 there + be/have 82
 what-clause, as subject 80
all (of), whole, every, each
 time expressions 102
 whole/entire, before nouns 102
among and **between** 178
amounts 104
any *see* **some** and **any**
apostrophe, for possessives 210
articles
 additional exercise 235–36
 definition of 219
 grammar review 211
 study guide 245–46
 see also **a/an, the,** and **zero article**
auxiliary verbs 219
 in inversion 198
 leaving words out after 128
  be as main verb in previous
   clause/sentence 128
  have as auxiliary + **done** 128
  modal auxiliary + **do/be** 128
  more than one auxiliary 128
  no auxiliary 128
  substitute **do** 128
 negative questions 54, 207
 substitute **so** and **not** 124
 see also modal verbs

B

bare infinitive 221
being + past participle clause 220
between and **among** 178

C

can *see* ability; permission;
 possibility
change, process of 42
'choosing' verbs 68
classifying adjectives 132, 134,
 136, 219
clauses
 definition of 220

study guide 247
types of 220
cleft sentences 196, 220
climate 90
collective nouns 80, 221
colon 174, 226
colour adjectives 122
comma 226
comment adverbs 150, 156, 219
comparative forms 217
  adjectives with comparative/
    superlative meaning 144
  comparative adjectives, linking
    with **and** 136
  more + one-syllable adjective 144
  more/less + two-syllable adjectives
    144
  one-syllable adjectives and
    adverbs + **-er** 144
  phrases and clauses
    as + adjective + **a/an** + noun
      146
    as + adjective/adverb **as** 146
    go so/as far as + to-infinitive
      146
    less + adjective + **than** 146
    as little/few as 146
    as much/many as 146
    not + adjective/adverb + **enough**
      + to-infinitive 146
    so + adjective/adverb + **as** + to-
      infinitive 146
    so + adjective/adverb + **that**-
      clause 146
    sufficiently + adjective 146
    too + adjective + **a/an** + noun
      146
    too + adjective/adverb + to-
      infinitive 146
  see also **few, little, less,** and **fewer**
complaining 12
complement
  adverbial phrases as 220
  definition of 220
  and linking verbs 42, 220, 221
  and object 220
  prepositional phrase as 220
  and subject 220
  transitive/intransitive verbs 56
  see also verb complementation
compound adjectives 138, 220
compound nouns
  countable compound nouns 86
  definition of 220
  grammar review 210
  hyphenated phrases, before nouns
    86
  noun + noun 86
  noun + preposition + noun 86
  one word, separate words,
    hyphenated 210
  plural forms 86
  possessive forms 86
  two- and three-word verbs, nouns
    related to 86
conclusions, drawing
  grammar review 205–6
  must 36, 74

present perfect continuous/present
  perfect 12
will/would 32
conditional clauses
  definition of 220
  real and unreal conditions
    217–18, 220
  real conditionals, tenses in 20,
    166, 168, 172, 218
  unreal conditionals, tenses in 166,
    170, 172, 218
conditional sentences 220
  conjunctions 174
  sentence connectors 174
conjunctions
  additional exercise 238–9
  conditions 174
  definition of 220
  noun phrases, adding information
    to 112
  reasons and results 174
  study guide 250
  time 174, 217
connecting adverbs 150, 219
contrasting
  although, though, while and
    whilst, with participle clauses
    164
  although and **though** 164
  conjunctions 174
  even though and **even if** 164
  sentence connectors 174
  in spite of the fact that 164
  while/whereas 164
  while/whilst 164
could *see* ability; permission;
  possibility; reporting; unreal past
countable/uncountable nouns
  definition of 220
  generalisations about classes of
    things 90
  grammar review 209
  with **there + be** 190
  see also **a/an, the,** and **zero article;
    a/an** and **one;** agreement, subject
    and verb; **all (of), whole, every,
    each; few, little, less,** and **fewer;
    much (of), many (of), a lot of,
    lots (of); one** and **ones; some**
    and **any**
criticising 12
  **might/could + have + past
    participle** 34
  negative questions 54, 207
  will/would, use of 32

D
dash (–) 174
days of the week 94
declarative sentences 220
defining relative clauses 222
  see also relative clauses
definite article 219
  see also **a/an, the,** and **zero article**
degree adverbs 219
  much, very much 154
  with **owing to** 160
  position of 150, 154

very, too 154
determiners 220
  grammar review 211–12
  study guide 245–46
direct object 58, 221
  see also complement; object;
    transitive/intransitive verbs; verb
    complementation
direct speech 220
direction adverbs 150, 152, 198,
  219
disapproval 168
'disliking' verbs 60
distance 104
do, after negative adverbials 200
  see also auxiliary verbs;
    substitution
dynamic verbs 221

E
-ed clauses *see* past participle
each *see* **all (of), whole, every, each**
echo questions 54, 222
emphasising adjectives 132, 219
every *see* **all (of), whole, every, each**
exceptions 182
exclamation mark 226
expectations 40

F
festivals 94
few, little, less, and **fewer**
  (a) few, (a) little, as pronouns
    104
  the few, the little + noun, as 'not
    enough' 104
  few + personal pronouns 104
  few and **little,** as informal
    alternatives 104
  less (than) and **fewer (than)** 104
  a little, as informal alternative
    104
  what few/what little, as 'the small
    (number/amount)' 104
fewer *see* **few, little, less,** and **fewer**
finite verbs 223
focus adverbs 154, 219
focusing
  fronting, for emphasis 198
  it-clauses 196
  wh-clauses 196
  what-clauses 196
frequency adverbs
  with **have to** 36
  indefinite frequency 219
  past continuous with 4
  position of 148, 150, 152
  present continuous with 4
full stop 226
future continuous
  arranged events/activities 22
  grammar review 204
  imagining what is happening
    around now 22
  particular point in future, relating
    start of event to 22
  repeated/regular events 22
  willingness, avoiding 22

future events
  additional exercise 231
  be about to + infinitive 24, 26
  be going to + infinitive 20, 166, 203
  be to + infinitive 24
  common phrases for talking about 26
  grammar review 203–4
  past and present continuous for intention 8
  possibility, **can/could** 30
  present continuous for 20
    grammar review 204
    informal arrangements 22
  present simple for
    conditional clauses 20
    fixed events 20
    grammar review 203
    if- clauses 24
    suppose/supposing/what if … 20
    time clauses 20
  real conditionals 166
  seen from the past
    be supposed to 28
    intentions 26
    reporting 28
    was/were to + infinitive 28
    was/were to have + past participle 28
  shall/shan't *versus* **will/won't** 26
  study guide 241
  verbs + **to-infinitive**, for intentions 26
  will + infinitive 203
  will and **be going to** 18, 20
future perfect
  and future perfect continuous 22
  passive form 224
future simple 224

G
generalisations 90
geographical areas 90
glossary 219–23
going to *see* **will** and **be going to**
gradable adjectives 134, 136, 216, 219
grading adverbs 134, 219

H
have (got) to 36, 205–6
having + past participle (-ed) clause 62, 116, 220
holidays 94
however 174

I
-ing (present participle) form
  grammar review 214–15
  non-finite clauses 221
  prepositional object 222
  reduced relative clauses 222
  see also participle adjectives; verb complementation
if, in comparison clauses 168
if and **whether**

after certain verbs 172
after **preposition** 172
in clause acting as subject or complement 172
noun + adjective + as to whether 172
possibilities, talking about 172
reporting **yes/no** questions 64
before **to-infinitive** 172
whether … or not 172
if-clauses 220
  after **would/would like** 130
  future events 24
  inversion instead of 198
  should, were, had, and omission of **if** 168
  without main clauses 168
  see also conditional clauses
imaginary situations 32, 218
imperative clauses 42, 166, 221
indefinite article 219
  see also **a/an, the,** and **zero article**
indirect object 58, 221
  see also object; verb complementation
indirect questions 222
  see also reporting
indirect speech 223
  see also reporting
infinitive forms 221
instructions 24, 166, 196
  grammar review 204–5
  if-clauses, without main clauses 168
intentions 26, 78
interrupted past actions/events 8
intransitive verbs *see* transitive/intransitive verbs
introducing new topic 196
inversion
  additional exercise 239
  adverbs of direction of movement 198
  after negative adverbials 200
  after **neither** and **nor** 200
  after time adverbs 152
  fronting, for emphasis 198
  with **here comes, there goes** 198
  instead of **if-clauses** 198
  with **so + adjective** 200
  with **such + be,** for emphasis of extent/degree 200
  with **as** and **than,** in comparisons 198
  of verb and subject 221
irregular verbs 227–28
it
  it is/was no *versus* there is/was no 194
  as object of verb 194
  reporting with passive forms 50
  with viewpoint verbs 194
it, introductory
  to focus attention on sentence element 192
  it + be + adjective/noun 192
  it + verb + object + that-clause 192

it + verb + object + to-infinitive clause 192
it + verb + that-clause 192
it + verb + to-infinitive clause 192
not as alternative to **noun** as subject 192
where subject is **to-infinitive, that-clause, wh-clause** or **-ing clause** 192
it-clauses 48, 196, 220

J
jobs/job titles 92

L
less *see* **few, little, less,** and **fewer**
linking verbs
  adjective patterns with 138, 140, 164
  become and **get** 42
  'becoming' verbs 42
  'being' verbs 42
  and complement 42, 220, 221
  go and **turn** 42
  'seeming' verbs 42
  study guide 242–43
  superlatives 144
little *see* **few, little, less,** and **fewer**

M
main clauses
  definition of 220
  and relative clause 222
manner, adverbs of 148, 219
may *see* possibility
might *see* possibility; unreal past
modal verbs
  additional exercise 231–32
  auxiliary verbs 219
  definition of 221
  grammar review 204–6
  with performatives 2
  reporting to reported clause, summary of changes 74
  study guide 242
much (of), many (of), a lot of, lots (of) 100
must
  drawing conclusions 36
  formal rules, regulations and warnings 36
  and **have (got) to** 36, 205–6
  must/mustn't, in reporting 74
  need(n't), don't have to, mustn't 206
  proposing future arrangements 36

N
names, of people 80, 92
narrative 64
nationality adjectives 136
necessity 205–6
need
  in formal written English 38
  need(n't), don't have to, mustn't, don't need to 38, 206
  as ordinary *versus* modal verb 38
  in questions 38

negative questions 54, 207
newspaper writing
  be to + infinitive, for events likely
    to happen 24
  participle clauses, use of 112
  past perfect continuous, use of 14
no, none(of), and **not any** 98
nominal relative clauses 108, 222
  see also relative clauses
non-affirmative meaning 221
non-defining relative clauses
  for adding information 106
  definition of 222
  participle clauses, use of instead
    of 112
  prepositional phrases 114
  whose, clauses with 108
  see also relative clauses
non-finite clauses 221
non-finite verbs 223
non-gradable adjectives 134, 136,
  216, 219
non-grading adverbs 134, 219
noun phrases
  adding information to 112
  conjunctions 112
  namely, use of 112
  participle clauses 112
  prepositional phrases 114
  that is, use of 112
  to-infinitive clauses 112
  complements 42
  definition of 221
  nominal relative clauses 222
nouns
  additional exercise 234–35
  definition of 221
  study guide 245
  see also compound nouns;
    countable/uncountable nouns
number expressions 88

O
object
  and complement 220
  definition of 221
  position of in two- and three-
    word verbs 188
  transitive verbs 223
  see also transitive/intransitive
    verbs; verb complementation
obligations 40, 206
offers 18, 72, 166, 204–5
one and **ones**
  with countable nouns 122
  inclusion of 122
  not used after nouns used as
    adjectives 122
  omission of 122
  with possessive determiners 122
  referring to people 122
  see also **a/an** and **one**
opinions 62
orders 24, 72, 78
organisations, names of 80
organising information 251
ought to *see* **should** and **ought to**

P
participle adjectives 221
  -ing and **-ed** forms, as adjectives
    138
  after nouns, reduced relatives 138
  in compound adjectives 138
  with **much**, **very much** 154
  position of 138
  that/those before 138
participle clauses
  active and passive in noun phrases
    112
  with adverbial meaning 116
  contrasting 164
  definition of 221
  having + participle, and timing of
    action 116
  implied subject, and subject of
    main clause 116
  not, position of 116
  with own subject 116
  use of prepositions with 118
participles 221
particles 188, 222
passive forms 222
  active patterns 44, 46
  additional exercise 232–33
  agent, omission of 48
  'appointing' verbs 44
  'giving' verbs 44
  grammar review 206–7
  it-clause as subject of 48
  'liking/wanting' verbs 46
  modal verbs 224
  'naming' verbs 44
  reporting with 50
  study guide 242–43
  'telling' verbs 44
  tenses 224
  topic emphasis 48
  transitive two- and three-word
    verbs 44
  verbs with related nouns 48
past continuous
  with adverbs of frequency 4
  as/when/while 158
  grammar review 203
  passive form 224
  past perfect continuous, and past
    perfect 14
  and past simple 8, 16
    intentions not carried out 8, 10
    in narratives 8
    past events in succession 8
    past events over same period 8
    repeated past actions 8
past participle (**-ed**) 220, 221
  grammar review 215
  non-finite clause 221
  reduced relative clause 222
  see also participle adjectives;
    participle clauses
past perfect
  grammar review 203
  passive form 224
  past perfect continuous, and past
    continuous 14
  and past simple

additional exercise 230–31
  intentions not carried out 10
  ordering past events 10
  reporting past events 10
  review of use of 16
  time clauses 6
past perfect continuous
  additional exercise 230–31
  grammar review 203
  intentions not carried out 10
  past perfect and past continuous
    activity in progress recently
    versus finished 14
    number of times something
    happened 14
    particular past time, relating
    events to 14
    review of use of 16
    state verbs 14
past simple
  grammar review 202
  passive form 224
  and past continuous 4, 8, 10, 16
  and past perfect 10, 16, 230–31
  and present perfect 6, 230
past subjunctive 223
  as it were 170
  unreal conditionals, **were** in **if-**
    clause 170
  were, for imaginary situations
    170
  were, in comparisons 170
perfect forms 16
performative verbs
  definition of 222
  present simple 2
permission 34, 38, 204
  could, be allowed to 30
personal pronouns 222
persuading 54
phrasal verbs
  definition of 222
  word order 188
  see also two- and three-word
    verbs
place adverbs 219
possessive determiners 220
possessive nouns 210–11, 222
possessive pronouns 210, 222
possibility
  can and **could** 30, 34
  grammar review 204
  may and **might** 34, 205
predictions 18
preferences 170
prepositional objects 58, 222
prepositional phrases
  as complement 220
  definition of 222
prepositional verbs 222
  see also phrasal verbs; two- and
    three-word verbs
prepositions
  additional exercise 239
  after nouns 186
  after verbs 184
  definition of 222
  particles 222

phrasal verbs 222
of place 178
of position and movement 176
reasons, giving 160
in relative clauses 110
study guide 251
of time 180
present and past time, review 16,
229
present continuous
with adverbs of frequency 4
for future events 20, 22, 204
grammar review 202
intentions 26
passive form 224
and present simple 2, 4, 16
present participle (-ing) 220, 221
see also participle adjectives;
participle clauses
present perfect
grammar review 202–3
passive form 224
and past simple 6, 230
and present perfect continuous
12, 16, 230
real conditionals 166
present perfect continuous
grammar review 203
passive form 224
and present perfect
activities in progress until
recently 12
additional exercise 230
conclusions from what can be
seen/heard etc. 12
recently completed events 12
repeated versus one-off activities
12
results of circumstances/activities
12
review of uses of 16
situations existing until present
12
present simple
contents of books/films etc. 4
for future events 20, 24, 166,
172, 203
grammar review 202
intentions 26
newspaper headlines 4
passive form 224
phrases introducing news 4
and present continuous 16
immediacy 4
life commentaries 4
mental states 2
performative verbs 2
state verbs 2
real conditionals 166
time clauses 6
present subjunctive 78, 223
present tenses, in reporting and
reported clauses 70
product names 92
promises 18
pronouns
definition of 222
study guide 247–48

types of 222
purposes and results
in order/so as + to-infinitive 162
in order that and so that 162
so + adjective/adverb + that-clause
146
such that, in such a way that,
such ... that 162

Q
qualitative adjectives 132, 136, 219
quantifiers
definition of 222
grammar review 211, 212–13
study guide 245–46
with and without 'of' 212, 213,
214
quantity expressions 84, 88
see also some and any
question forms 225
grammar review 207
indirect questions 222
negative questions 54
study guide 242–43
with that-clauses 54
types of 222
see also wh-questions; yes/no
questions
question mark 226
question tags 207
quotation marks 226

R
real conditionals
if-clauses 166, 168
real and unreal conditions
217–18, 220
tenses in 20, 166, 168, 172, 218
unless and if not 172
reasons
cleft sentences 196
conjunctions 174
prepositions 118, 160
sentence connectors 174
reduced relative clauses 132, 138,
222
see also relative clauses
reflexive pronouns
definition of 222
for emphasis 120
formality 120
grammar review 215
inclusion/omission of, with some
verbs 120
in verb + object + adjective
complement structure 56
regret 170
relative clauses
additional exercise 236–37
defining 106, 108, 112, 222
definition of 222
grammar review 214
nominal 108, 222
non-defining 106, 108, 112, 114,
222
prepositions in 110
reduced 132, 138, 222
study guide 247

relative pronouns
definition of 222, 223
omission/inclusion of 106, 110,
190
as subject/object of relative clause
106
relative words 223
a/the reason why/that 108
nominal relative clauses, with
who/what 108
whatever, whoever, whichever
108
when, whereby, where, why 108
whose, clauses with 108
reported speech 223
reporting 64
additional exercise 234
grammar review 209
modal auxiliaries 74
negative forms 64
offers/suggestions/orders/
intentions/requests 72
passive forms 44
punctuation for 226
questions 64
quotations 64
study guide 244
tense choice in 70
that-clauses 66, 72, 76
using adjectives 76
using nouns 76
reporting/reported clauses 64, 72
definition of 223
past tenses 70
present subjunctive 78
reporting verbs 64, 223
requests
grammar review 204–5
if-clauses 168
reporting 72, 78
will and be going to 18

S
seasons 88, 94
semi-colon 174
semi-modal verbs 221
grammar review 204–6
see also modal verbs
sense verbs 30
sentence connectors 174, 223
short answers 124
should and ought to
be supposed to 206
expectations 40
had better, in spoken English 40
obligations/recommendations 40
questions/requests for
confirmation or advice 40
regret/criticism 40
should and shall 40
simple sentences 223
simple versus continuous forms,
summary of uses of 16
since and for 12, 14
since-clauses 220
some and any
with before 96
'approximately' 96

with comparisons 96
general statements about whole classes of things 96
grammar review 211–12
with negative words 96
non-affirmative contexts 96
non-specific, unspecified things 96
before plural and uncountable nouns 96
strong and weak forms 96
unknown/unimportant person or thing 96
state verbs 2, 12, 14, 166, 223
subject
  and complement 220
  definition of 223
  it-clause as 48
  passive, uses of 48
  placement of long 48
  relative pronouns as 106
  who or **what** as 52
  see also agreement; inversion
subjunctive 223
  past 170
  present 78
subordinate clauses 220, 222
  see also adverbial clauses; relative clauses
substitution
  to, for **to-infinitive** clause 130
  additional exercise 237
  do 128, 200, 207, 216
  do so and **such** 126
  so and **not** 124
  study guide 247–48
suggestions 54, 72, 78, 207
superlative forms
  the + adjective with **-est** 144
  the + most + adjective 144
  of + plural noun phrase, after superlative 144
  in + singular noun phrase, after superlative 144
  adjectives with **a/an, the**, and zero article 92
  most + adjective/adverb 144
  noun + of which 110

T
tenses
  grammar review 202–4
  study guide 240–41
that-clauses 220
  passive sentences 48
  reporting 66, 72, 76
  should in 78
  wh-questions with 54
the *see* **a/an, the**, and zero article
there + be
  change of topic, topic known to listener/reader 190
  introducing topics 190
  noun following, agreement of **be** with 190
  noun following, indefinite/non-specific meaning of 190
  with nouns followed by **that-**,

wh-, to-infinitive or **-ing clause** 190
'thinking' verbs 30, 60
three-word verbs *see* two- and three-word verbs
time adverbs 219
time clauses
  conjunctions 174
  tenses in 217
times, of day and night 94
titles, of newspapers, books, films 80
to-infinitive
  with **come** and **grow** 42
  definition of 220
  leaving out 130
  with linking verbs 140
  non-finite clauses 221
  noun phrases, adding information to 112
  see also verb complementation
transitive/intransitive verbs 56
  grammar review 207
  implied object 56
  intransitive verbs 56, 221
  passives, grammar review 206
  transitive or intransitive verbs 56
  transitive verbs 56, 223
  two- and three-word verbs, word order 188
  see also verb complementation
two- and three-word verbs
  definition of 223
  particle in 222
  position of prepositions in 110
  word order 188

U
uncertainty 76
unchanging states 12
uncountable nouns *see* countable/uncountable nouns
unless and **if not** 172
unreal conditionals
  but for 166
  if + past simple 166
  real and unreal conditions 217–18, 220
  unless and **if not** 172
  were in **if-clause** 166, 170
unreal past
  might/could have + past participle 218
  would have + past participle 32, 218
used to
  grammar review 204–5
  repeated events in past 32
  in reporting 74

V
verb complementation
  additional exercise 233–34
  direct and indirect objects 58
  negative forms 62
  prepositional object, with **for/to** 58

study guide 243–44
summary of common patterns 207–8
verb + -ing or **bare infinitive** 60
verb + object + bare infinitive 60
verb + object + to-infinitive 62
verb + object/possessive + ing 60
verb + preposition + object + to-infinitive 62
verb + to have + past participle 62
verb + to (preposition) + ing 60
see also transitive/intransitive verbs
verb phrases 223
verbs 221, 223
viewpoint adverbs 156, 219

W
wh-clauses 220
  focusing 196
  with linking verbs 140
  verbs with 68
wh-questions 52, 222, 223
  auxiliary verb 54
  how and **what** 52
  reporting 64
  with **that-clauses** 54
  what 52
  which 52
  who 52
  whom 52
  whose 52
  see also negative questions
wh-words 222, 223
what-clauses 80, 196, 220
whether *see* **if** and **whether**
whether-clauses 220
whole *see* **all (of), whole, every, each**
will, would and **used to**
  characteristic behaviour/habits 32
  conclusions/assumptions 32
  criticism 32
  grammar review 204–5
  repeated events in past 32
  unreal past situations 32
will and **be going to**
  be going to + go/come 20
  conditional sentences 18
  decisions 18
  formality/informality 18, 20
  offers/requests/promises 18
  planned/likely events 18, 20
  predictions 18
willingness 22
works of art 92
would *see* **if-clauses; will, would** and **used to**

Y
yes/no questions 64, 222
  see also question forms

Z
zero article 219
  see also **a/an, the**, and zero article

Index of lexical items

A

a/an 88, 90, 92, 94, 146, 190, 219, 220
a bit 134
a bit of 104
a few (of) 214
a little (of) 214
a lot (of) 82, 100, 213
a number of 82, 110
a/the majority of 82
ability 186
able 140
about 184
above 176
above all 174
absent from 120
absolute 132
absolutely 134
abusive 76
academic 136
accept 124, 194
accident 194
acclimatise 120
according to 156
account for 188
ache 202
acknowledge 2, 50, 66
acknowledgement 76
across 176
act on 188
active 144
adamant 76
adapt 60, 120
adapted 42
address book 86
adhere to 56
adjust 60
admiration 186
admire 154
admit 2, 58, 60, 62, 66, 124, 194, 208
adult 136
advice 76
advisable 78
advise 2, 46, 62, 66, 68, 72, 78, 130, 172
affected 138
afford 130
afraid 130, 132, 140, 144
after 6, 20, 118, 158, 174, 184, 220
after all 174
after that 174
afternoon 94
afterwards 174
agitatedly 142
agree 2, 26, 46, 50, 62, 66, 72, 124, 130, 202, 208
agree about/on/with 184
agreed 76
aim 26, 46, 186, 208
alarmed 140
alarmed/alarming 216

alert 144
alike 132, 144
alive 132
all 110, 220
all (of) 82, 102, 212, 213
all of a sudden 4
all over 176
all the same 174
allegation 76
allege 50, 62
alleged 138
allegedly 142
allocated 138
allow 46, 58, 62, 208
almost 102, 134, 150, 154
alone 132, 144, 154
along 176, 198
also 174
alternative 194
alternatively 174
although 118, 164, 174
altogether 154
always 4, 36, 150
amaze 192
amazed 78, 140
amazed/amazing 216
amazement 186
amazing 140
ambition 186
among 178
among other things 178
among others 178
amongst 178
amount of 100
amused 78
and 112, 174, 220
angry 76, 134, 140
announce 44, 50, 58, 66
announcement 76
annoy 192
annoyed 76, 140
annoying 140
annual 132
annually 152
another 122
answer 56, 66, 76
answer back 188
anticipate 2, 46, 202
anxious 78
any 96, 186, 211–12
any- 82
any (of) 82, 212
anybody 98, 212
anyone 96, 98, 190, 212
anything 96, 98, 212
anyway 174
anywhere 98
apart 182
apart from 182
apologetic 76
apologise 2
appalling 78
apparent 42
apparently 156

appeal 62
appear 2, 42, 46, 62, 124, 132, 140, 164, 190, 192, 207
apply 62
applying 138
appoint 44
appreciate 46, 154, 202
approve 60
approve of 60, 188
argue 66, 194
argue about/for/with 184
argument 76
arise 227
arms trade 86, 90
army 80
arrange 46, 62, 68
arrest 207
arts festival 86
as 144, 146, 158, 174, 198
as a consequence 174
as a result 174
as a rule 150
as if 170
as it were 170
as long as 174
as many 146
as much 146
as soon as 6, 20, 174
as though 170
as to 68, 76, 172
as well 174
ashamed 132, 140, 144, 186
aside 182
ask 44, 46, 56, 58, 62, 66, 68, 72, 78, 130, 208
ask about/after/for/of 184
ask of 184
asleep 132
aspire to 56
associate with 56
association 80
assume 50, 56, 66, 124, 202
assuming (that) 174
assure 66
astonish 192
astonished 140
astonishingly 156
astounded 78
at no time 152
at that time 174
at the same time 174
athletics 84
atmosphere 90
atomic 132
attempt 46, 186
attract 2, 202
attribute to 56
audience 80
autumn 94
avail of 120

available 132
average 136
avoid 46, 207, 208
awake 132, 227
award 44, 58
aware 42, 132, 140, 144
away 198
awful 134, 140
awkward 140

B

baby's bedroom 86
back 198
back to back 94
bad 140
bald 42
ban 186
barely 96, 200
base on 56
be 42, 128, 130, 132, 140, 164, 219, 227
be able to 30, 130, 204, 221
be about to 24, 26
be afraid 124
be allowed to 30, 204
be bound to 26
be certain 124
be due to 26
be going to 18, 20, 166, 203
be likely 34
be on the brink of 26
be on the point of 26
be on the verge of 26
be supposed to 28, 190, 206
be sure to 26, 124
be to 24
beach 90
bear 227
beat 227
beautiful 132
because 118, 160, 174, 220
because of 160
become 42, 132, 140, 164, 227
before 20, 96, 118, 158, 174, 200
before that 174
beg 2, 78
begin 46, 56, 60, 130, 208, 227
behave 120
believe 2, 30, 46, 50, 56, 62, 64, 66, 124, 194, 202, 208
belong 12, 166
belong to 202
belongings 84
below 176
bend 56, 227
beneath 176
besides 118, 174, 182

bet 227
between 178
big 134
bind 227
biologically 156
bird of prey 86
birds' nests 86
bite 227
bleed 227
blind 42
blow 227
book 58
bored 144
bored/boring 216
boring 144
both 110
both (of) 212
bother 38
boy's arm 86
brave 140
bravely 156
break 56, 227
break in 188
break-out 86
brick-built 138
briefly 148
bring 46, 58, 227
bring about 188
broadcast 227
broken 138
brother-in-law 86
brush up on 44
build 58, 227
building materials
   industry 86
burn 56, 227
burst 227
busy 134, 140
busy with 120
but 174, 182, 220
but for 166, 182
buy 58, 227
by 94, 118, 180
by air 94
by bus 94
by car 94
by contrast 174
by email 94
by phone 94
by plane 94
by post 94
by sea 94
by taxi 94
by the time 6, 20
by train 94

C
calculate 50, 68
calculated 132
call 44
call back 44, 188
call on 72, 188
call up 44
campaign 62
can 30, 74, 128, 204,
   205, 221
can't bear 46, 194
can't stand 194, 208

capable 132
care 150
care about/for 184
careful 140, 144
careless 144
carelessly 156
carry out 44
cast 227
cast back 44
catch 46, 58, 208, 227
catch out 188
cause 62, 208
caused 138
cautious 144
cease 208
certain 76, 140, 144
certainly 156
chance 102, 130, 186,
   194
change 56
cheap 144
cheap(ly) 142
check 66, 68
check into 188
chemical 132
chicken drumsticks 86
Chief of Staff 86
choice 194
choose 58, 68, 130, 172,
   227
chosen 138
civil 136
claim 50, 76
class 80
clean 136
clean up 188
clear 140, 144
clear away 188
clearly 148, 150, 156
clear(ly) 142
clever 134
climate 90
climb 46
cling 227
close 56, 60
clothes 84
clothes shop 86
club 80
coal mine 86
coffee 90
coincidence 194
cold 144
collect 58
college 80
come 42, 46, 152, 198,
   207, 208, 227
come about 192
come across 110
come in for 188
come to 188
come up against 44, 188
command 62, 72, 78, 208
commander-in-chief 86
comment 76
committee 80
common 134, 136
community 80
company 80

company director 92
complain 66
complete 132, 144
completely 134, 150
complex 144
complimentary 76
computer 90
computer keyboard 86
concentrate 60
concern 38, 186, 192
concern with 120
concerned 78, 132, 140,
   172
conclude 2, 68
conclusion 76
confess 2, 60, 66
confide 66
confidence 102
confident 140
conflict 172
confusion 172
congratulate 2
congratulations 84
consent 62
consequently 174
consider 2, 8, 10, 46, 50,
   56, 62, 66, 68, 172,
   194, 202, 208
consist of 2, 202
constantly 4
constitute 202
contain 202
content 132
continually 4
continue 46, 208
conversation 90
convince 66
convinced 42
cook 56, 58
cost 2, 58, 186, 192,
   202, 227
could 30, 34, 74, 128,
   204, 205, 218, 221,
   224
council 80
count 60, 62
count out 188
country(side) 90
cover up 188
cowardly 142
cow's milk 86
crazy 140
creased 144
creep 227
crew 80
criteria 84
critical 76, 136
crop up 188
crowd 80
crucial 78
culminate in/with 56
cup of tea 86
curious 140
curiously 150
customs officer 86
cut 227
cut back on 188
cut out 188

D
daily 152
dance 56
dare 60, 204, 221
dark 144
data 84
dawn 94
dawn on 192
day 102
day by day 94
day-to-day 86
deaf 42
deal 227
debate 68, 172
decide 30, 50, 62, 68
decision 76, 186
declare 2, 44, 56, 66
decline 208
decrease 56
deep 134
deep(ly) 142
definitely 156
delay 208
delighted 130
demand 66, 72, 78, 208
democratic 132
demonstrate 44, 50, 58
deny 2, 46, 58, 62, 66,
   96, 194, 208
department 80
depend 60, 62
depend on 172
describe 44, 46, 58
description 186
deserve 130
deservedly 142
desire 186, 202
despite 164
deter 60
determination 186
determine 68
determined 130
determinedly 142
detest 60, 208
detract from 56
develop 150
diabetes 84
differ 150
differ from 202
differentiate between 56
difficult 42, 140
dig 227
digital 132
dignified 142
diplomatic 136
direct 78, 144
direct(ly) 142
disagree 66
disagreement 172
disappointed 78, 140
disappointedly 142
disapprove of 44, 60
discourage 60
discover 50, 68, 208
discuss 68, 172
discussion 76, 172, 186
dislike 12, 46, 60, 194,
   208

Index of lexical items

dismissive 76
dive 227
do 126, 128, 192, 200, 207, 216, 219, 227
do out of 188
do so 126
domestic 134
don't have to 38, 206
doubt 2, 124, 166, 172, 202
doubtful 76, 140
down 198
downstairs 148
draw 227
dread 208
dreadfully 134
dream 227
dress 120
drink 56, 227
drink up 188
drive 56, 227
drop 56
duck's eggs 86
due to 160
during 180
dwell 227

E
each 82, 102, 110, 122, 214, 220
each of 82
each (of) 212
each other 215
eager 144
earlier 174
earnings 84
easy 140
easy-going 138
eat 56, 227
economic 132
economics 84
effect 186
either 122, 213
either ... or 82
either of 82
elderly 142
electorate 80
electric 136
emerge 192
emphasise 194
empty 136
enable 62, 208
encourage 50, 62, 72, 208
encouragement 76
end 60
end to end 94
end up 42
enemy 80
enjoy 46, 154, 166, 194, 207
enormously 150, 154
enough 146
enquire about/after 184
entire 102, 132
entirely 134, 150, 160
entitle 62, 208
environment 90
environmental 132, 134

environmentally 156
envisage 208
envy 58
equal 144
equate with 56
especially 154
essential 78, 134
establish 50, 68
estimate 50
even 154
even if 164, 170
even so 174
even though 164, 174
evening 94
every 82, 102, 186, 214
every few (months) 102
every now and again 102
every other (kilometre) 102
every single (day) 102
every so often 102, 150
everybody 82
everyone 82
everything 82
exact 144
excellent 134
except 182
except for 182
excepted 182
excited/exciting 216
excitedly 142
exclusively 134
expect 2, 8, 10, 26, 46, 50, 54, 64, 66, 72, 124, 130, 202
explain 44, 50, 66, 68
explanation 76
extremely 134, 154

F
face 46
face to face 94
fail 56, 62, 96, 130, 208
failure 186
fair 144
fairly 134
fall 207, 227
fall through 188
false 136
familiarise with 120
family 80
far-reaching 138
fashion 142
fast 134
fast-growing 138
favourite 144
fear 38, 90, 186
feed 227
feel 2, 30, 44, 46, 50, 60, 64, 66, 132, 140, 164, 194, 202, 208, 227
feel like 208
fetch 58
few 104, 146
few (of) 212
fewer 104
fight 227
fill in 110

finally 148
financially 150, 156
find 2, 46, 50, 56, 58, 66, 194, 202, 207, 208, 227
find out 46, 68
fine 132
fine(ly) 142
finish 56, 60, 208
first 122, 150, 152
fit 2, 227
fix 58
flat(ly) 142
flee 227
flick through 188
fling 227
fly 152, 198, 227
focus 60
follow 192
fond 186
fondness 186
foolish 140
foolishly 156
for 12, 14, 174, 184
for one thing 174
for (reasons) 160
forbid 2, 96, 227
force 62, 207, 208
forecast 76, 227
foreign 136
forest 90
forever 4
forget 46, 60, 62, 68, 130, 227
forgive 58, 227
formal 144
forwards 148
found 138
frankly 150, 156
free 140
free(ly) 142
freeze 227
frequent 144
friendly 134, 142
frighten 192
frightened 132
frightened/frightening 216
from my/his/her perspective 156
from time to time 150
fully 134
fun 144
furious 140
furniture 96
furthermore 174
future 90

G
gather 124
gather up 188
general 132
generally 156
generation 80
generously 156
genuine 136
get 42, 58, 132, 206–7, 207, 227
get down 44, 188

get up 188
girls' school 86
give 44, 58, 227
glad 132, 140
glasses case 86
go 42, 146, 152, 198, 207, 208, 227
go bad 42
go bust 42
go dead 42
go missing 42
go mouldy 42
go off 42
go on 62
go over 188
go rotten 42
go through with 188
go up 150
go wrong 42
goat's cheese 86
good 140, 194
good and 136
good-looking 138
goods 84
government 80
grab 207
grammar 90
grateful 76
greatly 150
ground 90
group 80
grow 42, 227
grow up 188
grumble 66
guarantee 2, 26, 58, 72, 76, 194
guess 68, 124
guess so/not 124
guilty 136, 140
gymnastics 84

H
habit 186
had better 40, 204, 221
hair 90
hair-raising 138
hand 44, 58
hang 152, 227
hanger-on 86
happen 168, 192, 207
happily 142
happy 134, 140
hard 140
hardly 38, 96, 150, 158, 200, 205
hardly ever 150, 152
hate 46, 60, 130, 194, 202, 208
have 2, 60, 62, 114, 128, 202, 219, 227
have got 128
have got to 36, 204, 205–6, 221
have to 36, 38, 74, 205–6
hear 30, 44, 46, 60, 124, 202, 208, 227
hear out 188
help 44, 60, 192, 208

help on with 188
help out 188
hence 174
her 122
here 82
here comes 198
herself 120, 215
hesitate 208
hide 120, 227
high(ly) 142
himself 120, 215
hit 192, 207, 227
hold 56, 227
hold out 188
hold over 44
holiday 180
home-made 138
honestly 150, 156
hope 8, 10, 26, 46, 50,
  54, 62, 72, 102, 124,
  130, 194, 202, 208
horizon 90
hourly 152
how 52, 68, 82, 146,
  196, 223
however 174, 223
huge 134
hugely 134
human 136
human race 90
hurriedly 142
hurt 192, 227

I
I bet 18
I expect 18
I gather 4
I hear 4
I hope 18
I imagine 18
I reckon 18
I see 4
I think 18
I understand 4
I wonder 18
idea 130, 186
ideal 144
identified 138
ideologically 156
if 20, 64, 166, 172, 174,
  200, 220
if not 172
if only 170
if so 174
ill 42, 132
illness 180
I'm sure 18
imaginable 132
imagine 2, 46, 60, 68,
  124, 170, 202, 208
immensely 134
imperative 78
importance 90
important 78, 134
impossible 96, 134, 140
improvement 186
in 118, 180, 198
in addition 174

in amazement 142
in any case 174
in case 20
in consequence 174
in contrast 174
in my/his/her opinion
  156
in order that 162
in order to 162
in spite of 164
in such a way that 162
in that 160, 174
inability 186
inappropriate 78
inasmuch as 160
incline to/towards 56
inclined 140
included 138
income tax 86
inconceivable 78
increase 56
indicate 66
indication 76
indifferent 172
individual 136
industrially 156
infected 42
inflict on 56
influence 186
inform 50, 66, 68
innocent 136
insist 60, 78
insistent 76
insofar as 174
instead 174
instruct 46, 68, 72, 78
instruction 76
insulting 76
intake 86
intend 8, 10, 26, 50, 64,
  72, 78, 130
intensely 134
intention 186
interested 42, 138
interested/interesting 216
interesting 140
interestingly 156
interview 186
introduce 44, 58
invaluable 134
invitation 76
invite 62, 72, 208
involved 132
iron 90
irrelevant 42
issue 76
it 50, 140, 192, 194
it says here 4
itself 215

J
joke 66
journalist 92
judge 56
jury 80
just 154
just(ly) 142

K
keep 42, 46, 60, 227
keep on 62
kind 140
kindly 142, 156
kneel 227
knit 227
know 2, 12, 50, 60, 68,
  124, 166, 202, 227
know about/of 184

L
lack 186
lamb chops 86
largely 134, 154, 160
last 150
late 136
late(ly) 142
later 174
lay 227
lead 227
lean 227
leap 227
learn 68, 227
learn about/of 184
least 144
leave 58, 194, 208, 227
leave out 188
lend 44, 58, 207, 227
less 104, 144, 146
less (of) 214
let 60, 227
let go 60
let in 44
let in on 188
let out 44
lie 152, 227
light 227
like 2, 46, 60, 130, 154,
  166, 194, 202, 207,
  208
likelihood 186
likewise 174
linguistics 84
lion's den 86
little 104, 146, 200
little (of) 212
little ones 122
live 152
live up to 188
lively 142
logically 156
London-based 138
lone 132
lonely 142
long 72
long-lasting 138
longest-serving 138
look 2, 42, 164, 202
look after 110, 188
look down on 188
look forward 60
look forward to 154
look out 188
look to 26
look up 188
look up to 188
looker-on 86

lose 227
lots of 100, 213
loud(ly) 142
love 2, 46, 60, 130, 194,
  208
loved ones 122
lovely 140, 142
lovely and 136
low 134
luckily 156
lucky ones 122

M
mad 140
made-up 138
mainly 134, 154, 160
make 44, 58, 60, 140,
  227
make up 188
manage 62, 208
manner 142
many 100, 110, 146
many (of) 212, 213
march 152
mathematics 84
matter 207
maximum 132
may 34, 74, 128, 205,
  221
me 222
meal 180
mean 8, 10, 26, 46, 130,
  140, 192, 202, 208,
  227
means 84
meanwhile 174
measles 84
measure 2, 202
media 84
medical 132
medically 156
meet 227
mend 58
mention 44, 50, 58, 66,
  194
mere 132
mess up 188
midday 94
midnight 94
might 34, 128, 205, 218,
  221, 224
mind 46, 208
mine 222
minimum 132
miserable 140
miss 208
mistake for 56
mobile 136
modern 144
money-making 138
month 102
monthly 152
morally 156
more 144
more and more 136
more wrong 144
moreover 174
morning 94

most 110, 144
mostly 154
most(ly) 142
mount up 188
move 56, 120
move off 188
mow 227
much 100, 146, 154
much (of) 212, 213
must 36, 40, 74, 128, 221
mustn't 36, 38, 74, 206
my 122, 220, 222
myself 120, 215

N
name 2, 44
namely 112
naturally 150, 156
nearby 150
nearly 102, 134, 150
need 38, 46, 130, 194, 204, 208, 221
needn't 38, 206
neither 122, 200
neither do I 200, 216
neither/nor 82
neither of 82, 110
neither (of) 213
nerve-wracking 138
nervous 140
never 36, 38, 54, 96, 98, 150, 200, 205
nevertheless 174
news 84
next 150, 152
nice 140
nice and 136
night 102
no 54, 98, 182, 186, 200, 213
no amount of 98
no bother 98
no chance 98
no comment 98
no idea 98
no longer 194
no-one 38, 98
no problem 98
no sooner 158
no sooner than 200
no way 98
no wonder 98
nobody 38, 54, 98, 182
no(body) 190
nominate 44
none (of) 82, 98, 110, 212, 213
noon 94
nor 200
nor do I 200
normally 36
northern 132
not 200
not a single 98
not any 98, 186
not certain 76
not many 104
not much 104

not once 152
not one 98
nothing 54, 182
notice 46, 60, 66, 68, 194, 202, 208
notify 66
now 152
nowhere 54, 98
number of 100

O
object 60
obligatory 78
observation 76
observe 44, 46, 60, 208
obvious 42
obviously 156
occasional 132
occupy ... with 120
odd 136, 140
oddly 150
of 144, 184
off 198
offer 44, 58, 62, 72, 207, 208
office-worker 86
often 150
old 136
on 118, 184
on condition that 174
on many occasions 150
on the contrary 174
on the other hand 174
once 6
once a week 152
one 88, 122
one another 88, 215
one of 82
ones 122
oneself 120
only 38, 154, 200, 205
only later 152
open 56, 60
opportunity 130, 186
opposite 132
opposition 80
option 186
or 112, 174
orchestra 80
order 2, 46, 58, 62, 72, 76, 78, 208
order about 188
original 136
otherwise 174
ought to 40, 128, 204, 206, 221, 224
ourselves 215
out 198
outcome 86
outskirts 84
outwardly 156
over 176, 180
overheads 84
overhear 60, 208
owe 58, 194
owing to 160
own 2, 202
own up 60

P
panic 38
park 56
part 110
particular 136
particularly 154
particulars 84
partly 160
pass 58
passer-by 86
past 90
pause 56
pay 58, 192, 207, 227
peace-keeping 138
peculiar 144
pen top 86
people 48, 84
per cent 84
perfect 134, 144
perfectly 134
permission 186
permit 2, 58
person to person 94
personally 156
persuade 50, 62, 66, 72, 208
phenomena 84
phone 56
phonetic 132
phonetics 84
physically 156
physics 84
pick up 188
plainly 150
plan 8, 10, 26, 50, 62, 64, 68, 186, 208
plans 130
play 56, 58
pleased 140, 144
pleased/pleasing 216
pleasure 90
plenty of 82, 100
point 194
point out 58, 66
pointedly 142
police 84
politically 156
politics 84
popular 134
population 80
positive 140
possess 202
possibility 186
possible 132
post 58
pour 58
practically 134
predict 2, 194
prefer 2, 46, 78, 130, 154, 194, 202, 208
pregnant 42
premises 84
prepare 120, 208
prepared 140
present 90
press 80
presumably 150, 156
presume 66, 124

pretend 62
pretty 134
prevail 62
prevent 60, 96
previously 174
pride 186
pride on 120
primarily 134
private 136
probability 186
probably 156
problem 76, 186
professional 136
prohibit 60, 96
promise 2, 26, 66, 72, 76, 124, 130
pronounce 56
proper 132
property 90
proposal 186
propose 26, 44, 50, 64, 66, 72, 78
prospect 186
proud 186
prove 42, 56, 58, 164, 227
provide for 188
provided 20, 138
provided that 174
public 80, 136
publications department 86
pull 207
pull to 188
push to 188
push-up 86
put 227
put down as 188
put out 44
put pen to paper 94
put up to 188
put up with 188

Q
quarterly 152
question 76, 172, 194
quickly 142, 148
quick(ly) 142
quiet 134
quietly 148
quit 227
quite 150, 217

R
rabies 84
rarely 36, 96, 150, 152, 200
rather 134, 150, 170
read 44, 56, 58, 227
read-out 86
ready 140
ready-made 138
real 144
realise 2, 68, 202
really 134, 154
reason 102, 108, 186, 194
reasonably 134
reassure 50, 66

recall 46, 60, 62, 208
recent 144
reckon 54
recognised 42
recommend 50, 66, 72, 78
recommendation 76
refusal 76, 186
refuse 2, 46, 58, 62, 72, 96, 130, 208
regard 194
regard as/with 56
region to region 94
regret 2, 62, 154, 202, 208
regularly 150
reluctance 186
reluctant 96
rely 60, 62
remain 42
remaining 138
remember 30, 46, 60, 62, 68, 166, 194, 208
remind 2, 50, 62, 66, 68, 72
remind of 56
repair 58
repeatedly 142
reply 66, 76
report 44, 46, 50, 56, 58, 66, 207
reportedly 142
reputedly 142
request 2, 72, 78
require 46, 66, 78
resemble 202
resent 46, 60, 194, 208
resolve 26
resort 60
responsible 132
result from 188
resulting 138
reveal 50
rich 134
riches 84
ride 227
right 144
right across 176
rightly 156
ring 227
rip 56
rise 227
risk 186, 208
roll 152
rough 144
rule of thumb 86
run 152, 227
run into 188
runner-up 86

S
sad 140
sadly 156
satisfaction 186
satisfied 186
save 58
savings 84
savings account 86
saw 227

say 50, 54, 58, 62, 66, 68, 72, 124, 209, 227
scarcely 96, 150, 158, 200
scare 192
school 80
scientific 136
scornful 76
sea 90
seaside 90
secret 194
see 30, 44, 50, 60, 68, 194, 202, 208, 227
seeing as 160
seeing that 160
seek 227
seem 42, 46, 62, 124, 132, 164, 190, 192, 202
seen 140
seldom 96, 150, 152, 200
self 120
sell 58, 207, 227
selves 120
send 44, 46, 58, 227
sense 186
seriously 150, 156
set 227
sew 227
shake 227
shall 40, 74, 128, 221
shall/shan't 26
shame 186
shampoo 90
shave 120
she 222
shear 227
shed 227
sheer 132
shine 227
shock 192, 207
shocked 78, 140
shoot 227
shoot down 188
shop around 188
short-term 138
short(ly) 142
should 40, 74, 128, 198, 205, 206, 221, 224
show 46, 50, 58, 62, 66, 68, 208
shrink 227
shut 56, 227
shut up 188
side by side 94
sign 186
similar 132
similarly 174
simple 140
simply 134, 154
since 6, 12, 14, 118, 174
since (because) 160, 174
sing 56, 58, 227
sink 227
sister-in-law 86
sit 152, 227
sky 90

sleep 207, 227
sleeping 132
slide 227
slightly 134, 150
sling 228
slowly 148
slow(ly) 142
small-scale 138
smell 30, 202, 228
smoke 56
so 146, 174, 200
so as to 162
so do I 200, 216
so far 180
so long as 174
so that 162, 174
soft 144
soft-spoken 138
solely 154
some 96, 110, 122, 211–12, 220
some- 82
some (of) 82, 212
somebody 48, 96, 212
someone 48, 96, 212
something 48, 96, 190, 212
sometimes 36, 148
somewhat 154
soon 174
sooner 158, 170, 200
sorry 132, 140
sort out 188
sound 2, 42, 90, 164, 202
sour-tasting 138
sow 228
speak 60, 228
special 144
specialise in 56
specifically 154
speculate 66, 68
speculation 76, 172
speed 228
spell 228
spend 228
spill 228
spin 228
spit 228
splash out 188
split 228
split up 188
spoil 228
spot 208
spread 228
spring 94, 228
staff 84
stairs 84
stand 152, 228
stand up 188
start 46, 56, 60, 62, 130, 208
start to finish 94
state-of-the-art 86
statement 76
statistics 84
stay 42, 180
steal 228

stick 228
sting 228
stink 228
stipulate 78
stolen 138
stop 60, 208
straight 136
strange-sounding 138
strike 192, 228
strive 228
strong 134
study 56
stupid 140
stupidly 156
subdued 142
subsequently 174
such 200
such that 162
suddenly 4, 142
suffer 150
sufficiently 146
suggest 2, 44, 50, 54, 58, 66, 72, 78, 124, 208
suggestion 76, 130
suitable 132
summer 94
sun 90
superb 134
suppose 20, 50, 54, 64, 124, 170
supposed to 28, 190, 206
supposedly 142
supposing 20, 170, 174
sure 76, 132, 140
surprise 192, 194
surprised 78
surprised/surprising 216
surprisingly 156
surroundings 84
suspect 124
suspicious 42
swear 72, 228
sweep 228
sweet-smelling 138
swell 228
swim 152, 207, 228
swing 228
sympathetic 76
sympathy 102

T
tactful 76
take 58, 192, 194, 207, 228
take after 44, 188
take against 188
take on 110
take over 188
take up on 188
taken 138
talk 60
talk about/of/on/with 68, 172, 184
talk down to 44
talk out of 188
taste 30, 192, 202
tea cup 86
tea leaf 86

teach 44, 46, 58, 62, 66, 68, 208, 228
team 80
tear 228
tear away from 120
technical 136
technically 156
tell 44, 46, 50, 58, 60, 62, 66, 68, 72, 124, 207, 208, 209, 228
tell apart 188
tend 46, 190
terrible 134, 140
terrific 140
than 198
thank 2
thanks 84
that 106, 110, 122, 138, 196, 209, 223
that is 112
the 92, 94, 122, 144, 219, 220
the affluent 122
the disadvantaged 122
the elderly 122
the homeless 122
the low-paid 122
the main 122
the majority of 82
the minute/second/moment 6
the number of 82
the only 122
the poor 122
the position of 92
the post of 92
the privileged 122
the rich 122
the role of 92
the slightest 186
the sole 186
the way 68
the wealthy 122
the whole of 180
the young 122
their 220
themselves 120, 215
then 152, 174
there 50, 82, 190
there goes 198
there is 190
therefore 174
these 122, 209
they 48
they say 4
think 2, 8, 10, 50, 54, 56, 62, 64, 66, 68, 124, 194, 202, 228
think about 8, 10, 172
think of 8, 10, 60
thin(ly) 142
this 92, 122, 209, 220
this morning/week/month 6
those 122, 138
though 164, 174
thoughtful 140
threat 76

threaten 62, 72
through 118, 176, 180
throughout 176, 180
throw 44, 58, 207, 228
throw away 188
thrust 228
thus 174
tidy away 188
till 180
tired 140
tired/tiring 216
title 44
to 130
to date 180
to my/his/her knowledge 156
today 6
tomorrow 150
too 146, 154, 174
total 132
totally 134
touch 207
town 90
transpire 192
travel industry 90
tread 228
treatment 180
tree-lined 138
tremendous 134
tremendously 154
trouble about/with 120
true 136, 144
try 130, 208
try out 188
turn 42
turn in 188
turn out 42, 192

U
unable 96, 140
unaware 140
unbelievably 156
uncertain 76, 140, 172
uncertainty 172
uncomfortable 140
undecided 172
under 176
underlying 132
underneath 176
understand 2, 12, 30, 46, 50, 66, 68, 124, 166, 194, 202, 228
undertake 26
undoubtedly 156
undress 120
unexpectedly 142
unhappy 42, 140
unique 134, 144
university 80
unknown 134
unless 20, 172, 174
unlikely 96
unnecessary 78
unprofessional 140
unreasonable 140
unsure 132, 140, 172
unsure, not sure 76
until 6, 20, 158, 174,

180, 200
until now 180
unwell 132
unwillingness 186
up 198
up till 180
up to 180
upset 78, 140, 192
upstairs 148
urge 72, 78
urgent 78
use 194
use up 188
used to 32, 74, 190, 204, 205, 221
usually 148
utter 132
utterly 134

V
vary 56, 150
very 134, 154
very much 154
view 194
violently 148
virtually 102, 134, 154
visit 180
visually 156
vital 78
volunteer 62, 72
vote 44
vow 72

W
wait 62, 207
wake 56, 228
walk 152
want 8, 10, 26, 46, 64, 72, 130, 207, 208
warn 2, 50, 62, 66, 68, 72, 78, 207, 208
warning 76, 78
wash 56, 120
wash up 56, 188
watch 60, 208
wave 56
way 142, 186
we 48
weak 134
wear 228
weave 228
week 102
weekly 152
weep 228
weigh 2, 202
welcome 140
well 132
well-behaved 138
well-resourced 138
were 170
wet 228
what 52, 64, 68, 76, 108, 207
what if 20
what with 118
whatever 108
what's more 174, 223
when 6, 20, 54, 68, 108,

158, 174, 196, 200, 223
whenever 118, 174
where 64, 68, 82, 108, 196, 223
whereabouts 84
whereas 164, 174
whereby 108
whether 64, 68, 76, 172
which 52, 64, 68, 106, 110, 122, 196, 207, 222, 223
whichever 108
while 20, 118, 158, 164, 174, 220
whilst 164
who 52, 64, 68, 106, 108, 196, 207, 222, 223
whoever 108
whole 102, 134
whom 52, 106, 110, 223
whose 52, 108, 207, 223
why 68, 108, 196, 223
wide(ly) 142
wild 136
will 18, 20, 26, 32, 128, 204, 221
willing 140
willingness 186
win 56, 228
wind 228
wind up 188
winter 94, 102
wisely 156
wish 170, 208
with 118, 184
with confusion 142
without 96, 118
woman's face 86
women's clinic 86
wonder 4, 8, 68
wonderful 134, 140
world 90
worn 144
worried 42, 140, 144
worried/worrying 216
worriedly 142
worry 38, 192
would 32, 74, 128, 204, 205, 218, 221
would like 130
would rather 170
would sooner 170
wring 228
write 56, 58, 228
wrong 144
wrongly 156

Y
yesterday 152
yet 174
you 48
young 134
your 122, 220, 222
yours 222
yourself 120, 215
yourselves 215